ECONOMICS TODAY

Second Edition

ECONOMICS

Roger LeRoy Miller

Professor of Economics   **Department of Economics**
and Associate Director
Center for Studies in Law and Economics

University of Miami

TODAY

Second Edition

Canfield Press **San Francisco**
A Department of Harper & Row, Publishers, Inc.

New York   **Hagerstown**   **London**

We gratefully acknowledge the following sources for information
and quotations used in the biographical sketches:

Newsweek Magazine
U.S. News and World Report
Fortune Magazine
New York Times
Times Magazine
Business Week
Who's Who in America
Time Magazine
Current Biography
The Nation
The New Republic

The New York Review of
 Books
Harpers
Science
Webster's American
 Biographies
Encyclopedia Brittanica Book
 of the Year 1973
American Economic Review
Ralph Nader Congressional
 Report, 92nd Congress

This book was set in Melior by Computer Typesetting Services.
The editors were Gerald Papke and Eva Marie Strock; the
designer was Paula Tuerk; the graphic illustrations were
done by Axya Art; the cover was designed by Michael
Rogondino; the index was prepared by Carol Talpers.
Nick Keefe supervised production.
The printer and binder was W. A. Krueger Co.

Economics Today

Harper & Row, Publishers, Inc.
10 East 53rd Street
New York, NY 10022

Library of Congress Cataloging in Publication Data

Miller, Roger LeRoy.
    Economics today.

    Includes bibliographies and index.
    1. Economics. I. Title.
HB171.5.M642 1974   330   75-40359
ISBN 0-06-385453-8

76 77 78 79 80   10 9 8 7 6 5 4 3 2 1

Contents in Brief

UNIT ONE

GETTING STARTED   **1**

Issue I-1   The Scarcity Society: Are We Running Out of Everything?   **3**

1   What Economics Is All About   8

A   Reading and Working with Graphs   18

Issue I-2   Does Money Mean Happiness? How Important Is Material Well-Being?   **23**

2   How Different Systems Solve the Economic Problem   25

Issue I-3   Is There a New Breed of People on the Mainland? China Today   **38**

3   Some Economic Tools: Demand, Supply, and Elasticity   43

Issue I-4   Illegal Activities: Prohibition in Retrospect   **64**

UNIT TWO

THE AMERICAN ECONOMY AND ITS PROBLEMS   **71**

4   Measuring the Economy's Performance: National Income and Product   73

Issue I-5   Does GNP Mean Gross National Promise? Are We Measuring the Wrong Thing?   **86**

Biography   JAMES TOBIN—Economic Growth and Income Redistribution   92

5   Government Spending and Taxation   94

Biography   ARTHUR OKUN—Young Man at the End of an Era   110

Issue I-6   What Are Our National Priorities? How Should Public Funds Be Used?   **112**

Biography   OTTO ECKSTEIN—Fiscal Policy and Trend Analysis   118

Issue I-7   The Rape of the Taxpayer: What Do Loopholes Cost the American Taxpayer?   **120**

6   Changing Business Conditions and Unemployment   126

Issue I-8	Does Unemployment Compensation Cause Unemployment? Does Our System Have a Built-In Incentive for Not Working?	**142**
7	Inflation and Stagflation	147
Issue I-9	Would Indexing Help Fight Inflation? The Use of Economywide Escalator Clauses	**163**
Issue I-10	Can Wage and Price Controls Work? Direct Attempts at Combating Inflation	**168**

UNIT THREE

INCOME AND EMPLOYMENT DETERMINATION MODELS 175

8	Consumption, Saving, and Investment	177
9	Income and Employment Determination	198
Biography	JOHN MAYNARD KEYNES—The Spirit of His Age	**214**
B	The Acceleration Principle and the Interaction between the Accelerator and the Multiplier	**216**
10	Fiscal Policy	219
Biography	WALTER HELLER—The Economic New Frontiersman	**231**
Issue I-11	Direct Fiscal Fine Tuning: Public Service Employment Programs	**233**
Biography	PAUL A. SAMUELSON—Economics in the Public Mind	**236**
Issue I-12	Is There a Burden of the Public Debt? The Long-Run Effects of Deficit Financing	**238**
11	Money and the Banking System	244
Biography	ARTHUR BURNS—Doctor of High Finance	**263**
Issue I-13	Should Commercial Banks Be Subsidized? Borrowing from the Federal Reserve	**265**
12	Money in a Keynesian Model	270
13	The Role of Money: Other Views	284
Biography	MILTON FRIEDMAN—The Iconoclast As Institution	**294**
Issue I-14	Is Short-Run Stabilization Possible? Policymakers' Problems	**296**

UNIT FOUR

THE INTERNATIONAL SCENE 303

14	Benefiting from Trade among Nations	305
Issue I-15	Does International Competition Pose a Threat? The Question of Job Protection	**320**
15	Financing World Trade	326

Issue I-16   Can Flexible Exchange Rates Halt Worldwide Inflation? The Changing World of International Finance   **345**

UNIT FIVE

MARKETS, THE FIRM, AND RESOURCE ALLOCATION   **351**

16	Demand and Consumer Choice	353
C	Looking at Consumer Choice with Graphs	361
Issue I-17	Why Was the Onions Futures Market Abolished? The Nature of Speculation	367
17	Analyzing the Costs of a Business	372
18	The Firm in Competition	387
Issue I-18	The Perpetual Investment Fraud: On Not Getting Rich Quick	407
Issue I-19	The Changing Agricultural Sector: Will the Past Be Seen Again?	416
19	Monopoly Management	424
Biography	JOAN ROBINSON—Heretic to the Orthodox	440
Issue I-20	Medical Care for All: Theory and Practice	442
Issue I-21	On Forming an International Monopoly: Can Economic Warfare Be Successful?	452
20	Regulating the Big Ones	458
Biography	PHILIP A. HART—Senate Voice for the Consumer	475
Issue I-22	Is the Post Office a Natural Monopoly? Competition Rears Its Ugly Head	477
Issue I-23	Consumerism: Are Consumer Protection Laws Justifiable?	482
Biography	RALPH NADER—The Fifth Branch of Government	488
21	In between Monopoly and Competition	490
Issue I-24	Should Large Corporations Be Broken Up? The Question of Economic Power	499
Biography	JOHN KENNETH GALBRAITH—Economic Statesman	504
Issue I-25	Should the Corporate Structure Be Changed? How the "Planning" Sector Affects Our Lives	506

UNIT SIX

DERIVED DEMAND AND INCOME DISTRIBUTION   **509**

22	Aspects of the Labor Market	511
Biography	GEORGE MEANY—Lobbyist for the Organized	525

Issue I-26   Sexism in the Labor Market: Employers' and Customers'
             Sexual Discrimination   527
        23   The Decision to Hire and Fire   534
Issue I-27   Crime and Punishment: The Economics of Criminal Deterrence   553
Issue I-28   Athletic Slavery: Monopoly and Monopsony in Sports   561
        24   Wealth, Capital, and Savings   568
Issue I-29   Restrictions on Rates of Return: Usury Laws and Selective
             Credit Controls   578
        25   The Distribution of Income   586
Issue I-30   Poverty and the Poor: Finding Alternatives to Welfare   602
Biography   GUNNAR MYRDAL—Economics As a Moral Issue   611

UNIT SEVEN

ECOLOGY, POLITICS, AND GROWTH   613

        26   Social Costs and the Ecology   615
Issue I-31   Who Gets the Ocean's Wealth? The Common Heritage of
             All Nations   626
Issue I-32   Conservation and Energy: How Should We Utilize Our Resources? 631
        27   Politics and Public Choice   638
Biography   KENNETH J. ARROW—The Mathematics of Uncertainty   646
Issue I-33   Should Political Campaigns Be Publicly Financed? On Preventing
             Future Watergates   648
        28   Population Economics   653
Issue I-34   Was Malthus Right? The Exploding Population   664
        29   Development of the Less-Developed Countries   671
Biography   BARBARA WARD—The Economist As Evangelist   678
Issue I-35   Can Foreign Aid Help Less-Developed Countries? Can
             Development Assistance Work?   680
        30   Economic Growth   686
Issue I-36   Should Growth Be Stopped? What Does the Future Hold?   696

Detailed Contents

UNIT ONE

GETTING STARTED   1

Issue I-1   The Scarcity Society: Are We Running Out of Everything?   3

Can We Preserve Our Way of Life?   3   *The Shortage Society*   3
The Energy Shortage That Started It All   3   *The Impending Food
Crisis*   3   *Our Dwindling Mineral Resources*   4   *Some Proposed
Solutions to Shortages*   5   *The Other Side of the Story*   5
Another View of Energy Shortages   6   *World Mineral
Supplies*   6   *Who Is Right?*   7

DEFINITIONS OF NEW TERMS   7   SELECTED REFERENCES   7

1   What Economics Is All About   8

Scarcity, Economic Goods, and Free Goods   8   *Exchange
and Choice*   9   *Voluntary and Involuntary Exchanges*   9
Markets—Where Exchanges Take Place   10   *Exchanges and
Specialization*   10   *A Simple Example of Specialization*   11
Comparative Advantages   12   *Opportunity Costs*   13
Economics As a Science   14   *Assumptions*   14   *The Role of
Assumptions*   14   *The Complexity of the World*   16

DEFINITIONS OF NEW TERMS   16   CHAPTER SUMMARY   17
QUESTIONS FOR THOUGHT AND DISCUSSION   17
SELECTED REFERENCES   17

A   **Reading and Working with Graphs**   **18**

A Basic Graph   18   *The Numbers on the Axes*   19

Issue I-2   **Does Money Mean Happiness? How Important Is Material Well-Being?**   **23**

The Difficulty of Measuring Happiness   23   *An Opinion Poll*   23   *Another Study Confirms*   23   Other Factors Affecting Happiness   23   Comfort to the Economist   24

QUESTIONS FOR THOUGHT AND DISCUSSION   24

2   **How Different Systems Solve the Economic Problem**   **25**

Society's Choices   25   *The Numbers*   26   *Putting the Numbers onto a Graph*   26   *Inefficiency and Underemployment*   26 Why the Production-Possibilities Frontier Is Bowed Outward (the Law of Diminishing Returns)   26   What Is an Economic System?   29   Alternative Economic Systems   29   Capitalism in Theory   30   *Difference between Capital and Capitalism*   30 *Private Property*   31   *Free Enterprise*   31   *The Price System*   31   *The Role of Government*   32   American Capitalism   32   *Restrictions in the American System*   32 *Competition and Capitalism*   32   Socialism in Theory   33 *Socialism As a Movement*   33   *Economics—the Core of Socialism*   33   *Key Attributes*   33   Russia Today   34 *Resource Allocation*   34   *The Problem of Coordination*   35 The Economic Problem Is Universal   35

DEFINITIONS OF NEW TERMS   36   CHAPTER SUMMARY   36 QUESTIONS FOR THOUGHT AND DISCUSSION   37 SELECTED REFERENCES   37

Issue I-3   **Is There a New Breed of People on the Mainland? China Today**   **38**

The Early System under Mao   38   *Maoist Economics*   38   *The Planning Operation*   38   The New Policy   38   Growth in the Chinese Economy   38   Goals of the New Men and Women   39 *Serving the Proletariat*   40   *Deemphasizing Careers*   41 *Keeping the Experiment Alive*   41

QUESTIONS FOR THOUGHT AND DISCUSSION   42 SELECTED REFERENCES   42

3   **Some Economic Tools: Demand, Supply, and Elasticity**   **43**

PART A: DEMAND AND SUPPLY   43   The Law of Demand   43
The Law in Words   44   *The Law in Numbers*   44   *The Law in Graphic Terms*   45   The Law of Supply   45   *The Law in Words*   47   *The Law in Numbers*   47   *The Law in Graphic Terms*   47   Putting Demand and Supply Together   47   *Supply and Demand in One Graph*   49   Movements Along the Curve   50   *Shifting the Curves*   50
PART B: ELASTICITY   53   Price Responsiveness   53   Price Elasticity of Demand   53   *Different Kinds of Elasticities*   54   *Extreme Elasticities*   55   Price Elasticity of Supply   56   Elasticity and Slope   57   The Long and the Short of Elasticities   57   *Demand*   58   *Supply*   59

DEFINITIONS OF NEW TERMS   60   CHAPTER SUMMARY   61
QUESTIONS FOR THOUGHT AND DISCUSSION   62
SELECTED REFERENCES   63

Issue I-4   **Illegal Activities: Prohibition in Retrospect**   **64**

Applying Supply and Demand   64   Alcohol Prohibition   64
From the Supply Side   64   *From the Demand Side*   65   *The Final Outcome*   67   A Graphic Analysis   68   The Case of Completely Inelastic Demand   68   Was Society Better Off after January 16, 1920?   68

QUESTIONS FOR THOUGHT AND DISCUSSION   69
SELECTED REFERENCES   69

UNIT TWO

THE AMERICAN ECONOMY AND ITS PROBLEMS

71

4   **Measuring the Economy's Performance: National Income and Product**   **73**

National Income ≡ National Product   74   The Circular Flow of Income and Product   74   Gross National Product   75   Deriving GNP with the Expenditure Approach   75   *Government Expenditures*   76   *Gross Private Domestic Investment*   77   *The Foreign Sector*   77   Getting Rid of the Gross   77   GNP with the Income Approach   78   *Indirect Business Taxes*   79   *Depreciation*   79   The Rest of National

Income Accounting   80   National Income   80   Personal
Income   81   Disposable Personal Income   81   Correcting
GNP   81   Per Capita GNP   81

DEFINITIONS OF NEW TERMS   82   CHAPTER SUMMARY   84
QUESTIONS FOR THOUGHT AND DISCUSSION   84
SELECTED REFERENCES   85

Issue I-5   **Does GNP Mean Gross National Promise?**
Are We Measuring the Wrong Thing?   **86**

National Income Accounting and Human Happiness   86   More
Corrections for GNP   86   Do-It-Yourself Activities   86
Housewives' Services   86   Illegal Activities   87   Income
Never Reported   87   Measures of Satisfaction   87   Gross
National Pollution   88   MEW: A New Measure of GNP   89

QUESTIONS FOR THOUGHT AND DISCUSSION   91
SELECTED REFERENCES   91

Biography   **JAMES TOBIN—Economic Growth and Income Redistribution**   92

5   **Government Spending and Taxation**   **94**

The Economic Functions of Government   94   Providing Public
Goods   95   Regulating Economic Activity   95   Redistributing
Income   96   Stabilizing the Economy   96   Administering
Justice   96   The Growth of Government   97   The Components
of Government Expenditures   97   The Federal Budget   98
State and Local Expenditures   98   Taxation   99   Theories of
Taxation   100   Types of Taxes   100   Income Taxes   101
Personal Income Taxes   102   Progressive Taxation and Income
Distribution   103   The Corporate Income Tax   103   Not a
Tax on All Profits   105   Do Corporations Really Pay Their
Taxes?   105   Taxes on Wealth   105   Estate Taxes   106
Property Taxes   106   Taxes on Economic Activities   106
Unemployment and Social Security Taxes   106   Problems with
Spending and Collecting   107

DEFINITIONS OF NEW TERMS   107   CHAPTER SUMMARY   108
QUESTIONS FOR THOUGHT AND DISCUSSION   109
SELECTED REFERENCES   109

Biography   **ARTHUR OKUN—Young Man at the End of an Era**   110

Issue I-6 **What Are Our National Priorities?**
How Should Public Funds Be Used?   112

Government and the Problem of Scarcity   112   Setting National
Priorities   112   *Trends in Government Expenditures*   112
Declining Priorities   112   *Advancing Priorities*   113   Income
Redistribution   113   Defense Spending Declines   114   The
True Cost of the Military   114   Government Subsidies   116

QUESTIONS FOR THOUGHT AND DISCUSSION   116
SELECTED REFERENCE   117

Biography **OTTO ECKSTEIN—Fiscal Policy and Trend Analysis**   118

Issue I-7 **The Rape of the Taxpayer: What Do Loopholes**
Cost the American Taxpayer?   120

Taxes and Best Sellers   120   *Progressive Taxes and
Loopholes*   120   *Why Congress Legislates Loopholes*   120
Tax-Exempt Bonds   121   The Oil Game   122   *Oil Depletion
Allowance*   122   *Dry Holes*   123   *IDCs*   124   *Capital
Gains*   124   You Can Lose Money in Tax Shelters   124
Tax Shelters and Opportunity Costs   124   Other Costs of Tax
Shelters   125   An Alternative   125

DEFINITIONS OF NEW TERMS   125   QUESTIONS FOR THOUGHT AND
DISCUSSION   125   SELECTED REFERENCES   125

6 **Changing Business Conditions and Unemployment**   126

The Business Cycle and Business Activity in the United
States   126   *Phases in the Business Cycle*   127   *Indicators of
Business Activity*   127   Earlier Business-Cycle Theories   130
The Sunspot Theory   130   *The Innovation Theory*   130   *The
Psychological Theory*   131   Marx's Theory of the Business
Cycle   131   *Economic Crises*   131   *Business Cycles*   131
Unemployment   132   *How Is It Measured?*   132   *Voluntary
Unemployment*   133   *The Business Cycle and the Duration of
Unemployment*   134   *Hidden Unemployment*   135   The Major
Types of Unemployment   137   *Frictional Unemployment*   137
Cyclical Unemployment   137   *Seasonal Unemployment*   137
Structural Unemployment   138   Reducing the Suffering   139

DEFINITIONS OF NEW TERMS   139   CHAPTER SUMMARY   140
QUESTIONS FOR THOUGHT AND DISCUSSION   141
SELECTED REFERENCES   141

**Issue I-8   Does Unemployment Compensation Cause Unemployment?
Does Our System Have a Built-In Incentive for Not Working?   142**

Helping Out the Jobless   142   The Low Opportunity Cost of Not
Working   142   The Benefits of Unemployment   143   *The
Effective Marginal Tax Rate   144   Inverse Seniority   144*
Seasonal Unemployment   144   The New Unemployment   145

QUESTIONS FOR THOUGHT AND DISCUSSION   146
SELECTED REFERENCES   146

7   **Inflation and Stagflation**   147

Inflation and the History of Prices   147   *Inflation in Other
Countries   148   How We Measure Inflation   149*   Real-World
Price Indices   150   *Consumer Price Index   150   Wholesale
Price Index   151   Implicit Price Deflator   152   The
Accuracy of Price Indices   152*   Theories of Inflation   152
*Quantity Theory of Money and Prices   152   Demand-Pull
Inflation   153   Cost-Push Inflation   153*   Who Bears the Bur-
den of Inflation?   154   *Creditors and Debtors   154   Wage
Earners   155*   Inflation and the Poor   155   *How Inflation Af-
fects Fixed Incomes   155   The Poor Man's Price Index   156*
National Income and Inflation   156   Unemployment and In-
flation   157   *The Phillips Curve   157   The Trade-Off   158
Unemployment and Inflation Added Together   159   Stagflation   159*   The Use of Models in Policymaking   160

DEFINITIONS OF NEW TERMS   160   CHAPTER SUMMARY   161
QUESTIONS FOR THOUGHT AND DISCUSSION   162
SELECTED REFERENCES   162

**Issue I-9   Would Indexing Help Fight Inflation? The Use of Economywide
Escalator Clauses   163**

Contracts That Take Account of Inflation   163   *Escalator Clauses
Today   163   A Short History of Escalator Clauses   163*
Brazil—A Case Study of Indexing   164   Indexing in the United
States   165   *Indexing Taxes   165   Government Bonds   165
The Private Sector   166*   The Pros and Cons of Indexing   166
Will We Have More Indexing?   167

QUESTIONS FOR THOUGHT AND DISCUSSION   167
SELECTED REFERENCES   167

**Issue I-10 Can Wage and Price Controls Work? Direct Attempts
at Combating Inflation**   **168**

The Past As the Future   168   *Controls in Times Past*   168
Controls in America during World War II   168   Controls in Other
Countries   170   *The Netherlands*   170   *The Rest of Western
Europe*   171   The American Experience   171   *Guide-
posts*   171   *Jawboning*   172   Controlling Prices and Wages in
the 1970s   172   *The Nitty-Gritty*   172   *Why Controls?*   172
The Expectations Argument   173

DEFINITIONS OF NEW TERMS   174   QUESTIONS FOR THOUGHT AND
DISCUSSION   174   SELECTED REFERENCES   174

INCOME AND EMPLOYMENT DETERMINATION MODELS   175

8   Consumption, Saving, and Investment   **177**

Definitions and Relationships   177   *The Difference between
Stocks and Flows*   178   *Relating Income to Saving and
Consumption*   178   *Investment*   178   *Who Does the Saving
and Investing?*   178   The Circular Flow with Saving and
Investment   179   The Classical Theory and Mr. Say   179
Determinants of Consumption and Saving   180   *Graphing the
Numbers*   182   *Dissaving and Autonomous Consumption*   182
Average Propensity to Consume and to Save   182   *Marginal
Propensity to Consume and to Save*   184   *Some Relation-
ships*   184   *Distinguishing between a Movement and a Shift*   184
The Historical Record   186   Short- vs. Long-Run Consumption
Functions   187   *Other Determinants of Consumption*   188
Liquid Assets   188   *Expectations*   189   Determinants of
Investments   189   *The Planned Investment Function*   190   *The
Elasticity of the Demand for Investment*   190   *Other Determinants
of Investment*   190   *Expectations*   191   *Cost of New Capital
Goods*   191   *Innovation and Technology*   191   *Business
Taxes*   191   The Equality of Saving and Investment   192

DEFINITIONS OF NEW TERMS   194   CHAPTER SUMMARY   195
QUESTIONS FOR THOUGHT AND DISCUSSION   197
SELECTED REFERENCES   197

9   **Income and Employment Determination**   **198**

Aggregate Demand   198   Aggregate Supply   200   Finding
Equilibrium   201   *What About Employment?*   202   *What
Happens When We Are Out of Equilibrium?*   202   Looking at
Saving and Investment   203   The Multiplier   205   *The
Multiplier in Graphical Terms*   206   *The Multiplier Form-
ula*   206   The Effects of More Saving   207   The Paradox of
Thrift   209   Inflationary and Deflationary Gaps   209

DEFINITIONS OF NEW TERMS   211   CHAPTER SUMMARY   211
QUESTIONS FOR THOUGHT AND DISCUSSION   212
SELECTED REFERENCES   213

Biography   **JOHN MAYNARD KEYNES—The Spirit of His Age**   214

B   **The Acceleration Principle and the Interaction between the
Accelerator and the Multiplier**   **216**

The Acceleration Principle   216   The Interaction between the
Accelerator and the Multiplier   218

10   **Fiscal Policy**   **219**

Adding the Government Sector   219   *Adding Government
Purchases to Aggregate Demand*   219   *Filling the Deflationary
Gap*   221   *Reducing the Inflationary Gap*   222   The Effects of
Changing Taxes   222   The Balanced-Budget Multiplier   223
Fiscal Policy   224   *Discretionary Fiscal Policy*   224   *Auto-
matic Fiscal Policy*   225   Fiscal Policy and a Full-Employment
Budget   226   Fiscal Policy and the Budget   226

DEFINITIONS OF NEW TERMS   228   CHAPTER SUMMARY   228
QUESTIONS FOR THOUGHT AND DISCUSSION   229
SELECTED REFERENCES   230

Biography   **WALTER W. HELLER—The Economic New Frontiersman**   231

Issue I-11   **Direct Fiscal Fine Tuning: Public Service Employment Programs**   **233**

Traditional vs. Nontraditional Fiscal Policy   233   The Position in
Favor of PSE   233   Why PSE Is So Popular   233   The Problem of Federal Fund Usage   233   The Multiplier at Work   234
Do the Disadvantaged Get Help?   234   PSE and Fiscal Policy in
the Future   235

QUESTIONS FOR THOUGHT AND DISCUSSION   235
SELECTED REFERENCES   235

Biography   **PAUL A. SAMUELSON—Economics in the Public Mind**   236

Issue I-12   **Is There a Burden of the Public Debt? The Long-Run Effects of Deficit Financing**   238

Operating in the Red   238   Growth of Public Debt   238   Gross and Net Debt   238   How Do We Measure the Burden?   238   *Changes in Capital Stocks*   239   *Alternatives to Debt*   239   Taxation vs. Borrowing   240   Borrowing from Abroad   240   How Big Is the Interest Payment on the National Debt?   240   Redistribution of Income   240   Conclusions   241

DEFINITIONS OF NEW TERMS   243   QUESTIONS FOR THOUGHT AND DISCUSSION   243   SELECTED REFERENCES   243

11   **Money and the Banking System**   244

Types of Monetary Standards   244   The Functions of Money   245   *Money As a Medium of Exchange*   245   *Money As a Unit of Accounting*   245   *Money As a Store of Value*   245   The Distinction between Money and Credit   246   Defining the Money Supply   246   The Federal Reserve System   248   *Organization of the Federal Reserve System*   248   *Member Banks*   248   *Reserves*   249   *Assets and Liabilities*   249   *Excess Reserves*   249   The Supply of Money   251   *Federal Open Market Committee*   251   *The Relationship between Reserves and Total Deposits*   251   *The Money Supply Expands*   253   *The Expansion Multiplier*   255   The Tools of Monetary Policy   256   *Open-Market Operatives*   256   *Member-Bank Borrowing and the Discount Rate*   257   *Reserve Requirement Changes*   258   The Dynamics of Monetary Policy   259

DEFINITIONS OF NEW TERMS   260   CHAPTER SUMMARY   260   QUESTIONS FOR THOUGHT AND DISCUSSION   261   SELECTED REFERENCES   262

Biography   **ARTHUR BURNS—Doctor of High Finance**   263

Issue I-13   **Should Commercial Banks Be Subsidized? Borrowing from the Federal Reserve**

Looking at the Discount Rate from a Different Perspective   265   *The Subsidy Aspect of the Discount Window Operations*   265

A Case History of Subsidization   266   Protecting the Banking System   267   The Federal Deposit Insurance Corporation   268 The Pros and Cons Summarized   269

QUESTIONS FOR THOUGHT AND DISCUSSION   269
SELECTED REFERENCE   269

12   **Money in a Keynesian Model**   **270**

The Demand for Money or Cash   270   *Transactions Demand for Money*   270   *Precautionary Demand for Money*   271   *The Speculative Demand for Money*   271   Interest Rates—An Introduction   271   Interest Rates and Bond Prices   271   The Demand for Money and the Interest Rate   272   Adding the Money Supply   274   *Excess Supply*   274   *Excess Demand*   274   Completing the Keynesian Model   275   Transmitting Monetary Policy   275   Closing the Inflationary Gap   278   The Transmission Mechanism   278   When Monetary Policy Doesn't Work   279   Other Views on the Subject   280

DEFINITIONS OF NEW TERMS   281   CHAPTER SUMMARY   281
QUESTIONS FOR THOUGHT AND DISCUSSION   282
SELECTED REFERENCES   282

13   **The Role of Money: Other Views**   **284**

Stressing the Transactions Demand for Money   284   The Transmission Mechanism   285   The Monetarists' Explanation of an Inflationary Recession   285   *Expectations*   287   *Resulting Unemployment*   288   The Phillips Curve   288   The Importance of Expectations   288   *Full Anticipation*   289   *Short-Run Effects*   290   *Graphic Analysis*   290

DEFINITION OF NEW TERM   292   CHAPTER SUMMARY   292
QUESTIONS FOR THOUGHT AND DISCUSSION   293
SELECTED REFERENCES   293

Biography   **MILTON FRIEDMAN—The Iconoclast As Institution**   294

Issue I-14   **Is Short-Run Stabilization Possible? Policymakers' Problems**   **296**

Keeping the Economy on an Even Keel   296   How Do We Define Full Employment?   297   Deciding What to Do   297   Time Lags for Short-Run Policies   298   *The Information*

Time Lag   298   *The Action Time Lag*   298   *The Effect Time Lag*   298   Taking Lags into Account   298 Coordination   299   Policymaking and the Public   300 The Final Word   301

DEFINITION OF NEW TERM   302   QUESTIONS FOR THOUGHT AND DISCUSSION   302   SELECTED REFERENCES   302

UNIT FOUR

THE INTERNATIONAL SCENE
303

14   **Benefiting from Trade among Nations**   **305**

Putting Trade in Its Place   305   *If Foreign Trade Stopped*   306   Exports   306   *Voluntary Trade*   307   Demand and Supply of Imports and Exports   307   *Imports*   307 *Exports*   308   The Quantity of Trade in a Foreign Country   309 International Equilibrium (in a Two-Country World)   310   The Gains from Trade   311   *Comparative and Absolute Advantage*   312   *Finding One's Comparative Advantages*   313 Comparative Advantage and Opportunity Cost   314   *Differing Resource Mixes*   314   *Advantageous Trade Will Always Exist*   314   *Costs of Trade*   315   *Japanese Miracle*   315 Arguments against Free Trade   315   *Infant Industry Argument*   315   *National Security*   316   *Stability*   316   *Protecting American Jobs*   317

DEFINITIONS OF NEW TERMS   317   CHAPTER SUMMARY   317 QUESTIONS FOR THOUGHT AND DISCUSSION   319 SELECTED REFERENCES   319

Issue I-15   **Does International Competition Pose a Threat? The Question of Job Protection**   **320**

The Tenets of Protectionism   320   Getting Hurt from Free Trade   320   How We Pay for Imports   321   How Trade Can Be Handled   321   *Quotas*   321   *Tariffs*   323   What the Future Holds   324

QUESTIONS FOR THOUGHT AND DISCUSSION   325 SELECTED REFERENCES   325

15 Financing World Trade   **326**

Flexible Exchange Rates   326   Equilibrium Foreign Exchange
Rate   327   *Demand Schedule of Francs*   327   *Supply Schedule
of Francs*   329   *Equilibrium*   329   *A Shift in Demand*   329
Constant and Floating Exchange Rate   329   *Balance of Pay-
ments*   332   *How We Measure the Balance of Payments*   332
The United States Deficit   333   The Hypothetical Pure Gold
Standard   333   *Inflation in France*   333   *Rise in American
Prices*   334   *Fall in French Prices*   334   *Real-Income Adjust-
ment Mechanism*   334   *Pure Gold Standard in Theory*   335
Monetary Policies Come into Play   335   *A Recap*   336   Cur-
rency Crisis   337   *Internal Policies*   337   *Devaluation*   338
Financial Assets   338   The Multiplier   339   *Sectoral
Effects*   339

DEFINITIONS OF NEW TERMS   340   CHAPTER SUMMARY   341
QUESTIONS FOR THOUGHT AND DISCUSSION   344
SELECTED REFERENCES   344

**Issue I-16   Can Flexible Exchange Rates Halt Worldwide Inflation?
The Changing World of International Finance**   **345**

Inflation—A Worldwide Problem   345   The International Mone-
tary Fund   345   *Lord Keynes—Head of British Delegation*   345
Harry White—Head of American Delegation   346   *The IMF
Quota System*   346   *Marshall Plan*   346   The United States
Develops a Deficit   346   *Dwindling Gold Stock*   346   *A
Two-Tiered Gold System*   347   *A Rise in the Official Price of
Gold*   347   Exchange Rates and Monetary Policy   348   The
United States Experience   349   Floating Exchange Rates and
Oil Prices   350

DEFINITIONS OF NEW TERMS   350   QUESTIONS FOR THOUGHT AND
DISCUSSION   350   SELECTED REFERENCES   350

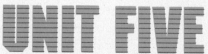

MARKETS, THE FIRM, AND RESOURCE ALLOCATION   351

16   Demand and Consumer Choice   **353**

Utility Theory   353   *The Law of Diminishing Marginal
Utility*   354   Reaching Equilibrium   355   Equilibrium and

Price Change   356   The Demand Curve Revisited   357   Using
Marginal Utility Analysis to Explain the Diamond-Water
Paradox   358   *The Supply*   359   *Total vs. Marginal
Utility*   359

DEFINITIONS OF NEW TERMS   359   CHAPTER SUMMARY   359
QUESTIONS FOR THOUGHT AND DISCUSSION   360
SELECTED REFERENCES   360

C   **Looking at Consumer Choice with Graphs**   361

On Being Indifferent   361   *The Shape of the Indifference
Curve*   362   *The Marginal Rate of Substitution*   363   The
Indifference Map   363   The Budget Constant   364   Consumer
Equilibrium Revisited   365   Income and Substitution
Effects   366

Issue I-17   **Why Was the Onions Futures Market Abolished?
The Nature of Speculation**   367

Onions and the Future   367   Commodities Today and in the
Future   367   Speculation and Total Utility   368   Maximizing
Total Utility   369   Speculation and Price Stability   370
Banning Futures Trading   371

DEFINITIONS OF NEW TERMS   371   QUESTIONS FOR THOUGHT AND
DISCUSSION   371   SELECTED REFERENCES   371

17   **Analyzing the Costs of a Business**   372

Defining a Business   372   *Corporations*   373   *Partnerships*
373   *Proprietorships*   373   The Firm   373   Profit   373   *Oppor-
tunity Cost of Capital*   374   *Forgetting the Opportunity Cost of
Certain Other Inputs*   374   *Accounting Profits ≠ Economic Prof-
its*   374   The Relationship between Output and Inputs   375
Diminishing Returns   375   *Measuring Diminishing Returns*
377   *An Example*   377   Short-Run Firm Costs   378   *Total Fixed
Costs*   378   *Total Variable Costs*   379   *Short-Run Average Cost
Curves*   379   *Marginal Cost*   381   *The Relationship between
Average and Marginal Costs*   382   *Finding Minimum Costs*   382

DEFINITIONS OF NEW TERMS   383   CHAPTER SUMMARY   384
QUESTIONS FOR THOUGHT AND DISCUSSION   385
SELECTED REFERENCES   386

18 **The Firm in Competition** 387

Characteristics of a Competitive Firm 387 Single-Firm Demand Curve 388 How Much Does the Perfect Competitor Produce? 389 *Total Revenues* 389 *Total Costs* 389 *Comparing Total Costs with Total Revenues* 389 Using Marginal Analysis 392 *Marginal Revenue* 392 *When Profits Are Maximized* 392 Finding the Firm's Short-Run Profits 393 The Break-Even Point 393 *The Meaning of Zero Economic Profits* 393 *Average Costs and Profits in the Long Run* 395 Distinguishing between the Short and the Long Run 396 The Shutdown Point 397 The Firm's Supply Curve 398 The Industry Supply Curve 398 Competitive Price Determination 399 The Long and the Short of a Competitive Supply Curve 399 Why Economists Are Fascinated with the Competitive Solution 399 Is Perfect Competition Possible? 401

DEFINITION OF NEW TERMS 403 CHAPTER SUMMARY 403 QUESTIONS FOR THOUGHT AND DISCUSSION 405 SELECTED REFERENCES 406

Issue I-18 **The Perpetual Investment Fraud: On Not Getting Rich Quick** 407

A Truly Competitive Market Situation 407 Making Money 407 Getting Advice on the Market 407 Some Facts on the Stock Market 408 Capital Gains and Losses 408 What Affects the Price of a Stock? 408 *Public Information* 409 *Inside Information* 409 *Capitalization* 409 Hot Tips 410 Why So Much "Research"? 410 The Random Walk 411 Charting the Future 411 What about Investment Plans? 412 Is There No Way to Get Rich Quick? 412 A Sure-Fire Scheme 414

DEFINITIONS OF NEW TERMS 415 QUESTIONS FOR THOUGHT AND DISCUSSION 415 SELECTED REFERENCES 415

Issue I-19 **The Changing Agricultural Sector: Will the Past Be Seen Again?** 416

The Farming Sector 416 Poor Farmers 416 The Growth in Demand for Farm Products 416 Low Price Elasticity of Demand 417 History of the Farmer's Dilemma 418 Price Supports 420 *How Can Supports Last?* 420 *Who Benefits from Price Supports?* 421 *Tobacco* 421 Moving

into an Era of No Surpluses   422   *Target Prices*   422
Graphically Speaking   422

DEFINITIONS OF NEW TERMS   423   QUESTIONS FOR THOUGHT AND
DISCUSSION   423   SELECTED REFERENCES   423

19   **Monopoly Management**   **424**

Definition of a Monopolist   424   *Monopolist's Demand
Curve*   424   *Some Examples of Monopolies*   425   On Becom-
ing a Monopolist   425   *Barriers to Entry*   425   *Economies of
Scale*   426   The Profit to Be Made from Increasing Pro-
duction   426   *Competitor's Marginal Revenue*   427
Monopolist's Marginal Revenue   427   *Marginal Revenues from
Marijuana*   428   Output and Price Determination for the
Monopolist   428   Marginal Revenue and Elasticity   430
Adding the Cost Curves   430   Figuring Out Profits   433   The
Cost to Society of a Monopoly   433   Can a Monopolist Make
Even More Money?   435

DEFINITIONS OF NEW TERMS   436   CHAPTER SUMMARY   437
QUESTIONS FOR THOUGHT AND DISCUSSION   438
SELECTED REFERENCES   439

Biography   **JOAN ROBINSON—Heretic to the Orthodox**   440

Issue I-20   **Medical Care for All: Theory and Practice**   **442**

Rising Costs of Medical Care   442   Medical Care Expendi-
tures   442   The Supply of Medical Care   443   *The
Production of Medical Doctors*   443   *Restrictions*   443
The Past   445   Why Did the AMA Seek Control?   446
AMA's Motives Not Satisfied   446   Jumps in Demand—
Medicare   447   *Price Discrimination*   447   *Graphic
Analysis*   448   Fighting the Group Health Plans   448
National Health Insurance   449   The Real Problem   450

QUESTIONS FOR THOUGHT AND DISCUSSION   451
SELECTED REFERENCES   451

Issue I-21   **On Forming an International Monopoly: Can Economic
Warfare Be Successful?**   **452**

Joining Together to Make More Profits   452   International
Commodity Cartels   452   *A History of OPEC*   452   *The Yom*

Kippur War   452   *Other Cartels Formed*   453   On Making a Successful Cartel   453   Assessing the Chances of a Cartel's Success   454   *The Desire to Cheat*   455   *Political Problems*   455   The Prospects for the Future   456

DEFINITIONS OF NEW TERMS   457   QUESTIONS FOR THOUGHT AND DISCUSSION   457   SELECTED REFERENCES   457

20   **Regulating the Big Ones**   **458**

One Way for a Monopoly to Arise   458   Regulating the Natural Monopolist   460   *Subsidization*   461   *Price Discrimination*   461   Methods of Regulating Monopolies   462   *Cost of Service*   462   *Controlling the Rate of Return on Investment*   463   *Problems with Inflation*   464   Quality of Service   464   Regulating Prices—the Case of the Airlines   465   *Nonprice Competition*   465   *Timing of Flights*   465   Antitrust Policy   466   *The Sherman Act*   467   *The Clayton Act*   467   *The Robinson-Patman Act*   468   *The Miller-Tydings Act*   469   *Other Exemption Laws*   469   The Enforcement of Antitrust Laws   470   When to Prosecute?   470

DEFINITIONS OF NEW TERMS   471   CHAPTER SUMMARY   472   QUESTIONS FOR THOUGHT AND DISCUSSION   473   SELECTED REFERENCES   473

Biography   **PHILIP A. HART—Senate Voice for the Consumer**   475

Issue I-22   **Is the Post Office a Natural Monopoly? Competition Rears Its Ugly Head**   **477**

The Postal Service Comes under Fire   477   History of Postal Service   477   *Private Express Statutes*   477   *Creation of the U.S. Postal Service*   477   The Natural Monopoly Argument   478   *Cream Skimming*   478   *Price Discrimination*   479   *Cream Skimming Already Exists*   479   What the Future Might Hold   480

DEFINITION OF NEW TERM   481   QUESTIONS FOR THOUGHT AND DISCUSSION   481   SELECTED REFERENCES   481

Issue I-23   **Consumerism: Are Consumer Protection Laws Justifiable?**   **482**

Straight Economics   482   The Need for Protection   482   The Case of the Fat Wienie   483   *Economic Analysis*   483

Marginal Analysis 484 *Truth in Labeling* 485 *Unsafe at Any Speed* 485 *Changing Quality* 485 *Commission on Product Safety* 485 *Costs and Benefits of Safety* 486 *Safety May Decline* 486

DEFINITIONS OF NEW TERMS 487 QUESTIONS FOR THOUGHT AND DISCUSSION 487 SELECTED REFERENCES 487

Biography **RALPH NADER—The Fifth Branch of Government** 488

21 **In between Monopoly and Competition** **490**

Monopolistic Competition 490 *Assumptions* 491 *Zero Profits* 491 *How Has Chamberlin's Theory Fared?* 491 *Advertising—a Way of Differentiating the Product* 491 *Arguments against Advertising* 493 Oligopoly 495 *Oligopoly vs. Pure Forms of Market Structure* 495 *Characteristics of Oligopolies* 497

DEFINITIONS OF NEW TERMS 497 CHAPTER SUMMARY 497 QUESTIONS 498 SELECTED REFERENCES 498

Issue I-24 **Should Large Corporations Be Broken Up? The Question of Economic Power** **499**

Oligopolies on the Run 499 Power and Concentration 499 *Concentration Ratios* 499 *The Meaning of Economic Power* 500 Wasted Efforts 501 The Question of Legislation 502 Finally—Looking at Costs and Benefits 503

QUESTIONS FOR THOUGHT AND DISCUSSION 503 SELECTED REFERENCES 503

Biography **JOHN KENNETH GALBRAITH—Economic Statesman** 504

Issue I-25 **Should the Corporate Structure Be Changed? How the "Planning" Sector Affects Our Lives** **506**

The Galbraithian System 506 *The Traditional Market System* 506 *The Planning System* 506 *The Technostructure* 507 Restructuring the Corporation 507 A Sweeping Change 508

DEFINITIONS OF NEW TERMS 508 QUESTIONS FOR THOUGHT AND DISCUSSION 508 SELECTED REFERENCES 508

UNIT SIX

DERIVED DEMAND AND INCOME DISTRIBUTION   509

22   Aspects of the Labor Market   **511**

Union Power and the Labor Movement   511   *American Labor
Movement   512   The Great Depression   513   The Wagner
Act—Labor's Magna Carta   513   The Congress of Industrial
Organizations   514   The Taft-Hartley Act   514   The Merging
of the Two Federations   514*   What Do Unions Attempt to
Do?   515   Demand Curve for Labor   515   The Supply of
Labor   516   Putting Demand and Supply Together   518
Limiting Entry   519   What Do Unions Maximize?   519   Has
the Labor Movement Helped Workers?   520   Problems in the
Labor Market   520   Seeking Highest Valued Employment   521

DEFINITIONS OF NEW TERMS   522   CHAPTER SUMMARY   523
QUESTIONS FOR THOUGHT AND DISCUSSION   524
SELECTED REFERENCES   524

Biography   **GEORGE MEANY—Lobbyist for the Organized**   525

**Issue I-26   Sexism in the Labor Market: Employers' and Customers'
Sexual Discrimination**   **527**

Women's Wages   527   Tastes for Discrimination   527   Other
Explanations for Male-Female Wage Differences   527   *Employer
As Chief Sexist   527   Customer Discrimination   528   Marital
Status and Age   530*   Role Differentiation   531   The Effects of
Legislation   532

DEFINITIONS OF NEW TERMS   533   QUESTIONS FOR THOUGHT AND
DISCUSSION   533   SELECTED REFERENCES   533

23   The Decision to Hire and Fire   **534**

A Competitive Market   535   Constant Factor Costs   535
*Marginal Physical Product   535   Value of Marginal Prod-
uct   535   Rule for Hiring   536   Denied Demand   536*
Input Demand Curve for All Firms Taken Together   537   Deter-
minants of Demand Elasticity for Inputs   541   Monopoly   542
Monopsony: A Buyer's Monopoly   544   *Marginal Factor*

Costs   544   *An Example*   544   The Monopsony Model and Minimum Wages   546   Bilateral Monopoly   548   *When There Are Other Factors of Production*   548   *Profit Maximization*   548   *Cost Minimization*   549

DEFINITIONS OF NEW TERMS   550   CHAPTER SUMMARY   550
QUESTIONS FOR THOUGHT AND DISCUSSION   551
SELECTED REFERENCES   552

Issue I-27   **Crime and Punishment: The Economics of Criminal Deterrence**   553

The Costs of Crime   553   Constraining the Chief of Police   553   *Eliminate Vice or Theft?*   555   The City Council   556   Deterring Crime   556   *Hard Drug Problems*   557   *Looking at the Margin*   557   Offensive Supplies   557   Increasing the Probability of Detection   557   The Courts   558   *No Compensation for the Innocent*   558   *Civil Suits*   558   The Victims   558   A Solution—Full Liability   559

QUESTIONS FOR THOUGHT AND DISCUSSION   560
SELECTED REFERENCES   560

Issue I-28   **Athletic Slavery: Monopoly and Monopsony in Sports**   561

"No Freedom, No Football"   561   Unrestricted Labor Market   561   *Coping with Excess Demand*   561   *Restricting the Market*   562   *Collusion*   562   The Baseball Market   562   *Reserve Clauses*   562   *Drafts*   562   *"Need" for Restrictions?*   562   Is the Distribution of Good Players Altered?   563   Monopsony and Monopoly   564   Graphic Analysis   564   Other Professional Sports   566   Conclusion   566

DEFINITIONS OF NEW TERMS   566   QUESTIONS FOR THOUGHT AND DISCUSSION   567   SELECTED REFERENCES   567

24   **Wealth, Capital, and Savings**   568

Concentration of Wealth   568   Wealth   569   How to Get Wealth   569   *Durable and Nondurable Goods*   570   *Saving*   570   *Net Worth*   570   Stocks and Flows   570   Present Values   571   Annuities   571   The Nature of Compound Interest   574   The Unkind Truth   576

DEFINITIONS OF NEW TERMS   576   CHAPTER SUMMARY   576
QUESTIONS FOR THOUGHT AND DISCUSSION   576

Issue I-29   **Restrictions on Rates of Return: Usury Laws and
Selective Credit Controls**   **578**

Savers and Borrowers Getting Together   578   Usury Laws   578
The Case of Washington State   578   *Supply and Demand
Analysis*   579   *Borrowing As a Form of Dissaving*   580   *Set-
ting the Maximum Rate below the Equilibrium Rate*   580   *The
Poor Lose Out Again*   580   *Who Benefits?*   580   The Lesson
to Be Learned   581   You Have to Pay to Get Money   581
Selective Credit Controls   582   *Graphic Analysis of Zero Interest
Rate for Checking Accounts*   582   *Competition in Bank-
ing*   583   *Destructive Competition*   584   *Housing Hunt*   584
Regulating Bank Credit   584

DEFINITIONS OF NEW TERMS   585   QUESTIONS FOR THOUGHT AND
DISCUSSION   585   SELECTED REFERENCES   585

25   **The Distribution of Income**   **586**

Income Distribution—Past and Present   586   Lorenz Curve   586
Measuring the Degree of Income Inequality   589   The Age-
Earnings Cycle   590   Marginal Productivity Theory   591
Process of Competition   591   *Full Adjustment Is Never Ob-
tained*   591   Earning Too Much   593   *Economic Rent Can-
not Be Eliminated*   593   *Joan Baez's "Peculiar" Habit*   593
Risk Factor   594   Exploitation and Discrimination   594
Exploitation   595   *Discrimination*   596   Investment in Human
Capital   597   Theories of Income Distribution   598
Need   598   *Equality*   598   *Productivity*   598

DEFINITIONS OF NEW TERMS   600   CHAPTER SUMMARY   600
QUESTIONS FOR THOUGHT AND DISCUSSION   601
SELECTED REFERENCES   601

Issue I-30   **Poverty and the Poor: Finding Alternatives to Welfare**   **602**

Poverty Still Around   602   The Low-Income Population   602
Defining Poverty   602   *The Relative Nature of Poverty*   602
Who Are the Poor?   603   *Minority Groups*   603   *The
Elderly*   603   *The Young*   604   *Rural Population*   604
Households Headed by Women   604   The Welfare Mess   604
Public Assistance   604   *Disparity of Payments*   605   Dis-
advantages of Current Public Assistance   605   *Incentives Not to*

Work   605   *Man-in-the-House Rule*   605   Social Insurance   606
Food Stamps   607   Some Alternative Ways to Eliminate
Poverty   607   *Guaranteed Annual Income*   607   *Negative*
Taxes   607   *Advantages of the Negative Income Tax*   608
Disadvantages of the Negative Income Tax   609   Taking into
Account Preferences of Taxpayers   609   A Final Note   610

DEFINITIONS OF NEW TERMS   610   QUESTIONS FOR THOUGHT AND
DISCUSSION   610   SELECTED REFERENCES   610

Biography   **GUNNAR MYRDAL—Economics As a Moral Issue**   611

UNIT SEVEN
ECOLOGY, POLITICS, AND GROWTH
613

26   **Social Costs and the Ecology**   615

Social vs. Private Costs   615   *Social Costs*   616   *Polluted*
Air   616   Externalities   616   Correcting the Signals   617
Property Rights   618   *Common Property*   618   *When Private*
Costs Equal Social Costs   619   Pinpointing Property
Rights   621   What about External Benefits?   621   External
Benefits and Nonpayers   622   Public Goods   622

DEFINITIONS OF NEW TERMS   623   CHAPTER SUMMARY   624
QUESTIONS FOR THOUGHT AND DISCUSSION   625
SELECTED REFERENCES   625

Issue I-31   **Who Gets the Ocean's Wealth? The Common Heritage of All Nations**   626

Resources from the Sea   626   Territorial Waters   626   Economic Zones   626   Suggestions for Mining Modules   627   The
Fishing Problem Revisited   627   Another Problem—Ocean
Spills   629   The Real Issue—The Distribution of Wealth   629

QUESTIONS FOR THOUGHT AND DISCUSSION   630
SELECTED REFERENCES   630

Issue I-32   **Conservation and Energy: How Should We Utilize**
Our Resources?   631

The Debate   631   What Conservation Really Means   631
Limited Resources   631   *An Operational Definition*   631

Discounting   633   Conservation Defined Operationally   633
Depletion of Nonrenewable Resources   633   *Correct Tim-
ing*   634   *Using Substitutes*   634   *Using Too Little May
Mean Less for the Future*   634   The Energy Question   635
The Problem of Dependency   636   *Further Energy
Considerations*   636

DEFINITION OF NEW TERM   637   QUESTIONS FOR THOUGHT AND
DISCUSSION   637   SELECTED REFERENCES   637

27   **Politics and Public Choice**   **638**

The Ideal Political Democracy   638   *Defining an Ideal Political
Democracy*   638   *The Equilibrium Point*   639   Actual
Democracies   639   *Tie-In Activities*   640   *Coalitions and
Cartels*   640   Politics and the Size of the Pie   640   The
Question of Ignorance   640   Bureaucracy and Public
Choice   642   The Gains to Political Entrepreneurship   642
Concluding Remarks   644

CHAPTER SUMMARY   645   QUESTIONS FOR THOUGHT AND
DISCUSSION   645   SELECTED REFERENCES   645

Biography   **KENNETH J. ARROW—The Mathematics of Uncertainty**   646

Issue I-33   **Should Political Campaigns Be Publicly Financed?
On Preventing Future Watergates**   **648**

The American Public Is Shocked   648   The Federal Campaign
Reform Act   648   Private Campaign Money   648   Does More
Money Ensure Winning?   649   The Problems of Regulating
Campaign Financing   650   Investments and Campaign Spending
Limits   650   Public Financing   650   *The Pros*   650   *The
Cons*   651   The Future of Reform   652

QUESTIONS FOR THOUGHT AND DISCUSSION   652
SELECTED REFERENCES   652

28   **Population Economics**   **653**

The Arithmetic of Population Growth   653   *Doubling
Time*   654   *Net Reproduction Rate*   655   Where the People
Are   655   The Population Curve   656   Why Has the S Curve
Gone Awry?   656   Birth Control   658   Investing in Chil-
dren   658   *Children as Consumption*   658   *Cost of*

Children   658   The Economic and Social Consequences of
ZPG   659   *Crowding*   660   *An Unexpected Result of ZPG—*
A Geriatric Population   660   *Depopulation*   661

DEFINITIONS OF NEW TERMS   661   CHAPTER SUMMARY   662
QUESTIONS FOR THOUGHT AND DISCUSSION   662
SELECTED REFERENCES   663

Issue I-34   **Was Malthus Right? The Exploding Population**   **664**

Essay on Population   664   A Product of Traditional
Europe   664   *Positive Checks*   664   *Key Assumption*   666
What Went Wrong?   666   *"Passion between the Sexes" Not the*
Answer   666   *Falling Mortality Rate a Mixed Blessing*   669
Breaking Out of the Malthusian Cycle   669

DEFINITIONS OF NEW TERMS   670   QUESTIONS FOR THOUGHT AND
DISCUSSION   670   SELECTED REFERENCES   670

29   **Development of the Less-Developed Countries**   **671**

How Do We Define an LDC?   671   The Problems of the
Information Explosion   671   Geographical Theories of Economic
Development   673   The Race Theory of Development   673
More Modern Theories   673   *Balancing Industry with*
Agriculture   673   *The Stages of Development*   674
Agriculture Subsidized   674   Planning Development in the
LDCs   675   Property Rights and Economic Develop-
ment   676   What Hope Is There for LDCs?   676

CHAPTER SUMMARY   676   QUESTIONS FOR THOUGHT AND
DISCUSSION   677   SELECTED REFERENCES   677

Biography   **BARBARA WARD—The Economist As Evangelist**   **678**

Issue I-35   **Can Foreign Aid Help Less-Developed Countries? Can**
Development Assistance Work?   **680**

The Rationale behind Foreign Aid   680   *Security*   680
Economics   680   *Politics*   680   *Humanitarianism*   680   A
Brief Rundown of American Foreign Aid   681   *The Marshall*
Plan   682   *A Shift in Emphasis*   682   The Case of
India   683   Problems with Assistance to Less-Developed
Countries   684   *The Situation in Less-Developed Coun-*

tries   684   *The Rate of Return on Investment*   684   *Destroying Relative Prices*   684   A Final Note   685

QUESTIONS FOR THOUGHT AND DISCUSSION   685
SELECTED REFERENCES   685

30   **Economic Growth**   **686**

What Is the Meaning of Economic Growth?   686   Growth and the Production-Possibilities Curve   687   The Importance of Growth Rates   687   Natural Resources and Economic Growth   688   Capital Accumulation   689   Why Is Capital Important?   690   Saving Decisions   690   *Saving and the Poor*   691   *The Hard Facts*   691   Improving Technology   692   Can We Tell Which Factor Is Most Important?   692   Economic Growth—A Policy Objective   693

DEFINITION OF NEW TERM   694   CHAPTER SUMMARY   694
QUESTIONS FOR THOUGHT AND DISCUSSION   695
SELECTED REFERENCES   695

Issue I-36   **Should Growth Be Stopped? What Does the Future Hold?**   **696**

The Economic Problem   696   Stopping GNP Growth   696   The Limits to Growth   696   Changing the Equation   698   The Problem with Gloom and Doom Projections   700   Planning for Planning   700

QUESTIONS FOR THOUGHT AND DISCUSSION   701
SELECTED REFERENCES   701

Preface

To the Instructor

Today there are indeed few people who would not agree that economic issues rank at or near the top of the list of problems confronting Americans. There is no news telecast, newspaper edition, or weekly news magazine that does not report on some new economic datum which shows that either things are getting worse or things are getting better. Those "things" obviously have something to do with the rates of inflation and unemployment, the length of food stamp lines, the number of individuals still on welfare rolls, the amount of racial discrimination still being practiced, the cost of cleaning up the air, or the handling of corporate profits.

Many, if not most, of the current social issues are involved with economics in some way or another. However, for students to understand and apply economic reasoning to social issues, they must have a solid foundation in economics. *Economics Today* was written both to provide that necessary foundation and to demonstrate the application of economic reasoning to the problems around us.

The Theory-Issue Interface

Economic reasoning requires a knowledge of basic theory. The thirty chapters in this book present that basic theory. However, the successful application of any theory requires continued demonstration of its usefulness. The thirty-six issues in this text serve that purpose; the issues are the topical applications and extensions of the theory presented in the chapters. Additionally, the issues provide an important component of the pedagogue's tool kit: a source that will generate interest among the students and stimulate discussion.

Economics Today is a flexible theory-issue text that lends itself to a variety of teaching uses. For example, many instructors find that their lecture time is best spent explaining the theory contained in the chapters while letting the students test their understanding of the theory by reading and perhaps discussing the issues associated with it. Other instructors use the opposite technique: class discussion centered only on the issues, with reading assignments to take care of the theory.

Organization of the Text

Although the basic organization of the text is from macro to micro, there is a common core of introductory chapters and issues in Unit One. This unit begins with an issue that discusses the scarcity society. Little actual theory is presented in this issue; the idea is to start students in their study of economics with a pressing problem always in the news. The rest of Unit One presents foundation materials for the study of economics at both the macro and micro level, including chapters on the science of economics, how different systems solve the economic problem, and supply and demand.

Unit Two presents some necessary background materials to the income and employment models that follow in Unit Three. Although the international materials are covered mainly in Unit Four, they can be used in the microeconomic part of the course if desired.

Unit Five (presumably read after Unit One) presents the basic models of consumer behavior and the firm. The theory of different industrial structures is also presented, accompanied by illustrative issues. The concepts of supply and demand are applied to resource markets in Unit Six.

Finally, Unit Seven treats ecology, politics, and growth.

Other Characteristics of the Text

In addition to its use of issues and its organization around those issues, the text offers six other useful features.

Biographical Sketches

Generally, the biographies consider living economists and industrial leaders. These sketches are presented for their intrinsic interest (students like to know what economists and economics are all about) and as historical background of what was involved in the policymaking at the national level.

Definitions of New Terms

All new economic terms are introduced into the text by bold type. At the end of each chapter and issue there is a glossary of definitions for these particular words. Also, in the index, page numbers indicating where these defined words appear in the text are shown in bold so students can immediately find the definitions of terms that are unclear to them.

Chapter Summaries

Chapter summaries are presented in a point-by-point format that allows for quick review of the preceding materials.

Questions for Thought and Discussion

There are selected questions for thought and discussion after every chapter and issue. Most of these questions are designed to elicit discussion either among the students themselves without the aid of an instructor or during classtime with the instructor's guidance.

Numerical Problems

Where appropriate, a numerical problem is presented as the last Question for Thought and Discussion. Answers to these problems are in the *Instructor's Manual*.

Selected References

There are selected references following each chapter and issue for those students who wish to further research any topic in the book. These references were selected with the students in mind. No specialized journal articles or books that would be understandable only to a trained economist are given; specialized references are included in the *Instructor's Manual*.

Teaching Aids and Supplements

Economics Today is part of an entire teaching package that includes the following five items:

Instructor's Manual

The *Instructor's Manual* presents an outline of each chapter and issue from which lecture notes can be drawn as well as additional comments for further points of discussion or additional lecture. There is a list of free materials when applicable; the instructor can send for these free materials and hand them out in class. Also included are extensive selected references for further research by the instructor, and, in some cases, films (and addresses) that relate to the topic discussed in the specific chapter or issue. As mentioned, there are answers for those problems that are at the end of certain Questions for Thought and Discussion in the text.

Student Learning Guide

The accompanying *Student Learning Guide,* written by Professor Lee Spector of S.U.N.Y. at Buffalo, started in a rather odd way. Spector asked himself what sort of materials students would need if they wanted to learn economics on their own. Starting from this unusual premise, Spector has written a truly different study guide: It not only provides tests of whether students are understanding the material, but it also gives substantial help to those students who are having trouble. Consequently, this supplement is called a learning guide, rather than merely a study guide. Included in this guide are such helpful features as learning objectives, hints on how to study the material, alternative explanations of difficult material, glossaries, and both pre- and posttests.

Independent Study Modules (ISMs)

A complete and heavily pretested audio/graphic learning system is available to instructors who have available classrooms or student learning centers that are equipped with tape playback facilities. These unique materials were independently developed in conjunction with the use of the first edition; they were further refined for the second edition by their authors, James Mason, Mike Melvin, and Craig Justice. The ISM package includes thirty separate cassettes, virtually one for each chapter in this book. Besides the graphic packets and cassette tape materials, there are self-tests that can be used in a programmed-learning manner.

The weekly ISM materials can be used in a variety of ways. One way is as a substitute for one lecture period. ISM materials can also be used to reinforce a full lecture schedule on an assigned or even a voluntary basis. The emphasis of the system tends toward integrating it with chapter theory while giving specific examples of problems that are different from those in the text.

We have found from extensive field testing that the ISM supplements develop positive responses to learning economic theory by the students. Students have a greater appreciation of the opportunity to learn the complex material objectively at their own individual pace. The instructors who have used the system contend that students come to lectures better prepared and with positive expectations.

Test Bank

The test questions, of which there are approximately 1,000, are quite different. They evolved from the audio/graphic learning system (ISM) developed by Mason, Melvin, and Justice. The test bank consists of both graphic and verbal multiple-choice questions that are divided by degree of difficulty. They are subdivided as to whether or not they treat concepts, problem solving, or institutional materials. There are also references to the text page number students should be referred to if they get any incorrect answers.

Transparency Masters

All the important graphs and charts are available in a set of transparency masters that are free to adopters.

The Second Edition

This edition of the text does not merely contain a few updated tables and graphs. Rather, I wanted to completely reorganize and redo sections of the text to increase its usability as a teaching device. To that end I have added eighteen new issues and eliminated those that seemed less interesting to today's students. The new issues are more serious and perhaps less ephemeral than those eliminated. Additionally, a great deal of the theoretical materials, particularly in the macro section, have been completely redone. In particular, the simplified Keynesian income and employment determination model is discussed in a more complete and easily learned manner. A number of materials were eliminated from the second edition because of their after-the-fact limited use by adopting professors.

Although not complete, the following summary indicates some of the substantial changes or additions to this second edition:

1. Inclusion of a brief **appendix** on reading and working with graphs, useful for those students who **are** unfamiliar with the techniques (Appendix A).

2. Expanded explanation of why the production-possibilities curve is bowed outward (Chapter 2).

3. Inclusion of elasticity in one basic supply-and-demand chapter (Chapter 3), which is, however, subdivided into Parts A and B; elasticity is treated exclusively in part B. Thus instructors who wish to postpone a discussion of elasticity have a definite cut-off point.

4. Stress on the distinction between relative and absolute prices when presenting the laws of supply and demand (Chapter 3). Chapter 3 includes an enumeration of determinants of demand other than price and numerical examples of how actual price elasticities can be calculated.

5. Application of supply and demand to one particular illegal activity—Prohibition—in Issue I-4.

6. Completely revised presentation of national income accounting presenting the expenditure and income approaches (Chapter 4).

7. A more complete presentation of unemployment, including duration of unemployment and hidden unemployment (Chapter 6).

8. An expanded presentation of stagflation (Chapter 7).

9. Greater distinction is made between anticipated and unanticipated inflation as well as the effects of the two different kinds of inflation on the wealth position of debtors and creditors (Chapter 7).

10. Expanded presentation of determinants of planned investment; stress on the difference between planned and actual values of aggregate variables.

11. Inclusion of a brief appendix on the accelerator (Appendix B).

12. Inclusion of T accounts to explain the multiple expansion of the money supply (Chapter 11).

13. A more complete explanation of marginal utility theory, with an application to the futures market and an appendix on indifferent-curve analysis (Chapter 16, Issue I-17, and Appendix C).

14. Throughout the discussion of the theory of the firm in Unit Five, numerical tables are always presented before graphs are shown.

15. Expanded presentation of the break-even and shutdown prices in Chapter 18. Addition of the explanation of the distinction between internal and external economies and diseconomies of scale.

16. Expanded section on antitrust legislation.

17. Inclusion of a chapter on politics and public choice (Chapter 27) as well as an accompanying issue on "Preventing Future Watergates" (Issue I-33).

18. Addition of the explanation of the distinction between internal and external economies and diseconomies of scale.

19. Eighteen new issues, including issues on the scarcity society, national priorities, the effects of unemployment compensation on the rate of unemployment, indexing, public service employment, subsidizing commercial banks, problems with short-run stabilization, the threat of international competition, flexible exchange rates and worldwide inflation, international cartels, the post office and natural monopoly, breaking up large corporations and restructuring them à la Galbraith, parceling out the ocean's wealth, preventing future Watergates, and what the future holds.

I received numerous comments from many adopters while preparing the second edition; these comments aided me greatly in improving the text and its supplemental materials. I welcome further comments on what is included in this edition. This edition, as with the first, is also available in two paperback versions: *Economics Today—The Macro View* and *Economics Today—The Micro View*.

Roger LeRoy Miller

Coral Gables

Suggested Outline for One-Term Courses

Macroeconomic Emphasis	Microeconomic Emphasis	Balanced Emphasis	Issue/Policy Emphasis
I-1	I-1	I-1	I-1
1	1	1	1
3	3	2	2
4	I-4	3	I-3
5	16	I-4	3
I-6	17	4	I-4
6	18	5	5
7	I-18	I-7	I-6
I-10	I-19	6	I-7
8	19	7	I-8
9	I-20	I-10	7
10	20	8	I-9
11	I-22	9	I-10
14	I-24	10	8
I-15	22	11	9
17	23	17	10
18	I-27	18	I-11
I-18	24	I-18	11
I-24	5	19	I-14
23	I-6	I-20	I-15
I-27	6	21	17
25	7	I-24	18
Choose from	I-10	23	I-18
Unit Seven	8	I-28	I-19
	9	25	I-21
	10	Choose from	I-22
	11	Unit Seven	I-23
	Choose from		I-24
	Unit Seven		I-25
			I-26
			23
			I-27
			I-28
			I-30
			Choose from
			Unit Seven

To the Student

Whether you are taking economics as a general course in a liberal arts education or, more specifically, as the foundation for further study of economics and/or business, the textbook you use can hopefully make the course more rather than less enjoyable. My comments should make the book a more useful aspect of the course you are now taking. Note, however, that my comments are secondary to the way your instructor wishes you to use the text.

The issues complement the theoretical points discussed in the chapters. Many of you may find that a quick first reading of the issues without attempting a thorough grasp of points not understood completely will be a good introduction to the particular topics at hand. Then, a quick reading of the appropriate theoretical chapter is in order, with a more careful later rereading of those points not understood. Finally, if the issue is skimmed again, any aspects of the theory not yet mastered will become apparent. Alternatively, first you can handle the theoretical chapters in more detail so you can find out, upon the initial reading of the issue, whether the application of theory is understandable.

This second edition covers a large number of new issues that have been included so you will keep abreast of the changing events in our economic world. Ideally, you will find the currency of these issues helpful in mastering the application of analysis to the real world.

For review, there are self-contained graphs, definitions of new terms, chapter summaries, and, in some cases, actual numerical or graphical problems that may be assigned by your instructor (who has the answers in the *Instructor's Manual*). You can, after having read all the text, go over one or more of the reviewing devices. If you want to do additional study on a particular topic, selected references are listed at the end of each chapter and issue.

An entirely new *Student Learning Guide* has been prepared for this edition. The guide not only reinforces the concepts and analysis presented in the text, it also helps you master particularly difficult aspects of economics without further help from your instructor or a tutor. In this sense, the *Student Learning Guide* is a self-contained learning program.

I sincerely hope you will become interested in the economic issues of our times, not in spite of, but with the help of, your textbook.

R. L. M.

Acknowledgements

The First Edition

The following people were responsible for critically commenting on the manuscript during its formation, writing, and rewriting. To them I owe my gratitude but certainly do not hold them responsible for any remaining errors:

John R. Aidem, Miami-Dade Junior College
Glen W. Atkinson, University of Nevada
Charles A. Berry, University of Cincinnati
Conrad P. Caligaris, Northeastern University
Warren L. Coats, Jr., University of Virginia
Ed Coen, University of Minnesota
Alan E. Ellis, De Anza College
Grant Ferguson, North Texas State University
Peter Frost, University of Miami
Martin D. Haney, Portland Community College
Timothy R. Keely, Tacoma Community College
Norman F. Keiser, California State University at San Jose
E. R. Kittrell, Northern Illinois University
John L. Madden, University of Kentucky
John M. Martin, California State University at Hayward
E. S. McKuskey, St. Petersburg Junior College
Herbert C. Milikien, American River College
Jerry L. Petr, University of Nebraska at Lincoln
I. James Pikl, University of Wyoming
Richard Romano, Broome Community College
Augustus Shackelford, El Camino College
Howard F. Smith, California Polytechnic State University at San Luis Obispo
William T. Trulove, Eastern Washington State College
Robert F. Wallace, Washington State University
Henry C. Wallich, Yale University
James Willis, California State University at San Jose
Shik Young, Eastern Washington State College

The Second Edition

Many first edition adopters were asked for specific comments on what changes they wanted in the second edition. These comments were taken into account when the revised Contents were made. An additional set of reviewers was then able to comment on the proposed changes in the second edition. All the following people participated in writing a review or answering a questionnaire:

Frank Emerson, Western Michigan University
Claron Nelson, University of Utah
Mike Ellis, North Texas State University
John Rapp, University of Dayton
E. L. Hazlett, Kansas State University
Travis Wilson, De Kalb Community College
Nicholas Grunt, Tarrant County Junior College
Glen Marston, Utah State University
Daniel Joseph, Niagara Community College
J. M. Sullivan, Stephen F. Austin State University
E. D. Key, Stephen F. Austin State University
Wylie Walthall, College of the Alameda
G. Jeffry Barbour, Central Michigan University
Ralph T. Byrns, Clemson University
James Mason, San Diego Mesa College
Robert P. Thomas, University of Washington
Mike Melvin, San Diego Mesa College
Craig Justice, Chaffey College
George Spiva, University of Tennessee
Barry Duman, West Texas State University
G. B. Duwaji, University of Texas at Arlington
Bruce Kimzey, New Mexico State University
Larry Ross, Anchorage Community College
Lee Spector, State University of New York, Buffalo
Maryanna Boynton, California State College, Fullerton
Demos Hadjiyanis, College of St. Thomas
David Jones, College of St. Thomas
Terrence W. Kinal, College of St. Thomas
Herbert Milikien, American River College

Before I started working on the second edition, Ronald Reddall of Allan Hancock College prepared a detailed, page-by-page critique of what was included in the first edition. My admiration for his tenacity is great.

The following people submitted detailed comments on drafts of the second edition. These reviewers were crucial in providing me with needed criticisms of my preliminary drafts of this edition. My admiration for their ability is unbounded.

Thomas Borcherding, Simon Frazer University
Raburn M. Williams, University of Hawaii
G. Hartley Mellish, University of South Florida
Thomas Curtis, University of South Florida
James Foley, University of Miami

I especially wish to thank Richard O. Sherman, Jr., of Ohio State University for his detailed participation in this project from the very beginning of the second edition. His comments were of immense help to me.

The biographies were skillfully developed by John Cobb. The issue (and occasional chapter) photographs were taken by Susan Vita Miller, who understood the concept of opportunity cost so well that she did not want to do the job jointly with me. Her photographs were all taken with a Nikon F-2.

R. L. M.

ONE
GETTING STARTED

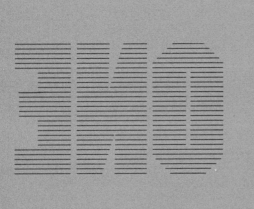

ARE WE RUNNING OUT OF EVERYTHING?

Can We Preserve Our Way of Life?

Americans have grown used to enjoying the highest living standard of any country in the entire world. But perhaps our way of life has become too wasteful and we can no longer take its preservation for granted. We are in an era of shortages, and scarcity seems to plague not only the American economic landscape but also that of just about every other country today. It was just a few years ago that a congressional survey of 258 major industries showed that 245 of them believed they confronted shortages of at least one commodity vital to their business. In fact, Honeywell, Bell & Howell, Utah International, and Stokely-Van Camp indicated that they were short of almost everything they needed. The list became impressive: 108 firms could not get an adequate supply of petrochemicals; 106 could not get all the steel they wanted; 74 said that they faced shortages of aluminum; and 62 lacked a sufficient supply of copper. All in all, the 245 corporations listed a **shortfall** of some 64 vital commodities.

The Shortage Society

The number of items considered in short supply began to grow rapidly after the first couple of years in this decade. By 1974, large companies were seeking alternatives for practically everything. General Foods was looking for a sugar substitute, Clorox was looking for a soda ash replacement to use in bleach, Alcoa decided to stop producing household aluminum foil, and Del Monte Corporation could not purchase enough glass for jars, fiberboard for boxes, or tin plates for cans.

The Energy Shortage That Started It All

People first became acutely aware of serious shortages throughout our economic system when the Persian Gulf oil-producing nations decided to boycott the United States in the fall of 1973. At the time, it was feared that the shortfall of petroleum products—mainly gasoline and heating-fuel oil—would greatly disrupt our economy. Indeed, some politicians and many concerned scientists told

us that because we had been profligate in the use of energy in the past, we now had to pay for our sins. Many spokespeople assumed that the scarcity of petroleum products would last indefinitely, even after the embargo was lifted, so they prescribed expensive long-run policies for research and development to make the United States self-sufficient in energy by 1980. They also exhorted the American people to change their basic life-style in order to conserve precious energy resources. In fact, some observers went so far as to state that the energy crisis suffered by Americans was "good." Why? Simply because it brought us to our senses, made us aware of our dependence on foreign sources for a vital resource, and showed us how wasteful our life-style had become.

Next on the list of actual and potential shortages that loomed large in the eyes of American consumers was food.

The Impending Food Crisis

In the 1950s, 1960s, and early 1970s, the United States was plagued with a problem that might be quite foreign to most of you reading this text. The American agricultural industry, the most productive in the world, produced not shortages but surpluses—year in and year out.

In fact, the surpluses became so embarrassing that the United States government at one time was dumping wheat into the Gulf of Mexico. Naturally, our less-developed neighbor nations, with untold numbers of undernourished individuals, found such activity appalling.

We obviously have solved the surplus problem—perhaps even for good. Thanks to unanticipated problems with agriculture throughout the world, shortages, not surpluses, are the order of the day. For a while, the specter of bread lines, similar to those for gasoline that occurred only a few years ago, seemed to be a real one. In fact, the Community Nutrition Institute of Washington stated that ''sooner, but probably reluctantly later'' the United States government would be forced to ration food. It's hard to believe, but the Los Angeles police force has been trained to handle riots that might occur over food shortages in this country.

If we look at what has happened to world grain reserves, we can get an idea of how serious the problem really is. In recent years the world has had to draw down its grain reserves with increasing frequency. This happened noticeably in 1966 and 1967 and has become much more pronounced in this decade. The number of days of grain reserves have been falling, on the average, since the early 1960s. Where we will go from here is indeed a serious question to be answered.

A study by the Ford Foundation came up with a proposal for a world food reserve, with the United States contributing a large amount but not 100 percent. This would be keeping in line with what the United States

government has done in the past because since 1954 this country has given away, under Public Law 480, $25 billion worth of grain to developing countries.

At a world food conference sponsored by the United Nations and the Food and Agricultural Organization a few years ago, 135 nations met to consider long-term measures to improve world food production. At the time this conference was meeting, an estimated 10,000 people a day were dying from starvation or diseases related to hunger. One of the attempts at the conference was to form a new system of international grain reserves similar to that proposed by the Ford Foundation. The international system would establish an emergency food aid bank and an agency to administer $5 billion worth of annual farm assistance. The con-

cern of the United States—far and away the largest producer of food —was that the burden of holding surpluses for the whole world would fall to it.

Our Dwindling Mineral Resources

When we look at mineral resources we find the same perplexing scenario—increasing shortages. Just look at Table I-1.1. Here we list some of the better-known and critical nonrenewable natural resources and the approximate number of years it will take to use up known worldwide reserves. Assuming no recycling, it is clear that we will one day run out of nonrenewable natural resources, no matter how slowly we use them. The problem, according to many, is that we are going to run out of critical natural resources in the very near

Table I-1.1

When Will the Day of Reckoning Arrive for Natural Resources?

By using a projection based on an ever-increasing rate of growth of consumption of nonrenewable natural resources, it is possible to predict how many years we have left before we exhaust today's known global reserves of these resources.

RESOURCE	WHEN KNOWN WORLDWIDE RESERVES WILL RUN OUT
Aluminum	31 years
Copper	21 years
Lead	21 years
Manganese	46 years
Mercury	13 years
Natural Gas	22 years
Petroleum	20 years
Silver	13 years
Tin	15 years
Zinc	18 years

Source: U.S. Bureau of Mines, *Mineral Facts and Problems,* Washington, D.C.: Government Printing Office, 1970, and D. L. Meadows et al., *Dynamics of Growth in a Finite World,* Wright-Allen Press, 1974.

future. Hence, we will be faced with increasingly disruptive shortages throughout the world economy, as well as in our own.

Some Proposed Solutions to Shortages

What can be done about the shortages that have been observed in the last few years? We have already touched on some long-term proposals for the energy crisis, including increased research and development for new energy sources and policies that would change our energy-consuming life-style. There are also numerous proposals for fixing limits on the amount of energy each person can use. These limits might come in the form of an allotment per individual or per family. Each family might, for example, be allotted a certain number of gallons of gasoline per month and would not be allowed to consume any more. This process is generally known as **rationing.** It was used during World War II for gasoline and other scarce commodities. At that time, ration coupons were given out and had to be used to purchase gas.

For the agricultural crisis that may occur, proposed solutions again draw heavily on improved production techniques to allow America, and indeed even underdeveloped countries, to dramatically increase their food production. However, there have been many suggestions to reduce the demand for food in years to come by drastically curtailing population growth, particularly in those countries where, if growth were to continue at current relatively high rates that cause the population to double every 20 years, there would hardly be enough room for every citizen to stand (let alone sit) by the year 2500.

With respect to nonrenewable natural resources, numerous conservation schemes have been suggested. These include limiting the extraction of certain nonrenewable resources so that we can lengthen the amount of time in which they will be available. Such a rationing, or allocation, procedure presumably would guarantee our grandchildren a continuing supply of such resources as natural gas and copper.

At issue, then, is really the question of whether we can continue our current American life-style, that is, whether we can keep consuming large quantities of many items that have been or threaten to be in very short supply. Americans represent only 6 percent of the world's population but consume more than 30 percent of the world's nonrenewable resources. The implication is that unless we are superbly successful in improving technology so we can simultaneously use fewer resources and increase the output of others, we will have to reduce our standard of material well-being.

The Other Side of the Story

Not all observers of the shortage situation in the United States and elsewhere agree with this doomsday analysis. In fact, if we examine what happened during past periods when energy was scarcer, we can get some inkling of the forces that may be acting to cure the current shortage problem. Perhaps ours will not become a society of empty market shelves and frustrated consumers.

Another View of Energy Shortages

When the supply of petroleum was temporarily reduced a few years ago, there was great expectation of chaos. Many commentators predicted freezing homes and automobiles abandoned for want of gas. There were indeed problems for motorists who, in some sections of the country, had to wait hours in line to get their gasoline, but in many sections of the country motorists did not have to wait at all. The heating-fuel situation too was bleak but not catastrophic. The Denver schools had to close for lack of fuel oil, and some houses did not have enough heat, but massive freezing did not occur. In fact, at the end of the so-called crisis, the amount of fuel oil in inventories of oil companies was greater than at any other time in the history of the United States. How could that have occurred during such a crisis?

For one thing, a powerful force was causing consumers of fuel oil to lower their thermostats, to close their windows, and to take all sorts of measures to reduce their total heating bills. That powerful force was a gradual, but nonetheless significant, rise in the price of heating oil.

At that time, the Federal Energy Office (now called the Federal Energy Administration) was allowing the price of fuel oil to be raised several cents a month. Several cents does not sound like much, but after a number of months, the price to consumers of fuel oil had risen approximately 50 to 70 percent over levels that prevailed the previous year. At the higher relative price, consumers voluntarily conserved fuel oil. (The publicity campaign waged by government officials to get Americans to use less fuel may also have had an effect.)

What we found out was that the "required" amount of fuel oil was related, at least partially, to how much consumers had to pay for it. When they had to pay more, they decided that they could live in a house at 68 degrees instead of 72 degrees, thereby freeing income that would otherwise have gone to paying higher fuel bills. The same thing happened with gasoline, but not as dramatically. In the first place, the Federal Energy Office did not allow the retail price of gasoline to rise as sharply, relative to the price charged in the previous year, as the Office had done for fuel oil. Nonetheless, within less than a year, the price of gas at the pump had risen and consumers had reacted—by cutting their consumption of gasoline by almost 10 percent. (Again, it could be argued that exhortations from government officials to Americans to drive less and to obey gas-saving lower speed limits were at work here. Speed limits, however, may have only been obeyed where there were enforcement efforts.)

Basically, then, the other view of shortages and increased scarcity indicates that after a while shortages may work themselves out because the products in short supply will sooner or later end up costing more and consumers will decide to conserve on those relatively more expensive items. And those who provide the items—the suppliers—will also react to the higher prices, but in the opposite direction. They will be willing to expend more effort and money to find ways to produce more in order to benefit from such higher prices. An understanding of how consumers and producers react when the cost of short-supply items rises is basic to understanding the other view of the supply of minerals in the world.

World Mineral Supplies

Refer to Table I-1.1. The second column is based on the assumption that known global reserves will run out simply because we will consume them all. But what do known global reserves really mean? Those reserve

Table I-1.2

The Amount of Minerals Contained in 1 Cubic Kilometer of Average Crustal Rock

The physical quantity of minerals contained in the earth's crust is indeed staggering and gives some idea of the extent of resources physically available.

RESOURCE	AMOUNT OF MINERALS CONTAINED
Aluminum	2,000,000,000 tons
Iron	1,000,000,000 tons
Zinc	800,000 tons
Copper	200,000 tons

Source: D. B. Brooks and P. W. Andrews, "Mineral Resources, Economics Growth, and World Population," Science, July 1974, vol. 185, no. 4145, p. 13.

we have seen, that as the relative price of a mineral goes up, the amount of proved reserves goes up also. Witness what happened with petroleum. We have more proved reserves today than we had in 1930, even though we have consumed a tremendous quantity of petroleum during that 45-year period.

Who Is Right?

Are we facing a shortage society? Must we suffer an inevitable decline in the quality of life, or will things work themselves out? In other words, will Americans respond to inevitable higher prices of items in short supply by consuming less and will industry respond to those higher prices by finding better ways to produce and by finding substitutes for the items in short supply?

Do not try to formulate your answer quite yet. Wait until you have gone through some of the economic theories presented throughout this book. Then come back to this introductory issue to see how you react to the problems posed.

figures are based on the amounts that would be taken out of the earth, given the current state of the arts, that is, technology, and given the current profitability of mining those amounts. But that current profitability certainly must, in part, be related to the price that those minerals can bring in the marketplace. Look at Table I-1.2. Here we show how many tons of some important minerals are contained in a single cubic kilometer of average crustal rock. If we were to multiply the numbers included in Table I-1.2 by the surface area of the earth that would, on the average, contain those amounts of minerals, we would come up with quantities of physical reserves many, many times those listed in any mineral tables. The reason we do not use those numbers is because at today's prices it would not be profitable to mine them, for at today's prices, only "proved" reserves are profitable to mine. We might expect, and indeed

Selected References	Brooks, D. B. and P. W. Andrews, "Mineral Resources, Economic Growth, and World Population," *Science,* vol. 185, no. 4145, July 5, 1974.
	Brown, Lester R., *In the Human Interest,* New York: W. W. Norton, 1974.
	Heilbroner, Robert L., *An Inquiry into the Human Prospect,* New York: W. W. Norton, 1974.
	Meadows, Dennis et al., *The Limits to Growth,* Washington, D.C.: Potomac Associates, 1972.
	Mishan, E. J., *Technology and Growth,* New York: Praeger, 1970.
	Olson, Mancur and Hans H. Landsberg (eds.), *The No Growth Society,* New York: W. W. Norton, 1973.

What Economics Is All About

Are we running out of food? Are we running out of energy? Are we running out of copper? These were the questions posed and partially analyzed in the introductory issue of this book. No one will deny that such problems are the crucial dilemmas facing our modern world. These and other modern-day problems, such as the urban crisis, overpopulation, pollution, and economic growth, will be our concern throughout the book. They are all areas of study in which you will be able to apply the tools of economic analysis.

Economic issues continue to be examined in the press, on radio and television, and in the halls of Congress. And the future will probably see even greater emphasis on economic issues and on the economic aspects of some supposedly noneconomic issues that have become worldwide problems. But before we can understand its relevance, we have to explain what economics is all about. The easiest way to begin is to relate the subject matter of economics to the scarcity society outlined in Issue I-1.

Scarcity, Economic Goods, and Free Goods

Economics and **scarcity** go hand in hand. We very loosely used the word scarcity in Issue I-1. What do we mean by scarcity? To begin with, we have always faced a problem of scarcity and always will, no matter how abundant natural resources are. If we didn't live in a world of scarcity, you wouldn't have to read about or even think about the economic aspects of anything because there wouldn't be any economic aspects. Scarcity presents us with a problem: How do we allocate the available resources to all the competing demanders; how do we make choices among limited alternatives? There are many people in competition for scarce goods and services, and even if they decided not to compete, they would still face the problem of how the available resources were to be allocated among members of society. So you see, it doesn't really matter what one's moral or political attitudes are. Everybody can love everybody else and want to help everybody else, but the decision still has to be made: Who gets what, how much, when, and by what means? Economics, then, attempts to answer such questions because it is concerned with the *allocation of scarce resources.* If a resource is not scarce, that is, if it is not an **economic good,** then economics has little to say about it.

There are, of course, some things around that are free. We call them **free goods,** as opposed to scarce, or economic, goods. Not many are left. Old economics textbooks used to call air a free good, but that is really no longer true because in many cities pollution makes air unfit to breathe. In many mountain areas clean air is still a free good (once you are there); you can have all of it you want, and so can anybody else who bothers to hike up to where you are. You and anybody else who hikes there do not have to worry about how free goods, including air and running water in many wilderness areas, should be or have to be allocated among competing demanders. There is no scarcity involved. Who is interested in free goods, then? Certainly not economists. Perhaps physicists, hydrologists, biologists, and chemists are interested in free air and water, but the economist steps in only when the problem of scarcity arises, as it does in cities, and people become concerned about allocating the scarce resource. We have seen throughout our history that as population and production increase over time, many "free" goods become "economic" goods, such as land for mining, water, and air for industrial uses, and water for hydroelectric power.

Exchange and Choice

Since individuals live in a world of scarcity, they are unable to obtain all that they might desire to have, even in our own country, the richest nation on earth, where people have a relatively high level of material well-being. We have unlimited wants, but we must make choices among the limited alternatives available to us. Economics is about these choices. You have the alternative of spending time reading this book or spending time in the student union having fun with your friends. You must make a choice because you are up against the problem of scarcity. In this particular case, the scarce good happens to be your time (and this resource is scarce no matter how rich you may be).

When you start trading with other individuals, choices arise because you have to pick among alternative *exchanges* that you could make. We know that people have been exchanging things since the beginning of time. For example, archeologists tell us that during the Ice Age, hunters of mammoths in the Great Russian steppe were trading for Mediterranean shells.

Voluntary and Involuntary Exchanges

In general, we will be talking about voluntary exchanges among individuals and nations. By necessity, every voluntary exchange has to make both parties in the exchange think they are better off: Exchange is mutually beneficial. If it were not, individuals and nations would not bother with it.

However, involuntary exchanges do occur, and some are pretty unpleasant for the losing parties. You find involuntary exchanges in situations where coercive power is used to alter another person's or nation's behavior. For example, when black persons were captured and shuttled aboard intolerably crowded slave ships going to the New World, they were forced to submit to a new economic arrangement whereby they provided labor power to their owners and in turn were given the necessities of life (barely that much in many cases). When individuals are robbed, they too are engaged in an involuntary exchange. Although it is true that the robber might present you with a choice to minimize your loss—you volunteer your money or your life—you are still a victim of coercive power and not in a choice situation to freely make up your mind about what to exchange and what not to exchange.

Markets—Where Exchanges Take Place

You and I make voluntary exchanges all the time. We usually do it by way of an intermediary good called money, but we could—not as easily, of course—trade things for things instead of using money to facilitate this trade. You exchange the purchasing power implicit in the price of this book for the book itself. If you hadn't used money, and we were in fact involved in a system of **barter,** you might have had to exchange a couple of records or another book to get this one. But the fact remains that you are always engaged in these sorts of exchanges whether or not you use money.

Voluntary exchanges take place in what we call a **market.** Markets are institutions that aid in the process of exchange by allowing communication between potential buyers and potential sellers of goods and services. This is the underlying function of all markets, no matter how primitive or sophisticated they might be. For example, in the formally structured New York and American Stock Exchanges, stockbrokers can immediately put potential buyers and potential sellers in touch with each other. The New York and American Stock Exchanges are highly centralized in terms of this function. At the other extreme are very decentralized, informal markets for such services as tutoring, babysitting, occasional home repair, and gardening. You can probably think of many other decentralized, informal markets that you often use.

The reason individuals turn to markets to conduct economic activities or exchanges is because markets reduce the costs of exchanging. These costs are generally called **transactions costs** because they are associated with transacting economic exchange. Certainly, the transactions costs in the most highly organized markets are relatively small. Take the example of the New York Stock Exchange. It is quite easy to obtain immediate information on the price of listed stocks and how many have been bought and sold in the last several hours, what the prices were the day before, and so on.

Generally, the less organized a market, the higher the transactions costs. We will see that no market can completely eliminate transactions costs, but some markets do a better job than others. And, as information-dissemination activity becomes less costly, transactions costs have fallen. Think how costly, in terms of time and money, it used to be for someone living in California to find out the price of stocks being sold in New York when our communications network was not as extensive as it is now.

Exchanges and Specialization

At first, Robinson Crusoe didn't exchange anything with anyone. And even though he had the problem of allocating his time and effort, he never had to worry, at least in the beginning, about making a choice between alternative exchanges with *other* individuals. Few of us, however, live in a Robinson Crusoe economy; we live in societies where many individuals with many different types of productive talents wish to engage in exchanges to make themselves better off. Herein lies the essence of economics and exchange. No one person makes a car or a house, or even a bushel of wheat. There is **specialization** in all our operations as producers of things or services because each of us undertakes only one or very few of the steps required to bring a commodity from its natural-resource state into the hands of the individual who ultimately uses that commodity. Robinson Crusoe was on a deserted island; most of us are not. Most of us specialize in doing one thing or another. Most of us do not attempt to be self-sufficient because if we did, we would be very poor indeed.

Just think about it. How well off could you be if you had to provide all your own food, shelter, clothing, recreation equipment, and so on? Look at an individual state. How well off would the residents of Delaware be if they could not obtain goods from other states but had to be self-sufficient?

It is fairly easy to figure out how any one individual can decide what he or she should specialize in doing. If the individual wants to be as well off as possible, he or she will apply productive talents to endeavors that yield the highest rewards. To figure out what you can do comparatively better than others, all you need analyze are your alternatives. In our society, where money is used, the easiest way to find out which productive endeavors give you the highest rate of return for your time spent working is by seeking out the job you can actually perform that yields the highest income or highest command over goods and services which you would like to consume. (We must add to this any nonmonetary returns received from a job.) Once this is accomplished, then specialization takes place. It is when individuals specialize, and then make exchanges, that material well-being is at its greatest, given the available amount of scarce resources. This is not a new idea, but it was made quite famous when the father of modern economics, Adam Smith, demonstrated the benefit of specialization in his famous pin example:

One man draws out the wire, another straightens it, a third cuts it, a fourth points it, a fifth grinds it at the top for receiving the head; to make the head requires two or three distinct operations; to put it on is a peculiar business, to whiten the pins is another; it is even a trade by itself to put them into the paper.[1]

Now, making pins this way allowed 10 men without very much specialized skill to make almost 48,000 pins "of a middling size" in a day. One worker, toiling alone, could have made perhaps 20 pins a day; therefore, 10 workers could have produced 200. Specialization, or the *division of labor,* as Smith liked to call it, allowed for an increase in the output of the pin factory from 200 to 48,000! Not only did the pin factory become more productive through specialization, by combining workers' talents and making 48,000 pins rather than a mere 200 per day, but workers became better off: Their wages could now reflect their much higher rate of output, and they could buy more goods and services with the relatively higher wages.

A Simple Example of Specialization

Perhaps another example will help convince you that specialization allows for a greater amount of goods to be obtained from a given amount of resources. For if you are not convinced, you will never think economics is very important because, as a science, it rests on this fact: Individuals desire to specialize and then exchange because in so doing they have found that they can be materially better off.

Look at Table 1-1. Here we show total output available for two productive workers in a small world where they are the only individuals. At first, they do not specialize; rather, each works an equal amount of time, 8 hours each day,

[1] Adam Smith, *An Inquiry into the Nature and Causes of the Wealth of Nations,* 1776.

Table 1-1	**Before Specialization**

Here we show the relationship between Ms. Jones' and Mr. Smith's daily work effort and the production of granola and ice cream. When Ms. Jones works on her own without specializing in any one activity, she devotes 4 hours a day to granola production and 4 hours a day to the production of ice cream. For her efforts, she obtains 2 pounds of each. On the other hand, Mr. Smith, again not specializing, will produce in the same two 4-hour periods 3 pounds of granola and 1 pound of ice cream. Their total output will be 5 pounds of granola and 3 pounds of ice cream.

DAILY WORK EFFORT	MS. JONES
4 hours	2 lb granola
4 hours	2 lb ice cream
	MR. SMITH
4 hours	3 lb granola
4 hours	1 lb ice cream

Total = 5 lb granola, 3 lb ice cream

Table 1-2	**After Specialization**

If Ms. Jones specializes in the production of ice cream, she can produce 4 pounds for every 8 hours of daily work effort. Mr. Smith, on the other hand, specializing in the production of granola, will produce 6 pounds. Their grand total of production will be 6 pounds of granola and 4 pounds of ice cream, a pound more of both goods than before they specialized.

DAILY WORK EFFORT	MS. JONES
8 hours	4 lb ice cream
	MR. SMITH
8 hours	6 lb granola

Total = 6 lb granola, 4 lb ice cream

producing granola and ice cream. Ms. Jones has the talent and chooses to produce 2 pounds of granola in 4 hours of work and an additional 2 pounds of ice cream with the additional 4 hours. Mr. Smith has the talent and chooses to produce 3 pounds of granola in his first 4 hours of work but only 1 pound of ice cream in his second 4 hours. The total amount that the two can and choose to produce without specialization is 5 pounds of granola and 3 pounds of ice cream.

Now look at what happens when they specialize. We see, in Table 1-2, that after specialization, when Ms. Jones spends all her time making ice cream, she can produce 4 pounds (since she produces 2 pounds in 4 hours). Mr. Smith, on the other hand, spending all his time making granola, produces 6 pounds (since he can produce 3 pounds in just 4 hours). The total output of this two-individual world has

now increased to 6 pounds of granola and 4 pounds of ice cream, an increase of 20 percent. Amazing, right? With the same two people using the same amount of fixed resources (no cheating was allowed), the total output of this little economy increased from 5 pounds of granola to 6 pounds, and from 3 pounds of ice cream to 4 pounds. Obviously, Ms. Jones and Mr. Smith would be better off (in a material sense) if they each specialized and exchanged between themselves. Ms. Jones would exchange ice cream for Mr. Smith's granola, and vice versa. (Our discussion, of course, has not taken into account the *disadvantages* of specialization—monotony and drudgery in one's job.)

After specialization, each individual would be doing what he or she could do *comparatively* better than the other. This leads us to the concept of **comparative advantage**.

Comparative Advantage

Specialization through the division of labor, as outlined in Smith's famous example of pin making and in our example of granola and ice cream production, rests on a very important fact—different individuals, communities, and nations are indeed different, at least when it comes to the skills of each in producing goods and services. In our simple two-person example, if these persons had been exactly the same in every respect, and therefore could do every job equally well, there would have been no reason for specialization since total output could not have been increased. (Go back to Table 1-1 and make Mr. Smith equally productive in producing both granola and ice cream, and then see what happens to our example after specialization.)

In fact, people are not uniformly talented. Even if they were, even if an individual or a nation had the talent to do *everything* better (for example, by using fewer resources, especially person-hours), individuals and nations would still want to *specialize in the area of their comparative advantage.* A good example involves former President William Howard Taft. Before he became President, he was probably the country's fastest stenographer. He might have been at the same time the country's best typist, best violin player, and best everything else, but he decided to become President when elected because that was where his comparative advantage lay. Had he declined the Presidency to remain a stenographer, the cost to him of that action would have been tremendous.

To continue the example, consider the dilemma of the president of a large company. He or she can type better than any of the typists, file better than any of the file clerks, drive a truck better than any of the truckdrivers, and wash windows better than any of the window washers. That just means that the president has an absolute advantage in all these endeavors. However, his or her comparative advantage lies in managing the company, not in doing the aforementioned tasks. How is it known that that is where the comparative advantage lies? The answer is quite easy: The president is paid the most for being president, not for being a typist or a file clerk or a window washer or a truckdriver for the company. The same is true of the simple two-person economy we previously discussed. If someone were paying Ms. Jones and Mr. Smith, Mr. Smith would obviously be paid more to specialize in producing granola rather than ice cream. In fact, he could figure that out all by himself. To get 1 more pound of ice cream, he would have to give up 3 pounds of granola. However, for Ms. Jones to get 1 more pound of ice cream, she only has to give up 1 pound of granola. She, therefore, has a comparative advantage in producing ice cream, and he, therefore, has a comparative advantage in producing granola, because in both cases the cost of *not* producing the other commodity is lower.

Opportunity Costs

We have a term for the cost of not doing something. That term is **opportunity cost,** defined as the *value of the highest forgone alternative.* What is the opportunity cost of Ms. Jones's making one more pound of ice cream? It is 1 pound of granola. What is the opportunity cost for Mr. Smith if he makes one more pound of ice cream? It is 3 pounds of granola. Since the opportunity cost of producing ice cream is lower for Ms. Jones than for Mr. Smith, Ms. Jones has a comparative advantage in producing ice cream. A useful way of looking at comparative advantage is to understand that it exists whenever opportunity costs are different for producing different things.

But the concept of opportunity cost is much broader and will be used more extensively in the rest of this book. What is the opportunity cost of sitting in an economics lecture? Since you are not working at some income-producing job, you do not have the opportunity to spend one more hour on the job and get one more hour's worth of pay. However, you have available other opportunities, such as playing tennis, or swimming, or reading a book for another class, or drinking coffee in the student union, or listening to records. The fact is you have numerous alternatives available to you, and you can measure the opportunity cost of an economics lecture by figuring out the value you place on the highest alternative among your available choices. Thus, the opportunity cost of your time is equal to its highest alternative use value. Hence, opportunity cost is sometimes called *alternative cost*.

Economics As a Science

Economics is a social science and, as such, shares many techniques and shortcomings with the other social sciences. Each of the social sciences is a special area of inquiry, but these areas overlap to some degree. These sciences are "social" to the extent that they deal, in the final analysis, with human behavior.

Assumptions

All sciences rest on some body of assumptions that form the basis for theories or hypotheses or *models*. A model is merely a simplified, interrelated set of ideas about how the world works. A sociologist will develop a theory or model to explain why a certain event occurred or why a certain subsector of the population acts in a specific way. A political scientist will develop a theory to explain why a nation acted in the way it did vis-à-vis an enemy. We can hope that the political scientist's theory can be used to predict (both forward and backward in time) what will happen in a similar situation in other countries. Of course, this is exactly the same thing that a physicist or biologist does.

Many people have the idea that in some real sense physics is a more exact science than economics, sociology, or psychology. This is an oversimplification of the differences between these sciences. Physics is the study of physical phenomena. Physicists hypothesize theories and test them either by running experiments or by observing physical phenomena in the real world. Economists examine the behavior of individuals and groups of individuals. Just as physicists build theories or models, so too do economists. Both are empirical sciences. One problem in economics is that well-controlled experiments are difficult to set up. Economists must usually be content with observing what has happened in the past in order to test theories that they have devised.

All theories rest on givens, or axioms, or assumptions. However, many students balk at the assumptions used in economists' models. In fact, that is what originally got us into this section. Implicitly, we have used the assumption that individuals prefer to have more than less, that individuals can be assumed to run their lives so as to maximize their ability to consume goods and services. Generally, we call this assumption *utility maximization*—where utility refers to satisfaction. In the following pages we will adhere to a narrower assumption, **wealth maximization.**

The Role of Assumptions

It may be true that the assumption of wealth maximization on the part of individuals is an oversimplification. But everything is a simplification in any explanation of what has happened. If it were not simplified, we would not be able to do anything with it; we would never be able to generalize from the particular to the whole and would therefore never be able to

predict anything. If a theory or hypothesis is so complex that it can refer only to a very specific situation, it cannot be used to analyze or predict what will happen in any other situation.

The assumption of wealth maximization generates the hypothesis that as the profitability increases in a specific area of economic endeavor, resources will flow into that area. And, conversely, if profitability is relatively low in a specific area, resources will flow out into other areas.

If you do not like the assumption that people are out to better themselves economically, that does not mean you will still not want to use it in your economic analysis, because what you would like to be able to do is predict how people will react to changes in their environment. If you can predict and analyze tolerably well using a model based primarily on an assumption of wealth maximization, you would not want, on moral grounds, to discard the assumption. This does not mean that social scientists are amoral but simply that, as scientists, they have to be very careful not to mix ethics with analysis. Some social scientists do become social reformers, but any successes they are able to effect are based on their knowledge of how people behave *in fact,* not on how they think people *should* behave.

The Complexity of the World

Because we have a finite capacity for reasoning and for understanding and because our brains can only hold a finite amount of data, we sometimes oversimplify and make assumptions that do not take everything into account when we analyze any situation. Economists have a tendency to leave out political, sociological, and psychological aspects when looking at any particular problem. This doesn't mean they consider those aspects irrelevant—indeed, more and more researchers are engaging in what are called interdisciplinary approaches to social science. However, only occasionally will we in this book step out of the economist's shoes into those of another social scientist. We are analyzing the economic events that have occurred and will occur in the United States and elsewhere.

Definitions of New Terms

Economics: The social science that is concerned with the way in which our limited resources are allocated—among alternatives today and also between today's uses and future uses. Economics involves making choices.

Scarcity: A condition that exists whenever all individuals taken together desire or want more of anything than exists. Scarcity forces us to make choices among limited alternatives.

Economic Good: Any good that is scarce; any good for which the quantity demanded exceeds the quantity supplied at a zero price.

Free Goods: The opposite of an economic good; any good for which additional quantities will yield no additional satisfaction to individuals.

Barter: A system of exchange in which a person trades one economic good directly for another economic good without the use of money.

Market: An institution that aids in the process of exchange. In any given market for any given good, the price of that good tends toward equality after transportation expenses and quality differences are accounted for.

Transactions Costs: All costs associated with engaging in economic exchange. Transactions costs include the cost of obtaining and disseminating information, the cost of initiating and policing contracts, and so forth.

Specialization: The act of dividing up productive activities among individuals, regions, and nations such that no individual is self-sufficient but rather specializes in certain productive activities and trades with others. Also called division of labor.

Comparative Advantage: A production advantage that arises out of different relative efficiencies in producing particular goods and services. Whenever opportunity costs are different for different individuals or different regions for doing the same productive activity, the one with the lowest opportunity cost will have a comparative advantage.

Opportunity Cost: The value of the highest forgone alternative; sometimes called alternative cost.

Chapter Summary

1. We live in a world of scarcity, which causes us to make choices among competing alternative uses of the scarce resources around us. Whenever we must make choices we are concerned with economics.
2. Economists study economic goods, that is, those which are scarce and those for which alternative competing uses exist.
3. Economics concerns itself mainly with voluntary exchanges and with the way in which individuals choose which exchanges to make from among alternative possibilities.
4. In a system without money as a medium of exchange, a barter system, in which goods are exchanged for goods, occurs.
5. Exchanges take place in a market, which is merely an institution that reduces transactions costs and allows for prices of similar products to tend toward uniformity.
6. Individuals have a comparative advantage in productive activities that yield a higher reward to them than to other people. Concentrating on this area leads to specialization or the division of labor.
7. As long as opportunity costs are different for different individuals, each individual will have a comparative advantage in some area and will be able, therefore, to benefit by specialization and trade.
8. The opportunity or alternative cost of an activity is the value of the highest forgone alternative. It tells an individual or a society the true cost of any action, whether that cost be implicit or explicit.
9. In any science a model is built based on a body of assumptions that can never be proved or disproved. The validity of that model or theory can be put to question, however, if that model or theory consistently predicts incorrectly.

Questions for Thought and Discussion

1. Can you think of any physical truths that are not theories?
2. What actions in your life do not have transactions costs?
3. Have you experienced the use of models in other social sciences, such as sociology or psychology?
4. Why do individuals specialize? What are some of the costs associated with specialization?
5. Do markets require for their existence that individuals engage in exchange through the intermediary good called money?

Selected References

Boulding, Kenneth E., *Economics As a Science,* New York: McGraw-Hill, 1970.
Maher, John E., *What is Economics?,* New York: Wiley, 1969.
Mundell, Robert A., *Man and Economics,* New York: McGraw-Hill, 1968, chap. 1.

Reading and Working with Graphs

Every day you read something containing a graphic display of an idea. For example, you probably have seen graphs showing the rapid rise in the cost of living or in taxes. We call those *descriptive* graphs because they are a means of describing some phenomenon that has occurred in our economy. The same is true of graphs that show how much unemployment there is over time, how fast the American standard of living has risen over time, and so on. Most students have little difficulty in understanding such diagrams.

However, when we move from the realm of descriptive diagrams to what we call *analytical* graphs, some confusion may arise. An analytical graph is merely a graphic representation of a theory or model. The theories and models that we discussed abstractly in the previous chapter can be presented in three different ways: in words, in equations (mathematically), or in graphs. We will present most of our theories with only words, but a lot of them can be more easily understood if they are also presented graphically. (We'll leave the mathematics for a more advanced course.) For those of you who have had little experience with graphs, this appendix should put you at ease so that, starting in Chapter 2, our graphic explanation of economic theories will not seem so foreign. As you will see, a graph may not be worth a thousand words, but it is certainly worth quite a few.

A Basic Graph

We have set out a graph in Figure A-1. It is merely two heavy lines denoted X for the horizontal one and Y for the vertical one. We have divided each into equal parts 10 units long. Each of the parts is numbered 1 through 10. In geometry, the horizontal axis or bottom line in the graph is called the X axis; the vertical one is the Y axis.

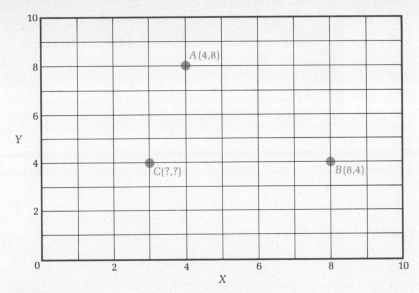

FIGURE A-1

The resultant criss-crossed graph resembles a sea captain's nautical chart, and in fact, if you had studied navigation, such a graph wouldn't be at all foreign to you. You would label the horizontal lines as latitude and the vertical lines as longitude. If somebody gave you a position, such as 38° longitude and 54° latitude, you would merely seek out the point on your nautical charts where the 54° latitude line intersected the 38° longitude line. We're not working with latitude and longitude, however, but with an abstract X and a Y. Later the X and the Y will be replaced by other things, like prices and quantities, interest rates and the amount of credit, and all the other things we study in economics. Right now, let's see if you can find the point at which X is equal to 4 and Y is equal to 8. That shouldn't be hard, and in fact we have labeled that point A. After the A we have put in parenthesis 4,8. This is a standard notation to show the coordinates of the point A. One other point is shown on the diagram also. It is labeled B, and its coordinates are 8 and 4, just the reverse of the above, meaning that it is a point where X is equal to 8 and

Y is equal to 4. We have also put in a point C. Can you find the coordinates of point C?

Charts or graphs using axes like those presented in Figure A-1 are generally used to show how one quantity of something varies with another. In Table A-1, we have shown a set of numbers giving the relationship between X and Y. That set of numbers is then plotted in the graph labeled Figure A-2. Here the resultant line or curve slopes downward from left to right. We say then that the two variables are inversely related. As X increases, Y decreases; and as X decreases, Y increases. (How would a positive relationship look?)

Charts or graphs are not limited to one curve or line. Figure A-3 shows the results of two relationships, one direct and the other inverse. The inverse one slopes downward, just as in the graph in Figure A-2, but the direct relationship slopes upward.

The Numbers on the Axes

We were careful in the first three diagrams to have both the X and the Y axes numbered

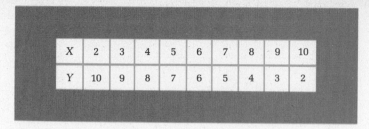

TABLE A-1

X	2	3	4	5	6	7	8	9	10
Y	10	9	8	7	6	5	4	3	2

exactly alike. This is not always the case. In fact, it would be impossible to number most axes exactly alike because we would be talking about two different variables. In descriptive graphs the variable on the horizontal, or X axis, is usually time in years, whereas the variable on the vertical axis might be the price level, standard of living, taxes, or something else. You must carefully label clearly on your graphs what the axes represent. You also have to pick a scale, and the scale will depend on the range over which you are graphing something. If you have a graph that is taking up, say, 2 inches of space on either axis and you want to graph a relationship between the price level and time for a period of, say, 10 years, the scale will be much different than if you take the same graph and put on the relationship between the cost of living and time over a period of 150 years. In the latter graph, you would have to have

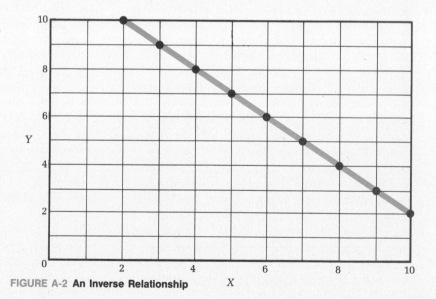

FIGURE A-2 **An Inverse Relationship**

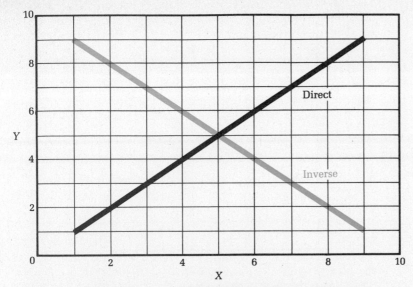

FIGURE A-3 **A Direct and An Inverse Relationship Shown on One Graph**

much smaller spaces between each year than in the former graph. There is no way to know ahead of time what your scale should be until you actually get to a graphic problem. Figures A-4 and A-5 show two possible scales that can be used for two separate problems using the same size graphs. Figure A-4 presents the historical relationship between time, labeled T on the horizontal axis, and the median family income in the United States for a 6-year period.

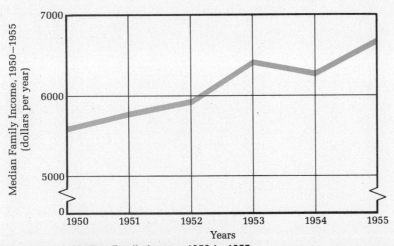

FIGURE A-4 **Median Family Income 1950 to 1955**

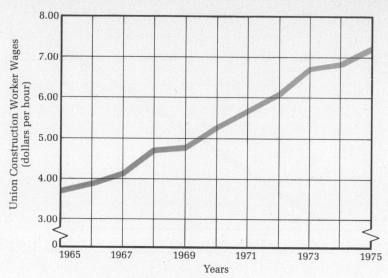

FIGURE A-5 Union Construction Worker Wages

Note that the vertical axis which used to be labeled Y is now labeled income, and everything is expressed in dollars. Now look at Figure A-5. Here we plot the average hourly pay for construction workers over an 11-year period. Again, the horizontal axis is time but the scale is different. The vertical axis is dollars, but it is labeled average wage, and of course its scale is vastly different than the one for the vertical axis in Figure A-4.

Does Money Mean Happiness?

HOW IMPORTANT IS MATERIAL WELL-BEING?

The Difficulty of Measuring Happiness

It is difficult, if not impossible, to measure how happy people are. Because happiness is a subjective state, there are no objective criteria that we can use to assess it. We simply have to ask people how they feel. Nonetheless, many of us hold common conceptions concerning what makes people happy. One common myth, probably partly based on idealized notions of the "simple life" or on Judeo-Christian teachings, is that the poor are really happier than the rich. However, we find out that no studies have given much support to the existence of "happy poverty."

An Opinion Poll

The American Institute of Public Opinion a number of years ago asked Americans whether they would rank themselves "very happy," "fairly happy," or "not very happy." They grouped the interviewees by income, level of education, sex, age, and other categories related to economic and social status.

The 1969 results were striking: 56 percent of those interviewed who had incomes in excess of $15,000 considered themselves to be "very happy." On the other hand, not even 30 percent of those in the income range of $3,000 and under considered themselves to be "very happy." Looked at another way, those who responded that they were "not very happy" numbered a mere 4 percent among the higher-income group but represented over 13 percent in the very low-income group.

Another Study Confirms

A study published under the auspices of the National Opinion Research Center confirms these findings: "To those who have the attributes that go with positions higher in the social structure, such as higher education and income, also go the psychic rewards of greater happiness.[1] The study suggested that there is a high correlation between level of income and general feelings of happiness.

[1]Norman M. Bradburn, *The Structure of Psychological Well-being*, Chicago, Ill.: Aldine, 1969, p. 226.

Other Factors Affecting Happiness

Now income per se is not really what we are talking about. Nobody has ever concluded from such poll results that individuals become happier simply because they have more income. Rather, happiness probably increases with income because higher income allows individuals to consume more goods and services. Note also that these goods and services do not necessarily have to be only big cars and fancy houses. They can include better health care, better diet, more education, more travel, more cultural activities, and freedom from worry, from overwork, or from working at boring jobs.

It is thus somewhat misleading to say that income itself leads to happiness. Rather, it is what income buys that may be causing the individuals' poll responses to indicate that they are happier when they have higher levels of income. In fact, when the pollsters asked more detailed questions of those being interviewed, they did indeed find out that happiness was highly correlated with such factors as health and family relationships. Note, though, that health is highly correlated with level of income because higher-income individuals spend more resources on better diet and medical care and are generally more educated so that they are aware of what is appropriate for improved health.

Comfort to the Economist

Since ''more is better than less'' is a key assumption in economists' theories and since much of what economists concern themselves with is the individual's quest for better material well-being, it is perhaps some comfort to know that there is an empirical correlation between higher levels of income and how happy individuals perceive themselves to be. At the very least, we can be sure that material well-being plays some role in people's happiness.

Questions for Thought and Discussion

1. ''Since it is virtually costless to dispose of undesired wealth, the question whether or not more income leads to more or less happiness does not seem like a very meaningful line of inquiry.'' Analyze this statement.
2. Is it possible to measure happiness objectively?

How Different Systems Solve the Economic Problem

The basic economic problem reared its head in the first issue of this book. Whether you consider nature stingy or generous, you must agree that human beings never have all they could conceivably desire. They have unlimited wants, and decisions therefore have to be made about who gets what and how much. The way such decisions are made depends on the economic and social system in which one is operating. We will look at the two major economic systems operating today—**capitalism** and **socialism**—and consider two of their real-world variants, American capitalism and Soviet socialism. Issue I-3 will provide a closer view of the Chinese method of solving the economic problem.

We will start the discussion by describing the output capabilities of any one nation, whether it be capitalist, socialist, or communist. In this way we can consider the connection between economic systems and the concepts of scarcity and opportunity costs, which were introduced in Chapter 1.

Society's Choices

Scarcity, or the limitation of the total resources needed for producing the different things which individuals and nations want, means that choices must be made between relatively scarce items. This can be easily demonstrated by use of a graph. (If that word scares you, go back to Appendix A.) To make the analysis simple, we'll look at a nation's production alternatives between, say, hamburgers and textbooks. Of course, this is an unrealistic example in the sense that no nation would produce only hamburgers and textbooks. It would be more realistic to talk about a nation's choice between military and civilian goods, agricultural and manufactured goods, and so on.

The Numbers

Table 2-1 shows five distinct alternatives for our hypothetical society. Notice that a *trade-off* occurs in each. To move from no hamburgers to 1 billion hamburgers, our economy must suffer a reduction of 10 million textbooks. The trade-off here, then, is between 1 billion hamburgers and 10 million textbooks. This trade-off, which changes as you go down the rows in Table 2-1, always means diverting resources away from textbook production and into hamburger production to get more hamburgers. We are assuming that the full resources available in the economy—labor, machines, natural materials, technology—are being used, so that the production alternatives in Table 2-1 represent the maximum technologically feasible alternatives there are.

Putting the Numbers onto a Graph

Let's see what happens when we turn the numbers in Table 2-1 into a graph. Look at points *A*, *B*, *C*, *D*, and *E* in Figure 2-1. The result is what we call the **production-possibility frontier,** a fancy name given to a graphical

Table 2-1 Alternatives Available

Here, the alternatives available to our society are hamburgers and textbooks. One alternative is to produce no hamburgers and 100 million textbooks. At the other extreme, we have no textbooks to read but 4 billion hamburgers ready to eat. In between the two extremes are several other alternatives open to this economy; each involves a trade-off and the diversion of textbook resources to the production of hamburgers.

	HAMBURGERS	TEXTBOOKS
A	0	100 million
B	1 billion	90 million
C	2 billion	70 million
D	3 billion	40 million
E	4 billion	0

depiction of a simple fact of life: In a full-employment economy, to produce one good you must direct resources from and therefore give up something of another good. All economic systems face this trade-off.

Note that the axes in Figure 2-1 are labeled with a time dimension, in this case "per year," because we have to specify the time during which the production of hamburgers or textbooks is going to take place. Certainly, the numbers would change if we were talking about production over a 10-year period rather than a 1-year period. After all, production occurs day in and day out. It is what we call a **flow,** as opposed to a **stock.** The number of textbooks waiting at your local bookstore we call a stock, but we refer to the production of textbooks over a year as a flow. When we draw a graph or talk about, for example, production and consumption, we have to specify the time period. Usually, it is a year if it is not specified.

Inefficiency and Underemployment

Look at point *U* in the production-possibilities frontier in Figure 2-1. What does it represent? It either represents a point of inefficient use of available resources in producing textbooks or represents a situation of less than full employment, or *underemployment,* in which workers as well as machines are idle. The problems of being inside the production-possibilities frontier are discussed in greater detail in later sections of this book.

Why the Production-Possibilities Frontier Is Bowed Outward (the Law of Diminishing Returns)

If you look at the curve *ABCDE* in Figure 2-1, representing the production possibilities for an economy, you will see that it is bowed outward.

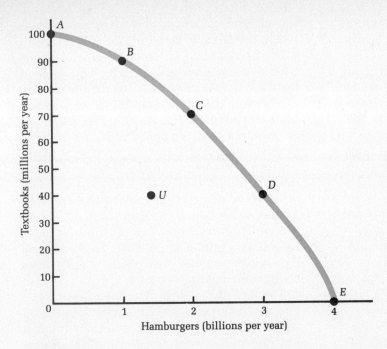

FIGURE 2-1 **Production-Possibilities Frontier**
On the horizontal axis we measure hamburgers per year expressed in billions. On the vertical axis we measure textbooks per year expressed in millions. We take the various alternatives open to society from Table 2-1 to give us points A, B, C, D, and E. That curve is called the production-possibilities frontier. It represents the maximum production possible if all resources are fully utilized. (There are, of course, an infinite number of combinations from which a society can choose.) Point U is inside the production-possibilities frontier and represents resource unemployment or inefficiency.

That is not an accidental shape but a graphic representation of a law which is a true in all economies. Briefly, the bulge shows that it is increasingly expensive to shift productive resources out of one good into the other. To see how relatively more expensive it becomes, let's go back to Table 2-1.

When we are producing no hamburgers, we can produce 100 million textbooks. If we shift just enough resources out of textbook production to increase hamburger production by 1 billion, we sacrifice only 10 million books. But how about at the other end of the scale? What about going from the production of 3 billion hamburgers per year to the production of 4 billion? Again, we have an increase of only 1 billion hamburgers, but now that increase costs us 40 million books. In other words, there is an increasing opportunity cost as we increasingly shift production from one activity to another.

What explains this increasing opportunity cost? First, the factors of production are specialized; that is, some resources are just plain better suited for producing one good than another. Resources are better combined in one way for producing, say, hamburgers and in another way for producing, say, textbooks. A compromise, to keep costs to a minimum, is therefore chosen. Thus, as resources shift from textbook production to hamburger production, the appropriate proportions of resources used for textbooks must be more or less employed for hamburgers. Hence, increasing costs and diminishing returns.

Second, we have the **law of diminishing returns.** The easiest way to understand this law, which we will meet over and over again, is to consider two broad categories of goods. Instead of hamburgers, we'll talk about all food products, and instead of textbooks, we'll talk about all manufactured goods.

This is what we do in Figure 2-2. We've merely redrawn Figure 2-1 with different labels on the axes. When we reduce the production of manufactured goods we shift workers from manufacturing into agriculture. We are going to assume here that workers are the only *variable input* to consider. The *fixed input* in the production process for agriculture is land.

At first, when we shift workers onto land there is lots of it around, and the increase in agricultural production is great. This can be seen by looking at the movement from *A* to *C* on the production-possibilities curve. All we had to give up in terms of manufacturing goods was the amount *AB*, and we got the amount *BC* in agricultural goods in return. However, look what happens on the next round. Again we have given up an amount, *CD*, which is just equal to the previous amount, *AB*, of manufacturing goods, but lo and behold, the increase in agricultural output is a far cry from *BC*. It is much smaller, actually only *DE*. This is what we would expect. We can get only a *diminish-*

ing amount of extra output when we successively add equal units of our variable input to a fixed amount of some other input. In our simple case, the variable input is workers, and the fixed input in agricultural pursuits is land.

Think of specific examples where you add more and more variable input to a fixed amount of another input. Suppose you owned some farmland and had 100 workers. If you added another 100 workers, do you think you would double output? If you're not sure, ask yourself what would happen if you added 4000 workers. Would your output be increased 40 times? Probably not, because some of those workers would start getting in the other workers' way, reducing the amount of output that each worker could contribute to the total.

The law of diminishing returns is generally operative everywhere. When you start producing, the law may be one of increasing returns, but returns will eventually diminish. Sometimes it is only after you add a considerable number of equal doses of the variable input

FIGURE 2-2 **The Law of Diminishing Returns**

This production-possibilities curve between agriculture and manufactured goods can be used to demonstrate the law of diminishing returns. What we do is start at point *A*, where we have no agricultural goods and all manufactured goods being produced. We now reduce the production of manufactured goods from *A* to *B* and shift those productive resources into the agricultural sector. The increase in agricultural production is relatively large—*B* to *C*. Now we reduce manufacturing production again by the same amount as before so that *CD* is equal to *AB*. What is our possible increase in agricultural goods? Only *DE*, which is certainly smaller than *BC*. The same is true throughout the rest of the graph. As we shift equal amounts of productive capacity from manufacturing to agriculture, we obtain smaller and smaller increases in agricultural output. This diminishing incremental increase can be attributed to the fixity of land, one kind of input.

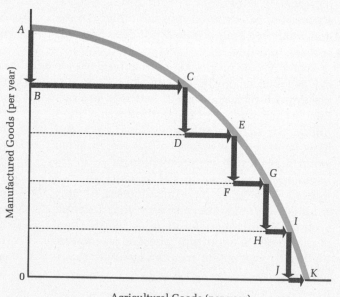

that diminishing returns set in and you get the bowed-out production-possibilities curve depicted in Figures 2-1 and 2-2. The curve is a reasonable and accurate representation of the trade-offs facing any economy.

But who decides at which point on that curve to operate? The answer depends on where one is because the economic system determines how and by whom that decision is made. Let us now ask the question, "What is an economic system?"

What Is an Economic System?

Any economic system must deal with the following fundamental questions: What is to be produced? How is it to be produced? Who is to receive what is produced? In analyzing economic systems, we will keep these fundamental questions in mind.

We might formally want to characterize an economic system as all the institutional means through which national resources are used to satisfy human wants. By institutions we mean principally the laws of the nation, but we may also mean the habits, ethics, and customs of the citizens of that nation.

It should be obvious that all economic systems are artificial; none of them is God-given or sent from the stars. All economic institutions are just what human beings have made them,

and when modifications of laws and other institutions occur, they are made by human beings: the judges, workers, government officials, consumers, and legislators are the ones who change, destroy, create, renovate, and resuscitate economic institutions.

These institutions are flexible and continually undergo change. After all, in the Middle Ages we had a feudal system. In the sixteenth and seventeenth centuries, mercantilism was the dominant system. After mercantilism came laissez-faire capitalism. The history of economic systems is one of constant change.

Alternative Economic Systems

One possible way of comparing alternative economic systems is to look at how decentralized their economic decision-making processes are. We can see in Figure 2-3 that on the extreme right-hand side is pure free-enterprise capitalism, where all economic decisions are made by individuals without government intervention. On the extreme left-hand side of the scale we see pure command socialism, where most economic decisions are made by some central authority. Somewhere in between would be the mixed economic systems such as we have in the United States and in the United Kingdom. The closer we go to a pure capitalist system, the less political centralization there is, and vice

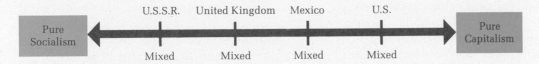

FIGURE 2-3 Scale of Decentralization

On the extreme right-hand side of the diagram we find pure capitalism, which no country follows. On the extreme left-hand side is pure socialism, which again no country follows. In the middle are all the mixed economies in the world. The U.S.S.R., the United Kingdom, Mexico, and the United States are shown, with the United States closer to capitalism, of course, than any of the others.

versa. Some economists like to distinguish economies according to whether or not they are planned, that is, whether or not the economy is a (political) **command economy** or a decentralized economy.

Four questions must be answered when analyzing different economic systems, and the answers to these questions indicate the attributes that each system has. If we want to know how any given economic system works, we must find out:

1. Who is permitted to own which items of wealth?
2. What kinds of incentives are presented to people to induce them to produce?
3. What forces determine the individual benefits that people get from producing?
4. Which lines of economic activity may individuals engage in on their own initiative and which lines are forbidden? What are individuals allowed to do with the proceeds of permitted activities?

Let's take a look at capitalism in theory and see how its economic institutions answer these four questions.

Capitalism in Theory

The theoretical concept of capitalism is usually associated with the father of laissez-faire[1] economics, Adam Smith, who wrote *The Wealth of Nations* in 1776. Smith described a system in which the government had little to do with economic endeavors other than enforce contracts between people. Individuals pursued their own self-interest and in so doing—according to his doctrine of the "invisible hand"—maximized the income and social welfare of the nation. Capitalism in its purest form may never

[1]The French phrase translates loosely as "let alone."

have existed, even though classical writers sometimes described theoretical capitalism as if it did exist.

Difference between Capital and Capitalism

At the outset, we should be careful to distinguish between *capital* and *capitalism*. In this book, *capital* has been used in two senses: One is *money* capital, and the other is *physical* capital. Money capital is a claim on resources, and business firms have to raise money capital either by borrowing, selling shares of stock, or using their own savings. Firms use the proceeds of those efforts to purchase physical capital for the production of goods and services that they later sell, hopefully for a profit. "Capital" can refer both to artificial things and to natural, tangible things that are not directly used in consumption. Capital goods assist in the production of other capital goods and of consumption goods. Obviously, every economic system, regardless of its label, has some sort of physical capital, if only the land on which individuals work.

To define capitalism, we must look to the economic institutions that characterize it and how these institutions answer the four questions we have posed. We shall use the following definition:

Capitalism is an economic system in which individuals privately own productive resources and possess the right to use these resources in whatever manner they choose, subject to certain (minimal) legal restrictions.

Notice here that we used the term *productive resources* rather than *capital*. This takes into account not only machines and land but also labor services. We see, then, that the definition of capitalism includes (at least implicitly) the right of individuals to use their talents in their own best interest. One of the most fundamental economic institutions in a capitalist system is that of private **property rights.**

Private Property

The ownership of property under a capitalist system is usually vested in individuals or in groups of individuals. That is, the state is not the owner of all property, as in some other systems which we might come up with in theory. In the United States, the government does own certain pieces of property, but in general we live under a system of private property rights. Private property is controlled and enforced through the legal framework of laws, courts, and police. Under capitalism, individuals have their property rights protected; are usually free to use their private property as they choose, as long as they do not infringe on the legal property rights of others; and are usually allowed to enter into private contractual agreements that are mutually satisfying.

These statements really apply to the realm of pure capitalism. In our **mixed capitalist system,** the government often intervenes in contracts between individuals, even when their private property is concerned. In some states, even if someone is willing, you cannot lend him or her money at an interest rate that exceeds a stipulated maximum. In some industries, you could not go to work for a wage rate below a specified minimum, even if you were willing to do so. You are prevented from using your private property—your personal labor services—in any manner that you see fit.

Under capitalism, the existence of private property rights makes the owners of productive resources the controllers of those resources. Exchanges of these resources are made between property owners who are largely private persons rather than government officials, bureaucrats, or politicians. Moreover, in a private property system, any accumulation of wealth that you as an individual amass throughout your life belongs to you and to no one else. You can decide who will get that accumulation of wealth upon your death. In fact, inheritance rights are a key aspect of capitalism in its purest form, for they provide an incentive for accumulation and conservation of wealth and thereby help keep the system going. In the United States there are taxes on inheritance, but there are few restrictions on how inherited wealth can be distributed.

Free Enterprise

Another attribute of a purely capitalistic system is free enterprise, which is merely an extension of the concept of property rights. Theoretically, free enterprise allows individuals to freely select economic activities for whatever resources they own and to seek whatever occupation they want; there are no restrictions. In the United States, however, people are not generally free to go into any occupation they wish. Try to become a doctor without first getting admitted to a medical school. Try to become a plumber without getting admitted to the plumbers' union.

Free enterprise is probably another way of stating laissez-faire. In a free-enterprise capitalistic system (at least in theory), productive resources are generally supposed to be directed toward their best uses. Presumably, workers will go where they can make the most money and, therefore, contribute the most to the social product.

The Price System

The way productive resources generally are directed to their best uses is via changing prices. We therefore talk about a price, or market, system in which just about everything that is exchanged has its price. There are virtually no legal restrictions on the prices for permitted goods or services. Prices are set only by the market forces that we will describe in Chapter 3, when we talk about supply and demand. Briefly, it is the interaction between buyers and sellers in a marketplace that results in changes in the prices of goods and services; prices, then, reflect *relative* scarcities.

The Role of Government

Even in a purely capitalistic system, there is still a role for government, for someone has to enforce private property rights. The government protects the rights of individuals and businesspersons to keep private property private, to keep the control of the property vested with the owners. Even the father of free enterprise, Adam Smith, described in some detail the role of government in a purely capitalist system. He talked about the need for government in providing national defense and in eliminating monopolies that would restrain trade.

American Capitalism

If America had a pure capitalist system, the economic problem would be solved forthrightly within the context of that system. Scarce goods would be allocated according to who wanted them most, evidenced by each individual's willingness to pay the market price for each item in question. In essence, individuals would vote in the marketplace with their dollars. When a good became relatively scarce, its price would rise, thus causing some consumers to cut back in their purchases of that good but at the same time encouraging some suppliers to increase their production of that good. Resources would seek out areas in which they yielded the highest reward. Individuals would not be restricted in seeking employment where they obtained the highest wages.

Restrictions in the American System

The American brand of capitalism, however, is not pure. All resources, for example, do not flow to areas where they yield the highest rewards for their private owners. There are numerous restrictions on economic activity in the United States by both government bodies and private organizations. Government restrictions make our system of capitalism a mixed one in which some elements of centralization or command by a political body enter into decisions on where resources should go, how they can be used, and who should get them. Moreover, the private sector in the economy obtains some of its goods and services—including fire and police protection and education—from the government. And most income-maintenance schemes are devices whereby some taxpayers put money into the general coffers so that that money can be redistributed to other individuals, not as a payment for services but rather as a gift, or income transfer.

Competition and Capitalism

In the purely capitalist system envisioned by Adam Smith, competition would always prevail. However, in the mixed American system it does not because some large firms control entire markets. Two well-known industries have no competition: the telephone company and the electric company. It has been argued that to a lesser extent large companies in the steel, aluminum, and rubber industries prevent competition.

In brief, although the American version of capitalism is based on free enterprise and private property rights, there are many exceptions. We cannot always be safe in applying the model of pure capitalism to our own country in order to answer the question "How is the economic problem solved?" Often, political decisions enter into the solution, and we must take these into account—especially when we try to understand how noncapitalist countries solve the economic problem. Most of these countries have systems that operate under some form of socialism.

Socialism in Theory

A socialist economy is often called a command economy because there is an authority, somebody in the government, who commands the means of production, such as land and machines. One of the most prevalent features in any theoretical socialist system is the attempt to redistribute income. The government will typically use its taxing powers to reduce inherited wealth and large incomes. Socialist systems usually have larger welfare services provided by the collective purse of the government than do even mixed capitalist systems.

Socialism As a Movement

"Socialism" usually refers to a movement that aims to vest in society, rather than in the individual, the ownership and management of all **producer goods** (capital goods used in any large-scale production). When we call socialism a movement, we imply that there exist organizations and programs at work to transform socialistic ideals into some concrete economy in which certain property rights—specifically property rights in producer goods—are vested in "society as a whole." However, to speak of "society as a whole" is to assume the continued existence of some form of *organized* society, that is, a society organized on "democratic" principles.

If the ownership of the means of production were vested in a group of people whose actions did not reflect the wishes of the masses, that would not be ownership by "society as a whole." Essentially, if the ownership and management of producer goods are to be vested in society as a whole, then the decisions concerning the use of those goods will be made "directly" by society rather than by individuals. Socialism as a movement, then, is really concerned with transferring decision-making powers from individuals to society. Most theories of socialism assume that this transference of power takes place only for large-scale, not for small-scale, production. Land and tools used personally by their owners, for example, are not usually subject to decision making by "society as a whole." Also implicit in the theoretical definitions of socialism is that a socialist economy will lead to increased output for the nation as a whole.

Economics—the Core of Socialism

Obviously, the heart of socialism is economic. The central issues include who should have the property rights in producer goods, who should make decisions about the use of these goods, and how income should be distributed once it is created. To be sure, around this central economic core there will be political, social, religious, and other types of issues. In fact, many of these issues seem to loom larger than the economic ones in current discussions of socialism. The central problem, however, is how to alter society's methods of producing, distributing, and consuming economic goods. We know—and socialists do not deny—that a change from a capitalistic system to the institutions necessary for a socialistic system will also entail many social, philosophical, religious, and even psychological changes.

Key Attributes

Perhaps we can best isolate the key attributes of a socialistic system by seeing how it answers the four questions outlined previously.

1. Although individuals are allowed to own many items of wealth, in a socialist system the government owns the major productive resources, such as land and capital goods. Individuals can own consumer goods and consumer durables, but they are not allowed to own factories, machines, and other things that are used to produce what society wants.
2. People are induced to produce by wage differentials. However, taxation of large incomes to redistribute income does reduce some of the incentives to produce a lot.
3. The forces that determine the reward people get from producing are usually set by the state, not by the market. That is, the government, rather than supply and demand, determines people's wage rates and who should be paid what in government-owned and operated factories.
4. In a socialist system, individuals are allowed to enter only certain endeavors. They cannot, for example, set up their own factories. They cannot become entrepreneurs or capitalists, for the state controls such enterprises.

This summary explanation of socialism is purely on the theoretical level. The real-world varieties of socialist systems seem to have only one thing in common: Their governments control more factors of production than do capitalist governments. We should not underestimate the importance of control of resources either because in many cases controlling resources is more important than owning them. In socialist countries such as the Soviet Union, ownership of resources is widely dispersed but very centrally controlled. In other socialist countries, such as Yugoslavia, both control and ownership of resources is widely dispersed because workers in individual factories largely control those organizations by assuming management functions. In the United States, both ownership and control of resources are widely dispersed, too, but government controls fewer factors of production.

Since we have taken a look at American capitalism, let's now take a look at Russian socialism and compare that system with socialist theory.

Russia Today

In the Soviet Union, the state owns almost all the factors of production. Workers receive wages, and they can choose what they want to spend their lives doing. However, Soviet citizens do not have as much geographic mobility as American citizens do, and they have to ask permission to take a job in another region or in another industry. They usually receive permission to move to a place where they think they can make higher wages; in fact, the current system now tries to attract workers to different locations by a system of wage differentials.

In the past, physical quotas were set for factories, but they caused too many problems: Factories would put out numerous items, all of poor quality, just to meet the physical quota. The typical Soviet factory is now generally evaluated according to some overall concept of profitability. The government does not measure profitability in the same way a factory in the United States measures it, but it is moving in that direction. Within the factory itself, the managers—in addition to getting a better-than-average paycheck—obtain special benefits that workers are not allowed to have, such as travel expenses, perhaps a car, and other privileges. This is a centralized system, and although there seems to be a change toward more and more decentralization, there is a continuous hierarchy within an individual firm and within economic life itself. Right now there are regional economic councils, above them a council of ministers, and beyond that, planners who decide which industries should do what.

Resource Allocation

Remember that in the United States, resources flow to where their relative rates of return are highest. If the highest rate of return is in making consumer goods, then resources will flow into making consumer goods. Individuals more or less decide how much should be saved and invested, how much put away and not consumed. And the amount of saving that the whole economy actually engages in follows these individuals' decisions.

Such is not the case in the Soviet Union. Generally, the planners decide how many of the economic resources available should be used in producing what consumers want, as opposed to producing what we'll call *capital equipment*—machines and the like. After the Bolshevik Revolution of 1917, there was a distinct drop in the amount of production that went to satisfy consumer wants. In fact, one of the reasons Russia grew so rapidly is that it spent a large amount of its resources in *capital formation* so it would have a higher level of living in the future.

Until recently very little market information was used to determine which consumer goods should be produced. The obvious result: lots of things in short supply and other things oversupplied or never bought at all. Today, however, central planners realize that when consumer goods are not purchased, production should be slowed down and that when goods are in short supply, production should be increased. Russian planners are even starting to engage in marketing surveys to see what consumers really want.

The Problem of Coordination

Since the Soviet Union is a command economy, it faces a fundamental problem of coordination. Even if a central plan mandates a 20 percent increase in steel production, planners must take additional steps to ensure that there are sufficient supplies, raw materials, and capital and labor for such an increase in steel output. For example, if the iron-mining industry does not achieve its quota, the desired goal for steel production will not be met. You can imagine what problems there might be in coordinating such economic endeavors nationwide.

Central planners somehow have to make sure that each of over 200,000 industrial enterprises in Russia today receives resources in correct amounts and at the right time to keep production moving smoothly. Millions, if not billions, of planning decisions must be made, and they are all interrelated. Mathematicians and computer experts have come up with advanced techniques to help the planners cope with such massive problems of coordination. For example, they analyze the relationship between inputs and outputs in different sectors of the economy and put their estimates into what are called input-output tables. The information in these tables tells planners how much input they require to change a specific output in a specific industry. This is one way they can avoid bottlenecks.

The planning techniques used in the Soviet Union are certainly too complicated to go into in this brief discussion. We know that priorities are established, with heavy industry given special status as a "leading link" and consumer goods assigned a lower priority. We also know that Soviet planners depend on large reserves or inventories of, for example, ball bearings, so that bottlenecks will be avoided. In any event, to get a command economy working, there is an enormous administrative problem.

The Economic Problem Is Universal

By now you should be convinced that the economic problem—scarcity—is common to all economic systems; only the solutions differ. Most of what we will discuss in the remaining pages of this book centers on the American capitalist system and a number of other mixed capitalist systems throughout the world. However, do not be surprised to find that you can apply the analysis you learn for our system to totally different systems—particularly to systems in which the assumption of individual wealth maximization is valid. Few economists would find it invalid. However, those visiting the Chinese mainland believe, to some extent, that this assumption is inappropriate for analyzing the behavior of Chinese citizens. This is such a fascinating possibility that we treat it in the following issue.

<table>
<tr><td>Definitions of New Terms</td><td>

Capitalism: An economic system in which individuals privately own productive resources and can use them in whatever manner they choose, subject to certain legal restrictions.

Socialism: An economic system in which producer goods for large-scale production are owned and controlled primarily by the state.

Production-Possibility Frontier: The line (or set of points) showing the boundary between that which can and that which cannot be produced at a moment in time, given the available resources in the community. At any point on the production-possibility frontier it is impossible to produce more of one good without producing less of another.

Flow: Those variables that are defined per unit time period. For example, income is a flow that occurs per week, per month, or per year.

Stock: The quantity of something, as measured at a point in time, for example, an inventory of goods and a bank account. Stocks are defined independently of time although they are assessed at a point in time.

Law of Diminishing Returns: A proposition stating that after some point, if all factors of production save one are fixed, an increase in that one variable input will yield a less-than-proportionate increase in output.

Command Economy: An economic system in which the central political authority allocates scarce resources.

Property Rights: Legal rights in property. We usually talk about private property rights where individuals have control over the use and disposal of whatever they legally own.

Mixed Capitalist System: A system that combines private property ownership with the ownership and control of certain aspects of the economy by government authorities.

Producer (Capital) Goods: Goods used in the production of other goods. Machinery and buildings are often called producer goods.

</td></tr>
</table>

Definitions of New Terms

Capitalism: An economic system in which individuals privately own productive resources and can use them in whatever manner they choose, subject to certain legal restrictions.

Socialism: An economic system in which producer goods for large-scale production are owned and controlled primarily by the state.

Production-Possibility Frontier: The line (or set of points) showing the boundary between that which can and that which cannot be produced at a moment in time, given the available resources in the community. At any point on the production-possibility frontier it is impossible to produce more of one good without producing less of another.

Flow: Those variables that are defined per unit time period. For example, income is a flow that occurs per week, per month, or per year.

Stock: The quantity of something, as measured at a point in time, for example, an inventory of goods and a bank account. Stocks are defined independently of time although they are assessed at a point in time.

Law of Diminishing Returns: A proposition stating that after some point, if all factors of production save one are fixed, an increase in that one variable input will yield a less-than-proportionate increase in output.

Command Economy: An economic system in which the central political authority allocates scarce resources.

Property Rights: Legal rights in property. We usually talk about private property rights where individuals have control over the use and disposal of whatever they legally own.

Mixed Capitalist System: A system that combines private property ownership with the ownership and control of certain aspects of the economy by government authorities.

Producer (Capital) Goods: Goods used in the production of other goods. Machinery and buildings are often called producer goods.

Chapter Summary

1. Every economic system must solve the economic problem of allocating scarce resources. In every economic system trade-offs must be made between producing one set of goods and services as opposed to an infinite number of other sets.

2. We can graphically show the concept of a trade-off by using a production-possibilities curve. At any point along that curve, society's resources

are being fully utilized. No point outside the curve is possible, and at any point inside the curve, underemployment of resources is implied.

3. The production-possibilities frontier is bowed outward for a number of reasons, the most obvious being that some resources are better suited for the production of particular commodities than other resources.

4. The law of diminishing returns is also operating. According to this proposition, after some point, less-than-proportionate increases in output will occur when one factor of production is increased in use.

5. An economic system deals with the questions of what should be produced, how should it be produced, and who is to receive what is produced. An economic system is a set of institutions that guides individuals in their use of resources. All economic systems are artificial.

6. We can look at the spectrum of systems in terms of how centralized (in a political sense) economic decision-making processes are. The United States has a less centralized economic system than the U.S.S.R.

7. It is important to distinguish between capital and capitalism. All economies have capital, but in a capitalist system individuals privately own productive resources and possess the right to use these resources in whatever manner they choose subject to certain legal restrictions.

8. A key aspect of a capitalistic system is the right to own private property and producer goods for large-scale production.

9. The capitalist system is sometimes called the free-enterprise system. This is merely an extension of the concept of private property rights. In a free-enterprise system, individuals can freely select economic activities for whatever resources they own.

10. American capitalism is certainly not a system of pure capitalism. Central authorities control and generate some resources throughout the economy.

11. In general, a socialist economic system is defined as one in which the major resources for production are owned by the state. The socialist system is often called a command economy.

12. In any command economy there is a problem of coordination. How does one coordinate the over 200,000 industrial enterprises in the U.S.S.R. today, for example?

Questions for Thought and Discussion

1. Since the means of production are owned by the state in a socialist system, would you expect to find less antisocial business behavior in the form of pollution in a socialist system?

2. The Soviet Union uses large amounts of capital. In one sense, is the Soviet Union capitalistic?

Selected References

Balinky, Alexander, *Marx's Economics: Origin and Development,* Lexington, Mass.: D. C. Heath, 1970.

Bornstein, Morris and Daniel R. Fussfeld (eds.), *The Soviet Economy,* 4th ed. Homewood, Ill.: Irwin, 1974.

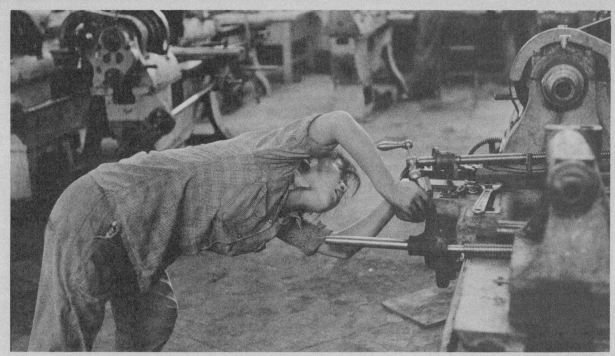

Photo by H. Cartier, Magnum

be not only to raise the level of material welfare of the population but also to develop the full human being. That is, each person in the economy should develop his or her creative powers (on an egalitarian basis).

In the United States we place a very high social and economic value on education, particularly higher education. The same is true in Maoist China, but the emphasis is a bit different: The aim of education is not just to make individuals more productive but to shape their values as communist citizens. Ideology, then, is a large part of each individual's education process.

There is a tendency toward nonspecialization in Maoist China—just the opposite of what has happened in the United States. Adam Smith once said specialization was determined by the extent of the market. In China, even though the market is huge, there is a tendency to *despecialize* workers so that there is no upper echelon of leaders, experts, authorities, and technicians. It appears, then, that Maoists are willing to pursue the goal of transforming workers into communist men and women, even if it means some slowdown in short-run economic growth.

However, as we have seen in Figure I-3.1, the slowdown is not at all apparent. According to Maoist thought, the elimination of specialization will increase workers' willingness to work hard for social rather than individual goals. Moreover, despecialization allows workers to get a broader view of the world around them because they are forced to participate in numerous production processes. The cost to the worker is struggle. According to Mao, "Unprincipled peace [gives rise] to a decadent philistine attitude. . . ." Progress, then, must be made by struggling with the world around oneself. One of the struggles is, of course, the same old Marxist class conflict: the proletariat versus the bourgeoisie.

Serving the Proletariat

According to social thinkers and decision makers in the new China, every individual must be devoted to the masses rather than to his or her own economic and personal ends. In other words, workers should be

Photo by Marc Riboud, Magnum

We have already noted the tremendous economic development in communist China. More impressive than that, however, is the conclusion Professor Gurley made:

> The basic overriding economic fact about China is that for 20 years she had fed, clothed, and housed everyone, has kept them healthy, and has educated most. Millions have not starved; sidewalks and streets have not been covered with multitudes of sleeping, begging, hungry, and illiterate human beings; millions are not disease ridden. To find such deplorable conditions one does not look to China these days but, rather, to India, Pakistan, and almost anywhere else in the underdeveloped world. These facts are so basic, so fundamentally important, that they completely dominate China's economic picture, even if one grants all of the erratic and irrational policies alleged by her numerous critics.[3]

What is important, according to Gurley, is that communist China is engaged in a social and economic experiment in which there is an attempt to develop industrially without dehumanization. The Marxist-Leninist goal is that eventually a communist man or woman will emerge in a classless society where every person works according to his or her ability and consumes according to his or her needs.

Is there a new breed of people

[3] Ibid., p. 31.

willing to serve the world proletariat. This differs little from the standard Communist Party line, "workers of the world, unite." The worker will work hard for the community or the nation rather than for his or her own selfish goals. To this end, Maoists deemphasize all material incentives because these lead to the decadence of bourgeois capitalist societies. Hence, workers must be disciplined and selfless. There must be unity. This is the aim of all teachings throughout mainland China.

Deemphasizing Careers

In keeping with the view that individuals should not specialize, Maoists have tried to eliminate the distinction between the city and the country. Consequently, most people who work in the city have to spend time farming in the country. Each person thus becomes a well-rounded communist man or woman, not a person who specializes in some specific type of career. And to avoid creating a hierarchy of bureaucrats and experts, much decision making is done by "the masses." This involves establishing new industries in rural areas even though the economic environment may not be the most favorable in those areas. The growth of cities as cultural and industrial centers has been discouraged for some time now. This, of course, imposes a loss in real output on the New China. But "So what," say the Maoists. "We are after the development of the communist man. And whatever development we have will be equitable, even if it is relatively inefficient."

Photo by Rene Burri, Magnum

in communist China? According to Professor Gurley, yes. One expert's account on the subject is hardly enough to answer the question, but it does give us a beginning. The Maoists claim that within each person numerous powers exist that can be released by proper ideological and economic planning. According to Gurley, ''If [the Maoists] are right, the implications for economic development are so important that it would take blind men on this side of the Pacific to ignore them.''

Time will tell.

Questions for Thought and Discussion

1. After reading this issue, do you think there is a new breed of people in China?
2. Is it possible to separate the social from the economic experiment in communist China?
3. Why do you think China isolated itself for so many years? Could this have been important for allowing the formation of the new men and women?

Selected References

Crook, F. W., ''Collective Farms in Communist China,'' *Monthly Labor Review,* March 1973, p. 45ff.

Eckstein, Alexander et al., *Economic Trends in Communist China,* Chicago: Aldine, 1968.

Galenson, Walter and Nai-Ruenn Chen, *The Chinese Economy under Communism,* Chicago: Aldine, 1969.

Hoffman, Charles, *Work Incentive Practices and Policies in the People's Republic of China, 1953–65,* Albany, NY: State University of New York Press, 1967.

Richman, Barry M., *Industrial Society in Communist China,* New York: Random House, 1969.

Wheelwright, E. L. and Bruce McFarlane, *The Chinese Road to Socialism,* New York: Monthly Review Press, 1970.

Some Economic Tools: Demand, Supply, and Elasticity

PART A: DEMAND AND SUPPLY

Market pricing makes up a good part of everyday activity in all countries. Crucial to understanding market pricing are the forces that underlie the determination of prices. Why does 1 pound of peanuts cost, say, $1, but 1 pound of macadamia nuts cost $3? Why does a steel worker earn, say, $10 an hour and a store clerk only $4 an hour? The only way to find out why the **relative price** of some things in our economy is high and that of other things is low is to understand what demand and supply are all about. We will first look at demand, then at supply, and finally put together the two concepts to show how prices are determined. After that, we will talk about some properties of demand and supply.

The Law of Demand

A commonsense notion of "demand" is simply "how much people want of something." You have a certain demand for records, Big Mac's, and textbooks, and so do I. In our analysis, however, we have to be careful about how we use that term because it can be confused with desire or want. Our desires, or wants, are unlimited; our demand for a particular scarce resource has to be limited because each of us has a limited income and therefore faces a personal scarcity problem. Since we all have limited incomes, we must solve our economic problem by allocating our incomes to various classes of expenditures. And here the pricing mechanism and **the law of demand** come into play. Since economic goods are provided to us only at a positive price (except where governments or other institutions provide the scarce resource at a zero price), it follows that none of us can completely ignore the price of things we buy. It also generally follows that at a higher relative price an individual will purchase less of most items. Why? Simply because if that person were to attempt to purchase the same quantity at a higher relative price than at a lower relative price, he or she would necessarily run out of income and be unable to buy the same quantities which could be bought at lower relative prices. Some people will decide that at a higher price a certain good, say, French fries, is just not worth it because they have to give up too much of other things they buy, such as Big Mac's and Cokes.

The Law in Words

The law of demand can now be stated succinctly:

> At higher (relative) prices, a lower quantity will be demanded than at lower (relative) prices, *ceteris paribus*.

Notice our use of "relative" before "prices." That's an important distinction to make when you want to study the demand for an individual commodity. Otherwise, you will get confused with problems involving all prices changing simultaneously in an up or down direction. Also notice that two funny Latin words were added at the end of the law of demand. *Ceteris paribus* simply means all other things are held constant. The reason we put it in the law of demand is fairly straightforward: All we are looking at is the relationship between prices and quantities demanded. Since we ignore, for the moment, all the other things which determine the demand for a good or service, we have to assume that all other things, such as income and the price of substitutes, do not change along with the relative price of the good or service in question.

The law of demand is not a law in the legal sense. Rather, it is a tendency that we commonly observe in the world around us, and it seems to accurately describe how individuals do behave when faced with a higher relative price for any commodity, *ceteris paribus*. After all, there are substitutes for most things that we buy, and if the price of those substitutes has not gone up, some of us will want to purchase them instead of paying a higher price for the alternative. If the price of butter goes up relative to the price of margarine, many households will sacrifice butter in favor of margarine.

The Law in Numbers

Let's take a hypothetical demand situation to see how the inverse relationship between the price and the quantity demanded looks. What we will do is consider the quantity of French fries demanded by American college students per year. Without stating the time dimension, we could not make any sense out of this demand relationship because the numbers would change if we were talking about the quantity demanded per month or per decade.

Look at Table 3-1. Here we show the price per constant-quality bag of French fries. Notice the words *constant quality*, which take care of the problem of varying quality in adding up all the bags of French fries that are sold, or could be sold, every year. After all, you would not count as equally valuable a bag of half-cooked, soggy fries and a bag of perfectly done, crisp ones sold at the same price.

What we see in Table 3-1 is that at a price of 10¢ per bag, 10 million bags would be bought by American college students each year, but at a price of 50¢ per bag, only 2 million would be bought. This reflects the law of demand. Table

Table 3-1 **Demand Schedule for French Fries by American College Students**

Column 1 presents the price per constant-quality bag of French fries. Column 2 presents the quantity demanded by American undergraduates, again measured in constant-quality bags per year of French fries. The last column merely labels these various price-quantity demanded combinations. Notice that as the price goes up, the quantity demanded per year falls.

PRICE PER CONSTANT-QUALITY BAG	QUANTITY DEMANDED OF CONSTANT-QUALITY BAGS PER YEAR	COMBINATION
$0.10	10 million	E
0.20	8 million	D
0.30	6 million	C
0.40	4 million	B
0.50	2 million	A

3-1 is also called a **demand schedule** because it gives a schedule of alternative quantities demanded per year at different prices.

The Law in Graphic Terms

We saw in Appendix A how tables expressing relationships between two variables can be represented in graphic terms. To do this here, we need only construct a graph that has the price per constant-quality bag on the vertical axis[1] and the quantity measured in constant-quality bags per year on the horizontal axis. All we have to do is take combinations *A, B, C, D,* and *E* from Table 3-1 and plot those points in Figure 3-1. Now we connect the points with a smooth line, and voilà, we have a **demand curve.** It is downward sloping to indicate the

inverse relationship[2] between the relative price of French fries and the quantity demanded per year by American undergraduates. Our presentation of demand schedules and curves applies equally well to all commodities, including toothpicks, hamburgers, textbooks, credit, and labor services.

Demand, of course, is only one side of the picture. The other side is supply, which we will now consider.

The Law of Supply

To derive a supply relationship for French fries, we can simply go back to the production-possibilities curves that we derived in Figures 2-1 and 2-2 on pages 27 and 28. We recreate that curve in Figure 3-2. On the horizontal axis we have French fries, and on the vertical axis we have all other goods. Now we measure equiva-

[1] Since we are really interested in the relative price of French fries, the vertical axis should be labeled "price for French fries/the price of other goods," not merely dollars and cents. The way around this problem is to standardize the units of all other goods so that a unit of all other goods costs exactly $1. Then, what we are showing on the vertical axis is essentially the relative price of French fries.

[2] An inverse, or negative, relationship (or correlation) is one in which an increase in one variable means a decrease in the other. A positive relationship (or correlation) is one in which the variables move in the same direction; an increase (or decrease) in one causes an increase (or decrease) in the other.

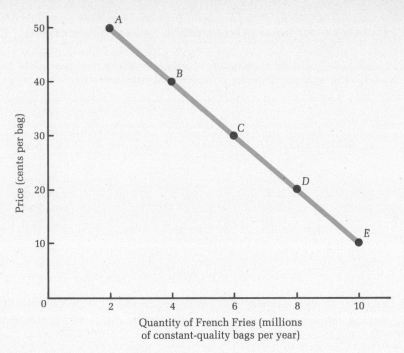

FIGURE 3-1 The Demand Curve for French Fries

We measure the quantity of French fries in millions of constant-quality bags per year on the horizontal axis and the price per constant-quality bag on the vertical axis. We then take the price-quantity combination from Table 3-1 and put them in this diagram. These points are *A*, *B*, *C*, *D*, and *E*. When we connect the points, we obtain a graphic representation of a demand schedule. It is downward sloping to show the inverse relationship between quantity demanded and price.

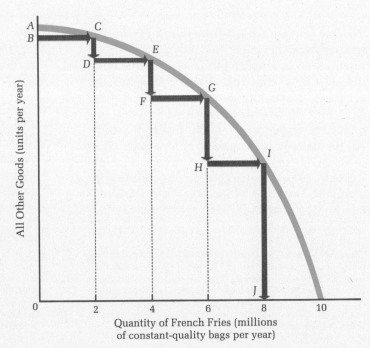

FIGURE 3-2 The Increasing Cost of Producing French Fries

Here we show a production-possibilities curve for all other goods and French fries. On the horizontal axis we measure French fries per year in millions of constant-quality bags, and on the vertical axis we give an unspecified measure of the production of other goods per year. Notice that as we increase French fry production by equal increments of 2 million bags per year, the reduction in the production of other goods becomes greater. As we move, for example, from 0 to 2 million French fries produced per year, the reduction of the output of other goods is only *AB*, but when we increase production by another 2 million, from 2 to 4 million French fries, the output of other goods falls by *CD*, which is greater than *AB*. We say, then, that because of the law of diminishing returns, opportunity cost rises as we increase French fry production.

lent units of French fries on the horizontal axis. As we go from zero to 2 million fries, we have to give up the quantity *A-B* of all other goods. Now, when we go from 2 to 4 million bags of fries, we have to give up the quantity *C-D* of all other goods.

The Law in Words

We continue this throughout the range of our experiment and find, not surprisingly, that as we attempt to produce more and more French fries, the opportunity cost of shifting productive resources into French fries production increases. What does this mean? Simply that for suppliers of French fries to be induced to supply more, and hence to incur higher opportunity costs, they must be paid more; that is, the only way to obtain a higher quantity supplied is by offering a higher price to suppliers. We see then that **the law of supply** is as follows:

> At higher (relative) prices a larger quantity will be supplied than at lower (relative) prices, *ceteris paribus*.

The Law in Numbers

We see this in our hypothetical **supply schedule** presented in Table 3-2.

The Law in Graphic Terms

We can easily convert the supply schedule presented in Table 3-2 into a **supply curve,** just as we earlier created a demand curve. All we do is take the price-quantity combinations from Table 3-2 and plot them in Figure 3-3. These we have labeled *F* through *J*. Now we connect them with a smooth line, and again we have a curve. This time it is upward sloping to show the *positive relationship* between price and the quantity supplied. Again we have to remember that we are talking about quantity supplied per year and measured in constant-quality units.

Now we are ready to put demand and supply together to answer the question, "How are prices determined?"

Putting Demand and Supply Together

Let's combine Tables 3-1 (the demand schedule) and 3-2 (the supply schedule) into Table 3-3. Column 1 shows the price; column 2 the quantity supplied per year at any given price; column 3, the quantity demanded. Column 4 is merely the difference between columns 2 and 3, or the difference between the quantity supplied and the quantity demanded. In column 5 we label those excesses as either an excess quantity demanded or an excess quantity sup-

---

Table 3-2 **Hypothetical Supply of French Fries**

At higher relative prices suppliers will be willing to supply more French fries. We see, for example, in column 1 that at a price per constant-quality bag of 10¢, only 2 million bags will be supplied, but at a price of 50¢ per bag, 10 million will be forthcoming from suppliers. We label these price-quantity combinations in the third column.

PRICE PER CONSTANT-QUALITY BAG	QUANTITY SUPPLIED OF FRENCH FRIES (MEASURED IN CONSTANT-QUALITY BAGS) PER YEAR	COMBINATION
$0.10	2 million	F
0.20	4 million	G
0.30	6 million	H
0.40	8 million	I
0.50	10 million	J

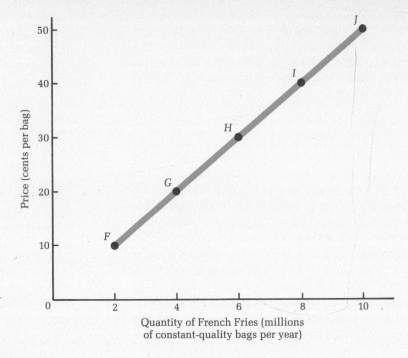

FIGURE 3-3 Supply Curve for French Fries

The horizontal axis measures the quantity of French fries supplied expressed in constant-quality bags per year. The vertical axis, as usual, measures price. We merely take the price-quantity combinations from Table 3-2 and use them as points *F*, *G*, *H*, *I*, and *J*. Then we connect those points to find the supply schedule for French fries. It is positively sloped, demonstrating the law of supply: At higher relative prices, a larger quantity will be forthcoming.

Table 3-3 Putting Supply and Demand Together

Here we combine Tables 3-1 and 3-2. Column 1 is the price per constant-quality bag, column 2 is the quantity supplied, and column 3 is the quantity demanded, both on a per year basis. The difference is expressed in column 4. For the first two prices, we have a negative difference; that is, there is an excess quantity demanded, as expressed in column 5. At the price of 40¢ or 50¢ we have a positive difference; that is, we have an excess quantity supplied. However, at a price of 30¢, the quantity supplied and the quantity demanded are equal, so there is neither an excess quantity demanded nor an excess quantity supplied. We call this price the equilibrium, or market clearing, price.

(1) PRICE	(2) QUANTITY SUPPLIED PER YEAR	(3) QUANTITY DEMANDED PER YEAR	(4) DIFFERENCE (2)–(3)	(5) EXCESSES
$0.10	2 million	10 million	−8 million	Excess quantity demanded
$0.20	4 million	8 million	−4 million	Excess quantity demanded
$0.30	6 million	6 million	0	Market clearing price = equilibrium
$0.40	8 million	4 million	4 million	Excess quantity supplied
$0.50	10 million	2 million	8 million	Excess quantity supplied

plied. For example, at a price of 10¢, there would be only 2 million bags of French fries supplied, but the quantity demanded would be 10 million. The difference would be a negative 8 million, which we label an excess quantity demanded. At the other end of the scale, a price of 50¢ per bag would elicit a 10 million quantity supplied, but quantity demanded would drop to 2 million, leaving a difference of 8 million, which we call an excess quantity supplied.

Now, do you notice something special about a price of 30¢? At that price, both the quantity supplied per year and the quantity demanded is 6 million bags of French fries. The difference then is zero. There is neither an excess quantity demanded nor an excess quantity supplied. Hence, this price, 30¢ is very special. It is called the **market clearing price**—it clears the market of all excess supply or all excess demand. There are no willing demanders who want to pay 30¢ but are turned away from hamburger stands, and there are no willing suppliers who want to provide French fries at 30¢ but who cannot sell all they want to sell at that price. The market clearing price is also called the **equilibrium price,** or price at which there is no tendency for change. Demanders seem happy with the quantity they are buying at that price; suppliers seem happy with the amount they can sell at that price.

Perhaps we can better understand the concept of an equilibrium, or market clearing, price by looking at the situation graphically. What we want firmly established is the understanding that in the market, a good or commodity will tend toward its equilibrium, or clearing price, and once that price is reached, unless something else happens, the price will remain in effect.

Supply and Demand in One Graph

Let's combine Figures 3-1 and 3-2 into Figure 3-4. The only difference now is that the hori-

zontal axis measures both the quantity supplied and the quantity demanded per year. Everything else is the same. The demand curve is now labeled *DD;* the supply curve *SS.* We have labeled the intersection of the supply curve with the demand curve as point *E,* for equilibrium. That corresponds to a price of 30¢, at which both the quantity supplied and the quantity demanded per year is 6 million. There is neither excess quantity supplied nor excess quantity demanded. Point *E,* the equilibrium point, always occurs at the intersection of the supply and the demand curves. Now let's see why we said that this particular price is one toward which the market will automatically tend to gravitate.

What if we were at a price of 10¢, where the quantity supplied was 2 million and the quantity demanded was 10 million. Demanders of French fries would find that they could not buy all the French fries they wanted at that price. We can surmise what would happen. Some demanders would sneak around the back of the hamburger stands and offer the owners a tip or a gift to get the French fries they wanted to buy. This would effectively raise the price received by the owner, and he or she could then be induced to supply a larger quantity (remember that the supply curve slopes upward). We would move from point *A* toward point *E.*

The process would indeed come to a halt when the price reached 30¢ per bag. The hamburger stand owners would not be getting any more orders for fries than they could handle, and French fry eaters would be able to buy all the French fries they wanted to buy at the going price of 30¢. We would move from a situation of excess quantity demanded at a price of 10¢ to a situation of no excess quantity demanded at a price of 30¢.

Now let's repeat the experiment with the price at 50¢ per bag. We draw a horizontal line at 50¢ to find out what the quantities de-

FIGURE 3-4 Supply and Demand on One Graph

The intersection of the supply and demand curves is E. It occurs at a price of 30¢ per constant-quality bag of fries, and at point E there is neither an excess quantity demanded nor an excess quantity supplied. At a price of 10¢ the quantity supplied will only be 2 million bags per year, but the quantity demanded will be 10 million. The difference is excess quantity demanded at price 10¢. There are forces that will cause the price to rise, so we will move from point A up the supply curve to point E, and from point B up the demand curve to point E. At the other extreme, 50¢ elicits a quantity supplied of 10 million, with a quantity demanded of 2 million. The difference is excess quantity supplied at a price of 50¢. Again, forces will cause the price to fall, so we will move from points Y and Z down the demand and the supply curves to the equilibrium point, E.

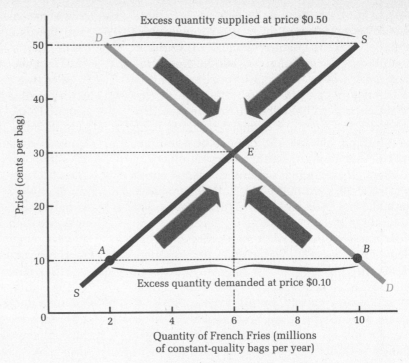

manded and the quantities supplied are. As can be expected, the quantity demanded has fallen and is now only 2 million bags per year, but the quantity supplied has risen greatly, to 10 million. There is one simple way for that excess quantity supplied to be eliminated. All that has to happen is for the price to fall from 50¢ to 30¢. As the price falls, that is, as the hamburger stand owners start offering French fries as a special to get rid of the excess quantities they want to supply consumers, consumers will indeed demand a larger quantity. The process will stop again at the equilibrium, or market clearing, price of 30¢.

Movements Along the Curve

Take note that when we dealt with a change in the relative price of French fries, we moved along curves which do not themselves change because the law of demand and the law of

supply are stated in such a way that the only thing that matters is the price. Hence, when there is a price change, the quantities supplied and demanded change also. We move to a different price-quantity combination in Table 3-3 or Figure 3-3. The table remains the same, as do the curves.

Shifting the Curves

If price determines *quantities* demanded and supplied, what causes changes in the curves and in the demand and supply schedules? The subtle difference here is important, as we will now see.

Shifting Demand How would we represent a dramatic increase in the quantity of French fries demanded at *all* prices because of a medical discovery that French fry consumption caused longer life? We could surely not move along the demand curve presented in Figure 3-4. What we have to do is *shift* the curve outward or to the right to represent an increase in demand, that is to say, an increase in the quantities demanded at *all* prices. We do this in Figure 3-5. The demand curve has shifted from *DD* to *D'D'*. Take any price, say, 30¢. Originally, before the great medical discovery, the quantity demanded was 6 million bags per year. After the discovery, however, the new quantity demanded is 10 million bags per year. Thus, we have witnessed a shift in the demand for French fries. We could use the same argument when discussing a shift inward, or to the left, of the demand curve for French fries. This might happen, for example, in the case of a medical discovery that French fry con-

sumption actually shortened life. We can list very briefly some obvious determinants of demand, that is, some factors which will cause the demand curve to shift:

1. *Changes in income* At higher incomes individuals generally buy more of most commodities.
2. *Tastes* A change in tastes, say, for miniskirts as opposed to maxis causes the demand curve to shift for both types of skirts.
3. *The price of substitutes* As the price of butter goes up, the demand schedule for margarine shifts upward, and vice versa.
4. *The price of complements* As the price of one item used together with another goes up, the demand schedule for the other will shift downward. For example, if the price

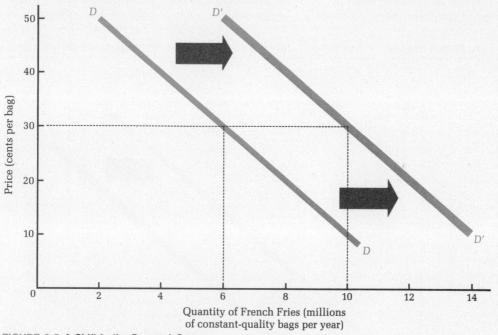

FIGURE 3-5 A Shift in the Demand Curve

If the relative price of French fries changes, we move along a given demand curve. However, if some factor other than price changed, the only way we can show its effect on the quantity demanded is by moving the entire demand curve from *DD* to *D'D'*. We have assumed in our example that the move was precipitated by a medical discovery showing that French fry consumption led to longer life. That meant that at *all* prices a larger quantity would be demanded. For example, at a price of 30¢, instead of 6 million bags per year being demanded, 10 million would be demanded.

of tennis balls went to $50 apiece, the demand curve for tennis rackets would undoubtedly shift inward (that is, decrease).

5. *Expectations*   If the relative price of a good is expected to go up in the future, consumers may buy more of it now than they would otherwise buy. If the relative price of a good is expected to fall in the future, consumers may buy less of it than they would otherwise.

Shifting Supply   Similar analysis can be applied to the supply curve. A change in price will cause a movement along a stable curve. However, anything that affects the entire supply schedule will shift the curve. Just take an example: If a new method of cooking French fries reduces the cost of cooking them by 98 percent, competition among sellers to produce more will shift the supply schedule of French fries outward to the right, as we see in Figure

3-6. At a price of 30¢, the quantity supplied was originally 6 million per year, but now the quantity supplied will be 9 million per year. Why? Simply because suppliers will now supply more at all prices because their cost of supplying French fries has fallen so dramatically.

The opposite case will make the point even clearer. Suppose that a new potato bug sneaks in from Iceland in somebody's backpack and that, within a matter of months, it has reproduced and destroyed 80 percent of the potato crop. When raw French fry makers go to buy potatoes, they will find an incredibly reduced supply. All of them—in competition, of course, with other businesspersons who want to sell potatoes in other markets—will bid up the price of potatoes. Ultimately, then, hamburger stand owners will have to pay greatly increased prices for raw, cut-up potatoes. The supply curve will shift inward. At all prices the quantity supplied will fall dramatically.

FIGURE 3-6 A Shift in the Supply Schedule

If the price changes, we move along a given supply schedule. However, if, for example, the cost of production of French fries were to fall dramatically, the supply schedule would shift outward from SS to S'S' so that at all prices a larger quantity would be forthcoming from suppliers.

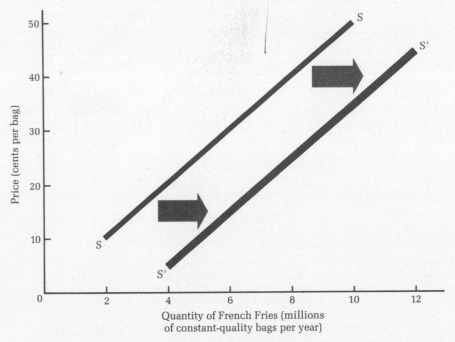

The factors affecting the position of supply curves are fewer than those affecting the position of demand curves. The cost of production basically determines the position of supply curves. Anything that affects the cost of production will therefore move a supply curve in or out. It is mainly technology and resources that affect the cost of production. Any technological improvement in the means of production or decline in resource prices will shift a supply curve outward. However, changes in the prices of other goods can also shift a supply curve for a product. A decline in the price of corn, for example, may cause a farmer to offer more wheat for sale at all possible prices. Expectations concerning the future price of a product also determine the position of the current supply curve. And lastly, if more and more new firms enter the industry, the supply curve will also shift outward.

We cannot overstress the importance of distinguishing between a movement along the curve, which occurs only when the price changes, and shifts in a curve, which occur only with changes in factors other than price. You should always ask yourself which situation you are analyzing:

If the price changes, we move along a curve; if something else changes, we shift a curve.

PART B: ELASTICITY

Price Responsiveness

When we talked about changes in the quantity demanded or supplied, we always talked in terms of prices. Now the question before us is "By how much will quantities demanded or supplied change as the price changes?" To figure this out, we must determine exactly *how responsive* demanders and suppliers are to changes in price. We would like to come up with a way to measure such *price responsiveness* and a way to talk about different degrees of price responsiveness. Do consumers change their spending habits a little or a lot when the price of gasoline goes up by 10 percent? Do suppliers change their production decisions greatly or hardly at all when the price of corn goes down by 10 percent?

We will look first at the demand side and then at the supply side.

Price Elasticity of Demand

If the price of French fries goes up by 1 percent, what will be the percentage reduction in the quantity demanded? If we can figure out the answer to that question, we will indeed come up with a numerical idea of what price responsiveness actually means. The technical term for price responsiveness is the **price elasticity of demand,** where the term elasticity is just the economist's way of saying responsiveness. A simple definition of price elasticity, which we will call e, will be the following:

$$e = \frac{\text{percentage change in quantity demanded}}{\text{percentage change in price}}$$

Here, we are comparing a change in the quantity demanded with a change in the price, and we have to express such comparisons in terms of percentage changes, not absolute changes. After all, the units of measurement of price are different from the units of measurement of quantity demanded. Moreover, if we tried to express price responsiveness in terms of absolute changes, a change in scale would give us a different number each time. By using percentages, we ignore problems of scale.

We have not indicated it in our definition, but by now it should not surprise you to learn that elasticity of demand will always be negative because the law of demand states that at higher prices, smaller quantities will be demanded, and vice versa. In other words, the change in price is always in the opposite direction to that of the change in the quantity demanded. We will not put the negative sign in front of our demand elasticities, but you should always keep in mind that *they are implicitly negative.*

Let's see if we can compute the elasticities from Table 3-1. We are going to have to use a modified form of our elasticity formula because we are measuring price changes over such a large range. What we have to do is essentially get an average percentage change of both price and quantity. We do that by computing the percentage change in price as follows:

$$\text{Percentage change in price} = \frac{\text{actual change in price}}{\text{av. of higher and lower price}}$$

We will do the same thing to compute the average percentage change in the quantity demanded. Using the data in Table 3-1, let's look at the numerical calculation of elasticity, *e*, presented in Table 3-4. Here we see that the computation of elasticity ranges from 3 down to 0.33. What does that mean? Simply that at very high prices for French fries, such as between 50¢ and 40¢ a bag, a 1 percent decrease in price will elicit a 3 percent increase in the quantity demanded. At the other extreme, at relatively low prices for French fries, say, between 20¢ and 10¢ per bag, the elasticity of minus 0.33 means that a 1 percent reduction in price will elicit only a one-third of 1 percent increase in the quantity demanded.

Different Kinds of Elasticities

We have names for the varying ranges of price elasticities, depending on whether a 1 percent change in price elicits more or less than a 1 percent change in the quantity supplied.

1. *Elastic demand* We call any price elasticity of demand in excess of 1 an **elastic demand.**

Table 3-4 **Numerical Calculation of Price Elasticity of Demand for French Fries**

Column 1 is the quantity demanded at different prices. Column 2 is the change in the quantity demanded. In other words, we merely subtract the smaller from the larger quantity. In each case, the change is 2 million bags per year. Column 3 is the price per bag, and column 4 is the change in the price, which happens to be 10¢ in each case. Columns 5 and 6 are the average quantities and prices. Column 7 presents an approximation of the price elasticity of demand, *e*.

(1) Quantity (Q)	(2) Change in Q	(3) Price (P)	(4) Change in P	(5) $\frac{Q_1+Q_2}{2}$	(6) $\frac{P_1+P_2}{2}$	$e = \dfrac{\text{change in } Q}{(Q_1+Q_2)/2} \Big/ \dfrac{\text{change in } P}{(P_1+P_2)/2}$
2		$0.50				
4	2	0.40	$0.10	3	$0.45	$2/3 \div 0.10/0.45 = 3$
6	2	0.30	0.10	5	0.35	$2/5 \div 0.10/0.35 = 1.4$
8	2	0.20	0.10	7	0.25	$2/7 \div 0.10/0.25 = 0.714$
10	2	0.10	0.10	9	0.15	$2/9 \div 0.10/0.15 = 0.333$

A 1 percent change in price causes a greater than 1 percent change in quantity demanded. Candidates for elastic-demand sections of our demand schedule in Table 3-1 are obviously an e of 3 and an e of 1.4.

2. *Unitary elasticity of demand*   In this situation, a 1 percent change in price elicits exactly a 1 percent change in the quantity demanded.

3. *Inelastic demand*   Here, a 1 percent change in price elicits a less than 1 percent change in quantity demanded. An elasticity of 0.33, as in the last line of Table 3-4, represents a situation of **inelastic demand.** In brief, a 1 percent change in price causes a less than 1 percent change in quantity demanded.

Extreme Elasticities

There are two extremes in price elasticities of demand: One is total unresponsiveness, which is called a *perfectly inelastic demand* situation, and the other is complete responsiveness, which is called an unlimited, infinite, *perfectly elastic demand* situation.

We show perfect inelasticity in Figure 3-7. Notice that the quantity of French fries demanded per year is 8 million, no matter what the price. Hence, for any percentage price change, the quantity demanded will remain the same, and thus the change in the quantity demanded will be zero. Look at our formula for computing elasticity. If the change in the quantity demanded is zero, then the numerator is also zero, and anything divided into zero is zero too. Hence, perfect inelasticity.

At the opposite extreme is the situation depicted in Figure 3-8. Here we show that at a price of 30¢, an unlimited quantity of French fries will be demanded. At a price that is only slightly above 30¢, none will be demanded. In other words, there is complete, or infinite price responsiveness here, and hence we call the

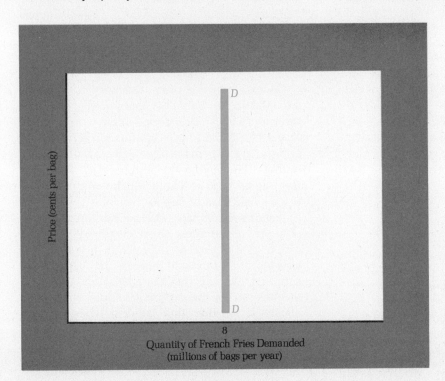

FIGURE 3-7 Price Unresponsiveness for French Fries

If people had to have their fries no matter what the price, the demand schedule would be represented by a vertical line, *DD*. Here consumers demand 8 million bags of fries per year no matter what the price. The elasticity of demand in this case is zero. We say that the demand is perfectly inelastic.

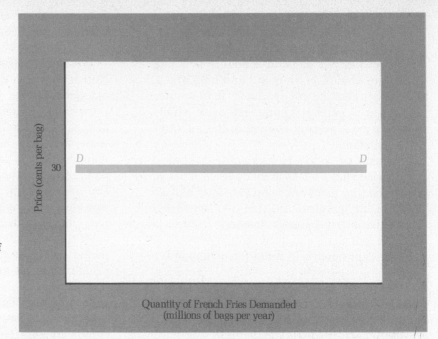

FIGURE 3-8 **Complete Price Responsiveness for French Fries**

Here we assume that even the tiniest increase in the price of fries will cause people to demand none. The demand schedule is a horizontal line at the price of 30¢. It is impossible to sell even one bag of fries at a higher price with this hypothetical demand schedule. There is total price responsiveness of demand. Here we say that the demand is completely, or infinitely, elastic at the price of 30¢ per bag.

demand schedule in Figure 3-8 infinitely elastic.

All demand-schedule elasticities lie between the two extremes. We present, for example, in Table 3-5 demand elasticities for selected goods. None of them is zero, and the largest one is 4.6—a far cry from infinity. Remember, again, that even though we are leaving off the negative sign, the inverse relationship between price and quantity demanded makes it implicit.

Price Elasticity of Supply

The price elasticity of supply is defined in exactly the same way as the price elasticity of demand. However, supply elasticities are generally positive because the law of supply indicates that at higher prices larger quantities will be forthcoming from suppliers. Our definition of the price elasticity of supply, s, is the following:

$$s = \frac{\text{percentage change in quantity supplied}}{\text{percentage change in price}}$$

To compute the price elasticity of supply from the data in Table 3-2, for example, or from the supply curve in Figure 3-3, we would have to use the same approximation presented for computing the price elasticity of demand. Rather than having the numbers worked out for you, go back to Table 3-2 and compute the price elasticities of supply.[3]

Just as with demand, there are different types of supply elasticities. They are similar in definition. If a 1 percent increase in price elicits a greater than 1 percent increase in the quantity supplied, we say that at the particular point in question on the supply schedule, supply is elastic. If, on the other hand, a 1 percent in-

---

[3]Starting with the lower prices, you should end up with 1.0, 1.0, 1.0, and 1.0.

Table 3-5 Demand Elasticity for Selected Goods

Here we have obtained the estimated demand elasticities for selected goods. All of them are negative, although we have not shown a minus sign. For example, the price elasticity of demand for onions is 0.4. That means that a 1 percent increase in the price of onions will bring about a 0.4 percent decrease in the quantity of onions demanded.

	ESTIMATED ELASTICITY
Food Items:	
White potatoes	0.3
Green peas, fresh	2.8
Green peas, canned	1.6
Tomatoes, fresh	4.6
Tomatoes, canned	2.5
Other Nondurable Goods:	
Shoes	0.4
Stationery	0.5
Newspapers and magazines	0.1
Gasoline and oil, short-run	0.2
long-run	0.7
Durable Goods:	
Kitchen appliances	0.6
China and tableware	1.1
Jewelry and watches	0.4
Automobiles, long-run	0.2
Tires, short-run	0.6
long-run	0.4
Radio and television receivers	1.2
Sports equipment, boat,	
pleasure aircraft, short-run	0.6
long-run	1.3
Services:	
Physicians' services	0.6
Legal services	0.5
Taxi	0.4
Rail commuting	0.7
Airline travel, short-run	0.06
long-run	2.4
Foreign travel, short-run	0.7
long-run	4.0

Sources: H. S. Houthakker and L. D. Taylor, *Consumer Demand in the United States, 1929–1970,* Cambridge, Mass.: Harvard University Press, 1966; U.S. Department of Agriculture, 1954.

crease in price elicits a less than 1 percent increase in the quantity supplied, we refer to that as an inelastic supply situation. If the change in the quantity supplied is just equal to the change in the price, then we talk about unitary elasticity of supply.

We show, in Figure 3-9, two supply schedules, *SS* and *S'S'*. Can you tell at a glance, without reading the caption, which one is infinitely elastic and which one is perfectly inelastic?

As you might expect, most supply schedules exhibit elasticities that are somewhere in between the range of zero to infinity.

Elasticity and Slope

It is important not to look at the slope of a demand curve as representative of its elasticity because the slope of a curve on a diagram can be easily changed merely by changing the scale of the axes. Remember from our initial discussion of elasticity that we had to abstract somehow from scale problems. We did this by expressing elasticity as a ratio of *percentage* changes in quantity demand over *percentage* changes in price. There is no way of picking up such information from the slope of a straight-line demand curve. As a matter of fact, the measured elasticity along, for example, a normal, or downward-sloping, straight-line demand curve goes from infinity to zero as we move down the curve. The only time we can be sure of an elasticity by looking at a curve is if that curve is either perfectly horizontal or perfectly vertical.

The Long and the Short of Elasticities

Elasticities do not come out of the blue. In almost all cases, the only way we can discover the elasticity of demand or supply for a particular good is by looking at what actually hap-

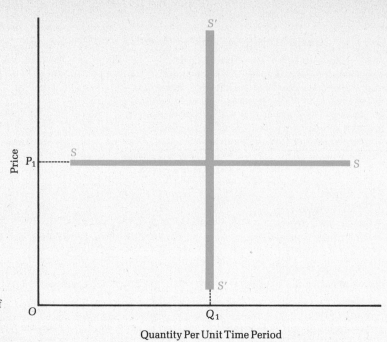

FIGURE 3-9 The Extremes in Supply Curves

Here we have drawn two extremes of supply schedules. SS is a perfectly elastic supply curve. $S'S'$ is a perfectly inelastic one. In the former, an unlimited quantity will be forthcoming at the price P_1. In the latter, no matter what the price, the quantity supplied will be Q_1. An example of $S'S'$ might be the supply curve for fresh fish the morning the boats come in.

pened in the marketplace in the past. That is, we have to look at real numbers which show us changes in quantities after there were changes in prices. Realizing this, we see that there are probably going to be different measures of elasticity for different time spans. One would assume, for example, that a change in the price of the good will elicit a smaller change in the quantity demanded and supplied *immediately after* the price increase than it would, say, after 1 year. One should distinguish, therefore, between *short*-run and *long*-run elasticities. Short-run elasticities are measured during the period immediately following the price change when people and firms don't have time for *complete* adjustments. Long-run elasticities are measured after people and firms have had time to adjust completely. In fact, we usually find that the demand schedule for a good in

question will pivot and become more elastic if more time is allowed for adjustment.

Demand

Let's take an example. Suppose the price of electricity goes up 50 percent. How do you adjust in the short run? You can turn the lights off more often, you can stop running the stereo as much as you used to, and so on. Otherwise it's very difficult to cut back on your consumption of electricity. In the long run, though, you can devise methods to reduce your consumption. Instead of using electric heaters, the next time you have a house built you will install gas heaters. Instead of using an electric stove, the next time you move you will have a gas stove installed. You will purchase fluorescent bulbs because they use less electricity. The longer you have to figure it out, the more ways

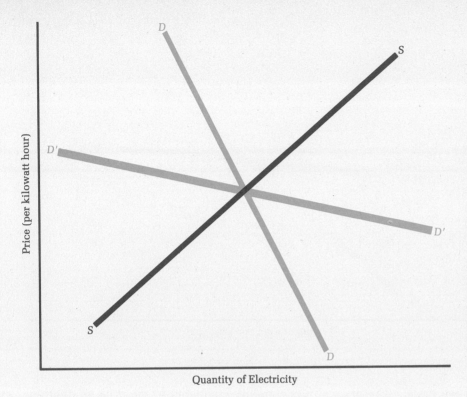

Price (per kilowatt hour)

Quantity of Electricity

FIGURE 3-10 **Short- and Long-Run Demand Curves for Electricity**
Here we have shown a supply schedule for electricity, *SS*. We have assumed that in the short run it is difficult to adjust to a change in the price of electricity. The demand schedule is therefore relatively inelastic, as shown by *DD*. However, as time goes on, adjustments can be made more easily. The demand schedule becomes relatively more elastic and pivots around to *D'D'*. In general, the longer the time allowed for adjustment, the more elastic demand will become.

you will find to cut electricity consumption. We would expect, therefore, that the short-run demand for electricity would be highly inelastic, as exhibited by *DD* in Figure 3-10. However, the long-run demand curve may exhibit much more elasticity, like *D'D'* in Figure 3-10.

Supply

The same holds for the supply curve. In the short run, the supply of umbrellas may be fairly inelastic because there are only several manufacturers and they would run into increasing costs per unit of production if they tried to expand their production rate very rapidly. However, in the long run, more and more firms can enter the market. They might be almost as efficient as existing firms. The long-run supply curve for umbrellas may nearly be the horizontal line *S'S'* in Figure 3-11. In fact, it has been asserted that in the long run, the supply curve for most manufactured goods is quite elastic because of the possibility of many new firms entering the market.

Once you distinguish between long-run elasticities and short-run elasticities, you will not be surprised to find that people's responsiveness to an increase in price is not very large immediately after the price change. As people learn to adjust and adapt to new methods of satisfying their wants, their responsiveness to the price increase will become larger. That is, the long-run elasticity of demand will be much larger than the short-run elasticity.

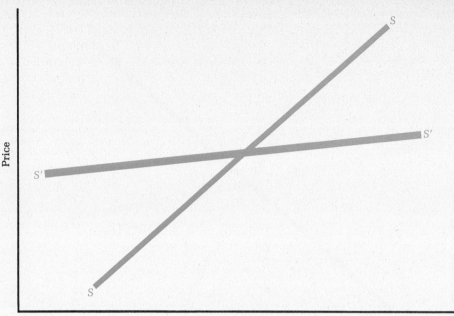

FIGURE 3-11 **Short-
and Long-Run Supply
of Umbrellas**

Here we assume that in
the short run, the
supply schedule for
umbrellas is *SS*.
However, if given a
long enough time to
adjust—that is, if given
enough time for new
firms to develop and
more plants to be
built—the supply
schedule may pivot
around to *S'S'*, which
is almost a horizontal
line.

Definitions of New
Terms

Relative Price: The price of a commodity compared to the price of another
commodity or a group of other commodities.

The Law of Demand: The law that states that the quantity of a good or
service varies inversely with the price.

Demand Schedule: The relationship between the prices for which a good
can be purchased and the respective quantities demanded at those prices.

Demand Curve: A line showing the demand schedule. The demand curve
shows the maximum price at which a given quantity will be demanded.

The Law of Supply: The law that states that the quantity of a commodity
supplied is directly related to its price.

Supply Schedule: The relationship between the various quantities that will
be forthcoming from suppliers at different prices.

Supply Curve: A line showing the supply schedule. The supply curve represents the minimum price at which a given quantity will be forthcoming.

Market Clearing Price: The price of a good or service at which the market
is cleared; that is, the quantity demanded equals the quantity supplied.

Equilibrium Price: Another term for the market clearing price or the price
at which the quantity supplied equals the quantity demanded.

Price Elasticity of Demand: The price responsiveness of the demand for a
commodity. The price elasticity of demand is defined as the percentage
change in quantity demanded divided by the percentage change in price.

Elastic Demand: A characteristic of a demand curve in which a given percentage change in price will be met by a larger percentage change in the quantity demanded in the opposite direction.

Inelastic Demand: A characteristic of a demand curve in which a given change in price will be met by a less-than-proportionate change in the quantity demanded in the opposite direction.

Chapter Summary

1. It is important to distinguish between the relative price of goods and services and their absolute price. During a period of rising prices, such as we are now experiencing in the United States, almost all prices go up, although some go up faster than others.

2. The law of demand is one of the most fundamental propositions in economics. It merely states that at a higher relative price individuals will purchase less of most commodities, and at a lower relative price they will purchase more.

3. When stating the law of demand we must be careful to add the phrase *ceteris paribus,* which means all other things held constant.

4. When discussing the law of demand (and supply), we must be careful to talk in terms of constant-quality units of the commodity in question. In other words, we have to correct for quality differences.

5. The law of demand can be seen in the demand schedule, which shows the relationship between the prices and quantities of an item purchased per unit time period. In graphic terms, the demand schedule is shown as a demand curve that is downward sloping.

6. To derive a supply curve or supply schedule, we can construct a production-possibilities curve, where we see that at a higher rate of production of one commodity, a higher opportunity cost is incurred. To induce producers to supply more, they must be paid more to cover these higher opportunity costs.

7. The supply curve is generally a positively sloped line, showing that at higher prices more will be forthcoming from suppliers. Again, we must talk in terms of constant-quality units of measurement and we must specify a time period for our analysis.

8. Where the demand and supply curves intersect, we find the equilibrium or market clearing price at which the quantity demanded equals the quantity supplied.

9. It is important to distinguish between a movement along a demand or supply curve and a shift in one of those curves. Whenever the relative price changes, we move along the curve. However, if something else changes, such as income, preferences, or population, then there is a shift in one or both of the curves.

10. We measure the price responsiveness of consumers to a change in the relative price of a commodity by use of the price elasticity of demand, which is defined as the percentage change in the quantity demanded divided by the percentage change in price.

11. The price elasticity of demand is always negative; this follows from the law of demand.

12. Price elasticity of demand can range from zero (perfectly inelastic demand) to a negative infinity (perfectly elastic demand). Most demand curves have price elasticities somewhere in between these two extremes.

13. Elasticity of supply is measured similarly to the elasticity of demand. In general, however, it is a positive number. Supply price elasticities can range also from zero to positive infinity. A zero price elasticity of supply indicates that there is a fixed quantity available no matter what the price. An infinite price elasticity of supply indicates that an unlimited quantity will be forthcoming from suppliers at a particular price.

14. The slope of a demand curve does not indicate its elasticity. Price elasticity is a ratio of percentage change in quantity demanded to percentage change in price. The slope of the curve, however, can change depending on the units chosen on the horizontal and vertical axes.

15. Both demand and supply price elasticities are greater in the long run than in the short run.

1. If the price of economics textbooks went up by 100 percent, is there any way you could adjust your purchase of them?

2. Why is it important to distinguish between relative and absolute prices?

3. Can you think of exceptions to the law of demand?

4. Can you think of exceptions to the law of supply?

5. What is the difference between demand and quantity demanded?

6. What is the difference between supply and quantity supplied?

7. Why is the supply curve generally upward sloping?

8. If the price of a commodity is set below the equilibrium price, what would you expect to occur?

9. "The price of margarine has nothing to do with the price of butter." Evaluate this statement.

10. Is it possible for all price elasticities of demand to be less than 1, that is, inelastic?

11. Can you think of any commodities that have a perfectly inelastic supply? Does the time period allowed for adjustment affect your answer?

12. If it is true that the price elasticity of the demand for heroin is, indeed, very low—if not zero—what happens when the government mounts a program to decrease the quantity of this illegal drug in the United States?

13. Use the following hypothetical demand schedule for marijuana to answer the following questions:

Quantity Demanded/week	Price/oz	(Elasticity)
1000 oz	$ 5	
800	10	
600	15	
400	20	
200	25	

(a) Using the above demand schedule, determine the elasticity of demand for each price change (Example: when price changes from $5 to $10, quantity demanded changes from 1000 to 800 oz, so the elasticity of demand is ⅓ or 0.33).

(b) The data given in the demand schedule would plot as a straight-line demand curve. Why is demand more elastic the higher the price?

Selected
References

Henderson, Hubert, *Supply and Demand,* Chicago: The University of Chicago Press, 1958.

Watson, Donald S., *Price Theory and Its Uses,* 3d. ed., Boston: Houghton Mifflin, 1972, chaps. 2 and 3.

Illegal Activities

PROHIBITION IN RETROSPECT

Applying Supply and Demand

We all know that illegal activities, including gambling, prostitution, and drug abuse, go on all the time despite legislation against them. Various estimates of the market value of all illegal activities taken together are around $50 billion for an average year.

What is interesting about illegal activities from an economic point of view is what happens because of their illegality. In this issue, we use the analysis of supply and demand that we developed in Chapter 3 to look at an actual case study in illegality: Prohibition.

Alcohol Prohibition

In 1808, Dr. Billy F. Clark met with citizens in Saratoga County, New York, who were opposed to hard liquor. Together, they organized the first American Temperance Society. At their second convention in 1836 they added beer and wine to their list of opposed intoxicants. In the 1850s, 12 states enacted dry laws, but most of these were repealed by 1900. The temperance forces then started to gain real momentum, and

by 1909, 5 states had again gone dry. By 1919, 29 states had adopted prohibition. On August 1, 1917, the Senate approved submitting the Eighteenth Amendment to the states. This amendment, along with the Volstead Act, was the fruit of temperance efforts.

Finally, on January 17, 1920, the Eighteenth Amendment to the United States Constitution was put into effect. It prohibited "manufacture, sale or transportation of intoxicating liquors within, or the importation thereof into, or exportation thereof from the United States . . . for beverage purposes." The Eighteenth Amendment, therefore, was a legislative attempt to eliminate the *supply* of alcoholic beverages.

We know, though, that there are two sides to every coin: No law is effective without enforcement, and Congress was aware of this. In 1919, while the Eighteenth Amendment was being ratified by the various states, the National Prohibition Act, or Volstead Act, was passed to enforce the amendment. This 73-section act tried to prevent trade in liquor by making it illegal to "manufacture, sell, barter, transport, import, export, deliver, furnish or possess any intoxicating liquor." Legislation therefore had also attacked the

demand side of the alcohol question by making possession illegal.

The days of speakeasies, the Feds, and Al Capone were quickly upon the nation. Admittedly, hindsight is always better than foresight, but economists would nevertheless have been able to predict many of the events that occurred during the Prohibition era. They would have used the simple concepts of supply and demand along with an analysis of the risks involved in transacting illegal business. As an introduction into the workings of economics, let's take a look at the supply and demand for liquor.

From the Supply Side

Before the passage of the Eighteenth Amendment, business people entered into the liquor business if they thought as large a profit could be made in distilling, importing, exporting, wholesaling, or retailing alcoholic beverages as could be made in some other line of commercial endeavor. Take, for example, the cost involved in distilling and wholesaling bourbon. A bourbon distillery usually consists of distilling, blending, and bottling plants; each plant contains highly specialized equipment such as stainless steel tanks (where the mash is heated to convert starch to sugars), cypress wood fer-

menting vats, large patent or column stills, and new charred white oak barrels for aging.[1] The owner has to pay for all this equipment and also must pay employees at least the amount they could earn by working for someone else in a similar job.

When the bourbon manufacturer goes to sell the product to wholesalers or even to retailers, if the manufacturer wants to eliminate the middleman, the bottles of whiskey must be provided with fancy labels that customers can use to identify this particular brand of spirits. The manufacturer has to package the trademarked bottles of bourbon in cartons so that they can be transported to the buyer. In order to make wholesalers, retailers, and the public aware of this particular product, the

[1]Old Carolina moonshiners assert that one can get by with considerably less equipment: a copper pot and worm, a section of garden hose, and some fruit jars, at a minimum. Suggested also is a rifle.

manufacturer also has to spend money on some sort of advertising. When wholesalers and retailers demand the product, the manufacturer either has to rent delivery trucks or purchase trucks. The manufacturer then has to pay the wages of the drivers. To guard against losses due to theft or accident, the manufacturer needs to purchase some form of insurance.

Before Prohibition, firms supplied an estimated 100,000 tax gallons a year at the going price of alcohol. At this price, it was not profitable for firms to expand their production of spirits. But what happened to the supply of whiskey when producing and selling it became illegal? We all know that the whiskey well did not dry up, despite the attempts of Congress to eliminate the source. Legislation against the manufacture, importation, and sale of alcohol merely changed certain aspects of the supply of that greatly demanded product. After prohibition, the cost of manufacturing and selling alcohol

suddenly shot up. For example, any distiller faced the possibility of a stiff fine or jail sentence if he were caught continuing his production process. From 1920 to 1930 alone, property worth over $136,000,000 in appraised value was seized by federal prohibition agents (71 of whom were killed while performing their duties).

One way to minimize the risk of being caught was to extend payoffs to the police and officials who were charged with preventing the illegal manufacture and sale of alcohol. In December, 1921—only 1 year after the start of Prohibition—about 100 federal agents in New York City were dismissed for the "abuse of permits for use of intoxicants." One New York speakeasy proprietor estimated that about 30 percent of his operating costs went for protection money to law enforcement agencies. Of course, it was no longer possible to buy insurance against economic losses from theft and accident. Apparently, the only insurance against theft was to pay off organized crime —the Mafia. Indeed, the Mafia's take in any individual's business dealings with alcoholic beverages was rumored to be substantial.

Briefly, as manufacturing and distributing spirits became illegal the cost of doing business increased. The amount of alcohol businesspersons were willing to supply at any given price thus had to decrease.

From the Demand Side

Even though the purchase and consumption of spirits became illegal after the passage of the Volstead Act, the demand for intoxicating beverages did not disappear. Before

Prohibition, the demand for alcohol was dictated, at least in part, by people's *preferences,* their *incomes,* and the *prices* they had to pay for what they wanted to drink. Let's look at the aspect of price first.

We all know that the price of any product or service represents what we have to give up in order to purchase it. Give up what? you might ask. Someone buying a fifth of bourbon in 1918 would have to give up $2 of purchasing power over other goods and services that were then being sold. For the price of a single fifth of bourbon, our whiskey drinker could have bought perhaps 12 bottles of beer, or 2 steak dinners, or 5 passes to the movies, or 6 new ties. The list of alternatives for the $2 purchase was large indeed. The higher the price, the more you have to give up of all other things; so you usually find that when the price of a commodity is high, you buy less of it. This is true for legal as well as illegal goods and services. Before Prohibition, the higher the price of alcohol, the less of it was sold. After Prohibition, the same relationship continued to hold.

When discussing the price of anything, we should be aware of the different qualities of the same product that can be purchased at any time. Before and after Prohibition, different qualities of alcoholic beverages could be bought. Connoisseurs could perhaps tell the difference, and those who desired high-quality alcohol were willing to pay a higher price. Those who were not so insistent upon high quality purchased cheaper spirits of a lesser quality.

Income was one of the other determinants of how much alcohol was purchased before Prohibition. Usually, the higher people's income is, the more goods and services they demand. For some, when income goes up even a little bit, the quantity demanded jumps a lot. For others, even when incomes goes up a lot, the quantity demanded doesn't change much at all. Historically we have seen that as incomes have been rising, per capita consumption of spirits has increased even more.

A third determinant of the demand for alcohol is preference. It is always correct to state that tastes determine what people buy. If I happen to prefer alcohol very very much, I may decide to forgo purchasing a large amount of other goods and services in order to satisfy my urge to drink. Even if my income is very small, I may demand a much higher quantity than, say, a multimillionaire who doesn't want to buy alcohol but who can obviously "afford" many times over what I could consume. Economists have very little to say about what determines taste. We have not come up with any generally accepted body of theory that explains how people form preferences, and consequently this text makes no attempt to present

FIGURE I-4.1

There has been a steady rise in liquor consumption since 1954. Because this graph shows total consumption rising faster than population (the line is steeper), per capita consumption is increasing. Can you explain why so much liquor was consumed in 1946? (*Source:* Adapted from *The Liquor Handbook,* New York: C. Frank Jobson, 1969.)

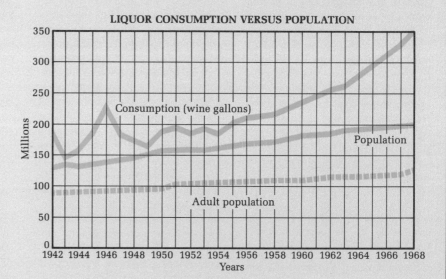

LIQUOR CONSUMPTION VERSUS POPULATION

a theory of preference formation. It's a fascinating topic, but one that few economists feel competent to discuss. Economists can assume that tastes remain constant, and then they can ask what happens if the price goes up or the income goes down. In this manner we are able to develop a usable theory that tells us what to predict in the future.

When Prohibition made consumption of alcohol illegal, certain of the determinants of the demand for spirits changed drastically. Costs that were unknown before Prohibition suddenly faced the potential drinker. When bourbon was legal, manufacturers advertised openly the various qualities that could be found in each individual product. The prices of different brands were well known and widely publicized. The courts upheld trademark laws, so consumers were fairly certain that a particular brand they bought was made by the same manufacturer. If the product was of high quality the last time it was purchased, it would probably be of the same quality the next time. Any manufacturers attempting to sell low-quality alcohol would not be successful in such a situation unless they lowered their price accordingly to induce buyers to buy their "inferior" product.

When Prohibition came, there was no more advertising. Brand names were not as numerous as before, and the possibility of fraudulent use of a brand name was now very high. A distiller couldn't very well go to the authorities to complain about some other bootlegger using his brand name. In a phrase, the cost of information about prices and

quality went up drastically after alcohol production and consumption became illegal. So, even if the price of a fifth of bourbon had remained the same, the actual cost to drinkers would still have gone up because they could not be sure about what they were buying. In fact, they risked the possibility of blindness or even death from drinking bootlegged liquor. Since information was so difficult and costly to come by, bootleggers could get away with producing an occasional batch of lethal bourbon and still stay in business—something that would have been much more difficult before Prohibition. Competitors would have made sure that consumers found out about such behavior, even if bourbon drinkers didn't take the time to inform themselves.

Another cost to imbibers was the risk of being involved in a speakeasy raid. After all, consumption of spirits was illegal, even though the authorities did not arrest all whiskey drinkers during the Prohibition period. In its first 10 years, the enforcement of the National Prohibition Act resulted in about 550,000 arrests. One might ask which people were most likely to be caught in a speakeasy raid. Who were the people least able to find out about the best whiskey? Or, who were the people most likely to pay intermediaries to go to Canada to purchase high-quality Canadian whiskey? Obviously, we would not be surprised to learn that richer whiskey drinkers ended up with consistently high-quality bourbon and did not run a very high risk of being jailed for consuming it. As we shall point out on

numerous occasions in this book, when the cost of information goes up, the people who suffer the most are usually those who are less well off. The poor are usually the ones who pay the most for our attempts to legislate morality.

The Final Outcome

What would economists predict as the final outcome? Would the price of liquor go up? Would the quantity demanded go down? Would society be better off? Very few things can be said with certainty in economics. However, predictive and analytical statements can be made with a high degree of reliability if qualifications are tacked on. We know that the cost of providing alcohol went up during Prohibition because of the risk of jail sentences or fines, the price of paying off the police or the Mafia to stay in production, and the difficulty of product differentiation in a market where open advertising was forbidden. Hence, if everything else had remained the same, we could state that the higher costs of production and distribution would have resulted in higher prices for alcoholic beverages, and smaller quantities of alcoholic beverages would have been demanded than before.

Everything else didn't remain the same, though. On the demand side, the implicit cost of purchasing spirits went up due to higher information costs and the possibility of being jailed or fined. In this case, if everything else had remained the same, less alcohol would have been demanded. We assume, for the moment, that income and preferences did remain the same. We see then that we could have predicted a *lower quantity both supplied and demanded* of alcohol after the passage of the Eighteenth Amendment.

A Graphic Analysis

It's fairly straightforward to translate our verbal analysis into a graph. We do that in Figure I-4.2, where we show the demand and supply of alcoholic beverages before and after prohibition. The "before" situation is represented by curves DD and SS; the "after" situation, by curves D'D' and S'S'. If our analysis is correct, what happened after prohibition was a shift of the supply curve inward because of the increased risk to the supplier, among other things. The shift in the demand curve inward is less certain. Presumably, because of

the stigma attached to the illegality of drinking, a lower quantity would be demanded at all prices, and hence the shift inward to D'D'. But demanders were rarely if ever punished like suppliers, so that the shift inward of the supply curve probably predominated. The market clearing, or equilibrium, price would rise from P_L to P_I because that is the price at which the relevant supply and demand curves intersect. That is to say, it is the forces underlying demand which yield these two market clearing prices. After prohibition, a smaller quantity would be both supplied and demanded at a higher price. Remember that we have to be talking in terms of constant-quality units per time period. In our case, we can talk about a constant-quality liter of alcoholic beverage per year.

The Case of Completely Inelastic Demand

What if the demand for alcoholic beverages were perfectly inelastic, as shown in Figure I-4.3? The decrease in supply from SS to S'S' would merely result in a higher price, but the quantity demanded would remain the same.

Was Society Better Off after January 16, 1920?

We cannot determine whether society was better off after January 16, 1920. People whose values included strictures against liquor were probably better off just knowing that the Eighteenth Amendment and the Volstead Act had been passed. If, in fact, the quantity of alcohol con-

FIGURE I-4.2 The Effects of Prohibition

We show the original supply and demand curves for alcoholic beverages as SS and DD. The equilibrium is established at their intersection, E. The market clearing price when alcoholic consumption is legal is P_L. Now prohibition comes into effect. The supply schedule shifts up to S'S', and the demand schedule, presumably, shifts down to D'D'. A new intersection occurs at E'. The market clearing price after prohibition is now P_I, which is greater than P_L.

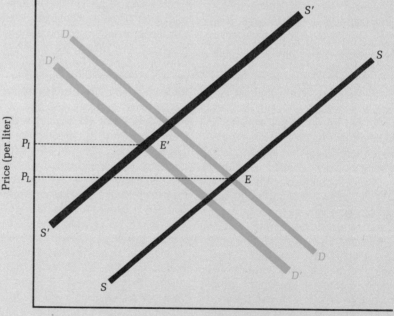

Price (per liter)

Quantity of Alcoholic Beverages (measured in constant-quality liters per year)

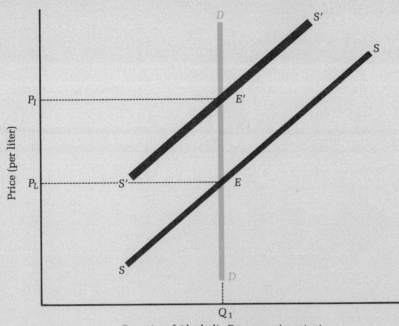

Price (per liter)

P_I — — — — — — — — E'

P_L — — — S' — — — — E

S

D

S'

S

D

Q_1

Quantity of Alcoholic Beverages (constant-
quality liters per year)

**FIGURE I-4.3 An Inelastic Demand
for Alcoholic Beverages**

What if the demand for alcoholic beverages were completely inelastic? Before prohibition, the intersection of the supply curve, SS, and the demand curve, DD, is at E, with a legal market clearing price of P_L. Now prohibition comes into effect, raising the cost of doing business and shifting the supply curve to $S'S'$. The new intersection occurs at E', with a market clearing price of P_I. However, the quantity demanded does not fall, as in the example depicted in Figure I-4.2. Rather, it stays the same at Q_1 because of the inelastic demand for alcoholic beverages. This is certainly a possibility, but it isn't very probable. After all, at some point some demanders of alcoholic beverages will seek less expensive substitutes.

sumed actually declined during Prohibition, these same people could have felt even more satisfied. If less consumption of spirits led to higher productivity, less social unrest, fewer barroom brawls, and so on, we could count these effects as benefits.

As for the costs to society, we must include the resources spent on increased law enforcement, court proceedings, and keeping people in prison. Also, we must not overlook the alcohol drinker's loss of happiness caused by the smaller amounts

he or she could drink. This is not an exhaustive list of the costs and benefits to society. To determine whether or not society benefited by Prohibition, we have to deal, in the final analysis, with value judgments.

Questions for
Thought
and Discussion

1. Why would you expect the price of a product to be higher when that product is illegal than when it is legal?
2. Some observers contend that more alcoholic beverages were consumed during Prohibition than before or after. If this is indeed true, how can you explain it?
3. What are the characteristics of an illegal good that distinguish its market from that of a legal good?
4. Who gains from making a good illegal? Who loses?

Selected
References

Severn, William, *The End of the Roaring Twenties: Prohibition and Repeal*, New York: J. Messner, 1969.
Sinclair, Andrew, *Era of Excess: A Social History of the Prohibition Movement*, New York: Harper & Row, 1964.

TWO

THE AMERICAN ECONOMY AND ITS PROBLEMS

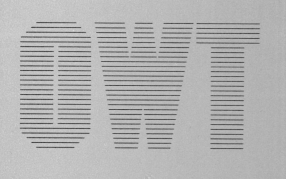

Measuring the Economy's Performance: National Income and Product

The American economy is gigantic and complex. It is composed of millions of businesses and even more millions of households. Workers do millions of different jobs, and there are innumerable ways households can spend their income. In this chapter, and in several following chapters, we will be concerned with **macroeconomics.** The study of macroeconomics entails the study of aggregates, that is, the total values of certain variables, such as income, employment, unemployment, and the like, for the entire economy. Macroeconomics concerns itself with the issues of unemployment and rising prices, whereas **microeconomics** concerns itself with the behavior of individual households, firms, and markets.

To study the aggregates in our economy, we have to both identify and define them. We also have to be able to measure the aggregates. This is where the study of **national income accounting** comes into play because it involves attempting to measure things like national income and its components, which we will discuss throughout this chapter and in the issue that follows. In addition, economists as scientists cannot know whether their theories are worthwhile and accurate until they test those theories with actual data.

Additionally, policymakers need information on our economy's performance in order to implement any given economic policy. This information may consist of such things as the unemployment rate, the rate of price rises (inflation), and changes in the total production of the economy. There are several ways that we can go about measuring total production and total income for the entire nation. Let us first see how production and income are related.

National Income ≡ National Product

What would a good definition of **national income** be? If you answered "The total of all individuals' income," you would be right. But all income is actually a payment for something, whether it be wages paid for labor services, rent and depletion to owners of natural resources, or interest and depreciation to owners of capital; therefore, national income is better defined as the total *cost* of producing the entire output of *final* goods and services.

Now what would your definition of **national product** be? Wouldn't it involve the aggregate of everything that was produced? Yes, it would. National product, then, can be formally defined as the total monetary value of all national output of final goods and services. National income, on the other hand, consists of the receipts from the sale of all the products comprising national output. National income must always equal national product, and this is what is illustrated by Figure 4-1. It shows the **circular flow of income** and product in any economy.

The Circular Flow of Income and Product

The concept of a circular flow of income involves two very simple principles: (1) In every economic exchange the seller receives exactly the same amount that the buyer spends, and (2) expenditures and resource payments flow in the opposite direction to products and to the services used to make those products (factor services).

In the simple economy presented in Figure 4-1, there are only two participants: businesses

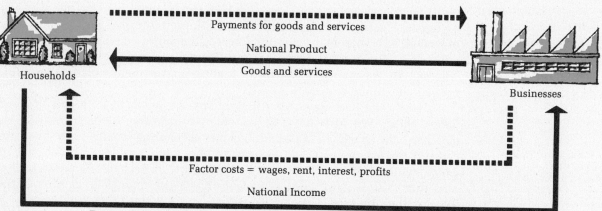

FIGURE 4-1 Circular Flow of Income, Or Why National Income ≡ National Product

This diagram shows a simple, two-sector economy comprised of just households and businesses. Households sell their factor services to businesses in return for which they obtain wages, rent, interest, and profits, which are called factor costs. This is national income. On the top of the diagram, we see that businesses provide households with goods and services (products) in return for which businesses receive payments. The broken lines are money flows, and the solid lines are real flows—goods and factor services. The nation's flow of output in the upper half of the diagram must equal the nation's flow of income in the lower half. (Actually, profits act as the residual, or balancing, item that brings about this identity.)

and households. It is further assumed that firms sell their entire output immediately to households and that households spend their entire income immediately on consumer products. Households receive their income by renting out whatever factors of production they own, such as labor services.

There are a number of things that may puzzle you about the simplified circular-flow-of-income diagram in Figure 4-1. We have listed profits as a factor cost. The commonsense view is that profits are not part of the cost of producing goods and services, but profits are indeed a part of this cost because the owners of capital anticipate being rewarded for providing that capital. Their reward is profit. If there were no expectation of profit, some owners would consume their stock of capital rather than invest it. That is why we consider profits a cost of doing business.

We have obviously simplified the world by leaving out the government sector, the foreign sector, taxes, investment, and depreciation. We will explain these elements in this chapter. Now let us try to get a clearer picture by looking at the makeup of the most widely used measure of total, or aggregate, economic activity: **gross national product.**

Gross National Product

Gross national product (GNP) represents the total money value of the nation's annual final product, or output. We will formally define GNP as the total market value of all final goods and services produced in an economy during a year period. We must specify a time period when we refer to any measure of a flow. We discussed the distinction between stocks and flows in Chapter 2, but it is worthwhile to mention it again. A nation produces at a certain rate, and you receive income at a certain rate.

It might be at a rate of $5,000 per year or $50,000 per year. In any event, the income you receive is a flow. You must contrast this with, for example, your total accumulated savings, which is a stock measured at a point in time, not across time. Implicit in just about everything we deal with in this chapter, and throughout the rest of the macroeconomic section of the book, is a time period—usually a year. All the measures of national product and income are specified as rates measured in billions of dollars per year.

As we have noted, GNP measures the value of *final* output; it ignores intermediate goods, or goods used up entirely in the production of final goods, because to include them would be to double-count. The way to understand this is to define GNP as the total of all *value added* at each stage of production. We can see what "value added" means by looking at Table 4-1. Here we show the respective sales values and values added at each stage in the production of a donut. You can see that the value added is equal to the sum of all incomes generated from the production of that donut. Those incomes are equal to profit, wages, rent, and interest.

There are two different ways of computing gross national product: the **expenditure approach,** in which we add up the dollar value at current market prices of all final goods and services produced by the nation's economy, or the **income approach,** in which we add up all the national income, including wages, interest, rent, and profits. Let's first look at the so-called expenditure approach.

Deriving GNP with the Expenditure Approach

How do we spend our income? As households or individuals we do that through consumption expenditure (C), which falls into three catego-

Table 4-1 Sales Value and Value Added in Cents Per Donut at Each Stage of Production

(1) STAGE OF PRODUCTION	(2) SALES VALUE	(3) VALUE ADDED
Stage 1: Fertilizer and seed	$0.01	$0.01
Stage 2: Growing wheat	0.02	$0.01
Stage 3: Flour milling	0.04	0.02
Stage 4: Donut baking	0.10	0.06
Stage 5: Donut retailing	0.15	0.05
Total sales value	$0.32 Total value added	$0.15

Stage 1:   A farmer purchases a penny's worth of fertilizer and seed that are used as factors of production in growing wheat.

Stage 2:   The farmer grows the wheat, harvests it, and sells it to a miller for 2¢. Thus, we see that the farmer has added 1¢ worth of value. That 1¢ represents income paid in the form of rent, wages, interest, and profit by the farmer.

Stage 3:   The flour miller purchases the wheat for 2¢, and adds 2¢ to the value added; that is, there is 2¢ for him as income to be paid as rent, wages, interest, and profit. He sells the ground wheat flour to a donut baking company.

Stage 4:   The donut baking company buys the flour for 4¢ and adds 6¢ as the value added. It then sells the donut to the final retailer.

Stage 5:   The donut retailer sells fresh hot donuts at 15¢ apiece, thus creating additional value of 5¢.

We see that the total sales value resulting from the production of one donut was 32¢, but the total value added was 15¢, which is exactly equal to the retail price. The total value added is equal to the sum of all income payments, including payments to rent, wages, interest, and profit.

ries: **durable consumer goods, nondurable consumer goods,** and **services.** Durable goods are arbitrarily defined as items that last more than a year; these include automobiles, furniture, and household appliances. Nondurable goods are all the rest, such as food and gasoline. Services are just what the name suggests, medical care, education, and the like.

You should be aware of the fact that there are some goods and services which do not pass through the marketplace. For example, food grown on the farm for household consumption by the farmers' families is certainly a consumption expenditure, but it does not show up in the usual way. In fact, government statisticians

have to estimate it to put it into gross national product. Additionally, the implicit rental value[1] of owner-occupied homes is also estimated and put into personal consumption expenditures (rental payments on apartments and the like are automatically included).

Government Expenditures

In addition to personal consumption expenditures, there are government expenditures on goods and services (G). Generally, we value

[1]If you own a home, you do not actually pay rent. However, whatever you would have to pay to some other owner of that same house is called the implicit rental value.

goods and services at the price at which they are sold. But many government goods and services are provided at no direct cost to the consumer. Therefore, we cannot use their market value when computing GNP. The value of these goods is considered to be equal to their cost. For example, the value of a new road is considered to be equal to its construction cost and is included in the GNP for the year it was built.

Gross Private Domestic Investment

Now we come to an expenditure that we haven't yet talked about—**investment** *(I)* on the part of business firms. We have to be careful when using the term "investment" because it has one meaning in everyday life but has another when it refers to the national economy. You know that an investment occurs when you buy a stock or a bond or a piece of property. However, from our national-accounting point of view, that is not an investment but merely a *transfer* of asset ownership among individuals. For our purpose here, we will define investment as the addition to or replacement of physical assets that can add to the productive capacity of the nation. Investment, therefore, includes new capital goods, such as factories and machines. It also includes newly built housing since the consumption of the shelter provided by a house lasts for a long time after it is built. Note the new housing is the only good bought by consumers that is included in "*I.*" Investment also includes changes in **inventories.** Inventories are defined as finished goods a firm has on hand for sale at a later date. An inventory is a stock concept that is measured at a moment in time. The investment aspect of inventories is the flow to or from that stock, that is, any increase or decrease in it over time.

The Foreign Sector

To get an accurate representation of gross national product, we must include the foreign sector, which we treat at length in Chapter 14. We, as Americans, purchase foreign goods called imports. The goods that foreigners purchase from us are our exports. To get an idea of the increase in total expenditures from the foreign sector, we subtract the value of our imports from the value of our exports to get net exports for a year:

Net exports = total exports − total imports

To get an idea of the relationship between *C, G,* and *I,* just look at Figure 4-2. Here we show gross national product, personal consumption expenditures, government purchases, gross private domestic investment, and net exports from 1929 to 1975.

Note that when we sum up the expenditures of the household, government, business, and foreign sectors, we get GNP, which is sometimes called GNE, or gross national expenditure.

Getting Rid of the Gross

We have used the terms gross national product and gross private domestic investment without really indicating what "gross" means. The dictionary defines it as "without deductions," as opposed to "net." Deductions for what? you might ask. Deductions for something we call **depreciation** is the answer. In the course of a year, machines and structures wear out as they are used in the production of national product. For example, houses deteriorate as they are used, and machines need repairs or they will fall apart and stop working. Most capital, or durable, goods, if not all, therefore suffer a form of depreciation. Expenditures on repairs and other means of replacing the existing capital stock are often netted out of gross national product to arrive at a figure called **net national product** (NNP), which we define as:

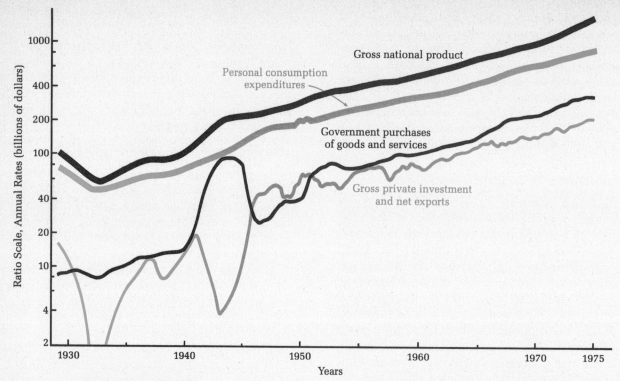

FIGURE 4-2 **GNP and Its Components**

Here we see a time-series display of gross national product, personal consumption expenditures, government purchases, and gross private domestic investment with net exports for the years 1929 to 1975. *(Source:* U.S. Dept. of Commerce. Data for 1975 are preliminary.)

NNP = GNP − depreciation (capital consumption allowances)

Depreciation is also called a capital consumption allowance because it is the amount of the capital stock that has been consumed over a year. Two other ways of defining NNP are:

NNP = *C* + gross *I* + *G* + net exports − depreciation

NNP = *C* + net *I* + *G* + net exports

Net investment measures changes in our capital stock over time and is positive nearly every year. Since depreciation does not vary dramatically as a percentage of GNP, you will get a similar picture about what is happening to our economy by looking at either one—NNP or GNP.

Let us now turn to the second approach of calculating GNP.

GNP with the Income Approach

We can calculate GNP in terms of the flow of costs or payments that firms make in order to produce the things they sell to households. We previously defined national income as the total amount of national factor payments to the owners of the factors of production that are utilized. Stated in other words, national income is the total income earned by the owners of resources who put their factors of production to work. Using this approach we have four categories:

1. *Wages* The most important category is, of course, wages, including wages and salaries and other forms of labor income, such as income in kind, incentive payments, and so on. We also count Social Security taxes (both the employees' and the employers' "contributions").
2. *Interest* Here, interest payments do not equal the sum of payments for the use of money capital in a year. Rather, interest is expressed in net rather than in gross terms. In other words, the interest component of national income is the difference between interest paid by the domestic business sector and interest received by that sector from all other sectors (plus the net interest received from other countries).
3. *Rent* Rent is all income earned by individuals for the use of their real (nonmonetary) assets, such as farms, houses, and stores. As we stated previously, we have to include here the implicit rental value of owner-occupied houses. Also included in this category are royalties received from copyrights and patents and things like oil and gas wells.
4. *Profits* Our last category includes total gross (pretax) corporate profits and so-called proprietors' income. Proprietors' income is that income earned from the operation of unincorporated businesses, which include sole proprietorships, partnerships, and producers' cooperatives.

These four components, added together, give us national income at factor cost. To get gross national income, which will then be equal to gross national product, we have to add two other components: **indirect business taxes** and depreciation.

Indirect Business Taxes

Excise taxes, sales taxes, and property taxes incurred by businesspersons make up what are called indirect business taxes. Think of it this way: Businesses are actually acting as the government's agent when they collect a sales tax. They collect it from you and turn it over to the government. The tax is a business expense, but the real burden is likely to be on the customer, who pays a higher price. Because of this, such indirect taxes are included in gross national income as a cost item.

Depreciation

Just as we had to look at depreciation in figuring out why NNP differed from GNP, to go from net national income to gross national income, we must add depreciation. Depreciation can be thought of as that portion of the current year's GNP which is used to replace physical capital consumed in the process of production. Since somebody is paid to do the replacement, depreciation must be added as a component of gross national income.

The last two components of GNP are called nonincome expense items.

Look at Table 4-2. Here we show a comparison between gross national product and gross national income for 1975. Whether you decide to use the expenditure point of view or the income point of view, you will come out with the same number. There are sometimes statistical discrepancies, but they are usually extremely small.

Now let us consider the other variants of GNP and GNI.

Table 4-2 Gross National Product and Gross National Income, 1975 (in Billions of Dollars Per Year)

By using the two different methods of computing the output of the economy, we come up with gross national product and gross national income, which are, by necessity, equal. One viewpoint is through expenditures, or the flow of product; the other viewpoint is through income, or the flow of costs.

EXPENDITURE POINT OF VIEW—PRODUCT FLOW		INCOME POINT OF VIEW—COST FLOW	
Expenditures by Different Sectors:		**National Income (at Factor Cost):**	$1,168
Household sector		*Salaries/wages*	
Personal consumption expenses	$ 938	All salaries/wages and supplemental compensation to employees	886
Government sector		*Rent*	
Payments for goods and services	339	All rental income of individuals plus implicit rent on owner-occupied dwellings	27
Business sector		*Interest*	
Gross private investment—domestic	147	Net interest paid by business	72
Foreign sector		*Profit*	
Net exports—goods and services	9	Business, professional, and farm income Corporate profits before taxes deducted	97
		Expenses not classified as income	265
		Indirect business taxes	138
		Depreciation (capital consumption allowance)	127
Gross national product	**$1,433**	**Gross national income**	**$1,433**

Source: U.S. Department of Commerce, preliminary data, 2d quarter.

The Rest of National Income Accounting

Table 4-2 shows the remaining components of the national income accounts. We have already defined gross national product and net national product. The difference is depreciation, or capital consumption allowances.

National Income

We know that net national income represents the total market value of goods and services available for both "consumption," used in a broader sense here to mean "resource exhausting," and net additions to the economy's stock of capital. NNP does not, however, represent the income available to individuals within that economy because it includes indirect business taxes, such as sales taxes, which we talked about in the last section. We therefore deduct these indirect business taxes from NNP to arrive at the figure for all factor payments to resource owners. The result is national income, or NI.

Personal Income

National income does not actually represent what is available to individuals to spend because some people obtain income for which they have provided no concurrent good or service and others earn income but do not receive it. In the former category are mainly recipients of **transfer payments** from the government, such as welfare, food stamps, and the like. These payments represent shifts of funds within the economy by way of the government, where no good or service is rendered in exchange. For the other category, income earned but not received, the most obvious examples are undistributed corporate profits that are plowed back into the business, contributions to social insurance, and corporate income taxes. When transfer payments are added and when income earned but not received is subtracted, we end up with **personal income,** or PI.

Disposable Personal Income

Everybody knows that you do not get to take home all your salary. To get **disposable personal income,** DPI, subtract all personal income taxes from personal income. This is the income that individuals actually have available for consuming or not consuming (saving).

We have completed our somewhat complicated rundown of the different ways GNP can be computed and of the different variants of national income and product. What we have not yet even touched on is the difference between national income measured in this year's dollars and national income representing "real" goods and services. This is an important distinction to make, especially now that we have significant increases in all prices every year.

Correcting GNP

If an eight-track stereo tape costs $5 this year, 10 tapes will have a market value of $50. If next year they cost $10 each, the same 10 tapes will have a market value of $100. There will have been no increase in the total quantity of tapes, but the market value will have doubled. Apply this to every single good and service produced and sold in the United States and you realize that GNP, measured in "current" dollars, may not be a true indication of economic activity. After all, we are really interested in variations in the real output of the economy. What we have to do, then, is correct GNP (and just about everything else we look at) for changes in overall prices. Basically, we need to generate an index which approximates the changes in overall prices and then divide that estimate into the value of output in current dollars to get the value of output in what are called **constant dollars.** This price-corrected GNP is called *real* GNP. Current price indices in the United States are compiled by the Department of Labor, Bureau of Labor Statistics, and have a 1967 base year. We present, in Figure 4-3, deflated, or price-corrected GNP (real GNP), with a base year of 1967. In Chapter 7, when we talk about inflation and how to measure it, we will go into some detail about the actual price indices used in the United States. However, correcting for prices is not the only analytical problem we should be concerned with. Another one involves how many people there are to share in GNP.

Per Capita GNP

If "real" GNP over a 10-year period went up 100 percent, you might immediately jump to the conclusion that the material well-being of the economy had increased by that amount. But what if, during the same period, population increased by 200 percent? Then what would you say? Certainly, the amount of GNP per person, or per capita, would have fallen, even though total deflated, or real, GNP would have risen. What we must do to account not only for price changes but also for population

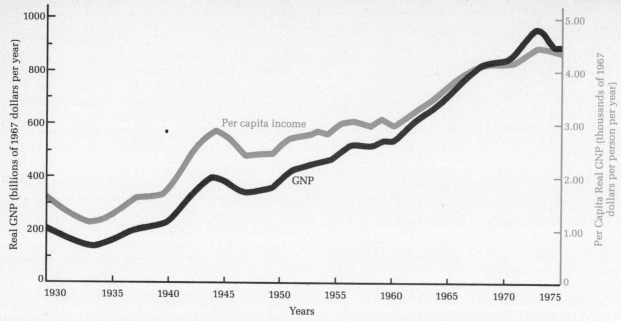

FIGURE 4-3   **GNP and Real Per Capita GNP over Time**

Here we see real GNP from 1929 to 1975 expressed in constant 1967 dollars. That is, the base year is 1967. We also put in the same diagram real GNP per capita, which is merely real GNP divided by the population for each year. (*Source:* U.S. Dept. of Commerce.)

changes is first deflate GNP and then divide by the total population, doing this for each year. This is what we have done in the bottom line of Figure 4-3. We show deflated, or real, GNP per capita in the United States over a 40-year period. If we were to look at certain underdeveloped countries, we would find that in many cases even though real GNP has risen over the past several decades, real GNP per capita has remained constant because population growth ate up all the gains in total output.

The difficulties in using GNP as an indicator of social well-being do not end here. In fact, there has been a running battle over the use of GNP statistics when recounting the material gains of our economy. What else is wrong with this measure, and what should be done to correct it? That is the topic of our next issue.

Definitions of New Terms

Macroeconomics: The study of economic aggregates, their movements, and the causes of their movements. In other words, the study of the economy as it functions as a whole.

Microeconomics: The study of the behavior of the individual economic agents in our society.

National Income Accounting: The science of measuring the theoretical concepts used in the study of macroeconomics. Specifically, national income accounting involves attempts at measuring national income and its components.

National Income: The total payment or cost to the economy of producing the entire output of final goods and services.

National Product: The total dollar value at current prices of all the final goods and services that are produced in a 1-year period.

Circular Flow of Income: The schematic representation of how real goods and services move among firms, households, and the government and the resulting receipts and payments from these movements.

Gross National Product (GNP):   The total market value of all final goods and services produced by the entire economy in a 1-year period.

Expenditure Approach: A way of computing GNP by adding up the dollar value of current market prices of all final goods and services; to be contrasted with the income approach.

Income Approach: A way of measuring GNP by adding up all components of national income, including wages, interest, rent, and profits.

Durable Consumer Goods: Goods, used by consumers, that have a life span, that is, goods which endure and can give utility over a longer period of time.

Nondurable Consumer Goods: Goods, used by consumers, that are used up more or less immediately.

Services: Commodities purchased by consumers that do not have physical characteristics. Examples of services are those purchased from doctors, lawyers, dentists, repair personnel, housecleaners, and educators.

Investment: The creation of new capital goods, such as factories and machines, that can yield production and hence consumption in the future. Also included in this definition are changes in business inventories.

Inventories: The stock of finished goods that a firm holds over from one period to another.

Depreciation: Reduction in the value of capital goods over a 1-year period due to physical wear and tear and also to obsolescence.

Net National Product (NNP):   GNP minus depreciation.

Indirect Business Taxes: All business taxes except the corporation tax on profits. Indirect business taxes include sales and business property taxes.

Transfer Payments: Payments to individuals for which no goods or services are exchanged in return. Examples are food stamps, unemployment benefits, and Social Security benefits.

Personal Income (PI):   The amount of income that households actually receive before they pay personal income taxes.

Disposable Personal Income (DPI):   Personal income after personal income taxes have been paid.

Constant Dollars: Dollars expressed in terms of purchasing power using a particular year as the base or standard of comparison.

1. National income accounting is the science (and art) by which economists attempt to statistically measure the variables with which they are concerned in their study of macroeconomics.

2. In any economy, there is a circular flow of income because every economic exchange involves a seller of a product or service who receives a payment in return. Thus, goods and services flow in one direction, and payments flow in the other direction.

3. One of the most often used concepts in national income accounting is gross national product, which is defined as the total market value of all *final* goods and services. The stress on "final" is important to avoid the double counting of so-called intermediate goods that are used in the production of other goods.

4. We can compute GNP by using the expenditure approach or the income approach. In the former, we merely add up the dollar value of all final goods and services, and in the latter we add up the payments for all those goods and services, or wages, interest, rent, and profits.

5. It is difficult to measure the market value of government expenditures because generally government-provided goods are not sold at a market clearing price. We have used the device of valuing government expenditures at their cost to include them in our measure of GNP.

6. It is important to realize that investment does not occur when there is merely a transfer of assets among individuals; rather, it occurs only when new productive capacity for the future is generated, such as when a machine is built to be used later.

7. Part of our capital stock is worn out or becomes obsolete every year. To take account of the expenditures made merely to replace such depreciation, we subtract depreciation from GNP to come up with net national product or NNP.

8. GNP has a number of components, including personal income, disposable personal income, and so on.

9. To correct for price changes, we deflate GNP in terms of constant dollars to come up with real GNP. To take account of rising population, we then correct for population and come up with real GNP per capita.

1. Is it possible to distinguish between final goods and intermediate goods?
2. What would happen if we double-counted when we tried to measure GNP?
3. What is the difference between gross private investment and net private investment? Which measure of investment would you be interested in if you were analyzing the growth of an economy or its potential growth?
4. Why do we include changes in business inventories as part of investment?

5. How could net private domestic investment be negative in 1933? What would happen if net private domestic investment remained negative for many years?

6. The following data are for a hypothetical economy:

$$
\begin{aligned}
\text{Consumption} &= \$400 \text{ Billion} \\
\text{Government spending} &= \$350 \text{ B} \\
\text{Gross private domestic investment} &= \$150 \text{ B} \\
\text{Exports} &= \$150 \text{ B} \\
\text{Imports} &= \$100 \text{ B} \\
\text{Depreciation} &= \$ 50 \text{ B} \\
\text{Indirect business taxes} &= \$ 25 \text{ B}
\end{aligned}
$$

(a) Based on the data, what is the value of GNP? ____ NNP? ____ NI? ____.

(b) Suppose that in the next year exports increase to $175 B, imports increase to $200 B, and consumption falls to $350 B. What will GNP be in this year? ____

(c) If the value of depreciation (capital consumption allowance) should ever exceed that of gross private domestic investment, how would this affect the future productivity of the nation?

Selected References

Abraham, William I., *National Income and Economic Accounting*, Englewood Cliffs, N.J.: Prentice-Hall, 1969.

Rosen, Sam, *National Income and Other Social Accounts*, New York: Holt, Rinehart and Winston, 1972.

U.S. Department of Commerce, *The Economic Accounts of the United States: Retrospect and Prospect*, Washington, D.C.: U.S. Government Printing Office, 1971.

Does GNP Mean Gross National Promise?

ARE WE MEASURING THE WRONG THING?

National Income Accounting and Human Happiness

The United States Department of Commerce defines GNP simply as "the market value of the output of final goods and services produced by the nation's economy." But critics of the economic situation in the United States define GNP as "gross national promise," indicating that it does not measure what is actually happening in the United States. We can all agree that no measure of a nation's production or output, no matter how perfect, can be used to assess the happiness or satisfaction of its citizens. There is no way we can equate human welfare with either economic goods and services or the satisfaction derived from them. The best we can hope for is a measure of material well-being based on how much the population consumes. After all, it is consumption, not production, that generates satisfaction.

Noting the many deficiencies in GNP and the national income accounts, several economists have suggested that we come up with a better measure to gauge economic growth and improvements in economic well-being. At the end of this issue we will present one such measure.

More Corrections for GNP

In Chapter 4 we saw that several adjustments have to be made in our computation of GNP. Let us now consider some items that are not taken into account by government statisticians.

Do-It-Yourself Activities

When you decide to fix your own car, you engage in the production of a service that is not included in GNP. Had you decided to take your car to a garage, that same service would have been included in GNP because you would have paid a mechanic. Services in the home represent the biggest category under this heading of what is left out of GNP.

Housewives' Services

The value of the services performed by women in the home is substantial,

as can be seen in Table I-5.1. These services range from cooking, to food buying, to being a practical nurse. In fact, if an individual marries a paid housekeeper and that housekeeper leaves the labor force, GNP will fall.

However, the services of nonworking husbands or wives are becoming less significant with respect to computing GNP. As more services are contracted for with regular businesses and with individuals selling those services, they become part of GNP (assuming, of course, the income is reported). Cases in point are the purchases of laundry services and convenience foods. Since World War II, the purchase of household activities has increased markedly, so some of the growth in measured real GNP has been exaggerated relative

to previous growth before this phenomenon occurred.

Illegal Activities

A large number of illegal activities do not enter into our national income accounts. These include, but are not limited to, narcotics, gambling, bootlegging, and prostitution. Since these activities generate satisfaction, they certainly do contribute to the well-being of the consumers. It is impossible to estimate their total market value, but it is probably in the neighborhood of $50 billion.

Income Never Reported

A number of economic activities generate income that, in principle,

should be included in our national income accounts. However, for purposes of tax evasion, some people do not report this income. The general term for this activity is "skimming." It is alleged, for example, that professionals (doctors, lawyers, and so forth), often skim by not reporting a certain percentage of cash payments received from patients or clients.

Measures of Satisfaction

Assuming we were able to include every single economic activity that should be included to measure real GNP, we could come up with a perfect measure of output, or production. However, output does not nec-

Table I-5.1

Value of a Housewife's Services—1974–1975

The market value of housewives' services is not insignificant. In this particular survey, the estimated value per week was $306.82.

SERVICE	HOURS PER WEEK	VALUE OF SERVICE PER HOUR	VALUE OF SERVICE PER WEEK
Nursemaid	44.5	$2.50	$111.25
Housekeeper	17.5	3.50	61.25
Cook	13.1	3.50	45.85
Dishwasher	6.2	2.25	13.95
Laundress	5.9	2.60	15.34
Food buyer	3.3	3.75	12.38
Chauffeur	2.0	4.00	8.00
Gardener	2.3	6.00	13.80
Maintenance "man"	1.7	6.00	10.20
Seamstress	1.3	4.00	5.20
Dietician	1.2	5.50	6.60
Practical nurse	0.6	5.00	3.00
Total	99.6		$306.82

Source: Chase Manhattan Bank of New York. Data are based on updated rates of pay in the New York area for the occupations listed.

essarily equal satisfaction, and a higher level of output may not be associated with a higher level of satisfaction. For example, if output were to increase by 10 percent but population were to increase by 20 percent, the amount of output available per person would fall. As we noted in Chapter 4, we can correct for this problem by dividing real GNP by population to obtain per capita real GNP, but even then we are faced with another problem.

What if the rich get richer and the poor get poorer as GNP grows? Has the general level of satisfaction increased? Many people would say no because the distribution of income, even though we have no way of taking it into account, must surely play an important part in determining the level of satisfaction of society.

And what about leisure? Surely it is a scarce good. As such, it has value and generates satisfaction. Although it has recently leveled off, in the United States, the amount of leisure time has been growing since World War II. Figure I-5.1 shows that the number of hours worked on average fell by some 18 percent from 1943 to mid 1971. This increased leisure certainly has added to our satisfaction, but it is not included in any measure of the national income accounts.

Gross National Pollution

Environmental concern in the 1970s has focused attention on a large deficiency in our measurement of the nation's economic well-being. Numerous critics of the environmental degradation in our nation maintain that our standard definition of GNP is misleading. In fact, some regard GNP as a symbol of everything that is wrong with America. The idea is that if GNP growth were slowed or even halted, economic output would fall but so would pollution. Dr. Arthur F. Burns, Chairman of the Board of Governors of the Federal Reserve System, told Congress that he would like to see GNP adjusted to "take account of the depreciation in our environment." He indicated that there should be a "proper recording of the minuses as well as the pluses." In Burns' opinion, GNP, properly adjusted, would be a good deal lower than it now appears.

FIGURE I-5.1 Average Weekly Hours Worked, 1943–1975

Up until 1970 there was a fairly steady decline in the average weekly hours worked in America. In other words, Americans were enjoying more leisure as their real incomes rose. Recently, however, the trend has leveled off. (*Source:* Bureau of Labor Statistics.)

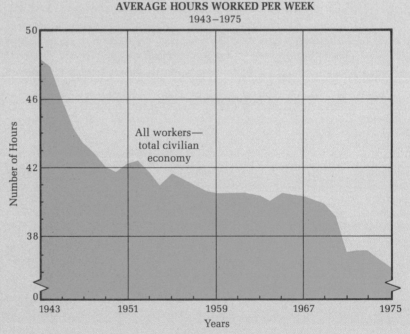

AVERAGE HOURS WORKED PER WEEK
1943–1975

All workers— total civilian economy

The trade-off between production and pollution is represented in Figure I-5.2. On the horizontal axis (output) are measured "good" goods, and on the vertical axis (pollution) are measured "bad" goods. The upward-sloping line is an odd sort of production-possibilities curve: Instead of having to give up more of one good when we produce more of the other, we get more of both. But we are not happy with an increase in the "bad" good.

A proper assessment of economic performance should probably include some type of subtraction for all the damages (expressed in economic terms) done by pollution. Moreover, we probably should not include the cost of pollution abatement in the measure of economic well-being because these services are not desired for their own sake.

Neither is police protection. Most people do not get any direct satisfaction or utility from services that are carried on in order to reduce illegal activities. With regard to our well-being, the inclusion of police protection in the national product is an inappropriate entry. Consider what would happen to our general level of happiness if, all of a sudden, robberies were to increase fivefold: We would need increased police protection; we would have to pay for it with additional taxes; and we would therefore have lower material well-being. The reduction would not show up in the national income accounts because the taxes would be used to pay the salaries of additional police personnel.

Given all the deficiencies in our national income accounts, is it possible to come up with a new measure of GNP? Yes, say two innovating experts in the field, James Tobin (whose biography follows this issue) and William Nordhaus.

MEW: A New Measure of GNP

Professors Tobin and Nordhaus a few years back presented their view of what GNP would look like if it were to actually take account of many of the deficiencies we have outlined. They called it "measure of economic welfare," or MEW. You get MEW by modifying GNP in three ways:

1. Subtracting certain costs or "bads," such as pollution
2. Excluding "regrettable necessities," such as police services
3. Adding activities that are not

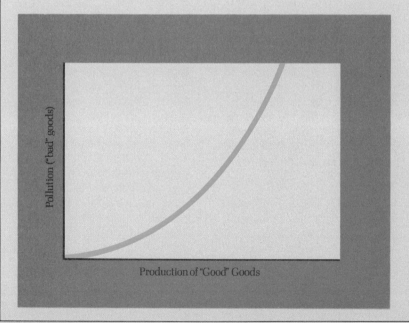

FIGURE I-5.2 The Pollution Costs of Increased Production

This graph represents a peculiar production-possibilities frontier since more "good" goods are associated with more of the "bad" goods—pollution. At very small rates of production, there may be little or no pollution. Nature can handle it in small doses. However, at higher rates of production, more pollution results, increasing even more rapidly than output.

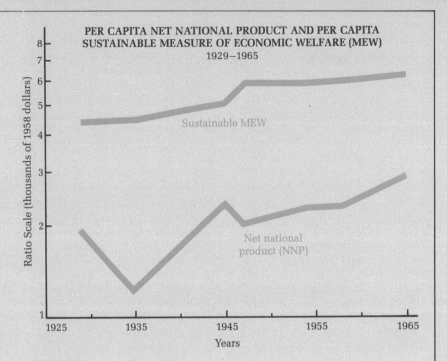

PER CAPITA NET NATIONAL PRODUCT AND PER CAPITA
SUSTAINABLE MEASURE OF ECONOMIC WELFARE (MEW)
1929–1965

FIGURE I-5.3
As we can see, the measure of economic welfare, MEW, is much greater than net national product, NNP. However, the growth rate of MEW is significantly less than the growth rate of NNP.

included in GNP, such as household services, home repairs, and leisure

Figure I-5.3 shows MEW compared with NNP. The results are interesting. MEW has been growing—but at a considerably lower rate (1.1 percent per year) than per capita real GNP (1.7 percent per year).

Using MEW instead of GNP is considered by many to be a step in the right direction. MEW is a good measure of consumption, but it is not, unfortunately, a measure of economic welfare. The two concepts are related, but economic welfare depends on the amount of total satisfaction that each of us actually receives from our consumption. Nordhaus and Tobin are certainly aware of these problems. The intent and the conclusions of their study are best summarized in their own words:

We recognize that our proposal is controversial on conceptual and theoretical grounds and that many of the numerical expedients in its execution are dubious. Nevertheless, the challenge to economists to produce relevant welfare-oriented measures seems compelling enough to justify some risk-taking. We hope that others will be challenged, or provoked, to tackle the problem with different assumptions, more refined procedures, and better data. We hope also that further investigations will be concerned with the distribution, as well as the mean value, of a measure of economic welfare, an aspect we have not been able to consider.[1]

[1]William Nordhaus and James Tobin, ''Is Growth Obsolete?'', in *Economic Growth*, Fiftieth Anniversary Colloquium, vol. 5, New York: National Bureau of Economic Research, 1972, p. 26.

Questions for Thought and Discussion

1. Do you think that the statistical measurement problems in deciding what MEW is are significant? If they are, is MEW still a better measure of economic welfare than GNP?
2. How would your ideal measure of economic welfare be constructed, assuming there were no problems of statistical measurement with any of its components?

Selected References

Goldsmith, Raymond and Christopher Saunders (eds.), *The Measurement of National Wealth,* International Association for Research, in Income and Wealth, ser. VIII, Chicago: Quadrangle Books, 1959.

Lekachman, Robert, *National Income and the Public Welfare,* New York: Random House, 1972.

Economic Growth and Income Redistribution

JAMES TOBIN

Former Member, Council of Economic Advisers (CEA) 1961–1962

When asked to make sacrifices for the defense of their nation, the American people have always responded. Perhaps some day a national administration will muster the courage to ask the American people to tax themselves for social justice and domestic tranquility.

Sentiments such as these appealed to George McGovern during the 1972 campaign when he called upon their author, 54-year-old Yale professor of economics, James Tobin, to help frame a viable economic program that would broaden the candidate's platform. Among the group of McGovern's advisers, Tobin was, in the words of *Time*, "the intellectual giant" and the economist who had "most influenced McGovern personally."

Best known for his schemes for income redistribution through changes in the tax system, former CEA member James Tobin devised for McGovern a negative income tax plan based on his article in *Agenda for the*

Nation, "Raising the Incomes of the Poor" (1968). In that article he proposed that all tax exemptions, exclusions, and standard deductions be eliminated and replaced with a system of taxation whereby every individual making under $2,250 would be reimbursed one-third of the difference by the federal government, and every individual making over $2,250 would pay one-third of the excess in taxes. Such a program could be financed, Tobin thought, through "the normal growth of tax revenues" and government funds freed by peace in Vietnam.

Tobin has written many other articles on income redistribution and economic growth. Aside from his recommendation with William Nordhaus for a new "measure of economic welfare" to replace GNP, the traditional measure of economic growth, Tobin has written on the costs and benefits of faster economic growth. In a 1969 article coauthored with Leonard Ross, Tobin proposed the creation of a "National Youth Endowment" that would make government credit available to the young for educational purposes and shift the burden of cost from parents to the students themselves. More recently, in September 1974, Tobin criticized the Nixon administration's economic policies and called for a new "social contract" to help reduce the rate of inflation. Among other proposals, he suggested that workers' take-home pay could be increased without inflationary consequences by reforming the Social Security tax structure to make it more equitable and progressive.

Educated at Harvard, Tobin worked as an economist for the Office of Price Administration and the War Production Board before joining the Yale faculty in 1950. He served as a consultant to the Board of Governors of the Federal Reserve System from 1955 to 1956. In early 1961, President Kennedy ap-pointed Tobin to the Council of Economic Advisers, where he stayed until August 1962. Like other economists associated with the Kennedy administration, Tobin has been a firm believer in what has become known as the "new economics," which is actually based on the Keynesian idea that economic growth can be stimulated and unemployment reduced by a combination of tax cuts and deficit spending. Tobin discussed elements of this strategy in his 1966 book *National Economic Policy.*

In his latest book, *The New Economics: One Decade Older* (1974), Tobin reassesses the idea of the "new economics" and attempts a qualified defense of the economic policies of the 1960s. Though admitting that the "new economics" was "oversold," he asserts that the economic growth of the early 1960s "did more to lift the incomes of the poor and disadvantaged than any conceivable redistribution program." The "new economics" provided the basis for successful policy through 1965, he believes; "then things began to fall apart." Tobin attributes the federal budget increases and the late 1960s surge in inflation to the Vietnam conflict and the timing of Johnson's tax increase, adding that "the validity of New Economics as science is not impaired but rather reinforced by the fact that bad things happened as predicted when the advice of its practitioners was rejected."

In defending the "new economics" against charges that its policies are inflationary, Tobin says "Our economy, like all others of the modern world, has an inflationary bias. When it operates without socially intolerable rates of unemployment and excess capacity, prices will drift steadily upward." Tobin suggests that the lapse of the "new economics" is only "partial and temporary" and believes it would retain its relevance if a number of fiscal and monetary reforms were adopted.

Government Spending and Taxation

Can you think of any aspect of your life that is not in some way influenced by the government? Almost every time you buy something, the government takes its cut in the form of sales taxes. Almost every time you produce something, the government takes its cut in the form of income taxes. Most of you have had your education provided by the government, and even if you are now going to a private college or university, it may be receiving government grants. This textbook might have been mailed to your college bookstore using the government's postal services. It would be difficult, if not impossible, to make a list of every way that the government influences your life. It seems appropriate, then, for us to spend this chapter finding out about the economic functions of government, the ways in which government spends its revenues, and the ways in which it obtains those revenues. Let us first look at the functions of government in our economy.

The Economic Functions of Government

The complex functions of government can be classified into five broad categories:

1. The provision of public goods
2. The regulation of economic activity
3. The redistribution of income
4. The stabilization of the economy
5. The administration of justice

These categories are not all-inclusive, but they do cover the bulk of government activity. After we have talked about these functions, we will look at the growth of government in our nation.

Providing Public Goods

Until now we have generally talked about private goods, such as French fries, hamburgers, and manufactured commodities. But some other goods—**public goods**—are in a class by themselves. National defense and police protection, for example, are public goods. If you partake of them, you do not necessarily take away from anybody else's share. The principle of exclusion does not apply as it does, for example, to an apple pie because if you eat the pie, no one else can do the same.

Pure Public Goods   We can list several distinguishing characteristics of public goods that set them apart from all other goods.

1. Public goods are usually indivisible. You can't sell $5 worth of our ability to annihilate the world with bombs. Public goods cannot be produced or sold very easily in small units.
2. Public goods can be used by increasing numbers of people at no additional cost. Once a television signal has been emitted, turning on your tube does not cost the TV station anything.
3. Additional users of public goods do not deprive other users from any of the services of the good. If you turn on your radio, no one gets weaker reception because of your action.
4. It is very difficult to charge people for a public good on the basis of how much they use. How does one determine how much any person uses or even values national defense?

Free Riders   This last point leads us to the free-rider problem, in which people either think

that others can take the burden of paying for public goods, such as national defense, or argue that they receive no value from such government services. For example, they will tell interviewers they are unwilling to pay for national defense because they don't want any of it—it's of no value to them. We all want to be free riders when we think we can get away with it.

Look at the problem as it is schematized in Table 5-1. How much national defense will you benefit from if you agree to pay and everyone else also pays? $90,000,000,100. How much will there be if you don't pay but everyone else does pay? $90,000,000,000. If you think everyone else will pay, wouldn't you be tempted to get a free ride?

However you view it, when government steps in, more public goods are provided than would have been provided by the private sector. Since many products and services in our economy are public goods, there is a strong case for the government's financing them. In some cases the private sector might not produce these goods at all.

In our discussion of government-provided goods, do not, however, confuse public goods with government-provided ones. Not all goods financed by the government are public goods, as we have defined them. Furthermore, not all public goods are provided by the government. TV and radio wave emissions are good examples.

Regulating Economic Activity

Another major function of the government is the regulation of economic activities. Governments at federal, state, and local levels are engaged in setting certain prices throughout the economy. Governments regulate the price of electricity, natural gas, and telephone service; they attempt to regulate illegal activities, such as prostitution and narcotics consumption; and

	If you pay	If you don't pay
If everybody else pays	$90,000,000,100	$90,000,000,000
If no one else pays	$100	$0.00

Table 5-1 **Scoreboard for National Defense**
The free rider is the one who will gladly let everyone else pay the bill. If you don't pay your share of national defense but everyone else does, there will still be $90 billion available for the country's defense. Whether you pay or not seems to make very little difference.

they attempt to foster competition by enforcing antitrust laws.

Moreover, the government has attempted to regulate economic activities that generate **negative externalities,** or harmful spillover effects, such as pollution. Government acts in this area by setting standards on air and water quality and by prohibiting certain production methods from being used altogether.

Redistributing Income

A third major government function is the redistribution of income from certain groups of individuals in our society to other groups of individuals. This is generally done through a system of transfer payments, direct payments to individuals who provide no concurrent goods and services to the government. Foremost among these payments are Social Security benefits, veterans' benefits and services, unemployment compensation, and aid to families with dependent children (AFDC). Other types of government transfers include food stamps, public housing, rent supplements, welfare, and medical care payments. Public education can be viewed as an indirect transfer to members of

lower-income groups who receive more benefits from public education than they pay for. We will have more to say about income redistribution in our section on taxes in this chapter.

Stabilizing the Economy

Our economy is presently plagued with the twin problems of unemployment and rising prices. The government, especially the federal government, has taken on the task of attempting economic stabilization, or smoothing out fluctuations in economic activity. The following chapters in this macroeconomic section of our book are all about this task of government. Suffice it to say here that economic stabilization occupies a relatively large amount of government policymaking. To a lesser extent, state and local governments have started considering stabilization as one of their roles also.

Administering Justice

Our legal system is based on the government provision of a police force, courts, and jails. The role of government in such a system has been to enforce private property rights and to prevent, or at least discourage, private individuals from using force in their dealings, whether they be economic or otherwise, with other citizens.

The Growth of Government

Look at Figure 5-1. Here we show the percentage of GNP accounted for by total government purchases at all levels of government—federal, state, and local. Up until the 1930s, government purchases accounted for less than 10 percent of GNP. Today they account for more than 25 percent, and if we look at total government expenditures, which include not only government purchases of goods and services but also transfer payments, the growth in government is even more startling. This can be seen in Table 5-2, where we also break down the percentage of GNP expended by the three levels of government.

The Components of Government Expenditures

Government is growing; of that there is no question. What is less obvious is where it has grown and, more specifically, which individual components make up total expenditures by governments. Where does government spend most of its revenues? This is a topic we will now look at, first at the federal level and then at the state and local levels.

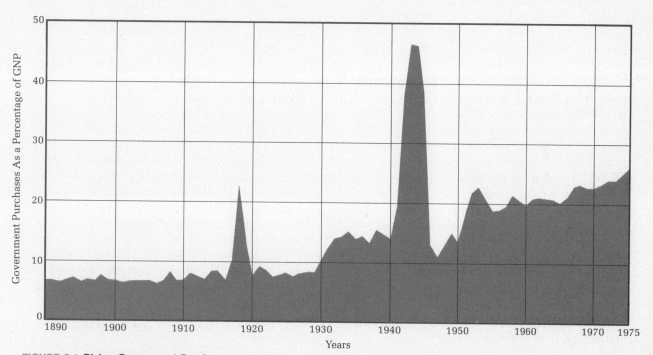

FIGURE 5-1 **Rising Government Purchases**

Here we show government purchases at all levels—federal, state, and local—of goods and services as a percentage of total gross national product. The big jump occurred during World War I, and the upward trend has continued ever since. (*Source:* U.S. Dept. of Commerce.)

Table 5-2 Outlays of Government As a Percentage of Gross National Product

This table shows the percentage of GNP accounted for by total government outlays, *including* transfer payments. Upon close examination, we see that although the federal government accounts for the major share of government outlays, the expenditures of both state and local governments are growing also.

YEAR	ALL GOVERN- MENTS	FED- ERAL	STATE	LOCAL
1950	25	15	4	6
1955	28	18	4	6
1960	30	18	4	8
1965	30	17	5	8
1970	34	19	6	9
1975	39	22	7	10

Source: U.S. Bureau of the Census, *Statistical Abstract of the United States*

The Federal Budget

The federal budget is big and is getting bigger. We see in Table 5-3 that Uncle Sam spends over $300 billion a year. The trends in the categories of federal budget outlays are interesting because they show the direction of the national priorities. This is such an important topic that we will cover it in the following issue when we discuss what are and what should be national priorities. Right now we will explain the particular categories enumerated in Table 5-3.

Defense   Defense includes all outlays for the military or space program and for foreign affairs. Many critics of defense spending contend that the official government estimate is biased downward because it does not include *all* money spent on defense affairs.

Cash Income Maintenance   These programs provide cash benefits, including Social Security benefits to the aged, unemployment compensa- tion, and public assistance to the poor and disabled.

Helping People Buy Essentials   This category includes vouchers or cash that allows individuals to buy *specific* goods and services. The most obvious specific service is medical care for the aged under the various Medicare and Medicaid programs. In addition, this category includes food stamps and housing supplements.

Aid for Social Programs   This category includes all the funds that the federal government expends to assist state and local governments in providing such services as education, manpower training programs, community revitalization, and regional development.

Investment in Physical Environment   Federal programs in this area are for environmental recreation, water, and transportation development.

Revenue Sharing   These programs provide nonearmarked funds to state and local governments. General revenue sharing was initiated in 1972. It is also called tax sharing, whereby states and localities share in the federal taxes.

Direct Subsidies to Producers   This category includes all federal programs intended to expand output and/or stabilize income in specific industries, such as in agriculture, the postal service, and maritime shipping.

Net Interest   These are interest payments paid to the public on the federal debt and are sometimes called interest payments on the national debt. We discuss the national debt in detail in Issue I-10.

State and Local Expenditures

By far the biggest category in state and local expenditures is education, as can be seen in

Table 5-3 Federal Budget Outlays by Major Category (Fiscal Year 1976)

Here we see the components of the federal budget for 1976. The individual categories are explained in detail in the text. It is obvious, however, that redistribution of income plays an important part in federal activities since cash income maintenance, aid for social programs, and helping people buy essentials added together overshadow any other budget category.

CATEGORY	AMOUNT (IN BILLIONS PER YEAR)	PERCENTAGE OF TOTAL
Defense, space, foreign affairs	$104.9	29.1
Cash income maintenance	118.7	32.8
Helping people buy essentials	42.2	11.7
Aid for social programs	24.4	6.8
Investment in physical environment	23.1	6.4
Revenue sharing	7.2	2.0
Direct subsidies to producers	3.1	0.8
Net interest on public debt	26.1	7.2
Other programs plus financial adjustments	11.6	3.2
Total	$361.3	100.0

Source: Budget of the United States Government, and B. M. Blechman et al., *Setting National Priorities: The 1976 Budget*, Washington, D.C.: The Brookings Institution.

Table 5-4. This should not be surprising since most elementary and secondary education, as well as a good amount of higher education, is provided by public funds. The other significant

Table 5-4 State and Local General Expenditures

The largest category for state and local expenditures is education, mainly for local schools below the college level. The "all other" category accounts for over one-fourth of state and local expenditures, and it includes parks and recreation, fire and police protection, public housing, and so forth.

FUNCTION	FISCAL 1975 (IN BILLIONS OF DOLLARS)
Education	$80.7
Highways	23.0
Public welfare*	27.1
Cash payments	13.4
Medical care	10.0
Health and hospitals	17.6
All other	66.3
Total	$214.7

*Includes items not shown separately.
Source: Tax Foundation, Inc.

categories for state and local governments are public assistance, hospitals, and health. Then come highways and a variety of other items. Note that "all other" general expenditures constitute a large category, absorbing perhaps one-fourth of state and local outlays. It includes parks and recreation, public housing, fire and police protection, public sanitation, and other such goods and services.

Now we know how government revenues are spent, but we have yet to explain how the government gets its revenues. The vast majority of them are obtained by taxation, which has become inevitable for just about everybody everywhere.

Taxation

Governments obtain revenues principally by taxation. There are, however, many ways to tax the public. Income can be taxed, so can wealth, and so can certain types of economic activities. Each tax has its own peculiar attributes, and taxes affect differently the behavior of individuals in our economy. Before we go into a discussion of the specific types of taxes in our system, let's look at several theories of how taxes should be levied.

Theories of Taxation

Should the rich pay more taxes than the poor? Should some types of activities be taxed more heavily than others? What is the "best" tax? These are questions to which philosophers, scientists, politicians, and laypersons have addressed themselves for centuries. The two most popular theories of taxation that remain with us today are based on individuals' ability to pay and the benefits received from government.

Ability-to-Pay Principle A taxing principle which states that individuals should pay taxes according to their ability to pay has been popular for at least several thousand years. This principle of taxation may be simple to state, but it is certainly not easy to put into effect. We all agree that an individual who earns $20,000 per year is better able to pay taxes than an individual who earns only $2,000 per year. A serious question remains: "How much greater is the first person's ability to pay than the second's?" No one has yet come up with a functionally meaningful way of measuring ability to pay, and the same can be said of the next popular taxing principle.

Benefits-Received Principle According to this principle, people should be taxed in proportion to the benefits they receive from government services. If they benefit a lot, they should pay a lot; if they benefit little, they should pay only a little. This principle has problems in application, however. First of all,

what value do people place on government-provided goods and services? Can we ask them? Our discussion of the free rider suggested some of the problems of asking people what they feel. One way out of this dilemma is to assume that the higher a person's income, the more services he or she receives, and therefore the more value that person obtains from the goods and services provided by the government. Nevertheless, an individual's income is only a crude measure and may not be a good criterion to use for a taxing formula.

Types of Taxes

Without a reliable measure, we cannot say which type of tax we ought to use. All we can do is describe the various types of taxes in terms of the relationship between taxes paid and income. The three main types in all economic systems are proportional, progressive, and regressive.

Proportional Taxation A proportional system of taxation is just what you would think it would be: As an individual's income goes up, so, too, do taxes—in exactly the same proportion. A proportional tax system is also called a *flat tax*. Taxpayers at all income levels end up paying the same *percentage* of their income in taxes. In other words, if the proportional tax rate were 20 percent, an individual who had an income of $10,000 would pay $2,000 in taxes. An individual making $100,000, would pay $20,000 in taxes, the identical 20 percent rate being levied on both.

Progressive Taxation Under progressive taxation, the more a person earns, the more he or she pays, just as in a proportional system.

However, the taxes paid, expressed as a percentage of income, go up as more income is earned. In a progressive system, the **marginal tax rate** increases as income increases. Marginal merely means incremental. Thus:

$$\text{Marginal tax rate} = \frac{\text{change in tax bill}}{\text{change in income}}$$

We should compare the marginal tax rate with the average tax rate, which is defined as:

$$\text{Average tax rate} = \frac{\text{total tax bill}}{\text{total income}}$$

The difference between the marginal and the average tax rate can be seen in Table 5-5. Let's take the example in Table 5-5. Say the first $100 in income is taxed at 10 percent, the next $100 at 20 percent, and the third $100 at 30 percent. The average tax rate is always less than (or equal to) the marginal tax rate with a progressive tax system. With a proportional tax system, the marginal tax rate is constant and always the same as the average tax rate.

Table 5-5 **A Progressive Tax System**

The percentage of tax taken out of each additional dollar earned goes up; that is, the marginal tax rate increases progressively with income.

INCOME	MAR-GINAL RATE	TAX	AVERAGE RATE
100	10%	$10	
			$\frac{\$10}{\$100} = 10\%$
200	20%	$10 + $20 = $30	$\frac{\$30}{\$200} = 15\%$
300	30%	$10 + $20 + $30 = $60	$\frac{\$60}{\$300} = 20\%$

Regressive Taxation We have yet to talk about regressive taxes. Any tax that is regressive takes away a smaller and smaller percentage of additional income as income rises. The marginal rate falls and is below the average rate. As an example, imagine that all revenues of the government were obtained from a 99 percent tax on food. Since we know that the percentage of income spent on food falls as family income rises, we also know that the percentage of total income that would be paid in taxes under such a system would likewise fall as income rose. It would be a regressive system.

Figure 5-2 shows the relationship between the percentage tax rate and level of income for all these tax systems. It is important here to distinguish between the legal, or legislated, tax rate, and what we will call the **effective tax rate.** Taxes are generally levied on a base that does not include all income, as we will see when we talk about the American tax system and its oddities in Issue I-7. The tax bill is determined by multiplying the tax rate times the base. To find the effective tax rate, we merely divide total income into the tax bill. If the effective tax rate so described rises as income rises, the tax is progressive; if it is constant, the tax is proportional; and if it falls, the tax is regressive.

Now we will look at three broad areas of taxation in the United States: income, wealth, and economic activities.

Income Taxes

At the federal level, income taxes are by far the most important source of revenues. Income taxes take the form of either taxes on personal income or income from corporations. Increasingly, states and even some cities are also levy-

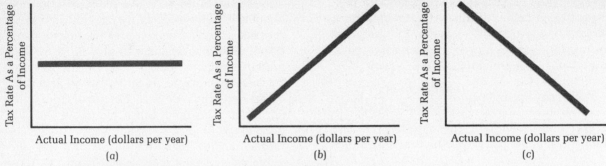

FIGURE 5-2 Proportional, Progressive, and Regressive Tax Systems

In *(a)* we see that the tax rate as a percentage of income remains constant as actual income rises. This, then, represents a proportional tax. *(b)* illustrates a progressive tax in which the percentage tax rate rises with income. With the regressive tax shown in *(c)*, the opposite is true: As income rises, the percentage tax rate falls.

ing income taxes, but the federal government is still the leader.

Personal Income Taxes

Most of us are aware that the personal income tax system in the United States is progressive.

In Table 5-6, we see part of the 1976 tax schedule. Notice that the marginal tax rate goes up as taxable income rises, even though the rate applicable to the previous lumps of income stays the same. Many students think that someone in a 50 percent tax bracket pays 50 percent

Table 5-6 Federal Personal Income Tax for a Childless Couple, 1976

Here we show the different income brackets and the marginal tax rates along with the average tax rates. As you can see, the marginal tax rates go up to a maximum of 70 percent. However, if income qualifies as being "earned," the maximum is 50 percent. All wages are considered earned income, but interest on bonds or dividends from stocks is not.

NET INCOME BEFORE EXEMPTIONS (BUT AFTER DEDUCTIONS)	PERSONAL INCOME TAX	AVERAGE TAX RATE, PERCENT	MARGINAL TAX RATE
Below $ 1,500	$ 0	0	0
2,000	70	3.5	14
3,000	215	7.2	15
4,000	370	9.2	16
5,000	535	10.7	17
10,000	1,490	14.9	22
20,000	3,960	19.8	28
50,000	16,310	32.6	50
100,000	44,280	44.3	60
200,000	109,945	55.0	69
400,000	249,930	62.5	70
1,000,000	669,930	67.0	70
10,000,000	6,969,930	69.7	70

Source: Internal Revenue Service

of his or her taxable income to the federal government. That is not the case, even for an honest taxpayer. Fifty percent may be paid on the last $15,000, for example, but certainly not on all the income.

At the federal level, personal income taxes account for over 40 percent of all federal revenues. We see in Table 5-7 that the federal budget tax receipts show over 45 percent coming from personal income taxes. In the same table, we see that at the state and local level only 20 percent comes from personal income taxes; however, this percentage has been rising.

Progressive Taxation and Income Distribution

Our progressive federal tax system on personal income is usually justified on the basis that it redistributes aftertax income. How effective has the federal government been in altering the distribution of income in the United States? A look at Figure 5-3 suggests that very little has actually changed. We have the same levels of income differences that existed after World War I. We will discuss why so little income redistribution has actually occurred in Issue I-7, when we discuss the ways that individuals can avoid paying taxes.

The Corporate Income Tax

Corporate income taxes account for over 15 percent of all federal taxes collected and for over 8 percent of all state and local taxes collected. Corporations are generally taxed on the difference between their total revenues or receipts and expenses. In 1901, the corporate tax rate amounted to a mere 1 percent of corporate profits, with the first $5,000 a year being exempted. By 1932, this exemption had disappeared and the rate had jumped to 13.755 percent. Since 1950, corporations have had to pay a "normal" tax on the first $25,000 of profit

---

Table 5-7 Government Revenues Accounted for by Personal Income Taxes

During the Depression, individual income taxes accounted for less than 20 percent of federal revenues. Now, however, individual income taxes account for almost 45 percent of federal revenues. The importance of the personal income tax has increased. The same trend is true at the state and local level.

FISCAL YEAR	PERCENT OF FEDERAL REVENUES ACCOUNTED FOR BY PERSONAL INCOME TAXES	PERCENT OF STATE AND LOCAL REVENUES ACCOUNTED FOR BY PERSONAL INCOME TAXES
1927	25.7%	
1932	19.0	
1936	16.7	
1940	15.5	
1944	39.5	
1950	40.7	12.3
1955	45.1	13.0
1960	45.6	14.6
1965	43.8	15.6
1970	45.0	18.1
1975	45.1	20.0

Source: U.S. Department of the Treasury

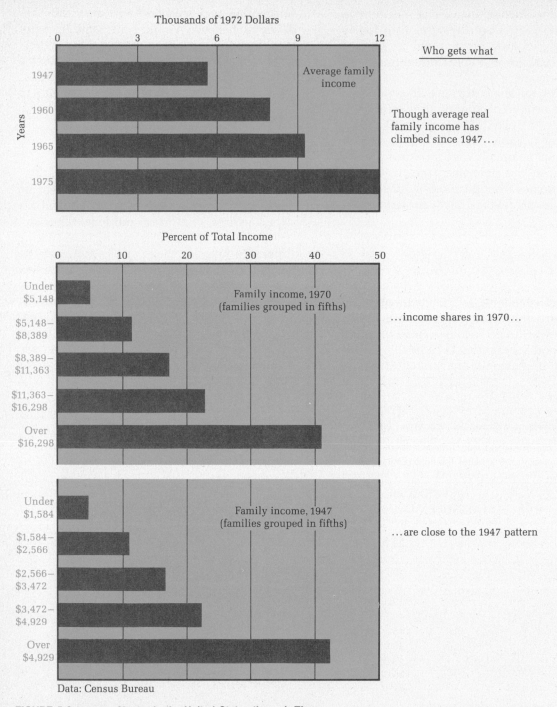

Thousands of 1972 Dollars

Who gets what

Average family income

Though average real family income has climbed since 1947...

Percent of Total Income

Family income, 1970 (families grouped in fifths)

...income shares in 1970...

Family income, 1947 (families grouped in fifths)

...are close to the 1947 pattern

Data: Census Bureau

FIGURE 5-3 Income Shares in the United States through Time

We see that the income shares in 1970 are quite close to the 1947 pattern. After 23 years of rising average incomes, the distribution of income has hardly changed at all in the United States. *(Source: Business Week,* Apr. 1, 1972, p. 56.)

per year, and a **surtax,** or addition to that normal tax, on profits in excess of $25,000 per year. Currently the "normal" tax rate is 22 percent and the "surtax" an additional 26 percent.

Not a Tax on All Profits

It is often suggested that the corporate income tax is a general tax on the income from capital. Remember that income comes from two sources: labor services and capital. In the United States, the income that goes to labor services has remained steady at about 75 percent of national income. The remaining 25 percent is comprised of profits, interest, dividends, and rent. Corporations pay out all the returns to labor in the form of wages, salaries, and special stock options to executives. After the corporation has subtracted all its other expenses, the result is profit. This profit, therefore, represents the income from the capital invested in the corporation (labor has already been paid its income). Therefore, when these profits are taxed, we are really taxing the income from capital.

Granted, the corporation income tax is a tax on the income from capital, but we know that not all income from capital is generated in the corporate sector of our economy. Fully one-half of capital's income comes from the noncorporate sector, for example, from housing and farming. The corporate income tax is, therefore, definitely *not* a general tax on the income from capital. All capital's income generated in the noncorporate sector is taxed at individual marginal tax rates that, on average, are lower than the corporate rate. Additionally, the aftertax profits of the corporation are taxed again when stockholders pay taxes on dividends or capital gains. If you receive $1000 in dividends, you have to declare them (except for the first $100, or $200 if married) as income, and you must pay taxes at your marginal tax rate. Before the corporation was able to give you those dividends, it had to pay taxes on all its profits, including any that it puts back into the company or does not distribute in the form of dividends. Eventually the new investment made possible by those **retained earnings** will be reflected in the increased value of the stock in that company. When you sell your stock in that company, you will have to pay a capital gains tax on the difference between what you sold it for and what you paid for the stock. In this sense, corporate profits are taxed twice.

Do Corporations Really Pay Their Taxes?

Corporations can only exist as long as consumers buy their products, employees make their goods, stockholders buy their stocks, and bondholders buy their bonds. Corporations, per se, do not do anything. They exist only insofar as they have employees, customers, bondholders, and stockholders. We must ask, then, who really pays the tax on corporate income. There is considerable debate on this subject. Some people say that corporations pass their tax burdens to consumers by charging higher prices. Other economists believe that it is the stockholders, the people who pay money to the corporation by buying stocks (shares of ownership), who bear most of the tax. Since the debate is not yet settled, we will not hazard a guess here as to what the correct conclusion should be. Suffice it to say that you should be cautious when you advocate increasing corporation income taxes. You may be the one who ultimately ends up paying the increase.

Taxes on Wealth

Wealth is defined as anything whose value is its ability to produce income in the future. In our tax system, certain types of wealth do not escape the tax collector's eye. These include taxes on property ownership, and on the transfer of ownership, the latter taking the form of estate taxes.

Estate Taxes

Estate taxes account for a mere 2 percent of total federal tax receipts, and about the same percentage for state government receipts. The federal and state system of taxing whatever wealth individuals own when they die is complicated and worthy of entire law school courses for would-be estate lawyers. There are, literally, thousands of ways to reduce potential estate taxes. If you are interested, just look in some of the legal treatises pertaining to this topic in your library.

Property Taxes

Real property has been taxed at the state and local levels for many years. The bulk of proceeds from property taxes goes to financing public education, streets and roads, and public safety facilities. The justice of the property tax, however, has often been challenged. As one student of property taxation once wrote, "The general property tax as actually administered is beyond all doubt one of the worst taxes known to the civilized world." Such were the words of Columbia University Professor Edwin R. A. Seligman in 1911. In colonial days a property tax was essentially a tax on wealth because most people's wealth was involved in farmland, livestock, buildings, and jewelry; today, however, a person's tangible property is not necessarily an index of his or her wealth or of how much income he or she makes. There are numerous other types of intangible property, such as stocks, bonds, savings accounts, mortgages, and so on. For the most part, intangible property is not touched at all by the property tax.

Taxes on Economic Activities

When you go to a store to buy a toothbrush, you usually have to pay a tax. It is called a sales tax, levied on the final sale of goods and services. In some states, certain necessary commodities such as medicine and food are exempted from the general sales tax.

In addition to general sales taxes, there are special sales taxes called **excise taxes.** These are levied on the manufacture, consumption, or sale of such commodities as gasoline and liquor. State governments rely most heavily on sales and excise taxes, in addition to special taxes on the gross receipts of businesses operating in the state. These three taxes on economic activity account for more than 50 percent of state government revenues.

Unemployment and Social Security Taxes

An increasing percentage of federal tax receipts are accounted for each year by taxes (other than income taxes) levied on payrolls. These taxes are for Social Security, retirement, survivors disability, and old-age medical insurance (Medicare). In 1975, the tax was imposed on earnings up to $14,100 at a rate of 5.85 percent on employers and 5.85 percent on employees. That is, the employer matches your "contribution" to Social Security. These taxes and the base on which they are levied will rise in the next decade. People who are self-employed must pay a self-employment tax equivalent to three-fourths of the combined employer and employee rate. These Social Security taxes came into existence when the Federal Insurance Contribution Act (FICA) was passed in 1935.

There is also a federal unemployment tax, which obviously has something to do with unemployment insurance. This tax rate is 0.5 percent on the first $4,200 of annual wages of each employee. It is only the employer who makes the tax payment. This tax covers the costs of the unemployment insurance system and the costs of employment services. In addition to this federal unemployment tax, some states also have an unemployment system and impose an additional tax of about 3 percent, or less, depending on the past record of particular employers. An employer who lays off workers frequently will have a higher state unemployment tax rate than an employer who never lays off workers.

Social Security and unemployment taxes seem to correspond with the benefits principle of taxation since it is the workers who pay the taxes and the workers who receive the benefits from the services made possible by the taxes. Critics of Social Security, however, note that the amount of Social Security taxes paid bears little relation to the payments individual workers receive. In fact, it has been argued that Social Security is a system whereby current workers subsidize retired workers. It is also argued that the system is not an insurance policy because Social Security benefits are legislated by Congress; they are not part of the original Federal Insurance Contributions Act. Therefore, future generations may decide that they do not want to give large Social Security

benefits to retired workers. Even if workers had paid in large amounts into Social Security, they could conceivably be denied the benefits in the form of large Social Security retirement income.

One last point about Social Security and unemployment: Most people think the employer pays part of the tax in the case of Social Security and all the tax in the case of unemployment insurance. This is not generally the case, however. In fact, in the long run, it can be argued that it is the employee who pays the entire tax. In other words, if employers did not have to contribute to Social Security on the behalf of their employees, the employees could now be making just that much more in wages.

Problems with Spending and Collecting

Government spending activities are large and numerous and extensive. How do we decide where government revenues should be spent? That is a problem of national goals and priorities. We turn to that problem in the next issue. Then we go on to look at problems associated with collecting the revenues that governments will spend. This leads us to the explosive issue of taxpayers' legal methods of avoiding taxes.

Definitions of New Terms

Public Goods: Goods that are not subject to the exclusion principle; that is, if one person uses public goods, the amount left for use by other persons is not reduced. Public goods are characterized by zero marginal costs once they are produced; they are generally indivisible.

Negative Externalities: The negative spillover effects of activities that harm individuals who are not compensated because no contract was made with the individuals who caused the negative externalities.

Marginal Tax Rate: The tax rate that applies to the last bracket of income earned. It should be contrasted with the average tax rate, which is merely the total tax bill divided by total income.

Effective Tax Rate: Actual taxes paid divided by actual total income.

Surtax: Any tax that is levied in addition to some normal tax.

Retained Earnings: Those earnings that a corporation saves or retains for use in investment in other productive activities. Earnings that are not distributed to stockholders.

Chapter Summary

1. The economic functions of government can be divided into the provision of public goods, the regulation of economic activity, the redistribution of income, the stabilization of the economy, and the administration of justice.

2. Public goods should be distinguished from government-provided goods, which do not have to be public goods. The former are defined as those goods of which additional users can partake at a zero marginal cost. When you turn on your television set, for example, you do not reduce the amount of TV available for other members of the community. The same is true when you use national defense.

3. With most public goods there is a free-rider problem in which individuals, if asked how much they want to contribute to the production of a public good, might usually indicate very little because they believe that others will pay for the provision of that public good.

4. Economic regulation involves the government setting certain prices throughout the economy, regulating illegal activities, and fostering competition by enforcing antitrust laws, as well as attempting to minimize negative externalities such as those caused by pollution-creating production activities.

5. From a macroeconomic point of view, much government activity is involved in stabilizing the economy, that is, attenuating relatively high rates of unemployment and preventing relatively fast rates of inflation.

6. Total government outlays have risen steadily since the end of World War II, expressed as a percentage of gross national product.

7. The federal budget includes expenditures on defense, cash income maintenance, direct subsidies to producers, net interest on the public debt, and others. Most of the state and local expenditures involve education, highways, and public welfare.

8. Government revenues are mainly derived by taxation. The ability-to-pay principle and the benefits-received principle are two principles of taxation.

9. Taxes can be classified as proportional, progressive, or regressive.

1. Would you want to live in a world where there was no government?
2. Do you expect the share of government expenditures in total national income to increase or decrease in the next decade? Why?
3. Sometimes taxes are less than total expenditures by the federal government. Critics then suggest that specific parts of the budget must be cut. Does it matter which part of the federal budget is cut to get it in line with taxes collected?
4. If you were in charge of scrapping our entire taxation system and coming up with an alternative, what principles of taxation would you use and what kind of system would you devise?
5. When you try to decide whether or not you should take on part-time work, do you look at your average tax rate or your marginal tax rate?

Selected
References

Anderson, William H., *Financing Modern Government,* Boston: Houghton-Mifflin, 1973.

Bureau of the Budget, *Federal Budget in Brief,* current ed., Washington, D.C.: U.S. Government Printing Office.

Carson, Robert B. et al. (eds.), *Government in the American Economy,* Lexington, Mass.: D. C. Heath, 1973.

Eckstein, Otto, *Public Finance,* 3d. ed., Englewood Cliffs, N.J.: Prentice-Hall, 1973, chaps. 3–5.

Groves, Harold M. and Robert L. Bish, *Financing Government,* New York: Holt, Rinehart and Winston, 1973.

Pechman, Joseph A., *Federal Tax Policy,* rev. ed. New York: W. W. Norton, 1971.

Young Man at the End of an Era

ARTHUR OKUN

Former Chairman, Council of Economic Advisers (CEA) 1968–1969

When Lyndon Johnson appointed CEA member Arthur Okun to succeed Gardner Ackley as Chairman of the Council in 1968, there was little surprise in the economic and business communities. Despite the fact that he was the youngest man to have ever been appointed chairman, Okun had been an important member of the Council staff since 1964. Yet, because of Johnson's change in plans in 1968, Okun served for only 1 year.

One of the most active of the "new economists" of the 1960s, Okun has been cited as a major force behind the success of Walter Heller's programs in the early part of the decade. It was Okun who did the "slide rule" work behind the 1964 tax cut. His influence was crucial because the cut was planned at a time of large federal budget deficits. As one Washington economist commented, "One of the reasons Heller was so successful was that he had Art Okun on his staff . . . Okun could do anything the whole Treasury could do and on the back of an envelope, if necessary."

Okun studied at Yale University and was serving on the faculty there in graduate economic programs when he joined the Council research staff in 1964. His work to that time had been concentrated in the area of economic forecasting, to which he contributed Okun's law, which relates changes in the gross national product to fluctuations in the rate of unemployment.

After leaving the federal government at the end of the Johnson era, Okun joined the Washington-based Brookings Institution, with which he has been affiliated ever since. From that vantage point he wrote *The Political Economy of Prosperity,* which was published by the Institution in 1970. While discussing the mechanism of the growth-inflation pattern of the mid-1960s, Okun argued that the Vietnam conflict had made broad analysis of the success or failure of the "new economics" virtually impossible. However, he felt that individual policies, like the 1968 tax hike, could be evaluated as conceptual and operational failures.

Okun was very skeptical of the Nixon administration's attempts to develop a workable fiscal policy. Yet, as an important planner of a highly active fiscal program, Okun is appreciative of the shortcomings of such policies. At the 1972 American Economic Associ-ation meeting, Okun commented, "Judged by its contribution to generating social welfare, to solve the big social problems, fiscal policy can be regarded as trivial and obsolete."

By the end of the 1960s, Okun felt that the major focus of administration action should be wage and price stability but that a planned recession would be like "burning down a building to get rid of termites." Okun believed that labor costs were the key to controlling inflation, so he became an advocate of wage and price controls, even though he had opposed these measures while he was chairman of the CEA. When the recession did come several years later, Okun noted that wage costs were indeed moderating. "But what a price to pay," he said. "It is like cutting off your hand and being consoled with the thought, 'Well, they cured your eczema.'"

Okun was a persistent critic of President Ford's gradualistic policies to cure the recession. Among liberal economists, he was one of those most afraid that the 1974 to 1975 recession would develop into a depression unless the government took more affirmative action. He was particularly critical of the restrictive monetary policies of Arthur Burns: "The Fed's policy this year [1975] seems to be the marriage-manual approach to monetary ease. Make it last, go slow, stretch it out, and you enjoy it better that way."

What Are Our National Priorities?

HOW SHOULD PUBLIC FUNDS BE USED?

Government and the Problem of Scarcity

We must eliminate poverty. We must give our children better education. We should extend health services to more Americans. We should create more adequate housing for lower-income families.

What do these statements have in common? At least two things: Each is a statement of value, not of fact, and each involves the use of scarce resources. From a purely scientific point of view, there is no way we can argue for or against the reduction of poverty, the improvement of housing, the extension of medical service, or any other social-reform program in our nation. These are not questions that you and I can resolve as scientists or economists. We react to them instead with our hearts, with our own values concerning what is and what is not appropriate for our society.

On the other hand, it does not require any value judgment to state that improvements in nearly all aspects of our economy require the use of scarce resources. This follows from the basic condition that scarcity is a pervasive phenomenon every-

where, even in the United States. That means one thing: Whenever the government—federal, state, or local—increases, say, health care services to the poor, we all have to give up something to pay for those increased services. And the government faces a scarcity problem just like you and I do. After all, at any moment in time the total amount of resources in our nation is fixed. If more resources go to the government for use in social-reform programs, less resources are available to the nongovernmental sector of the economy. A fundamental decision must be made concerning the degree to which the government allocates (exhausts) resources in our economy. This is where national priorities come into play.

Setting National Priorities

Because the government faces a scarcity situation, which we might call the government's budget constraint, it must decide on how to allocate its finite resources among competing ends. One way to do this is to set national priorities and goals. We can observe trends in national

priorities—even if politicians don't explicitly state them—by looking at what the government does with the tax dollars that it collects.

Trends in Government Expenditures

In Chapter 5 we looked at the budget of the United States Government for fiscal 1976. What we do now in Table I-6.1 is present that same budget by category for 1960, 1970, and 1975. Some fairly dramatic shifts have taken place in terms of *revealed* national priorities, that is, priorities revealed by the changing composition of the federal budget.

Declining Priorities

Some obvious examples of declining priorities make themselves known in Table 1-6.1. National defense, expressed as a percentage of total federal expenditures, fell from 53.7 percent in 1960 to 31.6 percent in 1975. This is a sufficiently important topic for us to devote a separate section to it later.

Another declining category of budget outlays is direct subsidies to producers, which fell from 5.9 percent of the federal budget in 1960 to 1.2 percent some 15 years later. However, compelling data indicate

Table I-6.1

Changing Federal Budget Priorities (Dollar Amounts in Billions)

Here we see some obvious shifts in federal budget expenditures. Defense outlays as a percentage of total expenditures are declining. Income redistribution programs seem to be on the upswing.

CATEGORY	1960		1970		1975 ESTIMATE	
	AMOUNT	PERCENT OF TOTAL	AMOUNT	PERCENT OF TOTAL	AMOUNT	PERCENT OF TOTAL
Defense, space, foreign affairs	$49.5	53.7	$ 87.7	44.6	$ 96.1	31.6
Cash income maintenance	20.6	22.3	46.6	23.7	98.2	32.2
Helping people buy essentials	1.1	1.2	14.2	7.2	33.2	10.9
Aid for social programs	1.3	1.4	10.3	5.3	18.2	6.0
Investment in physical environment	5.4	5.8	9.4	4.8	17.3	5.7
Revenue sharing	0.1		0.5		6.8	2.2
Direct subsidies to producers	4.5	4.9	6.7	3.4	3.7	1.2
Net interest	6.9	7.5	14.4	7.3	22.0	7.2
Other programs plus financial adjustments	2.8	3.0	6.7	3.4	8.9	3.0
Total	$92.2	100.0	$196.6	100.0	$304.4	100.0
Total as percent of gross national product	18.6		20.6		20.9	

Source: Budget of the United States Government, and B. M. Blechman et al., Setting National Priorities: The 1975 Budget, Washington, D.C.: The Brookings Institution.

that subsidies are much more widespread than figures in the federal budgets suggest.

Advancing Priorities

The major candidate for receiving greater priority, at the national level at least, is income maintenance. Cash income maintenance grew from 22.3 percent of the federal budget in 1960 to 32.2 percent in 1975. The category "Helping People Buy Essentials" grew from a mere 1.2 percent to over 10 percent in that same period, and aid for social programs grew from 1.4 percent to 6.0 percent. The Department of Health, Education, and Welfare budget (under which income maintenance, "Helping People," and aid for social programs fall) exceeds the budget of the Department of Defense. At least from these data, it is apparent that our national priorities have shifted away from military expenditures to social and income redistribution programs, such as aid for migrant children, aid to schools in "federally impacted" areas, expenditures for affirmative action employment policies, and so on.

Income Redistribution

A large portion of the federal budget is now going for cash income maintenance programs and such aids as food stamps and housing vouchers. Income redistribution, which we have already discussed, involves taxing higher-income individuals and transferring some of their tax dollars to lower-income individuals who perform no particular economic service in return. Have our programs of income redistribution worked? It would be difficult for us to say that they were a smashing success. Just look again at Figure 5-3 on p. 104. There we showed the income shares going to families grouped in fifths for 1947, just after World War II, and 1972. After 2½ decades of rising income and continued efforts to redistribute income, the distribution seems to have remained approximately the same. This evidence seems to suggest that national priorities, even if expressed by changes in federal budget outlays, can, in fact, be thwarted by opposing forces. We will discuss one of these opposing forces in the following issue when we examine the loopholes in our tax system that allow higher-income individuals to reduce their federal tax liabilities by reducing their taxable income.

Defense Spending Declines

We pointed out above that defense spending as a percentage of total federal expenditures fell dramatically in the last decade and a half. There is no doubt that a guns and butter choice exists here. Look at Figure I-6.1. Here we show a typical production-possibilities curve, with production of military goods and services on the vertical axis (guns) and production of civilian goods and services (butter) on the horizontal axis. What we have done over the last 15 years or so is move from a point such as *A* to a point such as *B*. We have moved toward the civilian-goods axis.

We can see the real trend in defense spending if we correct for changes in the price level. In Chapter 4, when we discussed GNP and national income accounting, we pointed out that real GNP (that is, GNP corrected for price changes) was the appropriate measure of physical output. The same is true for military expenditures. If we correct military expenditures by the federal government for changes in the price level, the result is the decline shown in Figure I-6.2. Military spending in real terms has fallen dramatically since our withdrawal from Indochina.

The True Cost of the Military

We know in economics that the true cost of anything is equal to its opportunity, or alternative, cost; hence, the direct, recorded outlays of the Defense Department do not include the entire cost of the military establishment to the American people. This was particularly true when we had a system of conscripted military labor, or draft. Involuntary military servitude means forcing individuals

Guns and Butter

It is true: We cannot have more guns and more butter at the same time when we have full employment at the outset. We have shown here a production-possibilities curve. The horizontal axis measures civilian goods, and the vertical axis measures war goods. If we want to have more war goods, we have to sacrifice civilian goods. There is always going to be a trade-off at any point in time. In the long run, however, as we increase our productive capacity, we can have more war goods and more civilian goods. In the United States there has been a fairly recent movement away from war production toward civilian production (shown here as a movement from *A* to *B*).

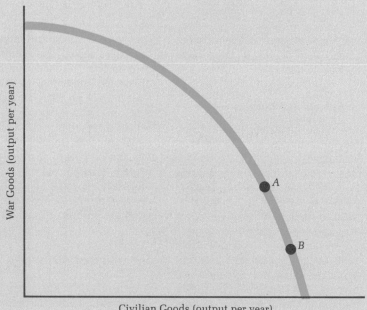

War Goods (output per year)

Civilian Goods (output per year)

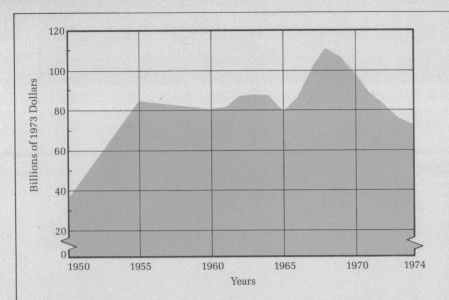

FIGURE I-6.2 Military Spending in Constant 1973 Dollars

The absolute level of military spending in real terms (corrected for inflation) has actually fallen over the last several years. *(Source:* U.S. Office of Management and Budget.)

to work in the military at a lower wage rate than would induce them to join voluntarily. The opportunity (true) cost of those working in the military is measured more or less by what they could be making in the civilian world. Thus, during the draft system the opportunity cost of military labor was significantly higher than the recorded outlays.

Many critics of defense spending contend that there are numerous costs which the public never sees, and therefore we citizens do not know the true size of the military budget. Should the cost to consumers of restrictions on trade with other nations for security reasons be included in the military budget? Should the cost of subsidizing specific industries to maintain strategic capabilities be included in the defense budget rather than in other categories? These are thorny and difficult questions to tackle. We leave them as nothing more than questions

for the moment. The general area of subsidization is, however, one on which we can put some numbers.

Government Subsidies

When the government subsidizes a particular economic activity, it either provides the good or service itself to the consumer at a below-cost (in some cases, zero) price, provides ancillary services at below-cost price, or provides credit or a guarantee of same at below cost. Federal subsidy programs are available for economic activities in agriculture, food, medical care, manpower training, education, international trade, housing, natural resources, transportation, and commerce and economic development.

A few years ago there was a massive effort on the part of the Joint Economic Committee (JEC) of the Congress of the United States. They

came up with the following conclusion:

Federal subsidies constitute an incredibly diversified and pervasive system of economic assistance to the private economy. Much of the information necessary to understand and evaluate this complex subsidy system is hidden from public scrutiny. Special effort is made to give subsidy programs some other label, such as aid, tax credit, loan, or loan guarantee. In many cases the budgetary costs of these programs are not reported or are incompletely reported in U.S. Budget documents; . . . .

The study went on to estimate that at the beginning of this decade, the cost of federal subsidy programs was of the magnitude of $63 billion per year, but, pointed out the study, "Even these enormous costs do not represent a complete accounting of federal subsidy programs."[1] The JEC's estimate for 1975 was $95 billion.

The authors of this particular study would probably disagree with the statement that direct subsidies to producers are on the downswing. What may be true, according to the Joint Economic Committee, is that an increasingly large number of subsidies are disguised as other types of outlays. It is certainly true that national priorities are all the more difficult to formulate if the na-

tion in fact has no clear picture of how current federal revenues are being expended. The Joint Economic Committee believes that "this absence of facts hides the enormous costs of the overall subsidy system and prevents the evaluation and elimination of inefficient and unfair subsidies."

We can only point out here that more information would allow for a better understanding of our subsidy program and enable us to see whether it coincided with our national priorities. However, as we shall see in Chapter 27, politics is not that simple. There is no such thing as a national consensus that can be accurately determined. We live in a democratic society where the ma-

jority rules. Elected representatives need only obtain 51 percent of the vote either to win or to remain in office. Those who are directly affected by such things as producers' subsidies can readily see the benefits from such subsidies in the form of higher incomes. They therefore form coalitions. Individuals in these well-organized and easily recognizable groups go to great lengths to influence legislation on their own behalf. Thus, it is perhaps only over a very long period of time that the desires of "the public" ever form such a thing as a national consensus which can ultimately work itself around to reordering the national priorities as expressed in the budget outlays of the federal government.

[1]United States Congress Joint Economic Committee, "The Economics of Federal Subsidy Programs," 92nd Congress, First Session, Jan. 11, 1972, Rept. no. 5270–1326, Washington, D.C.: U.S. Government Printing Office, p. 4.

Questions for Thought and Discussion

1. In this issue, changing national priorities have been inferred from changing government expenditure patterns. Can you think of any other way to assess changing national priorities?
2. Is it possible to obtain a consensus from Americans about what national priorities should be? How would you go about obtaining such a consensus?

Selected Reference

Setting National Priorities. Available every year, generally in May, from The Brookings Institution, Washington, D.C.; gives an analysis of each fiscal year's federal government budget.

Fiscal Policy and Trend Analysis

OTTO ECKSTEIN

Former Member, Council of Economic Advisers 1964-1966

The energy and food crises of 1973, economist Walter Heller told a conference of social scientists, had caught economists with their "parameters down." It was a relatively bad year for economic forecasters, and trend predicting, like the economy, seemed to go from bad to worse in 1974. Even Harvard professor Otto Eckstein, an often accurate and longtime respected forecaster of the nation's economic health, misjudged the duration and extent of the 1974 recession.

Using econometric models and information gathered by Data Resources, Inc., of which he is president, Eckstein simulates the effects of government policy alternatives and makes frequent predictions of trends in particular industries as well as the economy as a whole. Though now seen primarily as a skilled forecaster, Eckstein has conducted research on many aspects of the economy, ranging from a 1958 study of the merits of government intervention in water resource development to a recent study showing that the average corporate tax rate has declined from 43.3 percent in 1961 to 35.6 percent in 1973.

A graduate of Princeton and Harvard, Eckstein rose to prominence as an expert in fiscal policy during the early 1960s. He was an important contributor to Kennedy's "Let's get the country moving again" campaign in 1960 and served as a consultant to both the Treasury Department and the Council of Economic Advisers during the Kennedy administration. Drawing on his 1959 work as technical director of the employment, growth, and price-level study for the Joint Economic Committee of Congress, Eckstein suggested a remedy for the recession Kennedy had inherited in a 1961 article, "The World's Dollar and Ours." The government during the Eisenhower years was so concerned over the balance of payments and so afraid of inflation, he said, that the growth rate had declined but without curtailing inflation. The government needed to encourage economic growth in order to generate more profits, which would in turn stimulate business investment. Eckstein advocated a more flexible policy on consumer credit controls and tax revisions, using these as methods to promote economic stability. He argued that the government should launch "an offensive against trade restrictions and export subsidies and against high costs at home" in order to defend the dollar and stimulate the economy.

In September 1964, Lyndon Johnson appointed Eckstein to the Council of Economic Advisers, where he served until February 1966, overseeing the government's wage and price guidelines. During Eckstein's term on the CEA, indications of prosperity were everywhere in evidence: GNP, personal income, corporate profits, and employment all showed increases.

Like many economists associated with the administrations of Kennedy and Johnson, Eckstein has long believed in the necessity for government intervention in some areas of the free market system. He is an advocate of variable tax rates to control unemployment and inflation, not so much in the interests of income redistribution as in the interests of economic stability. In his 1964 book on taxation and government expenditure, *Public Finance,* Eckstein suggested the President might be given standby authority to adjust taxes up or down as conditions warranted. Two years later, he proposed a method Congress could use to achieve the same results.

Since rejoining the Harvard faculty in 1966, Eckstein's views on government economic policy and trends in the economy have been solicited frequently by both public and private interests. He has been a persistent critic of the "tight money" policies of the Federal Reserve Board. In February 1974, he worried that nations would adopt restrictive domestic monetary and fiscal policies aimed at fighting inflation and reducing demand, with high world unemployment as the consequence. A participant in President Ford's 1974 economic summit conference, Eckstein also criticized President Ford's 1975 economic program, seeing it as too conservative and contradictory in its proposed solutions to the recession that began in 1974.

WHAT DO LOOPHOLES COST THE AMERICAN TAXPAYER?

Taxes and Best Sellers

A few years ago a book appeared across the nation explaining what tax loopholes were: the ways in which taxpayers could legally avoid paying taxes. The author, P. M. Stern, contended that loopholes cost American taxpayers $77 billion every year.[1] Stern entitled tax loopholes "The Rich Welfare Program," presumably because loopholes only benefit higher-income individuals. Even if the annual figure of $77 billion turns out to be an exaggeration, there is little doubt that tax loopholes do exist in our system, and there is even less doubt that such loopholes effectively do much to negate the progressive structure of that system.

Progressive Taxes and Loopholes

You will recall from Chapter 5 on government spending and taxation that, in principle, we have a progressive, personal income tax system. Proponents of progressive income

taxes argue their necessity on many grounds, not the least of which is the goal of redistributing income from the more well-to-do to the less well-to-do. In other words, tax the rich proportionately more than the poor and transfer to the poor some of that income.

If we look at the effective rates of the combined federal, state, and local taxes from the latest detailed study computed by members of The Brookings Institution in Washington, D.C., the result is striking, as can be seen in Figure I-7.1. For the most part, our effective tax system can be described as proportional rather than progressive. The authors of the study from which this information was obtained conclude that the "United States tax system is essentially proportional for the vast majority of families and therefore has little effect on the distribution of income . . . the very rich pay tax rates that are only moderately higher than average."[2] The ability of individuals earning higher income to reduce their taxes

is a fact of life. It is largely through the use of tax loopholes, or "shelters" as they are sometimes called, that this is accomplished.

Why Congress Legislates Loopholes

Why would Congress ever knowingly legislate a loophole in our tax system that would defeat its progressive nature? The answer is twofold: In the first place, a tax loophole or tax shelter that is applied to a particular type of economic activity or investment will induce individuals and businesses who would otherwise not be interested to undertake that task. As such, a tax shelter affecting, for example, oil drilling, will cause more resources to be devoted to oil drilling than would otherwise have been the case. To the extent that Congress desires to expand such economic activities as, say, oil drilling, an appropriate tax shelter will bring about that result. An argument could be made that it is in society's best interest for certain activities to be encouraged to ensure a larger supply of oil, energy, meat, or eggs.

However, an alternative and perhaps less altruistic view of congressional activity would be that tax loopholes provide a method to reduce the tax liabilities of high-income individuals in our society. Given that

[1]P. M. Stern, *The Rape of the Taxpayer*, New York: Random House, Vintage Books, 1974.

[2]Joseph A. Pechman and Benjamin A. Okner, *Who Bears the Tax Burden?*, Washington, D.C.: The Brookings Institution, 1974.

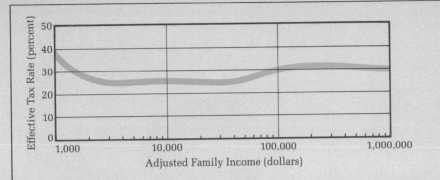

FIGURE I-7.1 Effective Rates of Taxation

We see that there is only a slight amount of progressiveness in our effective tax rates as incomes climb into the higher reaches. To a certain extent, tax rates are somewhat regressive over lower income levels. (*Source:* Joseph A. Pechman and Benjamin A. Okner, *Who Bears the Tax Burden?*, Washington, D.C.: The Brookings Institution, 1974.)

the incentive to influence legislation is directly correlated with the potential benefits, higher-income individuals, who are therefore in higher tax brackets, would be inclined to expend considerable resources seeking special legislation in the form of tax loopholes. This point cannot be overstressed—*a reduction in taxable income benefits the taxpayer directly in proportion to that taxpayer's marginal tax rate.* Perhaps the easiest way to see this is to examine one of the most common tax shelters—tax-exempt state and municipal bonds.

Tax-Exempt Bonds

The tax-exempt status of interest paid to holders of state and municipal bonds is well known to many investors. It is a form of tax shelter in the sense that the interest income which the investor obtains from a tax-exempt bond does not have to be reported on federal income tax returns. Hence, taxable income is reduced by the amount of income received from those bonds for it would otherwise have to be reported to the Internal Revenue Service. Now, what is the benefit to you of

tax-exempt income? You cannot answer that question unless you first determine what your marginal tax rate is. Let's say that it is 50 percent. Every dollar you get in tax-exempt interest from a municipal bond is a dollar on which you will *not* have to pay 50¢ in taxes. Therefore your tax savings from investing in municipal bonds is 50 percent. On the other hand, if your marginal tax bracket is only 20 percent, your tax savings is only 20¢ on every dollar of tax-exempt income.

Bond buyers are aware of this relationship, and what happens is that in their competition to obtain tax savings, that is, tax-exempt income, from these bonds they will bid up the price of the bonds, causing the yields to be relatively low. If you look in the financial pages of a newspaper that gives the yields on tax-exempt bonds and non-tax-exempt bonds of the same quality (risk), you will see that those yields will be different. The yield on the tax-exempt bonds will be lower. Usually, it is lower by between 30 percent and 40 percent.[3] Let's take a specific example. As-

[3]This difference represents the implicit taxes that you pay when buying a tax-exempt bond.

sume that tax-exempt municipal bonds are selling at a price which yields 7 percent per year and that the equivalent non-tax-exempt bond is selling at a price which yields 10 percent a year. Which one should you buy if you had to make the choice?

If you are in a relatively high tax bracket, you should buy the tax-exempt bond, but if you are in a relatively low tax bracket, you should not. Let's say you are again in the 20 percent bracket. If you buy a non-tax-exempt bond yielding 10 percent, the aftertax yield would be 8 percent. Of course the before- and aftertax yield on the municipal bond is the same, 7 percent, because no taxes are paid on the interest. You are obviously better off buying a non-tax-exempt bond and staying out of a tax shelter that benefits only those who are fortunate enough to be in the 50 percent tax bracket. A person in this bracket would not choose your non-tax-exempt bond whose yield is a mere 5 percent, certainly less than the 7 percent net yield on the tax-exempt municipal bond.

This simple example should demonstrate more clearly that it is be-

cause of our progressive tax system that tax shelters are beneficial only to those in higher income tax brackets. This is so because competition among investors drives up the price of tax-sheltered income-earning assets to reflect the tax savings.

The purpose of exempting income from state and municipal bonds was to subsidize state and local governments: The tax-exempt status of these bonds allows such governments to sell their debt (borrow) at a lower interest rate. The subsidy is real and may or may not be desirable, depending on your point of view. However, its distortion of the progressive nature of our tax system is perhaps an unwanted side effect.

The Oil Game

Oil exploration, drilling, and sales are areas of economic endeavor where individuals and corporations can shelter their income. Since the oil depletion allowance has been the most talked about of special tax gimmicks for the oil industry, that is the one we'll discuss first.

Oil Depletion Allowance

We know that the amount of oil found under each successful well is eventually going to be depleted by the pump put over it. Instead of having to pay taxes on all the income, owners of producing wells used to be able to choose a special tax program whereby they were allowed a

businesspersons use. One way of looking at it is to realize that if you pay $1 million for a machine, the most you can depreciate is $1 million. Suppose that an oil well costs $1 million but the oilperson opted for percentage depletion. That person ended up being able to deduct more than $1 million because the 22 percent of gross wellhead revenue depletion allowance was used year in and year out until the well was actually depleted. Twenty-two percent of the total amount depleted may far exceed the actual amount that was spent constructing the well or purchasing the mineral rights.

Dry Holes

There are other tax advantages bestowed on the oil industry. Let's look at oil exploration. We know that not all oil wells drilled are gushers. In the United States, probably only 20 percent are. But, of course, the only way to find out if you have a successful well is to drill. You may get a dry one. If you are going out to drill for oil, you have to expect that part of your costs will be spent on dry holes. Thus, in the United States, the true cost of finding one producing well includes the cost of drilling perhaps four dry ones.

The laws laid down by Congress in our tax code allow oilpersons to deduct all the costs of dry wells from other income. If you were a doctor, for example, who had invested money in oil exploration, you could deduct the full cost of all dry holes from your doctoring income. If your marginal tax bracket is 50 percent, every dollar you spend on a dry hole ends up costing you only 50¢.

percentage oil depletion allowance (a deduction) when computing their taxes. All businesspersons who buy machines are allowed to deduct the cost of *depreciation* on the machine. For example, if General Motors buy a $1 million bumper maker and the bumper maker is going to last 10 years, then every year GM can deduct part of the purchasing price of that machine from their income. This is done in such a way that by the end of 10 years they have deducted the entire purchase price from their income. This procedure is called *cost depreciation*. It is allowed because a percentage of the value of the machine is presumably used up each year while it is producing. Any legitimate cost deduction like this means the company has to pay fewer taxes. Obviously, businesspersons, if given the choice, would prefer as much depreciation as possible because that would mean valuable tax savings.

A businessperson who was pumping oil out of the ground could —instead of using cost depreciation—deduct 22 percent of the value of the oil from his or her income every year.[4] Now, you might be asking yourself why an oilperson would prefer a 22 percent depletion instead of the regular depreciation that other

[4]Oil depletion allowances for major oil companies were curtailed by 1975 legislation, which set a 3-year phase-out schedule. Small independents, however, retained the tax saving on the first 2000 barrels per day.

IDCs

Even for successful wells, about 70 percent of the costs can be deducted from other income because 70 percent of the cost of drilling a successful well is considered **intangible drilling costs** (IDC). These costs include expenses such as labor (as opposed to pipe), and all such IDCs are deductible in the year they are incurred. Thus, an oil company can plan its annual budget so as to pay zero taxes without planning to drill merely dry wells.

Capital Gains

In addition to percentage depletion and the dry-hole tax provisions outlined above, all exploration firms that sell successful wells are required to pay only the capital gains rate on the difference between the selling price and the total calculated cost of the wet well. (Remember that the costs of dry holes have already been deducted from other income.) Here the oil explorers get a double benefit. They can use the lower capital gains tax rate on the income from selling the gushers and still get the benefits of a higher tax-savings kickback by applying the cost deduction of dry holes to their other income, which is necessarily taxed at the higher-than-capital-gains rate.

Depletion allowances, deducting the cost of dry holes from other income, and capital gains concessions end up hurting the economy because they cause "excessive" use of resources in oil development. For example, investors would find and have found it profitable to spend $3 worth of resources to recover $2 worth of

oil. This is an inefficient use of our scarce resources.

You Can Lose Money in Tax Shelters

If you were Liza Minelli, Barbara Walters, Bob Dylan, Andy Williams, or Senator Jacob Javits, you would have learned a few summers ago that tax shelters are not always what they are cracked up to be. The so-called summer star-spangled swindle involved not only the above-mentioned luminaries but some 2000 other wealthy investors, including the President of the First National City Bank. They sank an estimated $100 million into an oil-drilling tax shelter called Home Stake Production Company. They all lost their shirts.

Obviously, then, not all tax shelters earn their investors a positive rate of return. The purpose of a tax shelter is to *show* a loss, for tax-accounting purposes, over a period during which the investor is in a relatively high income tax bracket. The ultimate purpose of a tax shelter is not to lose money but to eventually make a positive rate of return on the venture over a period of years. If someone were to offer you a tax shelter that only promised tax deductions, you would usually not be very interested. Say an oil-drilling scheme will allow you a 100 percent tax deduction on your investment, so you put in $10,000 and that year are allowed to deduct from gross income (in arriving at taxable income) $10,000. Even if you are in the highest tax bracket, your tax saving will not give you your money

back and certainly not allow you to have a positive rate of return. Eventually, the investment must make income or you won't even get your original outlay back, let alone any compensation for letting somebody else use your money.

Tax Shelters and Opportunity Costs

It would be a long list indeed if we were to write down every single tax shelter or loophole that exists in our system. They are all basically the same: a method of generating deductions so that taxable income is reduced, thereby reducing one's tax liability to the federal government. Tax shelters are involved in the purchase of professional athletes' contracts, Broadway plays, motion pictures, railroad tank cars, eggs, cattle, apartment buildings; the list goes on and on. All the shelters taken together constitute a reduction in revenues to the United States Treasury. However, that reduction is probably somewhat less than the number we gave in the beginning of this issue, the annual $77 billion estimated by P. M. Stern.

The reasons are fairly straightforward. In the first place, purchasers of tax-exempt municipal bonds do not walk away with no income reduction. After all, if the yield on tax exempts is 30 percent lower than non-tax exempts, those who buy tax exempts are implicitly paying a tax of 30 percent. More important, it would be unrealistic to assume that upper-income individuals would, in fact, make as high an income as they now make if they were actually as-

sessed for taxes in a truly progressive manner. Many of these high-income-earning individuals would opt for "the purchase of" more leisure since its price, or opportunity cost, would fall if they really only netted 30 percent of their income. What is the cost of forgoing a dollar's earnings? Not a dollar, but only 30¢. The opportunity cost, then, of not working is equal to the aftertax income that could have been earned. And when effective tax rates go up, the opportunity cost of not working goes down, and hence less work is performed. What would this mean for the government? Certainly we could not call those tax savings that upper-income individuals get a "raid" on the United States Treasury of $77 billion per year. If all those tax shelters were eliminated, $77 billion in additional taxes would not be reaped by the United States Treasury because the individuals now taxed at a higher rate would most certainly work less and earn lower gross and therefore taxable incomes.

Other Costs of Tax Shelters

Be that as it may, the loss to the United States Treasury is probably small compared to the sum of two additional costs: (1) the amount of resources used to obtain special legislation in the form of tax shelters, and (2) the resources that are squandered in tax-sheltered economic activities merely for the purpose of obtaining tax-sheltered income. The latter cost usually refers to an inefficient use of our available resources. In other words, if tax shelters were eliminated, fewer resources would be used in the now tax-sheltered investments and more resources would be used in other activities where they would have higher economic value.

An Alternative

Opponents of tax shelters contend that they subsidize the wealthy and cause an inefficient use of re-sources. As an alternative to tax shelters, they offer explicit subsidies to appropriate industries. For example, explicit subsidies to state and local governments (of exactly the same amount as the implicit subsidy they are now receiving as a result of the tax-exempt status of their bonds) would both save the United States Treasury billions of dollars and restore some of the progressiveness to our tax system, if that, in fact, is deemed desirable.

The same is true for tax-shelter-type subsidies to industries such as oil drilling and cattle raising. If Congress deems it desirable to increase production in a particular industry, let the subsidy be direct, say these observers, and eliminate the implicit subsidies in the form of special tax gimmicks. Politicians and their constituents would have the numbers laid out on the table so that more conscious decisions could be made about the social desirability of giving special treatment to particular industries.

Definitions of New Terms

Percentage Oil Depletion Allowance: The percentage of the value of oil that is taken out of the ground which is allowed to be deducted from income before taxes are paid.

Intangible Drilling Costs: Mainly the labor costs of drilling a successful well. These can be deducted from other income.

Questions for Thought and Discussion

1. Why do you think tax shelters get written into legislation?
2. Given our progressive system of taxation, who benefits the most from tax shelters?
3. How is it possible to lose money in tax shelters?

Selected References

Stern, Philip, *The Rape of the Taxpayer,* New York: Random House, 1973.

U.S. Congress, Joint Committee on the Economic Report, *Federal Tax Policy for Economic Growth and Stability,* Washington, D.C.: U.S. Government Printing Office, 1956.

Changing Business Conditions and Unemployment

Business activity in the United States has been moving ahead since this nation's economic life began. As we will see in this chapter, however, business activity has zigzagged rather than sloped smoothly upward. Studies of this movement are studies of the **business cycle,** the ups and downs that recur in our economy. Each of us personally feels the effects of inflation, unemployment, and other economic conditions that rise and fall with fluctuations in the business cycle. In this chapter we examine the nature of business cycles and consider several theories about why they occur. Using this information, we then move on to a detailed analysis of unemployment and its causes.

The Business Cycle and Business Activity in the United States

If we measure deviations from the upward trend line in overall business activity (real GNP) in the United States, we get an interesting picture. Figure 6-1 shows clearly that although American business cycles have been recurrent, they have varied greatly in intensity. The most obvious of the "downers" in Figure 6-1 (pages 128–129) falls a full 50 percent from the trend line. That was the period of the Great Depression, when, for a while, one out of every four Americans in the labor force was unemployed. The most visible of the "uppers" were the World War II boom and the prosperous period covering most of the 1960s. In fact, during the later 1960s, after the boom continued without interruption for 104 months, economists and government officials alike began to consider the whole concept of the business cycle old-fashioned. It seems that the history of business ups and downs had finally come to an end. Even the Department of Commerce, in November 1968, saw fit to change the title of its monthly publication from *Business Cycle Developments* to *Business Conditions Digest.*

As it turned out, the elimination of business ups and downs just wasn't in the cards because along came the recession of 1969 to 1970. Since then the American economy has been faced with the twin problems of unemployment and inflation, and students of the American economy are back to studying the ups and downs of business activity, that is, the business cycle.

Phases in the Business Cycle

As the name implies, a business cycle is an up-and-down motion in the economy's activity (real GNP) that takes place over time. Its fluctuations affect such aggregate variables as output, employment, income, and the price level. If we were to consult an *idealized* business cycle model, it would look like the one presented in Figure 6-2, in which the horizontal axis measures time, in years, and the vertical axis is a measure of business conditions.

There are four specific phases in an idealized business cycle, and we use these same phases to describe what happens in real-world business activity. The difference, of course, between an idealized business cycle and the actual ones is that the real world's changing conditions are not so neatly periodic and predictable. For example, real-life recessions do not come with unvarying intensity every X number of years, with boom time in between because actual business cycles and their phases are not periodic. The four phases depicted in the idealized model are nevertheless useful concepts and are fairly straightforward:

Recession   This is the downward phase of business activity. Real income, employment, and output are decreasing. Business and consumer pessimism is prevalent.[1]

[1] A depression is an *abnormally* severe recession. Very high rates of unemployment persist. Very few businesspersons or consumers feel that the economic outlook is rosy. We have had very few true depressions in this country compared to the number of recessions.

Bottom or Trough   The low point in business activity.

Recovery   This is the upward phase of the cycle. All aggregate variables, such as output, employment, and real income, are rising. Consumer and business optimism are rising.

Boom   This is the uppermost point of the cycle, generally associated with tight labor markets, that is, low unemployment, rising output and real income, and in addition, inflationary pressures as the economy approaches its capacity.

Indicators of Business Activity

In the real world we have indicators of business activity that either coincide with, lead, or lag behind the business cycle. These indicators are published by the Department of Commerce in *Business Conditions Digest.* Let's go to Figure 6-3 to see what they look like. Figure 6-3 shows the *leading, coincidental,* and *lagging* indicators from the period 1965 to 1975. Notice how well the leading indicators predicted the recession of 1969 to 1970. Some examples of leading indicators are the average work week for production workers, the average weekly overtime hours by production workers, the index of net business formation, new orders for machines, and changes in business inventories. Examples of coincident indicators are current dollar GNP and personal income, retail sales, unfilled orders, and an index of help-wanted advertising. Examples of lagging indicators are the unemployment rate, spending on new plant and equipment, labor costs per unit of output, and consumer installment debt outstanding.

Economists who are interested in predicting business activity in the United States sometimes rely on leading indicators for their information. However, economists attempting to predict the future of the price level, unemployment, con-

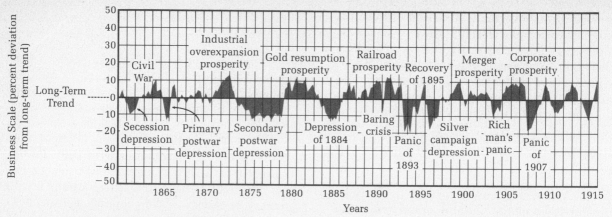

FIGURE 6-1 Business Activity in the United States

Here we see the ups and downs of business activity in the United States from before the Civil War until today. The prosperity during the 1960s, which was uninterrupted for almost 10 years, was the longest period of sustained rise in business activity that we have ever had. The ups and downs in business activity are measured as a percentage change compared to the long-run trend in the United States. *(Source: Cleveland Trust Company.)*

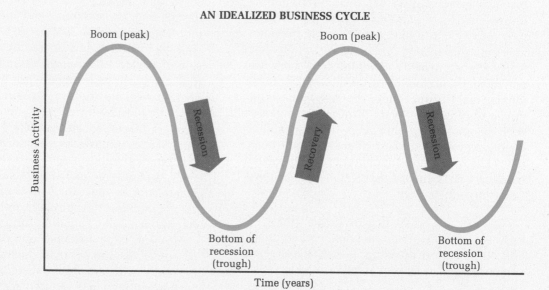

AN IDEALIZED BUSINESS CYCLE

FIGURE 6-2

The diagram shows that in an idealized business cycle there is first a boom period toward the end of the recovery, then a sliding off into recession and/or depression, which eventually bottoms out and another recovery begins.

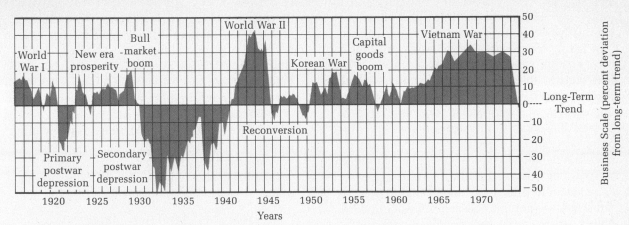

FIGURE 6-1 *(cont'd.)*

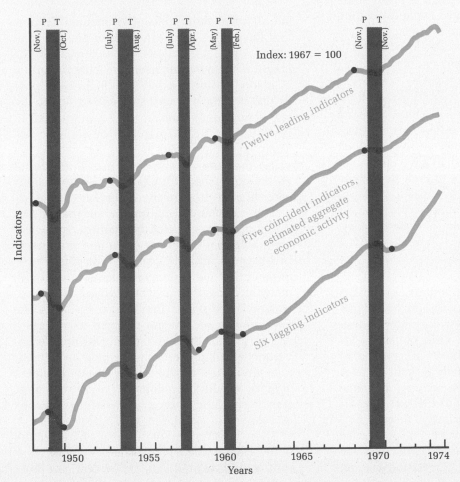

Index: 1967 = 100

Twelve leading indicators

Five coincident indicators,
estimated aggregate
economic activity

Six lagging indicators

Indicators

Years

FIGURE 6-3 **Leading Coincidental and Lagging Indicators**

Changes in leading business indicators usually signal the turns of the business cycle, but not always. Coincidental indicators move concurrently with business activity. On average, leading indicators peak about 5 months before the peaks in business activity. Lagging indicators usually turn down about 3 months after business activity has done so. (*Source:* U.S. Bureau of the Census, *Business Conditions Digest.*)

sumer spending, and other aggregate variables use much more sophisticated techniques. These forecasting techniques are usually based on a theory about how income is determined. The first step is to collect data for the relevant variables, such as past rates of change of prices, unemployment, and output. The next step is to feed these data into a computer. The computer analyzes the data, using an income-determination model based on a particular economic theory. The success of the theory, of course, depends on its ability to make accurate predictions. We are going to present a basic modern theory, or income-determination model, in the following unit. For now, we will see how some older theories of the business cycle—including Marx's theory—described it.

Earlier Business-Cycle Theories

In any field of study there have been as many theories as there have been theorists, and this is also true for the business cycle. We will look at a few of the theories that have stood out above all the others because of their popularity or success. Three theories that used to be popular based their predictions on very dissimilar things: sunspots, innovation, and psychology.

The Sunspot Theory

In the late nineteenth century, some economists believed that sunspots caused changes in business activity. Inane as this theory may sound, it did have some scientific basis. Sunspots affected the weather, and the weather affected the output of farmers. Since agriculture was such a large part of business activity, a change in agricultural output would affect overall business conditions. Historically, there was a fairly high correlation between sunspot cycles and agricultural cycles, but, unfortunately for the theory's advocates, the correlation seemed

to disappear just as the theory was gaining ground. The **sunspot theory** would have been a very useful predicting tool had the relationship between weather and business activity held, since we can *predict* sunspot activity accurately. Given the high accuracy of that prediction, the link to business activity could have been quite useful. Meteorological data would have led to sunspot prediction, which would have enabled weather prediction, which finally would have allowed business-activity prediction.

The Innovation Theory

We all know about some of the great *inventions* that have been made—the cotton gin, the telephone, and many others. An invention is the creation of something new. Once the invention is made, businesses have to figure out how to use it. That's where *innovation* comes in. We define innovation as the adaptation of an invention to actual production techniques. Many inventions never lead to innovations because they are never put to use; think about all the unsuccessful home inventors with their gadgets piled high to the basement ceiling.

The idea behind the **innovation theory** was that innovations caused fluctuations in investment, which ultimately caused ups and downs in business activity. As soon as one entrepreneur decided to innovate (use an invention), many businesspersons would hop on the bandwagon. In so doing, they'd also invest in the new production process, and we would see a rise in overall business activity as all this investment took place. Soon the new investment rage would die down, and aggregate business activity would slow down as a consequence. Hence, sporadic innovations would cause ups and downs in economic activity.

There is an important difference between the innovation theory and the sunspot theory. Sunspot activity is predictable; however, we don't know how to predict *when* innovations will occur. *After the fact,* we can hypothesize which ones caused the particular "take off" in economic activity, but we wouldn't have known beforehand what to predict. The innovation theory is therefore useful for *explaining* cycles, but not for *predicting* the *timing* of them.

The Psychological Theory

The **psychological theory** holds that the psychological reactions of businesspersons to changes in political, social, and economic events result in business-activity cycles. These decision makers ride waves of optimism, depending on the prospects for peace or war, on new discoveries of natural resources, and on many other factors.

Many stock market analysts maintain that swings in stock prices are due to psychological factors. The psychological theory may indeed prove useful in explaining stock market waves. Be careful, though: A dip in the stock market doesn't always precede a recession. In fact, one astute observer noted that the stock market has predicted nine of the last five recessions!

Marx's Theory of the Business Cycle

One of the key analyses offered by Marx in his economic works was his theory of the exploitation of laborers by capitalists. Marx came up with the notion of *surplus* value. In his theory, he pointed out that workers spend part of every working day earning the costs of maintaining themselves and their families. These are, in fact, their subsistence wages. The rest of the day it appears that they work without payment, creating for the capitalist some sort of surplus value, a source of wealth and profit for the capitalist class. In other words, in Marx's world the value of any good or service was directly proportional to the amount of labor used to

make it. That means that the worker will work all day to make, say, $50 worth of shoes, but will only be paid, say, $30. The difference is surplus value, and it accrues to the capitalist. It is this small group of lucky capitalists—that is, those who happen to own capital—who are able to garner this surplus. The reason the workers will not get more is because they supposedly only "require" wages that allow them to subsist. And because of an ever-increasing **reserve army of the unemployed** who seek work, the capitalists have always available to them a ready work force to exploit.

Economic Crises

According to Marx, the accumulation of capital would inevitably create contradictions. He predicted that as more and more things were produced and economic development continued, the reserve army of the unemployed would become depleted. Wage rates would have to rise. But capitalists would seek to increase their profits by introducing more sophisticated production equipment and techniques. Eventually, however, capitalists would no longer be able to sell their increased output because of deficient demand. Unemployment would result, thus reducing purchasing power. This would lead to a recession and depression. Marx saw continuous cycles of recessions and depressions in the capitalist economy, but these were different from the ones we've talked about in this book.

Business Cycles

Marx's theory of the business cycle describes the explosion and collapse of capitalism and the eventual revolution of the workers' class. He predicted that the rate of profit would fall in the long run. Industrial power would become increasingly concentrated in fewer and fewer monopolistic firms. Wealth also would become concentrated in the hands of fewer and fewer capitalists. Laborers would become more and more exploited as production became more and more capital intensive. Eventually, the workers of the world would unite and revolt. The whole system would be overthrown, and a more rational socialist economy would prevail:

> The revolt of a working class, a class always increasing in numbers and discipline, united, organized by the very mechanism of the process of capitalist production itself. Centralization of the means of production and socialization of labor at last reach a point where they become incompatible with their capitalist integument. This integument is burst asunder. The knell of capitalist private property sounds. The expropriators are expropriated.[2]

Marx's views caused considerable debate. His theories are still highly regarded by many economists, but his predictions about revolution in industrial capitalist societies have proved incorrect. His views on the inevitability of rising unemployment also have not been proved correct. Unemployment is still a problem in this country and elsewhere, but it seems to be more one of a cyclical nature rather than a secular increase in the percentage of the labor force that is unemployed. Let us now see how unemployment is measured and what different types of unemployment exist.

Unemployment

One of the major consequences of faltering business activity is the ensuing unemployment, particularly of workers, but also of other factors of production (resources). Unemployment has so many costs—in human suffering, in loss of dignity, in loss of savings—the list goes on and

[2]Karl Marx, *Das Kapital*, vol. 1, Moscow: Foreign Language Publishing House, 1961, p. 163.

on. That is why policymakers in our economy closely watch the unemployment figures published by the Department of Labor's Bureau of Labor Statistics. Unemployment is thought to be a social evil that must be kept at an "acceptable" level. We can see from Figure 6-4 that unemployment in the United States has been very low at times—1.2 percent in World War II—but has been intolerably high at other times—almost 25 percent at one point during the Depression.

How Is It Measured?

The Bureau of Labor Statistics, in cooperation with the United States Bureau of the Census, takes monthly surveys in an attempt to estimate unemployment rates. The government statisticians have designed a sampling method to collect the data. They have divided the country into almost 2000 primary sampling units, which generally consist of single counties or groups of counties with contiguous boundaries. They have further refined the sampling technique to take account of population density, rate of growth, percentage of minority groups, and principal industries. Out of each of these areas, called *strata,* statisticians, using demographic data available for all sample units, select one of the sampling units to represent that entire group. Then, within the unit, they randomly select a certain number of individual households and contact these households during each monthly survey. The households contacted change over time, so that no biases creep into the responses by those interviewed. All in all, the 1100 or more employees who go out into the field sample 50,000 households each month.

To be classified as unemployed, a person must meet the exacting official criteria. According to the definition used by the Bureau of the Census, an unemployed worker is a person who (1) did not work at all during the survey week but was looking for work and was available for work; or (2) was waiting to be

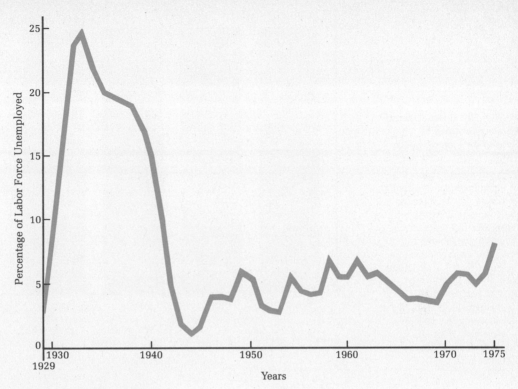

FIGURE 6-4 Unemployment in the United States

Unemployment has varied in the United States from a low of 1.2 percent of the civilian labor force at one point during World War II to almost 25 percent at the depths of the Great Depression. As can be seen, the cyclical variations in unemployment are irregular. (*Source:* U.S. Dept. of Labor, Bureau of Labor Statistics.)

called back after being laid off; or (3) was waiting to report to a new job within the next 30 days and was not in school; or (4) would have been looking for work but was temporarily ill.

The unemployment rate reported by the government lumps together everyone who meets these qualifications. However, the survey does reveal some interesting profiles on unemployed workers. For one thing, it allows us to distinguish between voluntary and involuntary unemployment.

Voluntary Unemployment

It's hard to imagine that unemployment may be voluntary, but a look at Figure 6-5 may

change your mind. The unemployed include quite a few individuals who have been neither laid off nor fired. Among the unemployed are those who quit their jobs, those who are looking for first jobs, and those who have decided to "reenter the labor force" after being out of it. At least three-fourths of the unemployment among youths and more than half the unemployment among females is voluntary. However, the unemployment rate determined by government sampling does not tell us how long unemployed individuals, whether they became unemployed voluntarily or involuntarily, remain unemployed. In fact, official statistics, by failing to take certain factors into account, can either overestimate or underestimate unem-

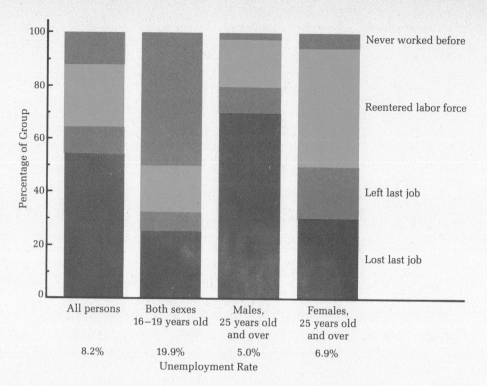

FIGURE 6-5 **Unemployment Persons Grouped by Reason of Unemployment, 1975**

It would appear that a lot of unemployment is actually voluntary. Those included in the voluntary category are those who have either quit their job, are looking for first jobs, or have "reentered the labor force" after having been a "nonparticipant." At least 44 percent of all unemployment in 1975 fell into these three categories. (*Source:* U.S. Dept. of Labor, Bureau of Labor Statistics.)

ployment rates. They can err on the upside by ignoring duration of unemployment. And duration of unemployment is an important factor that relates to our study of the business cycle.

The Business Cycle and the Duration of Unemployment

Look at Figure 6-6. It shows total unemployment broken down into three categories: people remaining unemployed for less than 5 weeks; from 5 to 14 weeks; and for 15 weeks or more. Actually, the average duration of unemployment is closely associated with the business cycle. In 1969, for example, at the end of the 1960s boom, the average duration of unemployment had fallen to a low of 8 weeks. However, as the recession set in, the average duration

of unemployment rose. In fact, much of what is seen as an increase in the unemployment rate is really a reflection of an increase in the average duration of unemployment. After all, if the *same* percentage of the labor force becomes newly unemployed each month, but all of a sudden those who are unemployed take several weeks *longer* to find a new job, survey results will show an *increase* in the unemployment rate. This suggests that care should be taken in interpreting monthly statistics that show slight variations in unemployment rates. Chances are that relatively small variations in the average duration of unemployment will fully account for these slightly inflated unemployment rates.

On the other side of the coin, official unemployment rates may seriously *underestimate*

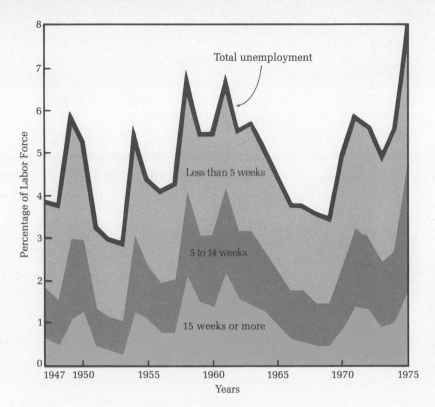

Total unemployment

Less than 5 weeks

5 to 14 weeks

15 weeks or more

FIGURE 6-6 Unemployment Rates by Duration

A very small percentage of the labor force that is unemployed at any given moment has actually been unemployed for 15 or more weeks. A rise in the unemployment rate often is merely reflecting an increase in the average duration of unemployment. (*Source:* U.S. Dept. of Labor, Bureau of Labor Statistics.)

the true rate of unemployment—particularly during periods of recession and depression—by not taking into account hidden, or disguised, unemployment.

Hidden Unemployment

A number of observers of the unemployment scene believe that official unemployment rates are biased downward because of the criteria used in the survey. To be marked down as unemployed, a person must be out of work yet looking for a job. But what about all those who would like to look for work but are discouraged? Should they not also be included in the unemployed category? This is a question we cannot answer. However, we do know that when Bureau of Labor Statistics personnel in-

terview individuals not in the labor force, they find there are several different reasons for this. Individuals indicate that they are not in the labor force because they think they will be unable to find a job or no jobs are available; an employer will turn them down because they are either too young or too old; or they lack sufficient education or training. If we lump together all these individuals and call them "discouraged" workers, we can see how evident the phenomenon of discouraged workers is in Figure 6-7. In any event, when individuals hold such attitudes, they drop out of the labor force and no longer look for a job—yet official surveys do not count them as unemployed.

In each case, however, the labor-force participation rate will fall for that potential worker's whole group. For example, every mid-

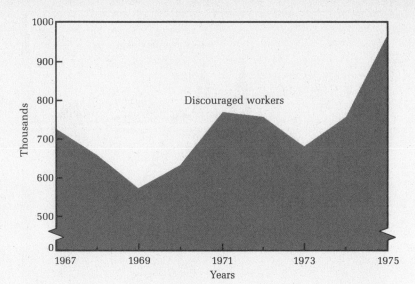

FIGURE 6-7 Discouraged Workers

There are many reasons why individuals want a job but are not looking. These reasons include thinking that jobs are not available, thinking that employers will not hire them because they are too old or too young, and so forth. (*Source:* U.S. Dept. of Labor, Bureau of Labor Statistics.)

dle-aged black male who drops out of the labor force lowers the rate of participation for all middle-aged black males. The labor-force participation rate is merely the percentage of available individuals of working age who are actually in the labor force. We show in Figure 6-8 total male and female labor-force participation rates over time. Notice that the male labor-force participation rate has been falling gradually over the past three decades, whereas the female participation rate has been rising gradually.

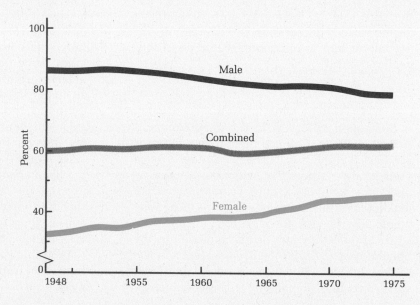

FIGURE 6-8 Labor-Force Participation Rates by Sex

The combined labor-force participation rate has increased slightly in recent years. However, over the same period, the male participation rate has fallen, and the female rate has risen. (*Source:* U.S. Dept. of Labor, Bureau of Labor Statistics.)

The Major Types of Unemployment

Unemployment has been categorized into four basic types: frictional, cyclical, seasonal, and structural. You often hear about these different types of unemployment, so you might want to know what they mean.

Frictional Unemployment

Here are the unemployment estimates for 1976: Of the 92 million Americans in the labor force, more than 10 million will have either changed or taken new jobs during the year; about 1 in 20 workers will have quit, been laid off, or been fired every single month; another 5 percent will have gone to new jobs or returned to old ones. In the process, more than 17 million persons will have reported themselves unemployed at one time or another. What we call **frictional unemployment** is the constant flow of individuals from job to job and in and out of employment. We know that some frictional unemployment cannot and probably should not be eliminated. (Notice that the "should" here is a value judgment.) To eliminate frictional unemployment, we would have to prevent workers from leaving their present jobs unless they had already lined up jobs elsewhere where they would start working immediately. It might be difficult for some workers to line up a better job while having to work at their current one. Besides, a complete elimination of frictional unemployment would probably reduce the rate of growth of our economy. One important source of advances in productivity is the movement of workers from sectors of the economy where labor productivity and wages are low to sectors where productivity and wages are high. The search for better job offers is the process by which workers discover areas where their productivity is highest—that is, where they can make the most income. Nonetheless, frictional unemployment can be reduced by getting better information about alternative sources of jobs and available workers.

The level of frictional unemployment determines our definition of "full" employment. If we assert that frictional unemployment is 4 percent of the labor force, then that is what we call full employment. And when governmental officials change their minds and say that full employment should be redefined as 5 percent rather than 4 percent unemployment, they are really saying that labor mobility, knowledge of job opportunities, and so on have changed so as to cause an increase in frictional unemployment. We really don't know how the magic number of 4 percent ever came into being. Perhaps the switch to 5 percent as our goal of "full" employment simply means that the government has learned better ways to estimate frictional unemployment.

Cyclical Unemployment

Cyclical unemployment is related to the business cycle. In fact, cyclical unemployment is defined as unemployment associated with changes in business conditions—primarily recessions and depressions. The way to lessen cyclical unemployment would be to reduce the intensity, duration, and frequency of ups and downs of business activity. Economic policymakers attempt, through their policies, to reduce cyclical unemployment by keeping business activity on an even keel.

Seasonal Unemployment

Seasonal unemployment is just that. It comes and goes with seasons of the year in which the demand for particular jobs rises and falls. Construction workers often can work only during the warmer months in northern climates. They are seasonally unemployed during the winter. Resort workers usually can only get jobs in resorts during the summer season. They, too, become seasonally unemployed during the winter; the opposite is true for ski resort workers. There is little we can do to reduce seasonal unemployment. It is unlikely that employers will begin to develop production techniques to allow, say, construction workers to work during winter months. For one thing, the costs would be prohibitive.

Structural Unemployment

Presumably, there have been structural changes in our economy that cause some workers to become permanently unemployed, or at least unemployed for a very long period of time. Structurally unemployed persons are usually those who simply can't find *any* job they can do. **Structural unemployment** has also been associated with **technological unemployment**— that is, unemployment resulting from the increased use of labor-saving machines.

Unlike cyclical unemployment, structural unemployment is not caused by the business cycle, although the business cycle may affect it. And unlike frictional unemployment, structural unemployment is not related to the labor mobility that occurs when workers move from low-productivity to high-productivity sectors of the economy. Rather, structural unemployment results when the demanding public no longer wants to buy an individual's services and instead of going through retraining, that individual persists in his or her search for employment with "obsolete" skills. According to theory, some of these people eventually will go into new industries. More often than not, in most urban settings this is precisely what happens. However, in some settings this does not happen. Often people refuse to move. They sit and wait for times to improve. The result is a kind of permanent depression in some geographic areas due to labor immobility.

The problem is widespread. Structural un-employment is not merely a matter of locale; it is something you carry with you if there is no demand for your skills. For example, vast numbers of blacks came to the northern cities from southern agricultural areas where they were structurally unemployed. In the cities blacks are now called "hard-core unemployables" because they have no skills that fit into the market demand. Usually, when these people are employed, it is in service jobs (like working in a car wash), and they are frequently the first ones to be hit by a business cycle. Although it may make very little difference to the person you're talking to, you can present a complex economic question by asking: "Are you cyclically or structurally unemployed?" It is sometimes hard to tell, but basically structural unemployment can be cured only by developing new skills for a changed market. For this reason, structural unemployment is a much tougher problem than the one brought on by simple cyclical swings.

One more point needs to be made: Don't assume that structural unemployment is a problem only for those with little formal education. Any time you specialize in something, you run the risk of having the market turn against you. Highly educated men who can build supersonic transports or rockets that go to the moon are in precisely the same jam when their demand (in this case, government) falls away. They are unemployed and must retrain. Much West Coast unemployment among so-called aerospace engineers in the early 1970s was very close in cause and cure to the problems of Appalachia.

It is interesting to note that worry over structural unemployment was quite intense during the 1950s but almost melted away to nothing during the 1960s. When the GNP growth rate finally increased in the 1960s, nobody spoke of structural unemployment as a problem. This leads one to be a little wary about the entire concept of structural unemployment.

Reducing the Suffering

In the United States we have a system of unemployment compensation that transfers income to those individuals who are unemployed and who qualify. This is one way of reducing the loss of income associated with unemployment. However, critics of unemployment compensation contend that such transfer payments, in spite of their positive benefits, have perverse results. How could this be? In Issue I-8 you will see why.

Business Cycle: A recurrent fluctuation in general economic activity. Business cycles usually are observed in such aggregate variables as gross national product and employment.

Sunspot Theory: A business-cycle theory according to which sunspots were believed to affect weather, which in turn affected agricultural output and, therefore, general business conditions.

Innovation Theory: A business-cycle theory attributing changes in business activity to the development of innovations that businesspersons can adopt to increase profits. Presumably once the innovation is successful, other businesspersons jump on the bandwagon, thus causing a rise in investment, which causes a rise in overall business activity. Later, investment peters out and investment activity goes down.

Psychological Theory: A theory which holds that business cycles are caused by the psychological reaction of businesspersons to changes in social and political events, as well as economic events, which cause changes in business activity.

Reserve Army of the Unemployed: In Marxian terminology, the unemployed workers, whose numbers will grow as workers become more and more exploited by the capitalist classes.

Frictional Unemployment: Unemployment associated with frictions in the system that may occur because of the imperfect information which exists.

Cyclical Unemployment: Unemployment resulting from business recessions that occur when aggregate demand is insufficient to create full employment.

Seasonal Unemployment: Unemployment due to seasonality in demand or possible supply of any particular good or service.

Structural Unemployment: Unemployment resulting from fundamental changes in the structure of the economy. Structural unemployment occurs, for example, when the demand for a product falls drastically so that workers specializing in the production of that product find themselves out of work.

Technological Unemployment: Unemployment caused by technologically superior equipment replacing labor in specific tasks.

1. The United States has a history of ups and downs in its business activity. Economists have tried to characterize these ups and downs by using business-cycle theories.

2. The business cycle is a recurrent up and down in economic activity. An idealized business cycle is periodic; that is, it goes up and down at regular intervals. No business cycles in the United States have been so regular. We therefore need a more sophisticated theory to predict turning points in economic activity.

3. There have been many business-cycle theories, including the sunspot theory, the innovation theory, the psychological theory, and Marx's theory of the business cycle. None of these theories are really used today. They have been supplanted by more modern theories.

4. Unemployment in the United States is composed of four types: frictional, seasonal, structural, and cyclical. It is difficult to discern what part of total unemployment is composed of any one of these four categories.

5. Frictional unemployment is caused by the temporary inability of workers to match their skills and talents with available jobs. Frictional unemployment could not be eliminated without passing a law that required employers never to fire a worker and that required employees never to quit a job unless they could go immediately to a new one.

6. Structural unemployment occurs when the demand for a product falls off abruptly. We have observed structural unemployment lately in the aerospace industry. Structural unemployment is often referred to as technological unemployment—that is, it occurs when machines put men or women out of work.

7. The hard-core unemployed are usually defined as undereducated members of particularly prominent minority groups. The hard-core unemployed are not necessarily unemployed because of structural reasons. They may be unemployed because of government legislation, discrimination in the labor market, and certain restrictive hiring practices on the part of unions.

8. The duration of unemployment in the United States varies dramatically over the business cycle. As business conditions worsen, the average duration of unemployment lengthens. As business conditions strengthen, the average duration of unemployment falls.

1. Why do you think the government would like to be able to predict the business cycle?
2. We have referred to unemployment only in terms of the labor force. Are there other unemployed resources in the United States during business recessions?
3. The United States Department of Labor defines unemployed people as those who are seeking work but have not found any. Do you agree with this definition?
4. Can you think of ways to reduce frictional unemployment?

Selected
References

Chandler, Lester V., *America's Greatest Depression: 1929 to 1941*, New York: Harper & Row, 1970.

Economic Report of the President, various issues, Washington, D.C.: U.S. Government Printing Office.

Gordon, R. A., *Economic Instability and Growth: The American Record,* New York: Harper & Row, 1974.

——, "How Obsolete Is the Business Cycle?", *The Public Interest,* Fall 1970, pp. 127–139.

Moore, Geoffrey H., *How Full is Full Employment?,* American Enterprise Institute of Public Policy Research, study no. 14, Washington, D.C., July 1973.

Does Unemployment Compensation Cause Unemployment?

DOES OUR SYSTEM HAVE A BUILT-IN INCENTIVE FOR NOT WORKING?

Helping Out the Jobless

The last chapter discussed unemployment in detail but made only passing reference to its costs to the unemployed. Now we will take a closer look at those "costs." During the depths of the Great Depression, the Roosevelt administration attempted to help out the unemployed with a system of unemployment compensation. We described it in Chapter 5, when we reviewed certain aspects of our tax system. Briefly, employers are required by state governments to collect a payroll tax whose proceeds are used to provide unemployment compensation benefits or "insurance" when employees become unemployed. Not all employees are eligible for unemployment compensation, but somewhere in the neighborhood of 60 percent to 70 percent of the work force is covered. Average unemployment compensation payments per week were 67 dollars in 1975. The average, however, doesn't tell the whole story because there are wide variations among the states. In addition to the wide variations in weekly benefits, the states also differ on the maximum number of weeks that an

eligible employee is entitled to draw benefits. The national maximum for this was 65 in 1975.

The unemployment insurance system now in effect has remained essentially unchanged since its inception in the 1930s. However, since World War II there has been a marked increase in the unemployment rate. Since the end of the war, annual unemployment rates have averaged in excess of 4.5 percent. In only one postwar year did the unemployment rate go below 3 percent of the labor force. Some observers contend that a structural shift in the economy has caused the rate of unemployment to go up: Increased complexity and "friction" have made it more difficult for workers who are out of a job to find appropriate employment.

Other observers disagree with this explanation of why average rates of unemployment have risen over the past few decades. They argue that what we are seeing is the "new" unemployment—joblessness induced by a combination of our unemployment compensation system and our system of taxes and transfers. What on earth could they be talking about? The analytics are

quite simple because they hinge upon the notion of opportunity cost, which we have discussed on several occasions.

The Low Opportunity Cost of Not Working

Recall from Chapter 5, when we talked about taxation, and from Issue I-7, when we discussed tax shelters, that the opportunity cost of not working was the forgone aftertax income. If an individual's aftertax income is $5 an hour and the individual becomes unemployed, the opportunity cost of being unemployed is then $5 per hour for each normal workday. Otherwise stated, the cost of leisure is the aftertax income forgone by not working.

What would the law of demand tell you about the quantity of leisure demanded if the opportunity cost of not working—leisure's price—were to fall? The quantity would rise. What does that mean? It means that some individuals will be induced by a lower price of leisure to accept unemployment more readily (that is, demand more leisure). What would lower the opportunity cost of not working? Unemployment compensation payments.

Look at Figure I-8.1. Here we show a downward-sloping demand

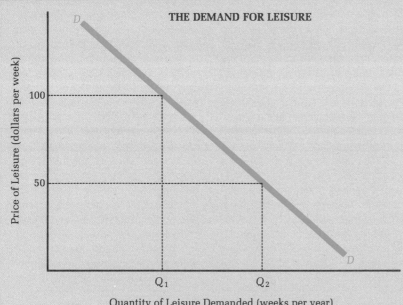

THE DEMAND FOR LEISURE

Price of Leisure (dollars per week)

100

50

Q_1 Q_2

Quantity of Leisure Demanded (weeks per year)

FIGURE I-8.1

The demand for leisure (not working) is related to its price. Its price, however, is basically an individual's aftertax income because when the individual stops working—that is, "buys" leisure—her or his opportunity cost is the aftertax income loss. We see that when aftertax income is $100 per week, the quantity of "leisure purchased" measured in weeks per year will be Q_1; however, if unemployment compensation makes up for $50 of the weekly aftertax income loss, then the price of leisure will be reduced to $50 per week, at which price the larger quantity, Q_2, will be purchased.

curve for leisure, where leisure is measured in weeks per year. A week of leisure is, of course, synonymous with a week out of work. The vertical axis shows the price per week of leisure. Let's assume that a worker is faced with the following choice: A job can be taken that yields $100 per week in take-home pay. If the job is not taken, the worker pays the price, for each week of leisure, of $100. At that price, the worker would demand a quantity of leisure, Q_1. However, if unemployment compensation of $50 per week were paid to this worker, the opportunity cost of not working would fall from $100 per week to $50. At the lower price of $50 per week, a larger quantity of leisure, Q_2 would be demanded per year. These are the simple demand analytics demonstrating how unemployment compensation will

increase the number of people choosing not to work.

But this is not the end of the story because unemployment compensation is often coupled with other benefits (food stamps, health insurance, and so on) that are lost when a worker goes *back* to work. What we want to determine now is the effective tax rate that is applied to an unemployed worker's potential income if that unemployed worker were to accept a job.

The Benefits of Unemployment

When workers become unemployed, they not only receive unemployment compensation but also are relieved of paying income and Social Security

taxes. Moreover, many may be eligible for food stamps, rent supplements, and even additional welfare payments. We will now look at the taxes one can avoid by being out of a job and accepting tax-free unemployment compensation. We will use the example given in an article by Professor Martin Feldstein of Harvard University.[1]

Consider a worker in Massachusetts in 1971. This worker has a wife and two children. If he remains employed all year long, he earns $500 a month, or $6,000 per year. The wife earns $350 per month, or a total of $4,200 per year if she works all year long.

What happens if the man be-

[1]Martin Feldstein, "The Economics of the New Unemployment," *The Public Interest*, no. 33, Fall 1973.

comes unemployed for 1 month? He obviously loses $500 in *gross* (before-tax) earnings. What does he lose in *net* (take-home) income? His federal income tax is reduced by $83. His Social Security payroll tax is reduced by $26. His Massachusetts state income taxes are reduced by another $25. The total tax reduction is $137. Now unemployment compensation comes into play to give him 50 percent of his gross wage, plus a dependence allowance of $6 per week for each child, totaling a tax-free $302 per month.

When working, his gross income was $500, but his take-home pay was $366. His take-home pay now is $302 because that is what unemployment compensation benefits total. For each month of unemployment (leisure), this man has a reduction in spendable income of only $64.

The Effective Marginal Tax Rate

In the above example, net income falls by $64 when 1 month of unemployment occurs. That means that net income, expressed as a percentage of gross income, falls by about 13 percent, implying an effective marginal tax rate on work effort of 87 percent. Go back to Table 5-6. Can you find 87 percent on that table? No, you cannot. The highest marginal tax rate that the highest income individuals have to pay in this economy is 70 percent, but for the low-income individual who might be eligible for unemployment, the effective marginal tax rate is higher than that paid by the most wealthy. Looking at this man's wife, we can

calculate the effective marginal tax rate to be over 93 percent. And in Massachusetts during the year for which the example was taken, if the family had had three children instead of two, the family's net income actually would have been higher if the woman had remained unemployed for 3 months than if she had worked for that period!

These startlingly high effective marginal tax rates certainly indicate a disincentive effect that may encourage workers to remain unemployed longer than they might otherwise be. After all, look at how much leisure they can buy for each week of unemployment and at what a low price. If we were to be more thorough in our example and include other transfer benefits that would be lost when an unemployed worker becomes employed—food stamps, housing supplements, and so forth—the effective marginal tax rate in many cases for low-income individuals would in some states exceed 100 percent. These individuals must see this, and not a few of them will realize that it pays to remain unemployed—particularly when the effective marginal tax rate is, in fact, in excess of 100 percent.

Inverse Seniority

For evidence that tends to confirm our analysis, we need only look at something new in labor agreements. Historically, seniority has been an issue, particularly in union contracts with employers. Those workers who had the most seniority (who had worked the longest) were the last to be fired or laid off. But in several industries, unions have negotiated

recent contracts that include *inverse* seniority provisions: Workers with more seniority have the option of being laid off earlier than other workers and rehired later. This would only be expected to occur if there were positive benefits attached to unemployment. These benefits are, of course, associated with unemployment compensation as well as with other transfer payments for which unemployed workers become eligible. Additionally, the unemployed worker has more leisure time and, in some cases, will invest part of that leisure time actually looking for a better job or "day-lighting" without reporting the income earned.

In a sense, then, unemployment compensation and the tax system, which taken together lead to high effective marginal tax rates, are subsidies to job searching. They allow workers to take longer to search for a job in the hopes of getting a better one than they had, or from which they had been laid off, or have been offered.

Seasonal Unemployment

We mentioned briefly seasonal unemployment in Chapter 6. Seasonal unemployment occurs whenever certain industries do not operate at specific times during each year. During the off periods, they lay off their workers. If no unemployment compensation were given to workers during these periods, employers who hire workers only seasonally would have to pay relatively higher wages to compensate for the anticipated periods of unemployment. However, with unemployment compensation

available, wages to seasonal workers do not have to be as high because these seasonal workers are partially compensated for their unemployment during the slack season. According to Feldstein, "Because the price of unstable labor has been artificially subsidized, employers organize production in a way that makes too much use of unstable employment."[2]

If there were no unemployment compensation, workers would have to be paid more to get them to accept unstable jobs. The differences in pay between stable and unstable jobs would then reflect the fairly certain probability of being laid off and the expected duration of unemployment. On the other hand, employers faced

[2]Ibid., p. 34.

with this wage differential would attempt to reduce unstable employment by many means, including inventory buildup during slack periods and the introduction of new techniques of production, such as improving outdoor work practices so that bad weather would not curtail employment to the extent it does now.

The results of a new unemployment compensation law in British Columbia offer some evidence for this proposition. In 1974 a new law was passed that allowed full unemployment compensation benefits to be paid to workers who had kept a job for a minimum of only 8 weeks. After the law was passed, the worker turnover rates in such seasonal jobs as logging increased 600 percent. After loggers had worked their requisite 8 weeks, many found it in their

interest to go on unemployment. The same was true among seasonal workers in resort areas. Their turnover rate increased dramatically; more workers had to be hired for the same work season than previously because of the increased turnover.

The New Unemployment

The above analysis leads one to conclude that unemployment compensation, coupled with the peculiarities of our tax and welfare system, is responsible for part of our frictional, cyclical, seasonal, and structural unemployment. In other words, there is a new type of unemployment that is induced by unemployment compensation. Feldstein estimates that the current structure of the unemployment compensation system accounts for at least 1.2 percent of the unemployment rate in the United States. That means that out of, say, a 6 percent unemployment rate, "new" unemployment accounts for over one-fifth of it. Studies done for the Canadian economy show similar results. New unemployment in Canada accounts for 1.5 to 2.5 percent of the total unemployment rate. Otherwise stated, a restructuring of the unemployment compensation system could reduce the unemployment rate by 1 percentage point or more. This is not, however, an argument in favor of abolishing unemployment benefits. Rather, it is presented by Feldstein and others as a case for restructuring the system of benefits paid to unemployed workers because so long as there is a strong incentive to remain unemployed, more workers will become and remain unemployed than they would if the benefits of unemployment were reduced.

One cannot immediately jump to the conclusion that just because unemployment compensation may have a serious effect on work incentives, it should therefore be abolished. We have analyzed some of the problems involved in providing benefits to unemployed workers. That is to say, we have deduced the likely consequences of such a system, furnishing some supportive empirical findings. We would need to step into the realm of normative economics to state that unemployment compensation systems should be abandoned, or even modified, for that matter.

Questions for Thought and Discussion

1. Is it possible to create a system of unemployment compensation that does not have a built-in work disincentive?
2. What are some of the arguments that can be used to counter the statistical findings presented in this issue? In other words, is it possible that, in fact, unemployment compensation as currently provided in the United States does not decrease work effort and hence increase the rate of unemployment?

Selected References

Feldstein, Martin S., "The Economics of the New Unemployment," *The Public Interest,* no. 33, Fall 1973.

——, *Lowering the Permanent Rate of Unemployment,* A Joint Committee Print of the Joint Economic Committee, Washington, D.C.: U.S. Government Printing Office, 1973. Also Hearings of the Joint Economic Committee published as *Reducing Unemployment to Two Percent,* Hearings before the Joint Economic Committee, Oct. 17, 18, and 26, 1972, Washington, D.C.: U.S. Government Printing Office, 1972.

Grubel, H. G. and D. Maki, "Real and Insurance Induced Unemployment in Canada," unpublished paper, Simon Frazer University, June 1973.

Sachs, Shelley, "Measuring the Induced Unemployment Rate in Canada," unpublished master's thesis, Department of Economics, Simon Frazer University, August 1973.

7 Inflation and Stagflation

The persistent increase in the cost of living in the United States has affected all of us. Rising prices now seem as inevitable as death and taxes. We are continually reminded by newspaper and magazine articles that today's dollar is only worth 30 percent of the 1939 dollar. Although prices have not always gone up at a rate of 5 to 15 percent a year, they rose at a compounded rate of almost 1 percent per year from 1867 to the 1960s. The pace of **inflation** (defined as a *sustained* rise in the general price level), however, has not been even.

Inflation and the History of Prices

The erratic behavior of prices is shown in Figure 7-1. After shooting up at a rate of 25 percent per year during and after the Civil War, the price index *fell* at the rate of 5.4 percent from 1867 to 1879. That is equivalent to a halving of the price level in less than 15 years. Farmers and businesspersons during those years of falling prices cried out, strangely enough, for higher prices— *greenbackism* as it was later called. Farmers thought that inflation would cause the prices of the products they sold to rise faster than those of the products they bought. Politicians apparently didn't listen very well, however, for prices kept falling, averaging a decline of 1 percent per year from 1879 to 1897. Prices then rose 6 percent a year continually until a few years after World War I. For a year or so after the war, prices fell drastically and then remained fairly stable until the Great Depression. Wholesale prices dropped at an average rate of 8 percent a year from the stock market crash in 1929 until Roosevelt declared a "banking holiday" in March 1933. Roosevelt's at-

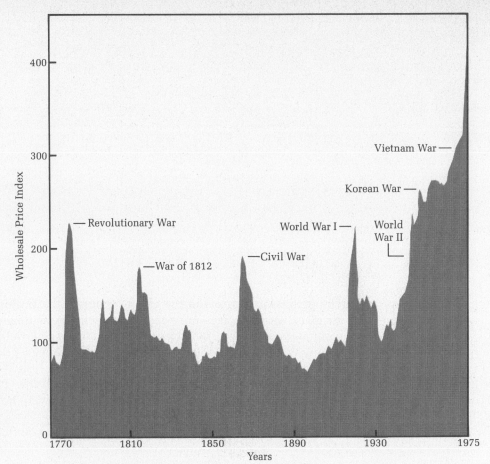

FIGURE 7-1 History of Prices in the United States, 1770 to 1973

Here we see the wholesale price index for the past two centuries. Prices have not always been rising, even though the experience of the past few years might lead us to that conclusion. Almost every war in our history has been associated with a rise in the wholesale price index. *(Source: U.S. Dept. of Commerce.)*

tempts to raise prices were moderately success-ful, and there was general inflation until 1937. Then prices leveled off until the beginning of World War II.

The rate of price increases during World War II was less than it had been during both the Civil War and World War I. The wholesale price index rose 118 percent from August 1939 through August 1948—about 9 percent per year. From 1948 until the mid-1960s, prices remained quite stable except for a jump during the Korean conflict. Since the Vietnam involve-ment, inflation has accelerated.

Inflation in Other Countries

The United States is not alone in its history of rising prices. Inflation seems to be a world-wide problem. In fact our rate of inflation has been mild relative to inflation in many other countries. Some countries have had waves of hyperinflation that make our wartime episodes look like ripples. In 1939, Hungary had a price index set at 100; by January 1946, it was almost 5,500,000. A half a year later it was 20,000,000,000,000, or 2×10^{13}! This means that a commodity with a 1939 price tag of 100 forints would have cost 5,500,000 forints in January 1946, and by August of the same year it would have cost 20,000,000,000,000 forints. Imagine having to carry a wheelbarrow full of money to the store just to buy a loaf of dark bread!

How We Measure Inflation

If inflation is defined as a sustained rise in the general price level, how do we come up with a measure of the rate of inflation? This is indeed a thorny problem for government statisticians. It is easy to determine how much the price of an individual commodity has risen: If last year a light bulb cost 10¢ and this year it costs 15¢, there has been a 50 percent rise in the price of that light bulb over a 1-year period.

Let's construct a hypothetical price index for light bulbs, using the information in Table 7-1. In the first column we show the year, where year 3 has been singled out as the base year, or period against which all comparisons will be made. Column 2 gives the number of light bulbs sold, and column 3 gives the price per light bulb. The fourth column presents a price index, which is merely the price per light bulb

each year expressed as a percentage of the base year's price. We created columns 5 and 6 to express the output of light bulbs in current dollars, that is, column 2 times column 3, and the value of light bulb output in constant (year 3) dollars. Column 6 is merely a simplification of what real GNP is all about, except here we are talking about "real" light bulbs. All that we have to do to obtain real GNP is correct for price changes, just as we have done in Table 7-1.

Now you should have a little better idea about the difference between *current* dollar or nominal GNP, which is expressed in today's dollars, and *constant* dollar or real GNP, which is expressed in the dollars of some base period. You can see in Figure 7-2 how much of the growth in current dollar GNP has been growth in real output and how much has been due to inflation. The real part was obtained by correcting for inflation as in the above simplified example.

A formal definition of a price index, which may be used for an entire economy, is as follows:

Table 7-1 Converting the Value of Output in Current Dollars to the Value of Output in Constant Dollars

We arbitrarily choose year 3 as our base period. We construct a price index in column 4. When we correct for price changes with this price index, we obtain output expressed in constant, year-3 dollars in column 6.

(1) YEAR	(2) PRODUCTION OF LIGHT BULBS	(3) PRICE ($ PER BULB)	(4) PRICE INDEX = EACH YEAR'S PRICE AS A PERCENTAGE QF THE BASE-YEAR PRICE	(5) VALUE OF OUTPUT IN CURRENT DOLLARS (2) × (3)	(6) OUTPUT IN CONSTANT (YEAR 3) DOLLARS (5) ÷ (4)
1	5	$0.10	50%	$0.50	$1.00
2	10	0.15	75%	1.50	2.00
3 = base year	11	0.20	100%	2.20	2.20
4	13	0.22	110%	2.86	2.60

$$\text{Price index} = \frac{\text{quantities of outputs in the current year valued at their current year prices}}{\text{quantities of outputs in the current year valued at their base-year prices}}$$

That is exactly the formula we use in column 4 in Table 7-1, except there the price index is for light bulbs only, not the entire economy.

Real-World Price Indices

A number of price indices are used in the United States. They are the consumer price index (CPI), the wholesale price index (WPI), and the implicit price deflator.

Consumer Price Index

The **consumer price index** attempts to measure changes in the average prices of all major categories of goods and services purchased by "typical" clerical workers and urban wage earners. The Bureau of Labor Statistics has its employees go to different parts of the country at regular intervals to buy a "market basket" representative of goods and services people buy in urban areas in the United States. It includes different types of food, clothing, appliances, services, and so on. The prices of approximately 400 different goods and services are currently included in this index. The base year has been rebased arithmetically to 1967. The construction of the current CPI however, involves using relative quantities based on a 1960 to 1961 sur-

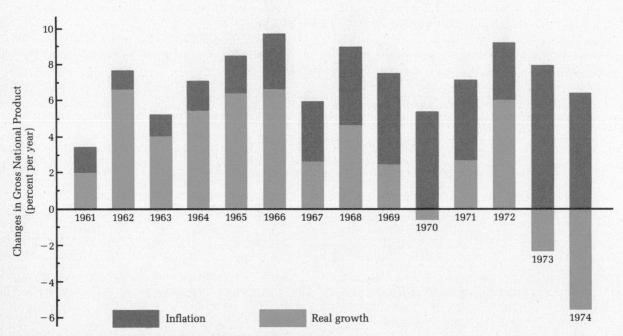

FIGURE 7-2 **How Much Has the Recent Growth in GNP Been Real?**

At various times the rate of growth in nominal GNP has consisted of more or less real growth and more or less inflation, or rise in the price level. In 1970, for example, all the growth was due to inflation. The real growth rate was actually negative in that recession year.

"I see a substantial upswing in the economy by October, but who knows? Maybe it's the Valium talking."

vey of consumer spending habits instead of using the current-year quantities. This saves a lot of time and money on the part of the Bureau of Labor Statistics (BLS) because only new price data have to be collected, expenditure patterns being implicitly assumed unchanged. The BLS updates the quantity computations about every 10 years.

Wholesale Price Index

The **wholesale price index** is similar to the CPI except that it measures changes in the average prices of goods purchased in large quantities by business firms. At present, price quotations are obtained for about 2500 items from producers and manufacturers. No services are included in the WPI market basket. It is calculated in the same manner as the CPI; that is, it employs base-year quantities at current prices and compares them with base-year quantities at base-year prices.

Implicit Price Deflator

The **implicit price deflator,** or GNP deflator, as it is called, is more akin to the original price index we discussed, the one that used current-year quantities at current-year prices compared with current-year quantities at base-year prices. The GNP deflator can be seen as a way of showing the average price level of all final goods and services. We call it a *deflator* because if we divide current dollar GNP by this price index, we get a measure of real or constant dollar GNP. We call it implicit because it is calculated after the fact—after current and real GNP are calculated. As Chapter 4 pointed out, we get today's GNP by adding up the current market value of all final goods and services. Then the dollar value of current output of final goods and services is evaluated at prices prevailing in the base year, which until recently was 1958. The implicit price deflator is then obtained by dividing the former by the latter.

The Accuracy of Price Indices

There is a continuous debate about how accurate the measured price indices really are. Do we have an accurate view of the rate of inflation? We cannot answer that question completely, but we can point out the biases in the price indices that are used.

The first bias has already been mentioned. The CPI and the WPI both use base-year quantities evaluated at today's prices. However, we know from the law of demand that when the relative price of a good goes up, a smaller quantity will be consumed and substitutes will be used in its place. Therefore, too much weight is given to those goods whose prices have risen since the base year relative to other goods; undoubtedly consumers spend a smaller proportion of their income on those relatively more expensive goods than they did in the base year. Nonetheless, the base-year quantities are used throughout the period between surveys on expenditure patterns. This discrepancy imparts an upward bias to both the CPI and the WPI. The opposite is true of the implicit GNP price deflator; since it uses current-year quantities, it has downward bias.

More important perhaps is the bias imparted to all three indices because of improper accounting for changes in quality. At the same nominal price a good is actually cheaper if its quality has been improved. It is difficult for government statisticians to take quality into account. This is also true for the introduction of new products, such as color TVs, that are not included in the market basket of goods because they were introduced after the market basket was made up. These problems probably cause an upward bias in the CPI, WPI, and GNP price deflator.

Theories of Inflation

There are as many theories of inflation as there are inflationary periods in our business history, and we could not hope to cover all of them in this brief chapter. We will limit our discussion to three main theories of inflation.

Quantity Theory of Money and Prices

Perhaps one of the oldest theories of inflation is the **quantity theory of money and prices.** This theory states that the level of prices in the economy is directly proportional to the quantity of money in circulation per unit of output, so that for any given percentage change in the stock of money, [1] there will be an equal percentage change in the price level (output remaining constant). The quantity theory of money comes from the classical equation of exchange.

$$MV = PQ$$

Here we find that M is the money supply, P is the price level, and Q is the output of goods and services. PQ is obviously going to equal output times prices, which is income or GNP. The letter V is called the *income velocity of money*. It is the average number of times per year that a dollar changes hands in purchasing a final good or service. We can define V by juggling the equation of exchange:

$$V = \frac{\text{income}}{\text{money supply}}$$

Let's take an example. Suppose that in 1976 income is $1.6 trillion and the money supply is $400 billion. The income velocity of money, V, would equal ($1.6 trillion)/($400 million), or 4. In other words, each dollar would change hands an average of four times a year. We might say, then, that the income velocity of money is a measure of the economy's output per dollar.

The quantity theory of money as expressed by the equation of exchange can, in fact, predict prices if V and Q remain constant. Obviously, any increase in the money supply is going to lead to an increase in the price level. Classical economists did, in a way, think that V and Q were fairly stable.

The evidence shows that the simple quantity theory of money and prices works pretty well for predicting the rate of inflation over a long period of time. For example, Spanish importa-

[1]We treat the money supply and its determination in Chapter 11.

tion of gold and silver from the New World caused large price increases in Spain and throughout Europe. The discovery of gold in Canada, South Africa, and the United States during the turn of the nineteenth century brought about drastic expansions in the supply of money and rapidly rising prices. However, in the short run, the quantity theory of money and prices as expressed by the equation of exchange does not work too well, mainly because V, the income velocity of money, does not remain constant in the short run. It may move by as much as 30 percent during a 5- to 10-year period.

Demand-Pull Inflation

This theory is summarized by the phrase "too many dollars chasing too few goods." Proponents of the theory of **demand-pull inflation** maintain that the only way we can have inflation (that is, a *sustained* rise in the price level) is for total aggregate demand to exceed the full-employment supply of goods and services at the existing price level. According to the quantity theory just presented, total aggregate demand will exceed the capacity of the economy to satisfy that demand whenever individuals in the economy taken together have too many dollars to spend. This can occur for any number of reasons. Expansionary policies on the part of the government, which we will treat in the following unit, are one of the major reasons cited.

Cost-Push Inflation

The **cost-push inflation** theory of why prices rise has recently reemerged as a popular theory. It attempts to explain why prices rise when the economy is *not* at full employment. Cost-push inflation apparently explains "creeping" inflation and the inflation that the United States experienced during its 1969 to 1970 recession and afterward. There are essentially two explanations of cost-push inflation: union power and big business monopoly power.

Union Power   Many people feel that unions are responsible for inflation. Their reasoning is as follows. Unions decide to demand a wage hike that is not warranted by increases in their physical output. Since the unions are so powerful, employers must give in to union demands for higher wages. When the employers have to pay these higher wages, their costs are higher. To maintain their usual profit margin, these businesspeople raise their prices. This type of cost-push inflation seemingly can occur even when there is no excess demand, even when the economy is operating below capacity at under full employment.

The union-power argument rests on the unions having monopolistic or market power in their labor markets. In other words, some unions are so strong that they can impose wage increases on employers, even when those wage increases are not consistent with increases in the productivity of their labor.

Big Business Monopoly Power   The other variant of the cost-push theory is that inflation is caused when the monopoly power of big business pushes up prices. Powerful corporations are presumably able to raise their prices whenever they want to increase their profits. Each time the corporations raise prices to increase their profits, the cost of living goes up. Workers demand higher wages to make up for the loss in their standard of living, thereby giving the corporations an excuse to raise prices again, and so goes a vicious cycle of price-wage increases.

Who Bears the Burden of Inflation?

Everybody agrees that inflation is a serious problem facing the entire world today. How-ever, as dispassionate observers of the economic scene, we should be able to measure inflation objectively. It is not enough to note that consumers are hurting because they are facing higher prices. After all, every higher price that someone pays is a higher receipt of income for someone else. Unless higher rates of inflation cause the total physical output of goods and services in the economy (real GNP) to fall, inflation's main effect must be to redistribute income and wealth from certain persons or sectors of the economy to others. We will not discuss in this section how inflation could affect the rate of production of goods and services either at a point in time or over time. That is a point on which few economists agree. However, we can point out, in historical perspective, who has been harmed and who has benefited at the hands of inflation. But, before we can adequately do that, we must distinguish between expected and unexpected inflation.

Expected and Unexpected Inflation

If prices rise by 10 percent next year and everyone fully knew that they would rise by 10 percent, then we call the 10 percent rate of inflation *expected*. However, if, for example, everyone expects prices to rise only at an annual 5 percent rate and, in fact, they end up rising by 10 percent, then we have suffered *unexpected* inflation. This distinction is crucial to understanding inflation's effect on the distribution of income and wealth. This distinction is brought out most clearly in analyzing the redistribution of wealth from creditors to debtors and vice versa during periods of unexpected inflation.

Creditors and Debtors

If you borrow money, you are charged an interest rate that presumably covers the cost of providing you with current purchasing power and gives the lender a profit. Let's assume that there is no inflation and, further, that none is anticipated. The lender charges you 5 percent per year for the use of his or her funds. If you borrow $100, at the end of the year you must pay back $105: $100 principal plus $5 interest.

Consider what would happen, however, if during the year there was a 10 percent rate of inflation. Now you give back the lender $105, but the value of that $105 has fallen by 10 percent. Effectively, then, the lender has lent you $100 and received back about $95 in purchasing power at the end of the year. You, as a debtor, gained; the lender, as a creditor, lost. The reason you benefited and the lender lost is because the inflation was unanticipated. Therefore, we can safely maintain that during periods of unanticipated inflation those who are, on balance, creditors will lose, and those who are, on balance, debtors will gain.

However, if the inflation were fully anticipated, the interest rate that you will be charged will include an inflationary premium which will compensate the creditor for the lower purchasing power of the dollars paid back. There would be no redistribution of wealth from creditors to debtors.

A recent estimate of how much inflation was expected by creditors puts it between one-half and two-thirds of the total inflation rate. That means that interest rates rose enough to compensate for between one-half and two-thirds of the loss in purchasing power of dollars paid back to creditors during the period of rising prices. This still leaves a net transfer of wealth from creditors to debtors. It has been estimated that from 1950 to 1975 this transfer was on the order of two-thirds of a trillion dollars.

Who gained in this situation? We know it was debtors, but who are the debtors? To find out we have to look at the net creditor or debtor status of households and businesses. Generally, the household sector has been a net creditor. That means households have had more assets in savings accounts and banks than they have had liabilities, or debts. Thus, households as

a group lost out during this period because they were net creditors. Businesses and governments gained because they were net debtors.

But what about the various income classes within the household sector? If we look at the net creditor or debtor position of various households, we find that both the very poor and the very rich are net creditors; that is, they have fewer debts than assets. We will discuss the poor and those on fixed incomes in a later section.

Wage Earners

Another group of individuals who lose out during a period of unanticipated inflation are wage earners, whose money incomes rise less rapidly than prices. To the extent that wage earners do not obtain wage increases at least equal to the rate of inflation, there will be a redistribution of income away from this class of individuals. On the other hand, to the extent that inflation is fully anticipated, contracts among wage and salary earners and their employers will take account of this anticipated inflation either explicitly by employing an escalator clause, or implicitly by scheduling nominal wage increases through the contract life.

Inflation and the Poor

It is always argued that inflation hurts the poor, especially those on fixed incomes, such as pensioners, retired persons, disabled people, and the like.

How Inflation Affects Fixed Incomes

However, if we look at the bottom line of Table 7-2, we find that transfer payments, defined as income provided by governments to individuals for which no productive activity is demanded, increased over the two periods studied. In fact, Social Security benefits have risen much faster

Table 7-2 Shifts in Percentage Shares of National Income Due to Inflation, 1950–1973

On average, wages and salaries increased as a percentage of national income during the period 1950 to 1971. However, during the inflationary period of 1972 to 1973, their share actually dropped by 0.4 percent. The reverse was true for corporate profits. Their share of national income fell by 6.2 percent over the period 1950 to 1971, but they rose by almost 1 percent during the 1972 to 1973 period.

INCOME	1950–1971	1972–1973
Wages and salaries	+6.6%	−0.4%
Unincorporated businesses		
Nonfarm	−3.8	−0.1
Farm	−3.7	+0.4
Rents	−1.0	+0.2
Interest	+3.4	0
Corporate profits*	−6.2	+0.7
Transfer payments†	+4.7	+0.1

*After inventory valuation adjustment, before payment of income taxes
†Not a part of national income

Source: U.S. Department of Commerce

than the rate of inflation. Moreover, since 1974 there has been a provision in the benefits system that links these benefits to the consumer price index. As the consumer price index goes up, so too do Social Security benefits without further legislation. It is largely due to this rapid increase in Social Security benefits that we cannot say inflation has hurt the aged more than other groups in society.

The Poor Man's Price Index

It has also been argued that the poor are hurt more than most by inflation. In fact, researchers at the Institute for Research on Poverty at the University of Wisconsin have tried to verify this contention. They have concluded that the prices of the commodities purchased by the poor have risen more rapidly than the general price level. What they have really done is come up with a Poor Man's Price Index.[2] Remember that the consumer price index measures the average change in prices based on the importance of various goods and services for an "average urban" family. This weighting scheme may be inappropriate for those who consume a disproportionate share of items whose price has risen relatively faster than that of other items. This would be true, for example, for medical care services since they have risen much more rapidly than the consumer price index has. The aged spend a disproportionately large share of their income on medical care services, and the consumer price index does not adequately reflect what the rate of inflation has been for them.

It is interesting to note that the price index for poor people rose less rapidly than the government consumer price index over the period from 1953 to 1967. However, if this comparison were extended through the mid-1970s, particularly over the years when the cost of food rose rapidly in comparison to other prices, the opposite would likely be true. That is, the price index for poor people has probably been rising during the first half of the 1970s at a faster rate than the CPI. Thus, the poor would be relatively worse off during this period, even if they received wage gains that took account of "the" rate of inflation as measured by the Bureau of Labor Statistics.

National Income and Inflation

What has happened to the share of national income going to different classes of income earners in our society? If we look at the data

[2]R. G. Hollister and J. L. Palmer, *The Impact of Inflation on the Poor,* sec. II, Madison, Wis.: Institute for Research on Poverty, 1969.

for various subperiods since 1950, we can see quite clearly the varying effects inflation has had on the distribution of income depending on whether inflation had been anticipated or not. We see in Table 7-2 that the percentage of national income going to wages and salaries actually increased by 6.6 percent during the period 1950 to 1971. If you look at Figure 7-1 you will see that during this period the rate of inflation was either effectively nil, or at best grew very slowly until 1965. Then inflation accelerated to a relatively high level at the beginning of this decade. It might be said, then, that in the early period the rate of inflation was more or less expected. At the same time, there was a reduction in the share of national income going to business profits.

However, if we look at the 1972 to 1973 period, just the reverse is shown. Wages and salaries dropped by 0.4 percent in terms of their percentage of national income. Nominal corporate profits went up 0.7 percent. The difference can, in part, be explained by the fact that the inflationary burst in 1972 to 1973 was largely unexpected.[3] Thus, labor incomes did not rise as rapidly as the rate of inflation.

What can we say about who bears the burden of inflation? We have seen that that depends on whether the inflation is anticipated or unanticipated and on which groups are net creditors and net debtors. Moreover, even for those on "fixed" income we must redefine our definition of *fixed* to take account of any increases in benefits such as those that occur with Social Security. That is the only way we can come to a reasonable conclusion about inflation's effects on individuals in our society.

[3]But we must be careful here because nominal corporate profits reflected inflationary adjustments in existing inventories, so that at least part of the gain in profits was an illusion.

Unemployment and Inflation

The last chapter pointed out that the business cycle involves ups and downs in both employment and price levels. According to many observers, there is a relationship between unemployment and inflation. If we look at the historical record in the United States and in other countries, we do indeed find some relationship between rising prices and high employment. In fact, we might consider this to be another theory of inflation. Price variation can perhaps be explained through changes in unemployment—low levels of unemployment indicate high economic activity, which puts pressure on wages and ultimately on prices; high levels of unemployment indicate slack economic activity, relatively fewer pressures on wages and prices, and hence less inflation. The policy question that arises is whether or not a definite relationship exists between inflation and unemployment. If there is a trade-off between the two, should we pursue a certain rate of inflation in order to reduce the rate of unemployment?

The Phillips Curve

Almost two decades ago Professor A. W. Phillips discovered that in Great Britain wages rose rapidly when the unemployment rate was declining and rose more slowly when it was rising. He drew a curve showing this relationship, and since the time his article appeared, that curve has been called the **Phillips curve.** Although Phillips' original analysis was in terms of wage rate increases and the unemployment rate, economists have contended that the relationship also holds between price increases and the unemployment rate; there seems to be a close relationship between wage rate change, and consumer price level changes.

We show a hypothetical Phillips curve in Figure 7-3.

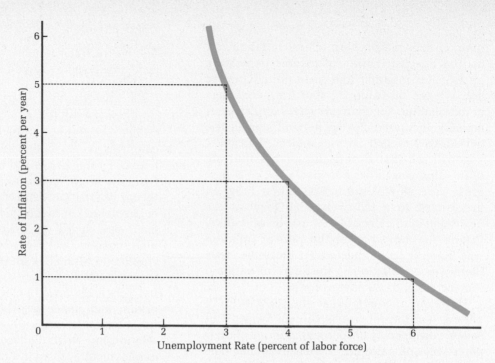

FIGURE 7-3 A Hypothetical Phillips Curve

The Phillips curve shows the relationship between the unemployment rate and the rate of inflation. If we want a 3 percent unemployment rate, we presumably have to live with 5 percent annual inflation. If we don't want to live with 5 percent inflation but only 3 percent, we will have to "buy it" with more unemployment since a 3 percent rate of inflation is associated with a 4 percent rate of unemployment.

The Trade-Off

The implication of Phillips' analysis is that a *trade-off* does exist between unemployment and inflation. Let's look again at our hypothetical Phillips curve in Figure 7-3. If we are at an unemployment rate of 6 percent, and we want to go to an unemployment rate of 4 percent, we have to allow for an increase in the rate of the rise in prices of 2 percent. This poses a dilemma. Inflation is assumed to be an economic "bad" and something that must be avoided. But so too is unemployment. The implication of Phillips' analysis is that one cannot simultaneously have full employment and no inflation; one must make a trade-off. Policymakers must decide what the trade-off should be and walk the line between an "acceptable" amount of inflation and a "tolerable" level of unemployment.

The Phillips curve relationship for the United States has not proved very stable over time. The trade-off numbers seem to be changing, so that policymakers can't really be sure that a given level of inflation will repeatedly allow the same rate of unemployment. The trade-off between unemployment and inflation has become increasingly worse since the mid-1950s. In 1955, for example, a 6 percent unemployment rate implied a 1 percent rate of rise in prices, but the same unemployment rate in 1974 was associated with a 12 percent rate of rise in prices. We will come back later, in our discussion of income-determination models, to the implications of this trade-off, which worsens every year. Here it is sufficient to say that the Phillips curve relationship has not stood up well in its original form. There are now a number of more refined views of what the Phillips curve might look like. These views take into account other variables besides actual rates of inflation and actual unemployment rates.

One of the most important other variables

is individuals' expectations of future inflation rates. The importance of distinguishing between expected and unexpected inflation was covered when we discussed the burden of rising prices and who bears it. The same argument holds when discussing the trade-off between inflation and unemployment.

Unemployment and Inflation Added Together

Almost everybody is convinced that unemployment and high rates of inflation are social evils. We might get a meaningful measure of economic discomfort from combining these two social evils. Arthur Okun of The Brookings Institution and former Chairman of the Council of Economic Advisers constructed such a discomfort index for the economy by combining the unemployment rate and the annual rate of change in consumer prices. Over the last two decades the discomfort index has grown dramatically. This can be seen in Table 7-3. Back in 1955 the discomfort index was only 4.0 percent. The estimate for 1975 was a whopping 15 percent. If we take Okun's index seriously, we must conclude that things seem to have gone awry in the American economy.

Stagflation

The combination of unacceptably high rates of unemployment and inflation has been commonly called **stagflation**—inflationary recessions, or periods when unemployment and inflation increase simultaneously. Economists and policymakers now see that the standard explanations of inflation and recession are no longer valid when both inflation and recession occur simultaneously.

Many policymakers believe that one of the main goals of an economic system should be to generate economic growth. Since we live in an era of continued inflation, the problem facing the nation during the 1970s has become one of preventing economic stagnation without allowing inflation to take off. To fight rising unemployment, or recession, policy tools could be put into effect, but these might increase inflation.

One solution to the problem, which we will talk about in Issue I-10, is wage and price controls. But as we shall see in that issue, controls

---

Table 7-3 An Index of Discomfort

Former Chairman of the Council of Economic Advisers, Arthur Okun, once suggested that we could measure "discomfort." All we need do is add the annual inflation rate and the rate of unemployment. If his measure of discomfort has any accuracy, then the economy is in a much worse position in the 1970s than it was in the previous 15 years.

YEAR	DISCOMFORT INDEX
1955	4.8
1956	7.0
1957	7.3
1958	8.6
1959	7.0
1960	7.0
1961	7.4
1962	6.7
1963	7.3
1964	6.4
1965	6.4
1966	7.2
1967	6.8
1968	8.3
1969	9.6
1970	10.4
1971	9.3
1972	9.0
1973	11.1
1974	16.6
1975	15.0

have not cured stagflation. Economists and politicians, as well as men and women in the street, cannot agree about which evil is the lesser one, unemployment or inflation. At the beginning of the Ford administration, inflation was the number-one enemy. However, within not too many months, recession became the number-one enemy, and all the policymakers were talking about what could be done to lower the rate of unemployment. By the time you read this text, inflation may again have become the number-one evil.

The Use of Models in Policymaking

Is there any way we can change the economic scene? Could we not somehow slow down the rate of inflation and cut out periods of severe cyclical unemployment? These are, of course, the dilemmas and the questions facing policymakers today. These policymakers, in coming up with answers and schemes to alleviate economic suffering, must rely on models. We have already presented several models of price-level determination, but we have yet to present a complete model of income determination. What is it that determines the level of income and output and hence the level of prices? We will turn to this question in the following unit. What we will do is set out the economic variables to be discussed and then construct some simple models of income and employment determination. You will then see what goes into the thinking of economists concerned with keeping our economic ship on an even keel.

Definitions of New Terms

Inflation: A sustained rise in prices.

Consumer Price Index: A statistical measure of the average of prices of a specified set of goods and services purchased by wage earners in urban areas.

Wholesale Price Index: A statistical measure of the average of prices of those commodities that firms purchase from other firms in large quantities.

Implicit Price Deflator: The general price level of all goods and services, found statistically by equating the ratio of GNP expressed in current dollars and real GNP.

Quantity Theory of Money and Prices: A classical proposition which predicts that changes in the price level are directly related to changes in the money supply. The quantity theory of money and prices is based on the equation of exchange.

Demand-Pull Inflation: Inflation caused by the aggregate demand exceeding the full-employment supply of goods.

Cost-Push Inflation: Rising prices caused by rising production costs.

Phillips Curve: A curve showing the relationship between unemployment and inflation. The Phillips curve gives the trade-off between unemployment and inflation.

Stagflation: A period of deficient aggregate demand and rising prices. In other words, a period of both economic stagnation and inflation.

1. The history of the United States has been a history of rising prices, although the rise in the price level has been erratic. It has almost always gone up during war periods. The rate of inflation in the United States is less than in almost all the other countries in the world. Some countries have experienced hyperinflations, where the price level has risen by phenomenal amounts.

2. We measure inflation by a change in some statistical price index. We can use either the consumer price index, the wholesale price index, or the implicit price deflator for GNP.

3. All price indices have biases.

4. There are many theories of inflation. One is demand-pull inflation, which is caused by aggregate demand exceeding the full-employment supply of goods, services, and productive workers. Demand-pull inflation can occur because of overexpansionary monetary and fiscal policy on the part of the government or because of overexpansionary investment activity on the part of individual businesspersons.

5. Cost-push inflation is a theory which asserts that inflation is caused by rising costs. There are two variants on the cost-push inflation argument. One involves union power; the other concerns big business monopoly power.

6. The union power cost-push inflation argument contends that due to the power of unions, employers must give in to union demands for excessive wages. These employers then pass on the higher wages to the consumer in the form of higher prices.

7. The big business monopoly power cost-push inflation argument maintains that powerful corporations are able to raise their prices whenever they want to increase their profits. Each time the corporation raises its prices to increase its profits, the cost of living goes up. Workers then demand higher wages to make up for the loss in their standard of living, thereby giving corporations an excuse to raise prices again.

8. During a period of unexpected inflation, creditors lose and debtors gain because the latter are able to repay debts in "cheap" dollars. Of course, if everybody anticipates rising prices, the interest rate will rise to take account of this future expected depreciation.

9. Anybody who holds cash during an inflationary period loses part of his or her real income as prices rise. The only way to avoid this loss is to not hold any checking account balances or currency in your pocket.

10. Historically, people with fixed incomes have suffered from inflation in the United States because most inflations have been unanticipated.

11. A British economist, A. W. Phillips, found an empirical relationship between the level of unemployment and the rate of wages and prices

in Great Britain. This relationship between unemployment and inflation has been called the Phillips curve. It shows the trade-off between inflation and unemployment.

12. Stagflation occurred in the United States and in many other countries in the world during the late 1960s and 1970s. It is probably the number-one problem of economists.

Questions for Thought and Discussion

1. You are a hard-working record store salesperson. You are given a raise of 10 percent at the end of the year. But during that year prices went up 10 percent. Are you any better off because of your raise?

2. People seem to be against inflation today, but they favored inflation in the 1880s. What is different about these two periods?

3. If you are sure that inflation is going to continue, what can you do to protect yourself against it?

4. Are there any groups in society that are helped by inflation? Does your answer depend on whether or not the inflation was anticipated?

5. Why would deflation or falling prices "hurt" lots of people in the United States today? Again, does your answer depend on whether the deflation was expected or unexpected?

Selected References

Brimmer, Andrew F., "Inflation and Income Distribution in the United States," *Review of Economics and Statistics*, vol. 53, no. 1, February 1971, pp. 37–48.

Economic Report of the President, various issues, Washington, D.C.: U.S. Government Printing Office.

Federal Reserve Bank of Philadelphia, Department of Research, *Economics of Inflation*, Philadelphia, 1974.

Lekachman, Robert, *Inflation: The Permanent Problem of Boom and Bust*, New York: Random House, 1973.

Morley, Samuel A., *The Economics of Inflation*, Hinsdale, Ill.: Dryden Press, 1971.

Okun, Arthur M., *The Political Economy of Prosperity*, New York: W. W. Norton, 1970.

Ozaki, Robert S., *Inflation, Recession . . . and All That*, New York: Holt, Rinehart and Winston, 1972.

THE USE OF ECONOMYWIDE ESCALATOR CLAUSES

Contracts That Take Account of Inflation

In the last chapter we pointed out several distinct problems associated with inflation. Unanticipated inflation seemed to affect different groups differently, in particular, debtors gain at the expense of creditors who are paid off with cheaper dollars. When we discussed the trade-off between unemployment and inflation, the policy implication was a clear one: Any reduction in the rate of inflation would lead to an increase in the unemployment rate.

A number of economic commentators have recently suggested a way out of these problems. Their solution is to institute widespread *indexing* of the economy. Indexing is nothing more than tacking a cost-of-living escalator clause onto a contract. That would mean, for example, that if you signed a contract to work for $10,000 per year this year and the contract had an escalator clause, you would be guaranteed increases in your nominal wages commensurate with increases in the cost of living. Additionally, you probably would have bargained for an increase in your real wages as well.

Escalator clauses are basically a method by which economic agents can contract in real terms rather than in nominal terms. In the preceding example the contract was for a level or annual growth in a level of real, as opposed to nominal, wages. The inclusion of the cost-of-living escalator clause, or indexing agreement, makes both parties to the contract indifferent to the rate of inflation; this is equivalent to both parties fully anticipating the rate of inflation.

Escalator Clauses Today

At least 50 million Americans are today covered in one way or another by escalator clauses. Under present law those individuals who receive benefits from Social Security are guaranteed increases that match the rate of inflation. This cost-of-living escalator was legislated into Social Security a few years ago. Today there are at least 6 million workers covered by employment contracts that have cost-of-living clauses. Benefits under the federal government's food stamp program are also linked to the rate of inflation. Moreover, it is virtually impossible to obtain a large long-term commercial loan at a fixed interest rate; rather, the interest rate to be paid is specified in relation to some market rate of interest that presumably will mirror the ups and downs in the rate of inflation.

A Short History of Escalator Clauses

Indexing is not a new idea. Back in 1707, a Cambridge don, William Fleetwood, made an attempt to estimate changes in the price level over a six-century period to set a limit on the outside income that holders of fellowships should be permitted to receive in 1707 money, as compared with 1107 money. In other words, he was trying to tie the outside-income limit of fellowship holders to the cost of living. Some 50 years later a form of indexing was used in Massachusetts Bay Colony, and during the same period Oxford and Cambridge Universities in England rented out their land for payments in grain, thus implicitly ensuring against price fluctuations (assuming that the price of grain moved in step with the overall cost of living). Again in England, payment of tithes to the Church was linked to an average of barley, wheat, and oat prices—a form of escalator clause, or cost-of-living index.

In 1886, the English economist Alfred Marshall enthusiastically supported what he called the "tabular standard."[1] Not too many years later the American economist Irving Fisher also came out in favor of the "tabular standard." He was, in fact, successful in persuading a manufacturing company (which he had taken part in founding) to issue securities paying interest (dividends) linked to some sort of cost-of-living index.

After World War I, in the United States changes in the cost of living were given much attention in wage adjustments. However, cost-of-living (escalator) clauses rapidly lost popularity when prices began to drop from their 1920 peaks. Apparently, workers wanted them when prices were rising but not when prices were falling.

The federal government inserted a cost-of-living clause in the Economy Act passed in March 1933. This act authorized the President to make federal salary reductions based on the cost of living.

In the early years of World War II at least 40 percent of all agreements between manufacturers and unions had wage-reopening clauses that permitted wage increases to match any price increases. However, the wartime wage stabilization program suspended most of these reopening clauses from 1942 to the end of the war.

There was little interest in escalator clauses during the 1950s, when prices were fairly stable. By the early

[1] Alfred Marshall, "Reply to the Royal Commission on the Depression of Trade and Industry," 1886, reproduced in *Official Papers by Alfred Marshall*, London: Macmillan, 1926.

1960s only 2 million workers were covered by escalators. This, however, was to rise to over 6 million by the middle of the 1970s, when workers saw their nominal wages lagging behind the double-digit annual increases in the cost of living.

Brazil—A Case Study of Indexing

Brazil is perhaps the one country that has been studied the most for its nationwide indexation. The Brazilians call this a regime of "monetary correction." It started with laws passed in 1964. Basically it involves adjusting the nominal value of such things as mortgage payments, savings account balances, and rentals to take account of changes in the cost of living. The adjustment formulas are based on estimated inflation rates. For example, wage increases are based on an average of *real*, that is, corrected-for-inflation, wages prevailing over the previous 24 months plus prospective increases in productivity and prices. Usually, the measure of the rate of inflation is taken from a general wholesale price index.

Take the example of a savings account. Say that the balance a Brazilian has in a savings bank is 10,000 cruzeiros. Say also that this person is receiving an annual 5 percent rate of interest on that savings account. At the end of 3 months, the cost-of-living increase has been 4 percent. What happens is that the Brazilian's savings account is increased by 4 percent, or 400 cruzeiros. This means that the interest rate being paid on the original account balance

will remain at 5 percent because nothing will have to be subtracted for losses in the purchasing power of that money left in the bank. The savings account is therefore indexed. Its nominal value increases sufficiently so that it does not lose any of its purchasing power.

Another important area where monetary correction is applied in Brazil concerns the value of machines and other items used by businesses. In a period of raging inflation, a machine will increase in nominal market value, even though it is wearing out, because its replacement cost will be rising so rapidly. This increase in the market value of machines and the like was, until the mid-1960s, taxed as part of profits by the Brazilian government. However, since monetary correction was applied to machines and other assets used by businesses, the government has not collected taxes on such fictitious aspects of profits, that is, on the rise in the value of business assets due to general inflation.

According to some observers, the Brazilian indexing experience has proved successful. While the rate of inflation has fallen, the rate of production growth in the economy has risen, and there has been little apparent trade-off between unemployment and inflation. This is not to say, however, that indexing is the cause of the reduced rate of inflation in Brazil; in fact, no one who supports indexing contends that, if adopted, it will reduce the rate of growth of prices. Indexing simply speeds the adjustment to changes in the rate of inflation, *either up or down*.

The Brazilian experience has prompted some economists and

politicians to suggest at least a modified form of indexing for the United States. Let's now look at some of those suggestions, which relate mainly to the government sector.

Indexing in the United States

Proponents of indexing suggest that at the very least our government should put its house in order by indexing its tax system and the way it borrows money from the public.

Indexing Taxes

Remember from Chapter 5 that we have a progressive income tax in the United States. That has important implications during an inflationary period.

Personal Income Taxes What if you had an increase in wages that just equaled the increase in the cost of living? You would probably consider your real standard of living, or real wage rate, unchanged because you would have just been compensated for the rate of inflation. But you would be wrong because if that wage increase put you into a higher income tax bracket, you would have to pay a larger percentage of your gross income in taxes to the federal government. What does that mean? Simply that during periods of relatively rapid inflation, when individuals' incomes are pushed into higher and higher income tax brackets, the percentage of income going to the federal government in the form of individual income taxes will rise without Congress having to legislate this rise.

Also consider the tax-saving benefits of a fixed exemption, say, of $750 per dependent. If you are allowed to exempt $750 of annual income from taxation for each person, including yourself, who depends on your salary, the exemption is worth less every year that the price level rises.

It has also been suggested that the base for calculating capital gains should be corrected for rises in prices. For example, if you bought a share of stock one year and sold it the next year for 10 percent more than what you originally paid for it, right now you would have to pay taxes on all of that 10 percent increase. However, if that 10 percent increase merely reflected a 10 percent rate of inflation, you are being taxed on a fictitious capital gain. The suggestion here, then, is to adjust the base, or "buying price," of capital assets for price-level changes before you figure out the capital gains taxes you must pay. In this simple example, your base would rise by 10 percent, so that the selling price would just equal the buying price (in constant dollars) and you would owe no capital gains taxes.

Essentially, then, indexing personal income taxes would merely take account of rises in the cost of living and hence would not allow the federal government to obtain an increasing share of personal income merely because there were high rates of inflation.

The Corporate Income Tax The corporate income tax would be altered in a similar manner to the personal income tax. The present $25,000 dividing line between the normal tax and the so-called surtax would be increased every year according to the rate of inflation. Capital gains would be altered as mentioned above, and so would some other technical aspects of how corporations are taxed.

Government Bonds

If you purchased a government bond that nominally yields 5 percent a year and the rate of inflation is 5 percent a year, what is your real rate of return? Zero percent. Actually, it is even less than that because presently you will have to pay federal income taxes on the 5 percent a year nominal rate of return. To counter this perverse incentive to savers, it is suggested that government bonds be indexed. This could be done in a variety of ways; however, the most often suggested idea is indexing the principal, that is, the face value of the bond. It would work as follows. If you bought a bond one year for $1,000 and it promised to pay you 3 percent a year, you would, in fact, receive $30 a year in income from that bond; when you redeemed it, you would also get a percentage of the principal equal to whatever the cumulative inflation percentage had been over the ensuing period. If the aggregated inflation had been 50 percent, instead of $1,000, you would get back $1,500. That would mean that your real rate of return would have been 3 percent no matter what the rate of inflation. You would not have to worry about losing out because the rate of inflation exceeded the interest rate being paid.

The Private Sector

Few economists have come out for any obligation on the part of the private sector to index its contracts. Indexing of private contracts has already occurred on a voluntary basis and will continue to occur as long as the rate of inflation remains variable. Some senators have, on occasion, suggested that all wage contracts in the private sector be indexed, but such proposals rarely have been taken seriously.

The Pros and the Cons of Indexing

Opponents of indexing claim that it will remove any pressure to reduce the rate of inflation. If everything were indexed, then no one would

have any incentive to reduce the rate of inflation, or so the argument goes. Still others believe that indexing will have an inflationary impact on the economy. After all, the reasoning goes, every increase in prices will be multiplied many times before there is any halt since it will automatically be spread throughout the economy. Lastly, it has been argued persuasively that, at least with the Brazilian experience, monetary correction leads to more rather than to fewer inequities throughout the economy. Specifically, according to one student of the Brazilian situation, the distribution of income has become more skewed in favor of the upper classes.[2]

On the plus side of indexing are equally compelling arguments. Indexing would allow relative prices to allocate resources naturally—without the distortion due to differential adjustments to our variable rates of inflation. In essence, any rate of inflation would affect the entire economy with equal speed because everything would be indexed to that rate of inflation. But perhaps more

[2]Albert Fishlow, "Indexing Brazilian Style: Inflation without Tears?", *Brookings Papers on Economic Activity*, I, 1974, pp. 261, 282.

important, according to this argument, would be the effect of indexing on the unemployment-inflation trade-off that we outlined in the last chapter. According to the proponents of indexing, if everything were indexed, the rate of inflation would have little impact on the labor market. We could effectively reduce the rate of inflation without paying the relatively high unemployment cost implied by the standard Phillips curve analysis. If one looks at the results in Brazil, one can obtain support for this view: Since 1964, the Brazilian rate of inflation has fallen dramatically, yet the rate of unemployment has beaten the Phillips curve; it has not risen in any systematic manner.

Indexing the government tax system would certainly lead to fewer government revenues unless they were specifically voted by Congress.

Taxpayers' take-home pay in real terms would not shrink just because of the inflation, nor would the real aftertax profits of corporations. The application of indexing to government bonds would give savers an outlet for their savings that would appear extremely attractive relative to other possibilities at the present time. This might encourage more saving and less consumption.

Will We Have More Indexing?

Is a "tabular standard" or "monetary-correction" system in the cards for the United States? Certainly, in the private sector we can safely predict that as inflation continues at historically high and fairly unstable rates, more indexing will occur because it protects both parties to a contract. (Don't forget that indexed contracts have to take account of lower rates of inflation too.) Whether the government will index its tax system is quite another matter. Finally, numerous government officials have suggested the indexing of some government securities, and that suggestion may be a reality by the time you read this.

Indexing has its costs, however, and it is not preferred to a situation of stable prices. After all, with a system of complete indexing, you have to have more contracts written, buy more bookkeepers' time, spend more money on price schedules and their revision, and so on. The economic world preferred by most would be one with stable prices.

Questions for Thought and Discussion

1. Can any argument be made that indexing changes the rate of inflation?
2. Who would gain and who would lose if nationwide indexing became a reality?
3. If the rate of inflation were relatively high but constant, would indexing be necessary?
4. How is indexing related to the difference between anticipated and unanticipated inflation?

Selected References

Jevons, Stanley W., *Money and the Mechanism of Exchange,* 1898 ed., New York: Appleton, pp. 318–326.

Krieger, Ronald A., "Inflation and the 'Brazilian Solution'," *Challenge,* September–October 1974, pp. 42–43.

Organization for Economic Cooperation and Development, Committee on Financial Markets, *Indexation of Fixed Interest Securities,* Paris: O.E.C.D., 1973.

DIRECT ATTEMPTS AT COMBATING INFLATION

The Past As the Future

On August 15, 1971, the United States government, by way of an executive order, froze prices, rents, wages, and salaries for a period of 90 days. This was the first instance in the peacetime history of the United States that wage and price controls had been instituted. These controls were to last, in one form or another, until April 30, 1974.

By now, most individuals are aware of what wage and price controls are—a form of legal limits on certain prices in our economy that have been used in the United States and elsewhere (particularly during wartime) to fight against inflation. Perhaps what many people do not realize is that wage and price controls have a lengthy history that dates back thousands of years.

Controls in Times Past

Price controls were, of course, not new to the American nation. They were first used during the Revolutionary War, and they date back quite a bit earlier than that. We know, for example, that in 1800 B.C. the ruler

of Babylonia decreed that anyone caught violating his wage-price freeze would be drowned. It seems that Babylonia endured more than 1000 years of such price fixing. Another example has been cited by historians in A.D. 301. The Roman Emperor Diocletian, in an edict called "Commanded Cheapness," fixed the maximum price on beef, grain, eggs, and clothing and prescribed the death penalty for violators. He also set wage ceilings for teachers, lawyers, physicians, tailors, and bricklayers. But, according to Lactantius, writing in 314, "There was . . . much bloodshed upon very slight and trifling accounts; and the people brought provisions no more to market since they could not get a reasonable price for them; and this increased the dearth so much that after many had died by it, the law itself was laid aside."

In 1636, during the early years of this nation, the American Puritans imposed a code of price and wage limitations. Anyone caught violating the code was considered as bad as "adulterers and whoremongers." Even before the Declaration of Independence, the Continental Congress

had set price ceilings. Later, a few states enacted price-control laws. General George Washington complained of excessive rates of inflation, as did others at the time. Sporadic attempts at price controls were highly controversial and certainly not comprehensive. All such efforts were largely abandoned by 1780.

Controls in America during World War II

After starting the huge war production effort in the early 1940s, Congress felt it necessary to pass the Price Control Act of 1942, which established the Office of Price Administration (OPA). The conditions for the implementation of direct controls were, of course, quite favorable. Most citizens were willing to make sacrifices to speed up a successful conclusion of the war.

Regulations During that time, numerous specific price schedules were established. In 1942, Price Emergency Regulation No. 2 noted that rents were climbing too fast for our good health and therefore established rent controls. Price Emergency Regulation No. 3 of October 1942, pointed out that despite regulations, farm prices and wages had moved up, thus forcing continuous amendments and additions to the regulations. By the middle of 1943, the OPA was overhauled: The authority for setting prices was taken away from the main office in Washington and given to the field offices. Advisory committees were appointed; ration books were issued with coupons that allowed you to spend your money only on an amount of the rationed commodity.

By 1944, there were almost 350,000 price control volunteers in addition to about 70,000 paid employees. The banking system was handling 5 billion ration coupons per month by 1944. Wholesale prices in the United States rose only 14 percent from November 1941 to August 1945. By 1946, however, people were no longer willing to make wartime sacrifices. Much of the wartime

price-control machinery was bypassed. It became extremely profitable to break the law.

The Black Market We can analyze the effect of a **black market** by using the supply and demand analysis presented in Chapter 3. Look at Figure I-10.1. Assume that this represents the demand and supply schedule for automobiles at the end of World War II. The equilibrium price would be at P_e, where the demand schedule and supply schedule cross each other. However, the government sets a maximum legal price of P_1. But at that price the quantity supplied by the manufacturers in Detroit would only be Q_s, and the quantity demanded would be Q_d. Obviously, there would be an excess

demand. The actual supply schedule, if the controls were properly enforced at the manufacturing stage, would now be equal to SS'—that is, the supply schedule slopes up until it gets to the intersection with the legal price, at which point it becomes vertical. The intersection of the new supply curve and the old demand curve is at E', or a price of $P_{\acute{e}}$. The black market price is obtained by customers making under-the-counter payments to retailers and other such gimmicks.

Repressed Inflation After the price controls were lifted in the United States, the wholesale price index jumped 55 percent from August 1945 to August 1948. Some economists maintained that the war

BLACK MARKETS

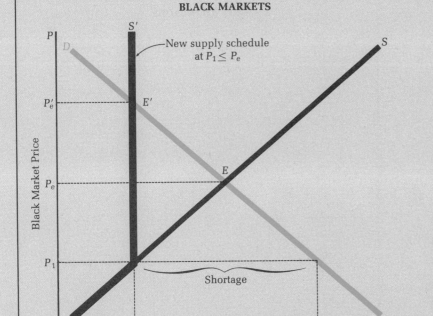

FIGURE I-10.1

The demand curve is *DD*. The supply curve is *SS*. The equilibrium price is P_e. The government, however, steps in and imposes a maximum price of P_1. At that lower price the quantity demanded will be Q_d, but the quantity supplied will only be Q_s. There is a shortage, and black markets develop. The price is bid up in the black market to $P_{\acute{e}}$ *because* that is where the new supply curve, *SS'*, intersects the old demand curve at *E'*. Black market prices can be obtained by any number of devices, such as under-the-counter payments to retailers.

period was one of *repressed* inflation because total aggregate demand was breaking at the seams while prices were not allowed to rise to cut off part of that demand. (Remember from Chapter 3 what happens when you move *up* the demand curve for goods and services.)

Controls in Other Countries

The United States is not the only modern country that has imposed wage and price controls during both wartime and peacetime. We look at the Dutch experience for an example of such controls.

The Netherlands

In 1945, the Dutch government passed a labor relations act that provided mediators with fairly strong powers to control wages and labor markets. At that time the socialists were in power, and the so-called incomes policy of the early postwar period seemed to be quite effective. Europeans have typically called direct wage controls an *incomes policy* because there is an attempt to maintain people's relative incomes at the same level. More specifically, there is an attempt to maintain the same distribution between the portions of national income that go to capitalists and to workers.

Labor Shortages By 1951 there was a high rate of inflation; with fairly static money wages, real wages (money wages divided by the price level) fell. The situation is shown in Figure I-10.2. On the horizontal axis is the quantity of workers and on the vertical axis is the *real* wage rate, W/P. If W goes up by 100 percent and P goes up by 100 percent, W/P remains the same. We start out in an equilibrium situation where there

FIGURE I-10.2

The demand for labor is shown as DD, downward sloping as always. The supply of labor is shown as SS. The equilibrium real wage rate (the money wage rate divided by the price level) is established at W_0 divided by P_0 or at E, where the demand and supply curves intersect. Prices have risen in this particular situation to P_1, where P_1 is higher than P_0. At the old nominal wage rate, the real wage rate falls with the higher price level. It falls to W_0 divided by P_1. At that real wage rate, there is an excess demand for workers on the part of employers. The excess demand is the difference between Q_d and Q_s. This is the situation that occurred in the Netherlands following 1951, during their *incomes policy*.

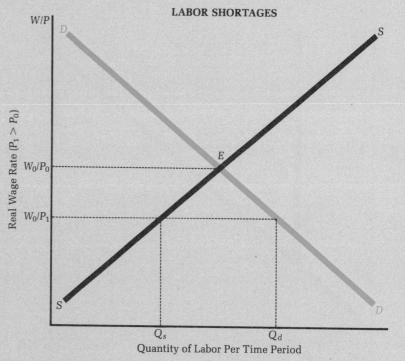

LABOR SHORTAGES

is no excess demand or supply of workers in Holland. That is a real wage rate of W_0/P_0. Now, W_0 is fairly constant because of the incomes policy, but prices are rising. Thus, real wages fall to W_0/P_1, where P_1 is a price level that is greater than P_0. At this real wage rate, the quantity of workers demanded by firms is Q_d and the quantity supplied is Q_s. The excess demand for workers is $Q_d - Q_s$.

Labor shortages inevitably developed, and there was considerable pressure for additional labor resources, especially in industries making a high profit. Employers who had the opportunity to make more money by producing more goods were willing to grant wage increases that exceeded the legal limits. This type of behavior on the part of employers started to undermine the guidelines. There followed a period of prosecutions, fines, and even jail sentences for employers caught offering black market wages.

The Result of Wage Controls The guidelines for wages became increasingly unrealistic throughout the 1950s as the economy of the Netherlands was booming. Finally, in 1959, a more conservative government was put into office. It allowed more flexible limits on wage settlements, and the increased use of collective bargaining was permitted at the industry level. But in 1961 there was a law passed that limited wage increases to increases in productivity. Throughout the 1960s, the government continued to attempt to curtail wage increases, but its ambitious attempts fell into complete collapse by the beginning of the 1970s.

The Rest of Western Europe

The Dutch experience is typical of other Western European countries. Rather than go into a detailed analysis of their experiences, we refer the interested reader to several studies on European income policies presented in the list of Selected References. The United Kingdom, Sweden, France, West Germany, Austria, Denmark, and a number of other countries have tried over and over again to use wage and price controls to combat inflation. If we judge from casual evidence—whether their rates of inflation are lower with than without an incomes policy—we do not get a picture that would support the use of controls. The same conclusion is generally reached by observers of the American scene. Let's now look at what has happened in the United States over the past decade and a half.

The American Experience

During the past 15 years or so, we have heard subtle and not-so-subtle exhortations from the government to restrain our wage and price demands. These exhortations have taken the form of guideposts and jawboning.

Guideposts

Even during the early 1960s, John Kennedy's Council of Economic Advisers came up with a set of **guideposts** for business and labor; these were rules of the game that would prevent inflation from taking off. In the 1962 *Economic Report of the President,* the Council of Economic Advisers presented a formal statement of guideposts for wage increases. The Council indicated that annual increases should not exceed about 3.5 percent, which was the annual rate of growth of productivity in the economy. The guideposts did not come out of the blue. From 1957 to 1961, every *Economic Report of the President* stressed, in one form or another, that private pricing should be tempered to create stable prices. In other words, restraint on the part of business and workers had been requested. The 1960 *Economic Report* was explicit in stating that wage increases should not exceed the growth in average *national* productivity. Further, the *Report* suggested that price reductions be made in sectors experiencing exceptionally rapid productivity growth since those sectors would be experiencing lower unit labor costs.

Jawboning

The guideposts did not have any legal standing; thus, the only means of enforcement available was public exposure by the Council of Economic Advisers or by the President. This process has been quaintly called **jawboning.** Kennedy did quite a bit of it, getting U.S. Steel, for example, to rescind a price increase in 1962 by making it a national issue. Johnson and Nixon both seemed to be less effective jawboners than Kennedy. In any event, business resented the selective political pressure that the President's Office brought against them, as this seemed to be an extralegal exercise of power.

Eventually, the guideposts broke down. In the President's *Annual Economic Report* of January 1969, the Council of Economic Advisers, although staunchly maintaining the indisputable correctness of the wage-price guidelines, finally admit-

ted that excess aggregate demand pressures had made the guidelines unenforceable—at least for the time being. In that portion of the report, no numerical price and wage guides were set for the coming year.

Controlling Prices and Wages in the 1970s

We started this issue with reference to the first wage and price controls ever instituted in the peacetime history of the United States. They lasted for a period of almost 3 years, taking on various forms, including absolute freezes on wages and prices as well as less-stringent, modified restraints on those same wages and prices.

Did they work? It is very difficult to answer such a question, even after the fact, because we do not know what the rate of inflation would have been had no controls been in effect. The only data we have are data on published prices during the period of control. Let's see what they look like. In Figure I-10.3 we show the rate of change of consumer prices before and after the nearly 3-year period of controls. We notice first that consumer prices were rising at a slower rate just prior to the imposition of the controls than they were during the middle of the control period. We also notice that immediately after the controls were removed, prices started rising at relatively higher rates. This is conflicting evidence. On the one hand, it shows that prices were rising faster during the controls than before, but on the other hand, it shows that prices were rising faster *after* the controls. Perhaps prices were just "catching up"

to where they would have been had no such controls been in effect.

The Nitty-Gritty

Everybody who tuned into what was happening during the wage-and-price-control period of the early 1970s knows about the problems that arose. It became literally impossible to effectively control all wages and prices, so the controllers focused on only the most critical prices and wages in our economy. Shortages began to appear not too many months after the controls were put into effect. Whether these shortages can be attributed to the black market variety of price control (exhibited in Figure I-10.1) is an open question because at the same time we had controls, we also had disruptions in normal supplies of such critical materials as petroleum. There was, however, widespread disappointment with wage and price controls, even by its most ardent supporters of earlier years. Apparently, such controls did significant damage to our system of relative prices, so that resources were not being allocated to their most valuable uses.

In spite of these problems, many politicians and economists alike often call for renewed or even more stringent price and wage controls in our economy. The question, then, is "Why would we want wage and price controls?"

Why Controls?

We have a problem of inflation. Few would deny it. We want to stop inflation—at least most of us do. How do we do it? Any solution, of course, has to attack the forces that drive

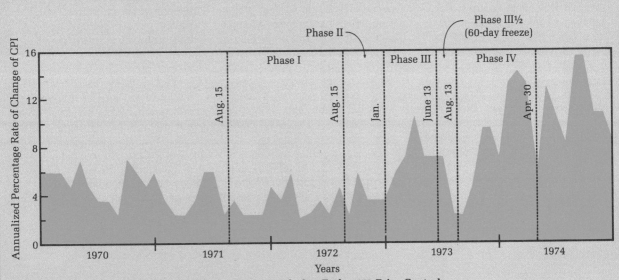

FIGURE I-10.3 Rate of Change of CPI before, during, and after Early 1970 Price Controls
If we look at the annual rate of change of consumer prices, as calculated monthly, we find that the rate of inflation reached a peak prior to the imposition of wage and price controls on Aug. 15, 1971.

inflation. We outlined several theories in the last chapter. They were under two general headings: demand-pull and cost-push. If inflation is in fact of the demand-pull type, then wage and price controls cannot succeed. What they do in such a situation is create shortages and black markets, as we outlined before. However, according to one view, if inflation is of the cost-push variety, wage and price controls can be an effective means of directly dealing with it.

We can further refine this argument, which makes a distinction between those industries where there is a high degree of competition and those dominated by a few firms. John Kenneth Galbraith, for example, has suggested that only the largest, say,

1000, firms in the United States should be subjected to permanent price controls. Such controls would presumably not be necessary for firms selling in more competitive markets. This argument suggests that such permanent price controls are the only way to eliminate price inflation caused by large firms administering relatively high prices.

The Expectations Argument

Is our inflation demand-pull or cost-push? Those who believe it is cost-push believe strongly in wage and price controls; those who believe it is basically demand-pull do not. Both, however, agree that wage and price controls can be effective to

some extent, no matter what the rate of inflation, if such controls alter individuals' expectations about the future change in prices. Otherwise stated, if wage and price controls are a signal to economic agents that wages and prices will be lower in the future, perhaps because the government has decided to institute contractionary policies, then this signal will change people's expectations about what wages and prices they should ask for in the future. Union leaders will not demand a 10 percent increase in wages to take account of an expected 7 percent inflation if they now think that inflation will be only 3 percent. They will demand a lower increase in wages for the next year. Unfortunately, the "expectations" argument cannot be taken too seriously in view of our past experience with controls. Perhaps the first set of controls in 1971 was a signal that prices would rise at a lower rate in the future, and therefore people lowered their price expectations. But today that probably would not be the case; we have a very recent experience that tells us otherwise. Controls did not signal an end to inflation then; therefore, a reimposition of controls will not likely change most individuals' expectations about the future course of prices.

Definitions of New Terms

Black Market: An illegal market that springs up whenever a legal maximum price is set below the market clearing price. Black markets occur during times of extreme price controls.

Guideposts: Official rules to which increases in wages were supposed to adhere during the early part of the 1960s. An official statement of guideposts for wage increases was mentioned in the 1962 *Economic Report of the President*. The Council of Economic Advisers indicated that they should not exceed 3.5 percent, which was the rate of growth predicted in the economy.

Jawboning: "Mouthing" by the President and his advisors against company increases in prices and excessive union wage settlements.

Questions for Thought and Discussion

1. Do you favor wage controls, price controls, or both? Why?
2. Would wage and price controls work if inflation were of the demand-pull type?
3. How do we assess whether or not wage and price controls have worked in a particular country at any particular time?
4. "Price controls cause shortages." Evaluate this statement.

Selected References

Feige, Edgar, L. and Douglas K. Pearce, "The Wage-Price Control Experiment—Did It Work?", *Challenge*, July–August 1973.

Moore, Thomas Gale, *U.S. Incomes Policy: Its Rationale and Development*, American Enterprise Institute, Special Analysis no. 18, Washington, D.C., December 1971.

Pohlman, Jerry E., *Economics of Wage and Price Controls*, Columbus, Ohio: Grid, 1972.

Schultz, George P. and Robert A. Aliber (eds.), *Guidelines, Informal Controls and the Marketplace*, Chicago: University of Chicago Press, 1966.

Sheahan, John, *The Wage-Price Guidepost*, Washington, D.C.: The Brookings Institution, 1967.

THREE
INCOME AND EMPLOYMENT
DETERMINATION MODELS

READ
UNDERLINED PARTS
DEF. OF TERMS AND SUMMARIES

Consumption, Saving, and Investment

In the last unit we looked at the measurement of economic activity, the role of government, and the problems of unemployment and inflation in the United States. It is now time to construct a model that will help us understand how the levels of income and employment are determined for the national economy. This is known as the *theory of income and employment determination*, or, simply stated, the *theory of income analysis*. The modern theory of income analysis depends on an understanding of consumption, saving, and investment. We touched briefly on the definition of these terms in Chapter 4 when discussing national income accounting. Just to make sure these concepts are understood, we will go over them again. Then we will take a brief look at the classical theory of income and employment, after which an analysis of the determinants of consumption and saving and investment will be presented.

Definitions and Relationships

There are literally only two things you can do with a dollar of income. You can consume it or you can save it. If you consume it, it is gone for good. However, if you save the entire dollar, you will be able to consume it (and perhaps more if it earns interest) at some future time. That is the distinction between **consumption** and **saving**. Consumption is the act of using income for the purchase of consumption goods. **Consumption goods** are those goods that are used up in a very short period of time. Consumption goods are such things as going to movies, food, clothing, and the like. By definition, whatever you do not consume, you save and can consume at some time in the future.

The Difference between Stocks and Flows

It is important to distinguish between saving and savings. Saving is an action that occurs continuously at a particular rate—for example, $10 a week or $520 a year. This rate is called a **flow.** It is expressed per unit of time period, just as we express demand and supply relationships with a time period—usually a year. Implicitly, then, when we talk about saving we talk about a flow or rate of saving. Savings, on the other hand, is a **stock** concept measured at a certain point or instant in time. Your current savings are the result of past saving. You may presently have savings of $2,000 that are the result of 4 years' saving at a rate of $500 per year. Consumption, being related to saving, is also a flow concept. You consume from aftertax income at a certain rate per week, per month, or per year.

Relating Income to Saving and Consumption

If we consider only aftertax or disposable income, we can see the relationship among saving, consumption, and disposable income quite clearly:

Consumption + saving = disposable income

This is called an "accounting identity." It has to hold true at every moment in time. From it we can derive the definition of saving:

Saving = disposable income − consumption

Investment

Investment is also a flow concept. "Investment" as used here differs from the common use of the term. Generally, it's used in relation to the stock market or real estate. However, in macroeconomics, investment is defined as expenditure by firms on things, such as new machines

and new buildings that are expected to yield a future stream of income. It also includes expenditures by households on such things as *new* houses. We must also include in our definition of investment changes in business inventories, a topic we referred to in Chapter 4 when discussing national income accounting. Obviously, if a firm increases its inventory of finished goods, it has accumulated items that are capable of yielding income in the future.

Now do you see why economists do not consider the purchase of a stock or a bond an investment? If you take $100 and purchase someone else's existing shares of stock in a company, you have not made an expenditure that directly creates the possibility of future income in the economy. Rather, you have engaged in a transfer of "paper" assets. You now do not have the $100, and the person who sold you the stocks no longer has the stocks. The $100 allowed you to obtain the ownership rights in those stocks. Wealth has been exchanged; none has been created.

When we refer to the inventory-change component of investment, we see again the clear distinction between stocks and flows. Firms, at any one time, have a certain level of inventories—a stock—of finished goods. However, over time they add to and subtract from those inventories. This net change is the flow of inventories; it is also the only part included in investment.

Who Does the Saving and Investing?

Primarily, it is households who save. Business firms save whenever they retain earnings that are later used for investing in either inventories or new plant and equipment (sometimes called **capital goods**). But on the whole, it is households who do the nation's saving. It is primarily business firms who do the investing. This distinction is crucial in understanding the modern theory of income and employment determination.

Now what happens if households plan a rate of saving that differs from the rate of investment planned by businesses? Don't try to answer that question until you have gone through the rest of this chapter and the following one.

The Circular Flow with Saving and Investment

If you go back to page 74 you will see a highly simplified circular-flow diagram. There is nothing in that diagram about saving and investment. Let's redo it as in Figure 8-1. Here, with two circles, we show two sectors in the economy: the household sector and the business sector. (We'll ignore the government and foreign sectors for the moment.) The flows are somewhat more specific in this figure than they are in Figure 4-1. Saving is funneled into the credit market, which channels the funds to firms that engage in investment expenditures which are added to the consumption expenditures that ultimately determine the demand for goods and services.

Keeping in mind this circular flow of income,

let's look very briefly at the classical theory of income and employment determination.

The Classical Theory and Mr. Say

One school of classical economists believed that a permanent unemployment situation could not exist. This classical theory was based on Say's law of conservation of purchasing power. The law states:

SAY'S LAW   Supply creates its own demand.

The idea behind the law was simple: People produce goods and services so they can use them in the market to buy other goods and services they want. Therefore, Say's law indicates there will always be sufficient aggregate purchasing power in the economy to allow everything that is produced to be demanded. In Say's own words (translated from the French):

The total supply of products and their total demand must, of necessity, be equal, for the total demand is nothing but the mass of commodities which have been produced; a general congestion would consequently be an absurdity.

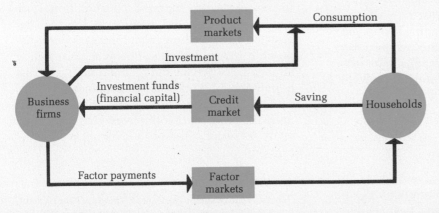

FIGURE 8-1 The Circular Flow of Income with Investment and Saving Added

Expenditures can travel from households to product markets in two ways: (1) directly by consumption expenditures and (2) indirectly by investment expenditures. Households do not make investment expenditures directly but rather provide funds via saving that are allocated by the credit market to business firms for investment projects.

By "general congestion," Say meant overproduction, leading to a situation whereby producers would have unwanted, unsold goods in their warehouses. Say's law predicts only temporary periods of excess aggregate supply in the economy, which will be automatically eliminated if prices are allowed to fall.

Say's law still makes some sense in a world of flexible prices. The classical model remains consistent with saving and investment done by different sectors, for example. If there is an excess of saving—that is, a provision for more saving than businesses want to invest—the credit markets would adjust. The price of credit (interest rate) would fall, inducing more investment and also less saving. In other words, no matter how much people save, at some interest rate businesses will borrow those savings to invest in new capital equipment and inventories. The interest rate, which is merely the price of credit, will see to it that saving and investment remain at equal rates. The classical model predicts full employment as a natural tendency. This aspect of the model conflicts with our actual periods of less than full employment and is perhaps the reason why modern economists, particularly in the 1930s, became disenchanted with the classical theory of income and employment determination.

The modern theory places more emphasis on the determination of saving and investment by factors other than the interest rate and the imbalances between the two leading to changes in the level of income and employment. For us to understand that theory, we must look into what determines consumption and finally what determines investment.

Determinants of Consumption and Saving

The major determinant of consumption expenditure is clearly expressed in the 1936 treatise that revolutionized economics: *The General Theory of Employment, Interest, and Money,* written by John Maynard Keynes. Lord Keynes' ideas underpin modern income analysis to an incredible degree. In fact, the modern theory of income and employment is usually called Keynesian. It was Keynes who asserted that to understand how aggregate demand is determined, we have to look at its separate components and how each is determined. According to Keynes, when we look at consumption we find

> ... the fundamental psychological law, upon which we are entitled to depend with great confidence both *a priori* from our knowledge of human nature and from the detailed facts of experience, is that men are disposed, as a rule and on the average, to increase their consumption as their income increases, but not by as much as the increase in their income.[1]

A relationship is suggested here between the planned consumption expenditures of households and their current income. This relationship is called the **consumption function.** Using for the moment only the first three columns of Table 8-1, we will present a consumption function for a hypothetical household.

We see from the table that as disposable income goes up, planned consumption rises also, but by a smaller amount, as Keynes suggested. Planned saving also increases with disposable income. Notice, however, that below an income of $5,000, the planned saving of this hypothetical family actually becomes negative. The more income drops below that level, the more the family either dissaves, going into debt or by using up some of its existing wealth.

[1] John Maynard Keynes, The General Theory of Employment, Interest, and Money, London: Macmillan, 1964, p. 96.

Table 8-1 Hypothetical Consumption and Saving Schedules

Table 8-1 presents a hypothetical consumption and saving function. Column 1 presents disposable income from zero to $10,000 per year; column 2 indicates planned consumption per year; and column 3 planned saving per year. At levels of disposable income below $5,000, planned saving is negative. In column 4 we see the average propensity to consume, which is merely planned consumption ÷ disposable income. Column 5 lists average propensity to save, which is planned saving/disposable income. Column 6 is the marginal propensity to consume, which shows the proportion of additional income that will be consumed. And finally, column 7 shows the portion of additional income that will be saved, or the marginal propensity to save.

COMBINATION	(1) DISPOSABLE INCOME Y_d	(2) PLANNED CONSUMPTION C	(3) PLANNED SAVING $S \equiv Y_d - C$ (1) − (2)	(4) AVERAGE PROPENSITY TO CONSUME $APC = C/Y_d$ (2) ÷ (1)	(5) AVERAGE PROPENSITY TO SAVE $APS = S/Y_d$ (3) ÷ (1)	(6) MARGINAL PROPENSITY TO CONSUME change in planned $MPC = \dfrac{\text{consumption (2)}}{\text{change in disposable income (1)}}$	(7) MARGINAL PROPENSITY TO SAVE change in planned $MPS = \dfrac{\text{saving (3)}}{\text{change in disposable income (1)}}$
A	0	1,000	−1,000	. . .	. . .	. . .	. . .
B	1,000	1,800	− 800	1.80	−0.8	0.8	0.2
C	2,000	2,600	− 600	1.30	−0.3	0.8	0.2
D	3,000	3,400	− 400	1.133	−0.133	0.8	0.2
E	4,000	4,200	− 200	1.05	−0.05	0.8	0.2
F	5,000	5,000	0	1.00	0.00	0.8	0.2
G	6,000	5,800	200	0.967	0.033	0.8	0.2
H	7,000	6,600	400	0.943	0.057	0.8	0.2
I	8,000	7,400	600	0.925	0.075	0.8	0.2
J	9,000	8,200	800	0.911	0.089	0.8	0.2
K	10,000	9,000	1,000	0.9	0.1	0.8	0.2

Graphing the Numbers

When we constructed demand and supply curves in Chapter 3, we merely plotted the points from a table showing price-quantity pairs onto a diagram whose axes were labeled price and quantity. We will graph the consumption and saving relationships presented in Table 8-1 in the same manner. In Figure 8-2 the vertical axis measures the level of planned consumption, and the horizontal axis measures the level of actual disposable income. In Figure 8-3 the horizontal axis is again actual disposable income, but now the vertical axis is planned saving. All these are on a dollars per-year basis, which emphasizes the point that we are measuring flows, not stocks.

As you can see, we have taken the income-consumption and income-saving combinations A through K and plotted them. In Figure 8-2 the result is called the "consumption function." In Figure 8-3 the result is called the "saving function." One is the mirror image of the other. Why? Because consumption plus saving always equal disposable income. In other words, what is not consumed is, by definition, saved. The difference between actual disposable income and the planned level of consumption per year must be the planned level of saving per year.

How can we find the rate of saving or dissaving (negative saving) in Figure 8-2? We draw a line that is equidistant between the horizontal and the vertical axes. This line is 45 degrees from either axis. Since it cuts the diagram in half and since we use identical scales for both axes, disposable income is exactly equal to planned consumption at all points along that 45 degree line. Thus, at point F, where the consumption function intersects the 45 degree line, actual disposable income equals planned consumption. Point F is sometimes labeled the break-even income point because there is neither positive nor negative saving. This can be seen in Figure 8-3, as well. The planned annual rate of saving at an actual disposable income level of $5,000 is indeed zero.

Dissaving and Autonomous Consumption

To the left of point F on either Figure 8-2 or Figure 8-3, this hypothetical family engages in dissaving, either by going into debt or selling off its existing assets. The amount of saving or dissaving in Figure 8-2 can be found by measuring the vertical distance between the 45 degree line and the consumption function. This simply tells us that if our hypothetical family temporarily finds its actual disposable income below $5,000, it will not cut back its consumption by the full amount of the reduction. It will instead go into debt in some way to compensate for the loss.

Now look at the point on the diagram where actual disposable income is zero but planned consumption per year is $1,000. This amount of planned consumption, which does not depend at all on actual disposable income, is called "autonomous consumption." In other words, the autonomous consumption of $1,000 is independent of the level of disposable income.

Average Propensity to Consume and to Save

Let's now go back to Table 8-1 and this time look at columns 4 and 5: **average propensity to consume** (APC) and **average propensity to save** (APS). They are defined as

$$APC = \frac{consumption}{disposable\ income}$$

$$APS = \frac{saving}{disposable\ income}$$

Notice that for this hypothetical family, the average propensity to consume decreases as

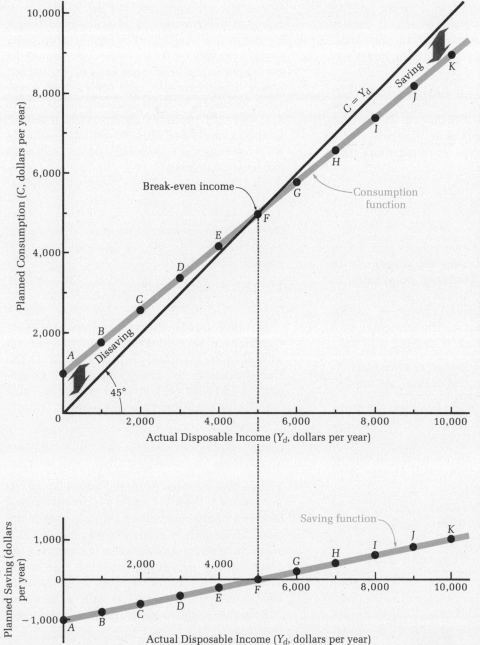

FIGURE 8-2 The Consumption Function

If we plot the combinations of disposable income and planned consumption from columns 1 and 2 in Table 8-1, we get the consumption function. Every point on the 45 degree line bisecting this diagram is equidistant from the horizontal and the vertical axes; thus, at every point on it, consumption equals disposable income. Where the consumption function crosses the 45 degree line, we know that consumption equals disposable income and there is zero saving. The vertical distance between the 45 degree line and the consumption function measures the rate of saving or dissaving at any given income level.

FIGURE 8-3 The Saving Function

If we plot the relationship between column 1, disposable income, and column 3, planned saving, from Table 8-1, we arrive at the saving function shown in this diagram. It is the mirror image of the consumption function presented in Figure 8-2.

income increases. This decrease simply means that the fraction of the family's disposable income going to saving rises as income rises. The same fact can be found in column 5. The average propensity to save, which at first is negative, finally hits zero at an income level of $5,000 and then becomes positive, never exceeding 1.00.

It's quite easy for you to figure out your own average propensity to consume or to save. Just divide your total disposable income for the year into what you consumed or into what you saved. The result will be your personal APC and APS, respectively.

Marginal Propensity to Consume and to Save

Now we go to the last two columns in Table 8-1. These are labeled **marginal propensity to consume** (MPC) and **marginal propensity to save** (MPS). We have already used the term "marginal." It means "small change in" or incremental or decremental. The marginal propensity to consume, then, is defined as

$$MPC = \frac{\text{change in planned consumption}}{\text{change in disposable income}}$$

Actually, if we wanted to be exact, the word "change" should be replaced by the mathematical symbol Δ (delta). We won't bother with that technicality now, but be aware that marginal generally refers to a small change, and not to just any change.

The marginal propensity to save is defined similarly:

$$MPS = \frac{\text{change in planned saving}}{\text{change in disposable income}}$$

What do the MPC and the MPS tell you? They tell you by what percentage of an increase or decrease in income will change consumption and saving. For example, you have an annual

salary of $8,000. At the end of the year your boss gives you a bonus of $1,000. What would you do with that additional $1,000 in income? If you were to consume $800 of it, then your marginal propensity to consume would be 0.8. By definition, then, your marginal propensity to save would be 0.2 because you would be saving an additional $200 out of the $1,000 bonus. The terms MPC and MPS sound somewhat imposing, but the concepts behind them are, you will probably agree, fairly intuitive. In the example in Table 8-1 the MPC and the MPS are constant; that is, they do not vary with the level of income.

Some Relationships

By definition, consumption plus saving must equal income. This allows us to make the following statements:

1. APC + APS = 1.00
2. MPC + MPS = 1.00

In other words, the average propensity to consume and save must total 1.00 or 100 percent as well as the marginal propensities. Check the two statements by adding the figures in columns 4 and 5 for each level of income in Table 8-1. Do the same for columns 6 and 7.

Distinguishing between a Movement and a Shift

Take a few minutes to reread pages 50 to 53 in Chapter 3. Here we made a clear distinction between a movement along a supply or demand curve and a shift in either of those curves. This same distinction applies when considering the consumption or saving function. Since the saving function is the reciprocal of the consumption function, let's just talk in terms of movements along, or shifts in, the consumption function.

Look at Figure 8-4. How do we represent the effect on consumption of a rise in actual disposable income of, for example, $2,500 per year, starting from the break-even income at $5,000 per year? We move upward along the consumption function, now labeled C, from point A to point B. Planned consumption per year will increase by the marginal propensity to consume (0.8) times the increase in income, or 0.8 × $2,500 = $2,000; that is, planned consumption will rise from $5,000 to $7,000 per year. The same analysis holds for a decrease in actual disposable income; planned consumption would fall by 0.8 times that decrease. These represent movements along a given consumption function, C.

How do we represent a decrease in autonomous planned consumption? We do this by shifting the entire consumption function downward by the amount of the decrease. For example, a $500 decrease in the autonomous component of consumption will shift the consumption function C down to C′. Notice that the break-even point moves from point A, or $5,000 to point F, or $2,500. (Verify this for yourself algebraically.) On the other hand, if the autonomous

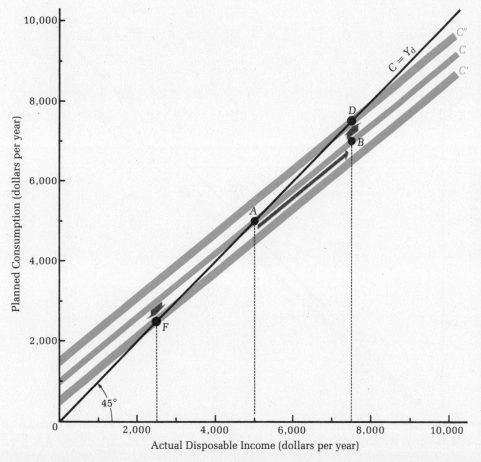

FIGURE 8-4

Distinguishing between Movements Along and Shifts in the Consumption Function

Starting at the break-even income at point A on line C, if actual disposable income increases by $2,500 per year, then we will experience a movement from point A to point B along that consumption function. Planned consumption will go up by a multiple of marginal propensity to consume and the increase in actual disposable income, or by 0.8 × $2,500 = $2,000. Planned consumption will rise from $5,000 to $7,000. On the other hand, if there were a $500 per year decrease in autonomous consumption, the entire consumption function would shift from C to C′. If there were a $500 per year increase in the autonomous component, the consumption function would shift from C to C″.

component of consumption shifts upward, for whatever reason, the consumption function will shift from *C* to, for example, *C″*. In this particular case, the autonomous component of planned consumption rose by $500. The new break-even income point, as you can see, is *D*, or $7,500. Another way of looking at this problem is by realizing that an increase in the consumption function means that at all income levels, more will be consumed than before. A decrease in the consumption function means that at each and every income level, less will be consumed than before.

We can summarize the difference between movement and shift in this way. If disposable income goes up or down, we *move* along a given consumption function to find the change in amount of planned consumption. But if there is a change in the autonomous component of consumption, we *shift* the entire curve. This is called a shift or a change in consumption.

The Historical Record

How does this consumption function hold up against the facts? Figure 8-5 is the historical

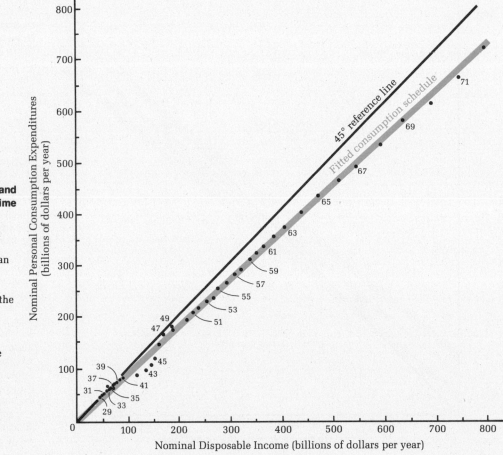

FIGURE 8-5 Income and Consumption over Time

Historically, the relationship between consumption and disposable income can be represented by a straight line passing through as many of the points as possible. Notice that the historically fitted crosses the 45 degree reference line at the origin where consumption equals disposable income. (*Source:* U.S. Department of Commerce.)

record for the United States from the Great Depression through 1975. It gives the disposable income for the entire nation and the *actual* personal consumption for the entire country. In a sense, then, this is the aggregate consumption of the United States over time. We have drawn a line to all the dots to show the so-called fitted consumption function. Almost all the points fall to the right of the 45 degree consumption-disposable income reference line, meaning that almost every year, aggregate or national saving was positive. Notice that the fitted consumption function lies above the observed points during the war years because rationing and the unavailability of a number of consumer items during that time. This perhaps encouraged consumers to save even though they might have desired to spend more of their incomes. Also notice that during the Depression there was *dissaving*.

Keynes' theory seems to have been borne out by the empirical evidence. Consumption is greatly dependent on disposable income, and, as income changes, so too does consumption, though by a smaller amount. However, there seems to be a difference between the historical consumption function represented in Figure 8-5 and the hypothetical household consumption function represented in Figure 8-2. In Figure 8-5 there is no autonomous consumption; that is, the consumption function never crosses the 45 degree $C = Y_d$ reference line. In fact, it intersects the vertical axis at zero. How can this be? These two different consumption functions can be reconciled by distinguishing between the short and the long run.

Short- vs. Long-Run Consumption Functions

The historical data show identical marginal and average propensities to consume of about 0.9 since autonomous consumption equals zero. Studies on household behavior, however, reveal significant amounts of autonomous consumption but a marginal propensity to consume that is, on the average, much lower than 0.9. This difference exists because the data, taken at a particular time, reveal the short-run consumption function, as represented in Figure 8-2. The data taken over a 40- or 50-year period, however, give us the long-run consumption function. These results can be explained by the permanent-income hypothesis.

Basically, the **permanent-income hypothesis** holds that consumption doesn't depend on *current* disposable income but rather on some measure of long-run, expected, or permanent income. The long-run may be anywhere from 2 to 3 to 5 years, depending upon people's expectations. According to this theory, consumption will not drop drastically even if, for some reason, people's income falls below what they think their permanent income is. Conversely, consumption will not increase very much even if people's income suddenly jumps above the level they consider permanent.

When we get data on families with different incomes and different levels of spending, we can assume that many high-income people are experiencing those levels of earnings only temporarily, not permanently. On the one hand, their rate of saving appears high because they assume they will not be able to maintain a high spending level when this income goes back to normal. Their rate of consumption, on the other hand, appears to be relatively low. Conversely, many people with low incomes may be at earnings levels that are abnormally low for them, when compared to a higher level they consider to be permanent. These people will probably be saving very little, or spending quite a bit, relative to their current income. Thus, we can imagine plotting a consumption relationship like the one in Figure 8-2. The permanent-income hypothesis would predict such a consumption relationship at any one point in time.

This hypothesis would also be useful in explaining the behavior of, for example, medical students. While they are in medical school, students' consumption expenditures, in general, greatly exceed their actual income. However, this is understandable since the medical student's permanent income will be much higher than the current income. Consumption is geared to expectations of permanent income rather than current levels of income.

This hypothesis also predicts the long-run consumption function found in Figure 8-5 since the permanent-income hypothesis assumes that the marginal propensity to consume is the same in the long run as the average propensity to consume. Proponents of the hypothesis contend that there is no difference between marginal and average propensities to consume if one looks at *permanent* income rather than *current* income. Accordingly, we would not expect to see the rich saving a larger percentage of their income (in the long run) than the poor.

Other Determinants of Consumption

The only determinant of spending in all the theories of consumption presented here is some form of income—whether it be current or permanent. Surely, other things must also help determine the level of consumption and saving in the United States. However, if one could get away with it, one would ignore these other determinants. If one variable—disposable income—were sufficient to predict the yearly level of consumption accurately, then (for the purposes of prediction) it wouldn't matter whether other variables were included. Researchers have found, however, that using just one variable does not yield highly accurate results for all periods of time. Specifically,

economists using the consumption function to predict levels of spending after World War II grossly underestimated what actually happened. After the fact, economists realized that several crucial variables had been left out of the relationship.

Liquid Assets

After World War II, Americans found themselves with a high level of **liquid assets.** A liquid asset is an asset that can be turned into money fairly rapidly and without much loss in value. Obviously, the most liquid asset is money itself. Other liquid assets are government bonds and shares in savings and loan associations. In 1946, many Americans found themselves with a large number of government-issued war bonds. This constituted a ready supply of liquid assets that people now turned in for cash and used to buy goods or services. At the same time, there was no longer a motivation to lend money to the government for the war effort, and consumers began to spend way beyond their regular take-home pay. The result was that the recession which economists predicted after World War II did not materialize.

If we had applied the permanent-income hypothesis to the situation during and after World War II, we probably would have predicted an increase in spending over and above what would have been predicted by just using the disposable-income hypothesis. During the war, people were saving more than they normally would have saved. After the war, this inducement disappeared. The permanent-income hypothesis would predict that after the war people would bring their average propensity to consume up to its normal level. In other words, people would dissave by getting rid of some of the savings they had accumulated during the war.

Expectations

Expectations also play a role in determining how much of their income people are willing to spend. For example, the expectation of future increases in prices may induce consumers to spend more of their current income than they would have spent otherwise. They would try to buy many goods now instead of waiting and paying higher prices in the future. Thus far, these possibilities have not been considered because we haven't really talked about the price level. We've actually been assuming implicitly that the price level remains constant. This, of course, is an unrealistic assumption that we will have to drop if our analysis is to fit the actual situation in the United States today. Expectations is a very subjective concept, however, and it is difficult for economists to come up with a measure of that variable. Therefore, we find it does not appear in many of the numerical studies of the consumption/disposable income relationship in the United States.

Determinants of Investment

Investment, you will remember, is defined as expenditures on new capital equipment and plant and changes in business inventories. As we can see from Figure 8-6, gross private domestic investment in the United States has been extremely volatile over the years. If we were to look at net private domestic investment, that is, investment after depreciation has been deducted, we would see that in the depths of the Great Depression the figure was negative—in other words, we were drawing down our capital stock—we weren't even maintaining it by replacing depreciated equipment.

If we compare investment expenditures historically with consumption and saving expenditures, we find that the latter are quite stable over time but the former are not. Why is this so? The answer is that the investment decisions of business people are based on highly variable, subjective estimates of how the economic future looks. We just discussed the role of expec-

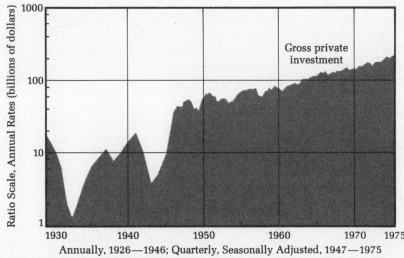

Annually, 1926—1946; Quarterly, Seasonally Adjusted, 1947—1975

Source: Federal Reserve Bank of St. Louis

FIGURE 8-6 Gross Private Investment

Gross private investment is extremely volatile as shown by the erratic movements in this figure. During the Great Depression it was barely above $1 million, and net private investment was actually negative. (*Source:* U.S. Department of Commerce.)

tation in determining the position of the consumption function. Expectation plays an even greater role in determining the position of the investment function. This could account for much of the instability of investment over time. Given this chronic instability, it is more difficult to derive a satisfactory theory of planned investment expenditures. We do not have the detailed knowledge of the causes of investment that we do of saving and consumption. Nonetheless, we'll make an attempt here to construct an investment function.

The Planned Investment Function

It seems reasonable to assume that the cost of obtaining investment funds to make investment expenditures is an important determinant of investment. Whenever a firm enters the credit market to obtain money capital for investment expenditures, it must pay the market rate of interest. The higher the rate of interest, the greater the cost—whether explicit, or implicit if retained earnings are used—to that firm of undertaking any given investment. Thus, a relatively higher or lower rate of interest cost will sometimes be the deciding factor as to whether or not the project will be undertaken.

It should be no surprise, therefore, that the investment function is the result of an inverse relationship between the rate of interest and the quantity of planned investment. A hypothetical investment schedule is given in Table 8-2 and plotted in Figure 8-7. We see from this schedule that if, for example, the rate of interest is 8 percent, the quantity of planned investment will be $225 billion per year. Notice, by the way, that planned investment is also given on a per-year basis, showing that it represents a flow, not a stock. The stock counterpart of investment is the stock of capital in the economy measured in trillions of dollars at a point in time.

Table 8-2 **Planned Investment Schedule**

The rate of planned investment is asserted to be inversely related to the rate of interest in this hypothetical schedule.

RATE OF INTEREST (PERCENT PER YEAR)	PLANNED INVESTMENT (BILLIONS OF DOLLARS PER YEAR)
5	$300
6	275
7	250
8	225
9	200
10	175

The Elasticity of the Demand for Investment

We talk in terms of interest elasticity in the demand for investment, just as we talked in terms of price elasticity in the demand for goods and services in Chapter 3. We show two extremes in (a) and (b) of Figure 8-8. In (a) we show a completely inelastic planned investment function. This means that regardless of the interest rate, planned investment will be $225 billion per year. In (b) we show a completely or infinitely elastic investment function. Here, at an interest rate of 5 percent, the quantity of investment demanded or planned is infinite; that is, the quantity is infinitely elastic at that interest rate.

Other Determinants of Investment

As with the consumption function, more than one main variable (which is the rate of interest in this case) may be important in determining the investment function. These other variables will have the effect of shifting the investment function up or down. The most important of these are now given.

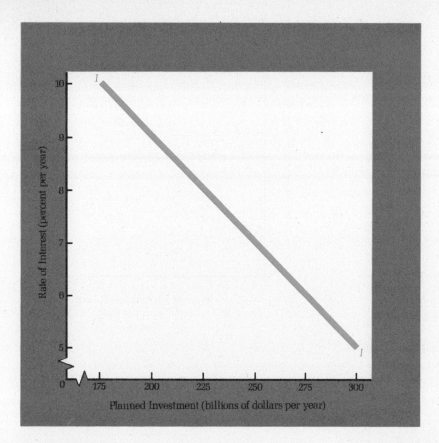

FIGURE 8-7 **Planned Investment**

If we plot the interest rate/planned investment data pairs from Table 8-2, we obtain the investment function, II. It is negatively sloped.

Expectations

Based on expectations as to the future demand for their product, business people may make projections about the future profitability of their investment decisions. If they expect a rosy future for their sector of the economy and for the economy overall, the investment function will shift outward to the right; that is, at each interest rate, more will be invested than before. If they expect the future to be grim, the investment schedule will move inward, to the left, reflecting less desired investment at each and every interest rate.

Cost of New Capital Goods

If the cost of new plant and equipment suddenly were to increase, the decisions of busi-

ness people as to the amount they should invest might change. In fact, we would expect the investment function to shift inward. The opposite would occur if there were an abrupt, unanticipated fall in the cost of capital goods.

Innovation and Technology

Both improvements in current productive technology and innovations could generally be expected to shift the investment function to the right since both would stimulate a demand for additional capital goods.

Business Taxes

Business people calculate rates of return on investments on the basis of aftertax profits. If

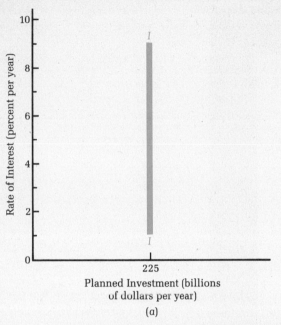

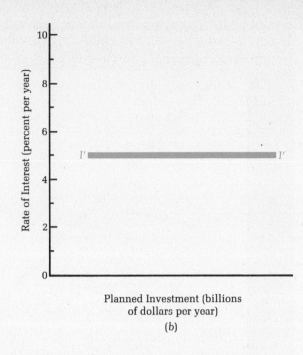

FIGURE 8-8 Two Extreme Planned Investment Functions

In (a) we show a planned investment function that is completely inelastic with respect to the rate of interest. In (b) we show a planned investment function that is completely elastic with respect to the rate of interest at 5 percent per year.

there is an increase in business tax rates, *ceteris paribus,* we expect a shift in the planned investment function inward. If there is a decrease in tax rates, we expect a shift outward.

That completes our discussion of the determinants of investment. To end this chapter, we demonstrate how actual saving must always be equal to actual investment.

The Equality of Saving and Investment

It is often perplexing to students of economic principles to learn that saving must always equal investment. After all, we started this chapter with a statement that those who do the

investing and those who do the saving are different people. How can different people make decisions that always come out alike? To understand the answer, we must look at the difference between planned and actual values. Thus far, we have spoken generally in terms of planned consumption, planned saving, and planned investment. The statement we are making now is in terms of actual saving and actual investment. It is actual values that must be equal—planned values do not have to be.

To better understand this distinction, look at Tables 8-3 and 8-4. Table 8-3 shows the planned rates of production for firms and the planned rates of expenditures for households and firms. We should notice immediately a

Table 8-3 **Planned Rates of Production and Expenditures for Firms and Households: Disequilibrium**

PLANNED RATE OF PRODUCTION (PER YEAR)		PLANNED RATE OF EXPENDITURE (PER YEAR)	
Consumer goods	$ 900	By households for consumption	$800
Investment goods	100	By firms for new capital goods	100
		By firms for inventory changes	. . .
Total planned production (per year)	$1,000	Total planned expenditures (per year)	$900

discrepancy: Total planned production is $1,000 per year, but total planned expenditures are only $900 per year.

What happens in actuality? The answer lies in Table 8-4. Firms do indeed purchase $100 worth of investment goods that other firms produced that year, and consumers purchase $800 worth of consumption goods for that year. This means that businesses are left with an unplanned inventory increase of $100. Thus, the actual rate of "expenditure" is $1,000, even though the planned rate was only $900. The difference was made up by the residual increase in actual inventories. Firms did not plan to increase their inventories but were forced to do so.

Now you can see why it is important to distinguish between planned and actual values. Now you can see better why actual saving and actual investment must always be equal, by definition.

If we ignore for the moment taxes and government spending, as well as the foreign sector of our economy, we can say that total expenditures ($1,000 in the above example) equal total income (or Y), but we know that total income *(Y)* is equal to actual consumption expenditures plus actual investment expenditures. Using the symbols C and I for consumption and investment, the equation becomes

$$Y \equiv C + I$$

On the other hand, income can be disposed of in only two ways: by consumption *(C)* or by saving *(S)*. This must mean that total income is equal to consumption plus saving, or

$$Y \equiv C + S$$

But if this is the case, then I must be equal to S. Note that these terms are applied here to actual consumption, saving, and investment figures.

Table 8-4 **Actual Rates of Production and Expenditures for Firms and Households: Equilibrium**

ACTUAL RATE OF PRODUCTION (PER YEAR)		ACTUAL RATE OF EXPENDITURE (PER YEAR)	
Consumer goods	$ 900	By households for consumption	$ 800
Investment goods	100	By firms for new capital goods	100
		Unplanned inventory changes	100
Total actual production (per year)	$1,000	Total actual expenditures (per year)	$1,000

Look at the above example and you can see how it works. Planned saving equaled total income ($1,000) minus planned consumption ($800), or $200 per year. But planned investment was only $100. Planned investment did not equal planned saving. After all the cards are dealt, however, we see that actual saving was $200 because households consumed only $800 of the total $1,000 per year of income, but actual investment was $100 a year in capital goods, plus $100 a year in unplanned inventory changes, or a total of $200. Hence, in the end, actual saving equals actual investment. In other words, unplanned inventory changes will always bring actual saving and actual investment into equality. To increase your understanding, you might want to work out some examples similar to the one given in Tables 8-3 and 8-4. To summarize, we note that

1. The actual rate of investment always equals the actual rate of saving.
2. When the planned rate of investment is greater than the planned rate of saving, inventories decrease (unplanned).
3. When the planned rate of investment is less than the planned rate of saving, inventories increase (unplanned).

Now that we have developed a theory of the determinants of consumption, saving, and investment, we have the basis for constructing a model of income and employment determination. This we will do in the next chapter.

Definitions of New Terms

Consumption: That which is spent on new goods and services out of a household's current income. Whatever is not consumed is saved. Consumption includes buying food, going to the movies, going to a concert, and so on.

Saving: The act of not consuming all of one's current income. Whatever is not consumed out of spendable income is, by definition, saved. Saving is an action measured over time, whereas savings is an existing accumulation resulting from the act of saving in the past. We usually talk about how much we save out of our paycheck every week or every month.

Consumption Goods: Goods that are bought by households to use up, such as movies, food, and clothing.

Flow: A process that occurs over time, measured in units per unit of time. Income, for example, is a flow, measured in dollars per month or dollars per year.

Stock: An accumulated quantity that exists at a point in time, such as a stock of wealth, the amount of money you have in your savings account today, and so on.

Investment: The spending by businesses on things like machines and buildings, which can be used to produce goods and services in the future. The investment part of total income is that portion which is not consumed this year but rather will be used in the process of producing goods in the future.

Capital Goods: Another name for producer goods, or goods that are used by firms to make other goods.

Consumption Function: The relationship between the amount consumed and the amount earned. A consumption function tells us how much people will consume out of various income levels.

Average Propensity to Consume: Consumption divided by disposable income for any given level of income.

Average Propensity to Save: Saving divided by disposable income.

Marginal Propensity to Consume: The ratio of the change in consumption divided by the change in disposable income. A 0.8 marginal propensity to consume tells us that an additional $100 earned will see $80 consumed.

Marginal Propensity to Save: The ratio of the change in saving divided by the change in disposable income. A 0.2 marginal propensity to save indicates that out of an additional $100 earned, $20 will be saved. Whatever is not saved is consumed. Therefore, the marginal propensity to save plus the marginal propensity to consume must always equal 1.00, by definition.

Permanent-Income Hypothesis: A theory of the consumption function that states that people's desire to spend is a function of their permanent or long-run expected income rather than of their current disposable income.

Liquid Assets: Assets that can be transformed into money quite readily without significant loss of value. The most liquid of assets is, of course, money itself. Government bonds and savings and loan shares are nearly as liquid.

Chapter Summary

1. For analytical purposes, the economy is split up into two sectors: the household sector and the business sector. We assume that these two sectors are entirely separate.

2. The act of saving is an act of not consuming. If you earn $100 in a week and buy food and entertainment and spend on other living expenses equal to $80, you have consumed $80 of your income. The rest you save; you put it in a savings and loan account or something of that nature. Saving is the difference between income and what is consumed. Saving equals what is left over after consumption expenses.

3. We can represent the relationship between income and consumption by a consumption function. A consumption function, in its simplest form, shows that current consumption is directly related to current income. The reciprocal of a consumption function is a saving function. A saving function also shows the relationship between current saving and current income.

4. The marginal propensity to consume shows how much consumption there is out of additional income. We have set the hypothetical marginal propensity to consume at 0.8. That means out of every additional $100 earned, $80 will be consumed and $20 will be saved. The marginal propensity to save is the difference between 1 and the marginal propensity to con-

sume. Otherwise stated, the marginal propensity to save plus the marginal propensity to consume must equal 1.

5. We must be careful to distinguish between the average and the marginal propensities. The average propensity to consume is the amount of total consumption divided by total disposable income. The average propensity to save is the total amount of saving divided by total disposable income for a certain period. The marginal propensities, on the other hand, relate increases in consumption and saving to increases in disposable income.

6. If the marginal propensity to save schedule or consumption function does not start out at the zero point on our typical consumption-income graph, but starts out at some positive subsistence level of consumption, then the average propensity to consume will fall throughout the entire schedule. This falling average propensity to consume implies that rich nations should save more than poor nations and that rich people should save more than poor people. The rich should become richer relative to the poor.

7. There are numerous other theories of the consumption function. One of them is the permanent-income hypothesis, which states that people's desire to consume is a function not of their current income but of their permanent or long-run income.

8. We have discussed one determinant of consumption and saving income. There are also other determinants such as liquid assets and expectations.

9. Investment is done by the business sector of the economy. Investment is the spending by businesses on such things as machines and buildings that can be used later to help produce goods and services which people want to buy for consumption purposes. Investment is the use of resources to provide for future production.

10. Obviously, the only way to provide for future production is not to consume everything today. That means that the only way businesses can invest is for people to save—not consume all their income. Thus, saving must equal investment. This is an accounting necessity that cannot be denied at any time. For investment to occur, households must save some of their income to make resources available for business people to use for investment purposes.

11. There are numerous determinants of investment. We showed the planned investment schedule to be related primarily to the rate of interest. Additionally, investment is a function of changes in expectations, the cost of new capital goods, innovation and technology, and business taxes.

12. After the fact, actual saving must always equal actual investment. This is an accounting identity.

1. The marginal propensity to consume plus the marginal propensity to save must equal 1. Must the average propensity to consume plus the average propensity to save also equal 1?

2. What are some of the reasons people save? Do you ever save? Do you ever dissave?

3. Draw consumption and saving schedules, under the assumption that you consume every last penny of your income.

4. Benjamin Franklin said that a penny saved is a penny earned. Was he right?

5. What do you think would happen to the saving schedule if there was an increased threat of nuclear holocaust?

6. Why does any upshift in the consumption schedule necessarily involve an equal downshift in the saving schedule?

Selected
References

Lekachman, Robert, *The Age of Keynes,* New York: Random House, 1966.

Peterson, Wallace C., *Income, Employment, and Economic Growth,* 3d ed., New York: W. W. Norton, 1974, chap. 4.

Stewart, Michael, *Keynes and After,* Baltimore, Md.: Penguin, 1968.

Income and Employment Determination

Why is the level of income what it is? Why is the resulting level of employment what it is and not lower or higher? To answer these questions, we must construct a model of income and employment determination. To do this, we will first employ the relationships developed in the last chapter to construct an aggregate demand schedule (again leaving out government and foreign dealings). Then we will construct an aggregate supply schedule and from there find out how an equilibrium is set.

Aggregate Demand

The aggregate demand function for the entire economy will ultimately relate everyone's planned expenditures to some variable. The variable we used for the consumption component of **aggregate demand** in Chapter 8 was disposable income. Now we will look at consumption as a function of aggregate or national income. We see this as the C curve in Figure 9-1. Notice that it is now slightly different from the ones we constructed before—here the horizontal axis is now labeled aggregate income. This means that the C function must be shifted downward to account for the amount by which taxes have cut into planned consumption at each level of income. Notice also that we use a C function having an autonomous component. In other words, we are using a short-run, as opposed to a long-run consumption function in this model. Since this model is basically concerned with short-run problems and policies here, this is appropriate.

We add the other component of private aggregate demand: investment spending *(I)*. Instead of using the planned investment function, which relates

Aggregate Income Per Year

FIGURE 9-1 **The Aggregate Demand Function**

If we assume no government, no exports and imports in our model, then planned consumption plus planned investment will equal aggregate demand, all measured in billions of dollars per year. This is represented by the vertical summation of the C line and the autonomous investment obtained from Figure 9-2.

investment to the rate of interest, we will simplify things by considering all investment to be autonomous. The autonomous nature of the investment function is depicted in Figure 9-2. In other words, investment spending is represented by the horizontal distance of the arrow in Figure 9-2 no matter what the level of aggregate annual income. How do we add this amount of investment to our consumption function? We simply shift up the C line in Figure 9-1 by the vertical distance equal to the amount of autonomous investment. That is shown by the arrow in Figure 9-1, which is exactly the same length as the arrow in Figure

FIGURE 9-2 **The Autonomous Investment Function**

In this simplified model of income and employment determination, we assume that investment spending is autonomous (or exogenous) with respect to aggregate income. It is represented by the vertical arrow, which is exactly the same length as the vertical arrow in Figure 9-1.

9-2. Our new line is labeled $C + I$ and is called the consumption + investment line. For the moment it is also our aggregate demand curve because we are leaving out the government and foreign sectors.

Now, to obtain an equilibrium level of aggregate income, we have to find out what the aggregate supply schedule looks like.

Aggregate Supply

Aggregate supply is the total value of all *final goods and services* sold by all firms in the economy. But you'll recall from national income accounting in Chapter 4 that this is identical to national product. Aggregate supply, then, must always equal actual national product.

How does aggregate product or supply vary as actual aggregate or national income varies? The answer is "They are the same!" Remember that national product and national income are identically equal. This is so because the aggregate market value of all final goods and services is, by definition, equal to the actual aggregate factor costs incurred in their production, which is, by definition, equal to aggregate or national income. [In the real world, *gross national product,* (GNP) is the aggregate we use.] It therefore follows that the value of aggregate supply is equal, by definition, to aggregate income.

Thus, the aggregate supply curve is going to be a straight line, as shown in Figure 9-3, that bisects the diagram forming two 45 degree angles.

Now we can establish equilibrium in the goods and services market in our economy: by

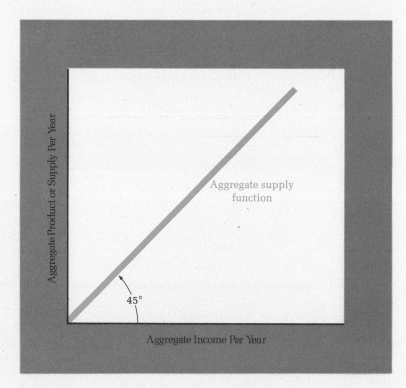

FIGURE 9-3 **The Aggregate Supply Function**

If we plot aggregate annual income on the horizontal axis and aggregate annual product or supply on the vertical axis, the aggregate supply curve will be a line, every point on which is equidistant from the two. This is because national product and national income are always identical at any and all levels of output.

putting together the aggregate supply curve and the aggregate demand curve on a single diagram.

Finding Equilibrium

What we do is lay out some hypothetical values for aggregate supply, planned consumption, planned saving, planned investment, aggregate demand, and then unplanned changes in inventories.

We are assuming a consumption function with an autonomous component equal to $220 billion per year. As in Chapter 8, the assumed marginal propensity to consume is 0.8 or four-fifths. Thus, planned consumption at an income level of $1 trillion will equal $220 billion plus 0.8 times $1 trillion or $1.02 trillion, as indicated in the first line of column 2 in Table 9-1. The planned saving is negative (in this case, −$20

billion per year). Planned investment in column 4 is assumed to be autonomous at a level of $100 billion per year no matter what the level of national income. Column 5 adds planned consumption and planned investment to get aggregate demand. Ignoring for now the last two columns in Table 9-1, let's plot actual aggregate supply and aggregate demand in Figure 9-4. The horizontal axis measures national income in billions of dollars, and the vertical axis measures consumption and investment in billions of dollars per year. When we plot the consumption function, we obtain the C line as shown. When we add autonomous investment to that C line, we get the C + I line, which is labeled "aggregate demand."

Where do the aggregate demand curve and aggregate supply curve intersect? At point E. Point E is called the "equilibrium point," just as it was in our study of the supply and demand curves for particular commodities. At point E

Table 9-1 **The Determination of Income Equilibrium**

When aggregate demand equals aggregate supply, national income will be in equilibrium. This occurs in our hypothetical example at a GNP level of $1.6 trillion per year. Here, planned saving equals planned investment, and thus unplanned inventory changes are zero.

(1) ACTUAL AGGREGATE SUPPLY (IN BILLIONS OF DOLLARS PER YEAR)	(2) PLANNED CONSUMPTION	(3) PLANNED SAVING	(4) PLANNED INVESTMENT	(5) AGGREGATE DEMAND (2) + (4)	(6) UNPLANNED INVENTORY CHANGES	(7) DIRECTION OF CHANGE IN INCOME
1,000	1,020	−20	100	1,120	−120	Increase
1,200	1,180	20	100	1,280	− 80	Increase
1,400	1,340	60	100	1,440	− 40	Increase
1,600	1,500	100	100	1,600	0	Neither (equilibrium)
1,800	1,660	140	100	1,760	+ 40	Decrease
2,000	1,820	180	100	1,920	+ 80	Decrease
2,200	1,980	220	100	2,080	+120	Decrease

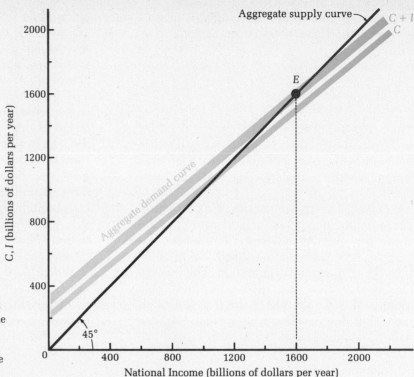

FIGURE 9-4 **The Equilibrium Level of National Income**

The equilibrium level of national income will be established at the output where aggregate demand equals aggregate supply. This occurs where the $C + I$ line intersects the 45 degree aggregate supply curve at point E with an equilibrium level of national income of $1.6 trillion per year.

there is neither an excess aggregate quantity of products supplied (output) nor an excess aggregate quantity of products demanded (spending). This can be seen also in Table 9-1, where aggregate supply at $1.6 trillion is equal to aggregate demand at $1.6 trillion. This figure is called the "equilibrium level of income."

What About Employment?

Now that we've obtained the equilibrium level of income from our aggregate supply and demand model, we would like to know the associated level of employment. This figure depends on the number of employees required to annually produce $1.6 trillion worth of national product. We show a hypothetical relationship between national production and re-

quired employment in Table 9-2. We call it a **production function,** relating input in terms of the number of employees to output in terms of the market value of national product. This relationship is fairly predictable in the short run when the amount of capital and level of technology are fixed.

We see then that at the equilibrium level of annual national income of $1.6 trillion, employment will be 100 million.

What Happens When We Are Out of Equilibrium?

What happens if the level of production is such that aggregate demand exceeds aggregate supply, or vice versa? Let's take two examples and work through the scenario.

Table 9-2 **Production Function**	
NATIONAL PRODUCT (IN BILLIONS PER YEAR)	REQUIRED LABOR INPUT (IN MILLIONS OF WORKERS PER YEAR)
1,000	85
1,200	90
1,400	95
1,600	100
1,800	105
2,000	110
2,200	115

Excess Aggregate Demand   Let's start with national income at $1.2 trillion. We see in Table 9-1 that at this income level, annual planned consumption will be $1.18 trillion. Adding planned investment, we get an aggregate demand of $1.28 trillion, which exceeds actual aggregate supply by $80 billion. The planned investment of firms exceeds the planned saving of households. In other words, goods and services are being bought at a faster rate than they are being produced. The result of that situation is seen in column 6. Inventories are being drawn down at the rate of $80 billion a year, exactly the rate by which aggregate demand exceeds aggregate supply. As a result, firms will seek to expand their production; they will hire more workers. This will create an increase in income, output, and employment. National income will rise toward its equilibrium level.

Excess Aggregate Supply   Now take the opposite situation. National income is at the $2 trillion level. We see from Table 9-1 that at that income level, planned consumption is $1.82 trillion and planned investment is still $100 billion. Aggregate demand $(C + I)$ now equals

$1.92 trillion, which is less than the aggregate supply. In other words, the rate at which households plan to save exceeds the rate at which firms plan to invest. This means that business firms will find their sales less than they had planned. They will accumulate inventories, as we see in column 6, by $80 billion per year. This unplanned accumulation of inventories will cause firms to cut back on their production and lay off workers. The result will be a drop in income, output, and employment toward the equilibrium level, E.

If we look at the mirror images of the consumption and investment schedules, we can get another view of why E is the equilibrium level of income. What we will do is look at the planned investment and planned saving functions. Then we can see clearly how planned and actual saving and investment differ when we are out of equilibrium.

Looking at Saving and Investment

Figure 9-5 shows the planned investment curve as a horizontal line at $100 billion per year. Investment is completely autonomous in this simplified model—it does not depend on the level of income.

The planned saving curve is represented by S. It is taken directly from Table 9-1, which shows planned saving in column 3 and national income in column 1. The planned saving schedule is the reciprocal of the planned consumption schedule, represented by the C line in Figure 9-4. For better exposition, we are looking at only a small part of the saving and investment schedules—outputs between $1.4 trillion and $1.8 trillion.

Why does equilibrium have to occur at the intersection of the planned saving and planned investment schedules? If we are at E in Figure 9-5, planned saving equals planned investment.

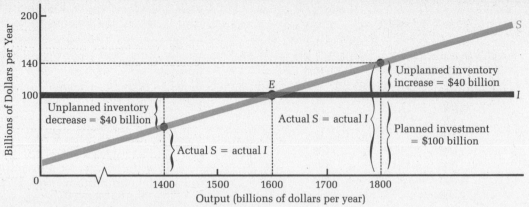

FIGURE 9-5 **Planned and Actual Rates of Saving and Investment**

Only at the equilibrium level of national income of $1.6 trillion per year will planned saving equal actual saving, planned investment equal actual investment, and therefore planned saving equal planned investment. At higher income levels, planned investment will be less than actual investment, the difference being made up of unplanned inventory increases. The opposite is true for all income levels less than $1.6 trillion per year.

All anticipations are validated by reality. There is no tendency for businesses to alter the rate of production or level of employment because they are neither increasing nor decreasing their inventories in an unplanned way.

However, if we are producing at an income level of $1.8 trillion instead of $1.6 trillion, planned investment, as usual, is $100 billion per year, but planned saving exceeds that. It is $140 billion per year. This means that consumers will purchase less of total output than businesses had anticipated. Inventories will now rise by $40 billion, bringing actual investment into line with actual saving. But this rate of output cannot continue for long. Businesses will respond to this unplanned increase in inventories by cutting back production and employment, and we will move toward a lower level of income.

On the other hand, if the national income is $1.4 trillion per year, planned investment

continues annually at $100 billion, but at that output rate planned saving is only $60 billion. This means that households will purchase more of the national output than businesses had planned. Business inventories will fall now by $40 billion, bringing actual investment into equality with actual saving. But this situation cannot last for long either. In their attempt to increase inventories to desired previous levels, businesses will increase output and employment, and the national income will rise toward its equilibrium value of $1.6 trillion.

Figure 9-5 demonstrates the necessary equality between actual saving and actual investment. Inventories adjust so that saving and investment, after the fact, are always equal.

The reason we can have a difference between the planned rate of saving and the planned rate of investment is that saving and investment are done by different individuals with different motivations.

The Multiplier

Look again at Figure 9-4. Assume for the moment that the only expenditures included in national income are those for consumption. Where would the equilibrium level of income be in this case? It would be where the consumption function (C) intersects the aggregate supply schedule, which, as we stated before, is at the $1.1 trillion point. Now we add the autonomous amount of planned investment, or $100 billion, and then determine what the equilibrium level of income will be. It turns out to be $1.6 trillion. In other words, adding $100 billion of investment spending increased the equilibrium level of income by five times that amount, or $500 billion.

What is operating is the multiplier effect of changes in autonomous spending. The **multiplier** is the number by which a change in investment, government spending, or taxation is multiplied to get the change in equilibrium income. In other words, any increases in in-

vestment or in any autonomous component of consumption will cause a more than proportional increase in income and output. The reverse is also true. To understand why this multiple expansion (or contraction) in the equilibrium level of income occurs, we'll look at a simple numerical example.

We'll use the same figures we used for the marginal propensity to consume and to save. MPC will equal 0.8 or 4/5, and MPS will equal 0.2 or 1/5. Now let's run an experiment and say that businesses decide to *increase* planned investment by $100 billion a year. We see in Table 9-3 that during what we'll call the first round, investment is increased by $100 billion; this also means an increase in income of $100 billion because the recipients of that spending obviously receive the spending as income. Column 3 gives the resultant increase in consumption by households who received this additional $100 billion in income. This, of course, is found by multiplying the MPC by the increase in

---

Table 9-3 The Multiplier Effect of a $100 Billion Increase in I

We trace the effects of a $100 billion increase in investment spending on the level of national income. If we assume a marginal propensity to consume of 0.8, such an increase will eventually elicit a $500 billion increase in the equilibrium level of national income.

ASSUMPTION: MPC = 0.8 or 4/5

ROUND	INCREASE IN INCOME	INCREASE IN PLANNED CONSUMPTION
1 ($100 B increase in *I*)	$100 B	$80 B
2	$ 80 B	$64 B
3	$ 64 B	$51.2 B
4	$ 51.2 B	$40.96 B
5	$ 40.96 B	$32.768 B
All later rounds	$163.84 B	$131.072 B
Totals	$500 B	$400 B

income. Since the MPC equals 0.8, during the first round, consumption expenditures will increase by $80 billion.

But that's not the end of the story. This additional household consumption will provide $80 billion of additional income for other individuals. Thus, during the second round, we see an increase in income of $80 billion. Now, out of this increased income, what will be the resultant increase in consumption expenditures? It will be 0.8 times $80 billion, or $64 billion. We continue these induced expenditure rounds ad infinitum and, lo and behold, we find that, on account of an initial increase in investment expenditures of $100 billion, the equilibrium level of income has increased by $500 billion. A $100 billion increase in investment spending has induced an additional $400 billion increase in consumption spending for a total increase in GNP of $500 billion. In other words, the equilibrium level of income has changed by an amount equal to five times the increase in investment. We are dealing here with figures much too large for our present economy, but using such large figures enables us to see the multiplier principle more clearly. By the way, this multiplier effect of a change in autonomous spending is a central point in Keynesian macroeconomic analysis.

The Multiplier in Graphical Terms

We can see the multiplier effect more clearly if we look at Figure 9-6. We are looking at only a small section of the aggregate demand and supply diagram we have been using. We start with the equilibrium level of national income at $1.6 trillion. This is the equilibrium given an aggregate demand of $C + I$. Now we increase investment (I) by $100 billion to I'. This shifts the entire $C + I$ curve up to $C + I'$. That is, the aggregate demand curve has shifted vertically upward by $100 billion. Now, aggregate supply

eventually catches up with increased aggregate demand. For each dollar increase in national income, supply has increased by $1, but demand increases by only a fraction of that dollar, that fraction being equal to the marginal propensity to consume or four-fifths. The new equilibrium level of income is established at E' at the new intersection of the new $C + I'$ curve and the aggregate supply curve. The new equilibrium level of income is $2.1 trillion. Thus the increase in income was equal to five times the increase in planned investment spending.

There's an easier way, however, to find the multiplier than by drawing a graph.

The Multiplier Formula

It turns out that the investment multiplier is always equal to the reciprocal of the marginal propensity to save—that is, the marginal propensity to save turned upside down. In our example, the MPC was 4/5; therefore, since MPC + MPS = 1, the MPS was equal to 1/5. If we turn 1/5 upside down, we get 5. Voilà! That was our multiplier. A $100 billion increase in planned investment led to a $500 billion increase in equilibrium income. Our multiplier will always be the following:

$$\text{Multiplier} = \frac{1}{\text{MPS}} = \frac{1}{1 - \text{MPC}}$$

You can always figure out the multiplier if you know either the MPC or the MPS.

When you have the multiplier, the following formula will then give you the change in the equilibrium level of national income due to a change in autonomous spending:

$$\text{Multiplier} \times \begin{array}{l}\text{change} \\ \text{in auton. spending}\end{array} = \begin{array}{l}\text{change in eq.} \\ \text{level of nat'l. inc.}\end{array}$$

The multiplier, as we mentioned, works both

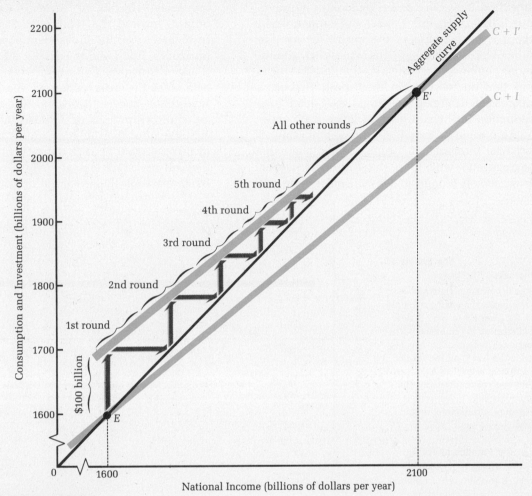

FIGURE 9-6 Graphing the Multiplier

We can translate Table 9-3 into graphical terms by looking at each successive round of additional spending induced by an autonomous increase of planned investment of $100 billion. The aggregate demand curve shifts from $C + I$, with an equilibrium level of national income of $1.6 trillion, to a new aggregate demand curve labeled $C + I'$. The new equilibrium level of national income is $2.1 trillion. It is established where aggregate demand equals aggregate supply at E'.

for an increase and a decrease in autonomous spending. In our previous example, if the autonomous component of consumption had fallen by $100 billion, the reduction in the equilibrium level of income would have been $500 billion per year.

The Effects of More Saving

We have talked about movements along schedules and shifts in those schedules. The multiplier effect occurs when there is a shift in the schedule because of a change in autonomous spending. Now we can see, by looking at movements in our schedules, what will happen when there is an increase in the desire to save. In other words, what happens when the autonomous component of consumption falls? It turns out that an increase in thriftiness, that is, a decreased desire to consume, may lead to a *reduction* in the equilibrium level of income.

An individual may feel financially better off because increased thriftiness leads to greater savings and wealth in the future. However, from society's point of view, if all individuals increase their rate of saving, a reduction in output, income, and employment may result. In Figure 9-7(a) the investment schedule is the horizontal line I and the saving schedule is the S curve. Since the equilibrium level of income occurs at the intersection of the saving and investment curves, it occurs here at E, giving an equilibrium level of national income of Y_1. Assume now that all individuals at all levels of income want to save more. This means that they all consume less at all levels of income. In other words, the consumption function shifts

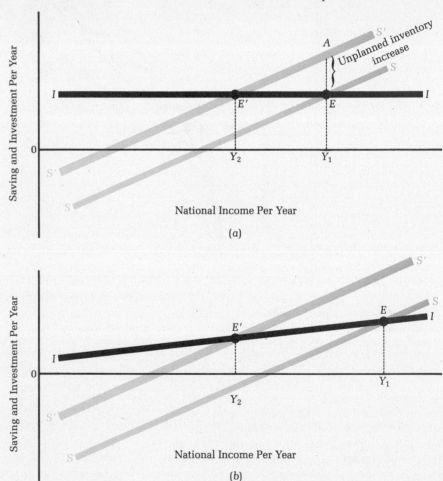

FIGURE 9-7 (a) The Effects of Increased Thriftiness

As all individuals attempt to save more, the saving schedule shifts from SS to $S'S'$. A new equilibrium is established at a national income of Y_2 per year, which is less than the former equilibrium level of Y_1. Although saving remains the same because investment is a constant, production, output, and employment fall.

(b) The Paradox of Thrift

If investment is positively related to the level of national income, then the investment function is shown with an upward slope, as II. An increased desire to save on the part of the population will shift the saving schedule to $S'S'$ from SS. The new equilibrium will be established at national income level Y_2, which is lower than the original equilibrium of Y_1. Notice that, even though all individuals want to save more, saving is lower at the new equilibrium than at the old.

downward and the saving function shifts upward from S to S'. At the old equilibrium level of income Y_1, however, desired or planned saving is equal to the distance from the horizontal axis to A on S'. Now, since firms do not sell as much as they anticipated, they accumulate inventories at a rate equal to the difference between A and E. As they accumulate these inventories unexpectedly, they respond by cutting back production, output, and employment. Because of these cutbacks, income eventually falls to a new equilibrium level of E', where the equilibrium level of national income is now Y_2. You see, then, that as all individuals attempt to save more, the equilibrium level of national income will fall and actual saving will remain unchanged.

The Paradox of Thrift

Now let's examine what has been called the **paradox of thrift.** If investment spending is not autonomous but rather is positively related to the level of national income, an increase in the desire of individuals to save will cause not only a reduction in production, output, and employment but also a reduction in investment and saving. This is an example of the fallacy of composition. What may be good for an individual may not be good for the economy as a whole. The paradox is that as each individual attempts to save more, all individuals taken collectively end up saving less!

We can see the paradox of thrift in Figure 9-7(b). The original saving function is curve SS intersecting the investment function II at point E, yielding an equilibrium national income of Y_1. Now an increased thriftiness occurs on the part of all individuals in the society; at each and every level of income they wish to save more than before. The saving function moves up to S'S'. Eventually, the equilibrium level of

national income is established at the intersection of S'S' and II, or point E', giving an equilibrium level of national income of Y_2. Notice that originally the rate of saving equaled the vertical distance between Y_1 and E and now equals the vertical distance between Y_2 and E'. All individuals have attempted to save and have ended up saving less—hence, the paradox of thrift.

Inflationary and Deflationary Gaps

We have presented in simplified form the modern theory of income and employment determination. We have also pointed out situations where the level of aggregate demand may be greater than, equal to, or less than the level of aggregate supply. If we have some notion of the full-employment level of national income, then we can label the situations. This is what we do in Figure 9-8. We put in the full-employment level of national income at Y_f. In the middle diagram, the C + I or aggregate demand curve intersects the aggregate supply curve exactly at that full-employment level of national income. However, in the top diagram, there is a gap. This is called the **inflationary gap** because aggregate demand exceeds aggregate supply at full employment.

On the other hand, if aggregate demand is less than aggregate supply at full employment, then the difference is called a **deflationary gap;** this is seen in the bottom diagram.

According to proponents of the simplified model we have used here, ways must be found to close the inflationary gap by reducing aggregate demand and the deflationary gap by increasing aggregate demand. Until now we have not really talked about prices changing. In fact, we have implicitly assumed all along that the price level has remained constant. When we

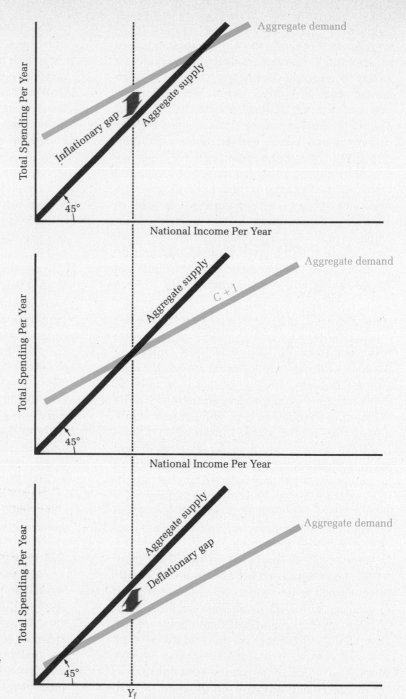

FIGURE 9-8 Inflationary and Deflationary Gaps

Here we show three possible situations. In the middle diagram, aggregate demand and aggregate supply are equal at the full-employment level of national income, Y_f. In the upper diagram, the aggregate demand curve intersects the aggregate supply curve to the right of the full-employment level of national income. The vertical distance between the aggregate demand curve and the aggregate supply curve at the full-employment level of national income is labeled the inflationary gap. In the bottom diagram, the opposite occurs. The aggregate demand curve intersects the aggregate supply curve at less than the full-employment level of national income. The vertical distance between the aggregate demand curve and the aggregate supply curve at the full-employment level of national income is labeled the deflationary gap. (This does not necessarily mean that prices will fall.)

talk about an inflationary gap, however, we refer to a situation where prices are rising, and so we must alter our model slightly to take account of this change.

In the following chapter we introduce the government component into our model and find out how changes in government fiscal policy (spending and taxation) can affect the equilibrium level of national income and help close inflationary or deflationary gaps.

Aggregate Demand: The dollar value of planned expenditures for the economy on all final goods and services per year.

Aggregate Supply: The total dollar value of all final goods and services supplied by firms to the market economy per year.

Production Function: The relationship between input and output. In the short run, if the amount of capital and the level of technology are assumed to be constant, we can use a simplified production function that relates output directly to labor input.

Multiplier: The multiplier is the number by which a change in investment, government spending, or taxation is multiplied to get the change in equilibrium income. The investment or government multiplier is the reciprocal of the marginal propensity to save—in other words, the marginal propensity to save turned upside down. If the marginal propensity to save is 0.2 or 1/5, the multiplier will be 5. A multiplier of 5 means that an increase in autonomous investment or in government spending will increase equilibrium income by a factor of 5.

Paradox of Thrift: A proposition demonstrating that, under certain circumstances, an increase in desired saving will not only lead to a reduction in the equilibrium level of income but also to a reduction in the rates of saving and investment. This concept was first introduced by Bernard Mandeville in the *Fable of the Bees,* 1714.

Inflationary Gap: The gap between full-employment spending and actual spending at full employment. It is usually measured by the vertical discrepancy at full-employment income between the $C + I + G$ schedule and the 45 degree line where spending equals income. The discrepancy is positive.

Deflationary Gap: The difference between actual spending at full employment and the full-employment level of spending. It is usually measured by the vertical discrepancy at full employment between the $C + I + G$ schedule and the 45 degree line. In this case, the discrepancy is negative.

1. When we first construct our aggregate demand schedule, it includes only consumption and investment spending.
2. The aggregate supply curve is merely a 45 degree line along which there is equality between aggregate income and aggregate product.

3. The equilibrium level of aggregate income occurs where the aggregate demand curve intersects the aggregate supply curve (spending = output).

4. To find the level of employment associated with the equilibrium level of income, we require a production function relating national product to required employment.

5. When there is excess aggregate demand, inventories will be drawn down more rapidly than planned. As a result, firms will expand production and, in the process, hire more workers, thus leading to an increase in income, output, and employment.

6. When there is excess aggregate supply, the opposite will occur—inventories will grow unexpectedly, production will be cut, and so too will employment and income.

7. We can look at the entire scenario from the point of view of planned saving and investment, which must be equal at the equilibrium rate of national income. Whenever the actual level of national income exceeds the equilibrium level, there will be an unplanned inventory increase triggering production cuts and layoffs. Whenever national income is less than the equilibrium level of national income, there will be an unplanned inventory decrease calling for increased production and employment.

8. A key aspect of simplified Keynesian analysis is that a change in investment will result in a multiple change in equilibrium income. This multiplier effect of a change in investment is positively related to the marginal propensity to consume. The higher the marginal propensity to consume, the greater the investment multiplier. We find the investment multiplier by first finding the marginal propensity to save (1 minus the marginal propensity to consume) and then turning the marginal propensity to save upside down. A marginal propensity to consume of 0.8 means that the marginal propensity to save is 0.2 or 1/5. Turning 1/5 upside down gives us 5. Thus, the investment multiplier equals 5.

9. If there is an increased thriftiness on the part of individuals, this will lead to a lower equilibrium level of national income. In the situation where investment is positively related to income, increased thriftiness will actually lead not only to a reduction in the equilibrium level of income but also to a reduction in the rate of saving and investment. Hence, the paradox of thrift.

10. If the equilibrium level of national income exceeds the full-employment level, there exists an inflationary gap. If the equilibrium level of national income is less than the full-employment level, there exists a deflationary gap.

Questions for
Thought
and Discussion

1. Why is the saving schedule the reciprocal of the consumption schedule?

2. Why does the break-even or equilibrium income level remain the same whether we draw the C line or the saving schedule?

3. What do you think the multiplier would be if the marginal propensity to consume were 1.1?

4. People tell you that it is wise to save for the future, but the paradox of thrift indicates that an increase in the rate of saving leads to a reduction in equilibrium income. What gives?

5. What is the difference between planned or desired saving and actual saving? What is the difference between planned or desired investment and actual investment?

6. Answer the following questions based on the table and graph.

National Income (Billions)	Consumption (Billions)
$100	$110
200	200
300	290
400	380
500	470

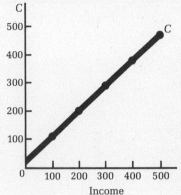

(a) If the linear function $C = a + bY$ describes this consumption function:
   (i) What is the value of a?
   (ii) What is the significance of a?
   (iii) What is the value of b?
   (iv) What is the significance of b?

(b) If national income in this model increased to $800 B, we would expect C to be _____.

(c) The multiplier consistent with this example is _____.

Selected References

Dillard, Dudley, *The Economics of John Maynard Keynes*, Englewood Cliffs, N.J.: Prentice-Hall, 1948.

Hansen, Alvin, *A Guide to Keynes*, New York: McGraw Hill, 1953.

Lekachman, Robert, *The Age of Keynes*, New York: Random House, 1966.

Stewart, Michael, *Keynes and After*, Baltimore, Md.: Penguin, 1968.

The Spirit of His Age

JOHN MAYNARD KEYNES

Economist, Cambridge University

The most influential economist of the twentieth century was John Maynard Keynes. During a 25-year period following 1919, he completely revolutionized economics—as a discipline, as an aspect of government policy, and as a way of looking at human society.

Raised in England and educated at Cambridge University, Keynes served as an economic adviser to the British Treasury during World War I. From this position, he was delegated chief economic counsel to the British representatives at Versailles. His distress over the harsh settlement exacted from the Germans inspired *The Economic Consequences of the Peace,* in which he predicted the collapse of the European economy, a prediction that proved tragically correct within 20 years.

During the next decade, Keynes studied interest rates, the gold standard, and the economic future of Europe. At the same time, he built a comfortable fortune in stock market speculation—purchasing on the basis of whim, instinct, and his own calculations, handling his transactions by telephone before getting out of bed each morning.

In 1930, he published *The Treatise on Money*, a book distinguished by a very broad view of economics. It explores the propelling and decelerating forces that seem to act against each other in an economic system.

Keynes' major yardstick of economic health was the rate of investment and capital expansion. In contrast to the classical view, Keynes considered thrift a deadening influence on economic growth: "it is Enterprise which builds and improves the world's possessions . . . if Enterprise is afoot, wealth accumulates whatever may be happening to Thrift; and if Enterprise is asleep, wealth decays whatever Thrift may be doing."

The General Theory of Employment, Interest, and Money was the major accomplishment of this prolific period. It remains the single most influential work of twentieth century economics. Opposing the classical view that employment fluctuates naturally around a "natural" level, Keynes presented a comprehensive approach to the problem of keeping populations working, fed, and housed. Only the maintenance of "effective demand"—that is, the maintenance of a desire for goods and services among people with sufficient income to act on their desire—can keep an economy out of a recession.

With this book, Keynes completely changed the vocabulary and fundamental principles of macroeconomic thinking. The book was greeted at first with confusion and controversy, but it effectively divided the discipline between economists who agreed with Keynes and those who rejected his theories. The division has been institutionalized in the past 40 years; but no matter how carelessly the term is used in the popular media, Keynesian economics remains a concrete school of thought.

Actually, it was Franklin Roosevelt who helped move Keynes' work into the spotlight. Keynes enjoyed a close personal relationship with the American president, and Roosevelt found several aspects of the economist's work that could be applied to the huge task of pushing the American economy out of the Depression.

By the time of his death in 1946, Lord Keynes had seen his theories become the basis of economic policy on both sides of the Atlantic. His close friend and biographer, Roy Harrod, wrote that some might attribute to Keynes a special power beyond the normal range of human capabilities. Keynes, however, had a more modest explanation: "The study of economics does not seem to require any specialized gifts of an unusually high order. Is it not . . . a very easy subject compared with the higher branches of philosophy or pure science? An easy subject, at which few excel! The paradox finds its explanation, perhaps in that the master economist must possess a rare combination of gifts. He must be mathematician, historian, statesman, philosopher—in some degree."

The Acceleration Principle and the Interaction between the Accelerator and the Multiplier

Business investment fluctuates to a much greater degree than does overall business activity. By the nineteenth century, economic observers were quite aware of this fact. By the early twentieth century, the idea had entered the main body of economic theory through the work of J. M. Clark.

The Acceleration Principle

Clark studied fluctuations in railroad traffic and in the orders for new railroad equipment. He noticed, for example, that the level of new car orders was more closely in relationship with *changes* in the level of traffic than in the level of traffic itself. Orders for new cars represent one form of investment by railroads. The empirical work that Clark did with railroads was used as evidence for what is now known as the acceleration principle, or the accelerator:

> The level of planned investment varies with *changes* in the level of output rather than with the level itself. Otherwise stated, the level of investment is related to the rate of change of output or sales.

We can see a simple example of the acceleration principle at work in the planned investment of the A & B Water Heater Company. Table B-1 shows the relationship between the company's investment and sales.

Table B-1 Relationship between Investment and Sales

(1)	(2)	(3)	(4)	(5)	(6)	(7) = (5) + (6)
			A & B WATER HEATER COMPANY			
YEAR	SALES (MILLIONS OF $ PER YEAR)	REQUIRED STOCK OF MACHINES (MILLIONS OF $)	ACTUAL STOCK OF MACHINES (MILLIONS OF $)	REPLACEMENT INVESTMENT (MILLIONS OF $ PER YEAR)	NET INVESTMENT ON NEW CAPITAL (MILLIONS OF $ PER YEAR)	GROSS INVESTMENT (MILLIONS OF $ PER YEAR)
1966	10	5	5	1	0	1
1967	12	6	5	1	1	2
1968	14	7	7	1	1	2
1969	16	8	8	1	1	2
1970	16	8	8	1	0	1
1971	16	8	8	1	0	1
1972	14	7	8	0	0	0
1973	14	7	7	1	0	1
1974	14	7	7	1	0	1
1975	18	9	9	1	2	3
1976	18	9	9	1	0	1

We begin by assuming that in 1966 the firm started with just the necessary amount of capital stock, that is, machinery valued at $5 million. This means that for every dollar of water heater sales (column 1), the required stock of capital is 50¢. In other words, for any level of sales, we can find the required stock in machines simply by dividing the level of sales by 2.

Let's see what happens when sales increase by $2 million, as they did from 1966 to 1967. The required stock in machines increases by $1 million. Therefore, in addition to an assumed replacement investment of $1 million a year to take care of depreciation in machines (column 5), the A & B Water Heater Company will have to invest an extra $1 million in new machines (column 6). That means that gross investment, which is replacement investment plus net investment (column 7), will be $1 million plus $1 million, or $2 million. So far so good. Now notice that the level of sales increases by

another $2 million per year from 1967 to 1968 and from 1968 to 1969 but that gross investment remains constant at $2 million per year. This is a demonstration of the acceleration principle. Gross investment is a function of the *rate* of change of sales. If that rate of change is constant, then gross investment will also be constant.

Now look what happens when sales decline from $16 million to $14 million per year as they did from 1971 to 1972. The required capital stock falls by $1 million, but the actual capital stock on hand is still $8 million. It is not necessary to add new capital equipment, nor is it necessary even to pay for depreciation. Therefore, we see that for 1972 the replacement investment is zero, net investment is zero, and, consequently, the total gross investment is also zero. In other words, if the rate of capital formation is a function of the rate of change of sales, a decline in sales can lead to a zero amount of gross investment (and in some cases, negative net investment).

We can also see that changes in sales result in magnified percentage changes in planned investment. For example, from 1966 to 1967 sales went up by 20 percent but gross investment went up by 100 percent. From 1974 to 1975 sales increased by 28.57 percent whereas gross investment increased by 300 percent.

The Interaction between the Accelerator and the Multiplier

Investment is a key determinant of the level of income in the model we are using in this unit. If the rate of planned investment follows the accelerator principle, this could explain, to some extent, the swings in business activity. After all, any change in investment, according to our theory in Chapter 9, leads to a multiple change in equilibrium income and employment.

Economists see this as a distinct possibility. Nobel Prize laureates Paul Samuelson and Sir John Hicks have both shown that the accelerator principle, combined with the multiplier, may produce the business fluctuations that are experienced in the real world.[1]

The combination would work as follows. We assume that the economy is moving toward full employment, national income is rising, and sales are expanding at an increasing rate. Because of the acceleration principle, this increase in growth results in a relatively high level of planned investment. Furthermore, because of the multiplier, this relatively high level of

planned investment provokes even greater increases in national income. Thus the accelerator and the multiplier tend to reinforce each other, resulting in a strong upward movement in national income. This is the expansion phase of the business cycle.

Eventually, however, the economy nears some level of full employment. That is to say, since we have only a certain amount of labor, land, and other factors of production, it is impossible to continue increasing national income at the extraordinarily rapid rate which was experienced during the recovery period of the business cycle. At some point, growth has to slow down. Sales too will not increase forever at the same fast rate—rather, they will begin to increase at a slower rate. This slowdown means that the rate of growth of planned investment is going to turn down abruptly, just as it did, for example, when sales of the A & B Water Heater Company maintained themselves at $16 million a year. However, because of the multiplier effect, this decrease in planned investment will lead to a magnified or multiplied decrease in the equilibrium level of income. The reduction in the rate of growth of national income will mean a further reduction in the rate of sales growth, leading to a further reduction in gross investment, and so on. Eventually, the economy will run into a recession.

At some point, the capital stock of firms gets into line with those firms' reduced sales rates. This is what happened between 1972 and 1973 for the A & B Water Heater Company. Now the stage is set for another upturn, another recovery, and the interaction again of the accelerator and the multiplier.

You will note that the multiplier-accelerator theory of the business cycle is one in which business cycles are self-starting and self-terminating. Each phase of the business cycle automatically leads into the next.

[1]Paul A. Samuelson, "The Interaction between the Multiplier Analysis and the Acceleration Principle," *Review of Economics and Statistics*, May 1939, pp. 75–78; and John Hicks, *A Contribution to the Theory of the Trade Cycle*, London: Oxford, 1950.

10 Fiscal Policy

Adding the Government Sector

The government sector in our economy is large indeed. Government purchases of goods and services account for a full one-fourth of GNP and total government spending, more than 40 percent. The difference between total government spending and government purchases of goods and services is what we call **transfer payments.** Social Security and unemployment compensation fall in this category. You'll remember that transfer payments include any payment the government makes to households or businesses for which no goods or services are concurrently rendered.

In this chapter we will add the government sector to our model of income and employment. We will consider the effects of changes in government purchases of goods and services on the equilibrium level of income and employment. We will also learn the effects of changes in taxes on equilibrium income. This can all be done by using the multiplier analysis we developed in the last chapter.

Adding Government Purchases to Aggregate Demand

In Chapter 5 we talked about the role of government spending in our economy and how it is financed. Although it perhaps would be appropriate here to consider the determinants of the rate of government purchases of goods and services, such consideration is beyond the scope of this text. What we will do for our macroeconomic model is assume the level of government purchases to be determined by political processes outside the economic system under study. In other words, we will consider G to be autonomous, just as, in the last chapter, we considered I, for simplicity's sake, to be autonomous.

Let's take the aggregate demand function from Chapter 9 and add $100 billion of government purchases of goods and services. We do this in Figure 10-1. The new aggregate demand curve is labeled $C + I + G$.

We started out in equilibrium at point E. That is to say, aggregate demand was equal to aggregate supply at an equilibrium level of $1.6 trillion per year in national income. Then we added $100 billion of autonomous government spending. This shifted the aggregate demand line vertically by $100 billion to become $C + I + G$. The new aggregate demand curve crosses the aggregate supply curve at point E'. And the equilibrium level of national income has gone up to $2.1 trillion.

How did the equilibrium level of national income increase by $500 billion when we added only $100 billion worth of government purchases? The answer is that new government spending had a multiplier impact on the equilibrium level of national income. Remember from Chapter 9 that the multiplier can be found by taking the reciprocal of the marginal propensity to save. Because we are still assuming a marginal propensity to consume of 0.8, the marginal propensity to save is 0.2 or 1/5. The reciprocal of 1/5 is 5, so our multiplier in this situation is still 5. Since we had an autonomous increase in spending by the government of $100 billion, we know that the equilibrium level of national income will increase by $100 billion times 5, or $500 billion.

We can use this new addition to our income and employment determination model to show how an increase in government purchases can

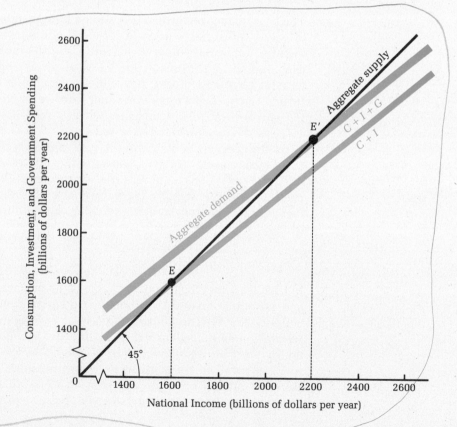

FIGURE 10-1 Adding Government to the Picture

If we add $100 billion of new government spending to the aggregate demand schedule we used in the last chapter, we get a new aggregate demand labeled $C + I + G$. The former equilibrium, without government spending, is labeled E, at an equilibrium level of national income per year of $1.6 trillion. When we add government, we get an increase in the equilibrium level of national income by $500 billion to $2.1 trillion per year, at point E'. In this case, as before, the multiplier is 5 because the marginal propensity to consume is assumed to be 0.8.

fill in the deflationary gap we mentioned in Chapter 9. That is, in a situation where the equilibrium level of income is below the full-employment level of income, an increase in government purchases of goods and services may be able to raise the equilibrium level toward the full-employment level.

Filling the Deflationary Gap

Look at Figure 10-2. Here we start out with the same $C + I + G$ or aggregate demand curve as in Figure 10-1, and the equilibrium level of national income is $2.1 trillion. However, the full-employment level of national income is greater than that—in our example, it is $2.3 trillion. The obvious gap between aggregate demand at the $2.3 trillion per year level of output and aggregate supply is what we have labeled the "deflationary gap" on this diagram. To fill the deflationary gap, which in this particular example is $40 billion, we increase government purchases of goods and services, and we do so by the full $40 billion. That raises the $C + I + G$ line to $C + I + G'$, where G' is now $40 billion greater than G. The new equilibrium level of national income is now at the intersection E', where aggregate supply now equals the

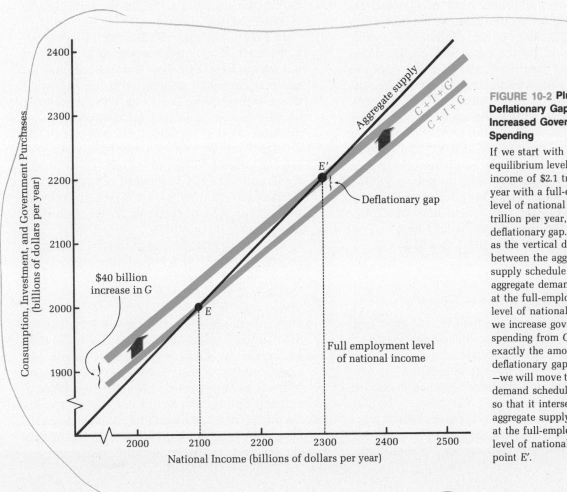

FIGURE 10-2 **Plugging the Deflationary Gap with Increased Government Spending**

If we start with an equilibrium level of national income of $2.1 trillion per year with a full-employment level of national income $2.3 trillion per year, we have a deflationary gap. It is labeled as the vertical distance between the aggregate supply schedule and the aggregate demand schedule at the full-employment level of national income. If we increase government spending from G to G' by exactly the amount of that deflationary gap—$40 billion —we will move the aggregate demand schedule upward so that it intersects the aggregate supply schedule at the full-employment level of national income at point E'.

new, greater aggregate demand, and the equilibrium level of national income is also the full-employment level.

Notice that this $40 billion increase in government spending led to a $200 billion increase in equilibrium national income. That's exactly what we would expect by the assumptions in this model. The multiplier is 5, and 5 times $40 billion equals $200 billion.

Reducing the Inflationary Gap

What if the situation in Figure 10-2 was reversed? What if $2.1 trillion was the full-employment level of national income and $2.3 trillion the equilibrium level of national income? Then we would have, as we labeled in the previous chapter, an "inflationary gap," which would be the same size as the deflationary gap described above. Now opposite measures would be needed. Government purchases of goods and services could be reduced by $40 billion so that the equilibrium level of national income would fall by $200 billion, that is, five times the reduction in G. The upward direction of the arrows in Figure 10-2 would now be reversed, and also, the labels for the two aggregate demand curves would be switched. The top one would now be $C + I + G$ and the bottom one would be $C + I + G'$, where G' was $40 billion less than G.

The Effects of Changing Taxes

We have been looking at only one aspect of government fiscal policy, that is, purchases of goods and services. What about the other aspect: taxation? What happens to the equilibrium level of national income when taxes are increased or decreased? The answer is that basically the same thing happens which happened when we altered the rate of government purchases of goods and services. The equilib-

rium level of national income changes by a multiple as taxes are changed, but it changes in the opposite direction. A reduction in personal income taxes, for example, gives consumers more take-home pay. And since disposable income is now increased, consumption spending, according to the consumption relationship, also increases. In other words, the C line shifts upward when taxes are reduced. That will also move the $C + I + G$, or aggregate demand schedule, upward also. The opposite occurs when there is an increase in personal income taxes. The consumption function shifts downward, bringing down with it the aggregate demand curve. A shift in the aggregate demand curve changes by a multiple the equilibrium level of national income.

In Figure 10-3 we change the full-employment level of national income to $2.1 trillion but leave the equilibrium level of national income at E, or $2.3 trillion, with the aggregate demand curve being $C + I + G$. The government decides to eliminate this inflationary gap. Its decision, in this particular example, is to increases taxes so that disposable income will fall and consumers will spend less. The ultimate result will be a shift downward in the aggregate demand schedule to $C' + I + G$, where C' is less than C. Now the question is "What should be the size of the tax cut?"

It turns out that the size of the tax cut necessary to eliminate the $40 billion inflationary gap is not $40 billion, but $50 billion. How can that be? Well, let's see what happens when taxes are increased. If taxes go up by $1, planned consumption falls, not by $1, but by the marginal propensity to consume times that $1 decrease in disposable income. Since in our example MPC = 0.8, for every dollar increase in taxes, planned consumption falls by 80¢ and planned saving falls by the remaining 20¢. In the initial spending round after the tax increase, then, planned consumption falls not by the full tax increase but only by MPC times the in-

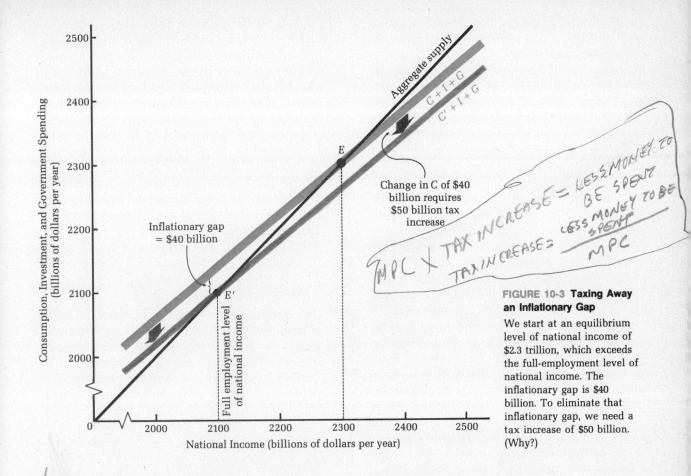

Handwritten notes on figure:

MPC × TAX INCREASE = LESS MONEY TO BE SPENT

TAX INCREASE = LESS MONEY TO BE SPENT / MPC

Figure labels: Aggregate supply, C + I + G, C' + I + G, E, E', Inflationary gap = $40 billion, Full employment level of national income, Change in C of $40 billion requires $50 billion tax increase

FIGURE 10-3 Taxing Away an Inflationary Gap

We start at an equilibrium level of national income of $2.3 trillion, which exceeds the full-employment level of national income. The inflationary gap is $40 billion. To eliminate that inflationary gap, we need a tax increase of $50 billion. (Why?)

crease. In other words, the change in autonomous consumption due to a tax increase is equal to the marginal propensity to consume times the tax change. Thus, in our example, the change in C of $40 billion requires a $50 billion tax cut because 0.8 × $50 billion = $40 billion.

How much of a tax decrease would be necessary to move the equilibrium level of national income from $2.1 trillion to $2.3 trillion? The answer, of course, would be a tax cut of $50 billion. This level of tax decrease would elicit a $40 billion increase in consumption, which would shift the aggregate demand schedule

upward so that it intersected the aggregate supply schedule at $2.3 trillion.

What happens when we change taxes and government purchases of goods and services in the same direction and by equal amounts? Since the taxation multiplier T is lower than the G multiplier, when the two are changed by equal amounts, we get what is called the "balanced-budget multiplier."

The Balanced-Budget Multiplier

Having included changes in government spending and changes in taxes in our simple multiplier model, we can now present a somewhat startling theorem that Keynesian economists developed using this analysis. Suppose that government spending goes up by $20 million and taxes are raised by that same amount. What happens to total spending? You probably think that spending remains the same since the change in government purchases seems to be just offset by an equal change in government taxation. However, the taxation multiplier is smaller than the government multiplier. If government spending goes up by $20 billion, total spending will increase by a multiple of that. When our marginal propensity to consume is 0.8, the multiplier is 5, so income will be expected to rise by $100 billion. Now we take away from disposable income by taxing $20 billion. Since the taxation multiplier is less than the government multiplier, the reduction in total spending due to increased taxes will be smaller than the increase in total spending due to increased government expenditures. In fact, the **balanced-budget multiplier** will be exactly equal to 1, which happens to be the algebraic summation of the government multiplier and the tax multiplier. If G is increased by $20 billion and taxes are too, income will also increase by $20 billion!

Notice that this analysis assumes something very important. We said that people's consumption decisions depend upon their disposable incomes. But when government expenditures come into the picture, there may be an influence on C when G changes. For example, if the new government expenditures consist of providing milk to children whose parents were already paying for the milk, the parents' consumption expenditures on milk will fall by approximately the same amount as the government increase in spending. If this is the case, then, the balanced-budget multiplier will equal zero. In fact, the balanced-budget multiplier can range from zero to a number even greater

than 1, depending upon the nature of the increase in government spending. If it is a *substitute* for private investment or consumption that would have taken place anyway, then the balanced-budget multiplier will be definitely less than 1. If government spending makes people desire to spend more than they would have otherwise, the multiplier will be greater than 1. An example of stimulated spending would be increased government spending on flood control; as a consequence of such spending, some people will not desire to save as much for the rainy day when they're flooded out of house and home.

Fiscal Policy

We just described the effects of changes in both government purchases of goods and services and in the level of taxes on the equilibrium level of national income. Changes in G and T that are legislated by Congress constitute the major areas of what is called *discretionary fiscal policy*.

Discretionary Fiscal Policy

Fiscal policy is usually associated with government spending and taxing activities. Discretionary fiscal policy results from the deliberate actions of Congress and, to some extent, the executive branch.

If we were to follow exactly the model presented in the preceding chapter, we would see that the "appropriate" discretionary fiscal policy during periods of less than full-employment levels of national income would be to increase government spending or reduce taxes, or employ a combination of the two. This is called *expansionary fiscal policy*. In periods when there are inflationary pressures on the economy and we are operating at or close to full capacity, the "appropriate" discretionary action, again assuming our model is correct, would be the opposite: reduce government spending and/or increase taxes. This is called *contractionary fiscal policy*.

Other fiscal programs in our economy occur automatically; that is, neither the Congress nor the President cause them to happen. These are called "automatic" or "built-in" stabilizers.

Automatic Fiscal Policy

In Chapter 5 we showed the 1976 personal income tax schedule. As taxable income went up, the marginal tax rate also increased—to a maximum of 70 percent. Or we can say that as taxable income decreased, the marginal tax rate went down. Think about this now for the entire economy. If the nation is at full employment, personal income taxes may yield the government, say, $375 billion per year. Now suppose that, for whatever reason, business activity suddenly starts to slow down. When this happens, workers are not allowed to put in as much overtime as before. Some workers are laid off, and some must change to jobs that pay less. Some workers and even some executives might take voluntary pay cuts. What happens to taxes when wages and salaries go down? Taxes are still paid but at a lower rate than before since the tax schedule is progressive. For example, a person who makes $15,000 taxable income a year is in the 39 percent marginal tax bracket. Now if this individual suddenly drops to only $10,000 taxable income a year and into the 32 percent marginal tax bracket, average taxes paid as a percentage of income also fall. And as a result of these decreased taxes, disposable income—the amount remaining after taxes—doesn't fall by the same percentage as before-tax income. The individual, in other words, doesn't feel the pinch of

recession as much as we might think if we ignored the progressive nature of our tax schedule. The *average* tax rate falls when less is earned.

Conversely, when the economy suddenly comes into a boom period, peoples' incomes tend to rise. They can work more overtime and can change to higher paying jobs. However, their disposable income does not go up as rapidly as their total income because their average tax rates are rising at the same time. Uncle Sam ends up taking a bigger bite. In this way, the progressive income tax system tends to stabilize any abrupt changes in economic activity. (Actually, the progressive tax structure simply magnifies any stabilization effect that might exist. Proportional taxation could stabilize also since its yield varies directly with GNP.)

Unemployment compensation works in the same direction as the progressive income tax: to stabilize aggregate demand. Throughout the business cycle, it mitigates changes in people's disposable income. When business activity drops, most workers who are laid off automatically become eligible for unemployment compensation from the state government. Their disposable income, therefore, remains positive, although certainly it is less than when they were working. During boom periods, there is less unemployment and, consequently, fewer unemployment payments made to the labor force. Less purchasing power is being added to the economy because few unemployment checks are paid out.

The key stabilizing impact of these two aspects of our taxing and transferring system is their ability to mitigate changes in disposable income. Many economists believe that disposable income—take-home pay—is the main determinant of how much people desire to spend and, therefore, is a key activator of general economic activity. It is felt that if disposable income is not allowed to fall as much as it would otherwise during a recession, the recession will be automatically cut off before it becomes a depression. On the other hand, it is felt that if disposable income is not allowed to rise as rapidly as it would otherwise during a boom, the boom will not get out of hand, causing prices to rise, among other things. The progressive income tax and unemployment compensation therefore provide automatic stabilization to the economy.

Fiscal Policy and a Full-Employment Budget

We earlier discussed the government increasing expenditures, but we did not discuss how those expenditures would be financed. If we assume no increase in taxes, we can conclude that when the government spends more it ends up with a **deficit.** If the government is already running a deficit, it will have an even larger one. Active fiscal policy has therefore been associated with **deficit spending** on the part of the government. Fiscal policy advocates point out that an increase in the deficit stimulates the economy, whereas a decrease in the deficit has the opposite effect. The government can also run a **surplus.** That is, it can take in more revenues than it spends. An increase in the government's budget surplus is supposed to have a depressing effect on the economy, just as would a decrease in government expenditures or an increase in taxes. The existence of, or increase in, the government budget surplus presumably reduces total aggregate demand and thereby depresses economic activity.

The government and many economists currently do not like to look at the government's *actual* deficit or surplus. They do not think it is useful to look at current levels of taxes and expenditures or the current budget deficit or surplus that results. Consider for a moment the following situation. Suppose the economy is at full employment and the government budget is in balance—no deficit and no surplus. Then the economy goes into a recession, and incomes fall. The government, however, does nothing. Spending on its part, *G,* remains the same; but, since some taxes, *T,* are based on income, government revenues fall. A formerly balanced budget goes into deficit since *G* is now greater than *T.* The budget deficit should certainly not be regarded here as an active stimulating policy decision on the part of the government. It is a *result* of the recession, not a counter-recessionary move. Therefore, economists now make calculations to determine whether *at full employment* the government budget would be in a deficit or a surplus position. The result is called the **full-employment deficit or surplus.** In Figure 10-4 the results of such calculations are presented for the years 1955 to 1975.

Economists now talk in terms of a *stimulating full-employment deficit* or a *depressing full-employment surplus.* The actual budget deficit may be $56 billion, as it was in fiscal 1975, but the full-employment deficit was much less. Many economists therefore maintained that the deficit was stimulating but not as *over-stimulating* as it would first seem because at full employment the deficit would have been much smaller.

Fiscal Policy and the Budget

Much of the content of fiscal policy debates is concerned with the advisability of actual federal budget deficits or surpluses or with the advisability of full-employment budget deficits or surpluses. Many economists, however, believe that in the long run the federal budget should be balanced. This is considered a "conservative" position because it requires that any deficits occurring during recessions be matched by surpluses at other times.

More recently, however, the notion of a

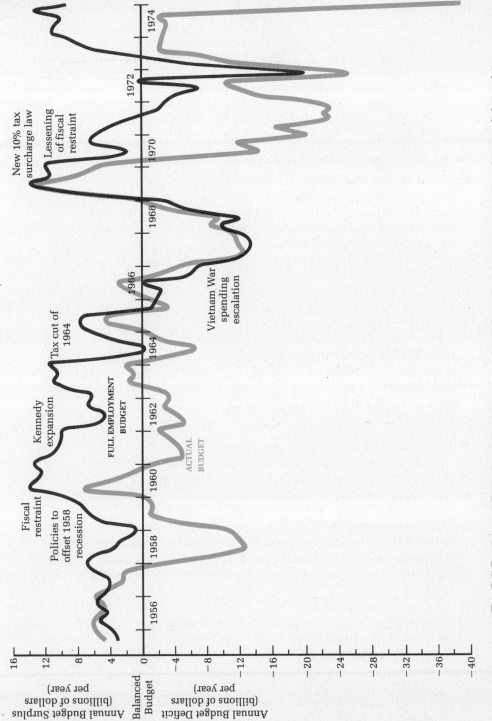

FIGURE 10-4 The Full-Employment Budget and the Actual Budget

Here we have drawn the actual budget of the United States government from 1955 to 1975. We have also put in the full-employment budget. We see that, for the most part, the federal budget has been in deficit for almost the last two decades. However, the full-employment budget has been in deficit for only a very few years. Presidents and their advisers like to talk in terms of the full-employment budget. (Source: A. M. Okun and Nancy H. Teeters, "The Full Employment Surplus Revisited," in *Brookings Papers on Economic Activity,* no. 1 (Washington, D.C.: The Brookings Institution, 1970); and Council of Economic Advisers, *Economic Report of the President* (Washington, D.C.: U.S. Government Printing Office, 1975).)

long-term fiscal policy that is related to a full-employment balanced budget has caught favor with a number of policy prescribers. For example, the Committee for Economic Development, an organization of business leaders and some economists, has come out strongly in favor of a long-run, full-employment balanced budget. If this were indeed to become the overall policy of the federal government throughout the business cycle, and if that cycle were symmetrical, the actual federal budget would become balanced in the long run.

Definitions of New Terms

Transfer Payments: Payments made to households that are not made in exchange for concurrently rendered goods or services. Unemployment compensation and Social Security benefits are examples.

Balanced-Budget Multiplier: The multiplier resulting from equal changes in both government spending and taxes. Under the most simplified assumptions, the balanced-budget multiplier is 1, meaning that an equal increase in both taxes and government spending will lead to an equal increase in the equilibrium level of income.

Deficit: The difference between government revenues and government spending (usually expressed in annual rates).

Deficit Spending: Government spending in excess of government tax yields.

Surplus: The excess of government revenues over government spending (usually expressed in annual rates).

Full-Employment Government Budget: What government revenues *would* be if the economy were at full employment.

Full-Employment Deficit or Surplus: The difference between actual government spending and what government revenues would be if the economy were operating at full employment.

Chapter Summary

1. When we add government spending to our model, the equilibrium level of output rises by a multiple of that government spending.
2. In the simplified model of this chapter, a deflationary gap can be reduced by increased government spending, and an inflationary gap can be reduced by decreased government spending.
3. The taxation multiplier is less than the investment or government multiplier. Thus, to eliminate a given inflationary or deflationary gap via a change in taxes, the change would have to be greater than the necessary opposite change in government or investment spending of equivalent impact.
4. The balanced-budget multiplier, simply stated, indicates that an increase in government spending matched by an increase in taxes will lead to an increase in the equilibrium level of national income by the same amount.
5. Automatic stabilizers include personal and corporate income taxes and unemployment insurance. Automatic stabilizers automatically counter ups and downs in business activity.
6. It is usually inappropriate to regard the actual government deficit or surplus as a policy variable. After all, if the government budget is balanced and,

for some reason, there is a recession, government receipts will fall and there will result a budget deficit. But budget deficits are usually associated with stimulative government fiscal policy. In this case, the deficit is purely passive. To take account of this possibility, economists have devised a concept called the full-employment budget.

7. The full-employment budget is the level of government revenues that would prevail if the economy were at full employment. Similarly, the full-employment surplus or deficit is the difference between actual government expenditures and the government revenues that would occur if the economy were operating at full employment.

Questions for
Thought
and Discussion

1. Analyze the early 1975 debate on the usefulness of a $20 billion to $60 billion tax cut. Use the diagrammatic tools we have developed in this and preceding chapters.

2. If all expenditures for defense were cut out, what alternative programs would you want the government to undertake to maintain full employment?

3. Taxes were raised during the Great Depression in an attempt to balance the federal budget. If you had been an economist at that time, would you have agreed with that policy?

4. Discuss the rationale underlying the 1975 tax rebate.

5. What do you think is the best method for financing the government deficit during a recession?

6. Can you think of any problems that the President might run into when he wants to change taxes?

7. In this problem, equilibrium income is $1,100 billion and full-employment equilibrium is $1,450 billion. The marginal propensity to save is 1/7. Using these data, answer the following:

(a) Is there an overfull employment gap or an underful employment gap? What is the size of the gap?

(b) What is the multiplier here?

(c) What is the MPC?

(d) By how much must new investment or government spending increase to bring the economy up to full employment?

(e) What is the tax multiplier in this problem?

(f) By how much must government cut personal taxes to stimulate the economy to the full-employment equilibrium?

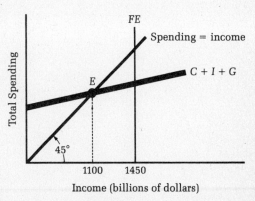

Selected
References

Economic Report of the President, Washington, D.C.: U.S. Government Printing Office, published annually.

Heller, Walter W., *New Dimensions of Political Economy,* New York: W. W. Norton, 1967.

Thurow, Lester C. (ed.), *American Fiscal Policy,* Englewood Cliffs, N.J.: Prentice-Hall, 1967.

The Economic New Frontiersman

WALTER W. HELLER

Former Chairman, Council of Economic Advisers

During the 1971 to 1972 academic year at the University of Minnesota, Walter Heller removed his own book, *New Dimensions in Political Economy,* from the introductory economics reading list. Heller quietly commented on why his book was no longer appropriate to the economic scene: "We were so pleased then [1966] to have accomplished the intellectual revolution of the 1960s. But we were expecting more than economics could deliver."

Walter Heller was one architect of the successful "new economics" of the Kennedy years. A combination of Keynesian economics and the social goals of the New Frontier, Heller's economic philosophy placed the federal government in a planning and channeling role that was completely different from the reserved, noninterventionist Eisenhower policies.

Heller first entered government service in 1942 as senior economic analyst for the Treasury Department. There he helped initiate the withholding tax system. During the 1940s and 1950s, he shuttled back and forth between his teaching job at the University of Minnesota and Washington, where he held several advisory jobs. In 1961, he was appointed chairman of the Council of Economic Advisers (CEA) by President Kennedy.

Under Heller's leadership of the CEA, more than advice in economics was given to the President. Heller also made statements to the press and various congressional subcommittees regarding housing, education, and other matters that eventually affect the economy. His approach was to stimulate economic growth rather than to balance budgets and keep prices stable: "Let's invest in education and scientific research and so forth. Let's get a defense establishment that will restore our position. Let's get an investment in space exploration. Then, if there's an inflation problem, by all means raise taxes and take the other necessary measures to curtail inflation."

Much of the impact Heller had was through his taxation plan. He viewed many taxes as potential economic levers and believed in selective programs to boost lagging sectors of the economy. In 1964, while still chairman of the CEA, Heller drafted an extensive revenue-sharing plan, a plan based on the belief that the Internal Revenue Service is a highly efficient tax-collecting device which could be used more effectively if it were to assume some of the tax-collection burdens now carried by the states. Moreover, Heller viewed the high interstate mobility of

corporations and citizens as a weakening influence on local tax bases, a weakness that would be offset by a central taxation clearinghouse.

Heller has been a vocal critic of the economic policies of Republican administrations since leaving government service in 1964. By the end of the 1960s, Heller, through his writings and speeches, was urging President Nixon to institute wage and price guidelines to slow down the inflationary pattern. At President Ford's economic "summit" conference in September 1974, Heller criticized the restrictive monetary policies of the Federal Reserve Board, and he was one of the liberal economists who encouraged Ford to accept a budget deficit and promote a substantial decrease in taxes. A designer of Johnson's successful 1964 tax cut, Heller, in early 1975, advocated a tax cut of over $25 billion annually to bring the country out of recession. "If we really want to reverse things," he said, "let's mainline it."

With the exception of the times he has worked in Washington, Heller has taught in the University of Minnesota economics department since the 1940s. He approves of the close ties between business and academia in the department, and he feels that the school offers a centralized position—both intellectually and geographically—that is particularly useful. As one of his colleagues commented: "His vision is of a great land-grant institution at one end of a boulevard and a state capital at the other, with an inevitable interplay of information between them."

PUBLIC SERVICE EMPLOYMENT PROGRAMS

Traditional vs. Nontraditional Fiscal Policy

In Chapter 10 we looked at traditional fiscal policy measures: changes in government spending *(G)* and changes in taxes *(T)*. Recently, the adequacy of such traditional policies has been questioned by many economists and politicians because of the persistently high inflation rates accompanied by significant amounts of unemployment. The cry in some circles has been that we need a new policy tool, one that is nontraditional and effective. The Emergency Employment Act of 1971 has provided just such a tool. The act provides for public service employment (PSE) and thereby not only adds fiscal stimulus to the economy but at the same time reduces the rate of unemployment.

Congress, at least, seemed sufficiently pleased with the results of the 1971 act to expand it with the comprehensive Employment and Training Act of 1973. Since then, massive expansions in the amount of money that can be provided for public jobs under the 1973 act have been requested by various senators and presidents.

The Position in Favor of PSE

Numerous economists are in favor of expanded PSE, including Harvard's John Kenneth Galbraith and the University of Minnesota's Walter Heller. And Yale Professor William Fellner was quoted, before he joined the Council of Economic Advisers, as saying that PSE "[is] not utopia, but it's at least a second-best solution for achieving low unemployment with price stability."

Of course, not everyone wants increased public employment. Dr. Ezra Solomon, while a member of the Council of Economic Advisers, remarked that "We already have an awful lot of public employment in this country—one in every five or six jobs. I'm not sure the outcry for more public services is as great as some assume."

Why PSE Is So Popular

To be sure, this nontraditional approach to fiscal policy has been tried in the past. During the Great Depression of the 1930s, there were numerous public service employ-

ment programs. The one that is now in effect, however, seems to differ from the typical old-style Works Progress Administration (WPA) programs. The jobs created by the new-style PSE are supposedly for services needed by the community. There has never been any talk of hiring workers to dig holes and then fill them up again, as is alleged to have taken place under the WPA.

Also, the net government budget costs of PSE are relatively low because every dollar budgeted goes directly into a job—presumably one that is filled by an unemployed person, thus saving unemployment insurance and welfare dollars.

Proponents of PSE go one step further. They see expanded PSE as a way to improve the incomes of disadvantaged workers and achieve a shift in output toward the public sector, thus helping to meet some of society's unmet "needs."

The Problem of Federal Fund Usage

If we look at the results of the various PSE programs, we find that the job-creating potential has not been completely fulfilled. We find, for example, that many state and local governments obtaining federal funds to create public service employment have simply substituted these funds for their own payroll budgets. They have then used the savings to reduce state and local taxes or to purchase additional buildings, computers, and the like. Estimates of the amount of federal money substituted for state and local money range from 40 percent to as high as 90 percent. This use of federal money means that the employment-creating effect of expanded PSE is not as great as its proponents contend.

The Multiplier at Work

However, even if this substitution does take place, the money that does go into job creation might have a multiplier effect on output, income, and employment. Various economists and congressional staffs have used the multiplier analysis presented in the previous chapters to estimate the actual net cost to the Treasury of creating a certain number of jobs by expanded PSE, assuming that output and income will rise. They do this by first calculating the number of PSE jobs to be created and then reducing this number by an estimate of the substitution discussed above. The effective number of new jobs created is multiplied by some estimated government-spending multiplier. The multiplier, you will remember, comes into play because the wages paid to the new workers hired under PSE sets off a chain of additional consumer spending that further increases the demand for goods and services, which, in turn, leads to an increase in employment in that sector.

Using this type of multiplier analysis, Congressman Richard Vander Veen (Dem., Mich.), predicted that an additional 2 million jobs could be created at a net cost to the Treasury of only $4.6 billion. This would mean that in the mid-1970s the unemployment rate could be reduced by over 35 percent at a net cost totaling less than 1½ percent of the federal budget.

Such estimates are not without their critics, however. Robert I. Lerman, a former staff member of the Congressional Subcommittee on Fiscal Policy of the Joint Economic Committee, pointed out that such estimates unrealistically assume that federal funds substitute for state and local payroll expenditures only to the extent of zero to 15 percent. Moreover, he contended that it was also unrealistic to presume that half the PSE jobs would go to persons who otherwise would be on unemployment or welfare.[1]

Do the Disadvantaged Get Help?

One of the major aims of PSE programs is to expand employment without adding to inflation. This is presumably accomplished by hiring disadvantaged persons who would otherwise remain unemployed. And, since these disadvantaged persons are hired, it is not necessary to bid up the wage rates of other workers. However, an analysis of the Emergency Employment Act of 1971 shows that only 17 percent of workers hired met the official criterion of "disadvantaged." Further analysis shows that those hired had a higher

[1]Robert I. Lerman, "The Public Employment Bandwagon Takes the Wrong Road," *Challenge*, January–February 1975, p. 12.

average educational level than the average of all workers in private employment.

It is not surprising that PSE seems attractive to other than disadvantaged workers. Most of the proposals for PSE call for jobs paying $7,000 and $8,000 per year. This is a salary level that exceeds the earnings of between 10 and 20 million full-time workers in the United States.

PSE and Fiscal Policy in the Future

Will PSE be expanded and become a major tool of fiscal policy in the future? It has been suggested by a number of economists that PSE be "triggered" automatically at predetermined levels of unemployment, thus hitting the problem immediately by providing new jobs. We have seen, however, that the total employment effect of PSE may not be as great as might be expected because of the substitution of federal funds for otherwise committed state and local expenditures. Moreover, we can be less than sanguine about the percentage of those newly employed who are actually "disadvantaged."

These criticisms, however, do not mean that PSE is necessarily ineffective or that it should be eliminated as a fiscal tool. Additional studies will undoubtedly be done to measure the impact of PSE on the equilibrium level of output, income, and employment.

Whatever the results of these studies, public service jobs provided by the federal government must be paid for out of government monies. In some cases (and, recently, in all cases) this involves increasing the federal government budget deficit. What is the effect of an increase in the budget deficit on the economy? We look at this topic in the next issue.

Questions for Thought and Discussion

1. What is the difference between traditional fiscal policy and PSE programs?
2. For fiscal policy to be effective, does it matter which sectors of the economy are stimulated?
3. What do the old Works Progress Administration and the new PSE programs have in common?

Selected References

Barnes, Peter, "Bringing Back the WPA," *New Republic,* Mar. 15, 1975, pp. 19–21.
Lerman, Robert I., "The Public Employment Bandwagon Takes the Wrong Road," *Challenge,* January–February 1975, pp. 10–16.

Economics in the Public Mind

PAUL A. SAMUELSON

**Economist, Massachusetts
Institute of Technology**

"They don't give Nobel Prizes for writing textbooks," commented Paul Samuelson, the 1970 Nobel Laureate in economics. Nor are Nobel prizes given for writing magazine columns, giving newspaper interviews, making congressional testimonies, or the many other activities by which this prominent American economist is known to millions of people outside academia.

Paul Samuelson was America's first Nobel prize winner in economics; he was awarded the prize for his work in applying mathematics to broad questions of static and dynamic equilibrium and for "raising the level of analysis in economic science." This statement, which appeared in the Stockholm press, is deceptively simple. During the 1940s and 1950s, Samuelson began to synthesize economic methodology on the basis of mathematical models of almost universal applicability. He was foremost in developing mathematical model building and in expanding quantitative analysis and prediction.

Samuelson has authored many books, including *Economics: An Introductory Analysis* (1948), *The Foundations of Economic Analysis* (1948), *Linear Programming and Economic Analysis* (1958), and a two-volume collection of articles (1967).

Of his own work, Samuelson said in his presidential address to the American Economics Association in 1961: "My own scholarship has covered a great variety of fields. And many of them involve questions like welfare economics and factor-price equalization; turnpike theorems and oscillating envelopes; non-substitutability relations in Minkowski-Ricardo-Leontief-Metzler matrices of Mosak-Hichs type; or balanced budget multipliers under conditions of balanced uncertainty in locally impacted topological spaces and molar equivalences. My friends warn me that such topics are suitable merely for captive audiences in search of a degree—and even then not after dark." Samuelson has been a popular spokesman for the economic profession. The wide circulation of his views on current economic policy, by way of his column in *Newsweek* magazine and his testimony before congressional committees, has made him a most public "private citizen."

Although he has never held a major government economic policy post, Samuelson—true to his belief that economists should be concerned with social issues—served as adviser to both John Kennedy and Lyndon Johnson. Kennedy appointed Samuelson to head an economic task force which was to recommend means of reversing the business slump of that period. Samuelson suggested a temporary 3 or 4 percent tax cut, improved unemployment compensation, defense spending, foreign aid, federal aid to education, urban renewal, health and welfare, but no large-scale emergency public works program. All was accepted by Kennedy, except the tax cut. Samuelson later worked on the Johnson task force that developed his Great Society program.

Samuelson was a harsh and consistent critic of the policies of the Nixon administration, and the economic programs of President Ford did not escape his disapproval. "If you turn this recession upside down," Samuelson commented in early 1975, "you will read clearly on its bottom, 'Made in Washington.' " The reason for it, he said, was that Nixon and Ford wanted to bring two-digit inflation to an end. Now, to bring the country out of recession, Samuelson favored a larger income tax cut to more than offset a stiff energy tax and an expansion of the money supply. "If economic conditions are deteriorating, what the economy needs is an infusion of purchasing power from a contrived higher deficit. You cannot take $30 billion in energy taxes from the American people and rebate some $16 billion in income taxes and thereby do anything except worsen the recession." When recovery was ensured, Samuelson predicted that "inflation will again be our primary concern."

Is There a Burden of the Public Debt?

THE LONG-RUN EFFECTS OF DEFICIT FINANCING

Operating in the Red

Everybody knows that if a business ends up in the red, year in and year out, it will eventually go bankrupt. It should follow from this that the United States government too cannot spend more than it receives year in and year out. The fact is, however, that it can and does. Moreover, the government hasn't yet gone bankrupt, and it never will. When the government spends more than it collects in taxes, it runs a budget deficit. That is to say, when G exceeds T, the government is running a deficit, and the national debt is thereby increased. It should be made clear that the national debt is a stock concept. The increase in the national debt due to federal government deficits exceeding surpluses is a flow concept.

Much of the deficit is made up by the government selling bonds to the public. In the process it increases this public or national debt—a debt made up of all the loans people made to the government by buying bonds. Many people think that an increase in the **public debt** imposes a burden on future generations. In this issue we will examine some of the arguments concerning the so-called **burden of the public debt.**

Growth of Public Debt

It is true that the public debt has grown continuously for many years. However, the total public debt is not what we should look at to analyze the burden of the debt. Let's consider the per capita public debt as shown in Table I-12.1.

We see that in 1945 the nominal public debt (expressed in current dollars) per capita was $1,849. In 1970 it was less than that, about $1,806. When we look at the *real* public debt per capita (that is, the public debt corrected for inflation), the decrease in recent years is even more drastic. Look at Figure I-12.1. Here we see that the real public debt per capita has actually fallen by more than one-half since 1945. Thus, although the total may be rising, the amount per capita is falling, and certainly the real amount per capita is falling rather noticeably.

Gross and Net Debt

We must also distinguish between the **gross public debt** and the **net public debt.** We will define net public debt as follows:

Net public debt = gross public debt − all intergovernmental agency borrowing

Let's look at one example of inter-agency governmental borrowing.

Suppose the Treasury is running out of money to pay the government bills. The Treasury decides to sell a $100,000 bond that the Social Security Administration has agreed to buy. The issuance of the bond by the Treasury and the purchase of it by the Social Security Administration will increase the gross public debt by $100,000. However, it will not increase the *net* public debt.

How Do We Measure the Burden?

We need to establish some method of measuring the so-called burden of the public debt. It is not sufficient to say merely that future generations will be worse off because they have to pay more taxes to cover the interest on the increased debt. Taxes may very well have to be raised by, for example, 10 percent over 25 years

Table I-12.1

The Public Debt of the Federal Government, 1915 to 1975

Here we show the gross public debt and the gross public debt per capita. Notice that per capita debt reached a peak in 1945 in terms of nominal dollars—that is, current dollars without correction for inflation. The gross public debt per capita was about the same in 1970 as it had been 25 years earlier.

YEAR	TOTAL (IN BILLIONS)	PER CAPITA
1915	$ 1.2	$ 12
1920	24.3	228
1925	20.5	177
1930	16.2	132
1935	28.7	226
1940	43.0	325
1945	258.7	1,849
1950	257.4	1,697
1955	274.4	1,660
1960	286.3	1,585
1961	289.0	1,573
1962	298.2	1,598
1963	305.9	1,615
1964	311.7	1,622
1965	317.3	1,631
1966	319.9	1,625
1967	326.2	1,637
1968	347.6	1,728
1969	353.7	1,741
1970	370.9	1,806
1971	409.5	1,978
1972	437.3	2,094
1973	468.4	2,226
1974	486.2	2,290
1975 (est.)	525.0	2,472

Source: U.S. Office of Management and Budget

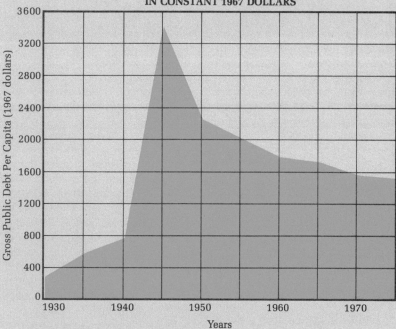

PER CAPITA PUBLIC DEBT OF THE UNITED STATES IN CONSTANT 1967 DOLLARS

FIGURE I-12.1

Here we have plotted the per capita gross public debt in the United States after correcting for inflation. We see that it jumped drastically during World War II but since then has fallen by more than 50 percent. (Source: U.S. Department of the Treasury.)

to handle the increased interest payments on a larger public debt. But this simply means that although people pay higher taxes, many of them (that is, United States citizens who are holders of government bonds) are receiving those monies as interest payments on money lent to the government.

Changes in Capital Stock

Let's instead describe the burden of future generations by looking at the size of the **capital stock** they will inherit from the present generation.

The capital stock consists of buildings, machines, and the like—all those things that help provide for future consumption by contributing to the production of future goods. If an increase in the public debt forces the present generation to hand down a smaller capital stock (wealth) to future generations, then we will say that these future generations are worse off; they are shouldering a burden.

Alternatives to Debt

What are the alternatives to increasing the public debt? Certainly, the government doesn't increase the public debt merely for the fun of it. The government seeks additional borrowing only if it has to make expenditures that are not covered by tax revenues. Now, if the public debt is increased only to cover expenditures, then the government has a choice. It can finance its expenditures either by taxation or by increasing the public debt—that is, by borrowing. (It can also finance its expenditures by what is called "money creation," but we'll cover this topic in the following chapter.) Let's compare the alternatives of taxation and increased government debt.

Taxation vs. Borrowing

To determine the burden of the public debt, we want to know whether a switch from taxation to government borrowing will decrease the wealth (capital stock) that our generation will pass on to the next. We shall assume that the economy is operating at full employment and that government expenditures are as productive as private expenditures.

When the government switches from taxation to debt financing, it increases the *future* tax liabilities of the nation because more government interest payments will be made to holders of new government bonds. Whether or not the nation takes full account of this increase in future tax liabilities is crucial in determining whether it will pass on a diminished capital stock. Suppose the present generation ignores the fact that it will have to pay more taxes in the future; the increased public debt will cause

people today to feel wealthier because they will own more bonds. As a result, they will consume more, save less, and therefore there will be less investment. This will result in a lower capital stock in the future, less wealth bequeathed by the present generation to future ones. Future generations will indeed suffer a burden of the public debt.

Suppose, however, that the present generation is fully aware of its future tax liabilities. It will not feel wealthier merely because it holds more bonds. In fact, people will want to save enough extra to pay for the increased tax liabilities in the future. There will be no change in the *net* investment of the community. In this particular case, investment and consumption will be the same whether the government taxes people or sells bonds. Future generations will inherit a capital stock that has not been diminished, and, by our definition they will suffer no burden of the public debt.

Borrowing from Abroad

Thus far, we have been concerned with the *internal* public debt. If part of it is held by foreigners, then it is no longer true that "we owe it to ourselves." Increased taxes for paying the interest on increased public debt will no longer be paid to ourselves. Currently, about 0.18 percent of the national debt is owned by foreigners. Far from being a burden, however, an increase in the public debt sold to foreigners can prove to be a boon to future generations.

Assume we are at full employment. It is impossible for us to increase either investment or consumption. We could, however, change the mix by altering savings behavior. Borrowing resources from abroad by selling public debt to foreigners can allow us to increase consumption today and also increase investment. Future generations must pay the interest that allows for this increased consumption today, but they will end up with a larger capital stock. Future generations will be better off if the additional income from the larger capital stock more than pays the interest owed to foreigners. If not, they will in fact be burdened by the increased **external public debt.**

How Big Is the Interest Payment on the National Debt?

Let's consider the size of the interest payments on public debt (the value of federal government bonds outstanding). In our Figure I-10.2 we show interest payments as a percentage of GNP. Even though interest payments have been rising steadily since before World War II, as a percentage of GNP, they have not gone much above 2 percent for the last two decades. Apparently, then, we are not getting future generations deeper and deeper into debt, relative to what their income is expected to be.

Redistribution of Income

It has been argued that the existence of a public debt on which interest

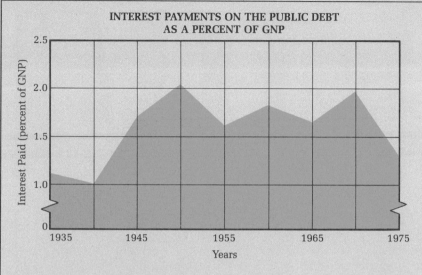

INTEREST PAYMENTS ON THE PUBLIC DEBT AS A PERCENT OF GNP

Interest Paid (percent of GNP)

2.5

2.0

1.5

1.0

0

1935   1945   1955   1965   1975

Years

FIGURE I-12.2

Here we see that the interest payments on the public debt vary between 1 and 2 percent as a percentage of GNP. *(Source: U.S. Department of Commerce.)*

is paid to bondholders tends to redistribute income. This presumably is true to the extent that those who receive interest are other than those who pay the taxes from which those interest payments are made. Whenever a situation exists where one group of heavily taxed taxpayers holds no bonds but another group of lightly taxed taxpayers does hold federal government bonds, there will be a net transfer of income from the first group to the second group. In other words, a minor redistribution of income might occur.

There is another effect of the public debt that is, perhaps, even more subtle than redistribution of income. The existence of a public debt requires taxes to be levied on American citizens. Most of these taxes, at least at the federal level, are in the form of taxes on income. If a larger public debt requires higher taxes to pay the higher interest costs of that debt, then Americans will pay higher rates of income taxation. But

higher rates of taxation are an incentive for individuals to work less because the opportunity cost of *not* working falls as the rate of taxation increases. Thus, even if income were not transferred from one American group to another, there could still be a burden in the sense that the higher tax rate needed to pay the interest payment on the public debt would lead individuals to choose more leisure (that is, to work less hard for shorter periods). We say in such a situation that the allocation of resources is distorted.

Note, of course, that debt financing really only *postpones* the tax burden. Basically, the financing decision is between present or future taxes.

Conclusions

It is impossible to determine exactly what type of burden might be be-

stowed upon future generations by increasing the national debt. First of all, we have to know whether we are talking about the gross or the net debt. Then we have to know whether individuals are going to discount correctly the increased future tax liabilities implicit in an increased public debt. Next we can determine whether investment will be altered and, therefore, whether the capital stock handed to future generations will be the same as it would be in the case of, say, taxation-financed spending. One thing is sure: We should be wary of editorials that decry the horrible, bankrupting increases in our national debt when, on the next page of the newspaper, an ad tells us to contribute to the public debt by buying U.S. Savings Bonds.

We should also note that there is much public outcry against the public debt, but no similar concern is expressed about private debt. Check the balance sheet of any company in the United States, and you will undoubtedly find that the company is in debt. This is a normal business practice. Part of the capital structure of a company is made up of debt, and part of it is made up of equity—that is, shares of stock. Company managers and investors will get concerned if the interest payments on the debt of a company get close to the operating income of that company, but no such problem has ever occurred in the federal government. Similarly, the interest on the public debt uses up a very small part of the total revenues collected.

Definitions of New Terms

Public Debt: The market value of all federal government securities outstanding.

Burden of the Public Debt: Expansion of the public debt will supposedly be a burden to future generations. This burden will be caused by our increasing the debt in this generation. More precisely, the burden will occur when future generations inherit a lower capital stock (wealth) than they would have had public debt not been expanded.

Gross Public Debt: The market value of all outstanding securities of the federal government, including those held by federal government agencies.

Net Public Debt: The gross public debt minus all interagency holdings. All debt concepts refer to a stock measured at a moment in time.

Capital Stock: The sum of all buildings, machines, and the like in the United States. Capital stock allows us to produce more in the future—that is, to provide more future consumption.

External Public Debt: Public debt owed to foreigners, as opposed to internal public debt, which is owed to ourselves.

Questions for Thought and Discussion

1. Some economists have likened the public debt to robbing Peter to pay Paul. Are they right?
2. Why can the federal government be forever in the red?
3. Adam Smith once said: "What is prudence in the conduct of every private family can scarce be folly in that of a great kingdom." Take out the words "that of a great kingdom" and insert "the United States." Was he right concerning the public debt?

Selected References

Anderson, William H., *Financing Modern Government*, Boston: Houghton-Mifflin, 1973, chaps. 22–29.

Bowen, William G. et al., "The Public Debt: A Burden on Future Generations?", *American Economic Review*, September 1960, pp. 701–706.

Okun, Arthur (ed.), *The Battle against Unemployment,* rev. ed., New York: W. W. Norton, 1972, parts II and IV.

Money and the Banking System

If someone were to ask you "How much money do you make?", you might answer so many dollars per week or per year. In this context, the term "money" really means income or the ability to purchase goods and services—in fact, the term money is most generally used to mean income. But in this sense it is being used incorrectly. Only counterfeiters and banks "make money." What you make is income. In this chapter and throughout the rest of the text, we will use the term money to mean only that which we use as our medium of exchange. Money is most often thought of as those pieces of paper and coins you have in your wallet, purse, or buried in the back yard. Our money supply, however, includes more than currency. At the very minimum, your checking account balance can be considered a medium of exchange because you can use it in exchange for the things you want to buy.

In this chapter we will examine the functions that money serves, the different types of money which are in existence today, the banking system, and how the supply of money in circulation is controlled.

Types of Monetary Standards

In the United States today we have a **fiduciary monetary system.** This means that the value of our currency rests upon the public's confidence in it. "Fiduciary" comes from the Latin *fiducia*, which means trust or confidence. In other words, in our monetary system the currency is not convertible into a fixed quantity of gold or silver.

Prior to the existence of a fiduciary currency, a **commodity currency** was used. A commodity currency is one in which a commodity such as cigarettes, beads, salt, or other items has a use other than as a medium of exchange.

Before money was used, transactions or exchanges took place by means of **barter.** Barter is simply a direct exchange—no intermediary good called money is used. Economic historians often suggest that the switch from bartering to the use of money allowed for the economic growth of the Western world since increased specialization was then possible. It was extremely costly (that is, the transactions costs were high) to make all exchanges via barter. Imagine the difficulty you would have today if you had to exchange your labor directly for the fruits of someone else's labor. Imagine the many exchanges that would have to take place for you to get from a position of owning, for example, 25 pairs of shoes to a position where you owned only two pairs but now also had bread, meat, a pair of pants, and so on. The use of money facilitates exchange, allowing for increased specialization and therefore higher material standards of living. (Remember, we are talking about money and *not* income.)

The Functions of Money

There are three traditional functions of money. The one most people are familiar with and the one we referred to above is as a medium of exchange. However, money also serves as a unit of accounting and as a store of purchasing power.

Money As a Medium of Exchange

As a medium of exchange, money allows individuals to specialize in any area in which they have a comparative advantage, receiving money payment for the fruits of their labor that can then be exchanged for the fruits of other people's labor. The usefulness of money as a medium of exchange therefore increases with the amount of a country's trade and specialization. Money would not be as important in self-suf-

ficient family units, for example, as it is in modern commercial economies.

For money to serve as a medium of exchange, it must first be generally accepted as a means of payment for all market exchanges. The fiduciary currency in our country works as a medium of exchange because it is accepted in payment for all debts and obligations. In fact, in the United States, individuals are required to accept our currency as ". . . payments for all debts public and private. . . ."

Money As a Unit of Accounting

As a unit of accounting, money is actually the common denominator that allows individuals to compare the relative value of different goods and services in our economy. In colonial times, our unit of account was not the dollar but the British pound sterling. Spanish pesos were also circulated, but prices were generally quoted in terms of pounds. The dollar became the official unit of account in 1792.

Money As a Store of Value

As a store of value, money is an asset that accounts for part of one's wealth. Wealth in the form of money can be exchanged later for other assets. Although it is not the only form of wealth that can be exchanged for goods and services, it is the one most widely accepted. This attribute of money is called **liquidity.** We say that an asset is liquid when it can easily be acquired or disposed of without high transactions costs and with relative certainty as to its value. Money is by definition the most liquid asset there is. Just compare it, for example, to a share of stock listed on the New York Stock Exchange. To buy or sell that stock, you must call a stockbroker who will place the buy or sell order for you. This must be done during normal business hours. You have to pay a percentage commission to the broker. Moreover, there is a distinct probability that you will get more or less for the stock than you originally paid for it. This is not the case with money. You can exchange a dollar for a dollar and exchange it for other assets at any time of the day or night. Therefore, most individuals hold at least a part of their wealth in the form of this most liquid of assets, money.

However, when we hold money, we pay a price for this advantage of liquidity. That price is the interest yield that could have been obtained had the asset been held in another form, for example, in the form of a savings and loan account. In other words, the cost of holding money (its opportunity cost) is measured by the alternative yield obtainable by holding some other form of asset.

The Distinction between Money and Credit

The distinction between money and credit is sometimes not very clear. Credit is funds or savings that are made available to borrowers. In other words, the credit market is basically a market where those who are willing to wait to have purchasing power provide funds at a cost (the interest rate) for those who want to have purchasing power now and are willing to pay a price to have it. It is through the interaction of supply (lenders) and demand (borrowers) in the credit market that saving provides funds for investment.

This is not the case with money per se. Money is merely the most liquid asset in which people choose to hold part of their wealth. We will see, however, that the ultimate amount of money supply is determined by credit expansions and contractions by banks. To *not* confuse money with credit, you should think of credit as a loan and money as that part of a person's wealth which is completely liquid.

Defining the Money Supply

There is not complete agreement about what should and what should not be included in the money supply. If we define money, functionally by its three roles: medium of exchange, unit of account, temporary store of purchasing power, then currency and checking account balances, which are also called demand deposits, should obviously be included. Currency has been defined as paper notes and coins. Demand deposits are accounts in commercial banks that can be transferred or converted into currency on demand—in other words, you can write a check at any time on your checking account. The most narrow definition of money includes demand deposits and currency in the hands of the nonbanking public. This total of currency and demand deposits held by the nonbanking public has been labeled M_1. Throughout the remainder of the macro portion of this text, we will talk in terms of M_1, even though there are broader measures of liquidity that could be used.

A second definition of money includes M_1 plus time deposits in commercial banks. Time deposits are savings account balances and small certificates of deposit held by commercial banks. They are called time deposits because, in principle, the bank can require notice of your intent to withdraw from your savings account. This second definition of money has been labeled M_2.

So, M_2 is circulating currency, plus demand deposits, plus time deposits in commercial banks. If we extend our definition of money even further to include deposits in noncommercial bank thrift institutions, such as passbook shares in savings and loan associations, then we obtain M_3. This M_3 is our broadest measure of the money stock. You can see in Figure 11-1 that there is a distinct difference between M_1, M_2, and M_3. However, we will talk only in terms of M_1 for the rest of this unit.

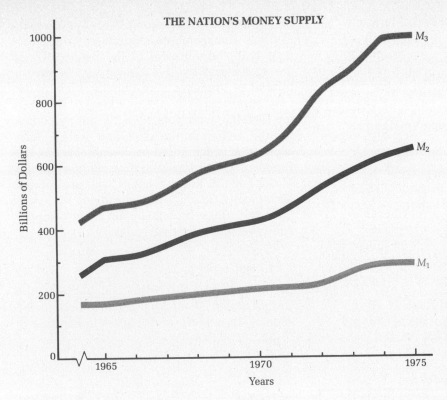

THE NATION'S MONEY SUPPLY

FIGURE 11-1 The Money Supply Defined Three Different Ways

Here we show for the last decade the money supply as defined in three different ways. The narrowest definition, M_1, includes only currency and checking accounts. If we add commercial bank time deposits, we get M_2. The broadest definition includes currency, checking deposits, commercial bank time deposits, and noncommercial bank thrift deposits. (*Source*: Board of Governors of the Federal Reserve System.)

Table 11-1 shows the components of M_1 for selected years. Although demand deposits account for over 75 percent of the money supply, even this figure underestimates their importance. Demand deposits are used for 95 percent of the dollar volume of all C, I, and G purchases in our economy.

Currency accounts for the remainder of M_1, but its percentage importance over time has been rising. Some observers contend that this shift toward a larger percentage of money being held as currency is the result of a rise in illegal activities. Since currency cannot be traced, illegal transactions demand the use of currency. And as more illegal transactions are undertaken, a higher percentage of the money stock will be demanded in the form of currency. Also, currency is used to conceal income from the IRS.

How does currency get into circulation? Who provides it? Who watches over the money supply? The answer is our central bank, which we call the Federal Reserve, or the Fed for short.

Table 11-1 **Components of M_1 (in Billions of Dollars)**

COMPONENT	1920	1950	1975 (MAY)
Demand deposits	18.66	90.20	219.48
Currency	4.49	25.00	69.52
Money supply (M_1)	23.15	115.20	289.0

Source: Board of Governors of the Federal Reserve System

The Federal Reserve System

Our central bank was established by the Federal Reserve Act, signed on December 23, 1913, by President Woodrow Wilson. The act was the outgrowth of recommendations from the National Monetary Commission, which had been authorized by the Aldridge-Vreeland Act of 1908. Basically, the Commission had attempted to find a way to counter the periodic financial panics that had occurred in our country. The Fed was set up to aid and supervise banks and also to provide banking services for the U.S. Treasury.

Organization of the Federal Reserve System

Figure 11-2 shows the Federal Reserve organizational chart. Basically, it consists of a Board of Governors, which is composed of seven salaried full-time members appointed by the President with the approval of the Senate. There are 12 Federal Reserve banks, which have a total of 24 branches. Additionally, there is the very important Federal Open Market Committee (FOMC), which decides the policy course for the Fed in future days and weeks. That committee is composed of the members of the Board of Governors plus five representatives of the Federal Reserve banks who are rotated periodically. The FOMC determines by its actions the future growth of the money supply and other important variables.

Member Banks

Of the 14,000 or so commercial banks in the United States, about 5700 are members of the Federal Reserve System. This is in contrast to

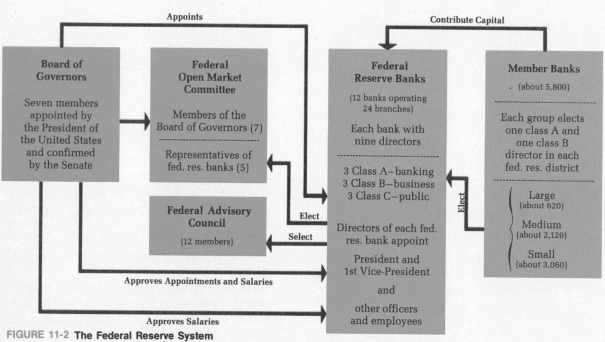

FIGURE 11-2 **The Federal Reserve System**

(*Source:* Board of Governors of the Federal Reserve System.)

the almost 7000 banks that were members of the system at the end of World War II. There has been an increasing movement of commercial banks away from membership in the Federal Reserve System to state bank status. All national banks have to be members of the system, but those banks that prefer to be regulated by state rules can, upon successful application, change their membership.

Banks belonging to the Fed do obtain significant privileges and prestige. They can borrow from the Federal Reserve banks and they can also obtain currency, information, and advice from those same banks. They can also use the check-clearing facilities of the Fed and transfer funds over the Federal Reserve's teletype wires.

There is, however, a cost for these privileges. The cost is that they must forgo certain profitable investment opportunities because of the higher requirements for non-income-producing assets, or "reserves" as they are called, which member banks must keep available in the form of vault cash or on deposit with the local Federal Reserve branch. State banks can keep a smaller proportion of their total assets in such non-income-producing reserves than can national banks in the Federal Reserve System.

Let's go into more detail now about the reserve system we have and see how it is used as a tool by the Fed to control the nation's money supply. In the process, we will see how the money supply can be expanded and contracted.

Reserves

Member banks of the Federal Reserve System are required to maintain a specified percentage of their customer deposits as reserves. If the required level of reserves is 20 percent and the bank has $1 billion in customer deposits, then it must have at least $200 million between the cash in its vault and the money in its account at the local Federal Reserve branch. Actually, the average required reserve level now is around 15 percent. Table 11-2 shows the reserve requirements that have been in effect since February 1975. Notice that there are lower reserve requirements for time deposits than for demand deposits and that there is a legal range within which the Fed's requirements must stay. That range has been legislated by Congress. To change it, new legislation would have to be passed.

Assets and Liabilities

Since required reserves are less than 100 percent of demand deposits, we have what is called a **fractional reserve banking system**—that is, only a fraction of customer account balances must be kept in reserve by banks. Note that a checking account balance, from a bank's point of view, is a liability since you own it, not the bank. However, the reserves the bank has in a Federal Reserve branch are part of its assets, and the Fed's liabilities.

We can see in Table 11-3 that the assets of member banks consist in large part of loans to customers and of securities such as stocks and bonds. On the other hand, their liabilities consist mainly of demand deposits and time deposits. These are liabilities because the banks must pay the former on demand and the latter essentially on demand. Table 11-3 is a composite or consolidated balance sheet, lumping all commercial banks together. The one term you may not be familiar with is *net worth*. This is the difference between assets and liabilities. It is put in the liabilities column because it is owned by the stockholders in the bank.

Excess Reserves

Member banks often hold reserves in excess of what is required by the Federal Reserve System. This difference between actual reserves and required reserves is called **excess**

Table 11-2 **Reserve Requirements of Member Banks**

Here we see the reserve requirements of all member banks. Notice that the reserve requirements for time deposits are less than for demand deposits.

EFFECTIVE DATE	NET DEMAND DEPOSITS					TIME DEPOSITS		
							Other Time Deposits	
	Under $2 Million	$2–10 Million	$10–100 Million	$100–400 Million	Over $400 Million	Savings Deposits	Over $5 Million	Under $5 Million
In Effect Feb. 13, 1975	7½%	10%	12%	13%	16½%	3%	3%	5%
Present legal requirements: Minimum Maximum			10% 22%				3% 10%	

Source: Board of Governors of the Federal Reserve System

reserves. Excess reserves can be negative as well as positive. Negative excess reserves indicate that banks do not have sufficient reserves to meet their legal requirements. Excess reserves are an important determinant of the rate of growth of the money stock for it is only to the extent that banks have excess reserves that they can expand their deposits by lending money to firms and individuals. Since reserves produce no income, banks have an incentive to minimize any excess reserves. They use them either to purchase income-producing securities or to make loans on which they earn income through interest payments. But we will see that the Fed itself is the primary determinant of the level of reserves in the banking system.

Table 11-3 **Consolidated Balance Sheet of Member Banks, January 1975 (in Billions of Dollars)**

ASSETS		LIABILITIES AND NET WORTH	
Total reserves	$ 36.95	Demand deposits	$180.95
Loans	414.40	Time deposits	316.70
Securities	135.80	Borrowings from Federal Reserve	0.39
Other assets	89.75	Other liabilities	130.12
		Net worth	48.74
Total	$676.90	Total	$676.90

Source: Federal Reserve Bulletin

The Supply of Money

What determines the number of dollars in circulation in the form of currency and demand deposit balances? We know that commercial banks must be an important part of our analysis because they hold the bulk of the money supply as liabilities in the form of demand deposits. We also know that the central bank, the Fed, must be an important part of the analysis because of its control over the commercial banks. What we will see is a very clear-cut relationship between the level of reserves and the level of demand deposits and hence the total money supply. We will see that whatever affects reserves affects the money supply.

Let's first talk about how the Fed affects the level of reserves in the most direct manner possible, and then we will discuss the process by which a change in the level of reserves causes a multiple change in the total money supply. We will begin with the Federal Open Market Committee since its decisions essentially determine the level of reserves in the system.

Federal Open Market Committee

Open-market operations involve the buying and selling of United States government securities in the open market (the private bond market). Most government bonds except U.S. Savings Bonds are negotiable. If the Open Market Committee decides that it wants the Fed to sell bonds, it instructs the trading desk at the New York Federal Reserve Bank to do so. Since the bond market is very well developed, this can be accomplished immediately. If the Committee decides it wants to buy bonds, it instructs the trading desk to buy.

But what happens when the trading desk of the New York Federal Reserve buys a $10,000 bond? How does it pay for it? To buy the bond, the New York Federal Reserve writes a check on itself. The person or bank selling the bond receives the check and deposits it in its own account. The depository bank gives it to the Fed and the Fed writes $10,000 in the reserve account of that particular bank. Therefore, if the Fed buys a bond, it expands reserves by the amount of the purchase. Conversely, if the Fed sells a bond, the person or bank buying the bond writes a check, and the Fed reduces the reserves of the bank on which the check was written. In other words, when the Fed sells bonds, it reduces the reserves in the banking system. It reduces the reserves of the commercial member bank by the amount of the sale. When the Fed buys bonds, the opposite occurs. We see, therefore, that open-market operations on the part of the Fed can increase or decrease commercial member bank reserves.

The Relationship between Reserves and Total Deposits

To show the important relationship between reserves and total deposits, we'll first look at a single bank. A single bank can make loans, that is, create deposits, only to the extent that it has excess reserves to cover those new deposits. Thus, the isolated individual bank can in no way alter the money supply. However, the banking system as a whole can. This will become obvious as we work through a set of what are called *T accounts,* showing the assets and liabilities of an individual bank and those of the banking system as a whole.

We'll begin by making some assumptions that will make the problem much easier to handle:

1. The required reserve ratio is 20 percent for all demand deposits.
2. Demand deposits are the bank's only liabilities, whereas reserves and loans are the bank's only assets. (Loans are pieces of paper promising that the bank will be paid back in the future or I.O.Us.) Net worth, therefore, is zero.

3. Banks desire to keep their excess reserves at a zero level.

Now look at the initial position of our representative bank. Liabilities consist of $1 million in demand deposits, and assets consist of $200,000 in reserves, either in the form of vault cash or in the account of the Federal Reserve branch, plus $800,000 in loans to customers. Assets of $1 million therefore equal liabilities of $1 million.

Bank 1

Assets		Liabilities	
Total reserves	$ 200,000	Demand deposits	$1,000,000
Required reserves	(200,000)		
Excess reserves	(—0—)		
Loans	800,000		
Total	$1,000,000	Total	$1,000,000

Now a new customer comes to the bank and deposits a check for $1 million. Demand deposits in our individual bank increase by $1 million; at the same time, total reserves increase by $1 million, leaving an excess reserve of $800,000. Reserves increase when the representative bank deposits the check it receives in its account at its local Federal Reserve branch.

Look at excess reserves. They used to be zero and now they're $800,000—$800,000 worth of non-income-earning assets. Our third assumption, however, was that the bank desires to have zero excess reserves. So, in this simple world, the bank will make additional interest-earning loans totaling $800,000. Now loans increase to $1.6 million, total reserves fall to $400,000, and excess reserves are again zero.

We see, then, that for any individual bank the amount of reserves it has is directly related to the amount of deposits it receives. In this example, a person came in and deposited an

Bank 1

Assets		Liabilities	
Total reserves	$1,200,000	Demand deposits	$2,000,000
Required reserves	(400,000)		
Excess reserves	(800,000)		
Loans	800,000		
Total	$2,000,000	Total	$2,000,000

Bank 1

Assets		Liabilities	
Total reserves	$ 400,000	Demand deposits	$2,000,000
Required reserves	(400,000)		
Excess reserves	(—0—)		
Loans	1,600,000		
Total	$2,000,000	Total	$2,000,000

additional $1 million that became part of the reserves of that bank. Since excess reserves now exceeded zero, further loans were possible, and these were made in order to earn interest.

There is no overall deposit creation (that is, money creation) because the $1 million check brought in to open a new account was probably written on another bank, which means that while this bank had its deposits and reserves increased and was therefore able to expand its loans, another bank was doing just the opposite.

Now let's look at the banking system as a whole and see the primary method by which the actual money supply is expanded. We do this by seeing how banks respond to an increase in reserves in the system, that increase being due to Federal Reserve actions.

The Money Supply Expands

We begin by making another assumption: The $1 million check deposited by the bank client was written not on another commercial bank but on a Federal Reserve bank. We'll further assume that this depositor obtained that $1 million check because the FOMC decided it wanted to purchase a $1 million bond from a private individual. When it did so, it gave the individual a check written on itself.

Let's go back now to our individual bank, Bank 1, and look again at the third T account, in which both liabilities and assets have been increased by $1 million and loans have been expanded from $800,000 to $1.6 million. Because of our new assumptions, the money supply has also been increased. The money supply increases by $800,000 when the bank expands its loans.

The process does not stop here. Let's assume that the additional $800,000 loan was given to a firm wishing to purchase a MacDonald's franchise. This firm takes the $800,000 check and deposits it in its bank account at bank 2. For simplicity, we'll ignore the assets and liabilities in that bank and concentrate only on the T account changes resulting from this new deposit. We add a plus sign to indicate that we are looking only at changes in the T accounts. We see that for bank 2 this new deposit becomes an increase in reserves. Since the required reserves are 20 percent or $160,000, excess reserves are $640,000. But, of course, excess reserves earn no income, so bank 2 will eliminate them by making loans, which do earn income, as shown. These loans increase the money supply again—by $640,000.

Bank 2

Assets		Liabilities	
Total reserves	+$800,000	Demand deposits	+$800,000
Required reserves	(160,000)		
Excess reserves	(640,000)		
Total	+$800,000	Total	+$800,000

Bank 2

Assets		Liabilities	
Total reserves	+$160,000	Demand deposits	+$800,000
Required reserves	(160,000)		
Excess reserves	(—0—)		
Loans	+ 640,000		
Total	+$800,000	Total	+$800,000

But we can't stop here. We assume that another firm has taken the $640,000 loan from the bank in anticipation of buying into an oil drilling fund later. This fund has a bank account at bank 3. Now look at bank 3's simplified T account, where again we look only at changes in the account.

When the depositor pays the $640,000 to the fund managers who bank in bank 3, total reserves go up by that amount. Required reserves are 20 percent, or $128,000, and excess reserves are $512,000. Bank 3, too, will want to lend out these non-income-earning assets. When it does, total reserves fall to $128,000, excess reserves become zero, and loans, increasing by $512,000, add the same amount to the money supply.

Bank 3

Assets		Liabilities	
Total reserves	+$640,000	Demand deposits	+$640,000
Required reserves	(128,000)		
Excess reserves	(512,000)		
Total	+$640,000	Total	+$640,000

Bank 3

Assets		Liabilities	
Total reserves	+$128,000	Demand deposits	+$640,000
Required reserves	(128,000)		
Excess reserves	(—0—)		
Loans	+ 512,000		
Total	+$640,000	Total	+$640,000

This process goes on and on and on. Each bank gets a smaller and smaller increase in deposits and each bank makes a correspondingly smaller amount of loans.

But what happened to the total money supply? In this simple model, the money supply was increased by the $1 million the Fed gave to the private individual in exchange for a bond; it was increased also by the $800,000 deposit in bank 2; and it was increased again by the $640,000 deposit in bank 3. Eventually, in fact, the money supply will be increased by a total approaching $5 million! This can be seen in Table 11-4, which is graphically represented by Figure 11-3.

The key to understanding how the money supply can be increased in this manner is remembering that the original new deposit in bank 1 was in the form of a check written on the Federal Reserve and therefore represented new reserves to the banking system. Had that check been written on another bank, bank 5 for example, nothing would have happened to the total amount of demand deposits and hence to the total money supply, for what one bank gained another bank would lose. This is not the case when the additional deposit that forms additional reserves comes from the Federal Reserve System itself. The commercial banking system, then, can increase the money supply primarily because excess reserves are created by the Federal Reserve System.

Table 11-4 The Maximum Potential Effects on the Money Supply of an Increase in Reserves of $1 Million with a 20% Required Reserve

BANK	NEW DEPOSIT	POSSIBLE LOANS (= EXCESS RESERVES)	REQUIRED RESERVES
Bank 1	$1,000,000	$ 800,000	$ 200,000
Bank 2	800,000	640,000	160,000
Bank 3	640,000	512,000	128,000
Bank 4	512,000	409,600	102,400
Bank 5	409,600	327,680	81,920
Bank 6	327,690	262,140	65,540
Bank 7	262,140	209,710	52,430
Bank 8	209,710	167,760	41,950
All other banks	838,870	671,110	167,760
Total	$5,000,000	$4,000,000	$1,000,000

The Expansion Multiplier

We can now make a generalization about the extent to which the money supply will increase when the banking system's reserves are increased. If we assume that no excess reserves are kept and that all loans are spent and deposited in other banks in the system, then the following equation applies:

$$\text{Maximum deposit expansion multiplier} = \frac{1}{\text{required reserve percentage}}$$

In our example, the required reserve level was 20 percent, or 1/5. Therefore, the maximum deposit expansion multiplier was 5, and that's exactly what we show in Table 11-4 and Figure 11-3: A $1 million increase in reserves due to a Federal Reserve purchase causing a $5 million increase in demand deposits and hence in the money supply.

The deposit expansion multiplier equals the maximum potential change in the money supply due to a change in reserves. Notice we use

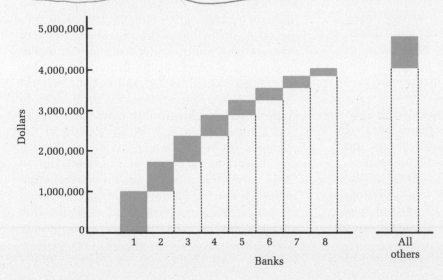

FIGURE 11-3 **The Multiple Expansion in the Money Supply Due to $1 Million in New Reserve**

The banks are all aligned in decreasing order of new deposits created. This is merely a graphical representation of Table 11-4.

the word "change" rather than "increase" because reserves can also be reduced by the Fed (when, for example, it sells a bond in the open market), and in that case we would see a multiple contraction in the money supply.

It may be easier to see this multiple expansion and contraction by picturing a monopoly bank that takes care of all banking services in the United States. In this case, an individual would deposit the proceeds from a bond sale to the Fed in the monopoly bank. The monopoly bank, since it receives all deposits and grants all loans, could immediately lend a multiple of its excess reserves, producing a 5 to 1 expansion in bank deposits, because every loan it made, whether spent or put into a checking account, would ultimately return to the monopoly bank, which would never lose reserves to any other bank. The T account of a monopoly bank would look the same as the consolidated balance sheet for all banks in the system.

Note that we made a number of simplifying assumptions to come up with the maximum potential deposit expansion multiplier. In the real world, however, the expansion (or contraction) multiplier is considerably smaller. Several factors account for this.

MULTIPLIER IS LESS BECAUSE

Leakages   The entire loan from one bank is not always deposited in another bank. Rather, some borrowed funds remain in circulation, as cash or currency. As a result, the expansion multiplier is smaller than the maximum.

Excess Reserves   Banks do not always keep excess reserves at zero. And to the extent that they want to keep positive excess reserves, the deposit expansion multiplier will be smaller. To test your understanding, go back to the example we used and find the multiplier, assuming required reserves of 20 percent and excess reserves of 5 percent at all times.

The Desire to Borrow   We have implicitly

PEOPLE MIGHT NOT WANT TO BORROW

assumed that individuals and businesses want to borrow whatever the banks want to lend. However, whenever or not this is the case, the deposit expansion multiplier will be lower. Borrowers, for whatever reason, may not want to borrow.

The actual relationship between the total money supply (which includes currency) and reserves is definitely smaller than its potential maximum.

The Tools of Monetary Policy

Monetary policy in the United States is carried out by the Federal Reserve System. We have already discussed one of the major tools of that monetary policy: changes in excess reserves by open-market operations. Now, we will go into more detail about open-market operations and discuss the other two major policy tools used by the Fed. In all cases, these policy tools are aimed at altering the supply of money in the United States.

Open-Market Operations

We have seen that if the Fed purchases a United States government bond, the money supply will increase by a multiple; similarly, if the Fed sells the government bond, the money supply will contract by a multiple. Federal Reserve monetary policy is concentrated in its open-market operations. When the Fed, through the Federal Reserve Open Market Committee, desires to "loosen up," it instructs the New York Fed to buy United States government bonds in the open market. When the Fed decides to "tighten up," it instructs the New York Fed to sell United States government bonds in the open market. In these ways, the supply of money is expanded or contracted. A multiple change (expansion or contraction) in the level of the money supply occurs with any change in the level of total reserves. Most changes in our money supply

TIME 3:15
TEMPERATURE 57
PRIME INTEREST RATE 11.75

Drawing by Bernard Schoenbaum; © 1974
The New Yorker Magazine, Inc.

are due to open-market operations like this.[1]

Member-Bank Borrowing and the Discount Rate

If a commercial bank wants to increase its loans but has reached the limit of its reserves, there

is only one way it can expand its deposits, and that is by borrowing reserve funds. One place it can borrow reserves is from the Fed itself. (This is another way the money supply is expanded.) The commercial bank member goes to the Federal Reserve Discount Window and asks for a loan of a certain amount of reserves. The Fed does not have to lend reserves to requesting member banks because it is not required to do so by law. Reserve borrowing by the member banks is a privilege—not a right. In any event, the Fed charges these member banks for any reserves that it lends them. The rate that the Fed charges used to be called the

[1]Actually, since Sept. 12, 1968, the Federal Reserve open-market operations do not work as simply as this. On that date, some new rules were put into effect. The most important one was that the current week's required reserves were to be calculated on the basis of average daily deposits 2 weeks *earlier.*

"rediscount rate," but now it is typically called the **discount rate.** In Canada and England, it is called the *bank rate*. When the newspapers report that the Fed has increased the discount rate from 7 percent to 8 percent, you know that the Fed has increased its charge for lending reserves to member banks. Note, however, that the discount rate is *not* the charge that banks must pay when borrowing money to lend you. The discount rate is applied to a very small percentage of total bank reserves.

Member banks actually do not often go to the Fed to borrow reserves because the Fed will not lend them everything they want. In addition, the Fed can always refuse to lend money to member banks even when the commercial banks need the money to make their reserve account meet legal requirements. There are, however, alternative sources for the banks to tap when they want to expand their reserves or when they need reserves to meet a requirement. If a commercial bank, for example, discovers that its required reserves are $200 million but that it only has $190 million in actual reserves, it can go to the **Federal Funds Market.** Since some banks are at the same time probably going to have excess reserves, banks wanting to borrow reserves can do so in that market. In fact, almost all reserve borrowing is done in the Federal Funds Market. Usually, the borrowing is for overnight only.

Reserve Requirement Changes

Another less-often used but still very important method by which the Fed can alter the money supply is to change reserve requirements. Previously, we assumed that reserve requirements were given. Actually, these requirements are set by the Fed within limits established by Congress. In Table 11-2 those limits were given along with the current reserve requirements.

What would a change in reserve requirements from 10 to 20 percent do (if there were no excess reserves)? We already discovered that the deposit expansion multiplier was the reserve requirement percentage turned upside down. If reserve requirements are 10 percent, then the deposit expansion multiplier *in principle* would be the reciprocal of 1/10, or 10. If, for some reason, the Fed decided to double reserve requirements to 20 percent, then the deposit expansion multiplier would equal the reciprocal of 1/5, or 5. The deposit expansion multiplier is therefore inversely related to reserve requirements. If the Fed decides to increase reserve requirements, then we will see a decrease in the deposit expansion multiplier. With a given level of reserves, the money supply will therefore contract.

Let's take a simple example. Suppose that the deposit expansion multiplier is in fact 10, and that reserves are $100 billion. We know then that the money supply is going to be $1 trillion. If the Federal Reserve decides to change member bank reserve requirements from 10 to 20 percent, we expect the money supply eventually to fall to only $500 billion because the deposit expansion multiplier will fall from 10 to 5 (if there are no excess reserves). What happens is that, as reserve requirements are raised, banks find they are in the red with the Fed. They must call in loans, for example, to increase their reserves to the new required level. When all banks attempt to do this, there will be a multiple contraction in the money supply.

Notice the difference between this method and the first two methods the Federal Reserve has for changing the total money supply in circulation. When the Fed makes open-market purchases or sales of bonds, it directly alters the bank reserves. When the Fed decides to lend more money at the discount window, it again directly alters the bank reserves. (Recall that the change in the money supply is equal to the change in the bank reserves times the

FEDERAL RESERVE POLICIES

EXPANSIONARY

Action	Result
Buy bonds in open market	Increase reserves
Lower discount rate	Increase reserves
Reduce reserve requirements	Increase deposit expansion multiplier

CONTRACTIONARY

Action	Result
Sell bonds in open market	Reduce reserves
Increase discount rates	Reduce reserves
Increase reserve requirements	Decrease deposit expansion multiplier

deposit expansion multiplier.) When the Fed alters reserve requirements, however, it does not change the bank reserves as we have defined it. Rather, it changes the deposit expansion multiplier. When the Fed changes the deposit expansion multiplier without any offsetting change in the bank reserves, a change in the money supply will result.

However, open-market operations allow the Federal Reserve to control the money supply much more precisely than do changes in reserve requirements. A small change in reserve requirements will result in a very large change in the money supply, if there are no changes in the bank reserves. That is why the Federal Reserve does not change reserve requirements very often. When requirements are changed, they are changed in very small steps. Usually the Fed will also offset at least part of the change in the money supply by engaging in open-market operations to change the monetary base in the direction opposite the expected money supply change.

The Dynamics of Monetary Policy

We live in a world of change. We live in a world of rising incomes and rising population. The money supply grows as the economy around us grows and monetary policy changes. The Fed is continually changing the rate of growth of the money supply. For example, the money supply may be growing at 6 percent a year when the Fed decides to "tighten up." Then, by its open-market operations, the Fed may cause the money supply to grow at only a 4 percent rate per year. Thus, when we talk about contractionary monetary policy, we are usually referring to decreasing the rate of growth in the money supply. When we talk about an expansionary monetary policy, we are usually referring to increasing the rate of growth in the money supply. The dynamics of monetary policy, however, do not essentially change the analysis we have given. Understanding the dynamic nature of monetary policy should pose no problems in later chapters.

Fiduciary Monetary System: A system in which currency is issued by the government, and its value is based uniquely on the public's *faith* that the currency represents command over goods and services.

Commodity Currency: A money supply composed of actual commodities, such as cigarettes or bottles of cognac. These commodities are used in place of bills and checking accounts.

Barter: A system where goods and services are exchanged without the use of a medium of exchange, or money.

Liquidity: A characteristic of any asset, it describes the degree to which the asset can be acquired or disposed of without much danger of any intervening loss in nominal value and without relatively high transactions costs. Money is the most liquid asset.

Fractional Reserve Banking System: A system of banking whereby member banks keep only a fraction of their deposits on reserve.

Excess Reserves: The difference between a member bank's actual reserves and the reserves required by law.

Discount Rate: The interest rate the Federal Reserve charges for reserves it lends to member commercial banks. Sometimes referred to as the rediscount rate or, in Canada and England, the bank rate.

Federal Funds Market: A private market (made up of member commercial banks) from which banks can borrow reserves from other banks that want to lend them. Federal funds are usually lent for overnight.

Chapter Summary

1. It is important to distinguish between money and income. Income is what you earn; money is a form in which you hold your wealth.

2. We use money as a medium of exchange and therefore do not use a barter system. Our monetary system is fiduciary in the sense that the currency is issued by the government, and its usefulness depends on the public's faith in its command over goods and services.

3. Money also serves as a unit of accounting and a store of value.

4. The money supply can be defined in many ways. Usually it is defined as currency in the hands of the public plus demand deposits or checking account balances in commercial banks. This definition is often labeled M_1. If we add time deposits in commercial banks, we get M_2. If we further add deposits in noncommercial banks and thrift institutions, we get M_3.

5. Our central bank is the Federal Reserve System, created by the Federal Reserve Act of December 23, 1913. The Federal Reserve is an independent agency of the federal government composed of a Board of Governors and 12 Federal Reserve banks, which have a total of 24 branches.

6. Members of the Federal Reserve System are required to keep reserves equalling a certain percentage of their deposits. Since this percentage is not 100 percent, we have a fractional reserve banking system.

7. A change in the reserves in the banking system will lead to a multiple change in the total money supply outstanding. The maximum increase is given by the deposit expansion multiplier, which is merely the reciprocal of the reserve requirement. However, the maximum deposit expansion multiplier is rarely reached because of leakages, excess reserves, and changing desires to lend and borrow.

8. The three tools in monetary policy are open-market operations, changes in the discount rate, and changes in reserve requirements. Open-market operations are by far the most important monetary policy tool.

Questions for
Thought
and Discussion

1. Do you think that actual reserves would fall to zero if there were no legal requirements?

2. Why would some people prefer that banks be required to hold 100 percent reserves?

3. Would you prefer to live in an economy without money? Why?

4. What is the difference between the money multiplier given by the reciprocal of the reserve requirement and the actual money multiplier? Why is there this difference?

5. How can banks get away with holding reserves equal only to a fraction of their total deposits?

6. If you ask a banker if he can create money, he will definitely tell you no. In fact, he is right; as an individual banker he cannot. Why is it, then, that the banking system taken as a whole can create money?

7. Since reserves earn no interest, why would a bank ever want to hold excess reserves?

8. Problem:

Multiple Money Supply Creation

Round	Deposits	Reserves	Loans
Bank 1	$1,000,000	$ _____	$ _____
Bank 2	$ _____	$ _____	$ _____
Bank 3	$ _____	$ _____	$ _____
Bank 4	$ _____	$ _____	$ _____
Bank 5	$ _____	$ _____	$ _____
All other banks	$ _____	$ _____	$ _____
Totals			

Bank 1 has received a deposit of $1,000,000. Assuming the banks retain no excess reserves, answer the following:

(a) The reserve requirement is 5 percent. Fill in the blanks. What is the money multiplier?

(b) Now the reserve requirement is 25 percent. Fill in the blanks. What is the money multiplier?

Selected References

Angell, N., *The Story of Money*, Philadelphia: Stokes, 1929.

Board of Governors of the Federal Reserve System, *The Federal Reserve System: Purposes and Functions*, 5th ed., Washington, D.C.: U.S. Government Printing Office, 1963; see chaps. 1 and 4 in particular.

Chandler, Lester V., *The Economics of Money and Banking*, 6th ed., New York: Harper & Row, 1973.

Maisel, Sherman J., *Managing the Dollar*, New York: W. W. Norton, 1973.

Ritter, Lawrence S. and William L. Silber, *Money*, 2d ed., New York: Basic Books, 1973.

Robertson, D. H., *Money*, 6th ed., New York: Pitman, 1948.

Doctor of High Finance

ARTHUR BURNS

**Chairman, Federal Reserve
Board of Governors**

Photo by Dennis Brack, from Black Star

Shortly after becoming chairman of the Federal Reserve Board of Governors, Arthur Burns was conducting a meeting of the Federal Open Market Committee. The staff members had prepared two alternative proposals for consideration by the full committee, as is standard procedure. Burns listened carefully to the presentation and then quietly pulled a third proposal out of his pocket. Long known for his independent thinking, Arthur Burns has been an influential economist for more than 20 years, especially during the Republican administrations of Eisenhower, Nixon, and Ford.

Burns first came into prominence in 1930 when he joined the staff of the National Bureau of Economic Research, an organization founded to provide factual background for the exploration of economic issues. There he began his study of business cycles, a field in which he is now considered an expert. In 1945 he became director of NBER.

Dwight Eisenhower brought Burns to

Washington when he appointed him chairman of the Council of Economic Advisers (CEA) in 1952, partially to restore the council's prestige, which had suffered during Truman's administration. Burns also served as chairman of the Advisory Board on Economic Growth and Stability during the Eisenhower years.

Burns' close association with Richard Nixon began in the early 1950s and was solidified during the 1960 presidential election campaign, when Burns correctly predicted the business slowdown that worked against Nixon's chances for election. During the Kennedy years, Burns returned to the National Bureau of Economic Research and taught at Columbia and Stanford. He returned to active political work as adviser on economic matters during Nixon's campaign in 1967 and 1968. After his election, Nixon created an advisory position in the Cabinet just for Burns.

The decision to move Burns from the White House to the Federal Reserve Board in 1970 was much more than an admiring gesture by a President who wanted to honor his close friend and trusted adviser. At that time, the Federal Reserve Board was a body appointed primarily by Democrats, and Nixon wanted his own man in charge.

Governments see themselves as having primarily two means of affecting the economy: changing the growth rate of the money supply as controlled by the Federal Reserve Board and using fiscal policies enacted by Congress. Burns' predecessor, William McChesney Martin, had resented the burden the Federal Reserve Board was forced to assume when Congress did not raise taxes to fund the Vietnam conflict. Burns was determined to avoid such a bind. He developed his own congressional contacts and emphasized that the Fed could not solve the country's economic problems by itself.

Like many of the President's appointees, Burns did not always see eye to eye with Nixon. In 1971, Burns publicly criticized Nixon's economic policies, which led Nixon in turn to threaten to expand the composition of the Federal Reserve Board. Burns was an early advocate of a wage-price review board because he felt that conventional fiscal and monetary tools were ineffective in combating inflation and unemployment.

Inflation has been Burns' driving preoccupation as chairman of the Federal Reserve Board. In June 1974, he warned that "the future of our country is in jeopardy" if inflation were not brought under control. At that time he imposed an even more restrictive monetary policy in the hope that this would return the country to an era of relative price stability. What was needed, for stability, he said, was a long period of slow growth to curb inflation.

During the Ford administration, Burns had come under increasing attack from both conservatives and liberals for his policies regarding the 1974 to 1975 recession. Since Burns became chairman of the Federal Reserve Board, the United States experienced its worst peacetime inflation and its worst slump since the Depression. Many economists argue that this is partially the result of Burns' policies—first, pumping too much money into the economy and then restricting the money supply too abruptly. Worried by the dangers of another Depression, critics of Burns have said the Federal Reserve Board, during a recession like that in 1974 to 1975, should expand the supply of money more rapidly and act more forcefully to lower interest rates.

Burns, whose term does not expire until 1984, has long since grown accustomed to criticism from all sides. "One of the functions of the Federal Reserve Board," he remarked, "is to be criticized."

Should Commercial Banks be Subsidized?

BORROWING FROM THE FEDERAL RESERVE

Looking at the Discount Rate from a Different Perspective

We pointed out in the last chapter that Federal Reserve member banks can, at the discretion of the Federal Reserve, borrow reserves from it at the discount rate to make up any deficiencies in required reserves. Or the bank in need of reserves can go to private sources where it must pay whatever is the going market rate. The primary source of additional reserves in the private market is the so-called Federal Funds Market, which we also discussed in the previous chapter.

In Table I-13.1 we present the average yearly Federal Funds Market rates from 1962 through 1975, along with the respective average discount rates posted by the New York Fed. Notice that there is a difference between the discount rate and the Federal Funds rate for many of the years. The difference has often been one in which the Fed has charged a lower rate of interest for reserves than has the private Federal Funds Market.

The Subsidy Aspect of the Discount Window Operations

Whenever a bank is allowed to borrow reserves from the Fed at an interest rate below the next best alternative, which is generally the Federal Funds Market, that bank is receiving a very definite subsidy. We can measure the actual amount of the subsidy by figuring the difference between the Federal Funds rate and the discount rate and multiplying that difference by the amount of the reserve loan. For example, if the Federal Funds rate is 10 percent per year and the discount rate is 7 percent per year, the difference is 3

Table I-13.1

The Difference between the Federal Funds Rate and the Discount Rate

Anytime the Federal Funds Rate exceeds the Discount Rate, any bank borrowing reserves from the Fed is obtaining an implicit subsidy equal to the interest saved.

YEAR	AVERAGE FEDERAL FUNDS RATE (PERCENT PER YEAR)	AVERAGE DISCOUNT RATE AT NEW YORK FED (PERCENT PER YEAR)
1962	2.68	3.00
1963	3.18	3.50
1964	3.50	4.00
1965	4.07	4.50
1966	5.11	4.50
1967	4.22	4.50
1968	5.66	5.50
1969	8.21	6.00
1970	7.17	5.50
1971	4.66	5.00
1972	4.44	5.50
1973	8.74	6.00
1974	10.51	8.00
1975 (January)	7.13	7.25

Source: Board of Governors of the Federal Reserve System

percent. Hence, for every $1 million loan the Fed makes through its discount window, the recipient member bank will receive an implicit subsidy at the rate of $30,000 per year. That means that if a bank were able to keep a Federal Reserve loan outstanding for 1 month, it would receive a subsidy equal to 1/12 × $30,000 or $2,500 per month for every $1 million borrowed. To get a better idea of the actual implicit subsidy given to the banking system as a whole, look at Table I-13.2. Here we take the difference between the Federal Funds rate and the discount rate as presented in Table I-13.1. Then we apply that difference to the average amount of Federal Reserve loans outstanding per year. You will notice, for example, that in 1974 the banking system as a whole obtained

an implicit subsidy of $50 million. This is not an insignificant sum.

This type of subsidy to the commercial banking system is something relatively new in the history of banking. If we look, for example, at the difference between the Fed's discount rate and the Federal Funds rate for years prior to the 1960s and 1970s, we find much less of a difference. In fact, when discounting first started, the Fed generally set the discount rate at a level that was slightly higher than alternative market rates. Any member bank that chose to go to the Fed for a loan was essentially punished by having to pay a higher rate of interest.

The question then remains, "Why is the Fed subsidizing member commercial banks today, and is such subsidization desirable from a policy

point of view?" The best way to find answers is to look at one of the best-known examples of the Fed using its power to help an individual bank.

A Case History of Subsidization

In 1974 the nation's twentieth largest bank, Franklin National, on Long Island, got into serious trouble. It had engaged in extensive foreign currency speculations and had lost money. There were also apparently other reasons why it had been mismanaged. In any event, the bank was in trouble. Some of its depositors started to sense impending doom and pulled out many of their deposits. This meant that Franklin started losing reserves at an alarming rate.

Table I-13.2

The Implicit Subsidy to Member Banks by the Fed

(1) YEAR	(2) DIFFERENCE BETWEEN AVERAGE FEDERAL FUNDS RATE AND AVERAGE DISCOUNT RATE	(3) AVERAGE AMOUNT OWED BY MEMBER BANKS TO THE FED (IN MILLIONS OF DOLLARS)	(4) IMPLICIT SUBSIDY (COLUMN 2 × COLUMN 3) (IN MILLIONS OF DOLLARS)
1962	−.0022	304	− 0.67
1963	−.0032	327	− 1.05
1964	−.0050	243	− 1.22
1965	−.0043	454	− 1.95
1966	+.0061	557	+ 3.40
1967	−.0028	238	− 0.67
1968	+.0012	765	+ 0.92
1969	+.0221	1,086	+24.00
1970	+.0167	321	+ 5.36
1971	−.0034	107	− 0.36
1972	−.0106	1,049	−11.12
1973	+.0274	1,298	+35.57
1974	+.0251	2,050	+51.46
1975 (Jan.)	+.0012	390	+ 0.47

Source: Board of Governors of the Federal Reserve System

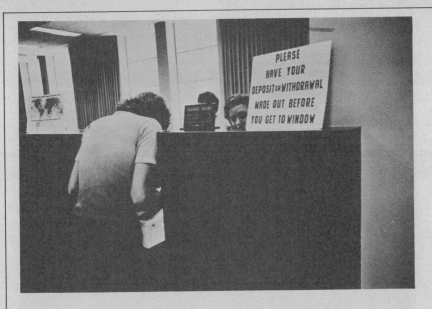

It had to go heavily into debt to make up these lost reserves. When it looked as if the bank might go under, the Federal Reserve stepped in and lent Franklin, through the Fed discount window, approximately $1.5 billion. The loan was made at the current discount rate of 7½ percent per year. At this same time, the Federal Funds rate ranged from 10.5 percent to 12.9 percent. The difference, and hence the implicit subsidy, was thus around 3 to 4 percentage points per year on whatever loans were made available. Since Franklin was given about $1.5 billion, the implicit subsidy was about $1 million per week! It should be noted that this subsidy was not voted on by Congress. It was given at will by the Fed.

This subsidy was provided to Franklin to prevent its demise; it was feared that if Franklin National went under, the banking system as a whole might suffer. The subsidy notwithstanding, however, Franklin

National was eventually forced into bankruptcy proceedings and was immediately taken over by another bank. It is interesting, nonetheless, to examine this reasoning that a large bank should be prevented from failing because of the potentially deleterious effect its failure would have on the entire banking system and hence on the economy in general.

Protecting the Banking System

A bank can fail for a variety of reasons. Today, however, a bank fails usually because of poor management. There is no difference in theory between operating a bank and operating a clothing store or a record shop. All three are profit-seeking enterprises. The main function of a bank is to provide checking and savings account services to its clients and to provide loans. Additionally, banks buy interest-earning securi-

ties. The business of running a bank involves choosing an appropriate portfolio, as it is called, of different types of earning assets. In the case of Franklin National, certain officers of the bank apparently felt that more earning assets should be held in the form of foreign currency balances which they hoped could be sold later at a higher price than they had paid. When instead the price dropped, the bank suffered a loss rather than a profit. This situation is actually no different from the bank making loans to customers who don't pay them off. If the bank makes too many "bad" loans, it may suffer a loss in its loan operations. Sound management of a bank requires the weighing of potential risks against potential gains. In the case of Franklin National and other banks that have failed, sound management did not prevail.

The above is merely a rundown of how a bank is managed and what can go wrong. What we are trying to understand is how one bank's demise might lead to a collapse in the entire banking system. In the early 1930s, at the beginning of the Great Depression, banks began failing right and left; when one bank failed, it would trigger the failure of another as depositors got cold feet and tried to withdraw all their funds. As an increasing number of depositors attempted to withdraw their bank deposits, an ever-increasing number became insolvent. If that were possible today, we could indeed understand the case for subsidizing banks with reserves from the Federal Reserve discount window at a below market rate of interest. However, times have changed, and the reason they have changed is because we now have federal deposit insurance, which protects depositors from the loss of their deposits even if the bank fails completely. It all involves the Federal Deposit Insurance Corporation.

The Federal Deposit Insurance Corporation

The Federal Deposit Insurance Corporation (FDIC) was established during the Depression in 1934. Its principal purpose was to insure commercial bank deposits. The establishment of deposit insurance has been considered by banking historians as perhaps the most significant banking legislation since the creation of the Federal Reserve System itself in 1913.

All member banks of the Federal Reserve System are required to belong to the FDIC, and most non-member banks also have joined. Presently, the FDIC insures the deposits of each individual or firm in each bank up to $40,000. Banks that have insurance must pay an annual premium equal to one-twelfth of 1 percent of their total deposits.

The FDIC has come to the rescue of depositors in a number of small bank failures, as well as in a number of more spectacular large ones. The number of banks that actually fail in any given year, however, is extremely small—on the order of 2 to 10. In most cases, depositors receive close to 100 percent of the funds they had in the bank. Generally, the FDIC will force the failing bank to merge with a more liquid bank.

The FDIC, in addition to providing almost complete insurance to individual depositors, also provides a

psychological barrier against a banking panic or a collapse because depositors no longer need fear the possible loss of their deposits. And since in all practicality there never again will be a general run on banks because of the existence of FDIC, many students of our banking system contend that there is little need to subsidize failing banks. They point out that if such subsidization continues as it has in the past couple of decades, the competitive control mechanism that weeds out bad management in banks will be seriously weakened. If bad management does not lead to the total collapse of a bank because the Fed steps in and props it up, then there is less incentive to minimize bad management; or rather, there is less of a check on the improper handling of a bank's portfolio, and bank managers will rationally opt for greater profit at excessive risk in their investment decisions.

The Pros and Cons Summarized

Should banks be subsidized by loans made at below market interest rates? Those who favor subsidization contend that banks in trouble should be at least temporarily bailed out to maintain confidence in the banking system as a whole and the economy in general. Additionally, those who favor subsidization feel that it provides for the smooth functioning of the banking system because it prevents precipitous collapses in individual banks.

Opponents of bank subsidization, however, contend that it is impossible for us ever to have a run on banks because the FDIC insures deposits. Therefore the subsidization of banks in trouble merely reduces the cost of bad managers to the bank's stockholders and leads to an inefficient use of our banking resources.

Perhaps you can think of other pro and con arguments. What conclusions can you draw from your arguments?

Questions for Thought and Discussion

1. "The banking system is the cornerstone of the American economy. The banking system must be preserved at all cost." Analyze this quote.
2. What is the difference between the Federal Funds rate and the Federal Reserve discount rate?
3. Member-bank borrowing from the Fed's discount window is considered a privilege and not a right. Does this have any effect on how much member banks feel they can use the discount window?
4. Why does lending money to member banks at a below market rate of interest constitute a form of subsidization?

Selected Reference

O'Bannon, Helen B. et al., *Money and Banking: Theory, Policy, and Institutions,* New York: Harper & Row, 1975, p. 356ff.

12 Money in a Keynesian Model

In Chapter 3, we discussed the elements of basic supply and demand. In the last chapter, we discussed what determines the supply of money. In this chapter we will discuss what determines the demand for money. Then we will integrate a simplified demand for money relationship into the income and employment determination model (generally considered a Keynesian model) used in Chapters 9 and 10.

The Demand for Money or Cash

Why do people want to hold money, rather than, for example, invest it in bonds, or savings and loan shares, or houses, or any of the other myriad assets that can replace money? One way of looking at the determinants of the demand for money is to look at the motives behind holding money. The British economist John Maynard Keynes outlined three motives: transactions, precautionary, and speculative.

Transactions Demand for Money

This is probably the most widely understood motive for holding money. It hinges on the use of money as a medium of exchange. Individuals desire to use money in order to handle the ordinary, day-to-day transactions in their lives. Without money, such transactions would be costly indeed. The amount of money desired for transaction purposes generally depends on the volume of purchases to be made per unit time. The amount needed will also depend on the frequency of income payments—that is, the more frequent the payments, the smaller the average amount of money needed to finance transactions.

Precautionary Demand for Money

The precautionary motive for holding money is related to the use of money's function as a temporary store of value. Money provides individuals with protection against certain risks. In other words, having completely liquid balances provides a cushion against abrupt reductions in income due to illness, accident, or unemployment. Businesses may need money or complete liquidity to meet unexpected payments for increased costs and also to take advantage of unanticipated opportunities for a quick expansion of profits.

The Speculative Demand for Money

Money provides individuals with the liquidity necessary to shift rapidly into other assets. This motive is called the speculative motive because it involves outguessing the movements in the prices of alternative assets such as bonds or stocks. If, for example, it is anticipated that bond prices will fall in the future, individuals may well want to hold more money today to take advantage of lower bond prices in the future.

In the remainder of this chapter we will concentrate on the speculative demand for money. For us to completely understand it, however, we must understand the role of interest rates in our economy and know the relationship between movements in the general level of interest rates and in the market value of bonds.

Interest Rates: An Introduction

The concept of interest dates back to the time of the Romans, when the laws stated that the defaulting party to a contract had to pay his creditor some sort of compensation. During medieval times, lawyers used the legal tactic of *damna et interesse* to extract such compensation. Thus, *interesse* became a charge for the use of money under the guise of indemnity for failure to fulfill a contract.

Indeed, interest rates have played a very special role in much of macroeconomic theory. The investment schedule is negatively related to the rate of interest. Actually, every specific lending market has its own interest rate. The bond market where the Federal Reserve sells and buys government bonds has its own interest rate. The housing (mortgage) market has its own interest rate and so do savings and loan associations. There is a particular interest rate for every type of market lending instrument.

Interest Rates and Bond Prices

Suppose you bought a bond for $1,000 which had an infinite lifetime—that is, it could never be turned in to the original issuer for the $1,000 face value. (You could, of course, sell it to another person.) In compensation for your loan of $1,000 to the bond issuer, you would get a large number of coupons that had the years 1977, 1978, 1979, and so on written on them, along with the following inscription: "Send this in on December 31 and you will get back $100 in the mail." The "coupon rate" on your **consol** (a bond with no maturity date) would, therefore, be 10 percent per year because you would get $100 interest per $1,000 invested every year. (Although consols exist in the United Kingdom, they are not used in the United States. We will use them in our own example only to simplify the analysis.) Let's say at the time you bought this $1,000 bond, with a coupon rate of 10 percent, other bonds of equal risk also yielded 10 percent per year. Assume also that *there had never been inflation in the past and that none was expected in the future.*

Now suppose, for some reason, prices suddenly started to rise at a rate of 10 percent a year and are expected to continue rising forever at that rate. Now would anybody pay you $1,000 for a bond with a coupon rate of 10 percent? Probably not because now $100 a year would just cover the loss in purchasing power of the bond you were holding. Most people would require an inflationary premium of 10 percent in addition to some real compensation for lending the money in the first place. That means that interest rates in the economy would rise from 10 to, say, 20 percent. The value of your bond would now be only $500 since that would make the $100 coupon give the current interest yield of 20 percent on a $500 investment. If you tried to sell your bond, you would get no more than $500. Notice that *the interest rate and the price of the bond are inversely related.* In fact, we have a formula for bonds with an infinite life; this formula is also approximately correct for bonds with very long lives. The value of $1 in interest payments per year *forever* is equal to $1 divided by *i*, where *i* is the nominal rate of interest:

$$\text{Value today of \$1 in interest payments forever} = \frac{\$1}{i}$$

In this example, $100 was paid out per year. With a market rate of interest of 10 percent, our formula tells us that the price of the bond was $100 divided by 0.10, or $1,000. When the market rate of interest rose to 20 percent, the market value of the bond equaled $100 divided by 0.20, or $500. Even if you could be absolutely sure of getting all your interest payments, you can never be certain that the price of the bond will equal what you paid for it. Any time market interest rates in the economy rise, the price of existing bonds fall. And of course, if interest rates fall, the price of your fixed-income-producing bond will rise.

The Demand for Money and the Interest Rate

In a simplified Keynesian analysis, we assume that people's demand for money—cash balances—depends mainly upon the cost of holding that money. What is the cost of holding money? The cost equals the earnings you could have had if you had invested that money. You have the opportunity, for example, to buy bonds with your money. If the interest rate on bonds is 10 percent per year and you decide to hold your cash rather than buy bonds, then the cost of holding that cash is 10 percent per year. We would expect that the higher the cost of holding money, the less money would be demanded. We can therefore construct on a graph a downward sloping demand function for money with the nominal interest rate on the vertical axis. We have done just that in Figure 12-1. The horizontal axis measures the quantity of money in billions of dollars; the vertical axis measures the interest rate yield on bonds. As interest rates go up, the quantity of money demanded falls. As interest rates go down, the quantity of money demanded rises. This is a demand schedule just like any other demand schedule except that the product in question happens to be the medium of exchange and the price happens to be the opportunity cost (interest rate) of holding that medium of exchange.

Keynes liked to call this the **liquidity preference function.** As we saw in Chapter 11, the most liquid asset around is money. You can purchase whatever you want with it, and it never loses its *face* value. A dollar is a dollar, today or tomorrow. The next most liquid asset might be savings deposits. You can take your passbook to the bank and get cash fairly rapidly.

Since money is the most liquid of all assets, the demand schedule for money can be thought of as the liquidity preference schedule. You show your preference for complete liquidity—

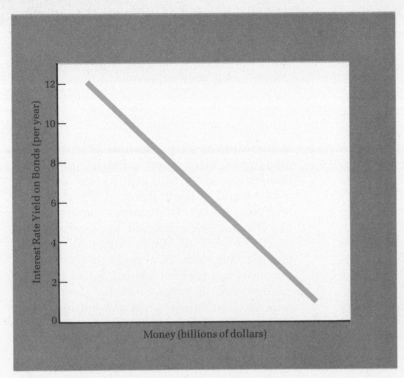

FIGURE 12-1 The Liquidity Preference Function: The Demand for Money
Here we show the liquidity preference function. The quantity of money demanded increases as the interest rate decreases. That is because the interest rate is the opportunity cost of holding money. As the opportunity cost falls, the quantity of money demanded will rise.

holding money—in accordance with the opportunity cost of holding it.

Another way to look at the liquidity preference function is to consider a person's *speculative motive* for holding money. Let's assume that the only alternative to holding money is buying bonds. Remember, there is an inverse relationship between the price of a fixed-income bond and the interest rate prevailing in the economy. If you are holding a bond and, for some reason, interest rates rise in the economy, you will suffer a capital loss. The value of that bond will depreciate. However, if you are holding the bond and interest rates fall, you will experience a capital gain; the value of the bond will rise. Think about how you might react to historically low interest rates in the economy. You might expect that the probability of interest rates falling is smaller than the probability of their rising. Therefore, you would not want to invest in bonds because you do not want to suffer a capital loss as interest rates rise. You would hold your speculative balances in money instead of bonds. At the other end of the spectrum, if interest rates prevailing in the economy are historically high, you might expect that the probability of interest rates falling is greater than the probability of their rising. Therefore, instead of holding your speculative balances in money, you would switch to bonds. Your demand for money would be smaller than it was at lower interest rates. Thus, the liquidity preference function slopes downward, as we have drawn it in Figure 12-1.

Adding the Money Supply

Now let's add the policy variable that can be used by the government—changes in the money supply. We can add the money supply to our liquidity preference diagram merely by drawing a vertical line wherever the money supply happens to be. Let's say the money supply is at M_s. We have drawn a vertical line at M_s in Figure 12-2. What we have in this figure is a demand schedule—liquidity preference function—and a supply schedule, which happens to be a vertical line. This means that the *supply* of money is completely insensitive to the interest rate. It is exogenous, assumed to be determined solely by the Federal Reserve. With a supply schedule and a demand schedule, we should be able to find an equilibrium point. As expected, the equilibrium is at the intersection of the supply schedule and the demand

schedule, or point E in Figure 12-2. At point E, the equilibrium interest rate happens to be 10 percent. This is the interest rate that equates the quantity of money demanded with the quantity of money supplied.

Excess Supply

If interest rates were somehow 11 percent, the quantity of money demanded would be less than the quantity supplied. Excess cash balances would be floating around. People would take those excess cash balances and buy bonds, but the increased demand for bonds would cause the price of bonds to rise. Remember, though, that there is a negative relationship between the price of bonds and the interest rate. As the price of bonds rises, the interest rate falls. In other words, when more people try to

FIGURE 12-2 Putting Together the Demand and Supply of Money

The demand schedule, *DD*, is downward sloping; the supply schedule is not only upward sloping, it is vertical at some given quantity of money supplied by the monetary authorities. The equilibrium rate of interest is at 10 percent. An interest rate of 9 percent could not prevail for very long because the quantity of money demanded would exceed the quantity supplied. For people to try to get more money, they would have to sell bonds, for example. But when they sell bonds, they must lower their price. They must offer higher yields to prospective buyers in order to get rid of the bonds; the interest rate would rise. Conversely, the interest rate couldn't last for long at 11 percent because there would be an excess supply of money. In the process of buying bonds, people bid up the price. When the price of bonds goes up, the interest rate falls because there is an inverse relationship between the price of a bond and the yield on it. The interest rate would fall to the equilibrium rate of 10 percent.

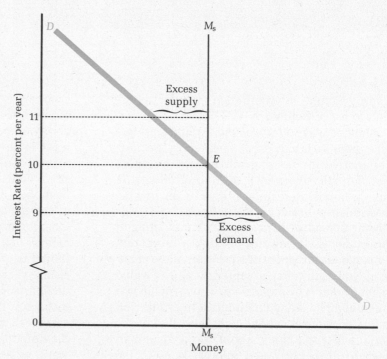

buy bonds, the only way they can do so is by accepting a lower yield—that is, a lower interest rate. Thus, when the interest rate is above the equilibrium level, the excess supply of money is translated into an increased demand for bonds, which in turn raises the price of bonds, thus lowering the interest rate.

Excess Demand

If the interest rate is lower than 10 percent or the equilibrium rate, there will be an excess demand for money. People will sell their bonds in an attempt to make up the deficiency between actual cash balances and desired cash balances; they will want to make up the deficiency between actual liquidity and desired liquidity. As people reduce their demand for bonds, the price of bonds falls. That is, the interest rate rises. Another way of looking at it is that since the demand for bonds has fallen, the only way people can be induced to hold them is by being offered higher yields—that is, higher interest rates. Hence, when the interest rate is below the equilibrium level, there is an excess demand for money that translates itself into a decreased demand for bonds; this causes the price of bonds to fall and the interest rate to rise until it reaches equilibrium.

Completing the Keynesian Model

How do we relate the monetary sector of this aspect of the Keynesian model to the rest of the model? Remember in Chapter 8 when we talked about the investment schedule? We drew it as a function of the interest rate and it sloped downward. We recreate that investment schedule in Figure 12-3. But the equilibrium interest rate has already been established by the liquidity preference function and the money supply in Figure 12-2. It is 10 percent. So we go from

the 10 percent equilibrium interest rate in Figure 12-2 to find out how much investment there is at that particular interest rate. As shown in Figure 12-3, the desired investment is $200 billion. We can now find out what equilibrium income will be given at that level of investment. We go to the $C + I + G$ diagram that we have drawn in Figure 12-4. C and G are already given. We add $200 billion worth of investment to get the $C + I + G$ schedule as shown in the figure. Equilibrium income turns out to be $2.0 trillion.

Transmitting Monetary Policy

You should now have some idea of how monetary policy works in a simplified Keynesian system. We assumed that the money supply was an exogenous variable, under the control of the Federal Reserve System. Suppose now that, for some reason, equilibrium income is less than full-employment income. Suppose, as shown in Figure 12-4, that the $C + I + G$ schedule intersects the 45 degree line (where total spending always equals total income) at only $2 trillion when the full-employment level of income is $2.125 trillion. We shall assume that the government decides monetary policy is the appropriate tool to use in stimulating the economy up to its full-employment level. The government decides therefore to increase the money supply; it goes out into the open market and buys government bonds. When the government buys bonds, it increases the reserves of banks. Those banks will not want to keep the excess reserves in the Federal Reserve banks; they will therefore start lending money. A chain reaction starts, whereby the money supply expands in a multiple of the change in reserves. If the money multiplier happens to be 3, then the money supply will expand by three times the original purchase of bonds by the Federal Reserve.

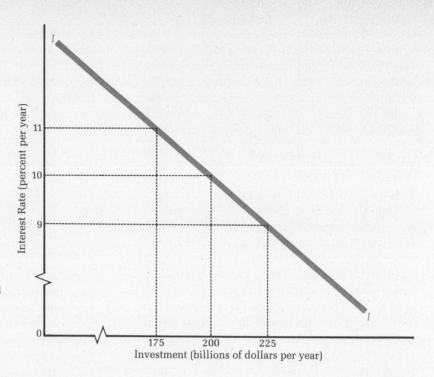

FIGURE 12-3 The Investment Schedule

The investment schedule represents the demand for investment. It slopes downward like all demand curves. The price, though, is not in terms of dollars but in terms of the interest rate measured on the vertical axis. At an 11 percent rate of interest, the investment schedule tells us there will be $175 billion worth of investment. At a 10 percent interest rate, there would be $200 billion, and, at a 9 percent interest rate, there would be $225 billion worth of investment.

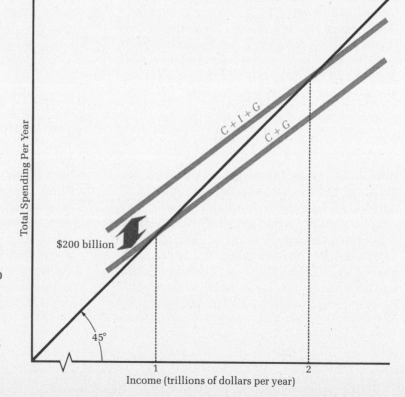

FIGURE 12-4 Finding the Equilibrium Level of Income

Without investment, the C + G schedule intersects the 45 degree spending-equals-income line at $1 trillion. We take the $200 billion of investment from Figure 12-3 and add it vertically to the C + G line to get C + G + I, which now intersects the 45 degree line at an equilibrium income of $2 trillion. Here we have assumed, as always, that the multiplier is 5 because the marginal propensity to save is assumed to be 0.2 or 1/5.

How do we show that on our graph for the demand and supply of money? In Figure 12-5, we have drawn the original supply curve of money as M_s, the vertical line. Now we increase M_s to M'_s and draw another vertical line to represent the larger money supply. But, at the same interest rate as before (10 percent), there is an excess supply of money in circulation. According to this particular Keynesian theory, people will therefore attempt to buy bonds with their excess money balances. When they all attempt to buy bonds with their excess money balances, they will bid up the price of those bonds; that is, the interest rate will fall. Obviously, it will fall to the point of equilibrium, where the liquidity preference function (demand for money curve) and the vertical supply of money function intersect. In our particular example, that happens to be at an interest rate of 9 percent.

Looking back at our investment schedule in Figure 12-3, we find that a decrease in the interest rate from 10 percent to 9 percent causes an increase in investment of $25 billion. We add that $25 billion of investment to our $C + I + G$ schedule in Figure 12-6 to get $C + I' + G$, which is $25 billion higher than the old schedule. Now look at where the new $C + I' + G$ schedule intersects the 45 degree line. If we assume that the marginal propensity to consume is 0.8, then the marginal propensity to save is 0.2 or 1/5. The multiplier is the reciprocal of the marginal propensity to save, or 5. A $25 billion increase in investment will eventually lead to a $125 billion increase in income, which is shown in Figure 12-6. Equilibrium income has been raised to a full-employment level of $2.125 trillion. As we can see, expansionary monetary policy has been successful in this particular model.

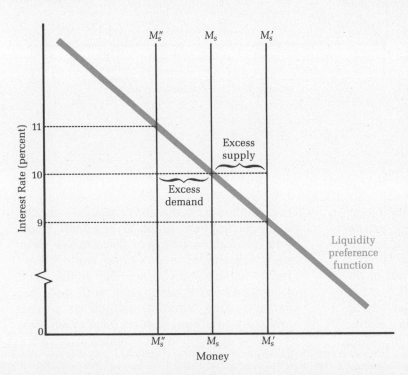

FIGURE 12-5 Effects of Changes in the Money Supply

If the money supply starts out at M_s, the equilibrium interest rate will be 10 percent. If the monetary authorities increase the money supply to M'_s, then at the old interest rate of 10 percent, there will be an excess supply of money. People's attempts at getting rid of this excess supply of money will cause the equilibrium interest rate to fall to 9 percent. That is, as people buy bonds with their excess supplies of money, they will drive up the price of bonds and thereby lower the interest rate. On the other hand, if the monetary authorities contract the money supply to M''_s, at the old equilibrium interest rate of 10 percent, there will be an excess demand for money. As individuals sell their bonds to get into equilibrium, they will be forced to accept a lower price for those bonds. That is, they will be forced to pay a higher interest rate to get rid of the bonds. The equilibrium interest rate will rise to 11 percent.

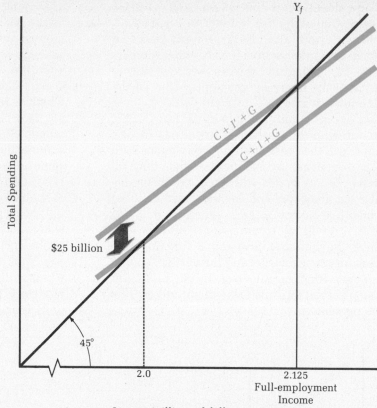

FIGURE 12-6 Effective Monetary Policy

Suppose that the economy finds itself in an underemployment situation where income is only $2.0 trillion. That is at the point where the $C + I + G$ curve intersects the 45 degree spending = income line. The Fed then decides to use monetary policy to increase equilibrium income and reduce unemployment. In a simplified Keynesian world such as we have outlined in this chapter, the Fed would increase the money supply by buying bonds in the open market. Having an excess supply of money, the public will demand more bonds. As it demands more bonds, the interest rate falls. As the interest rate falls, investment increases from I to I', where I' is greater than I by $25 billion. The $C + I + G$ schedule now shifts up to $C + I' + G$. Equilibrium income, that is, the intersection of $C + I' + G$ with the 45 degree spending = income line, is now at $2.125 trillion or full-employment income.

Closing the Inflationary Gap

To increase your understanding of the monetary mechanism in a Keynesian model, assume the economy is operating at more than full employment. Redo Figure 12-6, now labeling $2 trillion as the full-employment level of national income per year. Draw the $C + I + G$ line such that there is an inflationary gap. Assume that the equilibrium level of national income is $2.125 trillion. What should the monetary authorities do in this situation?

The Transmission Mechanism

One problem with the above analyses should be pointed out here. In our first example, there were no changes in prices because we were below *full* employment. Output could be increased without increasing prices. In the other example we were starting out with an inflationary setting. Therefore, when we moved from one equilibrium income level to another, prices changed, and in our example prices were the only things that could change since we started at full employment. It must be realized, therefore, that we weren't strictly correct in discussing all our variables in *nominal* terms. We probably should have talked about changes in the real money supply—that is, the nominal money supply divided by the price level. Also, we probably should have made the distinction between real and nominal interest rates. We can, however, forget about those problems for the moment and recapitulate the transmission mechanism of monetary policy in our model:

The transmission mechanism = a change in the money supply → a change in the interest rate → a change in investment → a change in income → a change in employment and/or price level

This transmission mechanism says nothing about the magnitude of a change in investment due to a change in the interest rate. In other words, we have to know something about the interest elasticity of the demand for investment. There is a general consensus among Keynesian economists that this interest elasticity of investment demand is not great. In other words, a change in the interest rate may indeed cause an increase in the rate of planned investment, but the increase will be rather small. In the extreme case, if the investment schedule in Figure 12-3 were completely vertical, monetary policy could have no effect; all it would do is change the interest rate. There would be no resulting change in investment and hence no change in income and employment.

When Monetary Policy Doesn't Work

In his *General Theory,* Keynes mentioned the possibility of a situation in which changes in monetary policy would have no effect whatsoever. Let's see whether we can analyze the situation he suggested. Imagine a period when interest rates are historically very low. Let's say

that the interest rate is only 2 percent. You might think that the probability of interest rates rising was much greater than the probability of interest rates falling. If so, you would probably not want to put your money into bonds because you would try to avoid a consequent capital loss. You would reason that there is a high probability that the value of those bonds will decrease. After all, there is an inverse relationship between the prevailing interest rate in the economy and the value of any fixed-income bonds you might be holding. If interest rates fall, you're better off. The value of your bonds will rise. But if interest rates rise, you're worse off. The value of your bonds will fall. We might expect, therefore, that at very low interest rates, people would be unwilling to exchange money—cash balances—for bonds.

This is the crux of what Keynes called the **liquidity trap.** He reasoned that at a particularly low interest rate, nobody would be willing to buy any more bonds. Therefore, increases in the money supply would be merely stashed away. There would be no mechanism by which an increase in the money supply would lead to a decrease in interest rates, thereby leading to increases in investment and output.

In Figure 12-7, we find that the liquidity preference function has changed shape. At a 2 percent interest rate, it becomes completely flat or horizontal. In other words, the demand for money at a 2 percent interest rate is infinite. This means that when bonds are yielding only 2 percent, nobody will be willing to buy any more. People will merely keep additional money in cash balances. This has very serious implications for the efficacy of monetary policy.

Imagine, as in Figure 12-7, that the money supply was at M_s. The interest rate is established by the intersection of the demand for money and the supply of money. In this case the equilibrium interest rate happens to be 2

FIGURE 12-7 The Liquidity Trap

The liquidity preference function is the normal shape until it reaches a 2 percent interest level. Then it becomes horizontal. At 2 percent the demand for money is infinite. Nobody is willing to buy any more bonds. Any money that is injected into the economy goes into people's cash balances. If the money supply is at M_s, the equilibrium interest rate will be at 2 percent. An increase in the money supply from M_s to M_s' leads to no lowering of the interest rate because the liquidity preference function is horizontal at 2 percent. The new intersection with the new larger money supply is at the same interest rate as the old intersection with the smaller money supply. In this particular case it is impossible for the unyielding interest rates to stimulate investment and thus increase output and employment. In short, monetary policy is ineffective in this model.

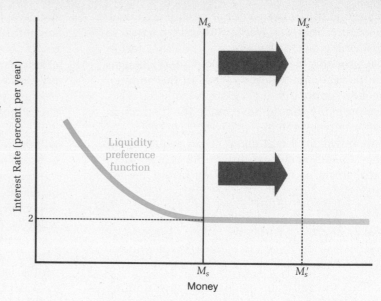

percent. Now suppose that the economy is languishing; there is unemployment. The government decides to use expansionary monetary policy. It therefore increases the supply of money by buying government bonds in the open market. There is a multiple expansion in the money supply. M_s moves out to M_s', the dashed vertical line in Figure 12-7. We know, however, that the demand for money is already in the liquidity trap. We are at an interest rate of 2 percent, and nobody wishes to buy any more bonds. All the extra money injected into the economy by the Federal Reserve is merely kept in checking accounts and in cash by the people who receive it. Nobody bothers to trade it in for bonds. The equilibrium interest rate remains at 2 percent because here is where we find the new intersection of M_s' and the liquidity preference function. *There will be no change in investment and no change in income or employment.* We're stuck in the liquidity trap. Monetary policy is useless. The only thing that can help out is fiscal policy—that is, increases

in government spending or decreases in taxes. So goes the most simplified theory of the liquidity trap.

However, you should be warned that few serious Keynesians today believe the liquidity trap has ever existed. Keynes himself never said he saw it. It turned out to be a cute analytical exposition of a possibility that never became a reality. Economists have not even found evidence that a liquidity trap of this kind existed during the depths of the Depression.

Other Views on the Subject

The way we have analyzed the role of money in this simplified income and employment determination model is certainly not the only way to handle its effects. We will see in the following chapter that there are significant disagreements among economists concerning the function of money supply changes in our economy.

Consol: A bond with no maturity date.

Liquidity Preference Function: A relationship between the opportunity cost of holding money and the quantity of money demanded—otherwise stated as the quantity of liquidity preferred.

Liquidity Trap: That part of the liquidity preference function which is horizontal. If the economy is in the liquidity trap—as the theory is most simply postulated—an increase in the money supply will not lower interest rates. People's demands for money or for perfect liquidity will be infinite. All increases in the money supply therefore will go into their pockets or into their checking accounts rather than into an increased demand for bonds.

Chapter Summary

1. Keynes outlined three different motives for demanding money or cash balances: the transaction demand, the precautionary demand, and the speculative demand.

2. The price of a bond and the prevailing interest rate in the economy are inversely related.

3. The interest rate is the opportunity cost for holding money. The liquidity preference function shows the relationship between the cost of holding money and the quantity of money demanded. It is otherwise called the demand for money function. It is negatively sloped; at lower rates of interest, more money is demanded.

4. Another way of viewing the demand for money function is that, at least in part, it is determined by people's speculative motives. They may wish to hold money because they think interest rates will rise in the future, in which case it would be better for them to wait to earn higher returns later and also to avoid a capital loss. If the market rate of interest rises while you are holding a bond, the value of that bond will fall. At low interest rates you expect that the probability for market interest rates rising would be relatively high. Therefore, you wish to hold money instead of bonds to avoid the possibility of a capital loss. The converse holds for high interest rates.

5. In our simplified model we assumed that the supply of money is completely exogenous. In our graphs it is a vertical line determined by the monetary authorities. The equilibrium level of interest is found at the intersection of the liquidity preference function and the vertical supply of money curve. At the equilibrium level of interest there is neither an excess demand nor an excess supply of money.

6. We can go from the equilibrium level of interest established in the money market by the intersection of the demand and supply schedules of money to find out what the equilibrium level of investment will be. We look at our downward sloping investment schedule to find out what the level of investment will be at the given equilibrium interest rate. Then we carry

over this amount of investment to our standard 45 degree line $C + I + G$ diagram to find out what the equilibrium level of income will be with that amount of investment. Remember, there is a multiple expansion in equilibrium income for any given increase in investment. The multiplier in our examples has always been 5.

7. In the model we have presented, monetary policy is transmitted through changes in the interest rate. If, for example, we're at less than full employment, the Fed might wish to engage in expansionary monetary policy. It would increase the money supply, thereby creating an excess supply of money. Individuals' attempts to rid themselves of those excess supplies will cause the interest rate to fall. That is, they attempt to buy bonds; in their attempt, they will bid up the price of bonds, which means the interest rate will fall. When the interest rate falls, the level of investment will increase. There will be a multiplier effect from the increase in the level of investment. Equilibrium income will go up by a multiple of that increase in I. Monetary policy can also be used to quell over full employment or inflation.

8. In our model the transmission mechanism of monetary policy goes from a change in the money supply to a change in the interest rate to a change in investment to a change in income to a change in employment and/or price level.

9. There are certain theoretical situations in which monetary policy doesn't work. One of them is the liquidity trap. The liquidity trap is the horizontal section of the liquidity preference function where the demand for money is infinite. The interest rate cannot be lowered by expansionary monetary policy. An increase in the money supply will not lead to a lowering of interest rates. Therefore, investment will not expand and neither will equilibrium income.

Questions for Thought and Discussion

1. During the Great Depression, the Federal Reserve stated that it could make sure there were enough reserves in banks to make money available to commerce, industry, and agriculture at low rates. However, the Fed stated that it could not make people borrow and it could not make the public spend the deposits that resulted when banks made loans and investments. Do you agree with that statement? Why or why not?

2. Can you think of any other reasons for wanting to hold money besides a liquidity preference or a speculative reason? (*Hint*: What do you use money for?)

3. What if the investment schedule were completely exogenous? (That is, it was not determined by the interest rate.) How would monetary policy work then?

4. Monetary policy has been criticized as being ineffective in the fight against inflation. One of the reasons is that "you can pull on a string but you can't push on it." Why would you expect monetary policy to be effective in increasing employment but ineffective in decreasing inflationary pressures? What is the string we are talking about?
5. Interest rates today are much higher than they were during the Great Depression. Does that mean that the possibility of the liquidity trap is less today?

Selected References

Bach, G. L., *Making Monetary and Fiscal Policy,* Washington, D.C.: The Brookings Institution, 1971.

Mayer, Thomas, *Elements of Monetary Policy,* New York: Random House, 1968.

Nichols, Dorothy M., *Modern Money Mechanics,* rev. ed., Chicago: Federal Reserve Bank of Chicago, 1971.

Ritter, Lawrence S. and William L. Silber, *Money,* 2d ed., New York: Basic Books, 1973.

The Role of Money: Other Views

We saw in the last chapter that in the most simplified of Keynesian models, monetary policy works through the mechanism of changes in excess reserves affecting the money supply altering the rate of interest; this then has an effect on the level of planned investment and hence on the equilibrium level of income and employment. The liquidity preference function was at the heart of this analysis. There are, however, many other ways of viewing the role of money in an income and employment determination model. In this chapter we briefly look at a variety of these views as outlined by macroeconomists who tend to call themselves monetarists because of their belief that changes in the money supply are the primary influence on the level of employment, output, and prices in the short run. That is not to say that the nonmonetarists, or Keynesians, as most would prefer to be called, who do not accept such a strong view of the role of money, believe that money does not matter. On the contrary, just about all economists talk in terms of both monetary and fiscal policy. Congress is important as it determines the level of government spending and taxation, and hence the size of the budget deficit or surplus, but so too is the Federal Reserve in its capacity as the controller of the money supply and hence the interest rates and economic activity that result from changes in it.

Stressing the Transactions Demand for Money

Rather than stress the speculative demand for money, or the liquidity preference function as Keynes preferred to call it, one alternative view puts more emphasis on the transactions motive. If individuals desire to hold a certain percentage of their income in cash, then as their income changes, their demand for cash balances will too. Moreover, if individuals with a certain level of income have larger cash balances than normal at that level, they will attempt to rid themselves of the excess. They do this by spending more than their current income. In the opposite situation, to build up their cash balances, they would spend less than their current income.

Although each of us can determine our own holding of cash, altogether we must hold the nation's money supply, by its definition. If, for example, the Federal Reserve buys United States government bonds and thereby increases the total amount of money in circulation, we, as the public, would be the holders of that increase in cash balances. The question is, in this case, what do we do with this increase?

In Chapter 12 it was hypothesized that the excess amount of cash balances would be an inducement to individuals to purchase bonds—the speculative demand. Looking at the situation from another viewpoint, that of the transactions demand, we could hypothesize that any increase in the money supply over that quantity demanded at the current level of income will cause households and firms to spend more than their current income. We can show this in our standard $C + I + G$ diagram by shifting the $C + I + G$ line upward by whatever amount autonomous investment and consumption expenditures increase due to an increase in the money supply. This is what is done in Figure 13-1.

We can now outline the transmission mechanism for this monetarist view of the role of money and income determination models.

The Transmission Mechanism

Let's suppose the quantity demanded and quantity supplied of money are equal, and

equilibrium exists. Now the Federal Reserve decides to buy bonds; in doing so, it increases the reserves of member commercial banks. Member banks then lend their excess reserves, causing a multiple expansion in the money supply. Now the money supply is greater than it was before, but the quantity of money demanded is less than this new, larger quantity supplied. According to the monetarists, people will attempt to get rid of their excess money balances. They will spend their money on a whole spectrum of possible assets—bonds, stocks, houses, cars, and myriad goods and services. The trade-off, then, is not just between money balances and bonds but between money balances and all possible avenues of spending. The monetarists, therefore, believe that the effect on interest rates is small—much smaller than the Keynesians expect. Certainly, part of the excess money balances will go into buying bonds, which will raise the price of bonds and thus lower the interest rate. However, the main influence is on income and employment, which are affected directly by people spending their excess cash balances on a variety of assets and goods and services. The monetarists maintain that spending will increase until income is such that the demand and supply of money are again in equilibrium. Equilibrium occurs when nominal income has risen sufficiently to cause people to want to hold all cash balances made available by the monetary authorities.

The Monetarists' Explanation of an Inflationary Recession

For a period of several years after the 1969 to 1970 recession, there were both high levels of unemployment and increasing prices. The United States experienced a phenomenon called an **inflationary recession.** We can use the monetarist theory presented above to explain this, if we add to it a little information

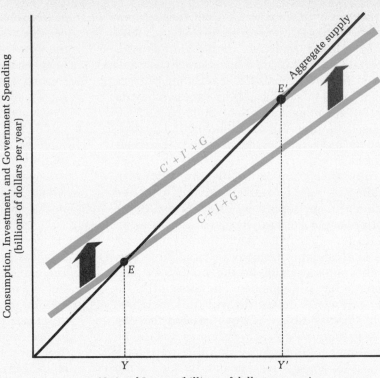

FIGURE 13-1 The Effects of an Increase in the Money Supply

This is one possible transmission mechanism for monetary policy. It is assumed that an increase in the money supply directly increases aggregate demand by increasing the autonomous component of planned consumption and/or planned investment and thus moves the aggregate demand function, $C + I + G$, up to a new aggregate demand function, $C' + I' + G$. The equilibrium level of national income moves from Y to Y'.

about the formation of expectations—on the part of both workers and business people.

In early 1960, we were at a period of under full employment. There were unemployed workers and there were machines that were not being used. The monetarists point out that, at this time, the rate of expansion of the money supply increased from 1.7 percent to 3.8 percent (see Figure 13-2). As people attempted to get rid of their excess cash balances, they spent more than their current income. As they spent more money for goods and services, they were increasing nominal aggregate demand. As people demanded and bought more, producers produced more because we were not at full employment. Prices rose hardly at all. By 1965, however, we were straining our available capac-

ities. The unemployment rate was 4.5, the lowest it had been in 8 years. But, at that time, the monetary authorities increased the rate of expansion of the money supply from less than 4 percent to about 7 percent per year except for a brief pause in 1966. As the private sector attempted to rid itself of the increased excess cash balances, the only thing that could go up were prices. The monetary authorities continued to increase the money supply until December 1968. Then there was an abrupt cutback in the rate of expansion of the money supply.

Using almost any demand for money relationship, we would now expect that the private sector would desire greater cash balances than it actually had, and this is what occurred. It was just the opposite of the situation in the

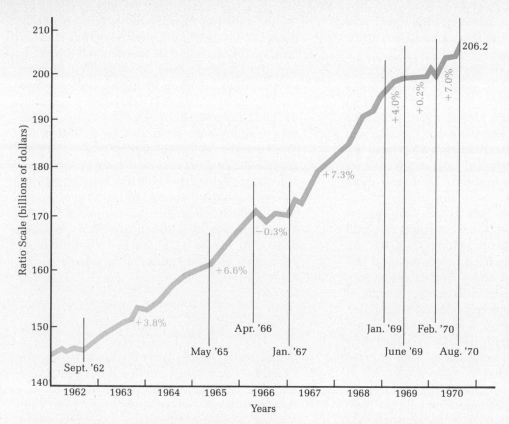

FIGURE 13-2 The Money Supply during the 1960s

Starting in September 1962, the growth of the money supply increased to 3.8 percent. Then in May 1965, it jumped up to 6.6 percent increase per annum. There was a temporary pause during the latter part of 1966. Then it shot off again, now at a higher rate of 7.3 percent. It finally slowed down at the end of 1968. Percentages are annual rates of change for periods indicated. *(Source: Federal Reserve Bank of St. Louis.)*

previous few years. To make up deficient cash balances, people spent less than they received. Total nominal aggregate demand fell.

Since prices increased when we were at full employment, when the situation was reversed, why didn't prices fall? Why did total output fall rather than prices? Why did we end up with continued rising prices and falling employment—that is, rising unemployment? The answer lies in the way workers and business people formulate their expectations about future prices and wages.

Expectations

From 1965 through 1968, workers found that every increase in their nominal wages was eaten up by increasing prices. In fact, blue collar workers experienced a slight drop in real income during that period. The purchasing power of their paychecks was actually smaller in 1968 than it had been in 1965. Workers had been continuously fooled into accepting wage increases they thought would compensate for rising prices but that, in the end, did not. Their expectations of how prices would change in the future were based on the experiences of past years. Workers refused to believe that prices were going to stop rising in the future, even when it was pointed out to them that the monetary authorities had switched to contractionary monetary policy. Due to their expectations, workers demanded increases in nominal wages not only to make up for *past* decreases in the real purchasing power of their paychecks but also as a hedge against anticipated price increases in the future.

In the beginning of the recession, business people were willing to give in to such wage demands because they too had experienced several years of being fooled. Every year they raised their prices but were still able to sell more than they had anticipated. That is, at the end of each year, they had smaller inventories than they felt were optimal. They sold more than predicted, even with the higher prices. Business people felt they could pass the increased labor cost on to the consumer and still make as much profit as before. They had no idea that total nominal aggregate demand had permanently shifted down, due to the restrictive action of the Federal Reserve. The rate of growth of nominal aggregate demand had fallen because the rate of growth of the money supply had fallen, thus inducing people to reduce their desired spending to get back to their desired level of cash balances.

We can now understand the monetarist analysis of the inflationary recession. Total aggregate demand fell because of restrictive monetary policy. However, prices did not fall but continued to rise due to *expectations* of rising prices that were built into the decisions of unions and business people. One can blame neither unions nor business people for their actions. They had no way of knowing that, in fact, the growth rate of aggregate demand had fallen.

Resulting Unemployment

The result was unemployment. Workers demanded higher wages and got them. Employers felt they could pass on the increased labor costs in higher prices, but they found that the demand for their products did not increase as they had expected. Inventories began to pile up, and workers were laid off as production slowed.

Output fell, but workers did not immediately accept lower wage offers because they did not believe the decrease in the demand for their services was permanent. So we see that, in some sense, the expectation of higher prices led to continuing increases in prices. However, sooner or later, the wage-price spiral had to peter out as unemployment grew and grew and grew. Workers eventually got the message, and employers refused to grant ever-increasing wages. We did not expect the price level to start falling, but we did expect the *rate* of increase of prices to fall, which is exactly what happened in 1970 when the rate of inflation finally peaked. As shown in Figure 13-3, the Fed continued its restrictive monetary policy, although at varying rates.

The Phillips Curve

When introducing the Phillips curve, in Chapter 7, we pointed out that it has been quite unstable over time; that is, the trade-off between inflation and unemployment hasn't remained constant. Professors Mary Hamilton and Albert Rees have commented upon the relationship: "We regard the construction of a plausible Phillips curve from annual data for a long period of time as a *tour de force* somewhat comparable to writing the Lord's Prayer on the head of a pin, rather than as a guide to policy."

Since 1965, the maintenance of a given unemployment rate has required higher and higher rates of inflation. The trade-off between unemployment and inflation has become increasingly worse.

The Importance of Expectations

The monetarists believe that, in fact, there can be no long-run trade-off between unemploy-

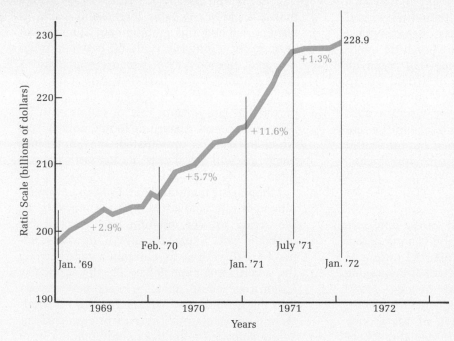

FIGURE 13-3 Restrictive Monetary Policy

In January 1969, restrictive monetary policy set in. From January 1969 to February 1970, the money supply increased at only 2.9 percent per year, compared to the 7.7 percent rate at which it had increased in the previous 2 years. Then the rate of growth picked up somewhat to 5.7 percent; it went crazy from January to July 1971 when it grew at 11.6 percent, and then became very restrictive between July and the end of 1971 when it grew at only 1.3 percent. (*Source:* Board of Governors, U.S. Federal Reserve System.)

ment and inflation. They don't believe that increasing the rate of inflation can forever "buy" less unemployment. Their reasoning relates to the fact that the original Phillips curve analysis completely ignored people's *expectations of future changes in prices.* Changes in the *expected* as opposed to the *actual* rate of inflation have an important impact upon the so-called trade-off between unemployment and inflation.

Ask yourself why inflation could reduce the level of unemployment in the first place. This assertion can be justified by assuming that workers always lag behind in their requests for higher wages. Employers are able to raise prices continuously and thereby make higher profits. Workers' anticipations of future increases in prices are not consistent with actual increases. Therefore, workers demand wage rates that fall behind actual increases in the cost of living (the price level). What, then, is the real wage rate

employers have to pay employees? The real wage rate is the money wage rate divided by the price level. If the price level goes up but the money wage rate does not go up proportionately, then the real wage rate falls. Since this is what employers actually look at in terms of their costs of labor, we would expect that, when the real wage rate falls, the quantity of labor demanded will rise. Therefore, unemployment will be decreased.

Full Anticipation

Now ask yourself what would happen if the rate of inflation were fully anticipated at every moment in time. Workers wouldn't be fooled; their demands for higher wage rates would take into account any expected inflation. Since the real wage rate would not fall, employers would not demand more workers; more workers would not be employed and output would not be increased. Therefore, any change in nominal aggregate demand due to, say, expansionary monetary policy would have very little effect on *real* output. The only thing that could be affected is nominal income. It would go up because prices would rise. Any change in the rate of expansion of the money supply would simply translate itself into a change in the rate of inflation. The growth in real output would remain the same as its long-run equilibrium.

Short-Run Effects

The monetarists contend that, in the long run, when the actual rate of inflation is anticipated, real output as opposed to nominal output is independent of the rate of growth of the money supply or of nominal aggregate demand. However, there can be short-run effects if there are abrupt changes in the growth of the money supply and nominal aggregate demand. There can be important effects on both output and employment. According to the monetarists, there can be temporary fluctuations in output and employment that are the results of unfulfilled expectations occurring during periods of adjustment to a new, previously unanticipated rate of inflation.

Suppose the Fed suddenly increased the money supply at a pace that was faster than it had been in the past. According to the monetarists, people would find themselves with excess cash balances. In their attempts to rid themselves of these excesses, they would cause nominal aggregate demand to rise. Businesses would find their inventories running low and would increase their production rates. New workers would be hired. In general, workers would find that they were able to find jobs faster than usual, even at the wage rates they had been used to asking. In short, a change in the rate of growth of the money supply would change the amount of employment, and, even-

tually, there would be an increase in prices as we approached full employment. This, however, is not a long-run trade-off between inflation and unemployment because expectations will eventually adjust to reality. Any stable rate of growth of nominal aggregate demand will permit the *equilibrium* rate of inflation to be fully anticipated. According to the monetarists, when inflation is anticipated, the unemployment rate will stabilize at its long-run natural rate.

Monetarists maintain that, to keep an unemployment rate below its long-run natural level, the actual rate of inflation must exceed the expected rate. Expectations will, however, adjust to reality; thus, to maintain a gap between the actual and expected rates, the monetary authorities would have to inject new money into the economy at ever increasing rates, affecting an accelerating rate of price increases. *What is needed to reduce unemployment is an accelerating inflation that is always underestimated.* We can translate the monetarist view of the Phillips curve into graphic analysis.

Graphic Analysis

In Figure 13-4, we see two curves similar in appearance to the standard Phillips curve. On the horizontal axis we measure unemployment; on the vertical axis we measure the *actual* rate of inflation. The Phillips curves, however, are drawn for two different levels of *expected* rates of inflation. The first one is drawn for an expected rate of inflation of 3 percent; the second one is drawn for an expected rate of inflation of 6 percent. The vertical line labeled U^* represents the so-called natural rate of unemployment, which we will assume to be 4 percent.

The monetarists assume that the unemployment rate will eventually settle at U^* when the future inflation rate is correctly anticipated—that is, when the actual rate of change

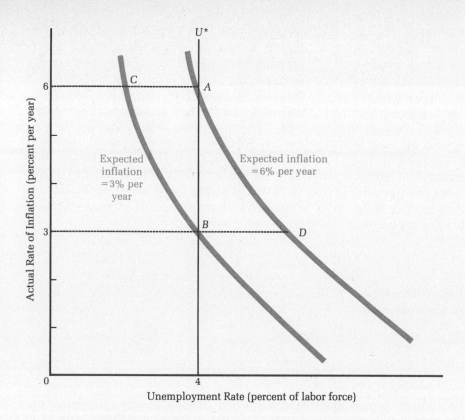

FIGURE 13-4 Hypothetical Phillips' Curves

Here we show two Phillips' curves. On the horizontal axis, the unemployment rate is measured. On the vertical axis is the rate of inflation. We assume that the "natural" or long-run level of unemployment is at U^*, or 4 percent of the labor force. There are two separate Phillips' curves: One is for an expected rate of inflation of 6 percent per year, and the other is for an expected rate of inflation of 3 percent per year. If the expected rate of inflation is 6 percent per year and the actual rate of inflation (which is measured on the vertical axis) is also 6 percent per year, then the long-run equilibrium unemployment level will be maintained at point A. However, if the expected rate of inflation remains at 6 percent per year, but the *actual* rate of inflation is only 3 percent per year, we will find ourselves at point D, where there is excess unemployment—that is, unemployment over and above the normal long-run U^* of 4 percent. Here we see that an actual rate of inflation less than the expected rate of inflation leads to unemployment. Now take the innermost curve, where the expected rate of inflation is 3 percent per year. If the actual rate of inflation is also 3 percent, then there will be no excess unemployment—that is, unemployment will be at its "normal" long-run level of 4 percent. We will be at point B. Suppose, however, that the actual rate of inflation is 6 percent. We will find ourselves at point C. We will be at over full employment—that is, unemployment will be less than its long-run or normal level of 4 percent. At point C, individuals *underestimate* the actual rate of inflation. Contrast this with point D, where individuals *overestimate* the actual rate of inflation. The underestimate causes unemployment rates to fall below U^*. The overestimate causes unemployment rates to be greater than U^*.

in prices is equal to the expected rate of change in prices. This would occur either at point *A*, if the actual rate of inflation was 6 percent, or point *B*, if the actual rate of inflation was 3 percent. Look at point *C*, however. Here, the anticipated rate of inflation is 3 percent, but the actual rate is 6 percent. Point *C* represents "over full" employment. Now look at point *D*. The actual rate of inflation is 3 percent, but the anticipated rate is 6 percent. Unemployment exceeding the natural rate thus occurs.

If the monetarists are correct in their interpretation of the Phillips curve analysis, the monetary authorities cannot be successful in forever keeping unemployment down by increasing the rate of inflation. If the monetarists are correct, it matters little in the long run what the rate of growth of the money supply is, provided that the rate remains stable through time. The monetarists believe that a continual rate of change of prices of 4 percent per year will yield the same long-run level of unemployment as a continual rate of change of prices of 10 percent. The only prerequisite for this outcome is that the rate of change of prices be correctly anticipated.

<table>
<tr><td>Definition of New Term</td><td>**Inflationary Recession:** A period of concomitant rising prices and relatively high unemployment.</td></tr>
</table>

Chapter Summary

1. Individuals in the economy determine their own holdings of cash balances, but together people must accept the total money supply offered by the monetary authorities.

2. Modern monetarists view the demand for money as part of the demand for all assets. Money is just one particular asset. Monetarists therefore maintain that the demand for money depends upon nominal income, the rate of return on alternative assets, and the rate of inflation. The rate of inflation is a determinant of the demand for money because it is equal to the rate of depreciation of cash balances. The faster cash balances depreciate, the more expensive they are to hold.

3. Monetarists and Keynesians alike predict that at full employment, any increase in the money supply will be translated into a rise in the price level. There will be no increase in output because that is impossible at full employment.

4. Expectations play a key role in monetarist analysis. Expectations, according to the monetarists, were responsible for the 1969 to 1970 inflationary recession. Workers demanded higher wages because of past inflationary experience; employers gave them higher wages, expecting to be able to raise prices without losing any business. However, since there was a drop in the rate of growth of nominal aggregate demand, at higher prices, employers could not sell all the goods they thought they could. Inventories built up; workers were laid off; unemployment and a recession resulted.

5. Monetarists maintain that there is no long-run trade-off between unemployment and inflation. They state that the Phillips curve will shift according to the expected rate of inflation. If inflation is fully anticipated, they maintain that there will be no employment effect from rising prices. It is only when the rate of inflation is completely unanticipated that it will have an employment effect.

Questions for Thought and Discussion

1. On the average, how much cash do you keep? (Remember to count not only the cash in your wallet but your checking account balances as well.) Do you think you would hold more cash if your part-time income or your scholarship or the money your parents send you were to double?
2. How can you increase your cash balances? How can you decrease your cash balances?
3. Why does the public have to accept the total money supply offered by the monetary authorities?
4. Do you think you would want to hold more or less cash if the rate of inflation increased from 5 percent per year to 500 percent per year?

Selected References

Federal Reserve Bank of Boston, *Controlling Monetary Aggregates*, Boston: Federal Reserve Bank of Boston, 1969.

Friedman, Milton, *Dollars and Deficits*, Englewood Cliffs, N.J.: Prentice-Hall, 1968.

Meiselman, David, Testimony before the Subcommittee on Fiscal Policy of the Joint Economic Committee, Congress of the United States, Oct. 13, 1969.

The Iconoclast As Institution

MILTON FRIEDMAN

Economist, University of Chicago

Milton Friedman has played a unique role in the continuing battle over the role of government in the economy. He has never held a major government post, but he has heard his ideas soundly condemned by the "new economists" of the early 1960s, eventually—if cautiously—adopted by the "gamesmen" of the Nixon administration, and then ignored shortly thereafter. Throughout, Friedman has hounded the economic watchmen about uselessly attending to invalid fiscal indices while ignoring what he considers the one crucial factor: fluctuation in the money supply.

One of America's major conservative economists, Friedman defends the modern "quantity" theory of money: changes in the amount of money in circulation shape short-run economic events. In his testimony before the Joint Congressional Economic Committee in 1959, Friedman said that the Federal Reserve Board, instead of tightening money during booms and loosening money during recessions (which doesn't work because of the lags), should simply increase the supply of money at a steady rate of 4 percent, "month in and month out, year in and year out."

An ideal economy, according to Friedman, is based on a free-market model; government's role should be little more than the maintenance of optimal competitive conditions. This concept has two important corollaries, both of which stand solidly in opposition to "liberal" economic thought in this country: (1) the obligation of the business community is the maximization of profit with direct responsibility to the stockholder, and (2) the economy is not a tool of social betterment, to be manipulated by the government in pursuit of social-welfare goals. Friedman explained, in "The Social Responsibility of Business is to Maximize Profit" (New York Times Magazine, 1970), that the use of corporate profits for environmental protection, safety and quality-control devices, and so on represents a direct tax on the stockholder; a board of directors that "levies" such a tax is acting as a legislative body. The way certain companies have timidly received the demands of consumer groups is, to Friedman, completely at odds with the valid economic role of the corporation. "When I hear businessmen speak eloquently about the 'social responsibility of business in a free enterprise system,' I am reminded of the wonderful line about the Frenchman who discovered at the age of 70 that he had been speaking prose all his life."

In Friedman's view, it is dangerous to regard the economic sector as a cure for social problems. It drives economists into roles of oracles and social magicians. As Friedman stated: "I believe that we economists in recent years have done vast harm—to society at large and to our profession in particular—by claiming more than we can deliver."

Friedman would, nonetheless, like to apply many of his free-market concepts to other areas of the society. He opposes protective tariffs, feeling that America has a good deal to gain by encouraging imports. "If Japan exports steel at artificially low prices, it is also exporting clean air. Why shouldn't we take it?" Other aspects of Friedman's approach are his distaste for subsidies (especially farm) and price supports and his dislike of government mandates for safety equipment in automobiles. He has advocated abandoning Social Security and welfare, to be replaced with a negative tax (a cash subsidy for those citizens in the lowest income group).

During Senator Barry Goldwater's unsuccessful bid for the presidency in 1964, Friedman served as chief economic adviser. Friedman also advised Nixon on economic matters during his campaign for the presidency in 1968, but Nixon broke with Friedman's theories when he instituted the wage and price freeze. In the first year of the Ford administration, Friedman advocated a substantial tax cut coupled with an equal cut in government spending. To cut income taxes without reducing government spending, Friedman argued, only means increased taxes later or higher inflation rates if the increased budget deficit is partly or wholly financed by the Fed.

Whether the American economy will ever turn in the direction Friedman proposes is perhaps not as important as Friedman's advocacy role in the economics establishment. Paul Samuelson said a few years ago: "To keep the fish that they carried on long journeys lively and fresh, sea captains used to introduce an eel into the barrel. In the economics profession, Milton Friedman is that eel."

Is Short-Run Stabilization Possible?

POLICYMAKERS' PROBLEMS

Keeping the Economy on an Even Keel

You have just been presented with the rudiments of income and employment determination models. One is characteristically labeled "Keynesian," the other "monetarist." Whichever model is used, the goal is the same: to understand and predict how our economy works. You should be aware that macroeconomic modeling, as it is sometimes called, is not done merely as an exercise in intellectual tinkering. Rather, we are in an era of applied macroeconomics, where policymakers rely on the results of sometimes simple and sometimes complicated macroeconomic models. How do they rely on those models? They use the models to make predictions of what will happen to the economy in the future; then they alter certain policy variables such as the rate of government spending, the rate of government taxation, or the rate of growth in the money supply in order to effect a desired change in future economic activity. Such policymaking is generally called short-term macroeconomic stabilization, since

it is concerned with changes in economic activity expected to occur over the subsequent 12-month period.

Short-run stabilization policymaking was virtually unheard of prior to the Great Depression. For one thing, the consensus among economists in those days was that the economy was self-regulating. For another, the importance of fiscal policy—changes in government spending and taxation—didn't really gain a foothold until after the publication of Keynes' *General Theory*.

At the end of World War II, Congress made explicit the federal government's "responsibility" to stabilize economic activity in the short run. The Employment Act of 1946 proclaimed:

The Congress hereby declares that it is the continuing policy and responsibility of the Federal Government to use all practicable means consistent with its needs and obligations and other essential considerations of national policy, with assistance and cooperation of industry, agriculture, labor and State and local governments, to coordinate and utilize all its plans, functions, and resources for the purpose of creating and maintaining, in a manner calculated to foster and promote free competitive enterprise and the general welfare, conditions under which there will be afforded useful employment opportunities, including self-employment, for those able, willing, and seeking to work and to promote maximum employment, production, and purchasing power.

Economic activism by the federal government was and continues to be the reality of the day.

However, is a proclamation that declares the federal government "responsible" for promoting maximum employment, production, and purchasing power sufficient to guarantee that the ups and downs in economic activity will in fact be smoothed out? Are there any reasons why short-run stabilization policies may work sometimes but not other times? Does the income and employment model used in predicting economic activity determine the success or failure of the policies based thereupon? These are the questions to which we address ourselves in this issue.

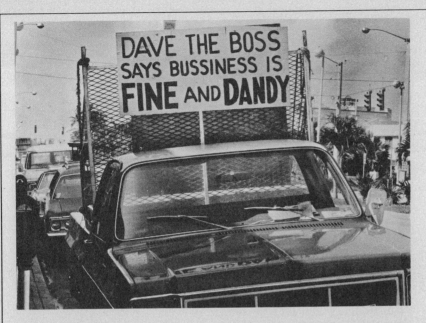

How Do We Define Full Employment?

Given the tenor of what is often called the "Full" Employment Act of 1946, it seems appropriate to start our discussion with a query—just what is meant by full employment? You might get an idea by reading the reports from certain government economists. They might define full employment these days as an employment situation where 5 percent —or even more—of the active labor force declares itself unemployed when surveyed by the Bureau of Labor Statistics. Presumably, that 5 percent level represents frictional unemployment which is "optimal" because of the transactions costs that exist in the real world labor market. However, if you refer back to statements by government officials, say, a period of 10 years ago, full employment was defined as 4 percent unemployment, and if you

go back even further, full employment was 3 percent unemployment.

Obviously, there is no objective way to come up with a definition of full employment. How much unemployment can we call frictional? There is no way of telling. The full employment level of unemployment has been defined in a very ad hoc manner and has been raised in recent years. Nonetheless, for any certain period of time, policymakers do accept, and work with some definition of full employment. Then, if their current definition is, for example, 5 percent unemployment and the unemployment rate rises to 6½ percent, policymakers can react to what is considered an unacceptably high rate of unemployment.

Deciding What to Do

Given the policymakers' tool kit, consisting primarily of the monetary

and fiscal policies we have discussed throughout this entire unit, how is the decision made that a particular policy should be put into play? Generally the decision is based on an admixture of data on the current economic scene: the current rate of inflation, the current level of unemployment, the current level of business capital formation, and so forth. Predictions about future economic activity based on current and past data will also be added. These predictions are not difficult to obtain for there are hundreds of business-forecasting organizations, both private and public. The government has, at its disposal, models employing elements of what you have learned in this unit that give projections on a monthly, quarterly, and yearly basis about future values of aggregate economic variables. The numerical values in these models are obtained by feeding past data into a computer that is programmed according to whatever the income and employment determination model in use indicates is appropriate. The subdiscipline used in this instance is called **econometrics,** which is basically the application of mathematics and statistics to the measurement of economic relationships. The models involved are called econometric models. They give predictions of future economic activity. However, ultimately, of course, theories are devised by economists. Therefore, when a particular econometric model doesn't work, that is, when the model doesn't predict well, it is rarely the fault of the computer. (In fact, there is a common saying among those people who use computers: Garbage in, garbage out.)

We mentioned already the first problem of policymaking—defining full employment. We now see a second difficulty—predicting with some accuracy the future course of economic activity. To a large extent this ability depends on using an income determination model that takes account of all the relationships necessary to do the job. Moreover, it depends on the availability of current accurate data on key aggregate variables. Models, for example, that use changes in inventories as a variable often go awry because the data on business inventory changes never seem to be right the first time they are collected. There are nearly always changes 3 or 6 months later.

The problem of information forms part of the larger problem called "time lags."

Time Lags for Short-Run Policies

Have you ever suddenly realized you had a cold when retrospect would indicate that you had felt it coming on for some time? In other words, have you ever experienced a time lag between displaying the first symptoms of a cold and your recognition of them? Short-run stabilization policymakers face not only a time lag like this but several others as well.

The Information Time Lag

Before any policy can be made, there must be information on the current state of the economy. However, we don't know concurrently what is happening to the rate of capital formation, the unemployment rate, changes in prices, and so on until after the fact and after a time lag. It is crucially important for us to obtain accurate information as quickly as possible, but sometimes accurate information about the entire economy doesn't come for months. In other words, it's possible that we will not recognize we are in a recession until, say, 6 months after it starts. This is often called the "recognition lag."

Another problem, one that particularly concerns fiscal policy, also faces policymakers.

The Action Time Lag

Once we discover we are indeed in a recession, a long period can sometimes elapse before any policy is put into effect. This is particularly true of tax cuts and tax increases that are desired for stabilization purposes. A tax cut was first suggested in the Kennedy administration in 1961. It didn't pass until 1964, a lag of 3 years. Monetary policy does not suffer the same action lag because the Board of Governors of the Federal Reserve System meet 13 times a year and can, almost instantaneously, put into effect any policy it decides upon. It must simply instruct the trading desk at the New York Fed how to proceed. The action lag, then, can be long and variable for fiscal policy but will generally be relatively short for monetary policy.

An effect lag also faces policymakers.

The Effect Time Lag

Even if there were no information lag or action lag, there would still be an effect lag because even the most perfect economic policy variable change will not have an immediate impact upon the economy. An increase in government spending, for example, takes time to work itself out; a change in taxes does too. A change in the rate of growth of the money supply may not have an effect for several months or several years. Economists have spent countless years attempting to estimate this effect lag. Some say that for fiscal policy the lag can draw out over several years. The initial lag in monetary policy, on the other hand, may be only months although it can draw out for several years after.

Taking Lags into Account

Now you can see the problems inherent in trying to stabilize the economy in the short run. Assume you are a policymaker and you have just discovered that the economy is going into a recession. You try to get taxes changed to counter that recession. What kind of problems will you encounter? First of all, we may have already been in a recession for 6 months or 1 year before you detected it. Secondly, it may take another year or two to get Congress to put the tax-change package into effect, and thirdly, it may take another year until the major effect of that fiscal policy change is felt in the economy. By that time, the economy may have already turned around and be on the upswing. Your fiscal policy change will then be inappropriate and only add fuel to a booming inflationary fire.

The long and variable lags in-

A monetary rule would require the money supply to grow at a fixed annual rate that would not be altered by the Federal Open Market Committee or anyone else for that money. In fact, that Committee would have no function if a monetary rule were instituted.

On the fiscal policy side, there are numerous advocates of a long-run commitment to a balanced full-employment budget. Essentially, there would be no discretionary fiscal policy to change the direction of economic activity in the short run.

Note that the adoption of a monetary rule and a long-run commitment to a balanced full-employment federal budget would, to a large extent, lessen the importance of macroeconomic models as a basis for short-run stabilization policies.

Coordination

Since stabilization policy can be instituted by using fiscal tools as well as monetary tools, there would seem to be a problem of coordination. What if the fiscal authorities—the President and Congress—decide on one policy, and the monetary authorities—the Fed—decide on another? As a matter of fact, we have observed occasionally conflicting policies being carried out by monetary and fiscal authorities. In 1968, for example, a fiscal policy of restraint was adopted by the Congress in the form of a temporary income surtax. Soon after that surtax went into effect, however, the monetary authorities began what would have to be considered an expansionary policy. It seems, therefore, that unless all

volved in short-run stabilization policy have prompted some critics of such policies to recommend essentially that no short-run stabilization attempts be made at all, either from a monetary or a fiscal policy point of view. The most outspoken proponent of stable, or nondiscretionary, monetary policy is Milton Friedman of the University of Chicago. He has been a proponent of the so-called monetary rule for many years now.

policymaking is put under one roof, so to speak, the problem of coordination will at times be serious enough to negate policies that might otherwise help stabilize our economy.

Policymaking and the Public

A relatively new school of macroeconomic thought is developing that, if right, will have serious repercussions on policymaking. This school of thought skirts completely the issue of monetary versus fiscal policy, or Keynesianism versus monetarism. In other words, according to this school, the debate between the effectiveness of monetary versus fiscal policy and the debate between the Keynesians and the monetarists about the role of money in income determination is irrelevant. To adherents of this school, the only way that short-run stabilization policy works is for the public to be temporarily fooled because if the public knew exactly what was going to happen, then it would be able to capitalize on that information and effectively negate it. This is similar to the argument that public information about a company is useless to an individual wishing to invest in that company because the information, if accurate, will already have been used by someone else and therefore the current price of the company's stock will reflect the information. If we look specifically at the trade-off expressed by the Phillips curve, we can apply the same argument. The employment effect depicted in the Phillips curve results from fooling individuals about the future rate of inflation.

If the same argument can be used for the economy as a whole, then government policymakers can suc-

ceed only to the extent that they are able to fool the public. However, somebody once said that you can't fool all the people all the time. Thus, the public will eventually catch on to what government policymakers are doing, and a new policy will have to be devised to have any effect. We can even extend this analysis to its ultimate conclusion; that is, even if policymakers use extremely complicated econometric models to make predictions on which to base their policies, economic agents in our society will find it profitable to decipher the models being used. Then they will be useless as prediction devices,

no matter how many equations or how long the computer works on them.

Such a view of economic policy is disconcerting to those who believe we can do better than essentially doing nothing, but, according to these critics, doing nothing really involves long-run stable monetary and fiscal policies such as those mentioned above—a monetary rule and a long-run balanced full-employment budget. If it is impossible to stabilize in the future, we may be better off doing nothing since then at least we won't exacerbate the ups and downs in business activity.

The Final Word

Economic debates sometimes go on for years. The debates on monetary versus fiscal policy and Keynesianism versus monetarism continue to occupy much of the time of numerous economists. However, a new debate has begun to surface that threatens to overshadow anything else which has come before. The debate concerns not only the appropriateness of short-run stabilization policy but the possibility that it is virtually impossible; that is, there is no way the federal government can do better than a stable long-run monetary and fiscal policy. The majority of economists and policymakers probably still believe strongly in our ability to dampen fluctuations in business activity. They can point to the longest peacetime expansion in United States history, which occurred in the 1960s under a regime of relatively active short-run stabilization policymaking. They can compare the ups and downs in business activity after the Employment Act of 1946 to what happened before that time and thereby demonstrate that the business cycle has not been as erratic as it was previously. For many years to come, you and I will be reading about government attempts to keep the economy on a fairly even keel. Now, however, you should have a good understanding of the macroeconomic models that form the basis for many of those government policies.

Definition of New Term

Econometrics: The measurement of economic variables and the use of statistics in economic model building for the purpose of explaining and predicting what happens in the economy.

Questions for Thought and Discussion

1. What goals are there in our economy besides full employment?
2. Do you know how to define full employment?
3. "You can fool some of the people all the time and all the people some of the time, but. . . ." Does this famous quote have anything to do with short-run stabilization policy?
4. Why are lags important in policymaking?

Selected References

McMillan, Robert A., "A Re-examination of the 'Full Employment' Goal," *Economic Review,* March–April 1973, pp. 3–17; pub. by the Federal Reserve Bank of Cleveland.

Miller, Roger LeRoy and Raburn M. Williams, *Unemployment and Inflation: The New Economics of the Wage-Price Spiral,* St. Paul, Minn.: West Publishing, 1974, chap. 8.

FOUR

THE INTERNATIONAL SCENE

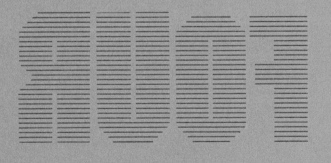

14 Benefiting from Trade among Nations

Most people regard trade as a gain when they are able to buy cheaper foreign products but as a loss when they see workers put out of jobs because of foreign competition. In this chapter, we hope to ferret out the real issues involved in international trade. It is certainly true that you as a consumer gain from cheaper foreign products. It is also true that employees and stockholders of industries hurt by foreign competition end up losing. The question is: "Are the gains from trade worth the costs?"

Putting Trade in Its Place

Trade among nations must somehow benefit the residents of each nation by more than it costs them. The volume of world trade has been increasing at a compound growth rate of between 5 and 10 percent per year for quite a while. In 1800, world trade was a mere $1.3 billion in terms of current purchasing power; just before the Great Depression, it reached almost $70 billion. That figure was again reached in 1950. Today, as seen in Figure 14-1, world trade on the average exceeds $300 billion a year. For the most part, the transactions involved take place voluntarily among individual citizens in different countries.

Table 14-1 shows that the size of international trade in different countries varies greatly when measured as a percentage of GNP. Some countries export and import more than one-third of their GNP. The United States ranks at the bottom of the list. In fact, the United States is the Western country that would suffer the least if foreign trade were completely stopped. The change, however, would not go unnoticed.

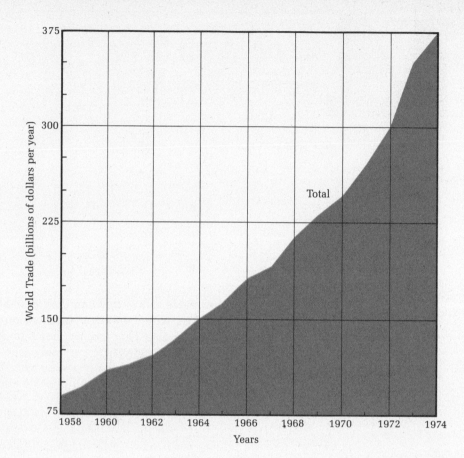

FIGURE 14-1 World Trade Per Year

World trade has grown rapidly over the last decade or so. In 1974, it had reached the $300 billion mark. *(Source: U.S. Department of Commerce.)*

If Foreign Trade Stopped

If imports stopped, tea and coffee drinkers would have to switch to Postum or Pero. Chocolate would be out of the question; you'd have to switch to carob. You would have no bananas, no pepper, no Scotch whiskey.

Many of our raw materials come from other countries. Over 90 percent of the bauxite from which we make aluminum is of foreign origin. All our chrome, cobalt, and the greater part of our nickel, platinum, tin, and asbestos are imported. If the world's trade stopped, we wouldn't be able to drink French wine; we wouldn't see Italian movies; and we wouldn't drive VWs.

Exports

Imports, of course, are only half the story. We pay for imports either by exports or through an extension of credit by other countries. Much of our employment comes from export industries. Twenty percent of our cotton, 25 percent of our grains, and 25 percent of our tobacco are shipped abroad. A third of our sulfur and a fifth of our coal is sold in foreign countries. Over 14 percent of our auto production, 25 percent of our textile and metal work machinery, and 30 percent of our construction and mining machinery are exported. And there are perhaps 35 other industries in which at least 20 percent of the output is regularly sold

Table 14-1 **World Trade in Different Countries**

Here we show the amount of world trade in different countries expressed as a percentage of their GNP. The United States, where world trade represents only 9 percent, is the lowest on the list. The Netherlands, on the other hand, where world trade is a whopping 44 percent of GNP, is at the top of the list.

COUNTRY	% OF GNP
Netherlands	44
Belgium-Luxembourg	37
Sweden	26
Canada	21
West Germany	19
United Kingdom	16
Italy	15
Japan	12
United States	9

Source: U.S. Department of Commerce

abroad. All told, there are 3 to 4 million jobs involved in the production of exports.

Of course, if world trade ceased to exist, all those jobs wouldn't be lost and all the imported goods wouldn't vanish from our shelves—we would simply alter our own production to take account of the situation. New industries would spring up to provide substitutes for the imported goods. Workers who lost their jobs in export industries would probably get jobs later as we readjusted.

Voluntary Trade

We engage in foreign trade for only one reason: We benefit from it. All trade is voluntary, and a voluntary exchange between two parties has to benefit both of them. Otherwise the exchange would not take place. The reasoning behind this argument is so simple that it often goes unnoticed by politicians who complain about for-

eigners "underselling" us by offering relatively cheap goods.

Demand and Supply of Imports and Exports

Let's explore the mechanism that establishes the level of trade between two nations. First we will need to develop a demand schedule for imports and a supply schedule for exports.

Imports

We will try to calculate graphically how many gallons of wine Americans will desire to import every year. We do this by deriving the **excess demand schedule** for wine. The left side of Figure 14-2 shows the usual supply and demand curves for wine in the United States. We draw consecutive price lines starting at equilibrium and going down. At the equilibrium price of $2 per gallon, there is no excess demand or excess supply for United States wine. In the right-hand portion of the figure, we again show that at the price of $2, *excess* demand is zero. If $2 were the world price of wine, there would be no net imports of wine. (In our two-country model, we're assuming the world is comprised of France and the United States.) In other words, at $2 per gallon, no wine trade would take place between these two countries.

But what about prices lower than $2? At a price of $1, there is an excess demand for wine in the United States. This is represented by the quantity (horizontal distance) between the domestic supply curve and the domestic demand curve at that price. We take that distance (indicated by the heavy arrow) and transfer it, at that price level, to the right-hand side of the figure. Here we draw the excess demand for wine at a price of $1 (the amount of wine represented by the length of the arrow).

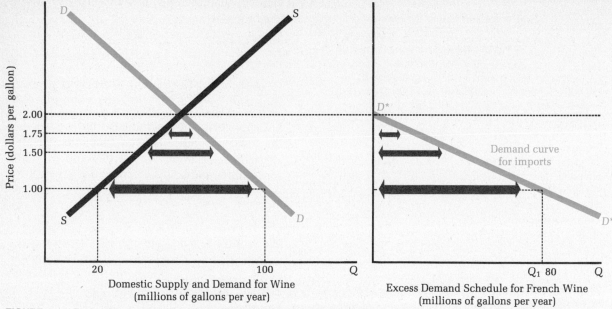

FIGURE 14-2 **Derivation of Import Demand Schedule for the United States**

On the left-hand side of the diagram, we draw the domestic supply and demand schedules for wine. The demand schedule is *DD*; the supply schedule is *SS*. The equilibrium price is $2. At $2 per gallon, there will be no excess demand for wine; therefore, the demand for imports will be zero. However, at a price of $1, there will be an excess demand for wine. The excess demand is represented by the longest arrow. We transfer that arrow to the right-hand graph to show the excess demand for wine at a price of $1. *D*D**, the excess demand for wine is, in other words, the demand for imports of wine. If the world price were $1, we would demand the quantity Q_1 of imported wine. The excess demand curve for French wine slopes down, starting at the domestic equilibrium price of wine—in this case $2.

The length of the arrow is the same on both sides of the graph. If we could continue doing this for all the prices below $2, we will come up with an *excess demand schedule for wine.* Whatever the world price is, we can find out how much the United States will import. If the price is established at $1, for example, we will bring in imports equal to Q_1. As we would expect, the excess demand schedule for imports is downward sloping, like the regular demand schedule. The lower the world price of wine, the more imports we will buy.

Exports

What about the possibility of the United States exporting wine? Europe, in fact, is starting to drink California wines. The situation is depicted graphically in Figure 14-3, where we derive the **excess supply schedule.** Let's look at prices above $2. At a price of $3, the *excess supply* of wine is equal to the amount represented by the distance between the demand curve and the supply curve (again represented by the bold arrow). The excess supply curve

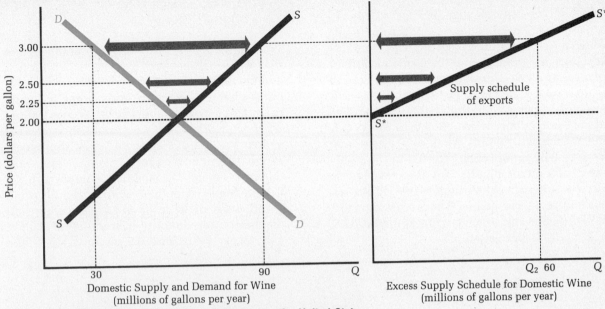

FIGURE 14-3 **Derivation of Export Supply Schedule for the United States**

The domestic demand and supply of wine is shown in the left-hand side of the figure. At an equilibrium price of $2, there is no excess demand or excess supply of domestic wine. In the right-hand graph, we show the excess supply of wine. At prices higher than $2, there is an excess supply of wine. The excess supply is represented by the bold arrows. We transfer these bold arrows over to the right-hand graph to derive the quantity of excess supplies that can be used for exportation purposes. In this manner, we derive the supply schedule of exports, $S*S*$. It slopes upward like all supply schedules. If the world price of wine were $3, we would export the quantity Q_2 to other countries.

is shown on the right side of the figure. The supply curve of exports slopes up, like all supply curves. At a price of $2, there are no net exports from the United States. At a price of $3, however, there are exports. The amount of these exports is represented by the length of the heavy arrow. Thus, if the world price rises above $2, the United States would become a net exporter of wine. The higher the world price, the more wine we would export. The lower the world price, the less wine we would export. Below a price of $2, we would start importing. The **zero trade point,** then, is $2. At

a world price of $2, we will not engage in world trade. (Note that the world price is established by the interaction of total world demand and world supply.)

The Quantity of Trade in a Foreign Country

We can draw the graph for France, our trading partner, in a similar manner. However, we have to establish a common set of measurements for the price of wine. Let's do this in terms of dollars, and let's say that the exchange rate is

20¢ for 1 franc. We place the excess demand schedule for imports and the excess supply schedule for exports on the same graph. Figure 14-4 shows a standard supply and demand schedule for French wine in terms of dollars per gallon. The equilibrium price of French wine is established at $1 per gallon. At a world price of $1 per gallon, the French will neither import nor export wine. At prices below $1, the French will import wine; at prices above $1 they will export wine. We see in the right-hand portion of Figure 14-4 that the excess supply schedule of French wine slopes up starting at $1 per gallon. The excess demand schedule for imports of wine slopes down, starting at $1 per gallon.

International Equilibrium (in a Two-Country World)

We can see the quantity of international trade that will be transacted by putting the French and the American export and import schedules on one graph. The zero trade point for wine in America was established at $2 per gallon, whereas in France it was established at $1 a gallon. We see in Figure 14-5 that the excess supply schedule of exports in France intersects the excess demand schedule for imports in the United States at point E with an equilibrium world price of wine of $1.50 per gallon and an equilibrium quantity of trade of 10 million gallons per year. Here we see how much and

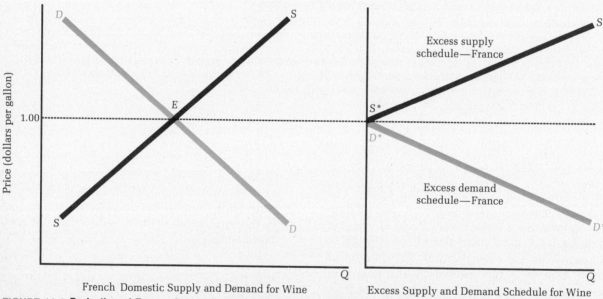

French Domestic Supply and Demand for Wine   Excess Supply and Demand Schedule for Wine

FIGURE 14-4 Derivation of Excess Demand and Supply of Wine for France

The left-hand side of the graph shows France's domestic demand and supply curve for wine. The domestic equilibrium price of wine in France, at an exchange rate of 20¢ per franc, translates into $1 per gallon. At $1 per gallon, France will have neither an excess demand nor an excess supply of wine. At higher prices, it will have an excess supply—that is, it will export wine. At lower prices it will have an excess demand—that is, it will import wine. On the right-hand side of the graph, we have drawn France's excess supply schedule and excess demand schedule. The export schedule is S*S*, and the import schedule is D*D*.

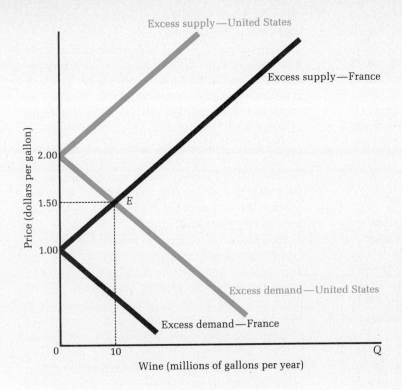

Price (dollars per gallon)

Excess supply—United States

Excess supply—France

2.00

1.50   E

1.00

Excess demand—United States

Excess demand—France

0   10   Q

Wine (millions of gallons per year)

FIGURE 14-5 International Equilibrium

We plot France's excess demand and supply schedule along with the United States' excess demand and supply schedule. France's excess supply schedule intersects our excess demand schedule at point E, which establishes an equilibrium world price of wine. That world price is $1.50, which will be the price of wine everywhere. America will import 10 million gallons of wine at that price and France will export 10 million gallons of wine.

the terms under which trade takes place. The amount is determined by the excess demand and supply schedules in each country and the point at which they intersect each other. If the tables were turned and America's no-trade point was below France's no-trade point, then America would be exporting wine and the French would be importing it.

The free-trade international equilibrium price will never fall below $1 per gallon, nor will it rise above $2 per gallon in this example. Moreover, you should realize that the equilibrium price in this example turns out to be $1.50 because of the particular way the curves were drawn. If we were to do the example differently, we might come out with a somewhat different equilibrium price—although it would still lie between $1 and $2 per gallon.

The Gains from Trade

We can once again mention that there are gains to be made from trade between the United States and France. Let's look at the United States first. After we started trading with France, the price of wine fell from $2 per gallon to $1.50 per gallon and the quantity demanded increased. Additionally, domestic wine production fell and the resources released when those firms went out of business could be used elsewhere. The increased satisfaction we received from the additional wine was *greater* than the cost to us in resources forgone. We are better off.

So, too, are the French. Their *consumption* of domestic wine fell, but their domestic *production* increased. The difference went to the

United States in the form of exports. With those exports the French could now purchase United States imports, the value of which to the French will be *greater* than the resources forgone to make additional wine for export to the United States.

Both countries gain in the free-trade situation. If, however, both countries had a no-trade point at the same price, there would, in fact, be no net imports or exports.

Comparative and Absolute Advantage

The reason there are gains from trade lies in one of the most fundamental principles of economics: A nation gains by doing what it can do best relative to other nations. The United States benefits by *specializing* in only those endeavors in which it has a **comparative advantage.** Let's take an example to demonstrate this concept.

Let's look at France and the United States. We show in Table 14-2 the comparative costs of production of wine and beer in terms of person-days. This is a simple, two-country-two-commodity world where we assume that labor is the only factor of production. As you can see from Table 14-2, in the United States it takes 1 person-day to produce 1 gallon of wine and the same for 1 gallon of beer. In France it takes 1 person-day for 1 gallon of wine, but 2 person-days for 1 gallon of beer. In this sense, Americans are more productive

than the French: They have an **absolute advantage** in producing beer.

However, trade will still take place. Let's assume first that there is no trade and no specialization and that the work force in each country consists of 200 workers. These 200 workers are divided equally in the production of wine and beer. We see in Table 14-3 that, in the United States, 100 gallons of wine and 100 gallons of beer are produced per day. In France 100 gallons of wine and 50 gallons of beer are produced per day. The total world production is 200 gallons of wine and 150 gallons of beer per day.

Now the countries begin to specialize. What can France produce most cheaply? Look at the comparative costs of production expressed in person-days in Table 14-2. What is the cost of producing 1 gallon more of wine? 1 person-day. What is the cost of producing 1 gallon more of beer? 2 person-days. We can say, then, that, in France, the opportunity cost of producing wine is less than that of producing beer. We allow France to specialize in the activity that has the smallest opportunity cost. In other

Table 14-2 **Comparative Costs of Production in Person-Days**

	UNITED STATES	FRANCE
Wine (1 gallon)	1	1
Beer (1 gallon)	1	2

Table 14-3 **Daily World Output before Specialization**

UNITED STATES		
100 workers on wine	=	100 gallons of wine
100 workers on beer	=	100 gallons of beer

FRANCE		
100 workers on wine	=	100 gallons of wine
100 workers on beer	=	50 gallons of beer

World total = 200 gallons of wine, 150 gallons of beer.

words, France specializes in her comparative advantage, which is the production of wine.

According to Table 14-4, after specialization, the United States produces 200 gallons of beer, and France produces 200 gallons of wine. Notice that the total world production per day has gone up from 200 gallons of wine and 150 gallons of beer to 200 gallons of wine and 200 gallons of beer per day. This was done without any increased use of resources. The world is better off when countries specialize in their comparative advantage and then trade, because world output is larger.

Finding One's Comparative Advantage

It is important to understand the difference between the concept of comparative advantage, which we covered before in Chapter 1, and the notion of absolute advantage. Any time a country can produce a product with fewer person-hours of labor than another country, we say that it has an absolute advantage over the other in the production of those products. You, for example, may have an absolute advantage in doing a large variety of jobs. This does not mean, of course, that you divide your time equally among all these jobs. What you do is discover your area of comparative advantage and specialize in that area.

In general, people discover their own area of comparative advantage by contrasting the return from doing one job with the return from doing another job. An executive in a large corporation may have an absolute advantage in doing 15 different tasks for that company. For example, he may be able to type better than all his secretaries, wash windows better than any of the window washers, file better than any of the file clerks, and carry messages better than any of the messengers. His comparative advantage, however, lies in being an executive. He knows this because he is paid more for being an executive than he would be for any other job. The company willingly pays his salary as an executive because the value of his output in that job is at least as large as the salary paid to him. They would not pay him the same amount if he wanted to be a typist. In fact, they might be able to pay 10 or more typists the amount of his salary.

The key to understanding comparative advantage lies in realizing that total resources are fixed at any moment in time. You have only so much time in a day. A nation has only so many workers and machines. An individual, a company, or a nation must decide how it will allocate its available resources at a given moment. No one can use a resource in two different jobs at the same time. Even if companies or nations are *absolutely* better at doing everything, they will still specialize in only those tasks in which they have a comparative advantage because in that specialization they maximize the returns for the use of their time and resources. The United States may have an absolute advantage in producing computers and roller skates in the sense that we can produce both goods with fewer person-hours of labor than any other nation in the world. However, we let other countries produce roller skates

---

Table 14-4 **Daily World Output after Specialization**

UNITED STATES
200 workers on beer = 200 gallons of beer

FRANCE
200 workers on wine = 200 gallons of wine

World total = 200 gallons of beer, 200 gallons of wine

because our comparative advantage lies in producing computers. We might be 25 percent more efficient in the production of roller skates but 60 percent more efficient in the production of computers—so we specialize in computers. We gain by exchanging the computers we produce for the roller skates that other countries produce.

Comparative Advantage and Opportunity Cost

We can also relate the concept of comparative advantage to the concept of opportunity cost. In fact, understanding comparative advantage will give you an important insight into all relationships involving exchange among individuals or among nations. Comparative advantage emphasizes the fact that cost means opportunities that must be forgone. If the United States decides to produce roller skates, it forgoes part of its opportunity to produce computers because the time and resources spent in producing roller skates cannot be used simultaneously in producing computers. The basic reason for the existence of comparative advantage among individuals, companies, and countries lies in the fact that opportunity costs vary. It costs less for different parties to engage in different types of economic activities. Opportunity costs for different countries vary just as they vary for different individuals. Let's examine some of the reasons why opportunity costs and, hence, comparative advantages differ among nations.

Differing Resource Mixes

We know that different nations have different resource bases. Australia has much land relative to its population, whereas Japan has little land relative to its population. All other things being equal, one expects countries with relatively more land to specialize in products that require more land. One expects Australia, for example, to engage in sheep raising but not Japan because the opportunity cost of raising sheep in Japan is much higher. Since land in Japan is scarce, its use represents a higher opportunity cost.

There are also differences in climates. We do not expect countries with dry climates to grow bananas. The limitations of a resource base, however, do not always prohibit a country's actions. Watermelons require tremendous amounts of water; they are, nonetheless, grown in Arizona. (The federal government subsidizes water to watermelon growers in that state.)

Advantageous Trade Will Always Exist

Since the beginning of recorded history, there have been examples of trade among individuals. Since these acts of exchange have usually been voluntary, we must assume that individuals generally benefit from the trade. Individual tastes and resources vary tremendously. As a consequence, there are sufficient numbers of different opportunity costs in the world for exchange to take place constantly.

As individual entities, nations have different collective tastes and different collective resource endowments. We would expect, therefore, that there will always be potential gains to be made from trading among nations. Furthermore, the more trade there is, the more specialization there can be. In most instances, specialization leads to increased output and—if we measure well-being by output levels—to increased happiness. (Indeed, we are using the term *well-being* very loosely here.) Self-sufficiency on the part of individuals undeniably means that they forgo opportunities to consume more than they could by not being self-sufficient. Likewise, self-sufficiency on the part of a nation will lower its consumption possibilities and, therefore, will lower the real-income level of its inhabitants. Imagine life in Delaware, if that state were forced to become self-sufficient!

Costs of Trade

Trade does not come without cost. If one state has a comparative advantage in producing agricultural crops, other states may not be able to survive as centers of agricultural production. Farm workers in states that are losing out will suffer decreases in their incomes until they find another occupation.

As tastes, supplies of natural resources, prices, and so on change throughout the world, different countries may find their area of comparative advantage changing. One example of this is the United States' production of steel. Japan has become increasingly competitive in steel products, and United States steelmakers are being hurt. The stockholders and employees in United States steel companies are feeling the pinch from Japan's ability to produce steel products at low prices.

Japanese Miracle

Japan is a good example of how a nation can benefit from exploiting its comparative advantage and engaging in a large volume of world trade. Japan's recovery from World War II has been called miraculous. Real income in that country has been growing at an average rate of about 10 percent a year. Foreign trade has grown at an even faster rate. While real incomes doubled between 1952 and 1960, exports from Japan more than tripled. During the early 1960s, Japan's exports were doubling almost every 5 years. Japan has used its comparative advantage in manufacturing to expand its export markets in cameras, automobiles, and steel products. One wonders how Japan can become a net exporter of steel products without already hav-

ing the raw materials needed to make them, but Japan's comparative advantage is in the machining of the steel and not in the exploitation of raw resources to make it. Japan, therefore, imports iron ore and exports cold rolled steel.

Obviously, you can see that many American steel producers would want to fight to *restrict* Japanese imports into the United States. Some industrialists claim that Japan has an absolute advantage (in the sense of person-hours consumed to produce a good) in the production of electronic equipment and steel products. Even in those areas where Japan must consume more person-hours than the United States to produce goods, the lower wage rates paid in Japan may still permit Japanese producers to undercut the prices of American producers. In any event, complaints about increased Japanese competition with American industries have produced pressures for hindering free trade among nations. We will discuss a few of the arguments against free trade here.

Arguments against Free Trade

The numerous arguments against free trade all have merit. However, most of the time, these arguments are incomplete. They mainly point out the costs of trade, but they do not consider the benefits or the possible alternatives for mitigating costs while still reaping benefits.

Infant Industry Argument

A nation may feel that, if a particular industry were allowed to develop domestically, it could eventually become efficient enough to be competitive in the world. Therefore, if some restrictions were placed on imports, native producers would be given the time needed to develop their efficiency to the point where they would be able to compete in the world market without any restrictions on imports. This **infant industry argument** has some merit and has been used to protect a number of American industries in their infancy. Such policy can be abused, however. Often the protective import-restricting arrangements remain even after the infant has matured. The people who benefit from this type of situation are obviously the stockholders in the industry that is still being protected from world competition. The people who lose out are the consumers, who must pay a price higher than the world price for the product in question.

National Security

It is often argued that we should not rely on foreign sources for many of our products because in time of war these sources may well be cut off and we would have developed few if any substitute sources. A classic example of this involves oil exploration. For national defense reasons (supposedly), President Eisenhower instituted at first a voluntary, and then a mandatory, oil-import **quota** system, thereby restricting the amount of foreign oil that could be imported into the United States. The idea was to create an incentive for more exploration of American oil; thus, in time of war we would have a ready and available supply of oil for our tanks and ships and bombers.

However, restricting the amount of foreign oil imported merely served to raise the price of oil in the United States. The people who benefited were, obviously, the stockholders in oil corporations; the people who lost out were the consumers of oil products. It has been estimated by various government officials that the oil-import quota program cost the consumer a staggering $7 billion a year in the form of higher oil product prices. Also, it was the poor who paid more, relatively, than the rich since the poor spend a larger proportion of their income on petroleum products than do the rich. And finally, it was absurd to think that restricting the amount of foreign oil imported would allow us to have more oil for a national emergency. Obviously, using more of our own would lead only to less for a national emergency.

Stability

Many people argue that foreign trade should be restricted because it introduces an element of instability into our economic system. They point out that the vagaries of foreign trade add to the ups and downs in our own employment level. However, if we follow this argument to its logical conclusion, we would restrict trade among our various states as well. After all, the vagaries of trade among particular states sometimes cause unemployment in other states. Things are sorted out over time, but workers suffer during the adjustment period. Nonetheless, we don't restrict trade among the states. In fact, there is a Constitutional stricture against taxing exports among the states.

As regards the international sphere, though, people somehow change their position. They feel that adjusting to the vagaries of *international* trade costs more than adjusting to the vagaries of domestic *interstate* trade. Perhaps people believe foreign trade really doesn't benefit us that much, and thus they argue against it, claiming that the stability of aggregate economic activity is at stake.

We should note one difference between the domestic and international situations, however, that lends some truth to this argument. Labor is mobile among our states, but it is not mobile among nations. Immigration laws prevent workers from moving to countries where they can make the most money. Therefore, the adjustment costs to a changing international situation may, in fact, be higher than the adjustment costs to a changing domestic situation.

"As Adam Smith so aptly put it . . ."

Protecting American Jobs

Perhaps the most often heard argument against free trade is that unrestrained competition from other countries will eliminate American jobs because other countries have lower-cost laborers than we do. This is indeed a compelling argument, particularly for Congresspersons from an area that might be threatened by foreign competition. For example, a Congressperson from an area with shoe factories would certainly be upset about the possibility of constituents losing their jobs because of competition from lower-priced shoe manufacturers in Spain and Italy. This argument against free trade is equally applicable, however, to trade among the several states. After all, if labor in the south is less expensive than labor in the north, southern industry may put northern workers out of jobs; but, again, we do not, and constitutionally cannot, restrict trade (at least not overtly) among states.

This is a sufficiently important topic for us to spend the next issue on it. There are numerous ways to hinder free trade, and there are even more arguments in favor of restrictions on trade. Which of the arguments is most meaningful from your particular point of view?

Definitions of New Terms

Excess Demand Schedule: A demand schedule for imports derived from the difference between the quantity of a product supplied domestically and the quantity demanded at prices *below* the domestic no-trade equilibrium price.

Excess Supply Schedule: A supply schedule of exports derived from the difference between the quantity of a product supplied domestically and the quantity demanded at prices *above* domestic no-trade equilibrium prices.

Zero Trade Point: The point on an excess demand and supply diagram at which there is no foreign trade. At this price the domestic demand and supply schedules intersect.

Comparative Advantage: An advantage arising out of relative efficiency, which follows from scarcity of resources. As long as the opportunity costs of doing the same job differ for different people or different countries, each will have a comparative advantage in something.

Absolute Advantage: The advantage that a person or nation has over other people or nations in the production of a good or service. If you have an absolute advantage in doing something, you can do it better than anybody else—absolutely.

Infant Industry Argument: An argument in support of tariffs: Tariffs should be imposed to protect from import competition an industry that is trying to get started. Presumably, after the industry becomes technologically efficient, the tariff can be lifted.

Quota: A specified number of or value of imports allowed into a country per year.

Chapter Summary

1. In terms of current purchasing power, trade has expanded from a mere $1.3 billion in the year 1800 to over $300 billion in 1975. Trade rates differ among nations. The United States has one of the smallest amounts of world trade (which is expressed as a percentage of GNP). Trade represents only 9 percent of our GNP, whereas it represents 44 percent of the GNP of the Netherlands.

2. Although it only represents 9 percent of GNP, we would, nevertheless, notice a substantial change in our life-style if we were to cease trading with other countries.

3. Trade is always voluntary among nations and among people. Therefore, it must benefit everyone concerned.

4. We can draw an excess demand schedule for foreign goods by looking at the difference between the quantity demanded and the quantity supplied domestically at prices below our domestic equilibrium price.

5. The excess supply schedule of domestic goods is found by looking at the difference between quantities supplied and quantities demanded at prices above our domestic equilibrium price. The excess supply schedule is our supply schedule of exports.

6. The equilibrium price and quantity traded are established at the point where one country's excess demand schedule intersects another country's

excess supply schedule. As long as the zero trade points of two countries are at different prices, there will be trade (in the absence of restrictions).

7. It is important to distinguish between absolute and comparative advantage. A person or country that can do everything better than every other person or country has an absolute advantage. Nevertheless, trade will still be advantageous because people will specialize in the things that they do relatively best. They will take advantage of their comparative advantage.

8. An individual's comparative advantage lies in that activity for which she or he is best paid. Comparative advantage follows from different relative efficiencies and from the fixed nature of our resources at a point in time.

9. Along with the gains, there are costs from trade. Certain industries may be hurt if trade is opened up. There are numerous arguments, therefore, against free trade.

10. There is also a national security argument for tariffs and import quotas. For example, the oil-import quota was imposed in the name of national security; presumably by keeping out cheap foreign oil, we increase the incentive for domestic exploration of oil resources. Therefore, in time of war we would have a sufficient amount of gas to put in our bombers and ships.

Questions for Thought and Discussion

1. Do you ever make trades in which you don't benefit? Why do you make them?

2. "Cheap foreign labor is ruining jobs for Americans. Therefore, we should stop all trade with other countries." Evaluate this statement.

3. If you believe in free trade among nations in reference to goods and services, do you also believe in the free movement of human resources? That is, do you think all immigration laws should be repealed?

4. If every state in the union had exactly the same productivity and efficiency, would there be any trade? Why?

5. Is it possible for a country to lose its comparative advantage in the production of a specific good or service? What happens then?

6. Why would you expect a newly discovered continent to have a comparative advantage in the production of food?

Selected References

Kenen, Peter B. and Raymond Lubitz, *International Economics,* 3d ed., Englewood Cliffs, N.J.: Prentice-Hall, 1971.

Pen, Jan, *A Primer on International Trade,* New York: Random House, 1967.

Snider, Delbert A., *Introduction to International Economics,* 5th ed., Homewood, Ill.: Richard D. Irwin, 1971.

Does International Competition Pose a Threat?

THE QUESTION OF JOB PROTECTION

The Tenets of Protectionism

. . . This bill would discourage American business investment abroad and limit the flow of imports into this country. We can no longer afford to export American jobs and technology at the expense of our own industry all in the name of "free trade". . . .

Such were the words contained in the preamble to one of the most talked about bills introduced into Congress in this decade: the Burke-Hartke Foreign Trade and Investment Proposal. The preamble went on to state that the statute under consideration was to be interpreted as attempting to "ensure that the production of goods which have historically been produced in the United States is continued and maintained." Moreover, "to the extent that production of such goods has been transferred abroad, it is the intent of Congress that this production be encouraged to return to the United States."

Such words seem to be at odds with the underlying principles of economics. We talked, in Chapters 1 and 14, about the virtues of trade. Specialization by people and countries in their area of comparative advantage, coupled with trade, presumably allows for increased standards of material well-being. Why, then, would Senators Burke and Hartke want to stifle free trade? How could other senators introduce numerous other bills along the same lines, that is, putting restrictions on the flow of goods and services between our nation and other countries? We already briefly touched on this phenomenon. It concerns protection—mainly what is called "job protection"—for those in industries hurt by foreign competition.

Getting Hurt from Free Trade

We have never said that free trade benefits everyone. What we did say on several occasions was that free trade allows for a higher *overall* material standard of living. This says nothing about how individuals may fare. Let's take a specific example.

Suppose you are a worker in a shoe factory in Massachusetts. Suppose, also, that the industrialization of Spain allows them to produce shoes at a lower cost per pair than is possible in Massachusetts. In other words, given the relatively lower wage rate in Spain, shoes can be produced there at a lower per-unit cost. The importation of these low-cost Spanish shoes into the United States might seriously threaten the profitability of the shoe manufacturing company for which you work. Suppose, in fact, there is no way for your Massachusetts company to effectively compete with the Spanish shoe imports. In this case, your company will go out of business. You, as a worker in that company, will suffer a loss of job. You will be upset and annoyed that "unfair" competition from "cheap" labor in Spain has taken away what was "rightfully yours."

This is the crux of the argument against free trade, and it is the backbone of such bills as the Burke-Hartke one mentioned. Free trade does put some Americans out of work. In a dynamic world where tastes change, resource bases change, technologies change, and everything else changes, the comparative advantages of individuals as well as states and nations will change.

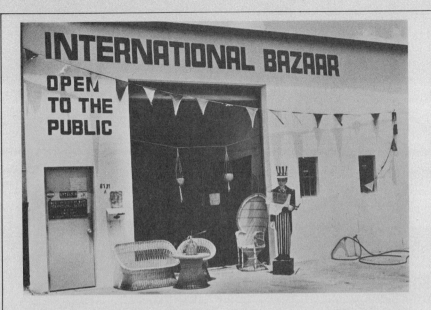

The fact, for example, that the United States has historically been a provider of high technology goods for the rest of the world does not mean that the United States' comparative advantage hasn't and won't change in the future toward some other good or service. This is essentially what has happened with the United States, Japan, and Germany. Historically, the United States has had a comparative advantage in high technology goods, but in recent years that comparative advantage has been eroded by the increasing sophistication of such countries as Japan and Germany. Naturally, jobs have suffered in the United States. But, this is what we call a *sectoral effect*. It affects a specific sector and not the entire American economy.

How We Pay for Imports

Strange as it may seem, if we reduce imports into the United States, we will also reduce exports out of the United States for we must ultimately pay for imports with exports. After all, the rest of the world is not interested in providing us with charity in the form of their exports (our imports). They want something in return. What they want in return ultimately is American goods and services. During certain periods of time, the rest of the world may be content to take, in exchange for the goods and services they provide the United States, such things as dollar bills, United States treasury bonds, and other financial assets. But ultimately, the rest of the world will want to exchange whatever liquid or illiquid United States assets they hold for United States goods and services. Thus, we know that the balance of payments must balance, and also that, in the very long run, the balance of trade must balance. Hence, if we stifle imports, we will, in effect, stifle exports. We will treat these topics in detail in the next chapter.

How Trade Can Be Hindered

There are many ways that international trade can be stopped, or at least partially stifled. These include, among other things, quotas and taxes—the latter are usually called tariffs when applied to internationally traded items. Let's talk first about quotas.

Quotas

In the quota system, countries are restricted to a certain amount of trade. Until 1973, we set a quota on the importation of oil into the United States. Let's look at Figure I-15.1. Here, we present the standard supply and demand graph for the product in question. The horizontal line, P_w, represents the world price line; this line also represents the world's supply of oil to the United States. We draw this line horizontally because we assume (somewhat unrealistically) that the United States buys only an extremely small fraction of the total world supply; therefore, the United States can buy literally all the oil it wants at the world price. In the absence of world trade, the price will be at the intersection of the domestic supply and demand schedules. The quantity demanded will be determined at that intersection also. With world trade opened up, Americans will buy 4 billion barrels of oil in total; domestic oil producers will provide 3.5 billion barrels of this total. The difference between 4 billion and 3.5 billion represents the imports. This is an equilibrium situation. The supply curve is the domestic one below the price P_w but becomes the horizontal P_w line at the price of P_w.

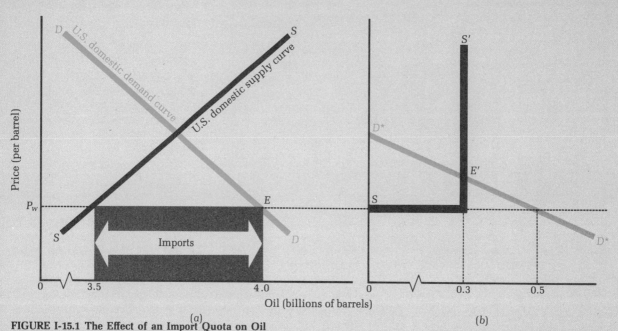

FIGURE I-15.1 The Effect of an Import Quota on Oil

The world price of oil is established at P_w. We assume that the United States buys a very small part of the total world supply of oil. The United States can buy all the oil it wants at the world price. The supply curve faced by the United States, in effect, is P_w. Our domestic supply curve is SS in the left-hand portion of the graph, and our domestic demand curve is DD. At the world price of P_w, we will reach equilibrium at E. This means we will consume 4 billion barrels of oil, of which 3.5 billion will be produced domestically. The difference is represented by imports. In the right-hand portion of the figure, we show the excess demand for oil as D^*D^*. That is, D^*D^* represents the demand curve for oil imports. At the world price of P_w, the quantity demanded will be 0.5 billion barrels of oil. The government, however, steps in and imposes an import quota of only 0.3 billion barrels. The supply curve remains P_w until it hits the quota line of 0.3 billion barrels. Then it becomes vertical. The new supply curve is then SS'. The new supply curve, SS', intersects the demand curve for imports, D^*D^*, at a new equilibrium of E'. The consumers of oil will end up paying the higher price represented by the vertical distance to E'. The stockholders in domestic oil-producing companies will benefit, however.

The intersection of the combined supply curve and the domestic demand curve is at E, where it will stay if there are no restrictions.

Let's now look at the right-hand portion of the graph. We draw the excess demand for imports. We put in the world price line, P_w, and we come up with the 0.5 billion barrels of oil imported at the world price.

Now we want to see what happens when a quota is instituted. Instead of allowing 0.5 billion barrels of oil to be imported, the government says that only 0.3 billion barrels may be brought into the United States. We draw a vertical line at 0.3 billion barrels per year. The supply curve effectively becomes the world demand price line until it hits the import

quota restriction at the vertical line. The supply curve then follows the vertical line up; it is now SS'. The new equilibrium point is at E', the intersection of the new supply schedule with the excess demand for imports. We see that at point E', however, there is a higher price for all oil consumed in the United States. This indicates that something in the situation has to change. Indeed—the price Americans must pay has to change. You, the consumer, lose. The importers (who get the quotas) and the import-substituting industries gain.

Tariffs

We can use our graphic technique to analyze the effect of a tariff. A tariff raises the price of a product—in this case oil—both foreign and domestic to United States residents.

Let's assume that the tariff is 10 percent of the price of the oil entering this country. In Figure I-15.2, we show the domestic supply and demand schedules for oil, with the world price at P_w. Now we add a

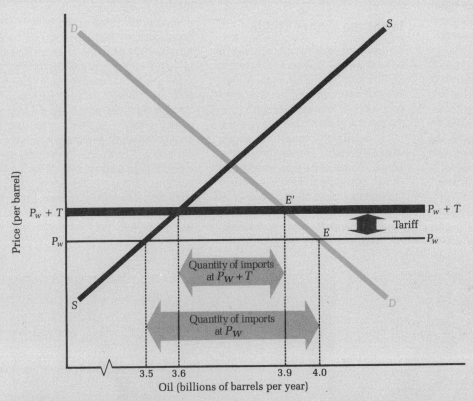

FIGURE I-15.2 An Import Tariff

The domestic supply curve for oil is SS. The domestic demand curve is DD. At a world price of P_w the United States can buy all the oil it wants. Equilibrium is established at E where the quantity demanded is 4 billion barrels. The quantity supplied domestically is 3.5 billion. The difference is imports, or 0.5 billion barrels. Now the government puts on a tariff, T dollars per barrel. The price at which Americans can buy oil now is equal to P_w plus the tariff. This shifts the effective horizontal supply curve up to the heavy solid line, $P_w + T$. Now, at this higher price the quantity demanded is at E', or 3.9 billion barrels. The quantity supplied domestically increases to 3.6 billion barrels. Imports, therefore, fall from 0.5 billion barrels to 0.3 billion barrels, as in the arbitrary example used for the import quota set at 0.3 billion barrels. However, in this particular case, it is the U.S. Treasury that reaps the benefits of restricting the supply of imports. In the case of import quotas, it was the stockholders in oil companies who benefited.

tariff. The tariff, T, is equal to the difference between the world price, P_w, and the heavy horizontal line above it $(P_w + T)$. Domestic demanders of oil must now pay the world price plus the tariff. They cannot get oil any cheaper because producers know that everyone must pay the tariff; no one can escape it. The quantity of oil demanded falls from 4 billion barrels to 3.9 billion barrels because of the higher price. The quantity supplied domestically rises from 3.5 billion barrels to 3.6 billion barrels. The level of imports decreases from 0.5 billion barrels to 0.3 billion barrels, as it did in the quota system we discussed. However, there are differences. Although in both cases the price is higher, the quantity demanded is smaller, and the domestic quantity supplied is greater. In this case, *the government is now in possession of tariff revenues.* These revenues can be used to reduce taxes or to increase government expenditures on public goods and services. These revenues did not result from the oil-import quota program. There, the beneficiaries of the higher oil price were the stockholders in oil corporations, not the United States Treasury. The United States has had a history of widely varying tariff rates as we can see in Figure I-15.3.

What the Future Holds

To be sure, the future will see a continuation of special interest groups lobbying for protection from international competition. It is difficult, though, for these groups to use the same arguments they have in the past—economic reality changes much too fast. For many years the cry of "cheap Japanese labor" was heard, particularly from the United States labor movement. Lower-paid Japanese workers were undercutting American workers, and, in essence, we were exporting jobs to Japan.

Japanese wages today, however, are far from being "slave" wages.

What we must realize is that every economic action has a cost. It is indeed rare when everybody can be made better off by some policy. But any time trade is stifled, there are gainers and losers. Economic analysis tells us that general material well-being will be reduced any time there are restrictions on trade. However, by the same token, specific groups will benefit by restrictions on foreign competition. It is impossible to argue, from a purely economic point of view, whether certain types of foreign trade should be restrained because to do so would require ultimately a value judgment as to who should benefit or gain from a particular policy. One thing is fairly certain, though: Free traders win all the arguments, but protectionists win all the votes. Do not be surprised, then, if some form of a highly restrictive Burke-Hartke bill is eventually passed in Congress.

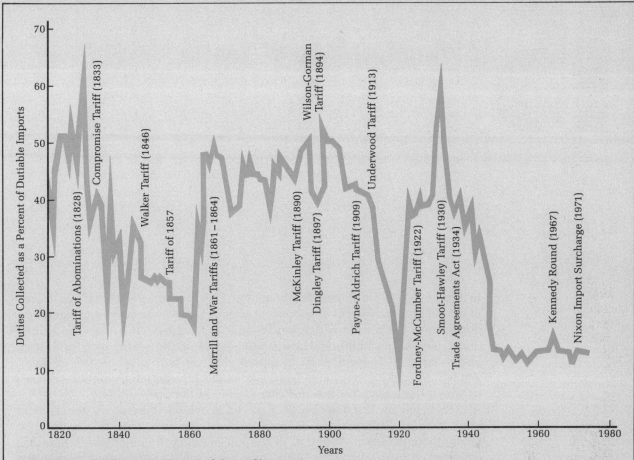

FIGURE I-15.3 Tariff Rates in the United States Since 1820

Tariff rates in the United States have bounced about like a football, and, indeed, in Congress, tariffs do represent a political football. Import-competing industries prefer high tariffs. In the twentieth century, the highest tariff we have had was the Smoot-Hawley Tariff of 1930, which was almost as high as the Tariff of Abominations in 1828. (*Source:* U.S. Department of Commerce.)

Questions for Thought and Discussion

1. What do we mean when we say that foreign trade is eliminating American jobs?
2. Is it possible for international trade not to create benefits for some and costs for others?
3. What is the argument in favor of a quota as opposed to a tariff?

Selected References

Adams, Walter, "The New Protectionism," *Challenge*, May–June, 1973.

Meier, Gerald M. *Problems of Trade Policy*, New York: Oxford University Press, 1973.

Financing World Trade

In Chapter 14 we outlined the benefits of trade among nations. We talked in terms of the movement of goods and services. We made very little reference, however, to the way in which world trade is financed. How does the United States pay for its imports? How does the rest of the world pay for United States exports? These are the questions that we will cover in this chapter. We will be looking at an area generally called *international finance*—an area in which there have been major disruptions in the last decade.

Let's begin by first looking at a world in which there is no government intervention in international monetary affairs. To an extent, this is the case today; there is less intervention in the international finance system than has occurred in many years. The 1970s have seen a more or less unrestricted international monetary market.

Flexible Exchange Rates

When you decide to buy foreign products—French wine, for example—you have only dollars with which to pay the French winemaker. However, that individual would be hard pressed to pay his workers in dollars. They're French; they live in France, and they need francs to buy goods and services. Obviously, then, there has to be some way of exchanging dollars for the francs the winemaker will accept. Normally, a **foreign exchange market** specializing in exchanging francs and dollars—that is, establishing a **foreign exchange rate**—would develop. In fact, these kinds of markets did develop very early in the game of international trade.

To get the Bordeaux wine you want, you go to the foreign exchange market.

Your desire to buy the wine therefore provides a supply of dollars to the foreign exchange market, and, at the same time, you demand francs. Every transaction concerning the importation of foreign goods constitutes a supply of dollars and a demand for some foreign currency and vice versa.

To simplify, we shall again consider only two countries: the United States and France. We will not worry about other currencies. We shall also assume only two goods are being traded: French wine and American bluejeans. The American demand for French wine creates a supply of dollars and a demand for francs. In France, the demand for American bluejeans creates a supply of francs and a demand for dollars. In the absence of restrictions—that is, in a freely floating exchange rate situation—these supplies and demands are going to reach an equilibrium level. The equilibrium level will be the equilibrium *exchange rate,* which tells us how many francs a dollar can be exchanged for (that is, the dollar price of francs).

Equilibrium Foreign Exchange Rate

We can easily demonstrate what the equilibrium exchange rate will be. The idea of an exchange rate is not different from the idea of paying a certain price for something you want to buy. If you like to buy cigarettes, you know you have to pay something like 70¢ a pack. At one time, cigarettes cost around 25¢. Usually, at such lower prices, you would demand more cigarettes. Therefore, the demand schedule of cigarettes expressed in terms of dollars slopes downward.

Demand Schedule of Francs

Now think about the demand schedule for francs. Let's say that today it will cost you 20¢

to purchase 1 franc. This is the exchange rate between dollars and francs. If you have to pay 25¢ tomorrow to buy that same franc, then the exchange rate has changed. When the dollar price of francs is higher, you will probably demand fewer of them. The demand schedule in terms of dollars for francs also slopes downward.

The easiest way to understand the derived demand (derived from the demand for final product) for francs is to take a simple numerical example. Below is the quantity of French wine demanded per week by, say, a representative wine drinker.

DEMAND FOR FRENCH WINE IN THE
UNITED STATES PER WEEK

Price Per Liter	Quantity Demanded
$10	1 liter
8	2 liters
6	3 liters
4	4 liters

If the price per liter of wine in France is 20 francs, we can now find the quantity of francs needed to pay for the various quantities demanded above.

Quantity Demanded	Francs Required to Purchase Quantity Demanded
1 liter	20
2 liters	40
3 liters	60
4 liters	80

If the exchange rate is 1 franc = 50¢, then a bottle of French wine costing 20 francs in France would cost $10 in the United States. The quantity imported would be 1 liter. If the exchange rate is 1 franc = 40¢, then a 20-franc bottle of wine would cost $8 and the quantity imported would rise to 2 liters per week. At an exchange rate of 1 franc = 30¢, the United States price would be $6 and 3 liters would be imported. And finally, at an exchange rate of 1 franc = 20¢, a bottle would cost $4 and 4 liters would be imported.

Now we can obtain the derived demand for francs in the United States with which to pay for imports of wine.

DERIVED DEMAND FOR FRANCS IN THE UNITED STATES WITH WHICH TO PAY FOR IMPORTS OF WINE

Price of 1 Franc	Quantity Demanded
50¢	20 francs
40¢	40 francs
30¢	60 francs
20¢	80 francs

As can be expected, as the price of francs falls, the quantity demanded will rise. The only difference here from standard demand analysis is that the demand for francs is derived from the demand for a final product called French wine.

We show an aggregate version of the demand for French francs in Figure 15-1. It represents the demand for francs or, in our hypothetical situation, the demand for all foreign currency. The horizontal axis represents the quantity of foreign exchange—the number of francs. The vertical axis represents the exchange rate—the price of foreign currency (francs) expressed in dollars (cents per franc). At the foreign currency price of 25¢, you know it costs 25¢ to buy 1 franc. At the foreign currency price of 20¢, you know that it costs 20¢ to buy 1 franc.

FIGURE 15-1 The Demand and Supply of French Francs

Here we have drawn the demand curve for French francs. It is a derived demand schedule—that is, a schedule derived from the demand by Americans for French wine. We have drawn the supply curve of French francs, which results from the French demand for American bluejeans. The demand curve, DD, slopes downward like all demand curves, and the supply curve, SS, slopes upward. The foreign exchange price, or the U.S. dollar price of francs, is given on the vertical axis. The number of francs, in millions, is represented on the horizontal axis. If the foreign exchange rate is 25¢—that is, if it takes 25¢ to buy 1 franc—then Americans will demand 80 million francs. The equilibrium exchange rate is at the intersection of DD and SS. The equilibrium exchange rate is 20¢. At this point 100 million French francs are both demanded and supplied.

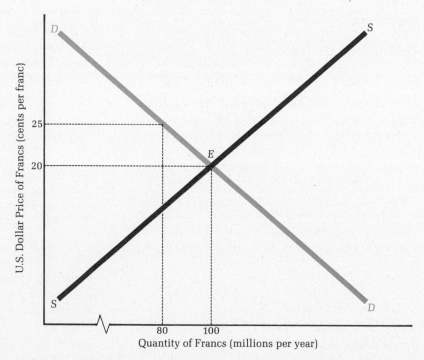

Supply Schedule of Francs

We now need to draw the supply relationship between French francs and their price in dollars. Obviously, the French want dollars in order to purchase American goods. When the dollar price offered for francs goes up, the French should be willing to supply more because they can then buy more American goods with the same quantity of francs. Let's take an example. A pair of bluejeans in the United States costs $10. If the exchange rate is 25¢ for 1 franc, the French have to come up with 40 francs to buy a pair of bluejeans. However, if the rate of exchange goes to 50¢ for 1 franc, they must come up with only 20 francs, thus inducing more purchases of bluejeans than before. Therefore, the supply schedule of foreign currency (francs) will be upward sloping.[1]

Equilibrium

As in all supply and demand diagrams, an equilibrium price will be established for the good in question—an exchange rate at which the French are happy to supply just the number of francs the Americans want to buy. The good in question here is foreign currency (French francs). The equilibrium price is established at 20¢ for 1 franc. This equilibrium is not established because Americans like to buy francs or the French like to buy dollars. Rather, the equilibrium exchange rate depends upon how many bluejeans the French want and how much wine Americans want (given their respective incomes, tastes, and the relative prices of wine and bluejeans).

[1]Actually, the supply schedule of foreign currency will be upward sloping if we assume that the demand for American imported bluejeans on the part of the French is price elastic. If the demand schedule for bluejeans is, however, price inelastic, the supply schedule will be negatively sloped. In the case of unitary elasticity of demand, the supply schedule for francs will be a vertical line. Throughout the rest of this chapter, we will assume that the demand schedule is elastic.

A Shift in Demand

Assume that a successful advertising campaign by American wine importers has caused the American demand (schedule) for wine to double. Americans demand twice as much wine at all prices. Their demand schedule for wine has shifted out and to the right. (Can you draw this?)

The increased demand for French wine can be translated into an increased demand for francs. All Americans clamoring for bottles of Bordeaux wine will supply more dollars to the foreign exchange market while demanding more French francs to pay for the wine. Figure 15-2 presents a new demand schedule, $D'D'$, for French francs; this demand schedule is to the right and outward from the original demand schedule. If the French do not change their desire for bluejeans, the supply schedule of French francs will remain stable. A new equilibrium will be established at a higher exchange rate. In our particular example the equilibrium is established at an exchange rate of 30¢. It now takes 30¢ to buy 1 French franc whereas it took 20¢ before. This is translated as an increase in the price of French wine to Americans and a decrease in the price of American bluejeans to the French.

Constant and Floating Exchange Rate

With *flexible* or *floating exchange rates*—that is, no regulations on the exchange rates—the number of francs demanded is always equal to the number supplied. Otherwise, the price will change until the quantities demanded and supplied are equal. With a floating exchange rate, there will always be equilibrium in the foreign exchange market. Actually, however, the foreign exchange market is merely a reflection of American desires for French wine and French desires for American bluejeans.

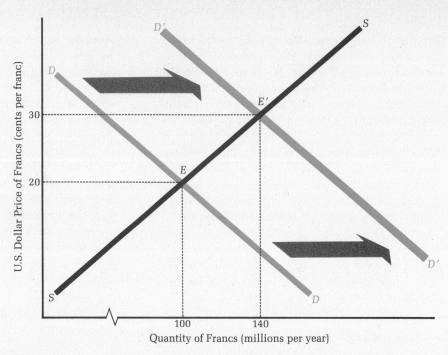

FIGURE 15-2 A Shift in the Demand Schedule

Americans experience a shift in their taste for French wine. The demand schedule for French wine shifts to the right, causing the derived demand schedule for francs to shift to the right also. We have shown that shift is a movement from *DD* to *D'D'*. We have assumed that the French supply schedule of francs has remained stable—that is, their taste for bluejeans has remained constant. The old equilibrium foreign exchange rate was 20¢. (It cost 20¢ to buy 1 franc.) The new equilibrium exchange rate will be at the intersection of *D'D'* and *SS*—or, *E'*. The new exchange rate will be higher than the old one. It will now cost 30¢ to buy 1 franc. The quantity of francs demanded is greater even at this higher price because the demand schedule has shifted out. The higher price of francs will be translated into a higher price for French wine.

In the above example, we assumed that Americans' taste for wine had shifted. Now let's assume that an inflation in France has caused the prices of everything there to double. The French now have to pay more for their wine. To Americans, prices in France have risen by 100 percent, while the price of bluejeans in the United States has remained constant. What would happen if exchange rates remained constant in such a situation? The price of French wine would rise relative to the price of American bluejeans in both countries. At the fixed exchange rate, the increase in French wine prices would reduce the supply of dollars in

the foreign exchange market because American citizens would buy less French wine at the new higher dollar price. The demand for dollars would increase because the French would want to buy more bluejeans that are now cheaper relative to French wine.

If we assume a *free* or floating foreign exchange market, this disequilibrium situation cannot last. What happens is that the exchange rate falls by 50 percent. We see in Figure 15-3 that the supply schedule for francs will shift to the right. (The demand schedule, for simplicity, is shown to be stable. However, this will occur only with a unitary demand schedule for

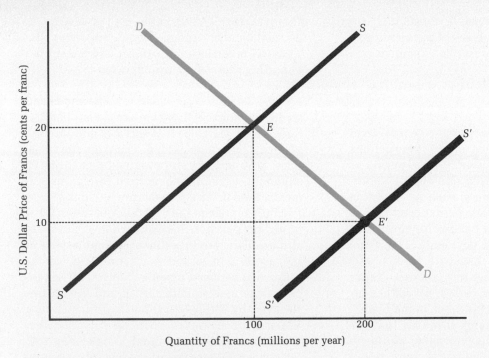

FIGURE 15-3 Free Foreign Exchange Market

An inflation in France causes prices there to double. As a result, Americans demand fewer francs than before and the French demand more dollars. (American prices are now cheaper relative to higher French prices.) A disequilibrium situation cannot last in a free or floating foreign exchange market, however, and the exchange rate falls. Now 10¢—rather than 20¢—will buy 1 franc. The supply schedule for francs will shift to the right. After the exchange rate adjustment, the amount of francs demanded will be 200 million. Thus, changes in prices due to inflation in one country bring about compensating changes in the foreign exchange rate so that the total amount of trade (measured in goods) remains the same.

exports.) The new equilibrium will be established at an exchange rate of 10¢. That is, 10¢ will now buy 1 franc, whereas before the rise in the price of wine, it took 20¢ to buy 1 franc. After the exchange-rate adjustment, twice as many francs will be demanded and sold as before. Notice the key point of this analysis: Changes in prices due to inflation in one country bring about *compensating* changes in the foreign exchange rate so that the total amount of trade remains the same.

This analysis did not hold in the first example because we assumed American tastes for wine had changed. Suddenly Americans were

willing to pay more for their wine than they had before. We ended up with a higher exchange rate and a larger quantity of francs being demanded and supplied. That is, the change in American tastes for foreign trade elicited an increase in foreign trade. In the present example, however, there is no change in tastes or in the underlying demand schedules for wine and bluejeans. Rather, there is an increase in the price of French wine relative to the price of American bluejeans at a fixed exchange rate. The final adjustment occurs in the foreign exchange market only. Our **balance of trade**—the value of goods bought and sold in the world market—remains constant. It remains in balance. The balance of payments also remains in balance because the exchange rate adjusts so that it will.

Balance of Payments

The **balance of payments** is a more general term used to reflect the value of *all* transactions made between nations, usually for a period of 1 year. Aside from buying and selling goods, we transact other business, such as investing and borrowing, with foreign nations. In our particular example, the balance of trade was equal to the balance of payments. The value of the transactions we had with France was equal to the value of the transactions France had with us. However, when a balance-of-payments deficit occurs (as it has in the United States for almost 20 years), it means that the value of our transactions with other countries is such that they are sending us more things than we are sending them. These "things" include all possible types of services, investments, and so on. Something very special is necessary for a balance-of-payments deficit to exist since with freely floating exchange rates, the balance of payments will, by definition, always be in balance. In fact, with a freely floating exchange rate it is meaningless to talk about a balance of payments since there can be no deficit or surplus.

How We Measure the Balance of Payments

Unfortunately for the beginning students, the balance of payments can be measured in a number of ways. In Table 15-1, we list six of the most common measures applied to the United States for various years over the last decade. These measures are described below.

Merchandise Trade Balance   This is merely the difference between our exports and imports of tangible items. For the better part of the last

30 years, the United States had a surplus in its merchandise trade account. However, the situation reversed in the 1970s, and we started importing more than we exported.

Goods and Services Account   The goods and services account is the same as the merchandise trade balance except that services and intangible items have been added. These are the invisibles; they include shipping insurance, tourist expenditures, and income from foreign investments. Note that these items are net in the sense that they represent the difference between what foreigners purchase here and what we purchase abroad. Thus the investment income aspect of the goods and services account tells us the difference between income received by Americans from investments abroad and the income received by foreigners from investments here. We see, for example, when we compare lines 1 and 2 in Table 15-1, that in the year 1961 the service balance in our balance-of-payments account was zero. Since then it has grown, primarily due to the growth in income from direct United States investment in other countries.

Table 15-1 **Our Foreign Accounts**

	1961	1966	1971	1975
Merchandise trade balance (goods)	5.6	3.8	−2.7	7.4
Goods and services	5.6	5.2	0.7	13.4
Current account	3.1	2.3	−2.8	8.6
Basic balance (current account and long-term capital)	0	−1.7	−9.4	−1.9
Net liquidity balance	−2.3	−2.2	−22.0	12.3
Official settlements balance	−1.3	0.2	−29.8	−12.9

Source: Federal Reserve Bank of St. Louis, *U.S. Balance of Payments Trends,* 1975 data are preliminary

Current Account This balance differs from the one in line 2 by the inclusion of net government and private transfers. In other words, it includes extension of foreign aid by the United States to other countries, charity to those living in other countries, and military expenditures.

Basic Balance (Current Account and Long-Term Capital Flows) The difference between the basic balance and the current account given in line 3 is the inclusion of long-term capital balances. Long-term capital flows relate to, for example, the purchase of foreign long-term bonds by Americans or the purchase of United States long-term bonds by foreigners.

Net Liquidity Balance Whenever there is a deficit or surplus in the basic balance, the difference must be made up by what are called short-term private capital flows and government actions. This is where we get the net liquidity balance. It tells us how much short-term debt (that is, debt investments having a maturity date of less than 1 year) we had to sell abroad to make up our basic balance (or vice versa).

Official Settlements Balance This balance differs from the net liquidity balance in that it includes private liquid-capital flows. In other words, it includes dollars that are accumulating in foreign banks (for example) instead of being spent in the United States because the United States has a balance-of-payments deficit.

The United States Deficit

However you look at it, the United States was running a balance-of-payments deficit at the beginning of this decade. Obviously, this is not possible in a freely floating exchange world, but at that time we weren't in a freely floating exchange world; rather, we were using **fixed exchange rates,** more or less, when transacting international business. To understand the adjustment mechanism for fixed exchange rates, we first have to consider a hypothetical world that is on a gold standard.

The Hypothetical Pure Gold Standard

Assume that many years ago, the world was on a pure **gold standard** and every nation's currency was tied directly to gold. Nations operating under this gold standard agreed to redeem their currency for a fixed amount of gold upon the request of any holder of that currency. Although gold was not necessarily the means of exchange for world trade, it was the unit to which all currencies under the gold standard were pegged. And since all currencies in the system were linked to gold, exchange rates between those currencies were fixed. Let's once again confine our discussion to two countries. Also, let's again assume that Americans buy French wine, and the French buy American bluejeans.

The value of a United States dollar is pegged to gold at a rate of $1 per 1/20th of an ounce of gold. The French have pegged their franc at a rate of 1 franc for 1/100th of an ounce of gold. Therefore, the exchange rate between francs and dollars is fixed at 1 franc for 20¢. Let's also assume that this is the equilibrium exchange rate at which the quantity of foreign exchange demanded is equal to the quantity supplied.

Inflation in France

Suppose an inflation raises French prices by 100 percent. At the fixed exchange rate, Americans will find wine is priced higher than before, and they will demand a smaller amount. Americans will supply fewer dollars to the foreign exchange market and demand fewer francs. On the other hand, the relative price of bluejeans will be lower for the French. (Everything they buy in France has gone up in price, but American bluejeans have not.) Wanting more bluejeans, the French will supply more francs to the foreign exchange market and demand more dollars.

Now, instead of an adjustment in the exchange rate, the exchange rates are fixed under the gold standard. There will be a balance-of-payments problem. France will run a deficit with respect to the United States, and the United States will run a surplus with respect to France. At the fixed exchange rate, the value of bluejeans sent to France is greater than the value of wines sent to America. This is a disequilibrium situation, and something has to give. Disequilibrium in the foreign exchange market (balance-of-payments imbalance) cannot last forever. Americans will find they have more and more francs, which, in themselves, are useless. Francs are only good if they can be exchanged for something. But French wine is too expensive, so Americans don't want to buy as much as before.

Rise in American Prices

Under the gold standard, the Americans can exchange their francs for French gold. Americans do this, and for every 1 franc they get 1/100th of an ounce of gold. The French are forced to ship the gold to America.

But what good is gold? Under our hypothetical gold standard, gold at that time was in circulation; it was used as money, as a medium of exchange. Thus, gold could be sent from France, and the Americans receiving it could spend it on goods and services. An increase in the supply of gold in the United States under the hypothetical gold standard, however, results in an increase in our money supply. In a full-employment situation, prices in the United States rise. As United States prices go up, French wine at the fixed exchange rate

becomes increasingly attractive. Even though the cost of French wine is higher than before, the price of French wine to a United States buyer remains the same (at least for a while) because of a fixed exchange rate. French wine therefore becomes less expensive *relative* to everything else in the United States, and Americans start to demand more.

Fall in French Prices

The French now see the price of bluejeans going up and up as United States prices rise. They start demanding fewer bluejeans. And since gold is leaving France, the money supply falls there and deflation ensues—falling prices. Eventually prices in the United States rise and prices in France fall to levels that induce French and American buyers alike to purchase the old quantities of bluejeans and wine. There would be equilibrium again in the foreign exchange market. The quantity of dollars supplied and francs demanded would just equal the quantity of dollars demanded and francs supplied.

With a fixed exchange rate under the gold standard in a full-employment situation, the adjustment mechanism is by way of changes in *internal prices*—not by changes in the exchange rate. How would the gold standard work in an under full employment situation? According to one analysis, it would work through adjustments in *real income*.

Real-Income Adjustment Mechanism

Let's assume the United States is experiencing unemployment. As gold flows in, people find they have excess supplies of cash balances. To rid themselves of these cash balances, they spend more than they receive. Desired expenditures rise. There is increased total aggregate demand, which results in an increase in output. Prices don't have to rise because unemployed people and resources are used to meet the increased demand. The increase in output can be translated to an increase in real income. Now, realizing that people's demand for goods and services is a positive function of their income, we know that, as incomes go up, more will be demanded even at the same price. The price of French wine in America would not fall. But the gold flow would result in increased real income, which would eventually cause Americans to demand more wine even at higher prices. As Americans demand more wine, they supply more dollars to the foreign exchange market and demand more francs. Eventually equilibrium is established when output rises high enough for Americans to want to buy the same quantity of wine they had purchased at a lower price. When equilibrium in the foreign exchange market is established, there ceases to be any more gold flows.

We have not considered the money supply, the price level, or the output in France. To test your understanding, analyze the situation at the same time in France as she loses gold. You will see that an offsetting situation establishes itself which also brings the foreign exchange market back to equilibrium.

Pure Gold Standard in Theory

Under the hypothetical pure gold standard outlined here, no country's money supply could be insulated from international balance-of-payments problems. Any difference between exports and imports alters a country's money supply. A country whose prices are relatively high in the world market at a fixed exchange rate will experience a decrease in her gold stock (money supply) and prices will fall. A country whose prices are relatively low in the world market will experience an increase in her gold stock (money supply) and prices will rise. Monetary control, as defined by alterations in the money supply, would not be under domestic control by domestic central banks. Such a situation would never be tolerated. Even a modified gold standard would fall apart sooner or later—as it did in the 1930s.

Monetary Policies Come into Play

During the 1930s, nations asserted their independence from the fixed-exchange-rate discipline. Nations refused to allow any excess demand or supply of their currencies in the foreign exchange markets to affect their own domestic money supplies. They would no longer give balance-of-payments problems the slightest priority over domestic economic considerations. What happens to a system of fixed exchange rates when there are not many shipments of gold? National governments, through their central banks, stabilize exchange rates by entering the foreign exchange markets themselves.

Let's take our two-country example again. Suppose the price of bluejeans has gone up. Suppose, in fact, there is a general rise in prices for everything in the United States. The French now will buy fewer bluejeans than before. They supply fewer francs to the foreign exchange market and demand fewer dollars at the fixed exchange rate. But Americans continue to demand French wines. In fact, they will demand more because, at the fixed exchange rate, the relative price of French wines has fallen. Americans will now supply more dollars in the foreign exchange market and demand more francs. As in Figure 15-4, the demand curve for francs will shift to $D'D'$. In the absence of any intervention by central banks, the exchange rate will change. The price of French francs in terms of dollars will go from 20¢ per franc to 25¢. That is, the value of a dollar in terms of francs will go down. The dollar will suffer a **depreciation** in its value relative to francs, and the franc will experience an **appreciation** in its value in terms of dollars. But the United

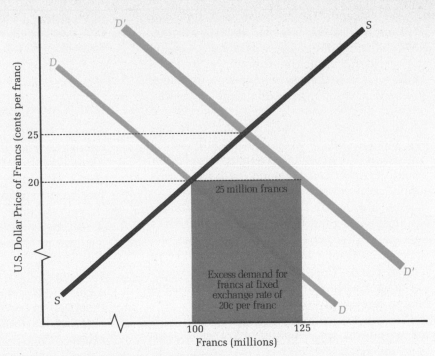

FIGURE 15-4 Supporting the Value of the Dollar in the Foreign Exchange Market

If there is inflation in the U.S., all prices go up. However, prices remain constant in France, so French goods become cheaper for Americans. The demand schedule for French goods shifts to the right as does the derived demand schedule for French francs, from *DD* to *D′D′*. Without exchange rate controls, the exchange rate would rise to 25¢—it would now cost 25¢ instead of 20¢ to buy a franc. The U.S. government, however, is committed to supporting the price of the dollar. Instead of allowing the dollar to equal 4 francs, the government maintains the price of a dollar at 5 francs—it keeps the price at 20¢ per franc. But at that exchange rate there is an excess demand for francs at the fixed exchange rate of 25 million. The U.S. government must step in and supply 25 million francs from its coffers in order to support the dollar in the foreign exchange market.

States government is committed to maintaining a fixed price of dollars in the foreign exchange market. When the French take their excess dollars and throw them onto the foreign exchange markets, the American central bank—the Federal Reserve—will be forced to go into the foreign exchange market and buy up those excess dollars. The Federal Reserve has to have foreign currency to buy up the excess dollars. That is, it has to have a reserve of francs in its coffers to get the dollars that the French want to sell. It must supply 25 million francs, as seen in Figure 15-4, to keep the exchange rate fixed. In the process, the money supply in the United States will fall because the dollars that left the country ended up with the Fed rather than in domestic circulation.

Just to make the process clearer, let's review it briefly.

A Recap

1. Prices in the United States have gone up.
2. French wine becomes a better deal for Americans at the fixed exchange rate;

American bluejeans become a worse deal for French buyers at the fixed exchange rate.

3. Americans buy more wine than before; the French buy fewer bluejeans than before.
4. At the fixed exchange rate, the value of American imports (French wine) exceeds the value of American exports (bluejeans). This is a trade deficit for the United States.
5. Americans send dollars abroad that are only partly returned as the French buy American bluejeans.
6. The French end up with excess dollars—those dollars are no longer in circulation in the United States.
7. The Federal Reserve buys up, with francs, those excess dollars in the foreign exchange market to support the price of the dollar; it now has dollars in its coffers.
8. The dollars in the coffers of the Federal Reserve do not constitute part of the money supply in the United States; therefore, the money supply falls.

Thus, we can see there are money supply alterations even without the gold standard if countries attempt to stabilize the price of their currency in the foreign exchange market.

Many countries finally tired of letting their money supplies be dictated by these balance-of-payments adjustments made in order to stabilize the fixed exchange rate. Instead of allowing the money supply to fluctuate, however, countries engaged in **sterilization policies.** A drop in the money supply due to a balance-of-payments deficit, for example, was made up by expansionary monetary policy.

In the last example, the money supply fell when there were more imports than exports because the Federal Reserve bought surplus dollars on the foreign exchange market in order to support their price. The Fed does not have to sit back and watch the money supply fall, however. It has the option of increasing the money supply by open-market operations. Therefore, every time the money supply falls because of a *deficit* in our balance of payments, the Fed can sterilize that fall by buying bonds from the commercial banks, thereby putting back in circulation all the dollars that flowed out of the country and into the coffers of the Federal Reserve as it stabilized the price of the dollar. This is essentially how each individual central bank can insulate its own money supply from the vagaries of world monetary events, when it does not opt for flexible exchange rates.

Currency Crisis

Notice that the only way for the United States to support the price of the dollar was to buy up excess dollars with foreign reserves—that is, with French francs (or with gold). But the United States might eventually run out of the francs (or gold). It would then no longer be able to stabilize the price of the dollar, and a **currency crisis** would ensue. A currency crisis occurs when a country can no longer support the price of its currency in foreign exchange markets. Many such crises have occurred in the past several decades. Deficit countries ran out of the wherewithal to stabilize foreign exchange rates.

Internal Policies

Deficit countries do have the option of following internal policies that will reduce the deficit in their balance of payments. This can be done by somehow lessening the demands for goods from other countries. Causing a deflation or reducing people's real incomes (belt tightening) are two possible actions. Surplus countries, on the other hand, can allow an inflation. Most countries, however, find this type of internal price and income adjustment to international payments problems too costly, although England has followed such policies on many occasions—much to the chagrin of most English citizens.

Devaluation

Another alternative is to unilaterally *devalue*. When this happens, a country states that it will now support the price of its currency at a lower value than before. Devaluation is exactly what would happen in a freely floating exchange-rate situation. With fixed exchange rates, though, it happens only after there has been a long period of balance-of-payments deficits—that is, only after the country has exhausted all the possible ways to support the price of its currency in the foreign exchange market.

There are several other possibilities that we have yet to discuss. One of these involves borrowing from abroad; others are using gold, "paper gold," or special reserves in the International Monetary Fund. We shall discuss these last three methods in the following issue. For now, we shall examine the alternative of borrowing abroad.

Financial Assets

In addition to buying and selling goods and services in the world market, it is also possible to buy and sell financial assets. There is really no difference in terms of the foreign exchange market. If, on the one hand, Americans decide to buy stocks in French companies, the demand for French financial assets will create a derived demand for francs and a supply of dollars. On the other hand, if the French decide they want to buy AT&T corporate bonds, that demand will result in a derived demand for American dollars and a supply of francs.

Suppose that, at the fixed exchange rate, there is a balance-of-payments deficit in the United States; the value of our imports exceeds the value of our exports to France. What happens if the American government gets the French government to purchase American financial assets? What if Americans somehow get the French to lend back some of those excess dollars? If we are successful, then the value of our imports at the fixed exchange rate can be made equal to the value of our exports including the export of debt—financial assets—to the French. This is one way of making up the difference between the value of imports and the value of exports.

If Americans have to cajole the French central bank into lending back dollars, then at present interest rates in the United States, *individual* French citizens will not find our financial assets attractive enough to purchase. If they did, it would alleviate the balance-of-payments problem. Their demand as *individuals* for our financial assets would provide a demand for United States dollars and a supply of francs so that equilibrium could be maintained in the foreign exchange market. The fact that it is not individuals but foreign central banks which lend us back our money by buying our financial assets indicates that these are *involuntary* loans. Germany and Japan have run a surplus with the United States for many years. Apparently, the Japanese and German citizenry has been "involuntarily" lending us back our dollars for a number of years. We can draw this conclusion because it is the central banks of those countries that have been buying our bonds to help our deficit with them.

There are ways, of course, to make our financial assets more attractive to foreigners. The easiest way is to increase the yield on those assets—that is, make the interest rate higher through monetary and fiscal policies. Thus, the government can temporarily get itself out of a balance-of-payments deficit by increasing its interest rates.

The Multiplier

Let's now try to analyze the output and employment effect of changes in exports or imports by using the multiplier analysis from past chapters. We now add to our $C + I + G$ schedule a **net export** factor. Let's call net exports X, so that

$$\text{Net } X = \text{exports} - \text{imports}$$

If X is negative, we are importing more than we are exporting; we're running a deficit in our balance of trade. If X is positive, we're exporting more than we're importing, which means we're running a surplus in our balance of trade. A change in our balance of trade will have a multiplier effect on output and employment.

Let's redraw our $C + I + G$ schedule to include net exports, X, which are considered to be autonomous, like G and I. There is also a **net export multiplier** of the same magnitude as the government multiplier and the investment multiplier. The reasoning behind this follows. With a positive X, foreigners demand more of our goods while we continue to demand the same quantity of their goods. There is an increase in net exports, and American exporters receive "fresh" income from the outside world. They pay this income to their workers (in part). Their workers save part of it and spend part of it. People who receive what these workers spend also save part and spend part, and so it goes. Thus, there is a multiple expansion in national income from any increase in exports without a concomitant increase in imports.

Look at our $C + I + G + X$ schedule in Figure 15-5. If X goes up, we have a new line, $C + I + G + X'$, which is higher by the amount of the increase in X, net exports. The increase in income, however, is a multiple of the increase in X. If our marginal propensity to consume is 0.8, the increase in NNP will be five times the increase in X.

Using this Keynesian analysis, we can see that the government would desire to increase exports relative to imports so as to have an increase in income. Also, the government would be concerned if there were an increase in imports over exports because it would fear a decrease in income and employment. In other words, using Keynesian analysis, one would predict that a rising balance-of-trade deficit (or a shrinking surplus) would lead to a reduction in output and employment. But corresponding changes in investment, government purchases, transfers, or taxes could compensate for any reduction in net exports, X.

Sectoral Effects

All economists readily agree that shifts in world trade will have effects on different sectors of the economy. For example, if Japan becomes more price competitive in the world market with her automobiles, Americans will demand more Japanese automobiles. The stockholders in General Motors and Chrysler will be hurt. Employment in the automobile industry in the United States will be lower than it would be otherwise. Workers who are laid off in that industry will experience the costs of unemployment even if it's temporary. If, however, IBM becomes more competitive in the world market, stockholders and workers in that company will be better off. Thus, whenever our balance-of-trade position worsens vis-à-vis the rest of the world, government officials become concerned because certain sectors of the economy suffer. Any time America's international competitive position weakens, the export sector as well as the import-competing sector will suffer. Any time America's world position in trade improves, the export- and the import-competing sectors will benefit (but there will still be offsetting changes in the nontraded goods sector).

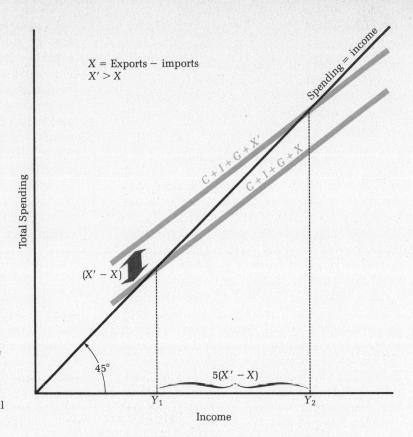

FIGURE 15-5 The Export Multiplier

Here is our usual multiplier graph. Income is measured on the horizontal axis; total aggregate spending, on the vertical axis. The 45 degree helper line is where total spending equals total income. We have added an X factor to our $C + I + G$ line. X equals exports minus imports, or net exports. We start out in equilibrium with the $C + I + G + X$ line intersecting the 45 degree spending-equals-income line at an income of Y_1. Now there is an increase in net exports. The schedule shifts up to $C + I + G + X'$, where X' is greater than X. The vertical shift in the schedule is the difference between X' and X. However, the new equilibrium income, if we assume a multiplier of 5, is going to be equal to the old equilibrium income of Y_1 plus five times the new increase in net exports, or $Y_1 + 5 (X' - X)$. The new equilibrium will be at Y_2.

Definitions of New Terms

Flexible Exchange Rates: Exchange rates that are allowed to fluctuate in the open market in response to changes in supply and demand. Sometimes called free exchange rates or floating exchange rates.

Foreign Exchange Market: The market for buying and selling foreign currencies.

Foreign Exchange Rate: The price of foreign currency in terms of domestic currency, or vice versa. For example, the foreign exchange rate for francs is 25¢. This means that it takes 25¢ to buy 1 franc. An alternative way of stating the exchange rate is that the value of the dollar is 4 francs. It takes 4 francs to buy $1.

Balance of Trade: The value of goods and services bought and sold in the world market.

Balance of Payments: The value of goods, services, financial assets, military transactions, and all other transactions in the world market.

Fixed Exchange Rate: A system of exchange rates that requires government intervention to fix the value of each nation's currency in terms of each other nation's currency.

Gold Standard: In its purest form (which is only hypothetical), an international monetary system in which gold plays a prominent part. Nations fix their exchange rates in terms of gold. Thus, all currencies are fixed in terms of each other. Any balance-of-payments problems could be made up by shipments of gold.

Depreciation: A lessening of the value of a domestic currency in terms of foreign currencies. Depreciation occurs in a freely floating foreign exchange market when there is an excess supply of the currency in question. In a fixed exchange market, depreciation can occur if the government allows it. Then it is called *devaluation*. Devaluation is an official lessening of the value of a domestic currency in terms of other currencies.

Appreciation: The increasing of the value of a domestic currency in terms of other currencies. This occurs in a freely floating exchange market when the demand for a currency exceeds the supply. In a fixed exchange-rate market, appreciation cannot occur naturally; it must be done officially. Then it is called *revaluation*.

Sterilization Policies: Central bank policies designed to mitigate or completely eliminate money supply changes due to the central bank's foreign exchange transactions. These transactions are necessary now and then to maintain a fixed exchange rate.

Currency Crisis: A situation in the international money market that occurs when a country no longer has the wherewithal (foreign exchange, gold, credit, and so on) to support the price of its currency. A currency crisis brings forced devaluation.

Net Exports: The difference between exports and imports.

Net Export Multiplier: The factor by which an increase in net exports will increase national income. Similar to the government and investment multipliers we discussed in previous chapters.

Chapter Summary

1. To transact business internationally, it is necessary to convert different domestic currencies into other currencies. This is done via a foreign exchange market, which specializes in exchanging different foreign currencies. If we were trading with France only, French producers would want to be paid in francs since they must pay their workers with francs. American producers would want to be paid in dollars since American workers are paid in dollars.

2. An American's desire for French wine is expressed in terms of a supply of dollars, which in turn is a demand for French francs in the foreign exchange market. The opposite situation arises when the French wish to buy American bluejeans. Their demand for bluejeans creates a demand for American dollars and a supply of French francs. We put the demand and supply schedules together to find the equilibrium foreign exchange

rate. The demand schedule for foreign exchange is a derived demand—derived, that is, from the demand for foreign products themselves.

3. With no government intervention, there will exist an equilibrium foreign exchange rate that clears the market. After a shift in demand or supply, the exchange rate will change so it will again clear the market.

4. Suppose Americans increase their demand for French wine. The demand schedule for French wine shifts outward to the right. The derived demand for francs also shifts outward to the right. The supply schedule of francs, however, remains stable because the French demand for American bluejeans has remained constant. The shifted demand schedule intersects the stable supply schedule at a higher price (the foreign exchange rate increases). This is an appreciation of the value of French francs (a depreciation of the value of the dollar against the franc). It now costs 25¢ instead of 20¢ to buy 1 franc. This causes the price of wine to Americans to rise and the price of bluejeans to the French to fall.

5. To take another example, assume there is an inflation in France. The price of all French goods goes up. The relative price of French goods increases, and American demand for French goods falls. French demands for American goods rise, however. In a freely floating exchange market, the supply curve will shift right so that a new equilibrium in the exchange market occurs. The new equilibrium will be at a lower price for French francs; the value of the French franc falls and the value of the American dollar in terms of francs rises. With freely floating exchange rates in this situation, the equilibrium quantity of trade remains the same while the exchange rate falls to take account of the inflation in France.

6. The balance of trade is defined as the value of goods bought and sold in the world market, usually during the period of 1 year. In the last example, it remained constant. The only thing that changed was the exchange rate. The balance of payments is a more inclusive concept since it includes the value of all transactions in the world market. In a world of freely floating exchange rates, it is impossible to have a balance-of-payments deficit or surplus. That is, the value of transactions in one country must equal the combined value of transactions in all the other countries it deals with. In essence, in a world of freely floating exchange rates, there is no such thing as a balance-of-payments imbalance.

7. With fixed exchange rates, however, there can be balance-of-payments deficits or surpluses. That is, the value of foreign transactions at the fixed exchange rate may be greater in one country than in another country. A deficit or surplus arises. One way to understand the fixed exchange rate is to go back to a hypothetical pure gold standard.

8. In a hypothetical pure gold standard situation, the American value of the dollar is pegged to gold at the rate of, say, $1 per 1/20th of an ounce. The French peg their franc to gold at the rate of 1 franc for 1/100th of an ounce. The fixed exchange rate, then, is 1 franc for 20¢. If there is inflation in France, a deficit in France's balance of payments results. American goods are more attractive at the fixed exchange rate. The French buy more American goods than Americans buy French goods. However, the French deficit means that Americans end up with surplus francs. Having no use for these francs, Americans ship them back to France and demand gold. Gold is shipped to America and is used as money, thereby increasing the money supply. In a full-employment situation, prices rise in America. In France the money supply falls and prices fall. Internal prices change so that equilibrium comes about again even at the fixed exchange rate.

9. It is also possible in a gold standard situation to have changes in real income. Such changes would lead to a contraction in the French demand for American products and an expansion in the American demand for French products. Equilibrium would be established again.

10. The pure gold standard has very high internal domestic adjustment costs and was, therefore, rejected long ago. Countries wanted to pursue their own independent monetary and fiscal policies. They sterilized money supply changes resulting from balance-of-payments problems and from their attempts to support a constant or fixed exchange rate for their currencies. Eventually, countries experiencing chronic deficits ran out of the foreign exchange or gold that they could use to support the price of their currencies in the world foreign exchange market. They experienced a currency crisis and were then forced to devalue. England has done this many times.

11. Americans purchase financial assets in other countries, and foreigners purchase American financial assets, such as stocks on a stock exchange or bonds in our bond markets. The buying and selling of foreign financial assets has the same effect on the balance of payments as the buying and selling of goods and services.

12. We can use a multiplier analysis to show the effects of a change in net exports. Net exports are defined as exports minus imports. Keynesian multiplier analysis indicates that an increase in net exports will increase income more than proportionally to the increase in net exports. In fact, there will be a multiple expansion. If the multiplier is 4, an increase in net exports of, say, $2 billion will equal an increase in income of $8 billion.

Questions for
Thought
and Discussion

1. What is the case for flexible exchange rates?
2. What is the case for fixed exchange rates?
3. Why have we had a balance-of-payments deficit for such a long period of time?
4. Is America as a nation better off if it has a balance-of-payments deficit? If so, is there anybody who is worse off?
5. Why aren't there balance-of-payments problems between New York and California, or, for that matter, between any two states in the United States?
6. Do you think that devaluation or revaluation should be used as a stabilizing policy to influence income and employment in the United States?

Selected
References

Economic Report of the President, various issues, Washington, D.C.: U.S. Government Printing Office.

Evans, John W., *U.S. Trade Policy,* New York: Harper & Row, 1967.

Friedman, Milton and Robert U. Roosa, *The Balance of Payments: Free versus Fixed Exchange Rates,* Washington, D.C.: American Enterprise Association, 1967.

Mikesell, Raymond F., *Financing World Trade,* New York: Thomas Y. Crowell, 1969.

Snider, Delbert, *International Monetary Relations,* New York: Random House, 1966.

Can Flexible Exchange Rates Halt Worldwide Inflation?

THE CHANGING WORLD OF INTERNATIONAL FINANCE

Inflation—A Worldwide Problem

Inflation is a problem in the United States and throughout the world. We show in Table I-16.1 the inflation rates for some industrialized countries. Inflation in the United States during the first half of the 1970s was

Table I-16.1

The Various Rates of Inflation in the World, 1970–1974

All industrialized nations have suffered inflation in this decade at rates equal to or greater than the United States.

COUNTRY	ANNUAL RATE OF INFLATION
Belgium	7.6
Canada	6.6
France	8.2
Germany	5.8
Italy	10.8
Japan	11.4
Netherlands	8.3
Switzerland	7.8
United Kingdom	10.5
United States	6.6

Source: Federal Reserve Bank of St. Louis

bad, but it certainly was not as severe as that of the other countries listed. There are, of course, many theories about what caused this worldwide inflation. We went into some of these theories in Chapter 7, and we also mentioned the monetarists' ideas concerning the importance of changes in the money supply in determining the long-run rate of inflation. In this issue, we will look at the relationship between inflation and the international monetary system.

Several years ago there was a great upheaval in the international monetary system. In 1973, world trade essentially began to take place on a flexible exchange rate basis. At that time there also occurred a great upsurge in our own rate of inflation. The natural conclusion seemed to follow—a switch to flexible exchange rates caused inflation. However, not all economists agreed. In fact, there was—and still is—a large group of international economic experts who firmly believe that a shift to flexible exchange rates will allow the world to reduce its high rate of inflation.

Before we discuss the pros and cons of this argument, let's look at the historical development of the

flexible exchange rate system that started in 1973.

The International Monetary Fund

In 1944, representatives of the world's capitalist nations met in Bretton Woods, New Hampshire, to create a new international payments system to replace the old gold standard that had collapsed during the 1930s. In 1944, Western Europe had been devastated by war and needed large amounts of imported capital—machines and raw materials—to rebuild its productive capacity. Also at that time, Western European countries were running large deficits with the United States. At the fixed exchange rates existing then, we were shipping more goods abroad than foreigners were shipping to us.

Lord Keynes—Head of British Delegation

At the head of the British delegation to the conference was John Maynard Keynes. He advocated a payments mechanism that would require surplus nations (the United States) to finance the deficits of other nations by lending them foreign exchange. The only other alternative was for the devastated Western European countries to reduce their imports so as to eliminate their trade deficits. Such a drastic measure would have made the recovery from war agonizingly slow. Lord Keynes rightly contended that if surplus nations were forced indefinitely to lend their foreign exchange to deficit nations, fixed exchange rates could be maintained. No country running a deficit would face a currency crisis. Any country could support the price of its currency with the foreign exchange lent to it by surplus nations.

Harry White—Head of American Delegation

The American delegation was headed by Harry Dexter White, who vigorously fought Keynes' proposal. America was the largest surplus nation in the free world, owning most of the world's gold stock. Keynes' proposal would have forced the United States into lending foreign exchange at a zero interest rate, thus forcing the country to continue subsidizing Europe for a long period to come. Harry Dexter White made a counterproposal that was finally adopted, and the **International Monetary Fund** (IMF) was created to help facilitate world financial exchanges.

The IMF Quota System

White's counterproposal called for fixed exchange rates but only a limited obligation to lend to deficit nations. The obligation was in the form of providing reserves for the International Monetary Fund. Upon becoming a member of the fund, each country was assigned a reserve quota. This quota was set according to a formula that took into account the economic importance of the country, its trade volume, and so on. The quota was paid to the IMF in a country's own domestic currency and in gold. The IMF was then able to lend foreign currency to any country that needed it in order to maintain a stable exchange rate.

When a country first borrowed from the IMF (within 25 percent of its quota), approval was given automatically. After the first borrowing, further borrowings were conditional. The IMF typically required deficit countries to take certain corrective measures (which would have occurred automatically under the gold standard) such as reducing their internal rate of inflation to make their goods more attractive internationally. In any event, the maximum amount a country could borrow was twice the quota assigned to that country. The unused portion of each country's automatic borrowing rights was called its **reserve position** in the IMF. Thus, America's limited obligation to lend to deficit nations was equivalent to the size of its quota in the IMF and no more.

Marshall Plan

The United States later solved Western Europe's deficit problems by voluntarily lending large quantities of dollars to Europe under the Marshall Plan. These loans enabled European countries to finance their imports from the United States. Consequently, the problem that Keynes feared concerning United States ability to finance imports was solved by voluntary loans from Uncle Sam.

The United States Develops a Deficit

Beginning in the late 1950s, the United States became chronically deficient in its balance of payments. Instead of a "dollar shortage," there was a "dollar surplus." By 1960 it was necessary for the United States to favor some arrangement whereby surplus nations, such as Germany and Japan, would be forced to lend exchange to deficit nations like the United States—just as Keynes had proposed in 1945.

The United States supported the creation of IMF Special Drawing Rights (SDRs), or "paper gold," that would enable deficit nations to borrow from surplus nations. A modified United States proposal was finally enacted and became effective January 1, 1970. The SDRs are different from the regular quota; they are a new international means of payment that has been *created* by the IMF. The original proposal was modified to give European nations a veto on the use of these pieces of paper gold. This, in effect, made the loans *voluntary* rather than obligatory on the part of the surplus countries.

Dwindling Gold Stock

Under IMF rules, the dollar was pegged to gold. The United States was obliged to redeem dollars in gold at $35 an ounce, if so requested by foreign holders of dollars. In effect, we were pegging dollars to the price of gold. Since foreigners had the right to demand gold for their excess dollars, we saw large outflows of gold during our period of balance-of-payments deficits. In Figure I-16.1

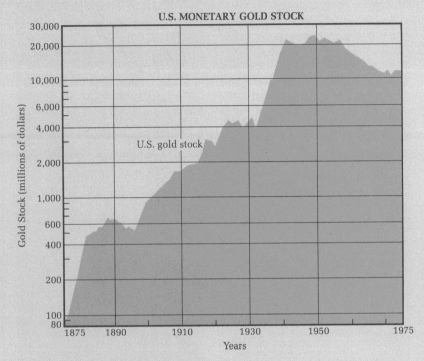

U.S. MONETARY GOLD STOCK

Gold Stock (millions of dollars)

30,000
20,000

10,000

6,000
4,000

U.S. gold stock

2,000

1,000

600
400

200

100
80

1875   1890   1910   1930   1950   1975

Years

FIGURE I-16.1

By the middle of World War II, we had amassed more than $20 billion worth of gold at the official price of $35 an ounce. By 1970, we had a little more than $10 billion worth of gold. Our chronic balance-of-payments deficit was responsible for this drain. *(Source: Federal Reserve Bulletin.)*

we see that our gold stock dwindled from $22 billion just after World War II to $11 billion in 1970. Many Americans were very distressed about our loss of gold.

In any event, during the 1960s, practically every Secretary of the Treasury spent part of his time trying to persuade foreign central banks to buy American financial securities rather than trade in their excess dollars for gold. In other words, we wanted surplus nations to lend back our dollars so we could continue our balance-of-payments deficit without altering our exchange rate and without cutting back our imports. Many countries went along with the American request, particularly West Germany. Other countries did not. We had much trouble with de Gaulle when he was in power in France because he kept turning in his excess dollars for gold.

A Two-Tiered Gold System

Finally, in March 1968, the United States announced it would no longer sell gold to foreign private holders of dollars. A two-tiered price system of gold developed. There was a private market (no central banks participated) in which the United States did not support the price of gold. Theoretically, however, we continued to sell gold to foreign central banks at $35 an ounce. From 1968 until August 1971, we lost very little of our gold. The reason for this was that we had made it clear to other nations that we would not allow a run on our gold. Essentially, we told other nations that they could buy gold from us at $35 an ounce, provided they did not ask for any.

A Rise in the Official Price of Gold

Although we were neither buying nor selling gold, the United States changed its official price for gold first from $35 to $38 an ounce, and then to $42.42 an ounce in February 1973. Throughout the world at that time there was a widespread adoption of floating exchange rates. This is not to say that the world financial community saw exchange rates moving up and down in response to the pure forces of supply and demand. Rather, governments entered foreign exchange markets to prevent changes in certain exchange rates, but the government intervention merely made the situation one of a **"dirty" float.** It did not, in effect, put us back onto the fixed exchange-rate system that had existed since the formation of the International Monetary Fund.

How would a floating exchange-rate situation affect a nation's rate of inflation? This is the basic question of this issue; we now turn our attention to it.

Exchange Rates and Monetary Policy

As we pointed out in Chapter 15, in a world of fixed exchange rates, a central bank can intervene any time there are forces that would alter the exchange rate from its pegged level. If, for example, there is pressure for an exchange rate to fall (depreciation), a central bank can enter the foreign exchange market and prevent such a fall by buying the currency with foreign exchange reserves. Normally, this would cause a contraction in the money supply and, in the long run, a reduction in the rate of inflation. However, a central bank, throughout the periods of large balance-of-payments deficits, prevents such a contraction in the money supply by expansionary open-market operations. On the other side of the picture, whenever there is pressure for a currency to go up in value (appreciate), then a central bank can enter the picture and prevent such a rise in value by selling its own domestic currency in

the foreign exchange market. Normally, this would lead to an increase in the domestic money supply because the central bank merely creates its own domestic currency for sale in the exchange market. This would have a tendency to cause an increase in the price level—at least in the long run.

Opponents of fixed exchange rates point out that during the period of rapidly rising prices in Europe and Japan, which started in the early 1970s, these surplus nations made a concerted effort to prevent the appreciation of their currencies and rapidly expanded their money supplies. However, the inevitable result was higher rates of inflation. Thus,

Table I-16.2

Percentage Rate of Change in Money Supply in Selected Countries*

DATE	MONEY
1960	9.94
1961	13.54
1962	12.02
1963	13.73
1964	9.43
1965	11.26
1966	8.83
1967	8.77
1968	9.24
1969	9.94
1970	9.74
1971	17.47
1972	17.31
1973	13.05
1974	10.10

*Weighted averages of data from France, Germany, Japan, United Kingdom, Italy, Belgium, Netherlands.
Source: The Phenomenon of Worldwide Inflation, David I. Meiselman and Arthur B. Loffer (eds.), Washington, D.C.: American Enterprise Institute, 1975, p. 86.

according to these same observers, switching to the system of floating exchange rates allows all nations to pursue independent monetary and fiscal policies without worrying about balance-of-payments problems because by definition they cannot exist in a world of floating rates. If we look at the data in Table I-16.2 in terms of changes in the money supply in selected countries, we do see some

evidence to support this position. We also see some evidence to support the position that worldwide rates of inflation did slow down when flexible rates became the rule rather than the exception in world financial dealings.

The United States Experience

The United States experience was somewhat different from that of Europe. When we essentially went on a system of free exchange rates, the dollar depreciated in world currency markets. We had to pay more for our imports than before—that is, we had to deliver more exports to pay for the same physical quantity of imports. Hence, depreciation of the dollar resulted in a decline of aggregate productivity and output. There is little doubt that the strong depreciation of the dollar in the early 1970s had an inflationary impact on the United States. However, the question is, "Will that inflationary impact be continuous and long lasting?" Or was it once and for all? Those who believe the former argue that we should go back to an international monetary system based on fixed exchange rates and in which the United States would be the world's central bank. Perhaps by the time you read this, more evidence will be available to support or refute such a view. Have worldwide rates of inflation finally slowed down in a world of flexible exchange rates? Or, does the argument in favor of an unrestricted international monetary system seem at odds with recent data?

Floating Exchange Rates and Oil Prices

Proponents of floating exchange rates point out that severe restrictions on oil production by leading oil exporters, particularly in the Middle East, and the resulting higher prices of oil, would, under a system of fixed exchange rates, have led to international monetary chaos. In fact, we can be fairly certain that if oil importing nations had attempted to maintain fixed exchange rates during the period when the Middle East oil-exporting countries effectively quadrupled the price of oil, there would have been recurrent currency crises. Flexible exchange advocates point with pride to the way in which the international monetary system was able to handle the perhaps unprecedented shock given to it by Persian Gulf oil politics.

Definitions of New Terms

International Monetary Fund (IMF): An institution set up to manage the international monetary system. It came out of the Bretton Woods Conference in 1944, which established, more or less, fixed exchange rates in the world.

Reserve Position: The unused portion of the automatic borrowing rights of IMF member countries.

"Dirty" Float: A freely floating exchange system that involves governments stepping in occasionally to prop up the value of their currency. To be contrasted with a "clean" float, where there is no government intervention in the foreign exchange market.

Questions for Thought and Discussion

1. "Fixed exchange rates impose the discipline necessary to keep the worldwide rate of inflation down." Evaluate this statement.
2. What does the IMF do today?
3. Does the official price of gold matter?

Selected References

Aliber, Robert Z., *The International Money Game,* New York: Basic Books, 1973.

Behrman, Jack N., "The Futility of International Monetary Reform," *Challenge,* July–August 1973, pp. 23–31.

Manne, Henry G. and Roger LeRoy Miller (eds.), *Gold, Money, and the Law,* Chicago: Aldine Publishing, 1975.

Stevens, Robert Warren, *A Primer on the Dollar in the World Economy,* New York: Random House, 1972.

Triffin, Robert, *Our International Monetary System: Yesterday, Today and Tomorrow,* New York: Random House, 1968.

Weil, Gordon L. and Ian Davidson, *Gold War: The Story of the World's Monetary Crisis,* New York: Holt, Rinehart and Winston, 1970.

FIVE

MARKETS, THE FIRM, AND RESOURCE ALLOCATION

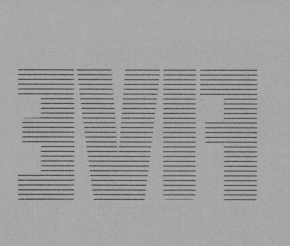

Demand and Consumer Choice

If the price of everything in the economy remained constant except the price of leather shoes, which went up by 500 percent, we might think twice about buying a new pair. We might instead have our old shoes repaired or buy shoes made out of material other than leather. This same reaction probably applies to just about anything else that we buy in our economy. When the *relative* price of a good or service goes up, the quantity demanded goes down. This statement, of course, is the famous law of demand that we talked about in Chapter 3. Given that everybody faces a limited budget, when one item in that total budget becomes more expensive, either less of that item will be bought or some other item in the budget must be cut back. Hence, at some point, a relatively higher price for one good will force some people to buy less than they did at the lower price.

Another way of deriving the law of demand and justifying the downward slope of a demand curve for any good or service involves an analysis of the logic of consumer choice in a world of limited resources. In this chapter, therefore, we will discuss *utility analysis*. As in Unit One, we will be dealing with a world of scarce resources, where individuals must make choices among alternative exchanges.

Utility Theory

When you buy something, you buy it because of the satisfaction or utility you receive from having and using it. And for just about everything you like to have, the more you have, the higher the level of satisfaction or utility you receive. In other words, for most goods and services, the larger the quantity you use, the greater your total utility from using those commodities. Let's look at an example. It is a very hot day and you are very, very thirsty. You walk into your house and you are offered, at a zero price, one Coke on ice. Assuming now that you like Coke, you drink it and receive a certain level of satisfaction or utility. Just as you finish drinking it, another is offered to you—again free of charge. You drink the second one and experience an increase in the total level of satisfaction. Your total utility has gone up. Now a third Coke is offered. And the free offers continue. Eventually, you refuse to drink any more Coke, even at a zero price. Why? Because your total utility from drinking the Cokes will diminish if you drink another one at that particular point. Until then, however, total utility rises. Does it rise at the same rate each time you drink another Coke? In other words, does the incremental or marginal increase in your total utility go up at a constant rate each time you are offered and drink another free Coke? We can surmise that the answer to this question is no. The additional or marginal utility you receive from drinking another Coke diminishes with each one. This is known as the **law of diminishing marginal utility.**

The Law of Diminishing Marginal Utility

For most people, as more is consumed, increases in total utility from the consumption of a good or service start getting smaller. Do you notice something familiar about the law of diminishing marginal utility? It's similar to the law of diminishing marginal returns, which we talked about in Chapter 2. In this case, however, the law concerns the psychological or subjective utility you receive as you consume more and more of a particular commodity. Let's state the law more formally:

The law of diminishing marginal utility As

an individual consumes more of the same commodity, total psychological or subjective utility increases. However, the extra utility added by an extra or last unit of that commodity does not increase at a constant rate. Rather, as successive new units of the commodity in question are consumed, total utility will grow at a slower and slower rate. Otherwise stated, as the amount of a commodity consumed increases, the marginal utility of the good or service tends to decrease.

Cokes and Diminishing Marginal Utility

Look at Table 16-1. In column 1 we show the quantity of Cokes consumed, in column 2, the total utility measured in some arbitrary unit. Notice that total utility rises up to three Cokes, remains constant at four, and then falls. Column 3 gives the incremental change in total utility

Table 16-1 **Total and Marginal Utility of Cokes**

If we were able to assign specific numbers to the utility derived from the consumption of Cokes, we could then obtain a measure of marginal utility. In column 1 is the quantity of Cokes consumed; in column 2, the total utility from each quantity; in column 3, the marginal utility, which is defined as the increment in total utility due to the consumption of one more Coke.

(1) QUANTITY OF COKES CONSUMED	(2) TOTAL UTILITY	(3) MARGINAL UTILITY
0	0	
1	4	4
2	6	2
3	7	1
4	7	0
5	6	−1

for each successive Coke consumed. It is called "marginal utility."

Figure 16-1 is a graphic representation of Table 16-1. In Figure 16-1(a), total utility as translated from columns 1 and 2 is shown. At three Cokes, total utility peaks at 7 units, stays at 7 for four Cokes, and then falls when five Cokes are consumed. We can see that total utility increases for the first three units of Cokes consumed, but at a decreasing rate. The increase is first 4, then 2, and then 1. This is seen more explicitly in Figure 16-1 (b), where we show marginal utility (depicted by the colored blocks). After the consumption of one Coke, total utility increases by 4 units. The second Coke adds 2 units to total utility. The third Coke adds 1 unit to total utility. If we connect these blocks with a line, we get the marginal utility curve showing the law of diminishing marginal utility.

Reaching Equilibrium

If you have a specific budget to spend—and who doesn't?—when will you reach equilibrium? That is, when will you maximize total utility from that budget? Will it occur when the mar-

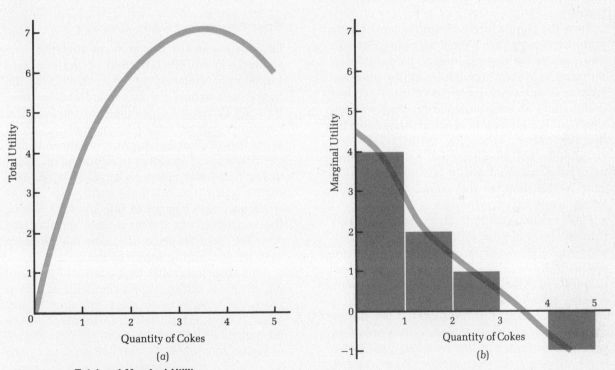

FIGURE 16-1 Total and Marginal Utility
In (a) we transfer the numbers given in columns 1 and 2 of Table 16-1. The result is a total utility curve. In (b) we measure marginal utility on the vertical axis. Transferring column 3 from Table 16-1 to (b) gives us the rectangles of marginal utility. If we draw a smooth line connecting the midpoints of those rectangles, we get a smooth curve called the marginal utility curve. Notice that, after the consumption of four Cokes, marginal utility becomes negative.

ginal utility you received from the last Coke you bought equals the marginal utility you received from the last pair of bluejeans you purchased? Probably not, for the price of bluejeans is usually much higher than the price of a Coke.

Wouldn't it make more sense if the marginal utility received from the last dollar spent on each item in a person's budget was equal all around? That way, the individual would be assured that there is no way to further increase total utility. However, if the marginal utility received from the last dollar spent on Cokes is greater than the marginal utility received for the last dollar spent on bluejeans, then the consumer can increase total utility by spending less on bluejeans, for example, and more on Cokes.

Now the choice is clear from the consumer's point of view. With a fixed income and with given prices for commodities to be purchased, the way to obtain maximum utility or satisfaction is to equate marginal utilities per last dollar spent on each commodity. This is sometimes known as the **law of equal marginal utilities per dollar.** According to this law, each commodity will be demanded up to the point where the marginal utility per dollar spent is exactly the same as the marginal utility per dollar spent on any other good.[1]

If we assume that individuals want to maximize the level of satisfaction or utility that they can receive from a given income or budget, the applicability of this law and its validity is hard to question. After all, why would a consumer remain for any period of time in a situation where the marginal utility received per dollar spent on, for example, tennis lessons was less than the marginal utility received per dollar spent on going to movies? The obvious thing to do would be to cut back on the tennis lessons and go to more movies.

This law is also applicable to activities other than the purchase of goods and services. We can apply it to the way people use their time. Every individual must make a choice among all possible uses of time. The marginal utility received from the last minute used, for example, to study economics should not be radically different from the marginal utility received from the last minute used to study English literature. If these marginal utilities are greatly out of line, then obviously you should change the time mix. You should spend more or less time with one than the other.

Equilibrium and Price Change

Let us assume for the moment that the consumer is in equilibrium; that is, the marginal utilities per dollar spent on each item in the consumer's budget are the same. Now one item, let's say Cokes, becomes more expensive. The consumer can no longer be in equilibrium. It is no longer possible for the marginal utility per dollar spent on Cokes to equal the marginal utility per dollar spent on anything else. At a higher price, the marginal utility *per dollar spent* on Cokes has got to fall. In other words, the consumer can get back into equilibrium after the relative price of Cokes has gone up only by purchasing fewer of them.

This situation is due to the law of diminishing marginal utility. When the price of Cokes rises, the only way to raise marginal utility again is to purchase fewer Cokes; that is, we move back up that marginal utility curve shown in Figure 16-1 *(b)*.[2] If the relative price of Cokes

---

[1]This can be written as $MU_a/P_a = MU_b/P_b = MU_c/P_c = \ldots$ where P_a refers to the price of commodity a, and so on.

[2]In equilibrium, MU_{Coke}/P_{Coke} equals the MU-to-P ratio of all other goods. But if P_{Coke} increases, this is no longer true. To get back into equilibrium, MU_{Coke} must increase also. This is accomplished by buying fewer Cokes.

falls, of course, the opposite would have to occur to bring the consumer back into equilibrium—more would have to be purchased. We move back down the marginal utility curve shown in Figure 16-1 *(b)*.

The Demand Curve Revisited

Linking together the law of diminishing marginal utility and the law of equal marginal utilities per dollar gives us a negative relationship between the quantity demanded of a good or service and its price. As the relative price of Cokes, for example, goes up, the quantity demanded will fall, and as the relative price of Cokes goes down, the quantity demanded will rise. Figure 16-2 shows this demand curve for Cokes. As the relative price of Cokes falls, the consumer can get back into equilibrium

only by purchasing more of them and vice versa. In other words, the relationship between price and quantity desired is simply a downward-sloping demand curve.

The demand curve we have been talking about is one that relates directly to an individual. But what about a market demand curve—that is, the demand curve that represents the entire market for a particular good or service? How can we derive a market demand curve from the individual ones we've looked at?

Actually, deriving a market demand curve from individual demand curves is not difficult. What we have to do is add together all the individual demands. We know that not all people are alike. We know, for example, that even at very, very low prices certain individuals will demand no Cokes whatsoever. We also know that at relatively high prices, other individuals will still demand a large quantity. So, to derive

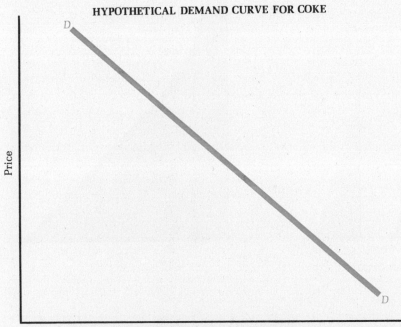

HYPOTHETICAL DEMAND CURVE FOR COKE

Price

Quantity of Coke Demanded (per day)

FIGURE 16-2
Here we have the quantity of Coke demanded per day on the horizontal axis, and the price per bottle on the vertical axis. The demand curve slopes downward by virtue of diminishing marginal utility. At a lower price, the last dollar spent on Coke will yield more utility than the last dollar spent on other things. To get the ratios in line with each other, we buy more Coke. As we buy and drink more Coke, the marginal utility falls—that is, we move back up the demand curve—until the marginal utility of the last dollar spent on Coke again equals the marginal utility of the last dollar spent on other things.

a demand curve for the entire market, we must add up each individual's demand. This is what we do in Table 16-2 and Figure 16-3. The figure shows explicitly that the demand curves are fitted together to obtain the market demand curve for Cokes by what we call "horizontal addition." Notice that the demand is expressed in quantity per time period. We have to add a time period to the demand analysis because we are talking about a flow through time of a demand for a specific good.

Table 16-2 **Cokes Demanded Per Day**

Individuals A, B, and C present us with the various quantities of Coke they demand at various relative prices: 20¢, 30¢, and 40¢. When we add quantities demanded by these individuals, we get the total or market demand at each of these various prices.

	20¢	30¢	40¢
Individual A's demand	4	3	2
Individual B's demand	2	1	0
Individual C's demand	1	0	0
Market demand	7	4	2

Using Marginal Utility Analysis to Explain the Diamond-Water Paradox

Adam Smith, the author of *The Wealth of Nations*, once asked the following question: "How can water, which is essential to life, be so cheap while diamonds, which are quite unessential to life, be so expensive?" This is called in eco-

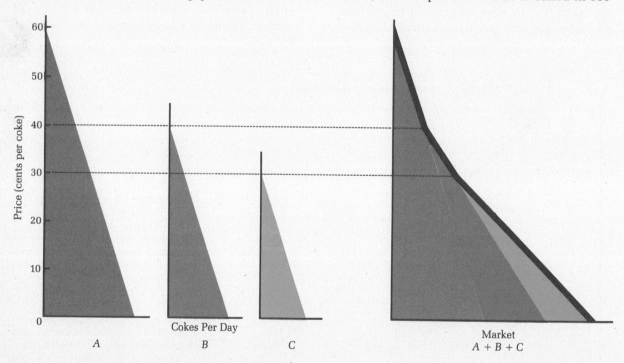

FIGURE 16-3 Deriving the Market Demand Curve

Individual A's demand curve is shown first, then Individual B's and Individual C's. By adding these three demand curves horizontally, we obtain the market demand curve represented by the heavily shaded line in the right-hand graph.

nomics the diamond-water paradox. The answer to this paradox is quite easily stated: The intersection of the demand and supply curves for water is at a lower price than the intersection of the demand and the supply curves for diamonds.

The Supply

From the supply side, the reason water is so cheap and diamonds so expensive seems almost trivial. Water, at least until recently, has been relatively abundant in the United States. The cost of getting an extra unit of water is almost nil in most situations, so the price of an extra unit is not going to be very high. On the other hand, diamonds are relatively scarce. The cost of obtaining an extra one, therefore, is quite high, and the market price is going to be high.

Total vs. Marginal Utility

But we can continue the analysis and use utility theory to tell us even more. It is not the total utility of water or of diamonds that determines the price of either. To be sure, the total utility of water must greatly exceed the total utility derived from diamonds. However, in economics what determines price is what happens on the margin, and what happens on the margin is quite simple. Since we have so much water, the marginal utility (because it is diminishing) is quite small, given the total quantity that we consume. Because we have relatively few diamonds, the marginal utility of that last diamond consumed is quite high. Moreover, since in most circumstances it is difficult to charge different people different prices for the same thing, we find that the price of water is the same, more or less, for everyone who buys it in a particular market situation. We find also that the price of the diamond, in another market situation, is the same for everyone who buys it. In other words, every unit must be sold for what the last (marginal), and hence least useful, unit sells for. By "least useful" we mean in terms of individual subjective or psychological marginal utility.

So the diamond-water paradox is only a paradox if one confuses total utility with marginal utility. Total utility does not determine what people are willing to pay for a particular commodity. Marginal utility does.

Another use of marginal utility analysis, for the futures market, is examined in the following issue. In particular, we will examine the market for onion futures—onions purchased today but to be delivered at some time in the future.

Definitions of New Terms

Law of Diminishing Marginal Utility: The increase in total utility from the consumption of a good or service becomes smaller as more is consumed.

Law of Equal Marginal Utilities per Dollar: Each commodity is demanded up to the point where the marginal utility per dollar spent is the same as the marginal utility per dollar spent on any other good or service.

Chapter Summary

1. As an individual consumes more of a particular commodity, the total level of utility or satisfaction derived from that consumption increases. However, the rate at which it increases diminishes as more is consumed. This is known as the law of diminishing marginal utility.

2. A consumer reaches equilibrium when the marginal utility per last dollar spent on each commodity consumed is equal. This is known as the law of equal marginal utilities per dollar.
3. When the relative price of a particular commodity goes up, the law of equal marginal utilities per dollar spent is violated. For the consumer to get back into equilibrium, he or she must reduce the consumption of the now relatively more expensive commodity. As this consumer moves back along the marginal utility curve, marginal utility increases.
4. It is possible to derive a downward-sloping demand curve by using the principle of diminishing marginal utility.
5. The market demand curve is merely the horizontal summation of individual demand curves.

Questions for Thought and Discussion

1. Do you think it is possible to measure utility objectively?
2. Do you think it is possible to talk in terms of one person receiving more utility from the consumption of a commodity than another person?
3. Is it possible to have increasing marginal utility?
4. How would you define a substitute?

Selected References

Bennett, Peter D. and Harold H. Kassarjian, *Consumer Behavior*, Englewood Cliffs, N.J.: Prentice-Hall, 1972.

Watson, Donald S., *Price Theory and Its Uses*, 3d ed., Boston: Houghton Mifflin, 1972.

Looking at Consumer Choice
with Graphs

It is certainly possible to analyze consumer choice verbally, as we did for the most part in Chapter 16. The theory of diminishing marginal utility can be fairly well accepted on intuitive grounds and by introspection. If we want to be more formal, and perhaps more elegant, in our theorizing, however, we can translate our discussion into graphic analysis with what are called "indifference curves" and "the budget constraint." Here we discuss these terms and their relationship and demonstrate consumer equilibrium in geometric form.

On Being Indifferent

What does it mean to be indifferent? It usually means that you don't care one way or the other about something—you are equally disposed to either of two choices. In this sense, we will again turn to the two choices we discussed in Chapter 16: Cokes and Seven-Ups. In Table C-1 we show several combinations of Cokes and Seven-Ups that our representative soft-drink consumer considers to be equally satisfactory. That is to say, for each combination, A, B, C, and D, this soft-drink consumer will have exactly the same level of total utility.

We can plot these combinations graphically in Figure C-1, with Seven-Ups on the horizontal axis and Cokes on the vertical axis. These are our consumer's indifference combinations—the consumer finds each combination as acceptable as the others. Each one carries the same level of total utility. When we connect these combinations with a smooth curve, we obtain what is called the "consumer's indifference curve." Along the indifference curve, every combination of the two goods in question yields exactly the same level of total utility. Every point along the indifference curve is equally desirable to the consumer.

Table C-1 Combinations That Yield Equal Levels of Satisfaction

The combinations *A, B, C,* and *D* represent varying numbers of Cokes and Seven-Ups that give an equal level of satisfaction to this consumer. In other words, the consumer is indifferent among these four combinations.

COMBINATION	COKES	SEVEN-UPS
A	1	7
B	2	4
C	3	2
D	4	1

The Shape of the Indifference Curve

Notice that the indifference curve is bowed inward. In mathematical jargon, it has a convex curvature when viewed from below. The reason for this is the law of diminishing marginal util-

ity, which we discussed in Chapter 16.* As the individual consumes more of a particular item, the marginal utility of consuming one additional unit of that item falls, or, in other words, as a good becomes relatively scarcer in a person's expenditure pattern, that good will have a higher marginal utility.

We said we could measure the marginal utility of something by the quantity of a substitute good that would leave the consumer indifferent. Let's look at this in Table C-1. Starting with combination *A* the consumer has one Coke but seven Seven-Ups. To remain indifferent, the consumer would be willing to give up three Seven-Ups to obtain one more Coke (as shown in combination *B*). However, to go from combination *C* to combination *D*, notice that the consumer would be willing to give up only one Seven-Up for an additional Coke. In other words, the quantity of the substitute con-

*Actually it can be shown that only diminishing marginal rates of substitution are required.

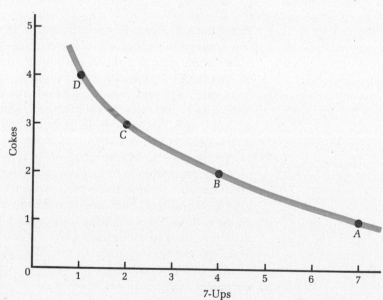

FIGURE C-1 An Indifference Curve

If we plot the combinations *A, B, C,* and *D* from Table C-1, we obtain the curve *ABCD,* which is called an indifference curve.

sidered acceptable changes as the relative scarcity of the original item changes.

Diminishing marginal utility exists throughout this set of choices, and consequently the indifference curve in Figure C-1 will be convex when viewed from below. If it were a straight line, then marginal utility would not be diminishing but constant; if it were curved the other way, then marginal utility would be increasing.

The Marginal Rate of Substitution

Above we discussed marginal utility in terms of the marginal rate of substitution between Cokes and Seven-Ups. More formally, we can define the consumer's marginal rate of substitution as follows:

MRS = the change in the quantity of one good which just offsets the unit change in the consumption of another good, such that total utility remains constant.

We can see numerically what happens to the marginal rate of substitution in our example if we rearrange Table C-1 into Table C-2. Here we show Seven-Ups in the second column and Cokes in the third. Now we ask the question: "What change in the consumption of Seven-Ups will just compensate for an increase in the consumption of Cokes and leave the consumer's total utility constant?" The movement from A to B reduces Seven-Up consumption by three and increases Coke consumption by one. Here the marginal rate of substitution of Cokes for Seven-Ups is 3-to-1. We do this for the rest of the table and find that the marginal rate of substitution goes from 3-to-1 to 1-to-1. The marginal rate of substitution of Cokes for Seven-Ups falls, in other words, as the consumer obtains more Cokes. This is sometimes called the *law of substitution*.

The *law of substitution* A good that becomes scarcer has a greater value in substitution. Its marginal utility rises relative to the marginal utility of another good that has become more plentiful.

In geometric language, the slope of the consumer's indifference curve (actually, the "negative" of the slope) measures the consumer's marginal rate of substitution. Notice that this marginal rate of substitution, or MRS, is purely subjective or psychological. We are not talking about financial capabilities, merely about a consumer's particular set of preferences.

The Indifference Map

Every consumer has more than one indifference curve for any two items that might be pur-

Table C-2 **Calculating the Marginal Rate of Substitution**

COMBINATION	SEVEN-UPS	COKES	MARGINAL RATE OF SUBSTITUTION OF COKES FOR SEVEN-UPS
A	7	1	3/1
B	4	2	2/1
C	2	3	1/1
D	1	4	

chased. In fact, the consumer has an entire indifference map. Figure C-2 shows several possible indifference curves. Indifference curves that are higher than others necessarily imply more of each good in question. That is, for any quantity of Cokes, indifference curve I_3 has more Seven-Ups and vice versa than any other indifference curve in the map. Thus, the higher a consumer finds himself or herself on the indifference-curve map, the greater that consumer's total utility—assuming, of course, that the consumer does not become satiated.

The Budget Constraint

Let's move from psychological preferences to preferences based on objective fact. Everyone has a budget constraint; that is, everyone is faced with a limited consumption potential. How do we show this graphically? We must find the prices of the goods in question and determine the maximum consumption of each allowed by our consumer's budget. For example, let's assume that Cokes cost $1 apiece and Seven-Ups cost 50¢. Let's also assume that our representative soft-drink consumer has a total budget of $3. What is the maximum number of Cokes the consumer can buy? Obviously, three. And the maximum number of Seven-Ups? Six. So we now have, in Figure C-3, two points on our budget line, which is sometimes called the "consumption possibilities curve." The first point is at b on the vertical axis; the second at b' on the horizontal axis. The line is straight because the prices do not change.

Any combination along line bb' is possible, and, in fact, any combination in the colored

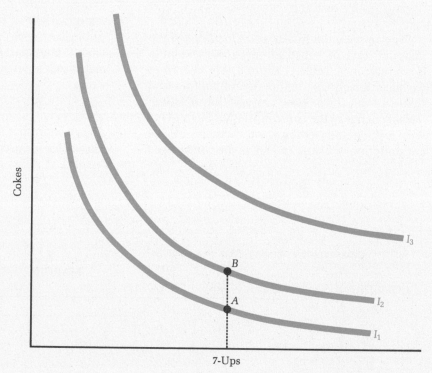

FIGURE C-2 **A Set of Indifference Curves**

There are an infinite number of indifference curves that can be drawn. We show three possible ones. You should realize that a higher indifference curve represents higher rates of consumption of both goods. Hence a higher indifference curve is to be preferred to a lower one. Generally we say that movement from a lower to a higher indifference curve represents an increase in real income. It is easy to see that a higher indifference curve is preferred to a lower one. Look at points A and B. Point B represents more Cokes than point A; therefore, indifference curve I_2 has to be a better position since the number of Seven-Ups is the same as at points A and B.

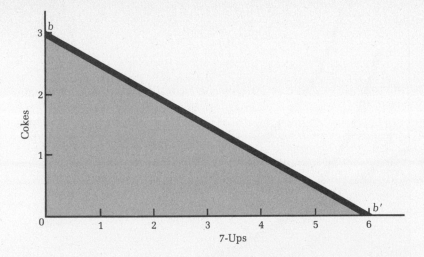

FIGURE C-3 **The Budget Constraint**
The line *bb'* represents this individual's budget constraint. Assuming that Cokes cost $1 each and Seven-Ups 50¢ and that the individual has a budget of $3, a maximum of three Cokes or six Seven-Ups could be bought. These two extreme points are connected to form the budget constraint. All combinations within the shaded area are feasible.

area is possible. We will assume, however, that the individual consumer completely uses up his or her available budget, and we will consider as possible only points along *bb'*.

Now we are ready to determine how the consumer achieves equilibrium.

Consumer Equilibrium Revisited

Consumers, of course, will attempt to attain the highest level of total utility possible, given their budget constraint. How can this be shown graphically? We draw a set of indifference curves similar to those given in Figure C-2 and we draw reality: the budget constraint, *bb'*. Both are drawn in Figure C-4. Now, since a higher level of total satisfaction is represented by a higher indifference curve, we know that the consumer will strive to be on the highest indifference curve possible. However, the consumer cannot get to indifference curve I_3 because his or her budget will be exhausted before any combination of Cokes and Seven-Ups represented on indifference curve I_3 is attained. This consumer can maximize total utility, subject

to the budget constraint, only by being at point *E* on indifference curve I_2 because here the consumer's income is just being exhausted. Mathematically, point *E* is called the tangency point of the curve I_2 to the straight line, *bb'*.

Geometrically, consumer equilibrium is achieved when the marginal rate of substitution (which is subjective) is just equal to the feasible, or realistic, rate of transformation. This realistic rate is the ratio of the two prices of the goods involved. It is represented by the absolute slope of the budget constraint. To see this, look carefully at the budget line in Figure C-3. How far up that line do we have to move to get a one-unit movement up the vertical axis? Well, when we move from four Seven-Ups to three Seven-Ups, there is a movement upward from 1 Coke to 1½ Cokes. This is a slope, in absolute terms, of 1-to-2, which is also the ratio of the prices of Cokes to Seven-Ups—Cokes cost $1 and Seven-Ups cost 50¢. That is, Cokes cost twice as much as Seven-Ups.

Point *E* then is the point of optimal equilibrium. At point *E*, the consumer maximizes total utility subject to the budget constraint.

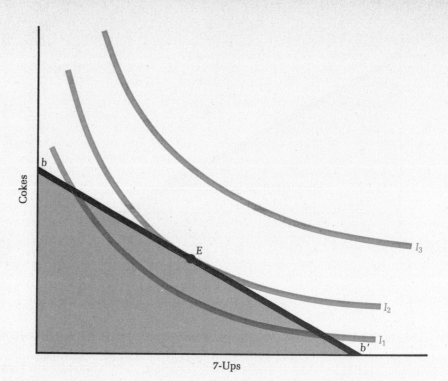

FIGURE C-4 Consumer Equilibrium
A consumer reaches equilibrium when he or she ends up on the highest indifference curve possible, given a limited budget. This occurs at the tangency between an indifference curve and the budget constraint. In this diagram, the tangency is at E.

Income and Substitution Effects

To firm up your understanding of the indifference-curve approach to the theory of consumer choice, see what happens when the price of Seven-Ups falls relative to the price of Cokes. You can show this by changing the slope of the budget constraint. What you will find is that more Seven-Ups are purchased as the relative price falls. However, in addition, the consumer's real income will go up. The consumer can now buy a larger number of Cokes and Seven-Ups with the same budget.

In the graphical analysis shown in Figure C-4, there are ways to get around this problem of a change in real income. In general, if we hold real income constant while changing the price of a good, we will see a substitution effect. More will be purchased of the good in question and less of other goods. If we then allow real income to change—in this case go up—we will see an income effect. In most cases, people purchase more goods when their real incomes go up. Together, the substitution effect and the income effect operate in the same direction—both cause the consumer to purchase more of the relatively cheaper good.

Now if you really want to test your understanding of this graphical analysis, try to derive a demand curve from the indifference-curve analysis presented in this appendix.

Why Was the Onions Futures Market Abolished?

THE NATURE OF SPECULATION

Onions and the Future

In 1957 a bill was introduced in the House of Representatives to amend prior legislation regulating the buying and selling of something called **futures contracts** so as to prohibit "futures trading in onions on commodity exchanges." According to the Committee on Agriculture's report,

> For the past several years there has been a growing conviction among onion producers that price variations on the futures markets have been adversely affecting the cash [current] price of onions. Violent fluctuations in the futures price of onions have tended to substantiate this position.

In 1958 a bill amending this prior legislation pertaining to trading in futures contracts was passed. Congress abolished the futures market in onions.

What's this all about? Why would Congress abolish the market? What are futures contracts? Can the existence of a market for futures contracts cause serious fluctuations in the price of the good in question?

To understand, and perhaps answer, some of these questions, we'll explain what a futures market is, how it operates, and why it exists—here we will apply marginal utility analysis. Then, finally, we can attempt to answer why Congress banned trading in onion futures.

Commodities Today and in the Future

You have probably heard about the commodities market, or the commodity futures market. It is the market where contracts for the future delivery of wheat, soybeans, corn, oats, cotton, barley, sugar, hides, lard, potatoes, frozen chickens, rubber, pepper, copper, and pork bellies, as well as gold, silver, and platinum, are bought and sold. A futures contract then is simply a commitment to deliver something at a specified time in the future at a price specified today. You could purchase today, for example, a futures contract for the delivery of wheat 5 months from now at the current price—say, $5 a bushel.

Why would anyone want to pur-chase futures contracts? Or, alternatively, why would anyone want to sell a futures contract? The easiest way to understand the futures market is to look at an example of the many individuals and firms who must use particular commodities in their production process throughout the year. A wheat miller uses wheat to make flour. If the wheat miller wants to specialize in milling and not in the purchase and storing of wheat over a long period, that miller might find it convenient to be able to get a commitment for delivery of wheat in the future at a specific price agreed on today. The miller, then, would enter into an agreement with someone else for the delivery of wheat. A futures contract would be purchased by the miller.

The miller is attempting to hedge against the possibility of a price rise between now and the time he will need the wheat for grinding. By purchasing a futures contract at today's price, this miller is insuring himself against a higher price of wheat in the future. But on the other hand, he is stuck with this price even if the price of wheat on the day of delivery (called the **spot price**—the current price on any given day) is lower. In other words, if the miller agrees to a price of $5 per bushel for wheat delivered 5 months from now, and if, 5 months from now, the spot price of wheat is only $4 a bushel, he is nevertheless obligated to pay the agreed upon price of $5. Therefore, in some sense the miller is taking a risk—the risk of having to pay a higher price than he would if he hadn't made the agreement and the price of wheat fell.

At the same time, the seller of wheat for delivery in 5 months is taking a risk because the spot price of wheat in 5 months may be greater than that agreed upon in the futures contract. This would mean that the wheat seller will lose out on potentially higher revenues. Of course, if the spot price 5 months from now is less than the price agreed upon, then obviously the seller of that futures contract for wheat will be better off. He will be receiving a higher price than he could without the futures contract agreement.

Why would anyone enter into such an agreement, since there are risks on both sides? The answer is that the seller believes the spot price of wheat 5 months from now *will* be lower than the price in the contract, but the buyer believes just the opposite.

Buying and selling wheat for delivery in the future, then, is actually a form of **speculation.** One party is betting that the price of wheat will go one way; the other party is betting that the price of wheat will go the other way. Of course, speculation is not limited to commodity futures markets. Speculation is involved whenever you own an asset that can change in value. For now, though, we will limit ourselves to an analysis of speculation as it applies to the commodities market. Also, don't forget that the futures market is used not only for speculation but by man-

ufacturers to ensure certain prices for their future input production.

Speculation and Total Utility

Let's shift our example from wheat to onions and restrict our analysis to 2 years of onion crops—this year and next year. How will total utility from the 2 years of onion crops be maximized?

Before we enter into the analysis, we'll make some more simplifying assumptions. We'll assume that the crop next year is going to be smaller than the crop this year and that we can store onions for at least a year. We'll also assume that there are no storage costs, insurance costs, or anything of the like (and a zero interest rate). That is, we can alter our rate of consumption of onions without cost. One rate of onion consumption would be to consume the

full crop this year and the full crop next year. We know, then, that the price of onions this year, since the crop is larger, will be relatively lower than the price of onions next year. This is shown in Figure I-17.1 *(a)* and *(b)*.

In *(a)*—Year 1—the supply curve is vertical—completely inelastic with respect to price. It is shown at 4 units of onions. The demand curve, *DD*, intersects this supply curve, S_1S_1, at price P_1. In *(b)* we show the reduced crop in Year 2 with only 2 units of onions available. This is represented by the supply curve, S_2S_2. The same demand curve, *DD*, prevails. Now the price in Year 2 will obviously be higher than in Year 1. We show it as P_2 in *(b)*.

Now think back to our discussion of consumer equilibrium in Chapter 16. You will remember that consumer equilibrium can be reached only when the marginal utility per

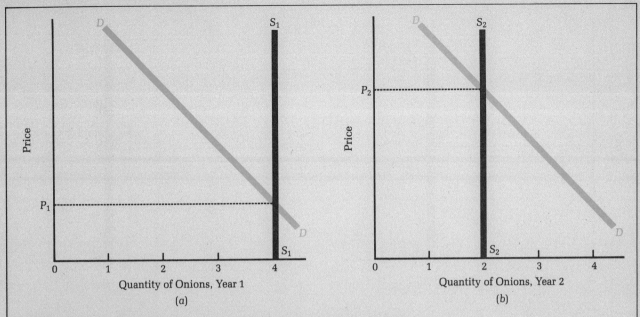

FIGURE I-17.1 Two Years' Demand and Supply of Onions without Speculation
(a) represents the demand and supply situation for onions in this year. The supply curve, S_1S_1, is vertical. The market clearing price will be P_1. A reduced crop occurs next year. This is shown in (b) by S_2S_2 being one-half the distance it was from the origin in (a). Next year's market clearing price will be higher than this year's. It will be at P_2.

dollar of all items is equalized. We can apply this same equilibrium condition to the two commodities in question here: onions in Year 1 and onions in Year 2. Obviously the equilibrium condition is not satisfied because in Year 1, due to the law of diminishing marginal utility, the marginal utility per dollar spent on onions is lower than the marginal utility per dollar spent on onions in Year 2. We can tell that right away just by looking at the difference in prices for the prices reflect the marginal utility of an additional unit of onion consumption (assuming no inflation and no change in real income).

Maximizing Total Utility

One way to achieve consumer equilibrium, and thus maximize total utility for a given onion crop in Years 1 and 2, is to store part of the crop from Year 1 and release it in Year 2. This way we can increase the marginal utility received from the crop in Year 1 and decrease the marginal utility received from the crop in Year 2, thus equalizing marginal utility per dollar spent on onions in Years 1 and 2. This is shown in Figure I-17.2 (a) and (b). In Year 1 the supply schedule of onions is at 3 units and labeled $S_1'S_1'$. The extra unit from that year is added to the

supply schedule in Year 2 to obtain $S_2'S_2'$. The quantities consumed in Years 1 and 2 are now equal so are the prices. Total utility is higher now than it was in the situation where no storage took place.

How does 1 unit of the onion crop get stored in order to be sold in Year 2? One way is for a planner, knowing the crop won't be as large next year, to decree that 1 unit should be stored. Another way is to allow speculators to withhold part of this year's crop in anticipation of higher prices next year. These buyers will be speculating that the stored onions will increase in value and they will make a profit.

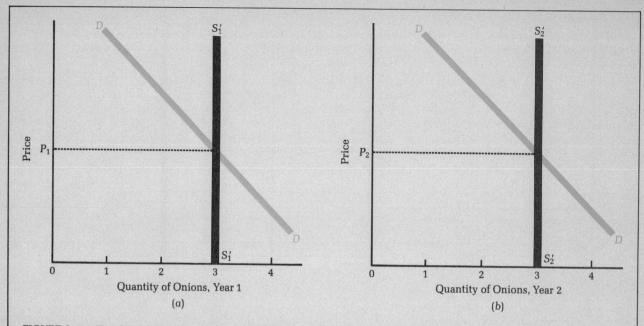

FIGURE I-17.2 Two Years' Supply and Demand in Onions—Equilibrating with a Futures Market

If a futures market exists for onions, speculators, in anticipation of next year's smaller crop, will bid up the futures price of onions. This will cause current owners of onions to put less on the market this year, thus raising the price and discouraging consumption. The supply curve this year will be $S_1'S_1'$; the supply curve next year will be $S_2'S_2'$. Under simplifying assumptions, the price this year will be equal to the price next year, or P_1 will equal P_2.

What do speculators do, then? They subtract from this year's supply and add to next year's. In the process, they raise this year's price and lower next year's price. They do this because they assume, either from intuition or from information they receive, that next year's crop will not be as large as this year's crop. If they assume otherwise, then they won't buy the current production of onions for storage into the future. Instead they will sell futures contracts (if the current spot price and future price are equal); that is, they agree to deliver onions at a specified future time at a price specified now. They are speculating, in other words,

that the actual spot price next year will be lower than the price they can agree upon in a futures contract. If enough speculators believe this to be the case, they will force down the futures price of onions. This will signal current owners of onion production to sell even more of their onion crop this year because next year's prices don't look as good anymore. The current price of onions will fall also. But to maximize total utility if the onion crop next year actually will be greater than this year's, then the current price should fall. In anticipation of an even larger crop in the future, why not use up more of this year's crop?

Speculation and Price Stability

In this simple example, we have seen that speculation leads not only to increased total utility from a given supply of a commodity over time, but also a reduction in price variations from year to year. When speculators are right about future crops, they gain, and so too do consumers. When speculators are wrong, they lose, but of course, in so doing they have given false market signals to the economy and have, thereby, lowered total utility. We can presume, however, that since speculators who predict incorrectly end up going bankrupt, then, on the average, speculators do more good than harm in the sense that price variations will be less with speculation than without and total utility will be greater with speculation than without.

Banning Futures Trading

This argument apparently went unheeded by Congress when it banned futures trading in onions. Looking at some of the behind-the-scenes maneuvering, Holbrook Working, an economist with the Food Research Institute of Stanford University, found that large onion dealers supported the legislation banning onions future trading. Working surmised that the banning of onions future trading would give increased bargaining advantage to large dealers as opposed to small dealers. He reasoned that, in a public futures onion market, all information about the future price of onions is public. The current or spot price of onions has to be influenced by this public knowledge of future prices. No matter how large the onion dealer, that dealer could not use his market power to obtain a cash price for onions today that was much out of line with any other dealer's price. Thus, legislation—the suppression of information that would otherwise be provided by the public onion futures market—allowed large onion dealers to benefit.

The evidence concerning price fluctuations leaves little doubt that futures trading was a stabilizer. The Department of Agriculture found that fluctuations in cash prices of onions tended to be slightly but significantly smaller in the years with futures trading than in the years prior to that trading when a market did not exist even though it was legal. Further evidence presented by Professor Working showed that "while there was in effect a futures market, extreme price fluctuations occurred only about half as frequently as in other years [when there was no futures market operating]."[1]

[1] H. Working, "Spoiling the Broth," *Barron's*, vol. 43, February 1963, p. 22.

Definitions of New Terms

Futures Contract: A contract specifying the future date of delivery of a certain amount of a commodity and specifying the particular price to be paid on that date.

Spot Price: The price for immediate delivery of a commodity—on the "spot."

Speculation: The buying and selling of assets in the hope of making a profit on their price fluctuations.

Questions for Thought and Discussion

1. How do you think those who favored the abolition of the onion futures market managed to convince Congress to vote for that legislation?
2. "Without an open futures market, information about onion conditions is not as widely dispersed; therefore, insiders such as firms specializing in onions can benefit by their more exclusive access to information and opportunity to buy and sell onions." Evaluate this quote.
3. Is it possible not to be a speculator? *(Hint:* Do you own any assets?)
4. Why does speculation have such a negative connotation?

Selected References

Sandor, Richard I., *Speculating in Futures*, Chicago: Board of Trade of the City of Chicago, 1973.

Stevens, Neil A., "The Futures Market for Farm Commodities—What it Can Mean to Farmers," *Federal Reserve Bank of St. Louis Review*, August 1974, pp. 10–15.

Analyzing the Costs of a Business

In the last chapter the main focus was on the behavior of consumers and households. To fully analyze many economic questions concerning microeconomic behavior, a theory of how businesses work is also needed. Much of this chapter will deal with some of the tools needed to complete a model of businesses. Since the object is to develop a model, the representation will be simplified. It may not be a 100 percent accurate representation of what actually goes on inside a working business. We want to be able to predict what will happen to a group of businesses—let's say to an industry—when its economic environment changes. We want to know what producers will do if, for example, the government increases taxes on business profits. We want to be able to predict what will happen if the government prevents firms from hiring college students for summer work at wages below a legal minimum. This chapter will equip us with the tools to answer these questions.

Defining a Business

What is a business? Everybody knows that. It's the supermarket down the street, the dress shop around the corner, General Motors, Playboy Enterprises, American Telephone and Telegraph. The list will get very large indeed if we attempt to name every business in the United States. Everybody also knows that there is a difference between a corporate giant like General Motors and the local dress shop. In terms of our analysis, however, we will not usually make a distinction between these types of firms—except with regard to the market power they have—that is, the extent to which they control the setting of their prices. There are legal differences, of course, between **corporations, partnerships,** and single-owner **proprietorships.**

Corporations

A corporation is a legal entity owned by stockholders in the company. Stockholders are those who have purchased shares in the corporation. They are legally liable only for the amount of money they put in to buy those shares. For example, if you buy $2,000 worth of General Motors stock and General Motors goes bankrupt, the most you can lose is $2,000. General Motors' creditors cannot come pounding at your door asking for more.

Partnerships

A partnership involves two or more individuals who have joined together for business purposes but have decided not to form a corporation. In most instances, if you are a partner in a business, you can be liable to the point where you lose all your personal wealth. That is to say, if your partnership goes bankrupt and your creditors are owed $50,000, they can legally get it from you; they can force you to sell some of your assets to pay off the amount the partnership owed. Another distinction in a partnership is that whenever one partner decides to leave the business or when one partner dies, the partnership must be dissolved and a new business must be started. A corporation, however, can last forever. The owners of the corporation may change constantly, but the corporation as a legal business entity continues to live.

Proprietorships

The third form of business organization is a single-owner proprietorship. You're probably familiar with the corner grocery store that's owned by one woman, or a gardening service owned and operated by one man, or a motorcycle repair shop owned and operated by one person. If you own a business yourself, you are legally liable for all the debts incurred by the business.

The Firm

We still haven't come up with a precise definition of what a business is, even though all of us have a pretty good idea. Let's define a business, or **firm,** as follows:

A firm is an organization that brings together different factors of production such as labor, land, and capital, to produce a product or service which can be sold for a profit.

A typical firm will have the following organizational structure: entrepreneur, managers, and workers. The entrepreneur is the person who takes the chances. Because of this, the entrepreneur is the one who will get any profits that are made. The entrepreneur also decides who to hire to run the firm. Some economists maintain that the true entrepreneur is the person who knows how to pick good managers. Managers, in turn, are the ones who decide who should be hired and fired and how the business should generally be set up. The workers are the ones who ultimately use the machines to produce the products or services that are being sold by the firm.

The workers are paid wages. So, too, are the managers. However, it is the entrepreneurs who make the profits if there are any, for profits in economics accrue to those who are willing to take a risk. The term "profit" will be used many times in this microeconomic section.

Profit

Most people—business people included—think of profit as the difference between the amount of money the business takes in and the amount it spends for wages, materials, and so on. In a bookkeeping sense, the following formula could be used:

$$\text{Accounting profits} = \text{total revenues} - \text{total costs}$$

The trouble with this bookkeeping identification of profits is that costs are usually incorrectly figured, at least from an economic point of view.

Opportunity Cost of Capital

We have occasionally mentioned a *normal rate of return*. By this term we mean that people will not invest their wealth in a business unless they obtain a positive competitive rate of return—that is, unless their invested wealth pays off. Any business wishing to attract capital must expect to pay at least the same rate of return on that capital that all other businesses in a similar situation are willing to pay. For example, if individuals can invest their wealth in almost any publishing firm and get a rate of return of 6 percent per year, then every firm in the publishing business must expect to pay 6 percent as the normal rate of return. *This is a cost to them.* It is called the **opportunity cost of capital.** Capital will not stay in industries where the expected rate of return falls below its opportunity cost.

Forgetting the Opportunity Cost of Certain Other Inputs

Often, single-owner proprietorships grossly exaggerate their profit rates because they forget about the opportunity cost of the time that the proprietor spends in the business. For example, you may know people who run small grocery stores. These people, at the end of the year, will sit down and figure out what their profits were. They will add up all their sales and subtract what they had to pay to other workers, what they had to pay to their suppliers, what they had to pay in taxes, and so on. The end result they will call "profit." However, they will not have figured into their costs the salary that they could have made if they had worked for somebody else in a similar type of job. For somebody operating a grocery store, that salary might be equal to $3 an hour. If so, then $3 an hour is the opportunity cost of the grocery store owner's time. In many cases people who run their own businesses lose money in an economic sense. That is, their profits, as they calculate them, may be less than the amount of money they *could* have earned had they spent the same amount of time working for someone else. Take a numerical example. If an entrepreneur can earn $3 per hour, it follows that the opportunity cost of his or her time is $3 $\times$ 40 hours $\times$ 52 weeks, or $6,240. If this entrepreneur is making less than $6,240 in accounting profits, he or she is actually losing money.

We have spoken only of the opportunity cost of capital and the opportunity cost of labor, but we could have spoken in general of the opportunity cost of all inputs. Whatever the input may be, its opportunity cost must be taken into account in order to figure out true economic profits.

Accounting Profits ≠ Economic Profits

You should have a good idea by now of the meaning of profits in economics. Economic profits as opposed to accounting profits, do necessarily include the opportunity cost of capital invested in a business and the opportunity cost of the owner's time.

The term *profits* in economics means the money that entrepreneurs make, over and above their own opportunity cost plus the cost of the capital they have invested in their business. Profits can be regarded as total revenues minus total costs—which is how the accountants think of them—but we must now include *all* costs.

In most instances, we will use a model which assumes that the goal of a firm is to maximize profits. The firm, then, is expected to attempt to make the difference between total revenues and total costs as large as possible. We are going to use this model because it will allow us to analyze a firm's behavior. Whenever that model produces poor predictions, we will examine our initial assumption that the goal of the firm is to maximize profits. We might have to decide that the goal is to maximize the prestige of the owners, sales, the number of workers, and so on. When the firm produces its products in the quest for profit, we must ask under what constraints (conditions) it will produce. One of the most important of these is contained in the concept of diminishing returns.

The Relationship between Output and Inputs

A firm takes numerous inputs, feeds them into a technological production process, and ends up with an output. In economics an output might be the level of understanding of a subject and the attitude that students have toward it. The inputs, in this case, would be textbooks, professors, classrooms, and all forms of the hardware used in the instructional process. There are, of course, many, many factors of production, or inputs. Here we will consider only two broad categories: capital and labor. The relationship is as follows:

> Output per unit time period = some function of capital and labor

The time period here is important. Throughout the rest of this chapter we will consider a "short" time period as opposed to a "long" time period. In other words, we are looking at short-run production relationships and short-run costs associated with production.

Since we are dealing with the short run, we will make the simplifying assumption that capital remains fixed and invariable. That's not an unreasonable assumption—in a typical firm, the number of machines in place will not change over several months or even a year. The input that changes the most is labor. In our production relationship, then, capital is given and fixed; labor is variable.

The relationship between physical output and the quantity of capital and labor used in the production process is sometimes called a **production function.** Look at the first two columns of Table 17-1. Here we show a production function relating total output in column 2 to the quantity of labor measured in worker-weeks in column 1. When there are zero worker-weeks of input, there is no output. When there are 5 worker-weeks of input (given the capital stock), there is a total output of 50 bushels per week. (Ignore for the moment the rest of that table.) In Figure 17-1 we show this particular, hypothetical production function graphically. Note, again, that it relates to the short run and that it is for an individual firm.

The shape of the production function in Figure 17-1 is not a straight line. In fact, it peaks at 6 worker-weeks and starts to go down. To understand why such a phenomenon occurs with an individual firm in the short run, we have to analyze in greater detail the law of diminishing returns (see page 377).

Diminishing Returns

The concept of **diminishing (marginal) returns** applies to many different situations. For example, you may get diminishing returns from drinking another glass of beer—that is, your satisfaction may not be as great as that from the previous glass. However, that doesn't nec-

Table 17-1 Diminishing Returns: A Hypothetical Case in Agriculture

In the first column we measure the number of workers used per week on a given amount of land with a given amount of machinery and fertilizer and seed. In the second column we give their total product; that is, the output which each specified number of workers can produce in terms of bushels of wheat. The last column gives the marginal product. The marginal product is the difference between the output possible with a given number of workers minus the output made possible with one less worker. For example, the marginal produce of a fourth worker is 8 bushels of wheat. With 4 workers, 44 bushels are produced but with 3 workers only 36 are produced; the difference is 8.

INPUT OF LABOR NO. OF WORKER-WEEKS	TOTAL PRODUCT (OUTPUT IN BUSHELS OF WHEAT)	MARGINAL PHYSICAL PRODUCT (IN BUSHELS OF WHEAT)
0	0	
		10
1	10	
		16
2	26	
		10
3	36	
		8
4	44	
		6
5	50	
		4
6	54	
		2
7	56	
		−1
8	55	

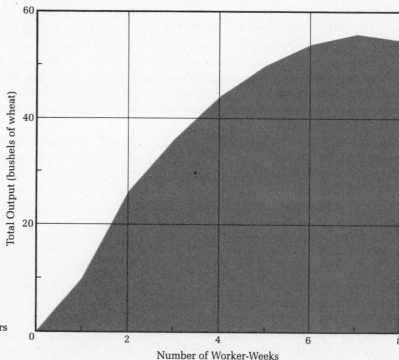

FIGURE 17-1 A Production Function

A production function relates outputs to inputs. We have merely taken the numbers off columns 1 and 2 of Table 17-1 and presented them here.

essarily mean you won't drink that glass of beer. In fact, if it is free, you'll probably drink it unless the returns you receive—pleasure or utility—are negative. You will continue drinking beer until the return in terms of happiness or utility is just equal to how much you have to pay for the beer. When beer is free, you'll keep drinking until the marginal return is zero. You certainly wouldn't stop just because you had reached the point of diminishing marginal returns.

The same is true of firms in the *use* of productive inputs. When the returns from hiring more workers are diminishing, it does not necessarily mean that more workers won't be hired. In fact, workers will be hired until the returns, in terms of the value of the extra output produced, are equal to the additional wages that have to be paid for those workers to produce the extra output. Before we get into that decision-making process, let's demonstrate that diminishing returns can be represented graphically and can be used in our analysis of the firm.

Measuring Diminishing Returns

How do we measure diminishing returns? First, we limit the analysis to only one factor of production (or input). Let's say that factor is labor. Every other factor of production, such as machines, must be held constant. Only in this way can we calculate the marginal returns from using more workers and know when we reach the point of diminishing marginal returns.

Marginal returns for productive inputs are also referred to as the **marginal physical product.** The marginal physical product of a worker, for example, is the increase in total product which occurs when that worker joins an already existing production process. The marginal productivity of labor, therefore, refers to the marginal increase in output caused by an increase in labor.

The marginal productivity of labor may increase from the very beginning. That is, a firm starts with no workers, only machines. The firm then hires one worker, who finds it difficult to get the work started. When the firm hires more workers, however, each is able to *specialize,* and the marginal productivity of those additional workers will actually be greater than it was with the previous few workers. Beyond some point, however, diminishing returns must set in; the firm will become so crowded that workers will start running into each other and will become less productive. Managers will have to be hired to organize the workers.

Using these ideas, we can define the law of diminishing returns as follows:

As successive equal increases of the variable factor of production, such as labor, are added to a fixed factor of production, such as capital, there will be a point beyond which the extra or marginal product that can be attributed to each additional unit of the variable factor of production will decline.

Diminishing returns merely refers to a situation where output rises less in proportion to an increase in, say, the number of workers employed.

An Example

The best example of the law of diminishing returns is found in agriculture. With a fixed amount of land, fertilizer, and tractors, the addition of more people eventually yields increases in output that are smaller than the increases in the variable input—the number of workers. A hypothetical set of numbers illustrating the marginal physical product of the law of diminishing marginal returns is presented in Table 17-1. The numbers are presented graphically in Figure 17-2. Marginal productivity (returns from adding more workers) first

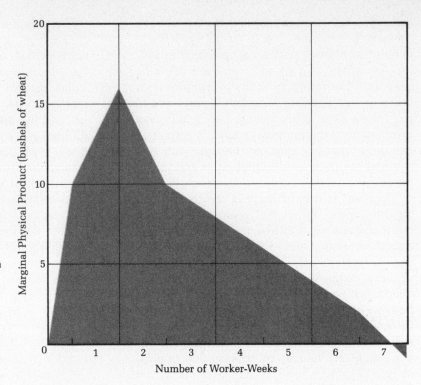

FIGURE 17-2 **Marginal Product— Diminishing Marginal Returns**

On the horizontal axis we plot the number of workers starting from 0 and going to 8. On the vertical axis we give the marginal product in bushels of wheat. With 0 workers there is 0 marginal product. With 1 worker, the marginal product is 10; with 2 workers, it is 16. Hence, at first we see increasing marginal returns to use of labor. But after 2 workers the marginal returns fall; there is diminishing marginal product. Diminishing returns have set in. Finally, the marginal return becomes negative after hiring 7 workers. The eighth worker's marginal product is −1 bushel. (We have approximated the curve by using the midpoints between the number of worker-weeks; that is why the curve peaks in between 1 and 2 worker-weeks.)

increases, then decreases, and finally becomes negative.

Short-Run Firm Costs

In the short run, a firm incurs certain types of costs. We will divide these **total costs** into fixed costs and variable costs. Then we will compute average and marginal costs.

Total Fixed Costs

Let's look at an ongoing business such as General Motors. The decision makers in that corporate giant can look around them and see big machines, thousands of parts, huge buildings, and a multitude of other pieces of plant and equipment that are in place, that have already been bought. General Motors has to take account of the wear and tear and technological obsolescence of these pieces of equipment no matter how many cars it produces. The payments on the loans taken out to buy the equipment will be exactly the same. The opportunity cost of any land that General Motors owns will be exactly the same. All costs which do not vary—that is, costs which do not depend on the rate of production—are called **fixed costs,** or *sunk* costs.

There is an old saying in economics that sunk costs are forever sunk. The cost of a lease, for example, is fixed for the duration of the lease. It is to be treated as a sunk cost; there is nothing the firm can do about it now. (Strictly speaking, a sunk investment is simply one that cannot be transferred to some other profitable use.)

Let's take as an example the costs incurred

by a manufacturer of leather purses. This firm's total costs will equal the cost of the rent on its equipment, the leather it buys, the thread it buys, the insurance it has to pay, the wages it has to pay, and so on. We see in Table 17-2 that total fixed costs per day are $10. In Figure 17-3, these total fixed costs are represented by the horizontal line at $10. They are invariant to changes in the output of purses per day—no matter how many are produced, fixed costs will remain at $10.

The difference between total costs and total fixed costs is total variable costs.

Total Variable Costs

Total **variable costs** are those costs whose magnitude varies with the rate of production per unit time period. The most obvious variable cost and probably the largest is wages paid. The more the firm produces, the more wages it has to pay. There are other variable costs, though. One is materials. In the production of leather purses, for example, leather must be bought. The more purses that are made, the more leather must be bought. The rate of depreciation (the rate of wear and tear) on machines that are used in the production process can also be considered a variable cost, if depreciation depends on how long and how intensively the machines are used. Total variable costs are given in Table 17-2 in column 3. These are translated into the total variable costs curve in Figure 17-3. Notice that it lies below the total cost curve by the vertical distance of $10. This vertical distance represents, of course, total fixed costs.

Short-Run Average Cost Curves

In Figure 17-3 we see total costs, total variable costs and total fixed costs. It is a matter of simple arithmetic to figure the averages of these

Table 17-2 **An Example of the Costs of Production**

TOTAL OUTPUT (Q/day) (1)	TOTAL FIXED COSTS (TFC) (2)	TOTAL VARIABLE COSTS (TVC) (3)	TOTAL COSTS (TC) (4) = (2) + (3)	AVERAGE FIXED COSTS (AFC) (5) = (2)/(1)	AVERAGE VARIABLE COSTS (AVC) (6) = (3)/(1)	AVERAGE TOTAL COSTS (ATC) (7) = (4)/(1)	MARGINAL COST (MC) (8) = $\frac{\text{Change in (4)}}{\text{Change in (1)}}$
0	$10.00	0	$10.00	0	0	0	
1	10.00	$ 5.00	15.00	$10.00	$ 5.00	$15.00	$5.00
2	10.00	8.00	18.00	5.00	4.00	9.00	3.00
3	10.00	10.00	20.00	3.33	3.33	6.67	2.00
4	10.00	11.00	21.00	2.50	2.75	5.25	1.00
5	10.00	13.00	23.00	2.00	2.60	4.60	2.00
6	10.00	16.00	26.00	1.67	2.67	4.33	3.00
7	10.00	20.00	30.00	1.43	2.86	4.28	4.00
8	10.00	25.00	35.00	1.25	3.13	4.38	5.00
9	10.00	31.00	41.00	1.11	3.44	4.56	6.00
10	10.00	38.00	48.00	1.00	3.80	4.80	7.00
11	10.00	46.00	56.00	.91	4.18	5.09	8.00

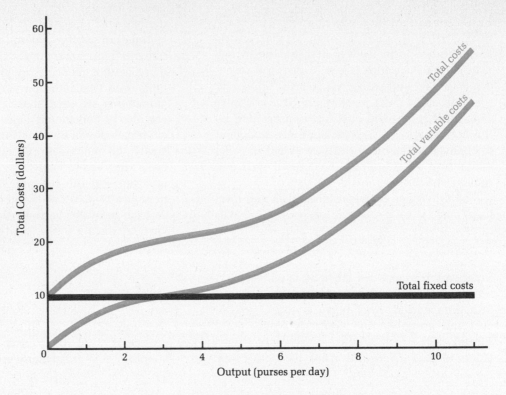

FIGURE 17-3 **Total Costs of Production**
This figure shows two total cost curves. The first one is total variable costs, obtained from column 3 in Table 17-2. When we add to total variable costs total fixed costs, which are represented by the horizontal line at $10, we obtain the total cost curve, which is merely the total variable cost curve moved up by a distance of $10.

three cost concepts. We can define them simply as follows:

$$\text{Average total costs} = \frac{\text{total costs}}{\text{output}}$$

$$\text{Average variable costs} = \frac{\text{total variable costs}}{\text{output}}$$

$$\text{Average fixed costs} = \frac{\text{total fixed costs}}{\text{output}}$$

The arithmetic is done in columns 5, 6, and 7 in Table 17-2. The numerical results are translated into graphical format in Figure 17-4. Let's see what we can observe about the three average cost curves on that graph.

Average Fixed Costs **Average fixed costs** continue to fall throughout the output range. In fact, if we were to continue the diagram farther to the right, we would find that average

fixed costs would get closer and closer to the horizontal axis. That is because total fixed costs remain constant. As we divide this fixed number by a larger and larger number of units of output, the result, AFC, has to become smaller and smaller.

Average Variable Costs The **average variable costs** curve has a U shape. First it falls dramatically, then it starts to rise. We can surmise that average variable costs start to rise after some point because, at some point in time, diminishing marginal returns will set in (the supply curve of the inputs is upward sloping).

Average Total Costs This curve has a shape similar to the average variable costs curve. However, it falls even more dramatically in the beginning and rises more slowly after it has

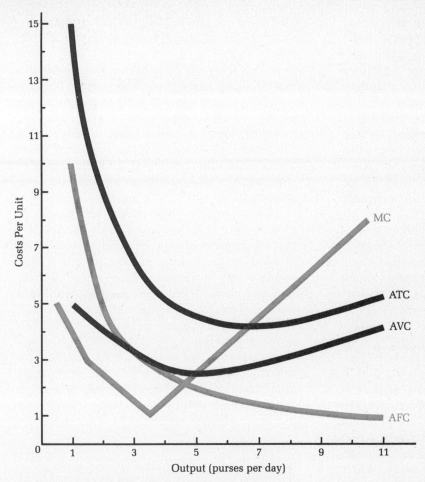

reached a minimum point. It falls and then rises because ATC is the summation of the average fixed costs curve and the average variable costs curve. Thus, when AFC plus AVC are both falling, it is only logical that ATC would fall too. At some point, however, AVC starts to increase while AFC continues to fall. Once the increase in the AVC curve outweighs the decrease in the AFC curve, the ATC curve will start to increase and will develop its familiar U shape.

Note that sometimes average total costs are called *average unit costs;* the word "unit" is usually implied and is not always given.

Marginal Cost

We have stated repeatedly in this text that the action is always on the margin—movement in economics is always determined at the margin. This dictum holds true within the firm also. Firms, according to the analysis we use to predict their behavior, are very interested in their **marginal costs.** Since the term "marginal" means additional or incremental, marginal costs refer to those costs that result from additional or incremental changes in production rates. For example, if the production of 10 leather purses costs a firm $48 and the production of 11 leather purses costs it $56, then the marginal cost of producing that additional leather purse is $8.

We find marginal cost by subtracting the total cost of producing all but the last unit from the total cost of producing all units, including the last one. We show the marginal costs of purse production per day in column 8 of Table 17-2, where marginal cost is defined as the change in total cost divided by the change in output. In our particular example, we have changed output by one unit every time, so we can ignore the denominator in that particular formula.

This marginal cost schedule is shown graphically in Figure 17-4. Just like average variable costs and average total costs, marginal costs first fall and then rise. It is interesting to look at the relationship between marginal costs and average costs.

The Relationship between Average and Marginal Costs

There is a relationship between average variable costs and marginal costs. When average variable costs are falling, marginal costs are less than average variable costs. Conversely, when average variable costs are rising, marginal costs are greater than average variable costs. When you think about it, the relationship is obvious. The only way for average variable costs to fall is for the variable cost of the marginal unit produced to be less than the average variable cost of all the preceding units. For example, if the average variable cost for two units of production is $4 a unit, the only way for the average variable cost of three units to fall is for the variable costs attributable to the last unit—the marginal cost—to be less than the average of the past units. In this particular case, if average variable cost falls to $3.33 a unit, then total variable cost for the three units would be three times $3.33, or $10. Total variable cost for two units is two times $4 or $8.

The marginal cost is, therefore, $10 minus $8, or $2, which is less than the average variable cost of $3.33.

A similar type of computation can be carried out for rising average variable costs. The only way for average variable costs to rise is for the average variable cost of additional units to cost more than that for units already produced. But the incremental cost is the marginal cost. Therefore, in this particular case, the marginal costs have to be higher than the average variable costs.

There is also a relationship between marginal costs and average total costs. Remember that average total cost is equal to total cost divided by the number of units produced. Remember also that marginal cost is not affected by fixed costs. Fixed costs are, by definition, fixed and cannot influence marginal costs. The above example can be repeated substituting the term *average total cost* for the term *average variable cost*. The arithmetic will be slightly different, but the result will be the same. Marginal cost equals average total cost when the latter is at its minimum.

Finding Minimum Costs

At what rate of output of leather purses per day does our representative firm experience the minimum average total costs? Column 7 in Table 17-2 shows that the minimum average total cost is $4.28, which occurs at an output rate of seven leather purses per day. We can find this minimum cost also by finding the point on Figure 17-4 at which the marginal cost curve intersects the average total costs curve. This should not be surprising. When average total costs are falling, marginal cost will be less than average total cost. When average total costs are rising, marginal cost will be greater than average total cost. At the point where average total costs stop falling and start rising, marginal cost must then be equal to average total cost.

When we represent this graphically, the marginal cost curve will intersect the average total costs curve at its minimum.

The same analysis applies to the intersection of the marginal cost curve and the average variable cost curve. When are average variable costs at a minimum? According to Table 17-2, average variable costs are at a minimum of $2.60 at an output rate of five leather purses a day. This is exactly where the marginal cost curve intersects the average variable costs curve in Figure 17-4.

Definitions of New Terms

Corporation: A legal entity owned by stockholders. The stockholders are liable only for the amount of money they have invested in the company.

Partnership: A business entity involving two or more individuals who join together for business purposes but who have not incorporated. In many instances the partners are liable for the debts of the business to such an extent that they can lose their personal wealth if the business loses money.

Proprietorship: A business owned by only one person.

Firm: An organization that brings together different factors of production, such as labor, land, and capital, to produce a product or service which can be sold for a profit. A firm is usually made up of an entrepreneur, managers, and workers.

Opportunity Cost of Capital: The normal rate of return or that amount which must be paid to an investor to induce her or him to invest in a business.

Production Function: The relationship between inputs and output. A production function is a technological, not an economic, relationship.

Diminishing (Marginal) Returns: Usually referred to as the law of diminishing marginal returns. After some point, successive increases in a variable factor of production, such as labor, added to fixed factors of production, will not result in a proportional increase in output.

Marginal Physical Product: The physical output which is due to the addition of one more unit of a variable factor of production—that is, the increase in total product occurring when a variable input is increased and all other inputs are held constant.

Total Costs: All the costs of a firm combined, including rent, payments to workers, interest on borrowed money, and so on.

Fixed Costs: Those costs that do not vary depending on output. Fixed costs include such things as rent on the building and the price of the machinery.

Variable Costs: Those costs that vary with the rate of production. They include wages paid to workers, the costs of materials, and so on.

Average Fixed Costs: Total fixed costs divided by the number of units produced.

Average Variable Costs: Total variable costs divided by the number of units produced.

Average Total Costs: Total costs divided by the number of units produced; sometimes called average per unit total costs.

Marginal Costs: The increment in total costs due to an increase of 1 unit of production.

Chapter
Summary

1. When analyzing a business, we define it as any organization that brings together different factors of production in order to produce a good or service which hopefully can be sold for a profit. Firms are typically made up of entrepreneurs, managers, and workers.

2. Accounting profits are the difference between total revenues and total costs. However, economic profits are usually different. We define economic profits as total revenues minus total costs where all costs are included. These would be, in addition to everything the accountant sees, the opportunity cost of capital (normal rate of return) and the opportunity cost of the owner's working time.

3. The normal rate of return on capital is the yield which is necessary to keep that capital in a particular business or industry. That rate might be 7 percent or 10 percent, for example. The 7 or 10 percent yield is a cost and is not part of economic profits.

4. When all factors of production are fixed except one, that one factor can be increased. But eventually, as that factor is increased, output will increase less than proportionately. This is called the law of diminishing marginal returns. At some point the marginal product attributable to an increase in the variable factor of production diminishes.

5. Marginal physical product is also a measure of productivity. We say that the productivity of workers has gone up if their marginal physical product increases—that is, if the amount of output that they can produce on the margin goes up.

6. The least cost production solution for a firm is to make equal the marginal product of every factor divided by its price.

7. A firm faces numerous costs. Economists like to separate these costs into fixed and variable, and then further into average and marginal costs.

8. Fixed costs are those that are sunk and cannot be eliminated. Average fixed costs are just total fixed costs divided by the quantity of production. Average fixed costs will forever fall.

9. Variable costs are those that vary with the amount of output. The most obvious, and usually the largest, variable cost is the cost of labor. As more laborers are hired, the wage bill goes up. Average variable costs are total variable costs divided by the number of units of output.

10. Marginal costs are those that can be attributed to an increase in production of one unit. Marginal costs are always below average costs when average costs are falling. Marginal costs are always above average costs when average costs are rising. Therefore, marginal cost is equal to average cost when average costs are at a minimum.

11. The average total cost curve is typically U shaped. Even though the average fixed costs are falling forever, at some point diminishing returns set in and variable costs start to rise, thus causing the average total cost curve to rise.

Questions for Thought and Discussion

1. If opportunity costs are not entered in the accounting records of a firm, what good are they?
2. Why do the average variable cost curve and the average total cost curve have a U shape?
3. It is sometimes said that in the long run there is no such thing as fixed costs. Can you figure out why?
4. We have shown that when average costs are falling, marginal costs are less than average costs, and when average costs are rising, marginal costs are more than average costs. Can the same relationship be applied to average product and marginal product?
5. Why do you think the corporation is such a popular form of business organization?
6. It is sometimes said that the most important thing is marginal cost. Do you agree or disagree? Why?
7. If you were setting up a new business, do you think you would expect to recoup your investment in the first year?
8. The effects of a unit tax on the cost curves of Sunshinesea Surfboards can be seen by comparing the tables below. Plot the data in Table 2, then compare the results. What happens to the AFC curve? The AVC curve? The ATC curve? The MC curve?

(a) Table 1: Sunshinesea Surfboards before the Unit Tax

	Total Costs Per Day			Unit Costs Per Day			
(a) TP	(b) TFC	(c) TVC	(d) TC	(e) AFC	(f) AVC	(g) ATC	(h) MC
0	$50	$ 0	$50				
1	50	40	90	$50.00	$40.00	$90.00	$40
2	50	75	125	25.00	37.50	62.50	35
3	50	105	155	16.67	35.00	51.67	30
4	50	130	180	12.50	32.50	45.00	25
5	50	150	200	10.00	30.00	40.00	20
6	50	165	215	8.33	27.50	35.83	15
7	50	185	235	7.14	26.43	33.57	20
8	50	215	265	6.25	26.88	33.13	30
9	50	260	310	5.56	28.89	34.44	45
10	50	330	380	5.00	33.00	38.00	70

(b) Complete the table.

Table 2: Sunshinesea Surfboards after the Unit Tax

	Total Costs per Day				Unit Costs per Day			
(a) TP	*(b)* TFC	*(c)* Tax Bill	*(d)* TVC	*(e)* TC	*(f)* AFC	*(g)* AVC	*(h)* ATC	*(i)* MC
0	50	0	0	50	. . .	. . .	. . .	45
1	50	5	45	95	50	45	90	
2								
.								
.								
.								
10								

Selected
References

Haynes, W. Warren, *Managerial Economics: Analysis and Cases*, rev. ed., Austin, Texas: Business Publications, 1969, chaps. 5 and 6.

Watson, Donald S. (ed.), *Price Theory in Action*, 2d ed., Boston: Houghton Mifflin, 1969, part III.

The Firm in Competition

In Chapter 17 we looked at the cost curves of an individual firm. Now we will look at how individual firms set their prices and how each firm decides the amount to produce. To do this, we must first have some information on the characteristics of firms. Usually, firms in our economy fit into one of two categories: competitive firms or monopoly firms. Of course, between these two categories lies an entire spectrum of possible degrees of competitiveness. For our analysis here, though, we'll concentrate on a more or less perfectly competitive market situation.

Characteristics of a Competitive Firm

Although there is no one definition of a purely **competitive firm,** most economists will agree with the following: The competitive firm is such a small part of the total industry in which it operates that it cannot greatly affect the price of the product in question.

This notion of competition relates in one sense to the number of competitors in an industry. A competitive industry usually has a large number of firms in it. Admittedly, no one knows exactly what this number must be. But the number must be large enough so as to ensure that no single firm has control over the price of the product. The number must be large enough so that each firm in the industry is a **price taker**—the firm takes prices as given, as something which is determined outside the individual firm.

The price that is given to the firm is determined by the forces of market supply and market demand. That is to say, when all individual consumer's demands are added together into a market demand curve, and all the supply schedules of individual firms are added together into a market supply curve, the intersection of those two curves will give the market price which the purely competitive or price-taking firm must accept.

This definition of a competitive firm is obviously idealized for, in one sense, the *individual* firm has to set prices. How can we ever have a situation where firms regard prices as set by forces outside their control? The answer is that even though every firm by definition sets its own prices, a firm in a more or less perfectly competitive situation will find that it will eventually have no customers at all if it sets its price above the competitive price. Let us now see what the demand curve of an individual firm in a competitive industry looks like graphically.

Single-Firm Demand Curve

In Chapter 3 we talked about the characteristics of demand schedules. We pointed out that for completely elastic demand curves, if the individual firm raises the price one penny, it will lose all business completely. Well, this is how we characterize the demand schedule for a purely competitive firm—it is a horizontal line at the going market price; that is, it is completely elastic (see Chapter 3). And that going market price is determined by the market forces of supply and demand. Figure 18-1 is the hypothetical market demand schedule faced by an individual leather purse producer who sells a very, very small part of the total leather purse production in the industry. At the market price, this firm can sell all the output it wants. At

FIGURE 18-1 **The Demand Curve for an Individual Leather Purse Producer**
We assume that the individual purse producer is such a small part of the total market that he or she cannot influence the price. The firm accepts the price as given. And at the going market price, it faces a horizontal demand curve, *dd*. If it raises its price even one penny, it will sell no purses. The firm would be foolish to lower its price below $5 because it can sell all that it can produce at a price of $5. The firm's demand curve is completely or perfectly elastic.

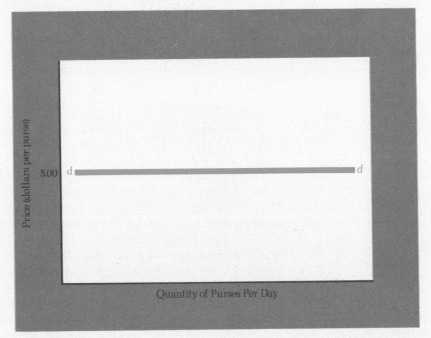

the market price of $5 each, which is where the horizontal demand curve for the individual producer lies, peoples' demand for the leather purses of that one producer is perfectly elastic. If the firm raises its price, they will buy from some other producer. (Why not worry about lowering the price?) We label the individual producer's demand curve dd, whereas the market demand curve is always labeled DD.

How Much Does the Perfect Competitor Produce?

As we have shown, a perfect competitor has to accept the given price of the product. If the firm raises its price, it sells nothing. If it lowers its price, it makes less money per unit sold than it otherwise could. The firm has only one decision variable left: How much should it produce? We will apply our model of the firm to this to come up with an answer. We'll use the *profit maximization* model, and assume that firms, whether competitive or monopolistic, will attempt to maximize their profits—that is, the difference between total revenue and total cost.

Total Revenues

Every firm has to consider **total revenues.** Total revenues are defined as the quantities sold multiplied by the price. They are also the same as total receipts from the sale of output. For a perfectly competitive firm, total revenues are quite easy to find. They equal total sales times the per-unit price—which the competitor cannot change because of the nature of the demand schedule facing the firm.

Look at Table 18-1. Much of the information comes from Table 17-2, but we have added some essential columns for our analysis. Column 3 is the market price of $5 per purse. Column 4 shows the total revenues, or TR, as equal to the market price, P, times the total

output in sales per day, or Q. Thus, TR = P × Q. We are assuming that the market supply and demand schedules intersect at a price of $5 and that this price holds for all the firm's production. We also assume that since our purse maker is a small part of the market, it can sell all it produces. Thus, Figure 18-2 (a) shows the total revenue curve as a straight line. For every unit of sales, total revenue is increased by $5.

Total Costs

Revenues are only one side of the picture. Costs must also be considered. **Total costs** are given in column 2 in Table 18-1. Notice that when we plot total costs on Figure 18-2 (a), the curve is not a straight line but rather a wavy line which is first above the total revenue curve, then below it, and then above it again. When the total costs curve is above the total revenue curve, the firm is having losses. When it is below the total revenue curve, the firm is making profits, or net revenues (revenues after costs are subtracted). We will use the term profits here and throughout the rest of this chapter.

Comparing Total Costs with Total Revenues

By comparing total costs with total revenues, we can figure out the number of leather purses the individual competitive firm should produce per day. Our analysis rests on the assumption that the firm will attempt to maximize total profits. In Table 18-1 we see that total profits reach a maximum at a production rate of between seven and eight leather purses per day. We can see this graphically in Figure 18-2 (a). The firm will maximize profits at that place on the graph where the total revenue curve exceeds the total cost curve by the greatest amount. That occurs at a rate of output and

Table 18-1 The Costs of Production and the Revenues from the Sale of Output: Finding the Profit-Maximization Rate of Output and Sales

Profit maximization occurs at a rate of sales of either seven or eight purses per day.

TOTAL OUTPUT AND SALES PER DAY (1)	TOTAL COST (TC) (2)	MARKET PRICE (P) (3)	TOTAL REVENUE (TR) (4) = (3) × (1)	PROFIT = (TR) − (TC) (5) = (4) − (2)	AVERAGE TOTAL COST (ATC) (6) = (2)/(1)	AVERAGE VARIABLE COST (AVC)* (7)	MARGINAL COST (MC) (8) = $\frac{\text{Change in (2)}}{\text{Change in (1)}}$	MARGINAL REVENUE (MR) (9) = $\frac{\text{Change in (4)}}{\text{Change in (1)}}$
0	$10.00	$5.00	0	−$10.00	0	0		
1	15.00	5.00	$ 5.00	− 10.00	$15.00	$5.00	$5.00	$5.00
2	18.00	5.00	10.00	− 8.00	9.00	4.00	3.00	5.00
3	20.00	5.00	15.00	− 5.00	6.67	3.33	2.00	5.00
4	21.00	5.00	20.00	− 1.00	5.25	2.75	1.00	5.00
5	23.00	5.00	25.00	2.00	4.60	2.60	2.00	5.00
6	26.00	5.00	30.00	4.00	4.33	2.67	3.00	5.00
7	30.00	5.00	35.00	5.00	4.28	2.86	4.00	5.00
8	35.00	5.00	40.00	5.00	4.38	3.12	5.00	5.00
9	41.00	5.00	45.00	4.00	4.56	3.44	6.00	5.00
10	48.00	5.00	50.00	2.00	4.80	3.80	7.00	5.00
11	56.00	5.00	55.00	1.00	5.09	4.18	8.00	5.00

*Taken from Table 17-2

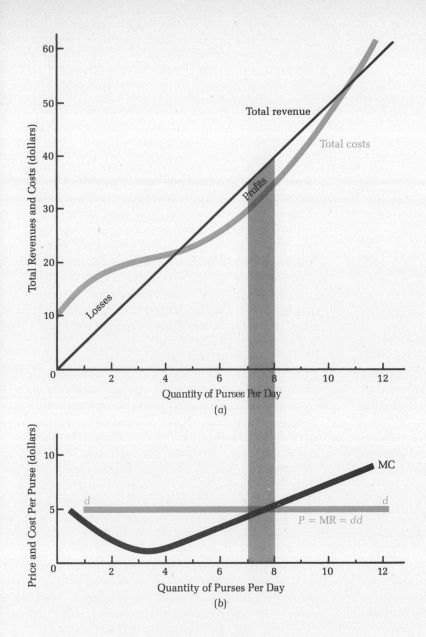

Total revenues are represented by the straight line, showing that each purse sells at $5. Total costs first exceed total revenues, then are less than total revenues, and then exceed them again. We find maximum profits where total revenues exceed total costs by the largest amount. This occurs at a rate of production and sales per day of seven or eight purses.

(b) **Profit Maximization Using Marginal Analysis**

Profit maximization occurs where marginal revenue equals marginal cost. Marginal revenue is represented by the individual firm demand curve, *dd*, which is a horizontal line at $5. The marginal cost curve is represented by MC. It intersects the marginal revenue curve at a rate of output in sales of somewhere between seven and eight purses per day.

sales of either seven or eight purses per day; this rate is called the *profit-maximizing rate of production*.

We can also find this profit-maximizing rate of production for the individual competitive firm by looking at marginal revenues and marginal costs.

Using Marginal Analysis

Marginal cost was introduced in Chapter 17. It was defined as the increment in total cost due to a one-unit increase in production. This leaves only **marginal revenue** to be defined.

Marginal Revenue

What amount can our individual purse making firm hope to receive each time it sells an additional (marginal) leather purse? Since the firm is such a small part of the market and cannot influence the price, it must accept the price determined by the market forces of supply and demand. Therefore, the firm knows it will receive $5 for every purse it puts on the market. So the additional revenue the firm will receive from selling one more purse is equal to the market price of $5; marginal revenue, in this case, equals price.

Marginal revenue represents the increment in total revenues attributable to selling one additional unit of the product in question. In a perfectly competitive market, the marginal revenue curve is exactly equivalent to the price line, which is exactly equivalent to the individual firm demand curve. Thus, in Figure 18-1, the demand curve *dd* for the individual producer is at a price of $5—the price line is coincident with the demand curve. But so too is the marginal revenue curve for marginal revenue in this case also equals $5.

The marginal revenue curve for our competitive leather purse producer is shown as a horizontal line at $5 in Figure 18-2 (b). Notice that the marginal revenue curve is equal to the price line, which is equal to the individual firm demand curve *dd*.

When Profits Are Maximized

Now we add the marginal cost curve, MC, taken from column 8 in Table 18-1. As shown in Figure 18-2 (b), the marginal cost curve first falls, then starts to rise, eventually intersecting the marginal revenue curve and then rising above it. Notice that the numbers for both the marginal cost schedule and the marginal revenue schedule in Table 18-1 are printed between the figures which determine them. This indicates that we are looking at a change between one rate of output and the next.

In Figure 18-2 (b), look at point A on the marginal cost curve. Here the marginal cost is obviously below what the leather purse firm can obtain if it produces and sells one more unit of output. Since it can receive $5 per purse, and since marginal cost is less than this marginal revenue, the firm has an incentive to increase production. In fact, it has an incentive to produce and sell until the amount of the additional revenue received from selling one more purse just equals the additional cost incurred from producing and selling that purse. This is how it maximizes profit. If marginal cost is less than marginal revenue, the firm will always make more profit by increasing production because the increased revenues will be greater than the increased costs.

Now, if the firm is producing at a point above the *dd* or marginal revenue curve—say, at B—it will be making smaller profits than it otherwise could. At B, marginal cost exceeds the price which can be received on that additional output. The individual producer is spending more to produce that additional output than it is receiving in revenues. The firm would be foolish to continue producing at this rate.

But where, then, should it produce? It should produce at point E, where the marginal cost curve intersects the marginal revenue curve. Since it knows it can sell all the purses it wants at the going market price, marginal revenue from selling an additional purse will always equal the market price. Consequently, it should continue production until the cost of increasing output by one more unit is just equal to the revenues obtainable from that extra unit. *Profit maximization is always at the point where marginal revenue equals marginal cost.* (To be strictly correct, we should add "and the MC curve cuts the MR curve from below.") For a perfectly competitive firm, this is at the intersection of the demand schedule, *dd*, and the marginal cost curve, MC. In our particular example, our profit-maximizing, perfectly competitive leather purse producer will produce at a rate of between seven and eight purses a day.

Notice that this same profit-maximizing rate of output is shown in both Figure 18-2 *(a)*, where the total revenue/total cost curve is drawn, and in Figure 18-2 *(b)*, where the marginal revenue/marginal cost curve is drawn. We can find the profit-maximizing output solution for the perfectly competitive firm by looking at either diagram.

Finding the Firm's Short-Run Profits

To find what our individual, competitive leather purse producer is making in terms of profits in the short run, we have to add the average total cost curve to Figure 18-2 *(b)*. We take the information from column 6 in Table 18-1 and add it to Figure 18-2 *(b)* to get Figure 18-3. Again the profit-maximizing rate of output is between seven and eight purses per day. If we have production and sales of seven purses

per day, total revenues will be $35. Total costs will be $30, leaving a profit of $5. If the rate of output in sales is eight purses per day, total revenues will be $40 and total costs will be $35, again leaving a profit of $5.

It is certainly possible, also, for the competitive firm to make short-run losses. We give an example in Figure 18-4. Here we show the demand curve shifting from *dd* to *d'd'*. The going market price has fallen from $5 to $3 per purse because of changes in market supply and/or demand conditions. The profit-maximizing price is still where marginal revenue equals marginal cost. Now it occurs somewhere between five and six purses per day. In this case, however, producing where marginal revenue equals marginal cost only minimizes losses.

The Break-Even Point

We now add the average variable cost curve (AVC) to our graph to get Figure 18-5 (see page 396). We again draw the two hypothetical demand curves, *dd* and *d'd'*.

Let's look at demand curve *dd*. It just touches the minimum point of the average total cost curve, which, as you will remember, is exactly where the marginal cost curve intersects the average total cost curve. At that price, which is about $4.30, the firm will be making exactly zero short-run profits. Thus, that particular price is called the short-run break-even price. And point E is therefore called the **short-run break-even point** for a competitive firm. It is the point at which marginal revenue = marginal cost = average total cost. The break-even price is the one that yields zero short-run profits.

The Meaning of Zero Economic Profits

Although we have been talking about profit maximization in the context of a perfectly

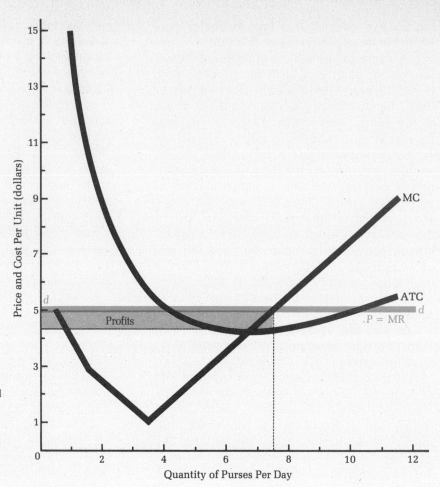

FIGURE 18-3 Measuring Profits

The profit-maximizing rate of output in sales is where marginal revenue equals marginal cost. Profits are the difference between total revenues and total costs. Total revenues will equal the rate of output in sales times the market price of $5. Total costs will equal the quantity produced and sold multiplied by average total cost (ATC). Profits are represented by the shaded area.

competitive situation, in strict economic terminology, a firm in a perfectly competitive industry, in the long run, will have a tendency to make zero economic profits. Why would any firm want to work for zero profits? Why would business people even bother?

Recall our definition of true economic profits. They were the returns over and above a normal or competitive rate of return. That is, profits in economics are defined as those returns in excess of the opportunity cost to the factors of production. Therefore, a firm in a perfectly competitive industry might make zero economic profits, while making 7 percent accounting profits at the same time. Those 7 percent accounting profits merely represent the rate of return on investment that is necessary to keep the businessperson from going into another business. Notice that we labeled the break-even price in Figure 18-5 as the short-run break-even price. This is because that price is actually necessary in the long run just to keep this particular firm in business. In the long run, we would have to call that price the going-out-

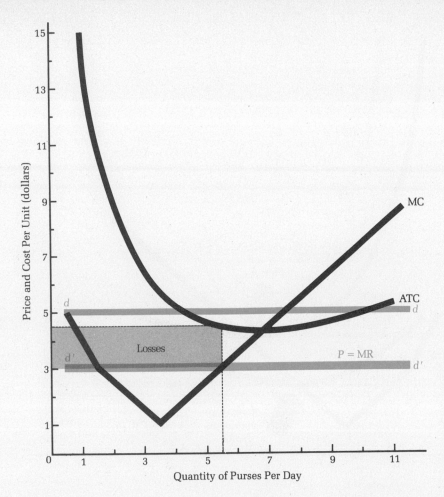

FIGURE 18-4 **Minimizing Short-Run Losses**

In cases where average total costs exceed the average revenue or price, profit maximization is equivalent to loss minimization. This again occurs where marginal cost equals marginal revenue. Losses are shown in the shaded area.

of-business price because it would not pay in the long run for the firm to remain in business if the price were to fall below the level which yields zero economic profits, that is, normal accounting profits.

Average Costs and Profits in the Long Run

We surmise, then, that, in the long run, firms will tend to have average total cost curves which just touch the price = marginal revenue,

or individual demand curve *dd*. That is, in the long run, in a competitive situation, firms will be making zero economic profits. Of course, in the real world, at a particular point in time, it would be pure luck for a firm to be making exactly zero economic profits because nothing is as exact as the curves we use to simplify our analysis. Things change all the time in the dynamic world, and firms, even in a very competitive situation, may, for many reasons, be making nonzero profits. But in our analysis, we say that, in the long run, competition leads to

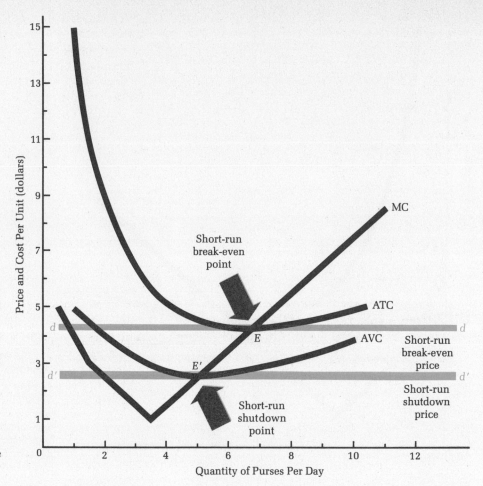

FIGURE 18-5 Short-Run Shutdown and Break-Even Prices

We can find the short-run break-even price and the short-run shutdown price by comparing the price with average total costs and average variable costs. If the demand curve is *dd*, then profit maximization occurs at point *E*, where MC = marginal revenue (the *dd* curve). Assuming now that the ATC curve includes all relevant opportunity costs, then point *E* is the short-run break-even point and zero economic profits are being made. If the demand curve falls to *d'd'*, then profit maximization (loss minimization) occurs at the intersection of MC and MR (the *d'd'* curve) or *E'*. Below this point, it does not pay the firm to continue in operation because its average variable costs are not covered by the price of the product.

zero economic profits. This is so due to the entry of new firms into the industry, which leads us to another market aspect that characterizes a perfectly competitive industry.

An industry that is perfectly competitive must have no **barriers to entry,** such as government restrictions on who can start a business, excessive capital costs, and so on. Other firms must be able to start a competing business without restriction. Thus, if we were to observe a situation such as that represented in Figure 18-3, where short-run economic profits were being made, we would expect firms to enter

the industry. Their entry would drive down the price so that eventually economic profits would not be made and then the short-run break-even price represented in Figure 18-5 would be reached. Profits would ultimately fall to zero as the *dd* curve (price line) fell.

Distinguishing between the Short and the Long Run

The long-run concept of zero economic profits being made in a competitive industry cannot be stressed too much. Although at any moment there may be nonzero profits accruing to a large number of firms, eventually free entry will allow other firms into the industry to seek those profits. This will cause the price to fall so that profits will no longer be made. Then entry will stop and the situation will be stabilized. We could look at it from another angle. If, instead, there were short-run economic losses as depicted in Figure 18-4, then firms would leave the industry. As firms left the industry, the supply would be reduced and the price would rise to the point where losses were no longer being made.

The Shutdown Point

Will a firm necessarily go out of business if it finds itself in a situation such as that depicted in Figure 18-4? No. It is, to be sure, incurring short-run economic losses, but it will not necessarily go out of business. In fact, it will not even necessarily shut down for a while. Look at the situation in Figure 18-5. Take a price below the short-run break-even price. As long as that price exceeds the average variable cost curve (AVC), and continues to produce at the profit-maximizing (or loss-minimizing) rate of output, then it will continue to minimize its losses. The profit-maximizing rate, of course, occurs at the intersection of the marginal cost curve and the marginal revenue (*dd* or price line) curve.

A simple example will demonstrate this situation. Let the price of a product be $8. Let average total costs equal $9 at an output of 100. In this hypothetical example, average total costs are broken up into average variable costs of $7 and average fixed costs of $2. Total revenues, then, equal $8 × 100 or $800, and total costs equal $9 × 100 or $900. Total losses, therefore, equal $100. However, this does not mean the firm has to shut down. After all, if it does shut down, it still has fixed costs to pay. And in this case, since average fixed costs equal $2 at an output of 100, the fixed costs are $200. Thus, the firm has losses of $100 if it continues to produce but has losses of $200 (the fixed costs) if it shuts down. The logic is fairly straightforward: As long as the price per unit sold exceeds the average variable cost per unit produced, the firm will be paying for at least part of the opportunity costs of capital invested in the business. Although the price is below average total cost and the firm is not making a normal or competitive rate of return on its investment, at least it's making some return—and in many cases, a small rate of return on an investment is better than no rate of return at all.

However, at some point, of course, it does become most profitable to shut down. Because in the long run no costs are fixed, there will be no replacement of depreciated capital.

Another potential demand curve in Figure 18-5 is represented by *d'd'*. Notice that it just touches the average variable cost curve at its minimum point, which is where the marginal cost curve intersects. This price is labeled the short-run shutdown price. Why? Because below this price it is most profitable to shut down operations. If the price does not even cover average variable cost, then not only is there nothing left over as a rate of return to capital, but there is not even enough to pay those expenses that are incurred only if production is continued—the variable costs. (Of course, if price falls below the short-run shutdown price, a firm may still continue in business in the short run, if it decides it can afford to wait until the price moves up again, and it can profitably reenter production.)

The intersection of the price line, the marginal cost curve, and the average variable cost is labeled E'. We called it the **short-run shutdown point.** This point is labeled short run because, of course, in the long run, the firm will not produce below a price that yields a normal rate of return and hence zero economic profits.

Now we are ready to derive the firm's supply curve.

The Firm's Supply Curve

What does the supply curve for the individual firm look like? Actually, we have been looking at it all along. We know that when the price of purses is $5, the firm will supply seven or eight purses per day. If the price falls to $3, the firm will supply five or six purses per day; and if the price falls below $3, the firm will shut down in the short run. Hence in Figure 18-6 the marginal cost curve becomes the individual firm's supply curve above the short-run shutdown point. This is shown as the heavily shaded part of the marginal cost curve. The definition, then, of the individual firm's supply curve in a competitive industry is its marginal cost curve above the point of intersection with the average variable cost curve.

The Industry Supply Curve

Now let's see what the market supply curve, or the supply curve for the entire industry, looks like. First, what is an industry? Isn't it merely a collection of firms producing a particular product? Yes, and therefore we have a way to figure out the total supply curve of, for example, leather purses. To do this, we merely add, for every price on the vertical axis, the quantities that each firm will supply. In other words, we horizontally add the individual supply curves of all the competitive firms. But the individual supply curves, as we just saw, are simply the marginal cost curves of each firm. Therefore, in Figure 18-7 we have drawn the industry supply curve as the horizontal sum of the marginal cost curves, where Σ stands for summation. In other words, ΣMC equals

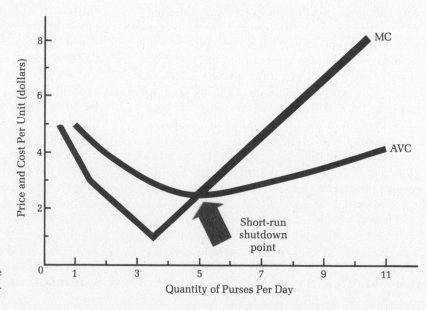

FIGURE 18-6 **The Individual Firm's Supply Curve**

The individual firm's supply curve is that portion of its marginal cost curve above the average variable cost curve.

(loosely stated) the MC curve of firm 1 plus the MC curve of firm 2 plus the MC curve of firm 3 and so on. Therefore, the supply curve is positively sloped.

Competitive Price Determination

How is the market, or "going," price established in a competitive market? This price is established by the interaction of all the firms and all the demanders. The market demand schedule DD in Figure 18-7 represents the demand schedule for the entire industry, and the supply schedule SS represents the supply schedule for the entire industry. Price P_e is established by the forces of supply and demand at the intersection of SS and DD. Even though each individual producer has no control or effect on the price of his product in a competitive industry, the interaction of all the producers determines the price at which the product will be sold. We say that the price P_e and the quantity q in Figure 18-7 is the competitive unrestricted solution to the pricing/quantity problem in that particular industry. It is the equilibrium where suppliers and demanders are content. The resulting individual demand curve dd is shown in Figure 18-8 at the price P_e.

The Long and the Short of a Competitive Supply Curve

In Figure 18-7 we drew the summation of all the marginal cost curves as an upward-sloping supply curve for the entire industry. We should be aware, however, that a relatively steep upward-sloping supply curve is really only appropriate in the short run. After all, one of the prerequisites for a competitive industry is that there are no restrictions on entry. We expect, therefore, that, if the demand schedule shifts out to the right (there is increasing demand for the product in question), eventually more firms will enter the market so that the quantity supplied can also be expanded. In fact, each time the demand curve shifts out to the right, the prices can be expected to rise. But this means nonzero economic profits for the current producers. Therefore, more producers will enter the market and force the price down to its old equilibrium level—assuming costs in the industry remain constant.

Such an industry is called a *constant-cost industry*. Its long-run supply curve is given in (a) of Figure 18-9. However, it is also possible that costs will not remain constant; they may either rise or fall. The first situation might occur because a large number of firms demanding more raw materials causes the price of raw materials to rise somewhat. In this case, the average cost curve for all firms (and the marginal cost curve as well) will shift up a little. Now, zero economic profits in the long run will be realized at a slightly higher price than before. This industry is called an *increasing-cost industry*. Its long-run supply curve is given in (b) of Figure 18-9.

It is also possible for a *decreasing-cost industry* to exist. This would be the case if more firms entering the industry caused a technological breakthrough that reduced costs for everyone. The long-run supply curve for a decreasing-cost industry is shown in (c) of Figure 18-9. As in (a) and (b), the long-run supply curve for the industry is labeled $S_L S_L$. We can define the long-run industry supply curve as the "path" of the industry's long-run equilibrium points as determined by the intersections of the short-run supply and demand curves, DD, $D'D'$ and SS, $S'S'$, in (a), (b), and (c).

Why Economists Are Fascinated with the Competitive Solution

Often, one will see economists using the competitive solution as the norm for what the econ-

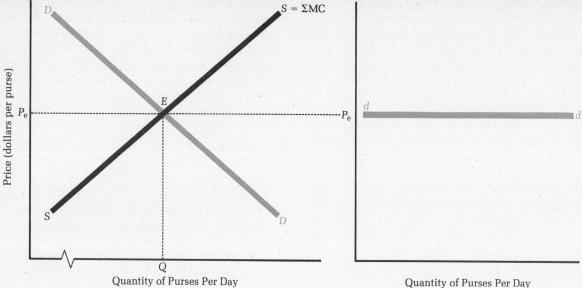

FIGURE 18-7 The Industry Demand and Supply Curve
The industry demand curve is a representation of the demand curve for all potential consumers. It is represented by *DD*. The industry supply curve is the horizontal summation of all the marginal cost curves of individual firms. We show it as *SS* and mark it as equal to ΣMC. The intersection of the demand and supply curve at *E* determines the equilibrium or market price at P_e.

FIGURE 18-8 Individual Firm Demand Curve
The individual firm demand curve is set at the going market price determined in Figure 18-7. That is, the demand curve facing the individual firm is a horizontal line, *dd*, at price P_e.

omy should be doing, for what an industry should be doing, or for what a firm should be doing. There is a reason behind this. However, we should note first whether the economist is stating a factual situation or recommending policy changes only because the current situation does not jibe with the desired situation. In other words, if an economist establishes the fact that a certain industry is pricing its products above the price that would prevail in a competitive situation, that is a positive economic statement. However, if the economist recommends that "something should be done" to make the industry more competitive, this is normative economics and involves subjective value judgments. Often, economists will declare

their desire for a competitive solution to an industry pricing problem without stating that this desire rests on personal value judgments.

Assuming an objective analysis, then, why are economists so fascinated with the competitive solution? First, what does marginal cost represent? It represents the cost of increasing production by one incremental unit. Suppose a marginal cost curve shows that an increase in production from 10,000 leather purses to 10,001 leather purses will cost $1.50. That $1.50 represents the *opportunity cost* of producing one more leather purse. It represents the opportunity cost of increasing production. Thus, the marginal cost curve gives a graphic representation of the opportunity cost of production.

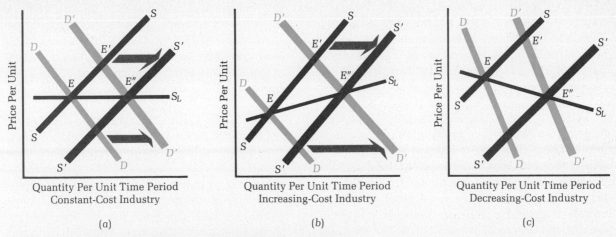

FIGURE 18-9 Constant-, Increasing-, and Decreasing-Cost Industries
In (a) we show a constant-cost industry in which the long-run supply curve, S_L, is a horizontal line. A shift outward in demand from DD to $D'D'$ initially moves the equilibrium from E to E'. However, the supply curve shifts outward to $S'S'$ as new firms enter the industry so that the new equilibrium is at E'', exactly at the same price as the prior equilibrium. In (b) we show an increasing-cost industry where the final equilibrium, E'', is at a higher price than the original equilibrium E. The long-run supply curve is upward sloping. In (c) we show a decreasing-cost industry where shifts in demand are more than met by shifts in supply. The new equilibrium, E'', is at a lower price than the original equilibrium E. The long-run supply curve, S_L, is downward sloping.

The competitive firm is faced with a price that just equals the marginal cost. Herein lies the element of the "desirability" of a competitive solution. It is called **marginal cost pricing.** The competitive firm sells its product at a price which just equals the cost to society—that is, the opportunity cost—for that is what the marginal cost curve represents.

When an individual pays a price equal to the marginal cost of production, then the cost to the user of that product is equal to the sacrifice or cost to society of producing that good as opposed to some other good. The competitive solution, then, is called *efficient*. It is efficient in the economic sense of the word. Economic efficiency means it is impossible to increase total production without lowering the total value of the output produced in the economy. No juggling of resources, such as labor and capital, will result in an output that is higher in value than the value of the goods and services already being produced. In an efficient situation, it is impossible to make someone better off without making someone else worse off. All resources are used in the most advantageous way possible. All goods and services are sold at their opportunity cost, and marginal cost pricing prevails throughout.

Is Perfect Competition Possible?

The analytic model presented here represents a situation that may never be seen in reality.

Perfect competition can exist only if information is also perfect. After all, the only way for a price to be uniform at every moment in time (corrected for quality changes and transportation costs) is for everybody to know what's happening every place else at every moment in time. Obviously, information is never perfect. In fact, the cost of trying to achieve perfect information would be prohibitive. A profit-maximizing firm will produce at the point where the additional revenues obtained from producing more goods exactly covers the additional costs incurred (where marginal revenue equals marginal cost). Similarly, if we are wealth maximizing, we would never spend more than we get in return from improving information flows. That is, we would improve information in the marketplace only up to the point where the marginal revenue from doing so is equal to the marginal cost. That is certainly at a point well below *perfect* information.

A purely competitive industry has been defined as one with many sellers. To satisfy the criterion of perfect competition where each seller has no control whatsoever over the price of his or her product, we would have to have a tremendous number of firms. There are many industries where the number of firms is not extremely large and therefore individually each firm has, at least in the short run, some control over its prices.[1] However, analyzing the industry in the *long run,* we might say that it was *tending* toward a competitive solution all the time because there were a sufficient number of firms *on the margin* attempting to increase their share of the total sales by undercutting the other firms. Notice we said that the industry might tend toward a competitive solution at all times. That is a **dynamic process**—which is to say that it never ends. At any time, an investigation of the particular industry would reveal that the industry was tending toward a competitive solution, but it would never reach that point.

Even if an industry is not perfectly competitive, it does not necessarily follow that steps should be taken to make it more competitive so as to ensure efficiency. After all, it is not possible to change an industry's structure from noncompetitive to competitive without using resources. We will discuss some of the ways of doing this, such as legislation against noncompetitive business practices, regulation of noncompetitive industries, and others. Remember that legislation and regulation involve the use of people who could be doing something else. That is, there is an opportunity cost involved in attempting to turn a noncompetitive industry into a competitive industry. Before engaging in such a campaign, we may want to be sure that the benefits of increased competition will outweigh the costs of getting the increased competition.

The fact that we use the model of perfect competition in an economic analysis does not mean that we should accept perfect competition as the only type of industry structure to be tolerated. Sometimes, however, the competitive model predicts well, even in noncompetitive situations and you may not wish to seek out alternative theories.

---

[1] Actually, more advanced students would point out here that all we require is constant returns to scale production functions and free entry, not a large number of firms.

Competitive Firm: A firm which is such a small part of the total industry picture that it cannot affect the price of the product it makes.

Price Taker: Another definition of a competitive firm. A price taker is a firm that must take the price of its product as given. The firm cannot influence its prices.

Total Revenues: The price per product times the total quantity sold.

Total Costs: All costs added together.

Marginal Revenue: The increment in total revenues attributable to selling one more unit of the product in question.

Short-Run Break-Even Point: The point where the firm's total revenues equal its total costs. In economics the break-even point is where the firm is just making a normal rate of return.

Barriers to Entry: Legal or other constraints that prevent the entrance of new firms into an industry.

Short-Run Shutdown Point: The point where the profit-maximizing price just covers average variable costs. This occurs at the intersection of the marginal cost curve and the average variable cost curve.

Marginal Cost Pricing: A system of pricing in which the price charged is equal to the opportunity cost of producing one more unit of the good or service in question. The opportunity cost is the marginal cost to society.

Dynamic Process: A situation that is always changing. We live in a world of dynamic processes. In some sense, prices are changing all the time, production is changing all the time, demand is shifting all the time. These changes make up the dynamic nature of our economy.

Chapter Summary

1. We define a competitive situation as one in which individual firms cannot affect the price of the product they produce. This is usually when the firm is very small relative to the entire industry. A firm in a perfectly competitive situation is called a price taker; it must take the price as given.

2. The firm, therefore, faces a completely elastic demand curve for its product. It can sell all it wants at the going market price. If it raises its price, it sells nothing. It will not lower its price because it would not then be making as much money as it could.

3. The firm's total revenues will equal the price of the product times the total quantity sold. Since the competitive firm can sell all it wants at

the same price (the "going" price), total revenues just equal the going price times whatever the firm decides to sell.

4. The firm decides to produce and sell wherever it maximizes profits. It maximizes profits when it maximizes the difference between total revenues and total costs. We can also find out where it maximizes profits by looking at its marginal cost curve.

5. You'll remember that the marginal cost curve is that curve which represents the increment in total cost due to an increase in production of successive units. The firm maximizes profits where marginal cost equals marginal revenue. The marginal revenue to the firm is represented by its own demand curve. This is because marginal revenue is defined as the increment in total revenues due to an increase in production by one unit. But the competitive firm can sell all it wants at the same market price; therefore, its marginal revenue will equal the price, which will equal its average revenue. The firm will always want to produce where marginal revenue equals marginal cost. If it produces above that point, marginal cost will exceed marginal revenue. If it produces below that point, marginal cost is less than marginal revenue, and it could be making more profits if it expanded production.

6. A perfectly competitive firm ends up in the long run making zero economic profits. However, it still makes a normal or competitive rate of return since that is the opportunity cost of capital. The competitive rate of return or normal profits are included in the costs as we have defined them for the firm. The point of maximum profits for the competitive firm is therefore also its break-even point; this is where total costs will equal total revenue. Business people like to talk of a break-even point that does *not* include a normal rate of return as a cost. Note that this differs from the economist's notion of a break-even point.

7. The firm will always produce along its marginal cost curve unless the price it charges to maximize profits will not cover average variable costs. This would be the shutdown point. It occurs at the intersection of the average variable cost curve and the marginal cost curve. Below that point it is not profitable to stay in business since variable costs will not be completely covered by revenue.

8. Economic profits are eliminated in a competitive situation because, in the long run, other firms will enter the industry if it is initially possible to make economic profits. These new firms increase the supply and lower

the market price. Conversely, if there are economic losses (negative economic profits), firms will leave the industry, thereby decreasing the supply and causing a rise in the market price.

9. The supply curve of the firm is exactly equal to its marginal cost curve above the shutdown point. The supply curve of the industry is equal to the horizontal summation of all the supply curves of the individual firms. This is a short-run industry supply curve, and it is upward sloping.

10. The equilibrium or market price is determined by the intersection of the market demand curve and the industry supply curve. That is how we determine the going price in the market.

11. In the long run the supply curve of the industry is probably quite elastic because firms can enter the industry and, therefore, cause the short-run supply curve to shift to the right.

12. The competitive solution is fascinating to economists because it is the most economically efficient one. That is to say, the competitive solution results in a situation where any change in the use of resources will result in a decrease in the economic value obtainable from a fixed amount of resources at any point in time. The competitive solution leads to what is called marginal cost pricing, where the price is set equal to the marginal cost, which is equal to the social opportunity cost of producing the good or service in question.

13. It is difficult to imagine many situations where perfect competition exists in the short run. However, we might say that in the long run there's a tendency towards a competitive solution, even if it will never be reached. That is because firms will constantly acquire new information and there will be entry and exit from the industry depending upon whether there are economic profits or economic losses.

Questions for Thought and Discussion

1. What is the meaning of zero profits in the economic sense?
2. How could a firm continue for years with negative economic profits?
3. Why would a firm be better off stopping production if the market price were less than the average variable cost?
4. Since pure competition has never existed and never will, why do we bother to study it?
5. "The leather purse producer must receive a living price for his or her leather purses." Discuss.

6. Is the price of leather purses determined by the cost of producing them, or is the cost of producing them determined by the price?

7. If the average total cost curve lies above the demand curve, why doesn't the profit-maximizing, competitive firm produce at the point where the marginal cost curve intersects the average total cost curve? Doesn't the marginal cost curve intersect the average total cost curve at its minimum? This means the intersection of the average total cost curve and the marginal cost curve is at minimum average total cost. Is this the best place to produce?

8. Can you think of any situation where it would be better not to produce when marginal revenue equals marginal cost?

9. If you were a businessperson, would you be content with just "breaking even"?

10. Do you think the concept of efficiency is in the realm of normative or positive economics?

Selected References

Knight, F. H., "Cost of Production and Price over Long and Short Periods," *Journal of Political Economy,* **29,** April 1921, pp. 304–335.

Robinson, E. A., *The Structure of Competitive Industry,* Cambridge: Cambridge University Press, 1959.

The Perpetual Investment Fraud

ON NOT GETTING RICH QUICK

A Truly Competitive Market Situation

If one were to look for an industry where almost pure competition prevailed, one would have to consider the stock market. Using this industry, we will see that in a very competitive situation, it is extremely difficult to make pure economic profits with any certainty. We will also see throughout this issue how the competitive model works in predicting the outcome of individuals' investment decisions, as each individual attempts to maximize his or her wealth.

Making Money

You've probably heard of J. P. Morgan. He was supposed to have made his fortune by manipulating the stock market. You've also probably heard of men becoming millionaires overnight by making astute investments in securities. You may even know someone who talks a lot about the stock market, follows the *Wall Street Journal,* reads the financial page of the local newspaper, and talks about the prices of various stocks going up or down. Making money in the stock market seems as easy as calling up your stockbroker for the latest "hot" tips.

Getting Advice on the Market

Try the following experiment: Look in your Yellow Pages under "Stock and Bond Brokers." Pick any one at random. Call up the broker. Ask to speak with a registered representative or an account executive. (In the old days, these people were called "customers' men.") Talk to this broker as if you had, say, $10,000 to invest. Ask this person for advice. The broker will probably ask you what your goals are: Do you want income from your investment? Do you want growth in your investment? Do you want to take a chance? Do you want to be safe? After you tell the broker the strategy you wish to pursue, he or she will tell you the best stocks to buy. If you ask the broker what he or she thinks the market in general will be doing over the next few months, that individual is bound to have an opinion, and an authoritative one at that.

Since you ask your local mechanic about your car, why not also seek out a specialist when you're interested in making money? Stockbrokers are specialists. You can get lots of useful information from them. They can tell you about the stock market; they can give you quotes on all the different stocks—that is, what their prices are and how many of them were sold in the last few days and what the history of the prices is. They can tell you about the various types of securities you can buy—common stocks listed on the big exchanges like the New York and the American, over-the-counter stocks that are sold only in very restricted sections of the country, preferred stocks, bonds, convertible debentures, puts, calls, warrants—the list goes on and on. Stockbrokers are the people you should ask concerning all these different avenues of investment.

But they are not the ones to ask when it comes to which particular stock to buy. *The probability of their being right is no higher than the probability of your being right.* In fact, the probability of their being right is about equal to the probability of your being right. One might just as well take a dart and throw it at a list of stocks in the New York Stock Exchange and then pick those stocks that the dart hits. The reason behind this perhaps shocking revelation is that the stock market is the most highly competitive market in the world and information costs are perhaps the lowest of any market in existence. That is the key to understanding why any investment advice concerning *which* stocks to buy is, in essence, a fraud—a fraud, however, that is perpetuated by people who do *not* know that they are unable to do better than a random dart thrown at a list of stocks.

Some Facts on the Stock Market

The *stock market* is the general term used for all transactions that involve buying and selling securities issued by companies. What is a *security?* A security is either a certificate giving the owner a certain right to a portion of the assets of a company issuing the security, or it is a certificate showing evidence of creditorship. Under the general title of securities are included both stocks and bonds. For the moment, we will ignore bonds, which represent the debt of a company, and concern ourselves with stocks.

The most common stocks are common stocks; these are called **equities.** A company may, for example, wish to expand its operation. It can obtain the money capital for expansion by putting up part of the ownership of the company for sale. It does this by offering stocks for sale, usually common stocks. Let's say that a company is worth $1 million. If the company wants $200,000, it may sell stocks. Suppose one individual owns the company and arbitrarily states that he or she owns

completely 100,000 shares of stock. The owner would then put about 20,000 shares of this stock on the market and sell them at $10 a share. The owner would get the $200,000 for expansion, and the people who paid the money would receive 20,000 shares of the stock. They would then have claim to one-fifth of the company's profits.

There are many different submarkets within the stock market. At the top of the ladder are the big ones: the New York Stock Exchange and the American Stock Exchange. Perhaps 80 percent of the value of all stock transactions are carried out at the New York and the American. Then there are regional stock exchanges throughout the country. Then there is the national over-the-counter market and regional over-the-counter markets. These markets are somewhat less organized than the actual exchanges. The stocks are usually not traded as often in the over-the-counter market as they are on the big exchanges. Also, the stocks usually traded in the over-the-counter market are the stocks of companies that are small and less well known.

Capital Gains and Losses

Stocks can go up and down in price. If you buy a stock at, say, $10 and sell it at $15, you make a **capital gain** equal to $5 for every share you bought and then sold at the higher price. This is called an appreciation in the price of your stock, which you realized as a capital gain when you sold it. If the value of your stock falls and you sell it at a loss, you have

suffered a *capital loss* because of the depreciation in the market value of your stock.

Some stocks pay dividends, but not all do. Those that do pay dividends mail out checks to the stock owners. Normally when you buy a stock that has never paid a dividend, you expect to make money on your investment by the stock's value going up. This is exactly what you would demand—if the company is making profits but not giving out dividends, it must be reinvesting those profits and a reinvestment could pay off in the future by higher profits. The value of the stock would then be bid up in the market. Your profit then would occur by capital gain rather than by dividend payments (current income from the stock that the company sends to you).

What Affects the Price of a Stock?

What affects the price of the stock? You might say that people's psychological feelings are the only things that matter. If people think a stock's going to be worth more in the future, they will bid up the price. If they think it will be worth less in the future, the price will fall. However, that is not a very satisfactory theory. What are psychological feelings based upon? Usually, such feelings are based upon the stream of profits that the company is expected to make in the future. Past profits may be important in formulating a prediction of future profits. However, past profits are bygones, and bygones are forever bygones. A company could lose money for 10

years and then make profits for the next 15.

If a company gets a new management with a reputation for turning losing companies into winning ones, people in the stock market might expect profits to turn around and go up. If a company develops and patents a new product, one would expect the profits to go up. If a company has a record number of sales orders given to it for future months, one might expect profits to go up. Whenever profits are expected to rise, we typically find a rise in the value of the stock. That is, people bid up the price of the stock. Any information about future profits should be valuable in assessing how a stock's price will react. However, we mentioned at the very beginning of this issue that the stock market was a market in which information costs are incredibly low; that is, news travels fast and accurately.

Public Information

Information flows rapidly in the stock market. If you read in the *Wall Street Journal* that International Chemical and Nuclear (ICN) has just discovered a cure for cancer, do you think you should rush out and buy ICN stock? You might, but you'll be no better off than you would be by buying any other stock. By the time you read about ICN's discovery (which will mean increased profits in the future for the company), thousands and thousands of other people will have already read it. A rule that you should apply and one which will be explained several times in this issue is that *public information does not yield an above-normal profit or rate of return*. Once information about a company's profitability is generally known, that information has a zero value in terms of being useful for predicting the future price of the stock. The only information that is useful is what we call **inside information.**

Inside Information

Suppose you happen to be the janitor at International Chemical and Nuclear. You make a habit of looking at some of the memos that are thrown in the wastepaper baskets. You've noticed recently there have been several memos about some miracle drug. Last night, you saw a memo that said: ''Success! We've done it.'' The note was a bit crumpled, but, being nosey, you straightened it out; and now you have inside information. Assuming that the scientists and corporation officers who knew about this discovery didn't tell anybody else, you have some very valuable information. You have it on the inside; no one on the outside knows about it. You should go out and buy as many shares of ICN as you possibly can—borrow on your house; borrow on your car; borrow on your life insurance and anything else, because you're going to strike it rich. When other investors hear the good news later, they'll bid up the price of ICN, and you'll be able to sell out at a big profit.

Capitalization

True inside information is just that: information that is not generally known. Information that becomes public is *capitalized* upon almost immediately; people consider what it means for future profits and bid up the price of the stock to a level that reflects the future expected increase in profits. Information is discounted almost immediately in the stock market because it flows so rapidly.

Studies on the value of information have appeared in the *Wall Street Journal* and the *New York Times*. These studies find that information is useless for assessing which stocks to buy. Even information about national or world events cannot tell you whether the market in general will go up or down. Reading that peace talks broke down does not give you any signals as to whether you should buy or sell in the stock market.

Studies have also been done on the profitability of information acquired by insiders in companies—that is, by corporate officers. Officers in a company are required to file statements of their transactions in their own company's stock with the Securities and Exchange Commission, the regulator of the stock market industry. Statistical studies have shown that most of the time when insiders (corporation officers) sell their stock, the price of the stock falls within 30 days. When insiders buy their own company's stock, the price of the stock rises within 30 days. Obviously there is a value to having inside information. (Note that it is illegal for officers to tell outsiders any inside information which can then be used to make money in the company's stock. In fact, it is illegal to trade any stock on the basis of inside information.)

research statements on different companies and industries in the economy. There are recommendations as to which stocks are underpriced and, therefore, should be bought. *The value of this research information to you as an investor is zero.* You will do no better by following the advice of research branches of your stock brokerage company than you will by randomly selecting stocks. This is particularly true for stocks listed on the New York and American stock exchanges. Nevertheless, the amount of research on those companies that is completed by firms, individuals, organizations, governments, and so on is indeed staggering. Since information flows so freely, by the time you receive the results of research on a particular company, you can be sure that thousands and thousands of other people have already found out. And

since so many brokerage firms employ research analysts, you can be sure that there are numerous analysts investigating every single company that has shares for sale in the open stock market.

Why So Much "Research?"

Brokerage firms are in competition with each other. Their competition leads them to do research as thoroughly as possible. That means it is highly unlikely that the research one company does is going to be substantially better than the research any other brokerage firm does. In any event, even if a particular brokerage firm does do exceptionally good research, by the time you read it or your broker tells you about it, any information of value will already have been capitalized. The informa-

Hot Tips

What about the hot tips your broker might have? It is highly unlikely that the broker will have inside information. After all, if it's really inside information, why would that individual be giving it to you? Why wouldn't the broker take advantage of it, get rich quick, and quit being a stock salesperson? The broker might get this information from the research department. Almost all stock brokerage companies have large research staffs, which investigate different industries, different companies, and the future of the general economy. These research departments issue

tion will already have been included in the price of the particular stock. It will have gone up or down depending upon whether the information was good or bad. The price of a stock at any moment includes or is directly related to every piece of information any potential or actual buyer has on the company or competing companies in the economy. Again, information flows freely in the stock market. In a competitive market, you can't make money by applying public information to investing decisions. But you can expect to make a normal rate of return on your investment. The normal rate of return seems to average about 8 to 10 percent per year if you randomly select some stocks and keep your money in them for a long time. This leads us to the controversial concept of the stock market known as a random walk.

The Random Walk

Think about a physics course where the Brownian motion of molecules was studied. This motion says that the molecules jump around randomly. There is simply no way to predict where a molecule will jump next. This is exactly what happens when something follows a **random walk;** it goes in directions that are totally unrelated to past directions. If something follows a random walk, no amount of information on the past is useful for predicting what will happen in the future. The stock market would be expected to exhibit a random walk merely because it is so highly competitive and information flows so freely. Examining past prices on the market as a whole or on individual stocks would not be expected to yield any useful information as to prices in the future. Years and years of academic research on the stock market have left little doubt that the stock market is, indeed, a random walk. (If you find out otherwise, you may be able to get rich very quickly.) Despite the industry's "technical analysts," you will find no useable information by examining past stock prices.

Charting the Future

Technical stock analysts believe that they can recognize patterns in stock prices. **Technical analysis** employs special terms and ways of **charting** the past behavior of stocks and the average of all stock prices. Technical analysts talk about "heads" and "shoulders" and "wedges" and "support" levels and "resistance" levels and so on. They will show you impressive x's and dots and dashes on sophisticated graphic charts like the one we have included here in Figure I-18.1 These analysts think they can predict which stocks will go up and which stocks will go down on the basis of the behavior of stock prices in the past. The random walk theory, however, says that this cannot be the case.

Suppose that an analyst could make accurate predictions. How much money do you think you could make on it? If you found a chartist who knew what he or she was doing, other people would soon find out as well. As soon as enough people found out about how well that individual's charting theory worked, his or her theory would become public information. And, of course, public information is useless for making profits in a competitive market where information flows freely. Actually, academic research on the value of charting or technical analysis has shown that it is not useful for predicting the future prices of stocks.

What about Investment Plans?

There are many investment plans and sophisticated investment counselors around. Looking at their advertising, you will see that they each guarantee you a higher rate of return on your stock dollars than anyone else. A typical piece of advertising might show, for example, the average rate of return for investing in all the stocks that make up the **Dow Jones Industrial Average.** The Dow Jones Industrial Average (shown in Figure I-18.2) is the most widely known indication of the level of average stock prices in use today.

It is made up of the price of 30 "blue chip" industrial stocks like General Motors, General Electric, and others. If you bought the Dow Jones Industrial Average, in the sense that you bought the same stocks that make up the average, you might make, on average, 8 percent a year. An investment counselor would show you that his or her stock portfolio made 15 percent a year. However, these investment counselors usually neglect to point out that the 15 percent rate of return does not take account of the investment counseling fees or the trading costs for buying and selling stocks. Investment services usually do much trading: they go in and out of the market—buying today, selling tomorrow. Each time someone buys or sells a stock, that person pays a commission to the broker. Thus, the more trading your investment counselor does for your account, the more trading costs you incur. In fact, in almost all cases that have been thoroughly examined, investments made through counselors do no better than the general market averages because any special profits they make are eaten up by brokerage fees and their own counseling fees.

This fact was confirmed in a study of **mutual funds.** Mutual funds use the money of many investors to buy and sell large blocks of stocks. Investors get dividends or appreciation from their shares of the fund. The mutual fund, then, is a company that merely invests in other companies but does not sell any physical product of its own. You can buy shares in mutual funds just as you can buy shares in General Motors. This study of mutual funds mentioned above concluded that mutuals which did

the *least* amount of trading made the highest profits, an expected result if one understands the competitive nature of the stock market.

Is There No Way to Get Rich Quick?

The general conclusion of our analysis of the stock market is that the investing schemes everybody talks about are really quite useless for getting rich. That does not mean, of course, that some people won't get rich by using them. Luck has a lot to do with making money in the stock market—just as it does with winning at poker or craps. Someone who does make money with a particular scheme is not necessarily smart, a better investor, a wise old person, or a prophet. Such an individual is probably just lucky.

Of course, an investor may make more than a normal rate of return on invested capital if a tremendous amount of time is spent finding areas of unknown profit potential. But in this case, then, resources are being spent—the individual's own time. The opportunity cost of any profits made is payment for the time spent analyzing the stock market and the different companies that could otherwise have been spent doing other things.

The question still remains: How can you make money? You know you can usually make a normal rate of return by randomly picking eight stocks on the New York Stock Exchange and buying them with your investment dollars. If you don't sell until you need money for retirement, over the long run, you'll probably

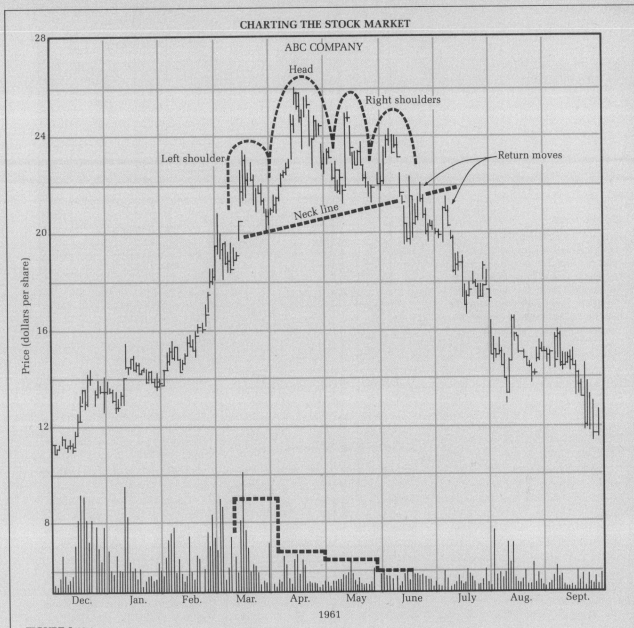

CHARTING THE STOCK MARKET

ABC COMPANY

Head

Right shoulders

Left shoulder

Return moves

Neck line

Price (dollars per share)

28

24

20

16

12

8

Dec. Jan. Feb. Mar. Apr. May June July Aug. Sept.

1961

FIGURE I-18.1

Here we see an example of the so-called technical analysis for charting. Chartists believe that they can make some sense out of the ups and downs in the price of any particular stock or group of stocks. According to their theories, certain patterns can be recognized so that the future course of the price of a stock can be predicted. Can you make heads or tails out of the above diagram?

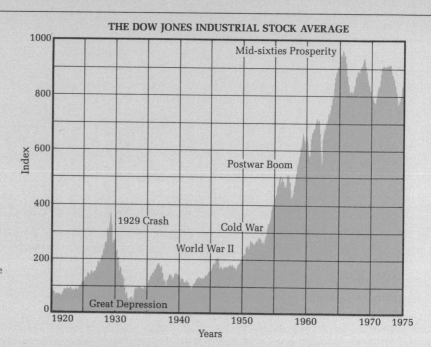

THE DOW JONES INDUSTRIAL STOCK AVERAGE

Mid-sixties Prosperity

Postwar Boom

1929 Crash

Cold War

World War II

Great Depression

FIGURE I-18.2

Here we have plotted the course of the stock market over the last half century or so. The ups and downs are tremendous, but the trend has been up. It would have been nice to buy during the low points and sell at the high points. Hindsight, however, is always more accurate than foresight.

make around an 8 to 10 percent rate of return. Or you might want to pick particular stocks if you have inside information or information that is better than anybody else's. In this case, you stand to gain more than by randomly picking stocks. Also, if you think you can somehow evaluate public information better than most, then you may want to do more than select random stocks. But before you decide whether you can evaluate better than others, consider how many others there are. The stock industry is huge and, by and large, everybody involved thinks he or she can evaluate better than anybody else.

There is one sure-fire method of making money in the stock market, but it is not by investing in stocks. Rather, it involves selling information

to investors who are hungry for advice.

A Sure-Fire Scheme

What you should do is start a newsletter. Call it the *Information Systems Associated Newsletter,* or the *ISA Newsletter.* In the first newsletter, expound the virtues of your information-gathering and evaluating investment system. Say you're using high-speed computers to analyze all the stocks in a selected region of the country. Say that you guarantee a higher rate of return than any other newsletter service in the nation. Then make a list of, say, 100 stocks. Mail out the newsletter free of charge to everybody in your city. Follow the price of the stocks. Throw out the

ones that fall in value. The next newsletter tells how successful your stock advice has been. Show how much in price all the winning stocks have gone up. Ignore what the other ones did. Repeat the blurb on how sophisticated your computer equipment is.

Do this for three newsletters in a row. You'll be able to show, most likely, some fantastic gains in some of the stocks you recommended from the very beginning. After doing this, send a fourth newsletter which includes a little announcement stating that you must now charge people for your service; the introductory free offer is over. Charge them, say, $1,000 apiece for a year's subscription. Quite a few people will buy your newsletter. After all, the stocks that you recommended have grown tremendously, right? (Recall that you ignored all the ones that didn't grow in price; you threw them out.) Once you collect the money, you continue with the newsletter so that you won't get sued. However, people will eventually find that your advice is no better than any random selection of stocks they could have made. They will already have paid their $1,000. They will be getting the product they requested, and you will be rich. In short, that's how to make money in the stock market—but don't tell a soul.

Definitions of New Terms

Equities: Another name for common stocks; shares in a company.

Capital Gains: The positive difference between the price at which a stock is bought and the price at which it is sold. When this difference is negative it is called a capital loss.

Inside Information: Information that is not public. It is usually acquired by insiders or those who have close contact with a company.

Capitalization: The process of taking account of all information about the future stream of profits for a company. This information is instantly capitalized in the current price of a stock whenever the information is public.

Random Walk: A theory about the movement of stock prices. In a random walk situation, the past movements of the stock have absolutely no ability to predict the future movements of that stock.

Technical Analysis: A way to analyze the past course of stock prices to predict the future course. Technical analysis usually involves charting.

Charting: A type of technical analysis in which the past price of a stock or a group of stocks is plotted or charted. The results of this charting are supposed to help the chartist predict the future price of the stock.

Dow Jones Industrial Average: The most widely known average of stock prices. It is a composite of 30 blue chip industrial stock prices.

Mutual Fund: A firm that buys the stocks of other firms and does not engage in the selling of products or services.

Questions for Thought and Discussion

1. If you had an extra $10,000, how would you invest it?
2. Why is the perpetual investment fraud perpetual?
3. When would it ever be worth your while to act on a "hot tip"?

Selected References

Cootner, P. H. (ed.), *The Random Character of Stock Market Prices*, Cambridge, Mass.: M.I.T. Press, 1967.

Engel, Louis, *How to Buy Stocks*, 5th rev. ed., New York: Little, 1971.

Sprinkel, Beryl Wayne, *Money and Stock Prices*, Homewood, Ill.: Irwin, 1964.

The Changing Agricultural Sector

WILL THE PAST BE SEEN AGAIN?

The Farming Sector

As another application of the competitive model, we turn now to the agricultural sector in our society. There are many, many farmers, each producing a relatively small part of the total farm output for any given crop. Every farmer, therefore, must take as given the particular price for a particular crop at a specific time of year. We will see, however, that the going price for certain crops is not always determined by the interaction of the market supply and the market demand curves. Government programs, even today, influence to some extent the price that farmers can receive for their crops.

Poor Farmers

Many farmers can be considered rather poor. In the mid-1970s, per capita farm income was only $4,060 as compared to $4,962 for the nonfarm population. Today there are more than 1.5 million farmers with annual product sales of less than $6,000 each. In fact, those 1.5 million farmers produce only 5 percent of the total output of the farming

industry. Table I-19.1 indicates the nature of the farming situation.

The farm problem is quite perplexing to most people. The agricultural sector is frequently referred to as the industry where technological progress has been more effective than anywhere else. Productivity has grown faster in agriculture than in any other major economic sector. Nonetheless, in terms of the percentage of the population engaged in farming, the agricultural sector is a declining industry. In Table I-19.2 we see the number of farms in the United States through the years. By 1964, the number of farms was less than the number existing before the turn of the century. Today the figure is even smaller.

The Growth in Demand for Farm Products

It is actually not surprising that the agricultural sector should decline as a proportion of the total economy. For one thing, productivity increases have been so great that the number of persons needed to produce even an increasing amount has fallen.

Additionally, we would expect that the rate of growth of demand for agricultural products will fall after a country has reached a certain standard-of-living level. That country will no longer increase its spending on food products as in the past. There is, after all, a limit to how much food people can eat—even if they can afford to buy a huge amount. We would expect, then, that in developed countries only a very small part of increases in income goes into increasing demands for food.

This is exactly what empirical evidence demonstrates. Look at Table I-19.3, where we show the **income elasticity** of the demand for agricultural products for various countries, some developed and some less developed. Income elasticity can be defined in the same way as price elasticity. The price elasticity of demand for a product is equal to the percentage change in the quantity demanded over the percentage change in the price. That is, elasticity measures the responsiveness of consumers to a change in the price of the product in question. Income elasticity will be defined as follows.

$$\text{Income elasticity} = \frac{\text{percentage change in quantity demanded}}{\text{percentage change in income}}$$

We see in Table I-19.3 that the

Table I-19.1

The Distribution of Total Farm Sales

The lowest 41.2 percent of farms produce less than 3 percent of total farm sales while the top 7.1 percent of farms produce over 50 percent of total farm sales. These farmers have annual sales in excess of $40,000 a piece.

ECONOMIC CLASS	VALUE OF SALES (THOUSANDS OF DOLLARS)	PERCENTAGE OF TOTAL FARM SALES, 1969	PERCENTAGE OF TOTAL NUMBER OF FARMS, 1969
I	40 and over	51.3	7.1
II	20–40	21.3	12.0
III	10–20	16.0	17.0
IV	5–10	6.3	13.1
V	2.5–5	2.4	9.6
VI	Less than 2.5	2.7	41.2

Source: Charles L. Schultze, The Distribution of Farm Subsidies: Who Gets the Benefits?, Washington, D.C.: The Brookings Institution, 1971.

income elasticity of the demand for food is much lower in wealthy countries than it is in poorer countries. This means that once a country becomes fairly well developed, farmers cannot expect the domestic demand for their product to go up as fast as the demand for other products. In the United States the income elasticity for food products is almost zero. That is, an increase in income of 1 percent yields a very small increase in the quantity of food demanded, holding everything else constant. Note that income elasticity is defined only with everything else held constant, just as with price elasticity. A price elasticity is measured holding income constant. An income elasticity is measured holding the price of the product constant. In both, tastes and the prices of substitutes are also held constant.

Low Price Elasticity of Demand

Not only is the income elasticity of demand for agricultural products low; so too is the price elasticity. Whereas the low-income elasticity was important for explaining the long-run downward trend in the farm sector, the low-price elasticity of demand is important for understanding the high variability of farmers' income in the short run.

Let's compare the change in price that results from an increase in supply due to extremely good weather conditions. In Figure I-19.1 we show the supply schedule shifting from SS

Table I-19.2

The Number of Farms in the United States

The number of farms in the United States rose from 1.4 million in 1850 to a high of 6.8 million in 1935. Today there are less than 3 million farms.

YEAR	MILLIONS OF FARMS	YEAR	MILLIONS OF FARMS
1850	1.4	1935	6.8
1870	2.7	1940	6.1
1900	5.7	1950	5.4
1920	6.5	1959	3.7
1930	6.3	1964	3.2
		1972	2.9
		1976	2.8 (estimate)

Source: U.S. Bureau of the Census

Table I-19.3

Income Elasticity for Food Products

The income elasticity of demand for food is defined as equal to the percentage change in the quantity demanded divided by the percentage change in real income. This income elasticity is quite low for the richer nations in the world. As real income rises, the demand for food products does not increase proportionally.

RICHER NATIONS	ELASTICITY	POORER NATIONS	ELASTICITY
United States	0.08	Italy	0.42
Canada	0.15	Ireland	0.23
Germany	0.25	Greece	0.49
France	0.25	Spain	0.56
Britain	0.24	Portugal	0.60

Source: Charles L. Schultze, The Distribution of Farm Subsidies: Who Gets the Benefits?, Washington, D.C.: The Brookings Institution, 1971.

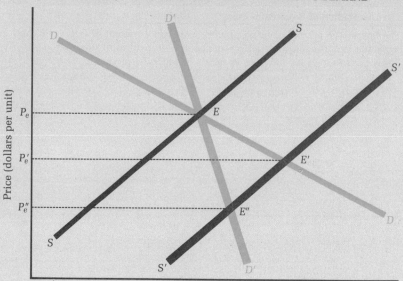

CONSEQUENCES OF A RELATIVELY INELASTIC DEMAND

FIGURE I-19.1

The quantity of food products per time period is on the horizontal axis and the price per unit on the vertical axis. Assume the original supply curve is SS. It is quite steep, indicating the relative inelasticity of supply in the short run. If the demand curve facing farmers is DD, a shift in the supply curve from SS to S'S' due to a good year of weather will lower the equilibrium price from P_e to P_e'. But if the demand curve is instead D'D', when the supply curve shifts to S'S', the new equilibrium price falls to P_e''. This accounts for the large variability in incomes of farmers in different years.

to S'S'. It has shifted out to the right, indicating a large increase in production. Notice that the supply schedule here is fairly vertical, indicating that the price *elasticity of supply* in the short-run period under consideration is quite small. After all, once the farmers have produced their crops, they can produce no more, no less—unless, of course, they decide to burn the crops.

What if the demand schedule is also very elastic, such as DD? The new equilibrium price in this case will be set at the intersection of the new supply curve S'S' and the demand curve DD, or at point E'. The old equilibrium price was established at point E, or at a price of P_e. The new price of P_e' obviously lies below the old price.

What if the demand curve is relatively less elastic, such as D'D'? The

new equilibrium will then be established at E'' and the new equilibrium price will be P_e'', which is even lower than P_e'. We see, then, that if the demand for agricultural products is relatively inelastic, a shift in the quantity supplied will result in a fairly drastic change in the market price. This is one reason why we see prices in a free agricultural market changing quite drastically in response to changes in weather or in control of pestilence. The situation can be reversed, in which case the price rise will be relatively more with a less elastic demand curve than with an elastic demand curve when the supply schedule shifts inward. If there is a drought, we expect prices to rise rather substantially due to the decreased supply in agriculture. Then, although the farmers could complain about a smaller crop, they could not

complain about the higher prices they could receive when selling it.

We see therefore that the relative inelasticity of demand for agricultural products has been one of the reasons that prices and, hence, incomes have fluctuated more in agriculture than they have in other industries from year to year.

History of the Farmers' Dilemma

Before World War I, there were at least 20 years of continuous agricultural prosperity in the United States. During the war, increased demand for agricultural products added to the "golden age of American farming." Many foreign countries demanded our agricultural products because they were using all their productive

facilities to fight the war. The sharp depression in 1920 brought the "golden age" to an abrupt halt. Even though the economy picked up by 1921 and we were into the roaring twenties, agriculture never did share in the remaining years of prosperity. European countries stopped demanding our agricultural exports as they increased their own productive capacity in farming. Also, the United States put high tariffs on all imported goods, thereby restricting the flow of imports. Since other countries were not able to export as many goods to us as before, they were in no position to import as much from us as before. Since exports are what any country uses to pay for its imports, the less you are able to export, the less you are able to import.

Then the Great Depression hit, and American farming was really hurt. Farm prices and farm income fell sharply. It was at this time that our massive farm programs began to be put into operation. In 1929 the Federal Farm Board was created and given a budget of $1.5 billion to begin price stabilization operations for poor farmers. The Farm Board was supposed to use the money to support the price of farm products so that farmers' incomes would not fall so much. Then, when the Great Depression got into full swing, a system of **price supports** came into being. At one time or another there have been some forms of price supports for wheat, feed grains, cotton, tobacco, rice, peanuts, soybeans, dairy products, and sugar. Let us now see if we can graphically analyze the effect of a price-support system.

Price Supports

A price-support system is precisely what the name implies. Somehow the government stabilizes or fixes the price of an agricultural product so that it can't *fall.* Look at our regular supply and demand curves in Figure I-19.2 showing the market demand and market supply of wheat. Competitive forces would yield a price of P_e and a quantity demanded and supplied of Q_e. If the government sets the support price at P_e or below, obviously there will be no change.

In many instances, however, the government will set the support price above P_e, say, at P_1. At P_1 the quantity demanded is only Q_d, but the quantity supplied is Q_s. That is, at the higher price, there is a smaller quantity demanded but a larger quantity supplied. The difference is the excess quantity supplied. Producers respond to higher market prices by producing more. That's why we show the supply schedule sloping up. At the higher prices, farmers are able to incur higher production costs and still make a profit. They will keep producing up to the point where the supported price cuts the supply curve. Since the government guarantees to purchase everything the wheat farmers want to sell at the price P_1, this price represents the marginal revenue to each farmer. Each farmer will continue producing until marginal revenue equals marginal cost, or until the price-support line intersects the summation of all the marginal cost curves (that is, the industry supply curve).

How Can Supports Last?

How can such a situation last? If producers are producing more than consumers want to buy at the support price, what happens to all the surplus production? The government buys it. (Actually, this is the only way for the price to stay up.) The government acquires the surplus wheat, or the distance between Q_s and Q_d in Figure I-19.2.

Back in the 1950s, things really

PRICE SUPPORTS

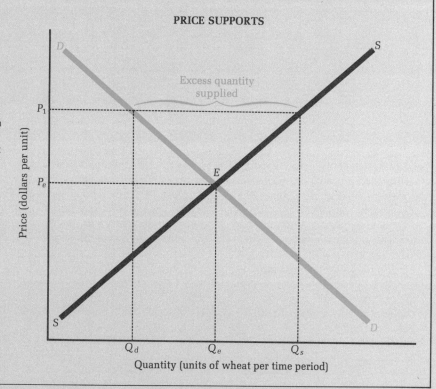

FIGURE I-19.2
The quantity of wheat is measured on the horizontal axis and the price on the vertical axis. The domestic market demand and supply curves are given by *DD* and *SS*. Equilibrium is established at *E* with an equilibrium price of P_e and an equilibrium quantity demanded and supplied of Q_e. However, the government steps in and sets a support price at P_1. At P_1 the quantity demanded is Q_d and the quantity supplied is Q_s. The difference is the excess quantity supplied, or surplus, which the government must somehow take care of. It usually does this by storing the surplus or giving it away to foreign countries under one of our "food for peace" programs.

got out of hand and the government was spending $1.1 million a day in storage costs for surplus wheat! The government acquired the wheat through the Commodity Credit Corporation (CCC). The Commodity Credit Corporation was given a **parity** or fair price that it was allowed to offer for different products. Let's say that Congress set a fair or parity price of $2 a bushel, but the market price, where supply and demand would cause an equilibrium, was $1.50 a bushel. Farmers would sell all the wheat they could to the public at $2 and the rest of it—the surplus—to the Commodity Credit Corporation. In principle, the Commodity Credit Corporation merely ''lent'' each farmer the fair price times the number of bushels the farmer gave the CCC. The loan, however, was a nonrecourse one. That is, the CCC could never ask the farmer for the money back.

In economics we find that the only way for a ''surplus'' to exist is for there to be some sort of price fixing. In an unrestricted market, a surplus can exist only temporarily. The forces of supply and demand will eventually eliminate the surplus by causing a decrease in the price.

Who Benefits from Price Supports?

The argument of those favoring price supports has always been that it is a method to guarantee a decent income for low-income farmers. However, the evidence does not show that the price-support system has ever done this, even during its heyday. The benefits of past price supports were greatly skewed toward the owners of very large farms.

Owners of farms with sales of less than $2,500, for example, received a mere 4.2 percent of the benefits from price supports in the late 1960s.

Even more importantly, however, any benefit that conceivably could have been derived from the price-support system would have ultimately accrued to landlords or owners of the land on which price-supported crops could be grown. Remember in the last issue when we talked about information being instantly capitalized into the value or price of the stock? This is exactly what happened with the value of land when price supports were announced and put into effect (maybe even before, if the owners and potential buyers of land knew that supports were going to be legislated). A recent study of past farm programs reached this conclusion. According to Professor D. Gale Johnson, ''Most of the benefit of the farm program has been capitalized into the value of farm land.''[1] This just means the price of land goes up in anticipation of higher profits in the future.

A clear example of this capitalization phenomenon is the tobacco program, which has been around for some time.

Tobacco

Support prices that are higher than market equilibrium entice more people into farming because of the lure of higher income. However, the threat of new competition was squashed by tobacco growers about

[1]*Farm Commodity Programs: An Opportunity for Change,* Washington, D.C.: American Enterprise Institute for Public Policy Research, May 1973, p. 3.

three decades ago. They got Congress to pass legislation that allotted the *then current* half million growers the right to grow tobacco on lands which were *then* in use. Since then, there has been no new land put into tobacco production and for a very good reason. Any tobacco grown on unlicensed land is taxed at 75 percent of its value. This tax is prohibitive: Potential tobacco farmers can not hope to make any money if they have to pay this tax—they're in competition with tobacco growers who do not have to pay it.

Perhaps, since tobacco farming is a monopoly today, you can make monopoly profits by buying some licensed tobacco growing acreage? If you think so, you're wrong. The price of that licensed land was bid up long ago to levels that yield new owners only a competitive rate of return. Who are the ones who benefit from the monopoly position granted by Congress? The owners of the land at the time the legislation was passed, of course; they reaped monopoly profits to the tune of $1,500 to $3,000 per acre because they could sell their land for more.

In addition to the restriction on acreage in tobacco growing, there are also tobacco price supports (that is, Commodity Credit Corporation nonrecourse loans), and, just to make sure that not too much reaches the marketplace, there are marketing quotas to keep output at a level consistent with price-support objectives. The net results of the tobacco program have been:

1. A smaller supply of tobacco leaves than otherwise would have been grown

2. A higher price for tobacco than would have prevailed under an unrestricted market situation

3. A higher price for tobacco products than would have otherwise prevailed

Moving into an Era of No Surpluses

The 1970s have indeed seen a shift in the farming situation. Now, instead of surpluses, there are domestic and worldwide shortages of farm products. Because of this changing situation, Congress passed a new farm bill in 1973. This farm bill provides for something new in the agricultural sector.

Target Prices

The Agricultural and Consumer Protection Act of 1973 provides a **target price** plan for grains and cotton for 4 years. Then Secretary of Agriculture, Earl L. Butz, called the bill a historic turning point in farm program philosophy, which, he said, is now "geared to expanding output."

The concept of target prices for major crops was first proposed by Charles F. Brannan back in 1949 when he was Secretary of Agriculture under Truman. The 1973 bill allows for target prices that are relatively low compared to market prices, or prices which are determined by the interaction of market supply and demand. If, at any time, the market price falls below the target price,

farmers will receive a direct payment from the government to make up for the difference. Thus, if the market price of wheat is $4 a bushel and the support price is $5 a bushel, farmers will receive $1 for every bushel they sell on the open market. That dollar will be paid as a subsidy to the farmer out of general tax revenues by the federal government.

Graphically Speaking

There are now essentially three possible prices: the target price, the support price, and the market price. We can put these different prices on one graph and explain their meaning. Look at Figure I-19.3. To begin, the market equilibrium price is P_e. It is determined by the intersection of the

FIGURE I-19.3 Three Different Types of Prices in the Farming Sector

There are basically three prices in the farm program: the market clearing price, determined by the intersection of DD and SS (P_e); the target price (P_t) determined by the government; and the support price (P_s), also determined by the government. If demand and supply are such that P_e is greater than P_t or P_s, we have an unrestricted market in agricultural products. But if the supply curve shifts to S'S', the new equilibrium is established at E', below the target price P_t. The difference between E' and P_t is given to the farmers as a pre-unit subsidy. If the supply curve shifts outward to W"S", the new equilibrium occurs at E". But the government will support the price of P_s; a "surplus" of the distance between B and A' will result, and presumably farmers might also be eligible for a subsidy of the difference between P_s and P_t.

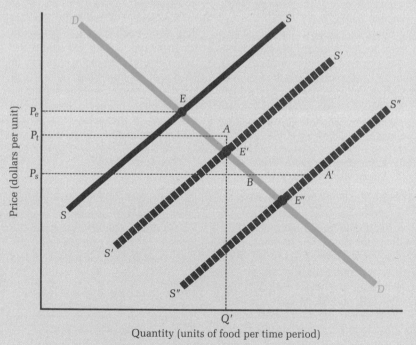

demand curve DD and the supply curve SS. Assume that Congress has legislated a target price of P_t and there still exists a potential support price of P_s. As long as DD and SS remain where they are, there will be no effect on the price by the government program, and taxpayers will not have to pay farmers anything.

However, what happens if the supply curve shifts out to S'S'? The new intersection will be at E', and that vertical distance Q'E' will represent the new market clearing price. In this particular situation, the market price will be below the target price, and the U.S. Treasury will make payments to farmers equal to the vertical distance between E' and the target price line at P_t, or E'A.

Now, what if the supply curve shifts farther outward to S''S''? (We could shift the demand curve inward and get the same effect.) Now the new market clearing price is the vertical distance to E''. This is below the support price. In this case, the government will support the price of P_s and the quantity supplied will be at A', the intersection of the support price with the new supply curve S''S''. However, the quantity demanded at that price will be at B, the intersection of the support price with the demand curve DD. The difference will be "surplus." Note that this raises the long-run expected price to farmers, however, and thus increases long-run production.

Definitions of New Terms

Income Elasticity: Percentage change in quantity demanded divided by the percentage change in real income. In general, income elasticities are positive.

Price Supports: A system that prevents the price of certain agricultural products from falling below a support level. If the government has a price support that is above the equilibrium price, it will end up with surplus agricultural products.

Parity: A price of agricultural products that gives the particular product a purchasing power in terms of the goods which the farmers have to buy. This price will be equivalent to what it was in some previous "good" year for farmers. A parity price is often called a "fair" price for food products.

Target Price: A price set by Congress for specified agricultural commodities. If the market price falls below the target price, farmers are paid the difference from the U.S. Treasury.

Questions for Thought and Discussion

1. Do you think there is an agricultural problem? Why?
2. If indeed there is a problem, is the system that's now helping the farmers one you would choose? What would be your alternative?
3. Do you mind paying higher prices for food in order to help out farmers?
4. There are milk strikes or potato strikes or pig strikes when the particular producers of these products refuse to sell them in order to demonstrate their desire for higher prices. Are these particular farmers acting rationally?

Selected References

Harshbarger, C. Edward and Richard D. Rees, "The New Farm Program—What Does It Mean?", *Monthly Review*, Kansas City: Federal Reserve Bank of Kansas City, January 1974.

Heady, Earl O., *A Primer on Food, Agriculture, and Public Policy*, New York: Random House, 1967.

Houthakker, Hendrik S., *Economic Policy for the Farm Sector*, Washington, D.C.: American Enterprise Institute, 1967.

Ruttan, Vernon W. et al. (eds.), *Agricultural Policy in an Affluent Society*, New York: W. W. Norton, 1969.

Monopoly Management

The world, of course, does not consist of purely competitive industries, and our predictions about the behavior of noncompetitive industries would be very poor if we did not take into account their special attributes. In this chapter we will present a model of a monopoly business and discuss how a monopolist decides what prices to charge and how much to produce. Fortunately, most of the analytical tools needed here have already been introduced.

Definition of a Monopolist

The words *monopoly* or *monopolist* probably bring to mind a business that gouges the consumer, sells faulty products, gets rich, and any other bad thoughts that one can have about big business. If we are to succeed in analyzing and predicting the behavior of noncompetitive firms, however, we will have to be somewhat more objective in defining a monopolist. Although most actual monopolies in the United States are relatively big, our definition of monopoly will be equally applicable to small businesses. Thus, a **monopolist** is formally defined as a *single supplier*. (This is the Greek origin of the word.)

Monopolist's Demand Curve

The term *true monopolist* refers to the original meaning of the word—single supplier of *one* product or good or service. A true monopolist faces a demand curve that is the demand curve for the entire market for the good. *The monopolist faces the industry demand curve because that person is the entire industry.*

A single corner drugstore in a small town is therefore just as much a monopolist as a corporate giant like American Telephone and Telegraph (Ma Bell).

There are other, less pure forms of monopoly. In the following chapter we will discuss other forms of monopoly such as monopolistic competition, and oligopoly (few sellers). Right now we want to talk about the case where one firm produces the entire output of the industry.

Some Examples of Monopolies

Everyone is aware of at least some of the forms of pure monopoly that exist in our economy. When you turn on the light to read this text, you are purchasing the output of the local monopoly power company in your area. There is only one company to which you can go to buy electric power, right? How did it get to be a monopoly? A government franchise gave it monopoly power. That is, the government certifies different electric power companies to operate in well-defined geographical areas. You and your friends could not pool your money, buy a small generator, and solicit electricity customers in your neighborhood. That is illegal; government regulations do not allow it.

When you mail a letter at the post office, you are purchasing the services of a government monopoly. Although various groups are now testing the legality of restricting first-class mail service to the U.S. Post Office only, for the moment, first-class service is a government-controlled and owned monopoly. There is a single seller of first-class service, and that is the government. (First class does not of course, necessarily, refer here to high quality.)

When you dial a number on your telephone, you are using the services of a monopolist—probably your local chapter of the American Telephone and Telegraph system. And until recently, the phone you used was produced by a monopolist because the government did not allow just anybody to produce and install telephone equipment. That is no longer the case, but it is still true that telephone services are sold by one of the largest monopolists in the country.

On Becoming a Monopolist

How does one obtain a monopoly? How can you, if you want to, become a monopolist? It isn't easy. There are many ways to become a monopolist but very few of them work in the long run. In the first place, for a monopoly to be able to exist, there must be **barriers to entry.** This means that somehow other people must be barred from setting up competing companies.

Barriers to Entry

The most obvious barrier to entry is government police power. It is impossible to enter the electric utility business in an area where someone else is already operating because the government does not allow it. The government creates a barrier to entry. It is impossible for you to set up an alternative telephone system because the government will prevent you from doing so. The most obvious barriers to entry, therefore, are legal barriers. Patents represent another type of legal barrier to entry into a business. The government grants an inventor the exclusive right to control a product for 17 years. Nobody else can produce that particular patented product unless that person obtains a license or a release from the owner of the patent.

There are also other barriers to entry. It may be that the cost of setting up a new electricity company—building a dam, buying generators, stringing power lines—might be so high that it does not pay to start a company to compete with an existing firm. Start-up costs can be overwhelming. In other words, this barrier to entry is excessive *capital* costs. You couldn't get enough people to lend you money to purchase the necessary equipment. More importantly, in a market where one large firm is the most efficient, the expected rate of return might be low for a new company just entering the field. And since capital is scarce, people will not invest in prospective businesses with low expected rates of return.

Ownership of essential raw materials can also lead to a monopoly situation. The classic example involves the diamond industry. The DeBeers Company of South Africa controls almost all the world's diamond mines. Another example used to be the Aluminum Company of America, which owned almost all the basic sources of bauxite, the major ore used in aluminum production. This company was able to retain its monopoly position in aluminum apparently because of its control over this essential raw material. It would not sell bauxite to any potential competitor.

Economies of Scale

A monopoly may arise because of a phenomenon known in economics as **economies of scale.** This term relates to *mass production*. It is generally assumed that bigger companies can produce things more cheaply than smaller companies because they can take advantage of mass production techniques, that is, they can realize **economies of mass production.** For a given amount of fixed costs, it is true that the more a firm produces, the smaller the average fixed cost. But production cannot continue indefinitely to get larger and average total costs, therefore, smaller. In any event, true economies of scale do not involve fixed costs at all. In the long run, all factors of production are variable.

Economies of scale refers to a situation where output increases more than proportionally to the increase in *all* inputs, including people *and* machines. That is, proportional increases in all factors of production yield proportionately larger increases in output. If all inputs are increased 10 percent and output goes up to 20 percent, those are known as economies of scale.

We should be sure that we are really observing economies of scale when looking at actual, big companies. General Motors sells $20 billion of products a year. However, it has many plants. Apparently then a firm may find economies of scale at the plant level, that is, in the production unit used. On the other hand, there may be much greater economies of scale at the firm level. These could be due to the economies of scale in management, for example.

We must also distinguish between **internal economies** (and diseconomies) **of scale** and external ones. The internal economies are those we just talked about. They are due to improved management techniques, production techniques, and so on, as all factors of production are increased. It is also possible, however, for external factors to allow for economies (or diseconomies) of scale. For example, as a firm grows larger, it will demand more and more supplies from supplier firms. As the supplier firms get larger orders, they may be able to improve their production techniques and lower their costs and prices. Hence, as a firm increases production, costs may actually fall. This would be caused by **external economies of scale**—due to factors beyond the control of each individual firm.

The Profit to be Made from Increasing Production

How do competitors and monopolists profit from increasing production? What happens to price in each case? We've already discussed the competitive situation.

Competitor's Marginal Revenue

Remember that a competitive firm has a horizontal demand curve. That is, the competitive firm is such a small part of the market that it cannot influence the price of its product. It is a price taker. If the forces of market supply and demand establish the price per bushel of wheat at $2, then the individual firm can sell all the wheat it wants to produce at $2 a bushel. The average revenue is $2, the price is $2, and the marginal revenue is also $2.

Let us again define marginal revenue:

Marginal revenue equals the change in total revenues resulting from the production and sale of one more unit.

In the case of a competitive industry, each time production is increased by one unit, total revenue increases by the going price, and it is always the same. Marginal revenue never changes; it always equals average revenue or price.

Monopolist's Marginal Revenue

What about a monopolist? Since the monopolist is the entire industry, that person faces the entire market demand curve. It is downward sloping just like the others we've seen. For the monopolist to sell more of the particular product, that person must lower the price. The monopolist must move *down* the demand curve. Usually, the monopolist must lower the price on all units sold; that person can't just lower the price on the last unit.

Here we see a fundamental difference between the monopolist and the competitor. The competitor doesn't have to worry about lowering prices in order to sell more. In a purely competitive situation, the competitor is such a small part of the market that he or she can sell the entire output, whatever that may be,

at the same price. The monopolist cannot do this. The more the monopolist wants to sell, the lower the price he or she has to charge on the last unit and on *all* units put on the market for sale. Obviously, the extra revenues the monopolist receives from selling one more unit are going to be smaller than the extra revenues received from selling the next to last unit. The monopolist has to lower the price on the last unit to sell it because he or she is facing a downward-sloping demand curve. The only way to move down the demand curve is to lower the price.

The monopolist's marginal revenue, therefore, is going to be falling. But it falls even more than one might think because to sell one more unit, the monopolist has to lower the price on all previous units, not just on the last unit produced and sold. This is because information flows freely; the monopolist will not be able to charge one consumer $2 and another consumer $3 for the same item. The consumer who could buy the product for $2 would buy lots of it and resell it to the one who was being charged $3 for a price of, say, $2.50. Unless the monopolist is successful in somehow separating (discriminating between) the different markets to prevent transactions among the consumers in those markets, she or he will have to sell all goods at a uniform price. Therefore, when the monopolist increases production, he or she charges a lower price on the last unit and on all previous units. We can, therefore, compute marginal revenue for the monopolist as follows:

A monopolist's marginal revenue equals the price for the last unit minus the reduction in price for all the previous units times the number of those units.

This is just another way of saying that marginal revenue equals total revenue for selling one more unit minus total revenue for sales without that last unit.

To drive home the concept of falling marginal revenues, we have presented in Table 19-1 a hypothetical demand schedule with total revenues and marginal revenues shown in the various columns. The demand schedule is for marijuana. It is assumed that the government has legalized and monopolized the industry; it has constructed a barrier to entry by making it illegal for private concerns to grow and distribute the euphoric. You can see for yourself that marginal revenue falls and is less than average revenue or the price.

This can be demonstrated graphically. In Figure 19-1, we have drawn a market demand curve for marijuana. The market demand curve is sometimes called the average revenue curve because at any point on the curve one can find the average revenues (price) from selling that particular quantity. The marginal revenue curve lies below the demand curve, as we have just explained. Notice that at point A the marginal revenue curve intersects the horizontal axis. After that point marginal revenues become negative.

Output and Price Determination for the Monopolist

We still haven't found the monopoly price and quantity solution to a monopolist's decision-making problem. The monopolist must decide at what rate to set production and sales and, at the same time, find out how much she or he can charge and sell at that rate. Let's assume that our monopolist faces no variable costs whatsoever in producing the product.

Take the example of a football stadium owner. The Superbowl is coming up. How much should he charge per ticket, if the tickets cost nothing to print? You would hardly expect the stadium owner to give the tickets away. You

---

Table 19-1 Hypothetical Revenue from the Government Selling Marijuana

In the first column we show the quantity of output; in the second column, the price or average revenue; and in the third column, total revenues. Total revenues equal the price times the quantity of output. Marginal revenue is shown in the last column. It is the difference between the two different total revenues when production is increased 1 unit.

QUANTITY OF OUTPUT (IN KILOS)	PRICE (AVERAGE REVENUE)	TOTAL REVENUE	MARGINAL REVENUE
1	$200	$200	
			$180
2	190	380	
			160
3	180	540	
			140
4	170	680	
			120
5	160	800	
			100
6	150	900	
			80
7	140	980	
			60
8	130	1040	
			40
9	120	1080	
			20
10	110	1100	
			0
11	100	1100	

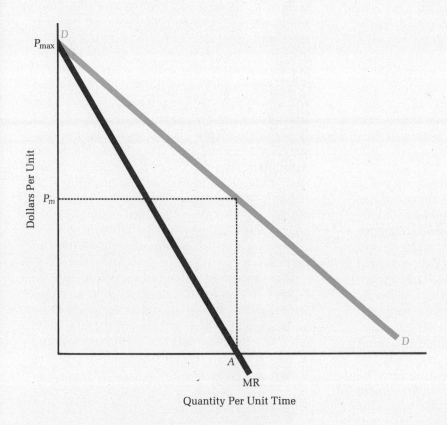

FIGURE 19-1 **The Monopolist's Marginal Revenue Curve**

The monopolist faces a downward-sloping demand curve. The demand curve is DD. Since the only way he or she can sell more units of the product is by lowering the price, the marginal revenue he or she receives from selling an additional unit is less than the average revenue or the price that he or she receives. The marginal revenue is equal to the price he or she receives on the last unit sold minus the reduction in price on all the former units sold times their number, so long as everyone is charged the same price. We have shown the marginal revenue curve as MR in this diagram. It intersects the horizontal axis at A; that is where marginal revenue equals zero. If a monopolist had no variable costs at all, he or she could figure out how much to charge to maximize profits by starting at P_{max}, the maximum price for which he or she could sell no units of the product. He or she could then see what happens as he or she charges successively lower prices. He or she would travel down the marginal revenue curve as he or she did this, going to the point where marginal revenue was equal to zero. He or she would charge P_m because that is how he or she maximizes his or her total revenues, and, since he or she has variable zero costs, his or her total profits. If he or she went to a price below P_m, marginal revenue would be negative; he or she would not be maximizing his or her profits because the benefit from selling additional units would be negative after P_m, or point A in the diagram. This diagram shows in a simplified manner that profit maximization occurs at the point where marginal revenue equals marginal costs. Here we have maintained that the marginal costs for our monopolist are zero—that is, his or her marginal cost curve is the horizontal axis. He or she will produce at point A and sell his or her product for P_m.

might expect him to sell tickets at near nothing. After all, if you multiply a very small number (the price) by a very, very large number (the quantity), you can come up with sizable revenues. Notice, however, that the demand curve we have drawn in Figure 19-1 slopes downward and will eventually cut the horizontal axis at some point. This means that to sell more than is indicated at the intersection of the demand curve and the horizontal axis (zero price), our monopolist would have to pay people to take his product. This certainly isn't any way for him to make money.

We will assume that the stadium owner is attempting to maximize profits. Since he has no variable costs, he should be merely looking at his total revenues. He should never set a price that yields less than a maximum. So he should never set a price that yields a negative marginal revenue. That is, no price below P_m in Figure 19-1 is correct for him. At a price below P_m his MR will be negative, thereby lowering total revenue and profits.

Look at it another way. The stadium owner has a fixed number of seats. The marginal cost of providing somebody with a seat is zero. He should continue selling seats until it is no longer profitable. It is no longer profitable when the marginal revenue falls below marginal costs. But marginal costs are zero. So seats should be sold until MR = 0.

Marginal Revenue and Elasticity

The point on the demand schedule directly above point A, where marginal revenue becomes zero, is a very special point. Here is where the elasticity of demand is equal to unity (−1). Look at Figure 19-2. Here at point A' on the demand schedule, the point corresponding to zero marginal revenues, we have marked $e = -1$. That portion of the demand schedule to the right of point A' we have labeled *inelas-*

tic. That is, to the right of point A', a change in price elicits a proportionately smaller change in quantity demanded. Contrast this with point A', where we have said that $e = -1$. That is, the elasticity of demand is such that a change in price elicits a proportionate change in quantity demanded.

That portion of the demand curve to the left and above point A' (above price P_m) we have labeled *elastic.* This means that to the left of A' a change in price will cause a proportionately larger change in quantity demanded. In our particular example, where the monopolist has no costs, we found that he would produce at point A' on the demand schedule. He would not go past that point because marginal revenues would become negative. Obviously, there is some relationship between elasticity and revenues.

We show that relationship graphically in Figures 19-2 and 19-3. Obviously total revenues are zero at a zero price and at P_{max} where no units are sold. Between these points, total revenues rise and then fall. The maximum revenue is where the elasticity of demand is unity as shown in Figure 19-3.

Adding the Cost Curves

We assumed there were no costs involved in producing the monopoly's product. Now we'll be more realistic. When costs are zero, production is expanded until marginal revenues equal zero. This should give you some hint as to how the monopolist will determine where he should produce. He's going to be looking at the difference between revenues and costs for each possible level of production and sales.

Let's draw some cost schedules in our monopoly diagram. In Figure 19-4, we have the same demand schedule and the same marginal revenue curve as before, but now we have drawn in a marginal cost curve. Remember that

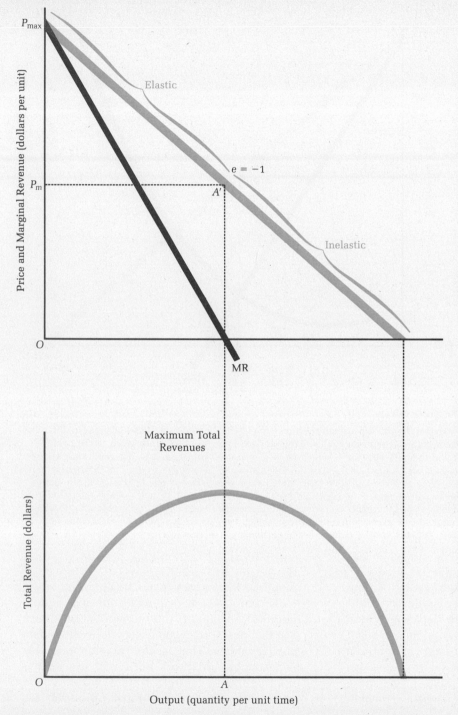

P_max

Price and Marginal Revenue (dollars per unit)

Elastic

e = −1

P_m ⌐‌‌‌‌‌‌‌‌‌ A′

Inelastic

O

MR

Maximum Total
Revenues

Total Revenue (dollars)

O   A

Output (quantity per unit time)

**FIGURE 19-2 Elasticity of
Demand and Total Revenues**

Here we show the relationship
between marginal revenue, the
demand curve, and the elasticity
of demand. From the point
where marginal revenue equals
zero—that is, point A′—demand is
inelastic to the right, and elastic
to the left. At point A, demand
has unitary elasticity, or −1. To
the right, the monopolist would
find that if he or she lowered
price, the quantity demanded
would not increase proportionally.
To the left of A′ as he or she
raised price, the quantity
demanded would fall more than
proportionally.

**FIGURE 19-3 Total Revenues
and the Demand Curve**

Here we show the relationship
between the demand curve,
elasticity of demand, and total
revenue. When the price is set at
P_{max} in Figure 19-2, the total
revenues are, of course, zero.
When the price is set at zero,
total revenues are also zero. In
between these two ends of the
price-possibilities scale we will
find some price that maximizes
total revenues. That price
happens to be where marginal
revenue equals zero, or at point
A′ in Figure 19-2. We have
shown here that the maximum
occurs at the output at which
marginal revenue equals zero.
If the monopolist had no
variable costs at all, he or she
would obviously want to
produce at point A because
that is where he or she would
maximize his or her total
revenues which, in essence,
would maximize total profits.

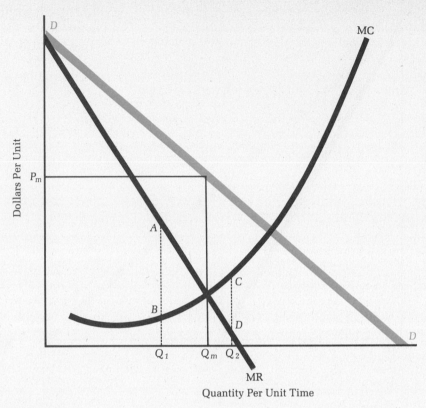

FIGURE 19-4 Maximizing Profits with Costs Added

Here we show the demand curve DD as before and a marginal revenue curve, MR. We add a marginal cost curve, MC. The monopolist will maximize profits where marginal revenue equals marginal cost; he or she will produce up to the point where MC equals MR and then will find the highest price at which he or she can sell that quantity. The profit-maximizing production rate is Q_m and the profit-maximizing price is P_m. The monopolist would be silly to produce at Q_1 because here marginal revenue would be Q_1A and marginal costs would be Q_1B. Marginal revenue exceeds marginal cost. If production is increased by one unit, the monopolist will obviously be better off because the extra revenues will more than cover the extra costs. He or she will keep producing until the point Q_m where marginal revenue just equals marginal costs. It would be silly to produce at Q_2 for here marginal cost exceeds marginal revenue. The benefits from selling the extra units here are outweighed by the additional costs. It behooves the monopolist to cut back production to Q_m.

the marginal cost curve was the key to deciding which output the perfect competitor would produce. It is also the key to deciding which output the monopolist will produce and sell.

The monopolist would be smart to continue production until the additional revenues received from producing and selling one more unit just cover the additional costs. *The mo-*

nopolist will continue increasing production up to the output at which marginal cost equals marginal revenue. If the monopolist produces past that point, marginal costs will exceed marginal revenues. That is, the incremental costs of producing any more units will exceed the incremental revenues. It just wouldn't be worthwhile. If the monopolist produces less than that, then he or she is not making maximum profits. That is, if production is increased by more units, the monopolist will increase total profit because marginal revenues still exceed marginal costs.

Look at Q_1 in Figure 19-4. Here the monopolist's marginal revenue is at A, but marginal cost is at B. The difference is the increase in profits on that particular unit of production. Why should the monopolist stop at Q_1? He or she won't. The monopolist will continue expanding output and sales until marginal revenue equals marginal costs. The monopolist won't go to Q_2 because here we see that marginal costs are C and marginal revenues are D. The difference between C and D represents the loss on producing that additional unit. It makes no sense to go that far.

How does the monopolist set prices? We know the quantity is set at the point where marginal revenue equals marginal cost. He or she then finds out how much can be charged—that is, how much the market will bear—for that particular quantity, Q_m. We know that the demand curve is defined as showing the *maximum* price that a given quantity can be sold for. So our monopolist knows that to sell Q_m and no more he or she can only charge P_m because that is where Q_m hits the demand curve DD. The monopolist can draw the vertical line up to the market demand curve. The monopolist can then reach over horizontally to the price axis to find the profit-maximizing price of P_m.

Figuring Out Profits

We can now easily figure out how much profit our true monopolist will make. Price is set equal to P_m, and the quantity which can be sold at that price is Q_m. The monopolist therefore receives total revenues equal to the price times the quantity, or P_m times Q_m. How much has

to be spent to produce all those goods? It is easy to find out: We add an average total cost curve to our diagram.

At the production rate of Q_m in Figure 19-5, the monopolist's average total cost per unit of production is at point F. Since that's the average or per unit cost, we can find out what our total costs are by multiplying the average cost times the quantity. This is exactly what is done graphically when the rectangle in the lowest corner of the diagram is shaded in. The difference between the total revenues and the total costs are the monopolist's profits, or the green area. There is no way for our monopolist to make larger profits than those shown by the shaded area. *The monopolist is maximizing profits where marginal costs equal marginal revenues.* If the monopolist produces less than that, he or she will be forfeiting some profits. If the monopolist produces more than that, he or she will also be forfeiting profits.

The same is true of a pure competitor. The competitor produces where marginal revenues equal marginal costs because he or she produces at the point where the marginal cost schedule intersects the horizontal *dd* curve. The horizontal *dd* curve represents the marginal revenue curve for the pure competitor for the same revenues are obtained on all the units sold. Pure competitors maximize profits at MR = MO, as do pure monopolists. But the pure competitor makes no true economic profits in the long run. Rather, all he or she makes is a normal competitive rate of return.

The Cost to Society of a Monopoly

Let's run a little experiment. We will start with a purely competitive industry with numerous firms, each one unable to affect the price of the product. The supply curve of the industry is equal to the horizontal sum of all the marginal cost curves of the individual producers.

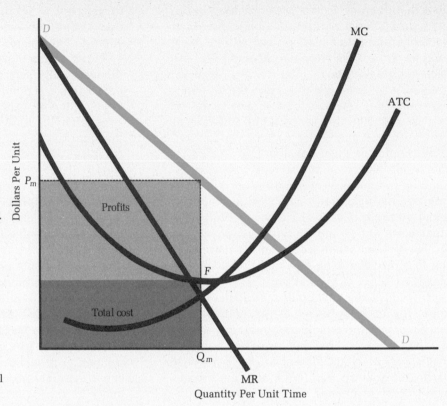

FIGURE 19-5 **Profits for the Monopolist**

The profit-maximizing monopolist will set the production rate at Q_m and charge all the traffic will bear—that is, P_m. Total revenues equal the price times quantity, or P_m times Q_m. Total costs will equal the quantity produced times the average total costs. Average total costs are found in this diagram at point F, so the gold-shaded area marked "Total cost" is just equal to Q_m times F, where F is the average total cost. Profits are marked as the olive-shaded area because they are the difference between total revenues, P_m times Q_m, and total costs, F times Q_m.

In Figure 19-6, we show the market demand curve and the market supply curve in a perfectly competitive situation. The competitive price in equilibrium is equal to P_e, and the competitive quantity demanded and supplied at that price is equal to Q_e. Each individual competitor faces a demand curve dd (which is not shown) that is coincident with the price line P_e. No individual supplier faces the market demand curve DD.

Now let's assume that a big monopolist comes in and buys up every single competitor in the industry. In so doing, we'll assume that the monopolist does not affect any of the marginal cost curves. We can therefore redraw DD and SS in the accompanying Figure 19-7. They are exactly the same as those in Figure 19-6.

How does this monopolist decide how much to charge and how much to produce? If the monopolist is smart, he or she is going to look at the marginal revenue curve and set the quantity produced at the point where marginal revenue equals marginal cost. But what is the marginal cost curve in Figure 19-7? It is merely SS because we said that SS was equal to the horizontal sum of all the individual marginal cost curves. The monopolist therefore produces a quantity Q_m and sells it at a price P_m. Notice that Q_m is less than Q_e and P_m is greater than P_e. A monopolist, therefore, produces a smaller quantity and sells it at a higher price. This is the reason usually given when one attacks monopolists. They raise the price and restrict production, compared to a competitive situation.

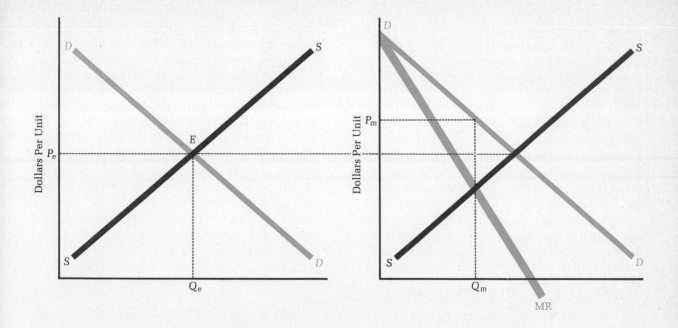

FIGURES 19-6, 19-7 The Effects of Monopolizing an Industry

In Figure 19-6 we show a competitive situation where *DD* is the market demand curve and *SS* is the market supply curve. The market supply curve is made up of the horizontal summation of the supply curves of all the firms involved. Equilibrium is established at the intersection of *DD* and *SS* at E. The equilibrium price would be P_e, and the equilibrium quantity supplied and demanded would be Q_e. Note that the demand curve *DD* is not the one facing each individual producer. Each individual competitive producer faces a demand curve that is a horizontal line at the market clearing price P_e. Nobody sees that industry demand curve *DD* except an observer looking from the outside at the entire industry. Now we assume that the industry is suddenly monopolized. We assume that the costs stay the same; the only thing that changes is that the monopolist now faces the entire downward-sloping demand curve. In Figure 19-7, we draw the marginal revenue curve. The monopolist will produce at the point where marginal revenue equals marginal costs. Marginal cost is *SS* because that is the horizontal summation of all the individual marginal cost curves. The monopolist therefore produces at Q_m and charges a price P_m. P_m in Figure 19-7 is higher than P_e in Figure 19-6. We see, then, that a monopolist charges a higher price and produces less than an industry in a competitive situation.

For a monopolist's product, consumers are forced to pay a price that exceeds the marginal cost of production. Resources are misallocated in such a situation—too few resources are being used in the monopolist's industry and too many are used elsewhere.

Can a Monopolist Make Even More Money?

In our preceding discussion we assumed that the monopolist sold all units at the same or uniform price. However, if the monopolist can somehow *price discriminate* according to the demand elasticities of different buyers, he or she can make even more profits. The monopolist then becomes a **price-discriminating monopolist.** This person will charge those consumers who really desire the product more than those consumers who have less desire for it. The monopolist will raise the price to those consumers with less elastic demand curves.

If the monopolist can somehow identify relatively less elastic demanders, he or she can raise the price to them and not realize much of a decrease in the quantity they demand and therefore he or she can transfer the amount demanded to the price-elastic consumers. If the monopolist lowers the price to consumers with relatively more elastic demands, he or she will attract more buyers. They'll substantially increase the quantity demanded. The monopolist will make more revenues, more profits, in both cases. Of course, he or she somehow has to prevent the elastic demanders who were charged a lower price from reselling the good to those who were charged a higher price.

Can you think of any examples of price discrimination? What about nightclubs that charge females less than males? It's easy to discriminate here and its pretty hard to transfer the product, right? Medical services are also hard to resell among patients. So we see doctors using price discrimination. We will cover this in our next issue.

Definitions of New Terms

Monopolist: The single supplier.

Barriers to Entry: Barriers that prevent new firms from entering an existing industry. Some barriers include government laws against entry and patents for research discoveries.

Economies of Scale: A situation where an increase in *all* factors of production brings about a more than proportionate increase in output. It is important in describing economies of scale to make sure that *all* inputs are increased proportionately. Economies of scale should not be confused with economies of mass production.

Economies of Mass Production: The term loosely applies to the reduction in average total costs as output is increased. Economies of mass production usually result in fixed costs being spread over a larger and larger number of units of output so that average fixed costs fall, thereby bringing down average total costs.

Internal Economies of Scale: A reduction in a firm's long-run average cost curve as a result of size adjustments within the firm as a unit of production. Internal economies of scale may result from greater specialization within the firm, improved managerial efficiency, and so on.

External Economies of Scale: A reduction in a firm's long-run average cost curve due to factors outside the control of the firm. These may occur, for example, because a large number of firms locate in one region and cause a reduction in the cost of the inputs used by all firms.

Price-Discriminating Monopolist: A monopolist who discriminates among classes of demanders with different elasticities of demand. This person will charge a higher price to those with relatively less elastic demands than to those with relatively more elastic demands.

1. We formally define a monopolist as a single supplier. A monopolist faces the entire industry demand curve because he or she is the entire industry. There are not too many examples of pure monopolists. In general, they have a government franchise to operate so that they can remain pure monopolists. We cite as examples electricity companies, the telephone system, and the post office. General Motors and U.S. Steel do not qualify as true monopolies under our restricted definition.

2. A monopolist can usually only remain a monopolist if there are barriers to entry; that is, if there is some reason why other firms cannot enter the industry and share in the monopoly profits. One of the most obvious barriers to entry is the government restriction. The government does not allow you to set up an alternative telephone system or an alternative electric utility. Patents on a discovery can also be an effective barrier to entry. A patent allows the owner of the patent to produce the product without fearing competiton for a period of 17 years.

3. A monopoly could arise because of economies of scale. Economies of scale are defined as a situation where an increase in *all* inputs leads to a more than proportionate increase in output. If this were the case, then average total costs would be falling as production and all inputs were increased to produce an increased output. In a situation where true economies of scale exist, the first person to produce a great deal and take advantage of those economies of scale can conceivably take advantage of the reduced average total cost by lowering price and driving everybody else out of the market.

4. The marginal revenue that a monopolist receives is defined in the same way as the marginal revenue that a competitor receives. However, there is one difference. Since the monopolist faces the industry demand curve, he or she must lower price to increase sales. He or she must lower price not only on the last unit sold but also on all the preceding units. The monopolist's marginal revenue, therefore, is equal to the price received on the last unit sold, minus the reduction in price on all the previous units, times the number of units.

5. The monopolist will produce where marginal revenue equals marginal cost. If the monopolist produces less than that, he or she is forgoing additional profits. Marginal revenue will exceed marginal cost; thus, it pays to continue production. If the monopolist produces at a point after marginal revenue equals marginal cost, marginal cost will *exceed* marginal revenues. The benefits from producing more are less than the costs.

6. The profit-maximizing price the monopolist charges is the maximum price he or she can get away with, while still selling everything produced up to the point where marginal revenue equals marginal cost. We find this price by extending a vertical line from the intersection of the marginal revenue curve and the marginal cost curve up to the demand curve and then over to the vertical axis, which measures price.

7. A straight-line demand curve can be separated into two sections. At the upper end is the elastic section; at the lower end is the inelastic section. Somewhere between is the point where elasticity is equal to −1, or unity. That can be found by extending a line vertically from the intersection of the marginal revenue curve with the horizontal axis. The quantity at which that line hits the demand curve is the quantity at which elasticity is unity. The elasticity is unity where marginal revenue equals zero. That is also the point where total revenues are maximized. If the monopolist had no variable costs at all, he or she would obviously want to produce where marginal revenue equals zero. That, in fact, is where the monopolist would maximize profits because he or she would be maximizing total revenues.

8. The monopolist's profits can be found easily. Profits are merely total revenues minus total costs. Total revenues are equal to the price of the product (the profit-maximizing price) times the quantity produced (the quantity found at the intersection of the marginal revenue and marginal cost curves). Total costs are equal to the quantity produced times average total costs. The difference between these total costs and total revenues is, as we stated, profits.

9. In general, it can be shown that a competitive industry, if monopolized, will end up with a higher price and a lower quantity supplied. That is why monopolies are "bad" in economic analysis. The monopolist will restrict production and increase price because he or she will look at the entire demand curve and realize that to sell more units of the product, the price must be lowered. The monopolist will look at the marginal revenue curve and produce where the marginal revenue curve intersects the marginal cost curve. Since the marginal revenue curve is below the demand schedule, we know he or she will produce less. Since the monopolist is producing less, he or she can obviously charge a higher price than can those in the competitive situation where more is produced.

10. If a monopolist can effectively separate different classes of demanders, grouping them according to their demand elasticities, he or she can become a price-discriminating monopolist. (But resale between groups charged different prices must be prevented.)

1. It is sometimes stated that pure monopoly never exists because there are always substitutes for whatever is produced. Do you agree? Why?

2. Do you think that a trademark gives a firm an effective amount of monopoly power?

3. Can you think of any reasons why a pure monopolist would not set the profit-maximizing price and produce the profit-maximizing quantity?

4. Will a monopolist ever produce at a point on the demand schedule that is to the right of where the elasticity is equal to −1, or unity?

5. It is often stated that the United States is run by large monopolists. Do you agree? If so, do you think you can utilize the model presented in this chapter to analyze and predict the behavior of most firms in the United States?

6. (a) Suppose the monopolist faces ATC_1. Define the rectangle that shows the monopolist's total costs at output rate Q. Also, define the rectangle showing total revenue. Is the monopolist showing an economic loss, a break-even (normal profit), or an economic gain situation? What is the significance of the MC = MR output?

   (b) Suppose the monopolist faces ATC_2. Define the rectangle that shows the monopolist's total costs. Also, define the rectangle showing total revenue. Is the monopolist showing an economic loss, a break-even (normal profit), or an economic gain situation? What is the significance of the MC = MR output?

   (c) Suppose the monopolist faces ATC_3. Define the rectangle that shows the monopolist's total costs. Also, define the rectangle showing total revenue. Is the monopolist showing an economic loss, a break-even (normal profit), or an economic gain situation? What is the significance of the MC = MR output?

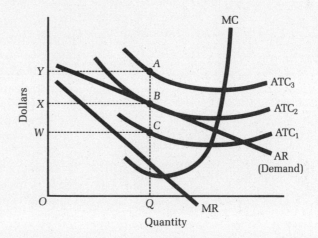

Selected References

Adams, Walter, *The Structure of American Industry*, 4th ed. New York: Macmillan, 1971, chap. 11.

Caves, Richard, *American Industry: Structure, Conduct, and Performance*, 3d ed., Englewood Cliffs, N.J.: Prentice-Hall, 1972.

Kefauver, Estes, *In a Few Hands: Monopoly Power in America*, Baltimore: Penguin, 1965.

Robinson, E. A. G., *Monopoly*, London: Nesbit, 1941.

Schumpeter, Joseph A., *Capitalism, Socialism, and Democracy*, 3d ed., New York: Harper & Row, 1950, chaps. 7 and 8.

Heretic to the Orthodox

JOAN ROBINSON

Economist, Cambridge University

Copyright Ramsey & Muspratt, Ltd.

Joan Robinson is one of the world's most important contemporary economists. A professor of economics at Cambridge University in England, where she has taught for more than 40 years, Robinson has written and lectured widely on economic theory and made significant contributions to the theories of imperfect competition and the accumulation of capital. She has called herself a "left-wing Keynesian," but she is knowledgeable in Marxist economic theory as well as in neo-classical economic theory. Eclectic in approach, but logical in thought, she draws on the insights of many of the great economists to develop critiques of modern capitalism and the current orthodox schools of economic thought. Her important books include *Introduction to the Theory of Employment* (1937, 1969), *An Essay on Marxian Economics* (1942, 1967), *The Accumulation of Capital* (1956, 1969), *Economic Philosophy* (1962), and *Freedom and Necessity: An Introduction to the Study of Society* (1970).

In *The Economics of Imperfect Competi-*

tion (1933, 1969) and later articles, Robinson developed a critique of the economic theory that is based on the notion of a static equilibrium. The growth of monopolies is inherent in the nature of competition in capitalist society, she says in one of her latest books, *Economic Heresies: Some Old-Fashioned Questions in Economic Theory* (1971). In the nineteenth century as well as today, "the majority of businesses are either growing, being forced out of existence by the growth of others, or being absorbed into some larger organization." Large corporations are able to grow even larger, she argues, through their great financial power rather than through technical economies of scale. Though the growth of monopolies has tended to reduce competition within individual countries, competition among the industries of different countries has increased. "In the textbook theory of the firm, a monopolist, faced by a known and stationary demand-curve for the commodity that he controls, restricts output to the level at which marginal revenue is equal to marginal cost and so extracts the maximum possible profit from the market." Noting that although there are some monopolies which conform to this pattern, Robinson argues that in reality most firms do not restrict their output, but are "continuously expanding capacity, conquering new markets, producing new commodities, and exploiting new techniques." The level of profit margins and the rate of profit on investment that they enjoy are in general higher than those in stagnant markets where competition still prevails because in expanding markets they can catch the profits that they need to finance expansion. "Modern industry," she says, "is a system not so much of monopolistic competition as of competitive monopolies."

The central assumption behind most economic thought since the time of Adam Smith, Robinson believes, is that "the pursuit of self-interest by each individual rebounds to the benefit of all." With this assumption, economists have thought they had solved the problem of moral values because morality would take care of itself in a perfectly competitive market. Although Keynes showed that the market did not provide a means for a harmonious reconciliation of conflicting interests, and the Depression gave ample evidence of the fallacy of this assumption, Robinson argues, the same assumption still pervades much contemporary economic thought.

The 1970s may prove a critical period for modern capitalism, Robinson thinks, not only economically but socially as well. Even if the capitalist countries can solve the problems of full employment without significant inflation and devise a viable international monetary system, other issues will remain. Modern capitalism has failed to eliminate poverty in its own countries, failed to seriously aid the development of the Third World countries, failed to be successful at all without an armaments race, and perhaps is in the process of making the planet uninhabitable in peacetime, she contends. "It should be the duty of economists to do their best to enlighten the public about the economic aspects of these menacing problems," Robinson says, but "they are impeded by a theoretical scheme which (with whatever reservations and exceptions) represents the capitalist world as a kibbutz operated in a perfectly enlightened manner to maximize the welfare of its members."

THEORY AND PRACTICE

Rising Costs of Medical Care

The woeful lack of adequate health care for large segments of the American population has been decried by those in Congress, presidents, laypeople, and even doctors. There have been many suggested solutions to our health care crisis, some of which have already been enacted in the form of Medicare and Medicaid. In addition, more comprehensive medical care insurance plans have been demanded by several senators.

In addition to the problems of inadequate supplies for medical care, concerned legislators and citizens cannot help noticing the rising costs of obtaining what medical care is available. In Figure I-20.1, we show the Consumer Price Index and a price index of health care services, which has risen considerably faster than the Consumer Price Index. This means, of course, that the relative price of health care services has been rising. Later, we shall present some plausible explanations for this phenomenon.

As one of his Phase II price-stabilization actions, President Nixon nominated a number of people to serve on a committee to oversee medical care prices. His hope was that this committee could encourage and perhaps obtain some price restraints on the part of the medical care industry. The success of Nixon's committee has not been overwhelming. Americans are still facing ever-increasing costs in health care services.

Medical Care Expenditures

Expenditures for medical care in the United States have increased dramatically in the last four or five decades. We spent only $4 billion on medical care in 1929; we increased our spending to $40 billion by 1965, and it is over $90 billion today. In 1929, expenditures on medical care represented 4 percent of total national spending; today's expenditures represent 8 percent. We can say, therefore, that the demand for medical care has been *income elastic*. As real incomes rose, Americans demanded not just more medical care, but more in proportion to the rise in real income.

While the proportion of total spending going to medical care has risen, the prices of medical care services have also risen. Since 1950, for example, health service costs rose at an annual rate of 4.6 percent, substantially higher than the annual percentage increase of all other prices in the economy for the same period.

For this to occur, the demand schedule for medical services must have shifted faster than the supply schedule of those services. We see this depicted in Figure I-20.2. Here we find that over time the demand schedule for health care has shifted from DD to $D'D'$. At the same time, the supply schedule has shifted from SS to $S'S'$. The shift in the supply schedule is much less than the shift in the demand schedule. The new equilibrium is at E', with a higher price than the old equilibrium of E. The key, then, to understanding why the price of medical services has risen more rapidly than other prices is to find out (1) why the demand schedule shifted to the right so fast and (2) why the supply schedule shifted so little. That is exactly what we will do in this issue. We will then discuss the possibilities of medical care for everyone in the United States.

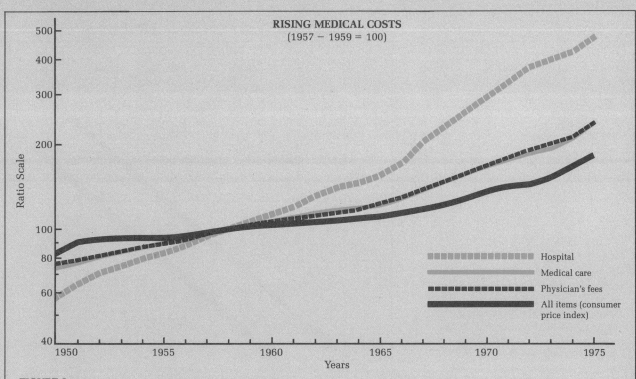

RISING MEDICAL COSTS
(1957 – 1959 = 100)

Legend:
- Hospital
- Medical care
- Physician's fees
- All items (consumer price index)

FIGURE I-20.1

Medical prices have risen faster than the average prices of all other goods. (*Source*: U.S. Department of Labor.)

The Supply of Medical Care

Medical care consists of a number of items including, but not limited to, the services of physicians, nurses, and hospital staff, hospital facilities, maintenance of the facilities, medications, and drugs. We will limit our discussion in this issue to what determines the supply of physicians' services (until now at least, the most important input).

The Production of Medical Doctors

In 1972, 50,000 people took the Standard Medical School Admissions Test; only 12,000 were accepted in medical schools. The number of applicants to Harvard's Medical School runs to almost 3500, but the class size remains at less than 150. Some students apply to as many as 10 different medical schools, and when turned down, reapply two or three times. The number of students who don't apply because they know the odds are so much against them is probably two or three times the number who actually do take the chance. Why is there such a large discrepancy between those who want to go to medical school and those who are accepted? If you compare the number of students who wish to attend law school with the number of students who actually go, the discrepancy is relatively smaller. The reason for this discrepancy is not hard to find; the number of medical schools in the United States is severely restricted, and the number of entrants into those schools each year is similarly restricted.

Restrictions

Restricted by whom? In principle, restriction on the number of medical schools is due to state licensing requirements, which universally prohibit proprietary medical schools

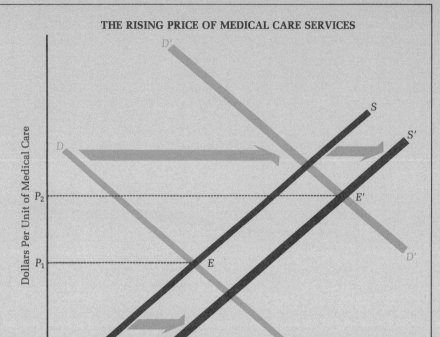

THE RISING PRICE OF MEDICAL CARE SERVICES

Dollars Per Unit of Medical Care

P_2

P_1

Quantity of Medical Care Services Per Unit Time

FIGURE I-20.2

The demand schedule for medical care services has been shifting outward faster than the supply schedule. Twenty years ago the demand and supply schedules were *DD* and *SS* and the price was P_1. Since then, the demand schedule has shifted to *D'D'* and the supply schedule to *S'S'*. The new equilibrium price is P_2 which is higher than P_1.

(schools run for profit). Also, it is difficult for a university that does not have a medical school suddenly to start one. A university can start a graduate department of romance languages without asking anybody, and it can start a law school without asking anybody. However, unless the medical school is accredited by the state, the graduates are not even allowed to take the licensing exam required for practicing medicine.

To understand why such restrictions have been put on medical schools, read the statements of Dr. John H. Knowles' article, in *Saturday Review,* August 22, 1970:

At the turn of the century, the AMA [American Medical Association] stood at the forefront of progressive thinking and socially responsible action. Its members had been leaders in forming much-needed public health departments in the states during the last half of the nineteenth century. It formed a Council on Medical Education in 1904 and immediately began an investigation of proprietary medical schools. Because of its success in exposing intolerable conditions in these schools, the Carnegie Foundation, at the AMA's request, commissioned Abraham Flexner to study the national scene. His report in 1910 drove proprietary interest out of medical education, established it as a full university function with standards for admission, curriculum development, and clinical teaching. Our present system of medical education, essentially unchanged since the Flexner (and AMA) revolution—and acknowledging its current defects—was accomplished through the work of the AMA. Surely this contribution was and is one of the finest in the public interest.

The Past

Looking back to the first decade in this century, we find there were 192 medical schools. By 1944 that number had declined to 69. The number of physicians per 100,000 people dropped from 157 in 1900 to 132 in 1957. Perhaps the American Medical Association and the so-called Flexner report lauded by Dr. Knowles were responsible for the reduction in the rate of growth of the supply of physicians. At least, this appears to be the case.

The AMA Wins Out The American Medical Association was started in 1847. It represented then and still does represent existing practitioners in the field of medicine. From 1870 to 1910 there was a struggle between the AMA and medical educators over who should control the output of doctors—that is, who should control the number of doctors allowed to practice. This became a battle over who should control medical schools themselves. The American Medical Association won the battle. It essentially has complete control over medical education in the United States. For a medical school graduate to become licensed in any particular state, the graduate must have obtained a degree from a "certified" medical school. The certification is nominally done by the states themselves; however, in all cases the states follow exactly the certification lists of the American Medical Association. If, for example, the American Medical Association were to decertify a particular medical school, you can be sure the state involved would decertify that same school. Graduates coming out of that decertified school would find themselves barred from legal medical practice.

The Flexner Report The regulation and certification of medical schools was, in all probability, based on the outcome of the famous Flexner Report. As mentioned, in 1910 the prestigious Carnegie Foundation commissioned Abraham Flexner to inspect the existing medical education facilities in the United States. Flexner's recommendations resulted in the demise of half the then existing medical schools. Flexner asserted that those schools were unqualified to teach medical education. It is interesting to note that Flexner had absolutely no qualifications himself for deciding which medical schools were to be rated class A. Flexner was not a physician, he was not a scientist, and he was never a medical educator. He had an undergraduate degree in arts and was the owner and operator of a for-profit preparatory school in Louisville, Kentucky. Moreover, his evaluation of existing medical schools consisted of a grand inspection tour—nothing more, nothing less. Sometimes Flexner evaluated an entire school in one afternoon. His method for deciding whether a medical school was qualified was to estimate how well it compared with the medical school at Johns Hopkins University.

It is also interesting to note that Flexner was examining the *inputs* and not the *output* of these particular schools. Instead of finding out how well or how qualified the *graduates* of the different schools were, he looked at how they were taught. This is equivalent to your instructor giving you a grade on the basis of how many hours you spent studying rather than how well you did on the final exam (even though you might find that preferable).

Discrimination Flexner's endeavor not only caused the number of medical schools to drop by half, but it also caused greater discrimination against blacks and women. Whereas the number of white medical schools fell by half from 1906 to 1944, the number of black medical schools went from 7 to 2, and the number of students admitted to the surviving two schools decreased. This should not surprise anyone reading the Flexner Report, in which Flexner states in all seriousness:

A well taught Negro sanitarian will be immensely useful; an essentially untrained Negro wearing an MD degree is dangerous. . . . The practice of the Negro doctor will be limited to his own race.

The number of women physicians reached a high point in 1910, just before the recommendations of the Flexner Report were put into effect. In 1940, the number of women physicians was less than it had been in 1910.

Discrimination in medical schools is not hard to understand. After all, the number of applicants greatly exceeds the number of vacancies. One easy way to ration out the available supply of slots in medical school is to weed out those persons with distinct characteristics like sex and race. One would also expect that the ability to discriminate increases as the discrepancy between the number of applicants and the number of available positions grows larger. Indeed, this is exactly what happened.

Why Did the AMA Seek Control?

It is not hard to find the motive behind the AMA's desire to control medical schools. We merely need quote from the former head of the AMA's Council on Medical Education, Dr. Beven, who said in 1928:

In this rapid elevation of the standard of medical education . . . the reduction of the number of medical schools from 160 to 80, there occurred a marked reduction in the number of medical students and medical graduates. We had anticipated this and felt that this was a desirable thing. We had . . . a great oversupply of poor mediocre practitioners.

Part of Dr. Beven's statement can be interpreted to mean that, if the supply falls, the price will rise, whereas if the supply increases, the price will fall. Figure I-20.3 shows that the reduction in the number of physicians during this period resulted in the supply curve of physicians shifting to the left. The demand curve was stable. Therefore, the price of the physicians' services went up, thereby allowing them to make higher incomes.

AMA's Motives Not Satisfied

If we look at the American Medical Association's avowed motives, we realize that even those were not satisfied. The AMA maintained that the qualifications of many doctors were deficient—that is, the public was being serviced by doctors who were doing damage to unsuspecting patients. The idea behind medical school licensing was to weed out the

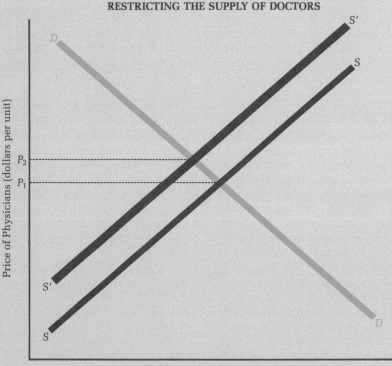

RESTRICTING THE SUPPLY OF DOCTORS

FIGURE I-20.3

The AMA's successful attempt at restricting the supply of doctors shifted the supply schedule from SS to S'S'. Even with a stable demand schedule the price of physicians goes up.

most unqualified students and to eliminate the possibility of an unsuspecting sick person being treated by an inadequately trained, yet licensed doctor. It is strange, therefore, that the AMA did not seek in 1910 to analyze the qualifications of the current crop of physicians. The closure of one-half of the medical schools resulted in the elimination of a *future* supply of supposedly unqualified doctors. The then current supply of supposedly unqualified doctors were allowed to continue practicing until retirement or death. Furthermore, the then current generation of unsuspecting citizens were supposed to seek the aid of whoever happened to have an M.D. degree before the implementation of the Flexner Report recommendations. Somehow this type of behavior does not seem consistent with the AMA's desire to raise the quality of medical services in the United States.

Moreover, it is difficult to understand why doctors are not reexamined periodically if they wish to continue practicing. Even a brilliant medical student from an excellent medical school can become very lax in medical practice and be unqualified after a period of years. Since there is no recertification procedure, the public can still be subject to the malpractices of unqualified doctors.

Additionally, it is not obvious that the quality of the medical care consumed by the public actually increased as much as the AMA professed. After all, there are two ways of obtaining medical services. One is self-diagnosis and self-treatment. The other is reliance on the medical care industry. If the price of a physician's diagnosis and treatment goes up, then one might expect that the quantity demanded would fall. An increased reliance on self-diagnosis and self-treatment would result. People would go to doctors only after their symptoms became alarming. It may be, then, that the increase in quality and, therefore, price of doctors' services resulted in a *decrease* in the *total* quality of medical care utilized because physicians were consulted less often. Moreover, we must presume that some people might forgo the services of a licensed physician in favor of some alternative method which may be of "inferior" quality, such as naturopaths or faith healers. When the price of the services of licensed physicians goes up, there is an increase in the demand for substitute healing services, and these substitutes may indeed be inferior to even a poorly trained M.D.

Jumps in Demand—Medicare

Another reason for large increases in the price of medical care relates to jumps in demand that aren't a function of rising real income. Prior to the introduction of Medicare ("free" medical care for the aged), congressional estimates of the cost of that particular program were many times less than the cost actually turned out to be. There is an easy explanation for this, and it partially involves the practice of *price discrimination* in the medical profession. Before we discuss this, we must realize that the demand for medical services is both income elastic and price elastic. When Medicare was instituted, the actual price of health care services to many were drastically lowered. In some cases, the price was reduced to zero. As the price fell, the quantity demanded rose. The quantity demanded rose so much that the available supply of medical care services was taxed beyond capacity. The only thing that could give was the price, and price did go up. Hospital room charges have skyrocketed since the imposition of Medicare—but this is not the only thing that has happened.

Price Discrimination

Previous to Medicare, a large percentage of poor, older patients were given free medical treatment. In other words, physicians did not charge these patients. After the imposition of Medicare, physicians did charge them. The patients still paid nothing, but the government started paying for what the patients had previously received free. The explanation of the change in the behavior of physicians has to do with their ability and desire to price discriminate.

We discussed price discrimination in the context of a monopoly. The same model can be applied to the medical profession. Doctors have a monopoly; the AMA controls the supply of doctors and, therefore, can be analyzed as a monopolist. Let's take a particular physician who wishes to maximize income. (We are not assuming this is actually the physician's motive; rather, we are applying an income-maximizing model to see what the results will be and to see if those results conform with what has actually happened.) Assume that the doctor is charging all patients the same price. Obviously, the doctor discourages patients with high price elasticities for medical services from buying those services by charging equal prices to all. The physician does not discourage very many potential patients with less elastic demands because, by definition, they are not very price responsive.

The doctor now decides more income might be obtained if some patients are charged lower prices and other patients higher prices for the same services. Let's assume that the doctor can separate the relatively less price-elastic demanders from the relatively more price-elastic demanders. One easy way to do this is to separate patients by their incomes. Apparently, high-income people have relatively lower elasticities of demand for medical services than do low-income people. If the doctor lowers the price of his or her services to low-income people—that is, those with elastic demands—his or her total revenues from these people will increase for the quantity demanded will rise more than proportionally to the decrease in price. If the price charged to high-income or less-elastic demanders is raised, total revenue will also rise. The quantity demanded will not fall as much as the increase in price.

Graphic Analysis

We see how our doctor does this in Figure I-20.4, where two separate market demand curves for the doctor's services have been drawn: one less elastic and one more elastic. We assume the doctor has a constant (horizontal) marginal cost curve. The

doctor will charge a higher price for the less-elastic demanders than for the more-elastic demanders. You might be asking yourself: "How can a doctor act as a monopolist?" The doctor is in competition with many more doctors. Unless this doctor is in a small city where no other doctor is practicing, he or she will not be able to price discriminate in a competitive situation. Other doctors will, in fact, undercut his or her expensive services to high-income patients. Eventually only a uniform price per constant quality unit can prevail in a competitive industry. Doctors, if left to their own devices, would actually be in competition with one another and price discrimination could not occur. So goes the reasoning, but the rules and regulations of the American Medical Association have prevented many doctors from competing by price cutting. It is "unethical" for doctors to advertise to compete for patients.

It is also difficult for price cutters to enter the specialties, the more lucrative aspects of medical care. The county medical board must certify a doctor before he or she can be allowed to specialize in, say, bone or heart surgery. Even doctors who are already certified in a specialty can be denied hospital privileges as punishment for overt price cutting. If a doctor cannot send patients to a hospital, he or she cannot perform lucrative operations unless, of course, they can be done in the office.

Fighting the Group Health Plans

Given that the American Medical Association has followed a policy

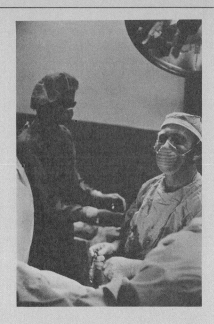

which we can equate with price discrimination, it is not surprising that the AMA has fought tooth and nail against prepaid medical plans, such as Kaiser, Group Health, and Ross-Loos. With these medical plans, everybody is charged the same for the same thing. These plans are all prepaid; the charges are not a function of subscribers' incomes. There is no way to price discriminate as there is with the typical "fee for service" method of payment that physicians usually use. The AMA has used various tactics to discourage doctors from participating in group medical plans. Many of these doctors have been run out of their county medical associations and, therefore, cannot practice specialties anywhere except

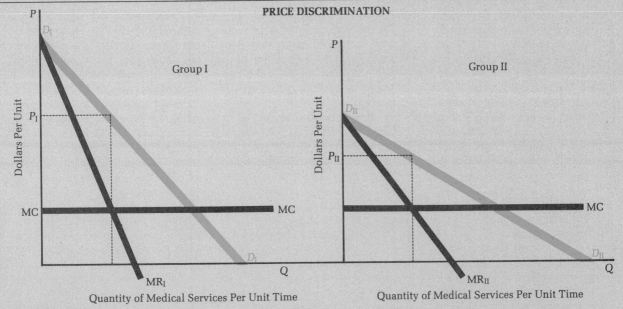

PRICE DISCRIMINATION

Group I

Group II

FIGURE I-20.4

Here the smart doctor has separated patients into those with relatively less elastic demand curves (group I) and those with relatively more elastic demand curves (group II). Profit maximization occurs when marginal revenue equals marginal cost. Therefore, our doctor sets marginal revenue equal to marginal cost in each individual category. We find that the doctor sets a price of P_I for group I and a price of P_{II} for group II. Those with the relatively less elastic demands end up paying more than do those with the relatively more elastic demands for the same service. In such a situation the doctor earns a greater income than he or she would by charging a single price to all patients.

with the group medical plan hospital. In some instances, the AMA was quite unsuccessful in its attempts to squelch budding medical establishments that promoted competition and didn't price discriminate. The AMA has been prosecuted under the Sherman Antitrust Act in Washington, D.C. and under other state antitrust acts; nonetheless, about one-third of the states have declared group health plans illegal.

National Health Insurance

Is a national health insurance policy the answer to our medical care problem? This is what many senators and numerous laypeople think should be done. After all, it has apparently worked in England. There, a limited national health insurance scheme was in effect from 1911 to 1948. In 1948, the present comprehensive national health plan was devised. Anybody in England can go to one of Britain's 23,000 family doctors and receive whatever health care is needed without paying the doctor a cent. If the family doctor is not equipped to handle the illness, the patient is sent to a nationally run hospital to see a specialist, again without paying directly. Britain has almost one-half million hospital beds available for those who are sick, whether rich or poor.

One might ask whether the national health plan in Britain is "free." It is certainly "free" to most people, although they pay for the "free" service with a weekly contribution of about $4 taken from everybody's paycheck. The plan costs England's taxpayers $8 billion a year, an amount that represents more than 10 percent of all public expenditures. The weekly contributions of employed individuals covers only 10 percent of the costs, and the rest is made up from taxes. Thus, medical care in England clearly is not free: It is paid indirectly via taxes that the government collects.

No matter *who* pays for medical care, however, the costs still have to be borne by *someone.* Don't think that medical services would somehow be sent from heaven if a national, all-inclusive health insurance plan were passed in the United States. Part of your taxes would go to pay for health care. To the extent that you took advantage of ''free'' health care, you would be repaid for your contribution. To the extent that you received more services than you paid for, you would be obtaining a subsidy from those taxpayers who received less than they paid for. Actually, this is a form of redistribution of income—not necessarily from the rich to the poor—but from the more healthy to the less healthy.

Britain's national insurance plan has not been without its problems. Currently, many doctors are leaving the country each year in search of greener pastures. The wages paid by the British government are not sufficient to keep all the doctors satisfied in England. This is a potential problem in the United States if a similar plan is instituted here. Our doctors probably couldn't find better jobs in other countries, but they could work less.

Let's assume that a national health care act is passed by Congress and anyone can obtain a physician's services if she or he wants—no matter what the income. The patient will not be billed directly. Rather, physicians will bill the government. If the government refuses

to pay what the physicians ask, then we might find that the quantity of health care in the United States may actually fall as physicians decide to work fewer hours because the rate of return for working more hours is not sufficient.

Another possible response to maximum rates for, say, office visits would be for physicians to cut down on the number of minutes spent per patient. This is apparently what has happened in certain circumstances. It has been discovered that a few doctors have made in excess of $200,000 a year in Medicare and Medicaid payments. The only way this can be done is by seeing a large number of patients each day; and the only way a doctor can see a large number of patients each day is by spending fewer minutes with each patient. Notice, however, that some patients still may be better off than they were before Medicare. If they have not been seeing a doctor at all, they have improved their lot even with only a few minutes of a doctor's attention at the expense of their fellow taxpayers.

The Real Problem

Apparently, there would still be a problem about adequate medical care even if a national health plan were passed in the United States. No doubt the supply of hospitals can be expanded. The supply of medical equipment and the supply of nurses can be expanded also. But the supply of licensed physicians would still be controlled by the American Medi-

cal Association. The only long-run means by which the wages of medical doctors can be brought down, without creating shortages, is to increase the rate at which new doctors are coming ''on line.''

Many suggestions have been made for increasing the supply of doctors, and the AMA has seen fit to implement some of these suggestions. For example, larger numbers of paramedics are being trained to assist physicians in medical tasks that do not require a high degree of training. Furthermore, there apparently has been some loosening up of the standards for entrance into medical schools.

An additional proposal involves elimination of licensing from medical school. Instead, there would be a licensing procedure at the *output* stage in the production of medical services. Potential doctors would have to pass a national examination before entering practice, and no questions would be asked about the doctor's training. This is similar to the bar examination that a potential lawyer must pass to practice in a particular state. The same examination given to potential doctors would also be given to practicing doctors at certain time intervals. In this manner, we would be assured that the supply of doctors would not deteriorate in quality. The current crop of doctors would write the examinations. They would know that with an extremely difficult examination, fewer doctors would enter the profession, but also fewer inferior colleagues would be able to pass the exam and continue in practice.

Questions for Thought and Discussion

1. In almost all cases, doctors with whom you come in contact will vigorously deny that the AMA has actually harmed the welfare of the nation by restricting the supply of doctors. Doctors will maintain that it is necessary to keep the quality of medical services as high as possible. Do you agree? If so, why shouldn't the argument hold for other products and services?
2. "Poor people would rather have low-quality, low-priced medical care than no medical care at all." Evaluate.
3. "The problem is not that poor people need medical care, but that they do not have the money to buy it. Therefore, it is a problem of a maldistribution of income." Evaluate.
4. Would you rather get medical services in England or in the United States? Does your answer depend on your income?
5. Small rural towns have difficulty in getting a doctor to live and work in them. Why? Can you think of a solution?

Selected References

Kessel, Reuben, "Price Discrimination in Medicine," *The Journal of Law and Economics,* **1,** October 1958, pp. 20–53.

——, "The A.M.A. and the Supply of Physicians," *Law and Contemporary Problems,* Spring 1970.

Rayack, Elton, *Professional Power and American Medicine,* New York: World, 1967.

On Forming an International Monopoly

CAN ECONOMIC WARFARE BE SUCCESSFUL?

Joining Together to Make More Profits

In the last chapter we outlined the theory of monopoly management. We pointed out that the basic difference between a monopolistic industrial structure and a purely competitive one is that higher profits are made in the former. In fact, in the long run, as we've seen, a monopolist can hope to make very significant economic profits (although they are not guaranteed), whereas a competitor can only hope to make a normal rate of return, that is, zero economic profits. Given, then, that a monopolistic situation is more profitable than a competitive one, it follows that firms would wish to band together to form a monopoly. A legal monopoly of firms is called a **cartel**. Recently, these attempts at forming a cartel have involved international commodity associations.

International Commodity Cartels

The most famous of these cartels is OPEC, the Organization of Petro-

leum Exporting Countries. This cartel has had a relatively short but highly successful history.

A History of OPEC

In 1960, OPEC started as an organization designed to assist the oil-exporting countries. By 1970 it included Abu Dhabi, Algeria, Indonesia, Iran, Iraq, Kuwait, Libya, Nigeria, Qatar, Saudi Arabia, and Venezuela. Then a few other countries, such as Ecuador, joined the group. When OPEC came into existence, its purpose was obviously to maximize the benefits of owning oil. During the 1960s its success was limited because an ever-expanding supply of oil kept just ahead of demand. As demand grew, new discoveries expanded the supplies so fast that wellhead prices for crude oil actually fell slightly from 1960 to 1970. Then in 1970 and 1971 the rate of growth of the demand for crude oil tapered off. Also in 1970, Libya, which had become a major supplier of crude oil to Western European markets, had a revolution. The successful regime cut output sharply in a partly political move against the oil companies whose concessions had been

granted by the previous regime. Libya's cutback made possible in 1971 sizable price increases. These increases were ratified by the other members in agreements drawn up in Tripoli and Teheran. Much of the success of this rise in prices was due to OPEC, but some observers contend that Libya was alone responsible and had no help from OPEC.

Besides these rising prices, there was an upsurge in demand in the United States. We increased our imports of crude oil from 1.5 to 3.5 million barrels a day from 1970 to 1973.

The Yom Kippur War

But the main ingredient in OPEC's success was the outbreak of war in the Middle East in 1973. In the wake of this war, Saudi Arabia, Kuwait, and a few smaller Arab countries greatly cut back their production of crude oil, thus allowing for large price increases. Remember that the only way to raise prices, even if one is a pure monopolist, is to cut back on production and sales. Thus, the OPEC countries could have an effective cartel arrangement only if some or all of them cut back on production and sales. Since Saudi Arabia, which accounts for the bulk of the oil production in the Middle East, did cut back greatly in 1973, the cartel arrangement was to work as it did for several years.

Other Cartels Formed

Perhaps because of the success of OPEC, other cartels, involved with other commodities, have formed.

Bauxite Seven leading bauxite exporters have formed the International Bauxite Association (IBA). Immediately after its formation, Jamaica, one of the leading exporters of bauxite to aluminum producers in the United States, forced a sixfold increase in price. Other members followed suit and have since attempted to raise prices even further.

Copper The Inter-Governmental Council of Copper-Exporting Countries (called, in French, CIPEC) has announced that it would attempt to market a greater share of world copper production. It has expanded its membership to increase market power.

Tin The International Tin Agreement signatories have attempted to get a 42 percent increase in the guaranteed floor price maintained by their buffer stocks. This cartel has existed since before World War II.

Coffee Leading coffee producers got together a few years ago through a series of interlocking marketing companies and stockpile-financing arrangements. They apparently seized control of world coffee prices.

Bananas The Organization of Banana-Exporting Countries has started leveling sizable taxes on banana exports to increase their earnings.

Phosphate Phosphate producers got together and agreed to triple their prices. Phosphate is an input of detergents and fertilizers.

Iron Ore, Mercury, Tea, Tropical Timber, Natural Rubber, Nickel, Cobalt, Tungsten, Columbian, Pepper, Tantalum, and Quinine Producer cartels—such as the Association of Natural Rubber Producing Countries and the Asian Pepper Community—have formed in all these commodities at one time or another.

The question now is, "What are the necessary ingredients to a successful cartel arrangement?"

On Making A Successful Cartel

A cartel must meet four basic requirements if it is to be successful:

1. The cartel must control a large share of total output. It must not face substantial competition from outsiders.
2. Available substitutes must be limited. In other words, the price elasticity of demand for the product in question must be fairly low; that is, demand must be relatively inelastic.
3. The demand for the cartel's product must be relatively stable, regardless of business conditions. If this is not the case, then the amount sold at any given price will be greater during economic expansions than during recessions, and the cartel will find it difficult to maintain any given price and output combination for very long.
4. Producers must be willing and able to withhold sufficient amounts of their product to af-

fect the market. Each member must resist the temptation to cheat. As a corollary to this, consumers must not be able to have large stockpiles of the product on which to draw.

There are probably other conditions that would make a cartel's success probability even greater, but these can be considered the basic ones.

Assessing the Chances of a Cartel's Success

We can analyze the success probability of the commodity cartels we mentioned before on the basis of these four requirements. Look at Table I-21.1. Here we show the production of selected metallic minerals giving United States imports as a percentage of consumption, the major foreign producers, and the major foreign producers' share of world production. If we were to look only at the last column, we would say that the bauxite cartel had a pretty good chance of being successful, but we should not be fooled. There may be a difference between the short-run price elasticity of demand for bauxite and the long-run price elasticity of demand. In other words, in the long run it may be possible to develop substitutes for

Table I-21.1

Mid-1970s Production of Selected Metallic Minerals

U.S. IMPORTS AS % OF CONSUMPTION		MAJOR FOREIGN PRODUCERS*	MAJOR FOREIGN PRODUCERS' SHARE OF WORLD PRODUCTION
Bauxite	84%	Australia, Jamaica, Surinam, Guyana, Guinea, Dominican Rep.	68%
Chromium	64	South Africa, Turkey, Rhodesia, Philippines	46
Copper	15	Canada, Chile, Zambia, Zaire, Australia, Peru, Philippines, South Africa	50
Iron Ore	29	Australia, Canada, Brazil, India, Sweden, Liberia, Venezuela, Chile	36
Lead	19	Australia, Canada, Mexico, Peru, Yugoslavia, Morocco, Sweden	41
Manganese	84	South Africa, Brazil, Gabon, India	42
Mercury	82	Spain, Italy, Mexico, Yugoslavia, Canada	56
Nickel	92	Canada, New Caledonia, Australia	59
Tin	81	Malaysia, Bolivia, Thailand, Indonesia, Australia, Zaire, Nigeria	74
Tungsten	56	Thailand, Bolivia, South Korea, Canada, Australia, Portugal	28
Zinc	53	Canada, Australia, Peru, Mexico, Japan, West Germany, Sweden	52

*Excluding China and Soviet bloc countries
Source: U.S. Bureau of Mines

the product in question. In the United States, for example, there are huge reserves of aluminum-bearing clays that could, and probably will, become an important substitute for bauxite as its price is raised by the producing countries, whether they do it in collusion or separately.

The other cartels that are being formed have similar problems. For example, the copper cartel looks like a good possibility for success, and it already has a very strong international organization, CIPEC. However, there is a definite substitute for copper: aluminum. The CIPEC members are well aware of this high degree of substitutability between copper and aluminum. The association charts the ratio between world copper and aluminum prices in both its quarterly and annual reports. According to a World Bank study, the short-run demand for CIPEC copper is so responsive to price changes—is so price elastic—that CIPEC could barely improve the export earnings of its members by price increases.

The Desire to Cheat

A big cause of cartel instability is cheating. When there are many firms or countries in a cartel arrangement, there will always be some that are unhappy with the situation. There will always be those who will want to cheat by charging a lower price than the one stipulated by the cartel. If there are geographical allocations for sales for each member firm in the cartel, any change in regional demand patterns will cause those cartel members who lose sales to be unhappy. The unhappy members will either require a bribe on the part of the happy members or will cheat on

the cartel by cutting prices and seeking customers outside their stipulated regions.

An individual cartel member is always tempted to cheat, to cut prices clandestinely. Any member who is producing a small percentage of the total output of the cartel essentially faces a very elastic demand curve if he cheats and no one else does. A small drop in price by the cheater will result in a very large increase in total revenues. The best analogy is the extreme case of the firm in a competitive industry. It can increase output without affecting the market price since it is such a small part of the industry. The lure of such increases in revenues is probably too tempting for cartel members to allow a cartel to last forever.

There will always be cartel members who figure that it will pay them to cut prices, to break away from the cartel. Each firm will try to do this, thinking that the others will not do the same thing. Obviously, though, when a sufficient number of firms in the cartel try to cheat, the cartel breaks up. We would expect, therefore, that as long as the cartel is not maintained by legislation, there will be a constant threat to its very existence. Its members will have a large incentive to price cut, and, once a couple of members do it, the rest might follow. We find numerous examples of cartels breaking up: Even the electrical conspiracy of the early 1960s seemed to be quite unstable since the agreements did not last too long. Apparently, overcapacity in the industry led numerous participants in the conspiracy to chisel in order to increase their profits. Because of the overcapacity, they felt they could do it without incurring very large

production costs and the potential profits seemed great. Apparently, one collusive agreement after another had to be reached because each preceding one broke down.

Indeed, cartel instability is not confined to business firms. Have you ever noticed how shortlived a housewives' boycott of supermarkets is? There are so many members in that particular cartel that it is difficult for one of them not to "cheat" and actually go out and buy some food from the supermarket. It is impossible to police the large number of housewives involved.

Political Problems

One area of problems we have not mentioned is the political reality. When the government owns many of the commodity production facilities in question, or the raw materials themselves, it becomes necessary for political units to agree about cartel arrangements. One strength of the OPEC cartel is the broad area of common interest among many of its members, due in part, perhaps, to the conflict with Israel. Such a commonality of interests is, indeed, rare. The world's chromium, for example, is produced by the Soviet Union, South Africa, Rhodesia, Turkey, and the Philippines. It seems very unlikely that these political units would ever agree on a common cartel arrangement for the marketing of chromium ore. The major producers of manganese, an ingredient in iron ore, are the Soviet Union, Gabon, Zaire, and Brazil, and South Africa and India. Again, it is hard to imagine these six countries getting together in a cartel arrangement.

The Prospects for the Future

Analysis tells us to predict that most cartels will break down eventually. The OPEC cartel now seems to be going strong; however, a number of member countries recently have not been getting what they want. For example, in the latter part of 1974, Ecuador, a country that had joined the OPEC cartel not even 2 years before, was having trouble selling its crude oil at $11.58 per barrel. Pro-duction was reported down from 220,000 barrels per day to 80,000 barrels per day, and storage tanks were reported full. Ecuador's National Oil Company had committed itself to building a refinery and a tanker fleet. Moreover, it looked like it would be merely a matter of time before oil came from the North Sea, Alaska, Greece, Mexico, and other places. Remember that at a very high price, the relative profitability of going into oil production increases.

The Middle East, in the 1970s, is producing more than 50 percent of the world's consumption of oil. Given that the cost per barrel of oil pro-duced in the Middle East ranges anywhere from 10¢ to $1.50, this is normal. The price received on a barrel, of course, is many times the cost. In such a situation something has to give. We can predict that individual countries in the OPEC cartel will begin cheating (as did Iran from the very beginning), and that other countries will start producing more oil. These reactions, of course, are in addition to the demand effect of a higher price. Experts in American oil companies were surprised to find out that the consumption of gasoline dropped not insignificantly when the relative price of gasoline rose. But this is what we would expect with just about any good or service. After all, the price elasticity of demand is not zero; it is usually quite substantial.

Like OPEC, the bauxite cartel and a few other cartels may be successful in the short run. However, it is, of course, very difficult for us to imagine that any international cartel can remain viable in the long run.

Definition of New Term

Cartel: An association of firms in the same industry established to allocate and regulate the market among the member firms. A cartel is an explicit form of monopoly organization. A cartel attempts to control prices by controlling the output of its members.

Questions for Thought and Discussion

1. Why do you think some cartels are successful and others are not?
2. Why did it take so many years for the organization of petroleum-exporting countries to form a successful cartel?
3. What are the incentives facing an individual member in a cartel that might cause the member to break the cartel arrangement?

Selected References

Bergsten, C. Fred, "The New Era in World Commodity Markets," *Challenge*, September–October 1974.

___, " 'Commodity Power' Is Here to Stay," *The Brookings Bulletin*, vol. 11, no. 2, 1974, p. 6ff.

___, "The Threat from the Third World," *Foreign Policy*, Summer 1974.

Mikesell, Raymond F., "More Third World Cartels Ahead?", *Challenge*, November–December 1974.

Miller, Roger LeRoy, *The Economics of Energy: What Went Wrong and How We Can Fix It*, New York: Morrow, 1974.

Trezise, Phillip H., "More OPECs Are Unlikely," *The Brookings Bulletin*, vol. 11, no. 2, 1974, p. 8ff.

20 Regulating the Big Ones

In our discussion of monopolies, we mentioned that there are actually very few examples of *pure* monopolies. In fact, almost all monopolies are supported or regulated by the government. However, certain conditions lead to **natural monopolies.** When these occur, government regulation steps in to protect consumers from the undesirable effects of monopoly. In this chapter, we will treat two separate issues involving monopolies. One is government regulation of natural monopolies and of industries deemed so important to the public good that they must be overseen. The second issue is antitrust legislation and theory. Antitrust legislation is a way of preventing monopolization in restraint of trade. Whereas regulation allows government to intervene directly into the decision-making processes of the regulated industries, antitrust legislation and enforcement seek to prevent monopolies from occurring in the first place and, therefore, to obviate the need for regulation.

One Way for a Monopoly to Arise

In many industries a tremendous amount of capital is required to produce the product or service in question. Think about how much money you would have to have to start an electric utility or a telephone company. Once you've started, however, the *marginal cost* of providing service is relatively small. Thus, in industries where large capital requirements are needed just to get started, average fixed costs fall dramatically with higher and higher production rates. That is, the average total cost curve would be downward sloping throughout a very large range of production rates.

In Figure 20-1 we have drawn a downward-sloping long-run average total cost curve (LATC) for electricity. (A long-run cost curve is one that relates to a time span long enough for all inputs to be freely variable; for example, when new plants can be built.) When the average total cost curve is falling, the long-run marginal cost curve (LMC) is below the average total cost curve. Since long-run average costs are falling over such a large range of production rates, we would expect that only one firm could survive in such an industry. That firm would be the natural monopolist. It would be the first one to take advantage of the decreasing average costs; that is, it would expand production faster than other firms. As its average total cost curve fell, it would lower prices and get increasingly larger shares of the market. Once that firm had driven all other firms out of the industry, it would set its price to maximize profits. Let's see what this price would be.

A monopolist will set the price where marginal revenue is equal to marginal cost. Let's draw in the market demand curve, *DD*, and the marginal revenue curve, MR, in Figure 20-2. The intersection of the marginal revenue curve and the marginal cost curve is at point *A*. The monopolist therefore would produce quantity Q_m and charge a price of P_m.

What do we know about a monopolist's solution to the price-quantity question? When compared to a competitive situation, we know that consumers end up paying more for the product, and, consequently, they purchase less of it than they would purchase under competition. In addition to these drawbacks, the monopoly solution is inefficient; the price charged for the product is higher than the opportunity cost to society. That is, people are faced with a price which does not reflect the true marginal cost of producing the good because the true marginal cost is at the intersection *A*, not at price P_m. Look at Figures 19-6 and 19-7 in Chapter 19. These figures demonstrate that, if a competitive industry were suddenly monopolized, the output would be restricted and prices would be raised. Thus, in a monopoly situation,

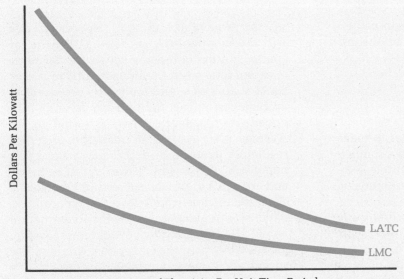

FIGURE 20-1 **The Cost Curves That Might Lead to a Natural Monopoly**

Here we show the long-run average total cost curve falling over a very large range of electricity production rates per unit time period. The long-run marginal cost curve is, of course, below the average cost curve when the average cost curve is falling. A natural monopoly might arise in this situation. The first firm to establish the low unit-cost capacity would be able to take advantage of the lower average total cost curve. This firm would drive out all rivals by charging a lower price than the others could sustain at their higher average total costs.

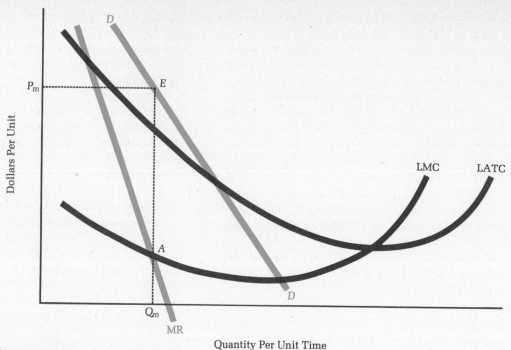

FIGURE 20-2 Profit Maximization

The profit-maximizing natural monopolist here would produce at the point where marginal cost equals marginal revenue—that is, at point A, which gives the quantity of production Q_m. The price charged would be P_m.

if we could somehow arrive at a competitive solution, prices would be lowered and the output would be increased.

Regulating the Natural Monopolist

Let's assume the government decides to make the natural monopolist produce as in a competitive situation. Where is that competitive solution in Figure 20-3? It is at the intersection of the marginal cost curve and the demand curve, or point A. Remember, the upward-sloping portion of the marginal cost curve represents the supply curve in the competitive industry. Now the regulatory commission forces the natural monopolist to produce at quantity Q_1 and

sell the product at a price P_1. Now how large will the monopolist's profits be? Profits, of course, are the difference between total revenues and total costs. In this case, total revenues equal P_1 times Q_1, and total costs are equal to average costs times the number of units produced. At Q_1, average cost is equal to P_2. Average costs are higher than the price the regulatory commission forces our natural monopolist to charge. Profits turn out to be losses and are equal to the shaded area in Figure 20-3. Thus, regulation which forces a natural monopolist to produce as in a competitive situation would also force that monopolist into negative profits. Obviously, the monopolist would rather go out of business than be subjected to such regulation.

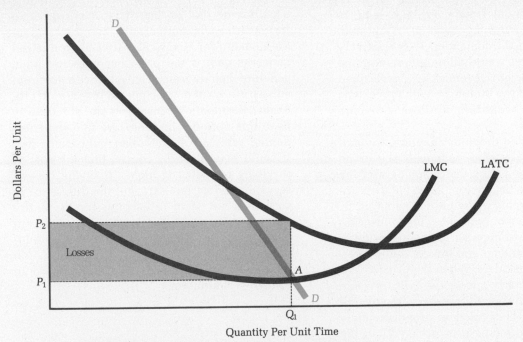

FIGURE 20-3 **Regulating Natural Monopolies—Marginal Cost Pricing**
If the regulatory commission attempted to regulate the natural monopolies so that a competitive situation would prevail, the commission would make the monopolist set production at the point where the marginal cost curve intersects the demand schedule because the marginal cost schedule would be the competitive supply schedule. The quantity produced would be Q_1 and the price would be P_1. However, the average total costs at Q_1 are equal to P_2. Losses would ensue equal to the shaded area. It would be impossible for a regulatory commission to force a natural monopolist to produce at a competitive solution without subsidizing some of its fixed costs because losses would eventually drive the natural monopolist out of business.

Subsidization

How do we get out of such a dilemma? There are several possible answers. The first is to have the government force the natural monopolist to produce at the competitive price and then subsidize the monopolist. That is, the government should give the monopolist a subsidy that will allow the person to break even (after a normal rate of return on investment has been included, of course). The subsidy per unit in this particular case would have to be equal to the difference between P_2 and P_1; it would have to match the natural monopolist's losses.

Price Discrimination

Another possible solution is to allow the monopolist to *price discriminate*. This means the monopolist would charge different prices to different customers who have different elasticities of demand for the product. The monopolist would charge a lower price to those who have very elastic demands and a higher price to those who have relatively less elastic demands. If allowed to perfectly discriminate, the monopolist will travel down the demand curve, making everybody who buys the product a marginal buyer. The monopolist will extract all the money possible from everybody who is interested in purchasing what is being sold. Essentially, then, the demanders with relatively less elastic curves would allow the monopolist to recover sufficient revenues to cover fixed costs. You might say that those with less elastic demands would be subsidizing those with more elastic demands.

As mentioned in previous chapters, any monopolist can make more money if she or he can discriminate among the demanders of the product. Assume the monopolist is not discriminating but charging everyone the same price. Now assume the monopolist begins to discriminate. First, the monopolist raises the price to less elastic demanders and lowers the price to more elastic demanders. When the price to less elastic demanders is raised, the total revenue received from them will rise because the fall in the quantity demanded is proportionately smaller than the increase in price. When the price to more elastic demanders, is lowered, total revenues from them will rise also. The increase in the quantity demanded will be proportionately greater than the decrease in price. The monopolist, therefore, makes out in both areas, and total revenues rise. The telephone company, for example, price discriminates against businesses and in favor of residential customers. Essentially the same service costs more if a business wants it than if a household orders it.

Although allowing a natural monopolist to discriminate results in more production than would otherwise be the case, most regulation does not condone such discrimination. It is usually felt to be unfair if those with less elastic demands are forced to pay more than those with more elastic demands; problems of equity arise. Many regulated utilities, however, do price discriminate. The extra charge for first-class service on airlines is also greater than the additional expenses involved in producing it.

Electric utilities price discriminate too. It is usually true that an industrial firm's demand for electricity is more elastic than the residential demand for electricity. After all, industrial concerns can, if the price becomes too high, generate their own electricity. Hence a potential substitute called user-generated electricity exists. Residential consumers do not usually have this option. Therefore, we find that residential rates are higher than industrial rates. It could be argued, of course, that the cost of servicing residents is higher than the cost of servicing industrial users, but the difference in cost does not seem to account for the entire difference in price. When prices to different people vary because of the different costs involved in servicing these people, the situation is called **price differentiation,** as opposed to price discrimination.

Methods of Regulating Monopolies

Since the government has decided to regulate the natural monopolies in our economy, it is faced with the problem of deciding how to regulate. There are many possible methods. We will name only a few and then talk about the problems involved and some of the more common methods of regulation.

Cost of Service

One way to regulate is to keep a lid on prices—that is, to keep prices at the level which would prevail in a competitive situation. This is usually called **cost-of-service regulation.** The regulatory commission allows the regulated companies to charge only prices that are in accord with the actual cost of providing the services to the customer. This was the standard practice for many years in the regulation of natural gas. Natural gas companies had to demonstrate exactly what their costs of service were, and it was on these costs that prices were based. It is not easy for any company, including regulated monopolies, to come up with an estimate of the costs involved for every service that they provide.

How does one allocate **joint costs** to several products or services that may be sold? For example, the post office can build a large building to handle incoming and outgoing mail. The post office sells various services: air mail, parcel post, first-, second-, third- and fourth-class mail. All these different classes of mail service utilize in some way or another the services of the building that the post office constructed. How can the post office attribute parts of the joint cost of the building to the various classes of services it provides? The answer is that it can't. The only way to allocate joint costs is to do so arbitrarily.

A reasonable expectation would be, therefore, that regulated monopolies which are forced to present costs of services in order to establish rate schedules would allocate more of the joint costs to services provided to less elastic demanders. In other words, we would expect the regulated monopoly to attempt some form of price discrimination. If the monopoly is successful, quantity demanded would not be reduced very much and total revenues would rise.

Controlling the Rate of Return on Investment

Another method of regulation involves allowing the regulated companies to set prices that ensure a normal or competitive rate of return on the investment in the business—**rate-of-return regulation.** (The investment in the business is usually called its *equity.*) Assume that the rate of return on investing in a competitive industry with risks similar to those of the regulated monopoly is 12 percent per year. The regulatory agency will attempt to keep the rate of return on investment in the regulated monopoly also at 12 percent per year. Therefore, in requesting rate changes, the regulated monopoly must demonstrate to the regulatory commission that the proposed rate schedule will just allow investors in the company to obtain a 12 percent rate of return. To do this, the company has to establish what its costs are going to be. In many instances, the regulatory commissions will allow the company to base these on its costs in an historic test year. Some regulatory commissions will allow a company to establish what its costs will be in a future test year. In any event, the problem of allocating joint costs again arises, in addition to the problem of which costs should be included in the computations and which costs shouldn't. As you can imagine, the rate-making proceedings that are carried out before regulatory commissions for most public utilities are extremely complicated. One sometimes wonders if the regulators themselves even understand all the technical material presented to them.

Many critics of this particular type of regulation point out that if the percentage rate of return on investment is fixed, then the regulated companies will have perverse incentives to overinvest. After all, the object of the game is to maximize total profits. If the rate of profit that can be earned on investment is fixed, then why not increase capital investment to get higher *absolute* profits? Although regulated companies staunchly deny that this actually happens, economic theory would predict that the ratio of capital to labor in regulated monopolies is higher than it would be without regulation.

It has also been pointed out by critics of regulation that when pecuniary or money profits are limited by regulation, unexploited monopoly profits may remain. How can the management take advantage of these unexploited profits? One way is to increase nonpecuniary gains. One can think of a thousand ways to do this. Managers can hire secretaries, have lavish offices, do a lot of entertaining at the company's expense, work shorter hours, have innumerable underlings do every conceivable task for them, drive company cars that are large, roomy, and always new, and so on.

Problems with Inflation

Regulation based on rate of return to investment will always run into problems in inflationary periods, particularly in cases where rate schedules are pleaded on the basis of costs that occurred in a past year. If the costs of operating a regulated monopoly are rising along with all other prices in an inflationary economy, a rate schedule based on a previous year's costs will be insufficient in future years. That is, rates based on historic costs will turn out to yield a lower than normal rate of return in future years when costs will have risen. This has been particularly burdensome to the public utilities in the United States since 1965, when inflation soared to heights that no one had been accustomed to. Until then, many regulated utilities had been asking for price *decreases* due to improved technology and economies of scale. After 1965, however, any increases in general productivity were swamped by the increases in costs due to the general inflation in the economy.

The utilities had to start asking for price increases. Regulatory commissions, which were used to granting price *decreases,* were against the idea of price *increases.* Many public utilities began to face serious capital problems by the beginning of the 1970s. They were faced not only with higher labor costs but with higher money capital costs and much higher fuel costs. Many of these companies had issued bonds in the past to get money for plant expansion at interest rates of 3 to 5 percent. Many of these bonds were coming due and had to be paid

off. The utilities then had to replace them with bonds that cost 7 to 9 percent. Their money capital costs were therefore increasing along with their labor costs. The price of physical capital was going up, too. Increased ecological awareness forced many utilities, particularly in electricity generation, to add expensive pollution-control equipment to their facilities.

Quality of Service

A major problem with regulating monopolies concerns the quality of the service or product involved. Consider the many facets of telephone service: getting a dial tone, hearing other voices clearly, getting the operator to answer quickly, having out-of-order telephones repaired rapidly, putting through a long distance call quickly and efficiently. The list goes on and on. But regulation of the telephone company usually deals with the prices charged for telephone service. Of course, regulators are concerned with the quality of service, but how can that be measured? Indeed, it cannot be measured very easily. Therefore, it is extremely difficult for any type of regulation to be successful in regulating the *price per constant-quality unit.* Certainly, it is possible to regulate the price per unit, but we don't really know that the quality remains unchanged when the price changes. And if regulation doesn't allow prices to rise, quality of service may be lowered surreptitiously, raising the price per constant-quality unit.

We must not overestimate the monopoly power that an "obvious" monopolist has. Nothing has a completely inelastic demand schedule; rather, most things do have substitutes in one form or another. It may be true that electricity for some uses does not have a substitute, but electricity for other uses does. For example, you can heat your house with gas, oil, or electric space heaters. You can cook with either gas or electricity. You can have a gas water heater or an electric water heater. And industrial users can generate their own electricity. There are perhaps fewer substitutes for telephone service, but there are still many: letters, person-to-person communication, and telegrams.

In some cases a supposed natural monopoly is not a natural monopoly at all. The post office is a good example. There are numerous entrepreneurs waiting to compete with the U.S. Post Office. (We will analyze this topic in the following issue.)

Regulation of natural monopolies will always have its problems. Regulation of whole industries that supposedly affect the public interest also has problems. We will treat several of these industries in subsequent issues. Right now, it might be useful to see what can happen when prices are regulated in an otherwise relatively competitive situation.

Regulating Prices—the Case of the Airlines

The airline industry could be quite competitive. The Civil Aeronautics Board (CAB), however, regulates the rates that commercial airlines can charge for their services. The CAB also regulates the routes that are awarded to the different airlines. If an airline wishes to fly a route which is not already scheduled, it must petition for that route. If the airline wishes to abandon service on a particular route, it must petition for that also.

The idea behind regulating the rates of commercial air carriers presumably is to prevent a monopoly rate from being charged and alternatively to prevent "destructive" competition. The idea behind CAB regulation is theoretically to provide the consumer with low-cost, high-quality air travel. We can see, though, that some detrimental effects result from across-the-board price regulation in the air transport field.

Nonprice Competition

There are quite a number of airline companies in the United States. In many cases, there are several competing airlines flying the same route. There are at least six competing companies flying to and from Honolulu and between major West Coast cities. Between New York and San Francisco or Los Angeles, there are at least four competing airlines. Since there is more than one company flying between two cities, we would expect some sort of competition. However, this competition has to take a very special form. The Civil Aeronautics Board does not allow companies to compete on the basis of price, so the airlines attempt to lure customers away from other airlines. They do this with improvements in the quality of service, which can be altered in many ways. There can be prettier stewardesses, better looking stewards, more champagne, better meals, wider seating, nicer music, instant computerized reservation scheduling, free additional travel arrangements, and so on. Occasionally, we find such quality wars among the airlines. For a while there was a "lounge" war among airlines flying between the West Coast and the East Coast. One airline started offering a lounge for its tourist-class customers. For a while it was taking away business from the other airlines; then they found ways to offer the same service. Then another airline started to offer live entertainment in its first-class lounge. And so went the lounge war. The CAB usually attempts to stop these wars before they get out of hand and will prohibit certain improvements in quality when it feels the time is ripe.

Timing of Flights

Another aspect of quality service is the timing of flight takeoffs and landings. Naturally, it would be better if you could leave New York at 4 in the afternoon and arrive on the West Coast at 8 P.M. than if you had to leave at 12 midnight and arrive at 4 in the morning. Moreover, an airline will probably seem more attractive if it has a larger number of flights leaving from your city than if it has a smaller number. The airlines have figured this out, and therefore competing airlines fly out of the same place at the same time headed for the same destination. For example, in Los Angeles you might find four different airlines leaving within 1 hour of each other, and all planes are going to the East Coast.

Most of those planes are probably not full. In fact, the airlines could be expected to add planes at different times until it was no longer worth their while. They would add planes until the marginal cost of doing so just equaled the marginal revenue. That is the reason why four half-empty planes leave Los Angeles at the same time, all headed for New York. At the present levels of regulated rates, a utilization rate of about 50 percent seems to be approximately the break-even point for airlines. Therefore, frequency-of-flight competition forces them to keep adding planes until the average load factor is 50 percent.

The Civil Aeronautics Board can set prices, but the Board has a difficult time in preventing competition via changes in quality. If price competition were allowed, however, then there would be decreases in certain quality aspects of air transportation. For example, there might be a reduction in the number of flights per day between big cities. But cut-rate economy classes would be offered, and it would be possible to travel at a lower cost between major cities in the United States. However, it might be impossible to travel by air at all between small cities. Under regulation, many companies are forced to maintain such unprofitable routes in order to be allowed to maintain profitable ones. In effect, then, those customers who use the airlines on the profitable routes are subsidizing those customers who travel the unprofitable routes.

Antitrust Policy

It is the expressed aim of our government to foster competition in the economy. To this end, numerous attempts at legislating against business practices that seemingly destroy the competitive nature of the system have been made. This is the general idea behind antitrust legislation: If the courts can prevent collusion among sellers of a product, then monopoly prices will not result; there will be no restriction of output if the members of an industry are not allowed to join together in restraint of trade. Remember that the competitive solution to the price-quantity problem is one in which no *economic* profits are being made in the long run and the price of the item produced is equal to its social opportunity cost.

The Sherman Act

The first antitrust law in the United States was passed during the period of the greatest merger movement in American history. A large number of firms were growing by acquiring or merging with other firms. When a number of firms merged together, the business organizations were then called "trusts." A copper trust, a steel beam trust, an iron trust, a sugar trust, a coal trust, a paper bag trust, and the most famous of all, the Standard Oil trusts, formed. However, there was an increasing public outcry for legislation against these large trusts.

The Sherman Antitrust Act was passed in 1890. It was the first attempt by the federal government to control the growth of monopoly in the United States. The most important provisions of that act are:

Section 1: Every contract, combination in the form of trust or otherwise, or conspiracy, in restraint of trade or commerce among the several states, or with foreign nations, is hereby declared to be illegal.
Section 2: Every person who shall monopolize, or attempt to monopolize, or combine or conspire with any other person or persons to monopolize any part of the trade or commerce . . . shall be guilty of a misdemeanor.

Notice how vague this particular act actually is. No definition is given for the terms *restraint of trade* or *monopolization.* Despite this vagueness, however, the act was used to prosecute the infamous Standard Oil trust of New Jersey. Standard Oil of New Jersey was charged with violations of Sections 1 and 2 of the Sherman Antitrust Act. This was in 1906, when Standard Oil controlled over 80 percent of the nation's oil refining capacity. Among other things, Standard Oil was accused of both predatory price cutting to drive rivals out of business and of obtaining preferential price treatment from the railroads for transporting Standard Oil products, thus allowing Standard to sell at lower prices.

Standard Oil was convicted in a district court. The company then appealed to the Supreme Court, which ruled that Standard's control of and power over the oil market created "a *prima facie* presumption of intent and purpose to maintain dominancy . . . not as a result from normal methods of industrial development, but by means of combination." Here, the word *combination* meant taking over other businesses and obtaining preferential price treatment from railroads. The Supreme Court forced Standard Oil of New Jersey to break up into many smaller companies.

The ruling handed down in the Standard Oil case came about because the judges felt that Standard Oil had used "unreasonable" attempts at restraining trade. The court did not come out against monopoly per se. The fact that Standard Oil had a large share of the market did not seem to matter; rather, according to the Court, the problem was the way in which Standard acquired that large market share. In any event, antitrust legislation had been used to break up one of the largest trusts in United States business at that time.

The Clayton Act

The Sherman Act was so extremely vague that in 1914 a new law was passed to sharpen its antitrust provisions. This law was called the Clayton Act. It prohibited or limited a number of very specific business practices, which again were felt to be "unreasonable" attempts at restraining trade. Some of the more important sections of that act are listed here.

Section 2: [It is illegal to] discriminate in price between different purchasers [except in cases where the differences are due to differences in selling or transportation costs].

Section 3: [Producers cannot sell] on the condition, agreement or understanding that the . . . purchaser thereof shall not use or deal in the goods . . . of a competitor or competitors of the seller.

Section 7: [Corporations cannot hold stock in another company] where the effect . . . may be to substantially lessen competition.

Notice that these provisions outlaw practices which tend to "substantially" lessen competition. It is not very clear, however, what the term *substantially* actually means. How are the courts to interpret this word?

The activities mentioned in the Clayton Act above are not necessarily illegal. In the words of the law, they are illegal only when their effects "may be to substantially lessen competition or tend to create a monopoly." It takes the interpretation of the court to decide whether one of the activities mentioned actually had the effect of "substantially" lessening competition. On the other hand, there is an additional provision in the Clayton Act that represents a **per se violation.** This activity is interlocking directorates. It is illegal per se for the same individual to serve on two or more boards of directors of corporations that are competitive and have capital surplus and undivided profits in excess of $1 million. The fact of the interlock itself is enough to allow the government to prosecute.

The Robinson-Patman Act

In 1936, Section 2 of the Clayton Act was amended by the Robinson-Patman Act. The Robinson-Patman Act was aimed at preventing producers from driving out smaller competitors by means of selected discriminatory price cuts.

The act has often been referred to as the "Chain Store Act" because it was meant to protect *independent* retailers and wholesalers from "unfair discrimination" by chain sellers.

The act was the natural outgrowth of increasing competition that independents faced when chain stores and mass distributors started to develop after World War I. The essential provisions of the act are as follows:

1. It was made illegal to pay brokerage fees unless there was an independent broker employed. Often chain stores would demand a brokerage fee as a form of discount when they purchased large quantities of the products they sold direct from the manufacturer instead of going through a broker or wholesaler. Thus, it was thought that the payment of a brokerage fee as a form of discount was a way that chain stores gained an unfair advantage over independents, who actually had to use a broker or wholesaler.

2. It was made illegal to offer concessions, such as discounts, free advertising, promotional allowances, and so on to one buyer of your product if you did not offer the same concessions to all buyers of your product. This provision was an attempt to stop large-scale buyers from obtaining special deals that would allow them to compete "unfairly" with small buyers.

3. Other forms of discrimination, such as quantity discounts, were also made illegal whenever they "substantially" lessened competition. Price discrimination as such was not made illegal if, in fact, price differences were due to differences in costs or were "offered in good faith to meet an equally low price of a competitor."

4. It was made illegal to charge lower prices in one location than in another, or to sell at "unreasonably low prices" if such marketing techniques were designed to "destroy

competition or eliminate a competitor." Thus, so-called predatory pricing was outlawed.

The Miller-Tydings Act

There are numerous other antitrust acts, many of which serve to exempt certain business practices from antitrust legislation! One of these is the Miller-Tydings Act, passed in 1937 as an amendment to Section 1 of the Sherman Act. This act allowed for "fair-trade" agreements. A fair-trade agreement is something that you are probably familiar with. A manufacturer can specify to all the people who sell his or her product that they cannot sell it below a listed or "fair-trade" price. This is called **resale price maintenance.** It is illegal for firms to lower the price of the product if the manufacturer has invoked a fair-trade price. One would think that this type of fair-trade agreement would violate antitrust laws aimed at preventing price fixing. Nonetheless, the Miller-Tydings Act made this type of price fixing legal. Some states skirted the Miller-Tydings Act by passing their own legislation allowing retailers to cut prices on fair-traded goods. If you look at advertisements for stereo equipment from different big stores around the country, you will notice that stereo stores advertising from Washington, D.C. will usually put on their ads "no resale price maintenance" or "no fair-trade laws here." These retailers are merely advertising the fact that they will cut prices on nationally fair-traded brands of stereo equipment.

In 1951 the Supreme Court declared invalid the "nonsigners' clause" of the Miller-Tydings Act. This clause required that even those who would not agree to sign a resale price maintenance agreement were still bound by it. Once the clause was struck down, resale price maintenance was essentially dead. The result was to be expected. In 1952, however, Congress passed the McGuire Act, which restored the nonsigners' clause.

Even with the McGuire Act still on the books, though, fair-trade pricing is disappearing gradually. Larger retailers and discount houses that use their own brands, and producers seeking mass markets by more aggressive pricing policies, have greatly reduced the importance of resale price maintenance. It may be eliminated completely by an act of Congress by the time you read this book.

Other Exemption Laws

Other laws besides the Miller-Tydings Act and the McGuire Act exempt business from certain anticompetitive practices.

Small Businesses Small businesses are allowed to engage in certain concerted activities without running afoul of the antitrust laws. This legislation started with the Small Business Act of 1953.

Oil Marketing In 1935, the Interstate Oil Compact was passed. It allows states to determine quotas on oil that will be marketed in interstate commerce.

Foreign Trade Under the provisions of the 1918 Webb-Pomerane Act, American exporters can engage in cooperative activity.

Labor and Agriculture Labor and agricultural organizations are exempt from the Sherman Antitrust Act by Section 6 of the Clayton Act. Agriculture's exemption from antitrust legislation is further extended by the Capper-Volstead Act, passed in 1922, the Cooperative Marketing Act, passed in 1926, and certain provisions of the Robinson-Patman Act. Labor's exemption was strengthened by the Norris-LaGuardia Act of 1932.

The Enforcement of Antitrust Laws

The enforcement of antitrust laws has been rather uneven. Of course, there have been many spectacular cases brought and won by the government, such as the case against the electrical companies' conspiracy in the early 1960s. Use of the Sherman Act did allow the government to break up the Standard Oil trust, and the government also broke up the American Tobacco Company. By and large, though, governmental efforts to prevent problems of monopoly have been concentrated in preventing mergers. A merger occurs when two companies join together and become one legal entity. It is very difficult for large companies today to merge without first seeking permission from the Justice Department of the United States government. Often, the Justice Department will deny the merger on the grounds that it will seriously lessen competition.

The uneven enforcement of antitrust laws reflects the political atmosphere more than anything else. Certain administrations are committed to big business; others are committed to doing as much as they can to thwart big business. For a while in the late 1960s and early 1970s, there was vigorous antitrust legislation against **conglomerates.** A conglomerate is a company that has many subdivisions dealing in totally different products. International Telephone and Telegraph (ITT) is a good example of how a conglomerate can get into numerous diverse fields of interest. It produces and sells houses, radios, books, insurance, hotel services, and rental car services. It is now a multibillion dollar corporation. In 1972, there was a scandal concerning ITT and the antitrust division of the Justice Department. There was going to be an antitrust proceeding against the large conglomerate, but government officials and the company's management worked out an out-of-court settlement.

Although the attack on conglomerates seems necessary to many students of antitrust policy, the empirical evidence as to the monopoly power of such large corporations is not overwhelming. In fact, a Presidential Commission on Antitrust Activities failed to support any attacks against conglomerates. It is alleged, for example, that conglomerates are so big they can wield market power in the separate submarkets in which they operate. However, ITT, despite its size, does not have market power in renting cars. Numerous car rental companies are in competition with ITT's Avis Rental Company. In fact, the competition seems to be getting even stronger as other rental companies "try harder" and as local rental companies pop up around the country.

When to Prosecute?

Even if we accept the premise that monopolies should not be allowed, how can the government come up with a policy rule that will help determine which mergers should be stopped? How can the government decide which companies should be dissolved? How will it know which business practices actually restrain trade? There have been numerous attempts by government officials and by interested academicians to derive specific policy rules. One of the most commonly mentioned rules states that the *concentration ratio* in a particular industry should not become too large. The concentration ratio is defined as the percentage of total industry output accounted for by a few leading firms—say the first four or five. No one knows, though, what this magic number should be. Does monopolization of the industry start when the four-firm concentration ratio becomes 50 percent, 60 percent, 70 percent, or 80 percent?

Another way to assess the degree of a firm's monopoly power may be to look at its profits. If the profits are higher than the "normal" rate of return elsewhere, then that company may be making monopoly returns. (On the other hand, it may just be more efficient.) However, it is difficult to find out what those profits really represent. They are accounting profits and, therefore, do not include risk or inflation. Also, the empirical findings on profits are usually for very short periods of time and may not demonstrate that the industry is tending toward a zero economic profit. Suffice it to say that it is difficult to establish any readily observable statistical procedures for determining when antitrust enforcement should be attempted.

There is also a problem involved with attempting new legislation to increase competition in our economy. Even if the legislation is exactly what it should be for bettering our competitive system, by the time it goes through the legislative mill, it will be vastly different. Moreover, legislation that calls for increased enforcement of antitrust laws leads to increased costs on the part of government and the firms involved. Only when we are fully convinced that the costs will be outweighed by the benefits might we then presume to proceed with our action.

Definitions of New Terms

Natural Monopoly: A monopoly that arises from the peculiar production characteristics in the industry. Usually a natural monopoly arises when production of the service or product requires extremely large capital investments such that only one firm can profitably be supported by consumers. A natural monopoly usually arises when there are large economies of scale.

Price Differentiation: Differences in price that depend on differences in cost, as distinct from price discrimination, which is not a function of costs but rather a function of relative elasticities of demand.

Cost-of-Service Regulation: A type of regulation based on allowing prices that reflect only the actual costs of production and do not include monopoly profits.

Joint Costs: Costs that are common to several products for a firm. The post office, for example, could be using the same building to service first-, third-, fourth-class and air mail. It is difficult to allocate joint costs to the various separate services or products that use them.

Rate-of-Return Regulation: Regulation that seeks to keep the rate of return in the industry at a competitive level by not allowing excessive prices to be charged.

Per se Violation: An activity that is specifically spelled out as a violation of antitrust laws. Whether or not competition is lessened does not have to be proved. A violation based on the facts only and not on the effects, which are taken as given.

Resale Price Maintenance: Sometimes called "fair-trade laws," a system whereby the manufacturer stipulates a specific retail price and the retailer is not allowed to sell the product at a lower price. Certain states have outlawed retail price maintenance because it is a form of price fixing; it prevents price competition.

Conglomerates: Large firms composed of numerous smaller divisions, each one in a different field. A conglomerate may be in automobile leasing, farming, airline travel, investment, and a dozen other types of economic activities.

Chapter Summary

1. Traditionally, there are two ways of regulating monopolies. One way is the actual regulation by some commission; the other way is by antitrust laws.

2. Regulation usually involves a natural monopoly that arises when, for example, the average total cost curve falls over a very large range of production rates. In such a situation, only one firm can survive. It will be the firm that can expand production and sales faster than the others to take advantage of the falling average total costs.

3. If regulation seeks to force the natural monopolist to produce at the point where the marginal cost curve (supply curve in the competitive case) intersects the demand curve, the natural monopolist will incur losses because when average total costs are falling, marginal costs are below average total costs. The regulators are faced with a dilemma. They can get out of this dilemma by (a) subsidizing the natural monopolist, (b) allowing the regulators to price discriminate to prevent losses, or (c) selling the rights to produce so that the price will be set equal to average total costs, where there will be zero economic profits.

4. There are several ways of regulating monopolies, the most common ones being on a cost-of-service basis or a rate-of-return basis. With a cost-of-service regulation, the regulated monopolies are allowed to charge prices that reflect only reasonable costs. With a rate-of-return regulation, the regulated monopolies are allowed to set rates so as to make a competitive rate of return for the equity shareholders.

5. In any type of regulatory procedure, there is always a problem of keeping the quality of the product constant. If a price is regulated, it may be possible for the regulated monopoly to lower the quality of its product in order to effectively raise the price above that which the regulators desire.

6. The airlines industry is a good example of what can happen with price regulation. Since the airlines cannot compete on the basis of price, they compete on the basis of nonprice or quality aspects of their product. This is why we find so many airlines leaving the same airport going to the same destination exactly at the same time of day, even though none are filled to capacity. That is also why we find that different companies will schedule their flights at prime times to bid away each other's customers. Hence, we get a tremendous amount of congestion at airports during the best times of the day.

7. Antitrust legislation is designed to obviate the need for regulation. The major antitrust acts are the Sherman, the Clayton, and Robinson-Patman Acts.
8. Although the legislation against monopolies may, in fact, be comprehensive, the enforcement of this legislation has been extremely erratic in the history of antitrust.

Questions for
Thought
and Discussion

1. If regulation was unsuccessful and the regulated monopolies were able to do exactly as they wanted to, how would the consumer lose out? Do you have any idea how we could measure losses?
2. If regulatory commissions are so against price discrimination, why do we, in fact, see price discrimination in almost all regulated industries?
3. It has been argued that if the Civil Aeronautics Board did not guarantee monopoly returns for airlines traveling profitable routes—usually between big cities—these same airlines would have to discontinue their unprofitable routes between smaller cities. Assume that this is true. Would you still favor the elimination of monopoly profits in the airlines industry?
4. Is there any way for regulation to be completely comprehensive and to take account of all aspects of the product or service being sold?
5. Our antitrust laws prohibit price fixing; yet for many years many state bar associations set minimum fee schedules for lawyers. This is a form of price fixing. To date it has not been prosecuted by the United States Justice Department. Can you think of a reason why?
6. Some economists maintain that conglomerates do not endanger competition because they involve the merging of totally unrelated companies. Others point out, however, that such mergers provide conglomerates with greater financial power and greater market power in general, thereby lessening competition. Which side do you agree with? Why?
7. During President Nixon's Phase II price-stabilization policies, the Price Commission came out with some rules for certifying rate increase requests by electric utilities. Many electric utilities maintained that if the rate increases were not granted, blackouts and brownouts would result in the United States. Do you think there is any truth in that statement? What is the relationship between price increases and the ability of an electric utility to meet its energy demands?

Selected
References

Berki, Sylvester E. (ed.), *Antitrust Policy, Economics and Law,* Lexington, Mass.: D. C. Heath, 1966.

Kahn, Alfred E., *The Economics of Regulation,* vols. 1 and 2, New York: Wiley, 1970.

Leonard, William N., *Business Size, Market Power, and Public Policy*, New York: Crowell, 1969.

MacAvoy, Paul W. (ed.), *The Crisis of the Regulatory Commissions*, New York: W. W. Norton, 1970.

Stelzer, Irwin M. (ed.), *Selected Antitrust Cases*, 4th ed. Homewood, Ill.: Irwin, 1972.

Wilcox, Clair, *Public Policies toward Business*, 4th ed. Homewood, Ill.: Irwin, 1971.

"And though in 1969, as in previous years, your company had to contend with spiralling labor costs, exorbitant interest rates, and unconscionable government interference, management was able once more, through a combination of deceptive marketing practices, false advertising, and price fixing, to show a profit which, in all modesty, can only be called excessive."

Drawing by Lorenz; © 1970
The New Yorker Magazine, Inc.

Senate Voice
for the Consumer

PHILIP A. HART
**Former United States Senator, Michigan
Chairman, Senate Antitrust
and Monopoly Subcommittee**

When Senator Philip A. Hart was chosen to succeed Estes Kefauver as chairman of the Judiciary Subcommittee on Antitrust and Monopoly in 1963, he said he was not out to change the economic system. The leaders of industry, after years of rigorous questioning by Kefauver, were generally pleased by the appointment of the Michigan Democrat. Senator Hart had a reputation for fairness and was the son of a banker and son-in-law of the millionaire industrialist who owned the Detroit Tigers. A decade later, in light of Hart's numerous investigations of corporate activity, the enthusiasm of business people had dimmed somewhat.

First elected to Congress in 1958, Hart was a consistent supporter of many liberal causes and active in their promotion. Hart cosponsored over 180 bills in the 1971 to 1972 session of Congress alone. From labor and from environmental and consumer groups, he consistently got high marks for his voting record; from conservative groups like the Chamber of Commerce and the National Associated Businessmen, he drew zeros.

Hart is perhaps best known for his support of consumer and environmental protection legislation. As chairman of the Commerce Subcommittee on the Environment, Hart held hearings and often sponsored legislation on herbicides and toxic substances, wildlife restoration, and pollution. As vice-chairman of the Commerce Consumer Subcommittee, he was a strong supporter of federal no-fault auto insurance, truth-in-packaging, and the automobile "bumper bill." Once he entered Congress, Hart's name was associated with almost every piece of consumer legislation. Many of Hart's investigations coincided with the concerns of consumer advocate Ralph Nader, who testified at numerous hearings conducted by Hart.

As chairman of the Judiciary Subcommittee on Antitrust and Monopoly, Senator Hart found another forum for his consumer-oriented interests. The function of this committee, Hart said, is to observe impartially the effects of the concentration of capital on the whole society and to provide a voice for the consumer in regulatory decisions. The connection between antitrust legislation and consumer protection legislation is an intrinsic one, according to Hart.

Although hampered by a coalition of Republicans and southern Democrats, the Subcommittee on Antitrust and Monopoly under Hart's leadership held many hearings and proposed legislation on the general economic consequences of the growth of monopolies and the supposed decline of industrial competition, as well as on specific industries such as life insurance, data processing, com-munications, automobiles, petroleum, and natural gas. Like Ralph Nader, Hart considers existing antitrust legislation and enforcement ineffectual and views the current government regulation of such industries as telephones, utilities, and aviation as serving to reinforce the power of large corporations in these fields.

In 1972 Hart first introduced his industrial deconcentration bill, which he reintroduced in successive years. Hart's bill marked a significant departure from previous antitrust legislation. Unlike existing antitrust statutes, which are concerned primarily with price-fixing among individual firms and require proof of collusion among competitors for conviction, Hart's bill contained a much broader definition of monopoly, one based on corporate size rather than on evidence of intent to restrain trade. Monopoly power would be presumed to exist, Hart's bill said, if a company's average rate of profit exceeded 15 percent of its net worth in each of five consecutive years; if there had been no substantial price competition between two or more corporations within an industry for three consecutive years, or if less than five corporations within an industry accounted for 50 percent or more of an industry's sales in any year.

The extensive nature of this bill can be gauged by the estimate of Hart's staff that between one-quarter and one-third of all United States corporations would fulfill the last condition alone. Although his bill was never expected to pass, Hart used it as a convenient way to open hearings on corporate giants and provide a forum for the public exposure of current corporate practices, thereby attempting to halt what he saw as further erosion of industrial competition.

Is the Post Office a Natural Monopoly?

COMPETITION REARS ITS UGLY HEAD

The Postal Service Comes under Fire

Postal service in the United States has been a government monopoly for more than 175 years. Recently, the U.S. Postal Service has been under fire. Competition has reared its ugly head in the form of actual and potential competitors who are attempting to take away the postal monopoly. Although the arguments both for and against a continued government monopoly are varied and complex, the major points are actually relatively simple and fit well into the theoretical analysis presented in the last chapter. What is at issue is the question of whether or not the post office is a natural monopoly, which is a question of whether or not economies of scale actually exist. Before we get into such theoretical arguments, let us first take a brief look at the history of postal service in America.

History of Postal Service

Prior to independence, various colonies set up their own postal system. This became known as the "Consti-

tutional Post" and effectively replaced the official British system. Then in 1775, the Continental Congress established a postal system, with Benjamin Franklin as postmaster general. Later, the Articles of Confederation gave Congress a "sole and exclusive" monopoly on interstate postal service. However, during that period after independence and before the enactment of our constitution, the official post office could not keep a monopoly.

In 1789 the Constitution gave Congress the power "to establish Post Offices and Post Roads" in Article 1, Section 8. Notice that the Constitution did not specifically require the government to establish a monopoly. By 1792, however, when a comprehensive postal law was passed, the notion of a United States government monopoly on mail transportation was firmly embedded. The new law specifically prohibited any private person from carrying letters or setting up a private post for hire.

The rest of the history of postal legislation can be summarized in one sentence: Changes in the postal laws restricted more and more any com-

petition that might hurt the United States postal system.

Private Express Statutes

The legislation that actually "sealed" the postal monopoly was passed in 1845 and was called the Private Express Statutes. Restrictions against "private expresses" were specifically laid down. Penalties for owners of vehicles who knowingly transported individuals employed as private letter carriers were spelled out. Numerous other restrictions were also given in this statute. It has remained basically unchanged since 1845, except for a few additional restrictions to shore up the postal monopoly.

Creation of the U.S. Postal Service

Perhaps because of continued complaints about the poor quality of postal service or perhaps because Congress wanted to relieve itself of the burden of managing the post office, the U.S. Postal Service was organized in 1970 as an "independent establishment of the Executive Branch" and was to be directed by a board of governors. It was the Postal Reorganization Act, or Public Law 91-375, that created the independent U.S. Postal Service. The legislation became effective July 1, 1971. The creation of a government corporation to run the U.S. Postal Service was the direct outcome of the report of the President's Commission on Postal Organization that had been submitted to the President in June 1968.

It is interesting to note that the Commission concluded that "the postal monopoly provided by the Private Express Statutes should be preserved, although not necessarily in its present form." This conclusion was based on two assertions: (1) The post office is a natural monopoly—having more than one post office would create waste and duplication of services, and (2) the post office is vulnerable to competitors taking away the most profitable routes and leaving the "dregs" to the government system.

Let's see if these two assertions really support the argument in favor of continuing the government monopoly.

The Natural Monopoly Argument

We defined a natural monopoly in Chapter 20 as a monopoly that arises from the existence of economies of scale, which is basically a long-run concept. The notion is that as output is expanded, long-run average total costs will continuously fall over a very wide range. Thus, the firm that expands output most rapidly will find its long-run average total costs falling most rapidly and will be able to undersell every other firm in the market and become the only profitable firm in the industry. This firm is the natural monopolist. The question is, does the post office have a downward sloping long-run average

total cost curve over a large range of outputs, and (which is essentially the same thing) does the U.S. Postal Service experience large economies of scale?

The empirical evidence on the existence of economies of scale in the post office is indeed scanty. The President's Commission on Postal Organization accepted as "apparent" the existence of economies of scale and the waste that would result from competition in postal services. The academic studies that have been done, however, show either no evidence at all of economies of scale or only slight, statistically insignificant, evidence.[1]

Furthermore, the actual technology of postal operations depends mostly on human beings, not machines. Eighty to eighty-five percent of all postal costs are still labor related, in spite of the post office's well-publicized attempts at mechanization. It is difficult to imagine such a labor-intensive industry exhibiting large economies of scale or even large economies of mass production.

If we look at the evidence in terms of the possible profitability of competitors to the post office, we find that rather small companies can be formed and can compete—where they are allowed by law. This is another suggestion that economies of scale do not exist in the post office.

But let us look at the question from another point of view. Let us assume that the post office is, indeed, a natural monopoly. If it is, then is there any necessity for the U.S. Postal Service to hide under the

[1]See, for example, Morton S. Baratz, *The Economics of the Postal Service*, Washington, D.C.: Public Affairs Press, 1962.

Private Express Statutes? If the natural monopoly exists, laws aren't needed to uphold it; it will occur by its own force. Given that the U.S. Postal Service is already in existence, already has buildings and trucks and other capital equipment, it would seem that if, indeed, postal delivery is a natural monopoly, then the U.S. Postal Service would remain the monopolist, even without the Private Express Statutes prohibiting competition for letter-carrying.

Cream Skimming

The second argument in favor of government monopoly is based on the assertion that competition cannot be allowed because the most lucrative routes would be taken over by competitors, leaving the U.S. Postal Service with the crumbs. This is known as a **cream skimming** situation. Competitors will come in and skim off the cream. In a competitive situation, there is generally no cream to skim from a market. In fact, that is the whole basis of zero economic profits existing in a long-run competitive industry. As soon as economic profits exist, competitors enter the industry and skim that cream away, leaving zero economic profits in the long run. The only way for the Postal Service to contend that competitors would skim off the cream is for the cream to actually still exist. And it can exist only in a monopoly situation. We show the argument graphically in Figure I-22.1.

Positive economic profits exist at a price of P_{cream} because that price is set above the competitive equilibrium price where the market supply

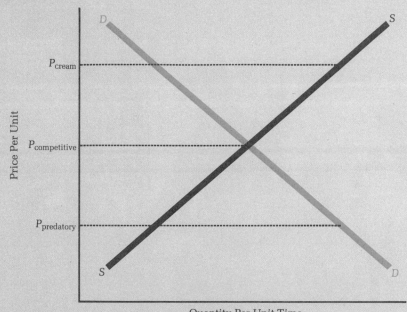

Price Per Unit

P_{cream}

$P_{competitive}$

$P_{predatory}$

D

S

S

D

Quantity Per Unit Time

FIGURE I-22.1 Skimming the Cream
Competitive price is given at $P_{competitive}$. If, however, price is set at P_{cream}, monopoly profits are being made. It is only in the case when monopoly profits are being made that there is any cream to skim off. The post office asserts that competitors would come in and set $P_{predatory}$, driving the post office out of business. However, it is more likely that the price would fall from P_{cream} to $P_{competitive}$, thus eliminating any monopoly profits.

curve intersects the market demand curve. If the U.S. Postal Service faced competition, competitors would come in and eventually force the price down from P_{cream} to $P_{competitive}$. The U.S. Postal Service no longer would be able to have any cream.

Price Discrimination

Cream exists in the U.S. Postal Service because price discrimination has been utilized for many years. First-class mail has been charged a price that exceeds its cost. The extra revenues have been applied to subsidizing other services, such as second-class mail, which consists mainly of magazines and periodicals. Moreover, there has been an implicit subsidy to certain types of mail service, in particular, mail service to

rural customers who live in out-of-the-way places.

For many years then, one class of mail users has been subsidizing other classes of mail users. Indeed, it would be true that, if the U.S. Postal Service were no longer a legal monopolist in the carrying of first-class mail, it would no longer be able to obtain the additional revenues to subsidize second-class mail users and rural areas. It would be forced either to obtain a larger subsidy from the U.S. Treasury, or it would have to raise the rates on other classes of mail service.

Cream Skimming Already Exists

To some extent, the exemptions to the Private Express Statutes have already allowed competitors to skim

some of the cream from the postal system. In particular, by the early 1970s, the U.S. Postal Service faced major competition in the delivery of parcels, the home delivery of advertising material, and the delivery of bills by the companies sending them.

The most well-known and, perhaps, most successful competitor in the parcel area of postal service is United Parcel Service, or UPS. By 1974, UPS was already delivering more parcels than the U.S. Postal Service. Moreover, it was delivering them faster and with fewer "accidents." The Postal Service has constantly referred to UPS's activities as "cream skimming."[2]

For third-class mail—the home delivery of unaddressed advertising

[2]See, for example, *Business Week*, July 18, 1970, p. 94.

circulars—there are at least a dozen private mail delivery companies competing with the post office. Such names as American Postal System, Independent Postal Service of America, Private Postal Systems of America, and Rocket Manager Services are seen more and more throughout the country. By the beginning of this decade, the Independent Postal Service of America already had 53 offices in 19 states and 1 in Canada, of almost 20,000 employees, and the ability to deliver materials to over 7 million homes.

Also, many companies are finding it cheaper to have their own employees deliver such things as bills to their customers. A number of large electric utilities, such as Virginia Electric and Power Company, found that it cost less to do it this way than to use the U.S. Postal Service.

What the Future Might Hold

What would happen if the U.S. Postal Service did lose its legal monopoly?

For one thing, we would immediately have more cream skimming. Private competitors would enter the most lucrative postal service markets, those mainly involving first-class mail, which, as we mentioned, is now overpriced to allow the Postal Service to subsidize other classes of users. The U.S. Postal Service would have to do one of two things: (1) improve its efficiency—that is, lower costs—to such an extent that it could profitably compete with the private companies, or (2) raise its prices on all classes of service to reflect their true costs. Ultimately, we will probably see a rise in rural delivery rates and delivery rates for magazines and newspapers. This rise in rates, however, presupposes that the Postal Service will not be able to greatly improve its efficiency. This is not a forgone conclusion. If the Postal Service were in competition with many private companies, it might be forced to become as efficient as those competitors seem to be already.

We would also find out if the post office is a natural monopoly. If it is, then it would be the only firm extant for certain types of mail services. Competitors would come and go because they could not compete with the natural monopolist.

What is most probable for the future, however, is that the U.S. Postal Service will retain its monopoly. There are strong forces lobbying for retention of that monopoly, one of the main ones being the union representing postal workers. They see the loss of monopoly power, due to repeal of the Private Express Statutes, as a serious threat to the Postal Service. Early in this decade, the union brought suit in a federal district court in Oklahoma to prevent the Independent Postal System of America from delivering Christmas cards. The suit stated that "the approximately 200,000 members represented by the union would be injured, in fact, by a significant loss of work time, overtime, employment opportunities, future pension and insurance benefits, and in morale." The union representing the U.S. Postal Service workers was no doubt correct. Once a monopoly is broken, workers in that previous monopoly will suffer some unemployment. Apparently the workers presently employed by the Postal Service believe they are getting a better deal from the government monopoly than they would get if the monopoly were eliminated and they were laid off and went to work for private competitors.

Definition of New Term

Cream Skimming: Competing for the most profitable areas of economic activity in a particular industry.

Questions for Thought and Discussion

1. Is the post office a natural monopoly?
2. Why do you think the post office is a government monopoly in just about every country in the world?
3. Why would postal service be different if there were competition from the private sector?

Selected References

"Is Business Subsidizing the Post Office?", *Dun's,* March 1974, pp. 67–70.

Johnston, Joseph F., Jr., "The United States Postal Monopoly." *The Business Lawyer,* vol. 23, no. 2, January 1968, pp. 389–397.

Rich, Wesley Everett, *A History of the United States Post Office to the Year 1829,* Cambridge, Mass.: Harvard University Press, 1924.

Scheele, Carl, *A Short History of the Mail Service,* Washington, D.C.: Smithsonian Institution Press, 1970.

Consumerism

ARE CONSUMER PROTECTION LAWS JUSTIFIABLE?

Straight Economics

What does standard price theory have to say about the "need" for legislation to prevent business people from defrauding the public with unhealthy food, unsafe products, and unsubstantiated advertising claims? Price theory tells us that the forces of market competition should obviate any need for regulation. Let's take an example. Suppose that, unknown to you, there is a fraudulent TV repairman in your neighborhood. When your set goes on the blink, you call him in. He says a lot more is wrong with your TV set than actually is. You, however, have no way of knowing whether he's telling the truth because you do not possess the necessary technical information. If you believe him, you are defrauded. He charges you a higher price than you "should" be charged. He takes your set, repairs it at a cost of about $5, brings the set back to you, and gives you a bill for $95. He tells you 3 transformers had blown out and 14 transistors had to be replaced. You may cry in anguish, but you pay the bill anyway. You have been defrauded.

If there's any competition, fraud-ulent, high-priced repair people would be expected to lose all their business. The competitive process takes time, however, and information costs are not zero. Nonetheless, according to our standard theory, competition among repair people will *eventually* lead to the elimination of "dishonest" ones since people will seek out the honest ones in time.

We know that competition will act faster in other circumstances. In this particular one, if we are in a community that is relatively small or has a relatively stable or fixed citizenry, we would expect that the dishonest repair people would be run out of business faster than if the community in question were unstable, with lots of people leaving and others moving in. In the former, the neighbors would all know which guys were the crooks. In the latter, the crooks could go to the unsuspecting newcomers to get business. We would expect, therefore, that there are fewer dishonest repair people in small towns than in large cities.

We would also expect manufacturers of TV sets to try to do something about reducing the repair costs of their products. After all, the higher the price you have to pay for repairs, the higher the price of service per unit time that you get from your set. If the price per constant-quality unit of service is artificially high due to costly repairs, then we would expect TV manufacturers to have an incentive to reduce the need for repairs in their machines. This would decrease the demand for repair services, which in turn would decrease the price. The effective price of television services would therefore fall, thus increasing the quantity of television sets demanded.

The Need for Protection

Why, then, is it necessary today to have consumer protection? First, even if we assume that competition will *eventually* lead to the elimination of fraudulent TV repair people, the adjustment time may be unacceptably long from a social standpoint. It may be socially cheaper for consumer protection agencies to take action and make spot checks on businesses suspected of defrauding the public.

Also, consumer protection may be more necessary now than in the past because the population has become more transient. In such a situation people would not know about dishonest business people. The ad-

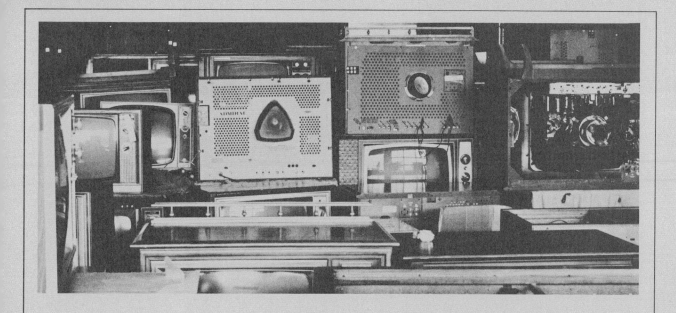

justment time needed for the eventual elimination of fraud would be greatly lengthened and, from a social standpoint, unacceptable.

There is another reason why information costs have increased and adjustment times have, therefore, become longer. Presumably, as products become more complex, it is more difficult for consumers to understand what they are buying. Therefore, consumers are easy prey for unscrupulous business people using technical jargon.

Another area in which consumers may be unable to protect themselves pertains to the ingredients in food products.

The Case of the Fat Wienie

For a number of years now, consumer protection agents, particularly the President's Aide on Consumer Affairs, have been concerned about the fat content in hotdogs. When the hotdog manufacturers wanted to raise the fat content, the President's Consumer Aide fought tooth and nail against them; consumer advocates also rallied to prevent hotdog manufacturers from increasing the amount of chicken meat in hotdogs. Let's use our standard microeconomic model to analyze this situation.

Economic Analysis

As with TV sets, we can talk about the price per constant-quality unit in the case of hotdogs. The price of hotdogs should be viewed as the price of a constant-quality unit hotdog. If the price of hotdogs remains the same and the fat content increases, then the price per constant-quality unit has gone up, assuming, of course, that the actual meat content of a wienie is important to the consumer.

Let's assume that the value of hotdogs to consumers is based both on taste and food content. Assume also that increasing the fat used in the hotdog does not change taste but does reduce food value. Thus, the true price of the hotdog goes up if manufacturers increase fat content. What does our standard supply and demand analysis say will happen? At a higher price with an unchanged demand curve, a smaller quantity will be demanded. But if this is the case, why would manufacturers want to raise the price? Obviously, the supply and demand curves must not remain stable; either the supply curve shifts to the left or it shifts to the right so that the equilibrium price is higher than it was. (This is obviously going to be true in an inflationary setting, but that's a macroeconomic issue.)

Let's take an individual firm, and assume for the moment that consumers are unable to assess the food value of hotdogs. If fat content does not alter taste, wouldn't a profit-maximizing producer try to make hotdogs that had 99.99 percent fat? Only the skin would be nonfat. If it could charge the same price and lower the cost of production, this profit-maximizing firm would make more profits. This is not the case, however, because obviously fat content *does* alter the taste; consumers can, at least on the margin, discover how much food value there is in a hotdog; and there is competition among wienie producers.

Marginal Analysis

Note that some sort of competition can exist if there is information *on the margin.* We must distinguish carefully between the average and the margin. The average consumer of wienies may not know what he or she is buying and not care, but there are marginal consumers who do take note. For example, dormitories and schools are usually highly critical of the food value they buy—but not the taste, right? They will not be fooled by higher percentages of fat in hotdogs. They will realize that it is an increase in the price per constant-quality unit.

Consumer protection in the form of preventing hotdog manufacturers from increasing the fat content can serve the purpose of increasing information in the marketplace and *decreasing* uncertainty. The search costs to the buying public can be reduced. One might wish, though, to assess the costs of such consumer protection as well as the benefits.

Moreover, one might distinguish between what one thinks people *should* buy and what people actually do buy. Such questions, however, are in the realm of normative economics.

Truth in Labeling

An alternative policy might be to enforce accurate labeling of the contents of food products. Then each consumer could buy exactly what he or she wanted and would know exactly what was being bought. Government regulation could seek to improve information about products rather than restricting their various characteristics to some governmentally "acceptable" norm.

Unsafe at Any Speed

It might be said that the current consumer movement started with Ralph Nader's book, *Unsafe at Any Speed,* a lambasting critique of the automobile industry and of General Motors in particular for its production of the apparently unsafe Corvair. (The Corvair is no longer being produced.) Partially as a result of Nader's unending assault on the unsafe automobiles being produced in Detroit, we now have a set of safety standards with which automobile manufacturers must comply when producing their cars. These safety standards involve collapsible steering wheels, dual-brake systems, over-the-shoulder seat belts, padded dashes, and crash-absorbing bumpers. The list of required safety features is growing. The apparent result is that we are now driving safer cars than we did 10 years ago. Let's see

what economic analysis can say about product safety regulations such as those imposed on automobiles.

Changing Quality

We should again be careful to distinguish between the price per unit and the price per constant-quality unit. Obviously, when an automobile is made safer, its quality is increased for most people. If the nominal price were to remain the same, the price per constant-quality unit would fall as quality increased. When viewed in this respect, safety is no different from any other aspect of a product. We can view the demand for safety the same way we can view the demand for ornamental trimmings on a car.

Remember that our object is to apply a simple economic model to our question. The question in this case is whether the effects of safety legislation actually protect the consumer.

Commission on Product Safety

The President's Commission on Product Safety once said that "The exposure of consumers to unreasonable product hazards is excessive by any standard of measurement." The report of the Commission also indicated that "Many hazards . . . are unnecessary and can be eliminated without substantially affecting the price to the consumer." If the President's Commission is correct and many safety hazards could be eliminated at substantially no cost to the producer or the consumer, then we must conclude that people do not care about safety.

After all, if people wished to have safer products, then profit-seeking producers would be motivated to provide safety aspects for their products since the costs for doing so would be negligible. However, we know that nothing is free; even safety has a cost. If we make cars safer, as we have been doing, the price of those cars will go up. It takes men and machines to make products that will last longer and that will be safer to use. This is a general rule that we can assume holds in most cases.

If a car has to have an airbag passive-restraint system to protect its occupants in a collision, then the car will probably cost more. In fact, the industry has estimated the cost of airbags will be several hundred dollars per car. From what we know about the resultant price of a product when the costs of production go up, we might say that safety legislation is essentially equal to a tax on products. The tax is only *nominally* paid by the manufacturer. The consumer will pay most of it.

Consumer Sovereignty Our competitive model would say that in the past the existing level of product safety was the one desired by consumers since they were the ones who actually determined what was produced. This model of **consumer sovereignty** may not be appropriate in certain circumstances, although it could conceivably be appropriate in many others. There is a tricky question as to whether consumer sovereignty actually exists. Do consumers determine what kind of products are made, or do producers? Do consumers, through their choice of products, determine what is actually produced and sold? If *not,* then there is an argument for product safety legislation. If consumers do not have control, even in the long run, over what they are actually sold, then producers may be selling products that are either unsafe or lack the greatest utility possible.

Costs and Benefits of Safety

Any increase in safety usually entails higher production costs and ultimately higher costs to the consumer. The question arises as to whether consumers benefit from the improvement of the products they buy if they have to pay more for them. In other words, are the benefits worth the costs? That sometimes depends on who bears the costs of *unsafe* products.

There is certainly a case for safety legislation when it involves so-called **third-party** or **external effects.** If you have faulty brakes, you might run over a pedestrian. Here, the pedestrian is an external party to your decision to drive with faulty brakes. There was no way for the pedestrian to get you to fix your brakes. Certainly you will be forced to compensate the injured pedestrian, or his or her dependents, since the accident was purely due to your negligence. However, in most instances, the compensation to the injured party is less than the injured party would have demanded before the fact of the accident. Thus, to avoid excessive third-party effects of faulty products, safety legislation may be appropriate. Such legislation would involve requiring good tires, good brakes, cars without knife-edged hood ornaments, windows that do not distort vision, and so on.

Safety May Decline

Let's assume that people demand a certain level of safety in their cars. When they are forced to buy an over-the-shoulder seat belt, they suddenly feel safer because they know that, in case of an accident, there is less probability of their being seriously hurt. Therefore, they drive faster to maintain their desired level of safety. This is particularly true with something like passive-restraint systems such as airbags. There is nothing that the occupants of a car can do to eliminate the safety feature of airbags, whereas there is something they can do with over-the-shoulder seat belts: They don't have to put them on. With airbags, however, the drivers feel they can increase recklessness and still maintain their formerly desired level of safety.

This argument may seem farfetched, but there are probably some of you who do, in fact, feel safer with a combination lap and over-the-shoulder seat belt and a large head restraint behind you. Would you perhaps be more timid when driving if you didn't have all that safety paraphernalia? Statistics from Sweden show that in the last few years no one wearing an over-the-shoulder belt has been killed in an accident at speeds of under 65 miles an hour. This is certainly impressive evidence that the probability of dying in an automobile crash is lower if you wear an over-the-shoulder belt. Might you not take a few more chances, given that new information? If the answer is yes, then the wild argument just presented does, indeed, have some relevance.

Some studies have shown that new auto safety standards have not had exactly the effect that was intended by the safety legislation. More specifically, one research project concluded that "... safety regulation has had no effect on the highway death toll. There is some evidence that regulation may have increased the share of this toll borne by pedestrians and increased the total number of accidents."[1]

What has happened, according to the author of this study, is that individuals have increased their driving "intensity"; that is, more people are driving more recklessly since they're in safer cars. Also, there has been an increase in drunken driving and driving by young people. And cars equipped with safety devices have been involved in a disproportionately high share of accidents.

Of course, there will be other studies that will reject or support these conclusions. The point is that we cannot take for granted the effects of regulation when only the supply side of the safety picture is regulated. The demand side has to be looked at also.

[1]Sam Peltzman, "The Regulation of Auto Safety," in H. Manne and R. L. Miller (eds.), *Administrative Power and Economic Costs: The Auto Safety Illustration,* Chicago: Aldine, 1976.

Definitions of New Terms

Consumer Sovereignty: A notion that the consumers register their preferences in the marketplace by their dollar votes. In a competitive economy, competition among suppliers will force them to adjust their particular production to whatever consumers demand.

Third-Party Effects: Sometimes called external effects; effects of a decision that bear on a third party who is not part of the decision-making process. When you buy a car from the dealer, you may make an agreement that is satisfactory to the two of you. However, if the brakes are faulty, you can run down a third party who is not part of the agreement.

Questions for Thought and Discussion

1. Many people contend that consumer sovereignty no longer exists in the United States because we do not have a competitive world. Do you agree? Why? What bearing does this have on consumerism?
2. Ralph Nader's study group has shown that the Volkswagen is a relatively unsafe car. Why do so many people still ride in Volkswagens?
3. It has been suggested that by 1985, only cars that meet very strict safety requirements will be allowed to drive on highways. All other cars will be restricted to city streets. Will you be better or worse off after this legislation is passed?
4. Do the requirements for sturdy bumpers relate to the safety of automobile occupants?
5. If all cars are required to have extensive safety features, do you think that the relatively less wealthy in the United States will benefit equally with the more wealthy?

Selected References

Nader, Ralph, *The Volkswagen: An Assessment of Distinctive Hazards,* Washington, D.C.: Center for Automobile Safety, 1971.

Stanford, David, *Who Put the 'Con' in Consumer?,* New York: Liveright, 1972.

Tomerlin, John, "Ralph Nader vs. Volkswagen," *Road & Track,* April 1972, pp. 25–33.

The Fifth Branch
of Government

RALPH NADER
**Founder, Center for the Study
of Responsive Law**

Photo by Steve Northup

Ralph Nader has been described as a public
official never elected by anyone, an unmoni-
tored watchdog accountable to no one, an institution unto himself. These observations
could also describe Nader's major targets: the
corporation executives, the utilities, the ineffective regulatory agencies, and the advertising media. Nader's focus for the past 10
years has been an anti-institutional one. He
has attacked the paradox of "crimes" that are
severely punished when committed by individuals but ignored or even subsidized when
committed by corporations. His research has
described the detailed way in which he feels
free enterprise has become a slogan rather
than an economic mode of operation.

While at Harvard Law School, Nader first
became conscious of the trend for bright
young lawyers to go into the lucrative fields
of corporation and tax law. After receiving
his degree, Nader began practicing law in
Hartford, Connecticut, specializing in automobile accident cases. By 1963 he had compiled a collection of data which he thought

refuted the myth that all accidents were caused by careless drivers. He discovered that the auto industry was sitting on plans for "safety cars" while pushing dangerous cars onto an unsuspecting public.

Two years later, *Unsafe at Any Speed* was published; probably few books have had as immediate and serious an impact on American industry. Its primary target was General Motors—the Chevrolet division in particular. With case studies and detailed engineering data and specifications, Nader had compiled a devastating attack. The company hired a private detective to trail Nader, tried to trap him into compromising situations with attractive young women, and generally harassed him at every turn. But General Motors could not have selected a less vulnerable target: Nader's idea of relaxation is "sitting down to discuss anthropology." Nader then sued GM, bringing even more attention to the book, and was awarded $280,000, money he used to continue his fight against harmful corporate practices. The book and subsequent trial established Nader's reputation as an uncompromising, incorruptible, skillful fighter.

Nader has spawned a number of institutions to further his causes. The Center for the Study of Responsive Law, one Nader creation, has produced reports on many facets of industrial production, federal regulation, and state government policy in the United States. Nader, who views "citizen action as a countervailing force" to corporate and governmental injustices, has moved increasingly from exposing these injustices to lawsuits and other legal actions. Under the auspices of Public Citizen, Inc., another Nader creation, Citizen Action Groups have been formed in various parts of the country to research and organize citizens around consumer and environmental issues.

At least five major regulatory and consumer protection laws can be ascribed directly to Nader's efforts: the Motor Vehicle Safety Act (1966), a direct result of *Unsafe at Any Speed;* the Wholesome Meat Act (1967); the Natural Gas Pipeline Safety Act (1968); the Coal Mine Health and Safety Act (1969); and the Occupational Safety and Health Act (1970). Nader has also produced a series of books on some of the federal regulatory agencies; he and his staff found absenteeism, featherbedding, inefficiency, incompetence, and a lack of commitment at the highest levels of the Federal Trade Commission and other agencies.

A staff report on the state of Delaware explored the broad political and economic influence of the duPont corporation that, in the view of the authors, completely compromises any semblance of a free market economy and electoral freedom in the state. And although it swallowed hard, the duPont corporation spent $450 to obtain copies of the report.

The oldest argument against Nader is that he would sell the free-enterprise system down the river to a series of megaagencies with absolute regulatory power. "Where is the free enterprise system?" he asks. "I'm trying to find it. Is it the oil oligopoly, protected by import quotas? The shared monopolies in consumer products? The securities market, that bastion of capitalism operating on fixed commissions and now provided with socialized insurance? They call me a radical for trying to restore power to the consumer, but businessmen are the true radicals in this country. They are taking us deeper and deeper into corporate socialism—corporate power using government power to protect it from competition."

21 In between Monopoly and Competition

Up to this point two extremes in market structure have been discussed: pure competition and pure monopoly. It was mentioned that there are variations between these two extremes. In this chapter we will discuss several of these variations, although cut-and-dried models are not possible because the theories of *monopolistic competition* and oligopoly are not as definitive as the theories of pure competition and pure monopoly. At any rate, the supposed harm to the buying public caused by monopolistic competition and oligopoly has been decried by numerous congresspersons and consumer advocates—including, of course, Ralph Nader. We will have a chance to analyze some of the recommendations and findings of the Nader study group on antitrust enforcement later. That group comes out very strongly against industries where economic power is concentrated in a very few large firms.

Monopolistic Competition

Back in the 1920s and 1930s, economists became increasingly dissatisfied with the polar extremes of market structure: competition and monopoly. Theoretical and empirical research was instigated to develop some sort of middle ground. The most popular and, at least for awhile, well-received theory was that of **monopolistic competition.** This theory was presented by Harvard's Edward Chamberlin, who wrote *The Theory of Monopolistic Competition* in 1933.[1]

[1]Essentially the same theory was also presented by Britain's Joan Robinson in her *The Economics of Imperfect Competition,* also in 1933.

Chamberlin defined the monopolistic competition structure as one in which there are a relatively large number of producers offering similar but *differentiated* products. The most obvious situation is reflected by the plethora of brand names for such things as toothpastes, soaps, and gasolines. Should you buy Crest, Colgate, Gleem, Macleans, Ultra-Brite, Stripe, Close-Up, or any of numerous other brand names? Each firm has some market power because it has product identity. The differences between the similar products may be very small indeed. However, Chamberlin still presumed that each firm selling its differentiated product faced a gently downward-sloping demand curve. The firm is still such a small part of the industry that it does not face the total industry demand curve, nor does it face a large part of it like an oligopolist does. It isn't a perfect competitor and, therefore, does not face a perfectly horizontal, completely elastic demand curve. Each monopolistic competitor firm has some control over the price of its product, but that control is very little because the availability of substitutes—other brand names—is very large. Chamberlin found it useful to group together all firms producing similar products and call them a *product group*. Obviously, the way we combine firms into different product groups has to be arbitrary; there is no way to decide how close substitutes must be to be included in the same product group. But Chamberlin did assert that meaningful groups could be formulated.

Assumptions

One key assumption in Chamberlin's theory was that the number of firms in each product group was large enough that every firm could expect its actions to go unheeded by all the other firms in that particular group. In other words, no retaliatory measures are expected.

Notice that this is different from the oligopolistic situation, where interdependence is usually presumed. Additionally, Chamberlin assumed that both the cost curves and the demand curves for all the firms would be the same in each group. Notice here that this is a very restrictive assumption: Since the products are, by definition, differentiated, would we not expect their demand and cost curves to be somewhat different?

Zero Profits

Since there is free entry into a monopolistically competitive industry, zero economic profits are going to result in the long run. The price will be just equal to the long-run average total cost. That is, price equals cost; there is no profit. But since each firm faces a slightly downward-sloping demand curve, it produces *less* than a competitive firm would produce. Compare Figure 21-1 with Figure 21-2.

How Has Chamberlin's Theory Fared?

A number of economists have pointed out some serious and some not so serious problems with Chamberlin's theory. We mentioned one of the problems. The definition of the product group must be completely arbitrary. The number of firms in a product group could be one or many. If you don't know how to distinguish the firms that should be in a product group from the firms that shouldn't, then how can you talk about a particular industry being monopolistically competitive? You can't.

Advertising—a Way of Differentiating the Product

In monopolistic competition, product differentiation plays a key role and, consequently, so

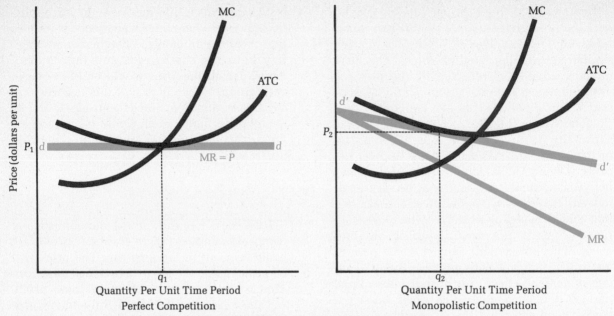

FIGURES 21-1, 21-2 Comparison of Perfect Competitor with Monopolistic Competitor

In Figure 21-1 the perfectly competitive firm has zero economic profits in the long run. Its long-run average total cost curve is tangent to the demand curve *dd* just at the point of intersection with the marginal cost curve. The price is set equal to marginal cost, and that price is P_1. There are zero economic profits. Also, its demand curve is just tangent to the *minimum* point on its average total cost curve, which means the firm is operating at its optimum rate of production. With the monopolistically competitive firm in Figure 21-2, there are also zero economic profits in the long run because the average total cost curve is tangent to the individual monopolistic competitor's demand curve, *d'd'*, at the point where production occurs. The price, however, is greater than marginal cost; the monopolistically competitive firm does not find itself at the minimum point on its average total cost curve—it is operating at a rate of output less than optimum, that is, to the left of the minimum point on the ATC curve.

does advertising. Advertising is an important part of the economic landscape, not only in America but in most other countries in the world. The economic analysis of advertising is fairly straightforward.

Since advertising takes money, firms are going to engage in advertising only if they think they will profit from it. We expect, therefore, that advertising will be undertaken only when marginal revenue exceeds the marginal costs of advertising. In an economic sense, firms actu-

ally hope to make higher profits when they decide to advertise. For one thing, they hope to increase their volume of business. Through advertising, a firm hopes to *shift* the demand curve for its product to the right. This is shown in Figure 21-3. Then, at the same price, it can sell a larger quantity of its product. (The firm may also be content if advertising prevents the demand curve from shifting to the left.)

Since the effects of advertising are usually felt over a period of time, it might be better

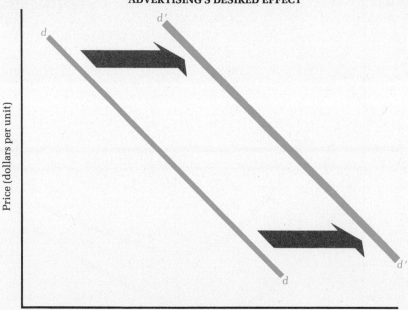

ADVERTISING'S DESIRED EFFECT

Price (dollars per unit)

Quantity Per Unit Time Period

FIGURE 21-3

The firm which advertises hopes that the advertising will shift the demand schedule for its product to the right. In other words, before advertising, the demand schedule is at *dd*; after advertising takes place, the demand schedule hopefully will shift to *d'd'*.

to analyze advertising as an investment rather than as a current business expense. And this is probably the way most businesses view it. Since advertising is an investment, the firm must decide whether the rate of return on that investment is adequate. This will depend upon the alternative uses the business could have found for that particular amount of money. The firm finds the rate of return by looking at the increased sales made possible by the advertising campaign over a period of time.

Another alleged reason for advertising is that the subsequent increased sales can lead to economies of scale. This is possible only if the economies of scale outweigh the advertising costs. Look at Figure 21-4. Here we find that the hypothetical average total cost curve without advertising is ATC. With advertising, it is ATC'. If production is at point A, then average total costs will be ATC_1. If advertising campaigns shift demand and production to point

B, then average total costs will fall to ATC_2. The reduction in average total costs will more than outweigh the increased expenses due to advertising. If the advertising campaign was not successful and demand and production remained where they were, then the firm would stop advertising. It would not be profitable to continue.

Arguments against Advertising

Many critics of advertising do not accept the argument that expanded production through advertising makes for a lower unit cost. These critics contend that much advertising is self-canceling, as in the cigarette industry. Although each advertiser must continue to spend money on flashy billboards and magazine ads, the tobacco industry as a whole gets no additional

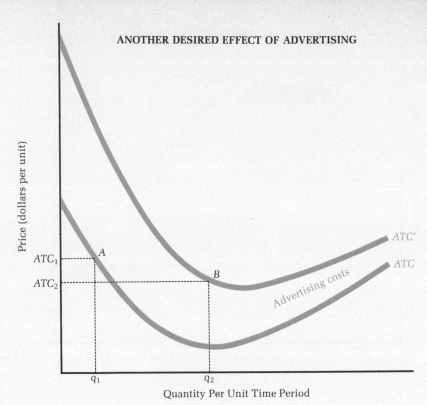

ANOTHER DESIRED EFFECT OF ADVERTISING

FIGURE 21-4

Advertising may be able to more than pay for itself. For example, in this diagram we start out on the average total cost curve ATC at point A with production of Q_1. Here average total costs are ATC_1. Advertising is added, and the average total cost curve shifts out to ATC'. However, we move out to point B with the quantity produced of Q_2 and an average total cost of only ATC_2, which is lower than ATC_1.

customers, with all members advertising at once. Moreover, if advertising can cause a firm to realize gains from mass production through increased growth, it seems that at some point the firm will incur diseconomies of scale.

Critics also contend that advertising expenditures divert human and other resources away from much more pressing needs. Advertising, in short, gives rise to a misallocation of resources. The most telling argument along these lines is the claim that advertising causes people to consume more private goods and fewer "public" goods—such as schools, hospitals, better streets, and so on. Although the critics may be right, we should realize that private businesses are not the only ones who advertise. Look at the amount of advertising done by universities in need of funds; look at the amount

of advertising that the government uses to ensure us we are being well cared for.

Advertising has also been attacked as the means by which producers can create artificial wants. Numerous books have been written about how advertising subtly and not so subtly alters the ways we think and the things we desire to consume. Analyzing this particular contention is difficult because economics can say very little about the creation of wants. However, we do know that advertisers compete, and, therefore, it would seem to be quite difficult for one manufacturer to induce consumers to buy a product they didn't want when numerous other manufacturers were attempting to do exactly the same thing. Moreover, there is plenty of advertising for nonconsumption—that is, for savings. How many times do you see ads on TV and in the newspaper about new savings and loan associations wanting your money? And don't we see ads for U.S. Savings Bonds? The fact is we find ads asking us to do everything imaginable with our income and our time. Thus, the question is whether some forms of advertising are more persuasive than others, and, if so, does one particular industry have a monopoly on that form of advertising? This is a question no one has yet answered.

Oligopoly

We define **oligopoly** as a market structure characterized by a few firms with a rather large amount of interdependence among them. Presumably, each oligopolistic firm makes its own pricing policies with an eye to how its rival producers will react. The main characteristic of oligopoly is that any change in one firm's output or price influences the profits and sales of its few competitors. This leads one to predict that an oligopolistic firm will attempt to anticipate impending changes in the pricing and output policies of other firms before it decides to change its own policies.

You can probably think of quite a few examples of an oligopolistic market structure. The automobile industry is dominated by three large firms: Chrysler, Ford, and General Motors. The steel industry has numerous firms, but the top four account each year for more than 60 percent of the industry's ingot capacity. Economists maintain that these major firms must take account of the reaction of the others each time a change in pricing policy is contemplated. One of the most blatant practices we find in oligopolistic industries is that when one large company changes its prices, others follow suit immediately.

In Table 21-1 we see that in a number of industries, the percentage of the industry output produced by the first four firms exceeds 80 percent. The mere fact that the four firms in

each of these industries produce a large amount of the industry output does not necessarily mean that "something" should be done. In fact, one of the most surprising aspects of attacks against oligopolies is that very little proof is usually given as to the detrimental effects of such an industry structure. Merely because we define an industry as oligopolistic does not mean we have said anything about what *alternative* market structures should be and what the cost of getting to those alternatives might involve.

Oligopoly vs. Pure Forms of Market Structure

We know that the demand curve facing an individual competitor is a horizontal line es-

Table 21-1 **Industry Concentrations**

This table shows the percentage of total output produced by the largest four firms in selected concentrated industries.

	PERCENT OF DOMESTIC INDUSTRY'S OUTPUT PRODUCED BY FOUR LARGEST FIRMS
Primary aluminum	100
Passenger cars	99
Locomotives and parts	97
Steam engines and turbines	93
Sewing machines	93
Electric lamps (bulbs)	92
Telephone and telegraph equipment	92
Gypsum products	84
Synthetic fibers	82
Cigarettes	80

Source: U.S. Senate

tablished at the going market price. The individual firm cannot influence the price of the product it sells—it takes the price as given; it is a price taker. On the other hand, we know that the demand curve of an individual monopolistic firm is the market demand curve, because a monopolistic firm *is* the entire industry. It can influence the price of its product. If it wants to sell more, it can do so by merely lowering its price. It is a price setter, not a price taker.

What about an oligopolistic firm? It does not face a horizontal demand curve because it is a large part of the market and can probably influence the price. It does not face the entire market demand curve because it is not the only firm in the industry. A graphic characterization of an oligopolist's demand curve is not easy. Although there are a few theories around—and we present one of them here—bear in mind that

there are numerous critics of any theory of oligopoly, no matter what the theory looks like.

Some economists believe that oligopolists face a downward-sloping *kinked* demand curve. Look at Figure 21-5. The oligopolistic firm is selling at P_e. If it lowers its price, it knows its competitors will follow suit because if they don't, they'll lose too much business. So the demand curve it faces is DD. It is relatively inelastic. Lowering its prices will not create many new customers for the firm because all its rivals will be charging the same low price. If it raises its price, however, the oligopolistic firm will face demand curve D'D'. All his rivals may *not* follow suit. Its higher price will send its customers fleeing to its lower-priced rivals. Thus, D'D' is more elastic than DD.

We might put DD and D'D' together to form a kinked demand curve D'D. It may not pay

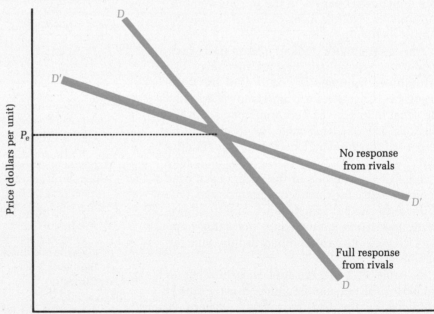

the oligopolistic firm to change price if it is profit maximizing at the kink. Only if its marginal cost curve changes drastically will it want to change prices.

One of the problems with the kinked demand curve is that we have no idea how the existing price, P_e, came into being. Seemingly, if every oligopolistic firm faced a kinked demand curve, it would never pay, in a stable environment, for it to change prices. The problem is that the kinked demand curve does not show us how supply and demand originally determined the going price of an oligopolist's product.

Characteristics of Oligopolies

We said that oligopolistic industries have few sellers who usually sell identical or similar products. Besides these characteristics, oligopolistic industries have others:

1. *Relatively high obstacles to entry* Oligopolistic industries are usually characterized as industries requiring large investments to enter. These investments may be high advertising costs to get a new firm known or high capital costs to build plant and equipment. Patents may also prevent entry.

2. *Mutual dependence* One way of showing an oligopolistic situation is by the kinked demand curve. This, basically, is mutual dependence—each oligopolist has to consider the reactions of rivals. The behavior of oligopolies in the marketplace may thus be akin to the behavior of players of checkers or chess: Every move by one leads to a move by the other or others.

3. *Growth through merger* The oligopolies that exist today have, in large part, been the result of the merging of competing firms. For example, U.S. Steel Corporation was formed out of a merger of 11 independent steel producers.

In the following issue we examine public policy alternatives for oligopolies.

<table>
<tr><td>Definitions of New Terms</td><td>**Monopolistic Competition:** A market situation where a large number of firms produce similar but not exactly identical products. There is relatively easy entry into the industry.
Oligopoly: A market situation where there are only very few sellers. Each seller knows that the other sellers will react to changes in prices and quantities.</td></tr>
</table>

<table>
<tr><td>Chapter Summary</td><td>1. Numerous market situations lie between the extremes of pure competition and pure monopoly. Monopolistic competition and oligopoly are two of these.
2. Monopolistic competition is a theory developed by Edward Chamberlin of Harvard University in 1933. It refers to a market situation composed of specific product groups in which the different companies involved have slight monopoly powers because each has a product slightly different from the others. Examples of product groups might include the toothpaste and soap industries. The monopolistic competitor ends up with zero economic</td></tr>
</table>

profits because there is free entry into the industry. However, according to Chamberlin, the monopolistic competitor does not produce where price equals marginal costs and, therefore, does not produce at the minimum point on the average total cost curve.

3. Advertising occurs in industries where the firms are not pure price takers. The basic goal of advertisers is to shift the demand curve for their product outward.

4. Oligopoly is a market situation where there are several firms. Each firm knows that its rivals will react to a change in price. Oligopolies are usually defined as those in which the four-firm concentration ratio is relatively high—for example, more than 70 or 80 percent. That means that we would classify all industries in which the leading four firms produce 70 percent or more of the value of the industry shipments each year as oligopolies.

5. Oligopolies are characterized by relatively high barriers to entry, mutual dependence, and growth through merger.

Questions for Thought and Discussion

1. Numerous market structures lie between the extremes of pure competition and pure monopoly. Which one do you believe prevails?
2. If you believe the kinked demand curve theory, how could you ever explain a change in the price of an oligopolist's product?
3. Do you buy soap on the basis of brand or price? Does it make any difference?

Selected References

Adams, Walter, *The Structure of American Industry,* 4th ed., New York: Macmillan, 1971, chaps. 2, 3, 5, 7 to 9.

Chamberlin, Edward H., *The Theory of Monopolistic Competition,* 8th ed., Cambridge, Mass.: Harvard University Press, 1962.

Galbraith, John K., *American Capitalism,* Boston: Houghton Mifflin, 1956, chaps. 7 and 9.

Mansfield, Edwin, *Monopoly Power and Economic Performance,* 3d ed., New York: W. W. Norton, 1972.

Robinson, Joan, *The Economics of Imperfect Competition,* New York: St. Martin Press, 1969.

Simon, Julian, *Issues in the Economics of Advertising,* Urbana: University of Illinois Press, 1970.

Weiss, Leonard W., *Case Studies in American Industry,* rev. ed., New York: Wiley, 1971.

Should Large Corporations Be Broken Up?

THE QUESTION OF ECONOMIC POWER

Oligopolies on the Run

Not many years ago the Nader task force on antitrust activity came up with the following recommendations:

1. Break up large companies in any industry with a four-firm concentration ratio of 50 percent or an eight-firm concentration ratio of 70 percent or more.
2. Require the top 500 corporations to divest an amount of assets equal to any firm they acquire.
3. Place an absolute asset size limitation of $2 billion on firms.
4. Levy a 100 percent tax on all advertising expenditures of firms possessing incipient market power in excess of a certain percentage of sales revenues.
5. Make into a public corporation any defense contractor that does more than 75 percent of its business with the government over a 5-year period.

They based their recommendations on the following assertions:

1. Large firms can set prices at a higher level regardless of consumer demand.
2. Antitrust violations have resulted in high prices for bread, gasoline, automobile parts, prescription drugs, and houses.
3. Antitrust violations have resulted in air pollution and faulty products.
4. Prices in oligopolies tend to be progressively going up, not down, regardless of consumer demand and economic climate.
5. High-concentration ratios lead to monopoly profits and the ability to set monopoly prices.
6. Approximately 33.4 percent of the value of manufactured goods is produced by industries with four-firm concentration ratios of 50 percent or more.
7. Large firms engage in internal subsidization whereby the larger entities shield the smaller from the usual pressures of the market by making money available as necessity exists.
8. Oligopolies engage in worthless product differentiation.
9. Monopoly has caused the loss in GNP of $60 billion yearly, which is enough to cover our annual crime bill and remove the major sources of pollution along with the elimination of poverty.[1]

Power and Concentration

There are many issues in question here. One issue involves the meaning of economic power and the way in which "too much" of it is detrimental to our society. Another issue is the definition of an oligopoly, an industrial structure in which a significant amount of economic power is vested in only a few large companies. Let us look first at the way in which a potentially oligopolistic situation can be defined.

Concentration Ratios

As we saw in the last chapter, concentration ratios are the statistics looked at the most. In particular, we saw that the Ralph Nader study group was concerned primarily with industries whose four-firm concentration ratio exceeded 50 percent. Remember that the concentration ratio measures the percentage of the

[1] *The Closed Enterprise System,* The Nader Study Group Report on Antitrust Enforcement, Mark J. Green, Project Director and Editor, 2 vols., preliminary draft, copyright June 1971 by the Center for the Study of Responsive Law, Washington, D.C.

value of total domestic shipments accounted for by the top four firms, for example, in an industry. The higher the concentration ratio, the larger the percentage of total output that is accounted for by the top four firms. It is a simple, straightforward calculation—but what does it mean?

Few economists can agree on an operational meaning of concentration ratio for policymaking purposes. The Nader study group came up with what would have to be considered a somewhat arbitrary cutoff point. How it arrived at that cutoff point is not explained in their study.

For policymaking, a cutoff point could be specified where concentration leads to excessive profits or monopoly profits. In other words, if an industry has a concentration ratio of 60 percent or more, then we might assume it is making higher than competitive rates of return. We then might be able to justify a policymaking rule which stated that no industry could have concentration ratios in excess of 60 percent. Whenever this cutoff point was approached, the Justice Department's antitrust division would step in and break up some of the largest firms into smaller, competing firms.

But what does the evidence tell us? It tells us that, yes, higher concentration ratios lead to higher profits and that, no, higher concentration ratios do not lead to higher profits. In other words, no agreed upon, definitive study has shown a positive relationship between the degree of concentration in an industry and the level of profits in that industry or the level of profits by the leading firms in that industry. A study by Professor Joseph Bain showed a distinct rela-tionship between industry concentration ratios and profit rates,[2] as did the White House Task Force on Antitrust Policy.[3] However, both these studies were criticized by Professor Y. Brozen.[4] Another researcher concluded that "part, probably all, of the observed positive relationships between profitability and concentration is in fact attributable to other factors which happen to be correlated with concentration."[5]

So, where are we? Little can be said about more concentrated industries making higher rates of profit. This does not necessarily mean that large firms in highly concentrated industries should not be broken up. In the mid-1970s, the Justice Department started prosecuting large, more or less true monopolies in an effort to make the industries more competitive. An example is American Telephone and Telegraph. The Justice Department filed suit against that company, a true monopoly because of its government franchise, in 1974. When we talk about monopolies that have been either created, fostered,

[2]Joseph Bain, "Relation of Profits Rate to Industry Concentration," *Quarterly Journal of Economics,* August 1951, pp. 293–324.
[3]*Trade Reg. Rept.* no. 1, sup. 2, no. 415, May 26, 1969.
[4]Y. Brozen, "Bain's Concentration and Rates of Return Revisited," *Journal of Law and Economics,* vol. XIV, no. 2, October 1971, pp. 351–370, and Brozen, "The Antitrust Force Deconcentration Recommendation," *Journal of Law and Economics,* vol. XIII, no. 2., October 1970, pp. 279ff.
[5]Sam Peltzman, "Profits, Data, and Public Policy," in J. Fred Weston and Sam Peltzman (eds.), *Public Policies toward Mergers,* Pacific Palisades, Calif.: Goodyear Publishing Company, 1967, p. 128.

or helped along by government regulations or legislation, we are talking about an entirely separate issue. If the monopoly would not exist except for the police power of the state, then it is probably true that breaking it up will lead to more competitive prices.

The question of the desirability of breaking up large companies into smaller ones may not, however, center around the issue of relatively higher profits being earned by these companies. Rather, such a question may center around the more nebulous, less easily identified question of excessive economic power.

The Meaning of Economic Power

What does it mean to say that firms in highly concentrated industries have a degree of economic power? Again, there is little agreement among economists as to the operational meaning of the term. It is not enough to say that firms in highly concentrated industries have economic power because they can set their prices wherever they want. In fact, that cannot be the case unless the demand curve facing the individual firm is completely inelastic. If it is not completely inelastic, then there is going to be a profit-maximizing rate of output and price that even the most powerful oligopolist will want to set. In other words, there are market forces determining the maximum price that any firm can charge for its product.

Even the demand curve facing a pure monopolist depends on the extensiveness and availability of substitutes for the product in question. Even General Motors has to pay

debate as to what firms do. Do they maximize profits? Do they maximize sales? Are the managers responsible to the stockholders? And so on. In the next issue, we will look at this topic from one important point of view.

Wasted Efforts

A major criticism of oligopolistic industries is that the leading firms can become sloppy and inefficient in their production techniques. They become so comfortable and fat-cattish that they do not attempt—that is, the managers do not make an effort—to minimize costs. This wastes economic resources. This criticism can be leveled particularly against large corporations in highly concentrated industries with motivating forces other than profit maximization. For example, if a large firm in a concentrated industry aimed at a target rate of return instead of profit maximization, then when that target rate of return was reached, fewer efforts might be made to further improve technological efficiency and thereby further lower costs.

How large is "large"? How large should a firm, in fact, be? Of course no one knows, but there is an implicit agreement among critics of large corporations that the largest of the corporations are "too" large. In fact, Ralph Nader's study group, as we mentioned before, concluded that "We also recommend an absolute asset size limitation of two billion dollars." In other words, the group feels that legislation should be passed limiting the total size of a corporation to one with assets of no

heed to the price of substitute products, namely, cars by Ford, Chrysler, Volkswagen, Renault, and Fiat. And taken together, all automobile manufacturers must take heed of substitutes such as bicycles, motorcycles, feet, buses, taxis and rickshaws.

But perhaps we are looking at the wrong issue. Perhaps economic power concerns a firm's ability to do

what it wants within a *very wide range.* What does this mean? Simply that managers can allocate part of a firm's budget to activities that might not go on in a highly competitive market. This might be true particularly if we are dealing with situations where the profit motive is not the basis of most decisions. Here we get into a methodological and messy more than $2 billion. However, even adding an inflationary factor onto this number, we still do not know whether this represents the optimal size of a firm from an efficiency point of view and thereby from a cost-minimizing point of view.

Again, how can the cutoff point be determined? Some groups and critics say $1 billion, some even say $250 million, and others say $5 billion. As of now, no consensus has been reached and no consensus will be reached unless the desired goals of society can be explicitly stated in terms of something operationally meaningful. If the goals are to minimize the cost of producing what is sold in the marketplace, then an effort must be made to find that size of firm which minimizes the cost of production. This task will not be easy and, in fact, may be impossible. The very large corporations produce literally thousands of products and have many plants. Should we talk about the optimal size of the firm for one product, two products, or five products? Or should we look at the optimal size of the plant in which the products are produced?

The Question of Legislation

Let us assume for the moment that society would benefit from the breaking up of large corporations in highly concentrated industries. How can it be done? It must be done by some operationally meaningful rule or law. But look at the history of legislation in the field of antitrust, for example. Antitrust legislation is filled with special exemptions given to specific types of monopoly activity.

There is also a problem about resale price maintenance. And there are the antitrust exemptions given to special industries. We will talk about the antitrust exemptions that labor unions and professional sports leagues have obtained. If the history of legislation in this area shows that exemptions will be granted, what is to prevent future legislators from de-

feating the intent of future legislation designed to break up large corporations by exempting certain industries?

Even more importantly, how can the legislation be enforced? Even if the best laws are passed, they must be enforced, and there must be rules as to when specific laws should be invoked. But the history of the Justice Department's antitrust activities is spotted. Sometimes the most blatant activities in restraint of trade have gone untouched by Justice, and the most trivial activities have been prosecuted and tied up in the courts for years. Will the future level of enforcement be appropriate for the intent of any legislation passed?

Finally—Looking at Costs and Benefits

As a final note to our question of whether or not large corporations in oligopolistic industries should be broken up, we point out that we must look not only at the benefits but also at the costs of any such action. There may be many benefits to breaking up large corporations. They might include increased efficiency, lower prices, more responsiveness to changing consumer tastes, and so on. But the costs might be large also. We have to consider the costs of legislation and litigation, the cost of enforcement, the actual cost of setting up separate corporations, and so on. Also, by breaking up large corporations, we may indeed be sacrificing true economies of scale, in which case the resource cost of the output after the corporation is broken up will be higher than before.

All these costs and benefits have to be considered before we can come to any conclusions. Both those who are certain that highly concentrated industries are detrimental and must be broken up and those who are against any meddling in the marketplace should have detailed, hard facts about at least the major costs and benefits of any proposed action before feeling fully confident of their conclusions.

| **Questions for Thought and Discussion** | 1. Which of the recommendations of the Nader Study Group on Antitrust Enforcement do you agree with? Which ones do you disagree with? Why?
2. Why would more highly concentrated industries tend to have larger profits?
3. What does economic power mean? |

| **Selected References** | Blair, John M., *Economic Concentration: Structure, Behavior, and Public Policy,* New York: Harcourt Brace Jovanovich, 1972.
Caves, Richard, *American Industry: The Structure, Conduct, Performance,* 3d ed., Englewood Cliffs, N.J.: Prentice-Hall, 1972.
Mueller, Willard F., *A Primer on Monopoly and Competition,* New York: Random House, 1970. |

Economic Statesman

JOHN KENNETH GALBRAITH
Economist, Harvard University

John Kenneth Galbraith has been one of the most conspicuously public figures in American academia today, and he is also probably the most widely read American economist. Two of his books, *The Affluent Society* (1958) and *The New Industrial State* (1967), have become best sellers. Through his associations with the administrations of Kennedy and Johnson, his writings and his speeches, Galbraith has been able to exert great influence on liberal economic thought.

Galbraith was educated at the University of Toronto and the University of California. He stayed in Berkeley through the 1930s as a research fellow studying price controls, both as an intrinsic aspect of the economy and as a part of government policy. After 3 years of teaching at Princeton University and 2 years as economic adviser to the National Defense Advisory Commission, Galbraith moved in 1942 to the Office of Price Administration, where he had his first taste of controversy. He later explained that most of the people around him based their ideas on an article he had written in the 1930s. He alone among them found fallacies in the article, and completely ignored it. He became so unpopular that, according to his own account, when Franklin Roosevelt accepted his resignation in 1943, "it was the most popular thing [Roosevelt] did that entire term." Galbraith then served on the editorial staff of *Fortune* magazine for 5 years. In 1948, he joined the faculty at Harvard University, and was affiliated with it until 1975.

During the Kennedy administration, the President could not appoint Galbraith Secretary of the Treasury or chairman of the Council of Economic Advisers because Wall Street simply would not accept him. However, he did serve as ambassador to India for 2 years, where he earned a reputation as a friendly but extremely unconventional emissary who ignored State Department protocol at every opportunity. *Ambassador's Journal* (1969) is a delightful diary in which Galbraith records his attempts to hold off rampant Dullesism and the cold war mentality of the United States Information Agency.

During the remaining years of the 1960s, Galbraith moved comfortably into the most influential levels of the liberal Democratic establishment. He helped Lyndon Johnson plan the War on Poverty. In retrospect, he feels that there were two basic problems with the program: Massive government aid should have been given to education and teacher-training programs, and the operating budget of the program was unrealistically low. In 1967, Galbraith became chairman of the Americans for Democratic Action, an organization that has been his major forum. He urged wage and price controls relatively early in the Nixon era, and when Nixon

eventually came around on the issue, Galbraith called it a "triumph of circumstance over ideology."

One of Galbraith's major areas of interest has been what he sees as the decline of the free-market economy in the United States. Our economic system, says Galbraith, has become "in substantial part a planned economy." Giant corporations have attained such power and influence that they now dominate large segments of the market, deciding what is to be produced, and bending the needs of consumers to fit corporate purposes. Corporations, Galbraith contends, have become so dependent on the state for regulation of aggregate demand, wage and price stability, research and development, and government contracts that the state and large corporations have tended to merge into one system, with corporate needs often predominating.

Unlike many who see in this trend reason to break up large corporations, Galbraith, in his book, *Economics and the Public Purpose*, urges that corporations which are heavily dependent on government contracts should be nationalized, along with the housing, medical care, and mass transport industries. Other companies should be disciplined in such a way as to bring their goals in line with public purposes. The danger to liberty, says Galbraith, lies not in the great size of some corporations but in their "monopoly of social purpose." Only by asserting its larger interests can the community put the industrial system in its proper place—subordinate to human needs instead of dominant over them. Through it all, Galbraith has become used to waiting to see his ideas gain favor. As he once said, "I got a reputation for being unsound for urging things that now seem extravagantly trite."

HOW THE "PLANNING" SECTOR AFFECTS OUR LIVES

The Galbraithian System

In this day and age, it is not unusual to hear cries for reforms. More specifically, it is not unusual to hear requests for changing the structure of industry. In the last issue we talked about proposals to break up large corporations in highly concentrated industries. In that issue and in Chapter 20 we discussed the use of antitrust laws to do this. We also discussed regulation as a means by which potential or actual monopolies can be "kept in line" (at least in principle). However, it is unusual for someone to tell us that our entire corporate structure is all wrong, that the corporation should be restructured because as it is now, it is "bad" for society. The most outspoken advocate of this total restructuring of our corporate system is John Kenneth Galbraith, whose biography was just presented. In this issue we further clarify his view of the world.

In his book *Economics and The Public Purpose* (Boston: Houghton Mifflin, 1973), the Harvard economics professor recapitulates much of his previous writing and also brings to the forefront his notions about the two-tiered economy we now live in. Let us now examine those two tiers.

The Traditional Market System

Much of what we have covered in this text so far has concerned the market system in the United States. Basically, we have made an assumption that individuals and firms attempt to income- or wealth-maximize. Moreover, we have assumed throughout that in the long run competition among individuals and firms will apply strong forces to prices and the allocation of resources. We have also discussed monopoly in its various forms, misallocating resources and charging a higher relative price for the monopolized product.

Galbraith in *The Public Purpose* reaffirms the applicability of market system economic theory in certain sectors of the economy, most particularly in the service sector and in the arts. In these sectors, the traditional economist's tools of supply and demand can be applied and will, indeed, predict well. However, Galbraith sees many economic agents acting within the market system in a way that he, at least, does not approve. More specifically, many of the individuals who own or work in small firms end up implicitly getting paid a very low wage rate. This is a form of what Galbraith calls "self-exploitation." He considers that if it were not for those who exploit themselves, the other system in the economy would not be able to function as profitably.

Moreover, he points out that in certain sectors of the economy, restrictions ensure that the small firm will continue to exist. This is true, for example, with lawyers and physicians. It is also true for those engaged in illegal and semilegal activities, such as pornographers, dope peddlers, and illicit gamblers.

The market system is not developing at a relatively rapid rate. It is the other system—**the planning system**—that is developing rapidly and is, in effect, exploiting those who are unfortunate enough to be only in the market system.

The Planning System

No matter how small the firm is, some planning, of course, has to be done, so it is not enough to talk about the planning sector or system in the economy as one involving firms that plan. Galbraith uses this term to refer to the giant corporations where this normal in-firm planning is most obvious and also to the big corporations that plan the use of their power to alter the behavior of consumers and government.

Echoing some of the same arguments from his *New Industrial State*, Galbraith asserts that large corporations dominate the affairs of advanced societies whether they be capitalist or socialist. It is these large corporations, he says, which are planning for the future of our society.

Although corporate managers first attempt to control only their own operations, they soon branch out and attempt to manipulate their customers by various marketing and advertising techniques and to regulate unions and smaller business firms that supply labor and materials—those presumably in the market system. The maturing corporation becomes more and more sophisticated at planning and altering the behavior of elected officials and regulatory agencies. The large corporations in the planning sector are run by what are called their **technostructures.**

The Technostructure

Presumably, no large corporation is controlled by the majority vote of its shareholders, or even by its board of directors; rather, the large corporation is generally ruled by its management. According to Galbraith, management constitutes a self-perpetuating group that selects the boards of directors rather than vice versa. But even the corporate managers do not have the skills to run a corporation; this knowledge must be obtained from a large group of specialists. Galbraith writes

> . . . to perfect and guide the organization in which the specialists serve also requires specialists. Eventually not an individual but a complex of scientists, engineers and technicians; of sales, advertising and marketing men; of public relations experts, lobbyists, lawyers and men with a specialized knowledge of the Washington bureaucracy and its manipulation; and of coordinators, managers and executives becomes the guiding intelligence of the business firm. This is the technostructure. Not any single individual but the technostructure becomes the commanding power [p. 82].

Thus, management, even though it is self-perpetuating, is subordinated to the much larger technostructure. The technostructure derives its power from its specialized knowledge, and it is in no way beholden to the ownership, that is, the stockholders.

Because the technostructure is so unresponsive to the stockholders and ultimately to the consumer, Galbraith gives us a blueprint for restructuring the corporation.

Restructuring the Corporation

Galbraith states that "the central tendency of the modern large corporation—and the source of the problems that increasingly provoke discussion—can be quickly summarized: With time, increasing size, and increasing technical and social complexity of task it loses its legitimacy as an entrepreneurial and capitalist institution; it becomes instead an instrument of its own organization.[1] If we accept this, then we must ask, as Galbraith does, "What should happen to the modern corporation?" Merely breaking it up into smaller units will not change the corporate structure, which according to his theory is at fault. What changes must be made?

In the first place, if the stockholder really ceases to have any power, then "the case for private ownership through equity capital disappears. . . ."[2] The change in the modern large corporation, then, must begin with the stockholders. Galbraith suggests that the state has to replace the "helpless stockholder" as a supervisory and policy-setting body. A public holding company must take over the common stock of each large corporation. Galbraith sees 100 or more of our largest industries as being eligible for this public holding company action. In addition, a fair number of the larger utility, transportation, financial, and merchandising corporations would also be eligible.

In other words, we're discussing the public ownership of large corporations. Since the state "will inherit the turkeys" (the big companies that are going to go bankrupt) any-

[1] John Kenneth Galbraith, "What Comes after General Motors?", *The New Republic*, November 2, 1974, p. 14.
[2] Ibid., p. 16.

way, why shouldn't the state take over some of the good companies as well? Or more specifically, why shouldn't the government inherit the predators rather than just the preyed upon in a planning system?

Now that private stockholders will have disappeared from these corporations, the board of directors will be replaced by what can be called a board of public auditors or public inspectors. Such a board would be composed of 12 members, with only a minority being selected by the management. The remaining members would be designated as public members by the state itself.

What would the board do differently from the now-existing board of directors? It would maintain continuing surveillance, a type of social audit, on any divergence from public and private purposes. The board of public auditors would appoint top management; it would also ratify investment plans and would reconcile these with public planning requirements. At the meetings of these auditors, there would be discussions of the public impact of major policies.

A Sweeping Change

So here we have it: The Galbraithian system comes down to a sweeping change in corporate structure. Of course, there is much more to the system—Professor Galbraith has described it throughout his many publications. He has been a frequent advocate of permanent wage and price controls for large corporations. He has commented extensively on the role of women in our society. But, perhaps more than any of his other suggested reforms, his idea for completely reorganizing private, for-profit corporations in America is startling.

Does the planning sector actually exist? If so, is it as bad as he says it is? If so, do his suggestions for the restructuring of the modern corporation make sense? These are questions that will be debated for years to come.

Definitions of New Terms

Planning System: In the Galbraithian view of the economy, that part of it in which large firms are able to plan how to use their power and how to alter the behavior of consumers and governments.

Technostructure: The decision-making part of large corporations in the planning sector. These decision-making units are guided, if not run, by those with specialized or technical knowledge of the production processes at hand.

Questions for Thought and Discussion

1. How would you decide which firms belong in the planning sector and which do not?
2. Do you think corporations would be run differently if they were restructured according to Galbraith's suggestions? How?
3. Was the technostructure evident in corporations 100 years ago?

Selected References

Andreano, Ralph L. (ed.), *Superconcentration/Supercorporation,* Andover, Mass.: Warner Modular Publications, 1973.

Galbraith, John Kenneth, *The New Industrial State,* 2d ed., Boston: Houghton Mifflin, 1971.

SIX

DERIVED DEMAND AND INCOME REDISTRIBUTION

Aspects of the Labor Market

One important factor of production used by firms is labor. The demand for labor, coupled with its supply, determines the wages that individuals obtain. Of course, the labor market is much like all other markets. In the following issue we'll look at some of its restrictions. Here we'll look at a broader view of it.

Union Power and the Labor Movement

The concept of **unions** goes back at least as far as the Middle Ages when guilds were formed. By the twelfth century, western European guilds were of four broad types: religious, frith (peace), merchant, and craft. Only the merchant and craft guilds had primarily economic goals. Although the guild merchant in England had unrestricted and monopolistic rights to regulate trade within his borough, this general guild category, nevertheless, disappeared by the thirteenth century.

The medieval craft guilds were the original occupational associations, formed by all the artisans in a particular field. Some strange partnerships resulted, however. For example, fourteenth century Italian painters found themselves in the same guild as surgeon apothecaries. The English named these early union ancestors *mysteries*, which seems rather appropriate. Although unable to obtain a monopoly because of the many crafts in each city, the mysteries did restrict membership by requiring an apprenticeship period before an artisan could become a journeyman; the journeyman was then required to provide proof of his technical competence (the "masterpiece") before he was judged a master craftsman.

American Labor Movement

The American labor movement started with local **craft unions.** These were groups of workers in individual trades, such as banking, shoemaking, or printing. Many of the efforts of the earlier craft unions were thwarted by unfavorable court judgments against them. In Table 22-1, we see that union membership remained small until the twentieth century. In most cases,

the conspiracy provisions of common law developed in England were used to squelch any incipient organization of trade workers.

The first permanent federation of labor on a national scale was the National Typographic Union, formed in Cincinnati in May 1852. It survives today in the form of the International Typographical Union and is still known as the most democratic of all the federations.

The Knights of Labor From the period following the Civil War to Roosevelt's New Deal during the Depression, labor's struggle for the right to join together in collective bargaining was a hard and slow road upward. The trend was toward national labor organizations. In 1869, the Knights of Labor was formed. By 1886, the organization had reached a membership of approximately 800,000. Among their demands, the Knights of Labor asked for an 8-hour day, equality of pay for men and women, and replacement of free enterprise with a socialist system. The organization was not very aggressive in carrying out its programs; in particular, the strike was to be used only after all other means of negotiation had failed. Apparently, many leaders within the organization were more militant than this, however, and the Knights of Labor slowly withered away until it disappeared altogether in 1917.

Public disdain for the Knights of Labor increased sharply after the famous Hay Market Riot in Chicago on May 4, 1886. On that day, approximately 100,000 workers demonstrated for their demands—the 8-hour day being one. The demonstration was held in front of the McCormick Harvester Works at Hay Market Square. A group of anarchists decided to throw a bomb into the crowd, killing seven policemen and injuring scores of other demonstrating participants. Even though the media disseminated the information concerning the anarchists' part in the bombing, the Knights of Labor and or-

---

Table 22-1 **Union Membership, 1830–1975**

We see here that it wasn't until the twentieth century that union membership exceeded 3 percent of the United States labor force. In terms of percentage of the labor force, membership hit its peak in 1960. Since then it has slowly but steadily declined.

YEAR	UNION MEMBERSHIP (THOUSANDS)	U.S. LABOR FORCE (THOUSANDS)	% ORGANIZED
1830	26	4,200	.6
1860	5	11,110	.1
1870	300	12,930	2.3
1880	50	17,390	.3
1883	210	. . .	. . .
1886	1,010	. . .	. . .
1890	325	23,320	1.4
1900	791	29,070	2.7
1910	2,116	37,480	5.6
1920	5,034	41,610	12.1
1930	3,632	48,830	7.4
1935	8,728	52,600	16.6
1940	8,944	56,290	15.9
1945	14,796	65,600	22.6
1950	15,000	65,470	22.9
1960	18,117	74,060	24.5
1965	18,519	77,177	23.9
1970	20,589	85,903	24.1

Source: L. Davis et al., *American Economic Growth* (New York: Harper & Row, 1972), p. 220, and U.S. Department of Labor, Bureau of Labor Statistics.

ganized labor in general were considered the cause of the "riot."

The American Federation of Labor   About this time, a group of craft unions became increasingly dissatisfied with the Knights of Labor and formed their own group, which they named the American Federation of Labor (AFL). The AFL was formed in 1886 under the leadership of Samuel Gompers, who ran the organization until he died in 1924. By 1900, the AFL boasted a membership of over 1 million workers, and by the start of World War I, the organization claimed that it was the voice of the majority of organized labor. For much of the period preceding World War I, the government supported business opposition to the union by offering the legitimate use of police power to break strikes. The courts upheld many of these police actions, ruling that unions were in restraint of trade.

During World War I, there grew up an increasingly favorable climate of opinion toward unions, and by 1920 membership had increased to over 5 million. But after the war, the growth of unionism suddenly stopped. The government decided to stop protecting labor's right to organize. Businesses refused to recognize labor unions, and membership began to fall. By the beginning of the Great Depression, union membership, as shown in Table 22-1, had dropped to 3.6 million, or only 7.4 percent of the labor force.

The Great Depression

Then came one of the worst periods of economic activity in the history of the United States. Franklin Delano Roosevelt was elected President. When he took office, the nation had seen output fall since 1929 by 36 percent. Roosevelt felt that the industrial depression could be reduced by getting rid of "wasteful, cut-

throat competition." He wanted to allow management organizations to collude on prices and quantities, and he also wanted organizations among workers to be encouraged. Roosevelt succeeded in passing the National Industrial Recovery Act. The act was originally intended to apply only to big industries, but the National Recovery Administration became ambitious and soon established a universally applied blanket code, known as the President's Reemployment Agreement. The National Recovery Administration was supposed to grant "justice to the worker." A section in the National Industrial Recovery Act allowed for the right of labor to bargain collectively. This was in line with Roosevelt's belief that the way to cure the Great Depression was to increase wages. He and his advisers reasoned that if wages were increased, the income of labor would also be increased; thus, workers would be able to buy more goods and services. When workers buy more goods and services, overall aggregate demand increases and even more workers are needed.

The Wagner Act—Labor's Magna Carta

The National Industrial Recovery Act was declared unconstitutional. Section 7a, which gave workers the right to organize, was replaced by the National Labor Relations Act (NLRA), otherwise known as the Wagner Act. The basis for the Wagner Act was the argument that the inequality in bargaining power between workers as individuals and large businesses depressed "the purchasing power of wage earners in industry" and prevented "stabilization of competitive wage rates and working conditions." Among other things, the NLRA guaranteed workers the right to start labor unions, to engage in **collective bargaining,** and to be members in any union that was started. The Wagner Act has been called labor's Magna Carta. It was declared constitutional by the Supreme Court in 1937, after which the strength of organized labor grew rapidly in our economy.

The Congress of Industrial Organizations

At the time the Wagner Act was passed, several discontented leaders within the AFL decided that they did not like the "craft bias" of that particular organization. John L. Lewis, the president of the United Mine Workers, was the head of this dissident group of union leaders. In 1938 he became president of the Congress of Industrial Organizations (CIO), composed of **industrial unions.** Both the AFL and the CIO were able to make large gains in their membership until the end of World War II. Then, in November 1946, John L. Lewis' United Mine Workers apparently added the straw that broke the camel's back by defying a court order to go back to work after a long violent strike. Even though the union and its leader were fined for contempt of court and the miners actually did go back to work, legislation against unions had already started in Congress.

The Taft-Hartley Act

The Taft-Hartley Act of 1947, otherwise called the Labor Management Relations Act, has been termed the Slave Labor Act by union people. Among other things, it allows individual states to pass their own **right-to-work laws.** A right-to-work law makes it illegal for union membership to be a prerequisite for employment in any individual establishment.

More specifically, the act makes a **closed shop** illegal; a closed shop requires union membership before employment can be obtained. A **union shop,** on the other hand, is legal; a union shop does not require membership as a prerequisite for employment but can, and usually does, require that workers join the union after a specified amount of time on the job. (Even a union shop is illegal in states with right-to-work laws.)

Jurisdictional disputes, sympathy strikes, and secondary boycotts are made illegal by this act as well. A jurisdictional dispute involves two or more unions fighting (and striking) over which should have control in a particular jurisdiction. A sympathy strike occurs when one union strikes in sympathy with another union's problems or another union's strike. A secondary boycott is the boycotting of a company that deals with a struck company. For example, if union workers strike a baking company, then boycotting grocery stores which continue to sell that company's products is a secondary boycott. The purpose of the secondary boycott is to bring pressure against third parties to force them to stop dealing with an employer who is being struck.

In general, the Taft-Hartley Act outlawed unfair labor practices of unions, such as "make-work" rules and forcing unwilling workers to join a particular union. Perhaps the most famous aspect of the Taft-Hartley Act is its provision that the President can obtain a court injunction that will last for 80 days for any strike believed to imperil the national safety or health. Presidents have, on occasion, used this provision, much to the chagrin of the unions involved. For example, President Nixon applied the 80-day injunction order to striking longshoremen in 1971. President Eisenhower did the same thing to striking steel workers in 1959.

The Merging of the Two Federations

In 1955 the AFL-CIO was formed under the presidency of George Meany. This amalgam of craft and industrial unions has not been without problems since its formation. In addition to internal problems, there have been problems with the International Brotherhood of Teamsters and with the auto workers. The United Automobile Workers, under the leadership of Walter Reuther, became disenchanted with the AFL-CIO in 1968 and decided to join the International Brotherhood of Teamsters. The merger of the UAW with the IBT started a federation that was called the Alliance for Labor Action.

What Do Unions Attempt to Do?

The constitution of the AFL-CIO includes the goals of that organization. Some of these goals are: to improve working conditions, to get better wages and better hours, and to allow employees to realize the benefits of unrestrained collective bargaining. These generalized goals of the AFL-CIO can hardly be used, however, in an analysis of the effects of unionism on our economy. Put yourself in the position of a worker who is a member of a union. What would you like the union to do for you? Certainly, you would like to have higher wages, better working conditions, more job security, a shorter work day, free health insurance, free life insurance policies, ad infinitum. But what you would like the union to do and what you can reasonably expect it to do are, of course, two different things.

First, you must realize that everything you want will most likely cost your employer money. For analytical purposes, we can translate any change in working conditions, fringe benefits, and so on, into a specific rise in your wage rate. In other words, we assume employers are indifferent to the choice between either a 10 percent increase in your paycheck or an equivalent increase in the form of fringe benefits (such as a new medical insurance program). Here, of course, we are ignoring the possibility that certain changes in working conditions will cause workers to produce more than before so

the true cost of that additional fringe benefit is less than the employer would initially think.

Demand Curve for Labor

It is useful to introduce a demand schedule for labor similar to the demand schedules presented in other chapters. The difference here is that the price of labor is the wage rate. The wage rate will be all inclusive; that is, it will include fringe benefits and so on. We will assume that the employee and employer are indifferent as to how the total (true) wage rate is made up; it can be either a high money wage with no fringe benefits or a moderate money wage with several fringe benefits. We will not go into the complete development of the demand schedule for labor since that will be treated in the next chapter. Suffice it to say that the demand for labor is a **derived demand** dependent on how much output each employer can sell. That is, it is derived from the demand for the products produced. Obviously, if the firm can't sell very much, it will not want to hire a lot of workers.

We see, in Figure 22-1, that the familiar downward-sloping demand schedule is used for the different quantity and wage rate pairs that represent some sort of equilibrium in the labor market. In Figure 22-1, we see that at a wage rate of $3 an hour, employers in the steel industry demand 800,000 workers. At higher wage rates they demand fewer, and at lower wage rates they demand more workers. The quantity of labor demanded is inversely related to the wage rate in our hypothetical example. In most cases we will assume that this is, in fact, the way the economy works.

We also need to establish constant-quality units of labor. Only in this manner can we represent the labor market on a single graph; otherwise, we would have to represent it on

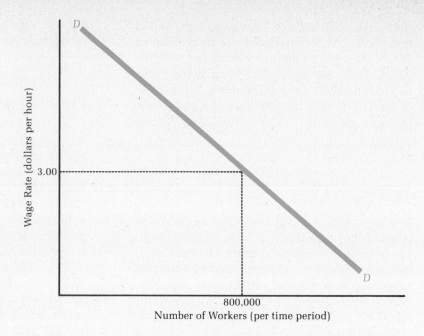

FIGURE 22-1 Demand for Labor in the Steel Industry

The demand schedule for labor in the steel industry is represented hypothetically by *DD*. The wage rate is on the vertical axis. On the horizontal axis are numbers of *constant quality* workers. At a wage rate, say, of $3 per hour, there would be 800,000 employees demanded.

many graphs. As we all know, there are different qualities of workers in any industry.

The Supply of Labor

Having developed the demand schedule for labor in the steel industry, let's now turn to the supply schedule. By filling in the whole picture, we'll be able to present a standard analysis of what unions can do. Our supply schedule for labor in the steel industry, as seen in Figure 22-2, will be upward sloping. At higher wage rates, more workers will want to enter the steel industry.

For the United States as a whole, at higher wage rates, people who are not in the labor force decide it is worth their while to enter it. In other words, as wages are raised, the **participation rate** increases for groups such as housewives, teenagers, and retired people.

Table 22-2 shows participation rates of different groups over time. There have been numerous studies attempting to explain phenomena such as why women enter the labor force during some phases of the business cycle but not during others. One of the main determinants of this phenomenon has been found to be higher wage rates during boom times and lower wage rates during recessions. We typically find higher participation rates during booms than during recessions. This is additional evidence that our labor supply schedule should slope upward.

From a purely psychological point of view, we would expect that most people put a positive value on their leisure time. Therefore, to induce them to work more, they have to be paid more. One would therefore expect that higher wage rates will induce more people to give up more of their leisure. Another way of looking at this leisure-labor choice is to con-

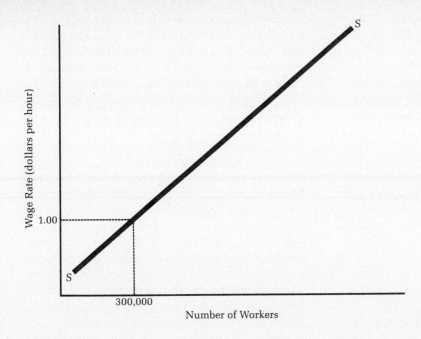

FIGURE 22-2 **Supply Curve of Workers for Steel Industry**

The hypothesized supply schedule of workers in the steel industry slopes upward. At higher wage rates, more people will want to work in steel. Remember that the horizontal axis is measured in *constant-quality* units of workers. At a wage rate of $1 per hour, 300,000 workers will be willing to work, for example.

Table 22-2 **Labor-Force Participation Rates by Race and Sex**

The participation rates expressed here are percentages of the total population actually in the labor force. Thus, in 1960, 59.2 percent of the entire population was actually in the United States labor force. We see that the projection through 1985 shows almost no change in the participation rates for the total population.

RACE AND SEX	PARTICIPATION RATES (PERCENT)					
	1960	1965	1970	1975	1980	1985
Total	59.2	58.8	60.3	60.1	60.5	60.8
White	58.8	58.5	60.2	60.0	60.3	60.6
Male	82.6	80.4	79.7	79.4	79.4	79.8
Female	36.0	37.7	42.0	41.8	42.5	42.7
Negro and other	63.0	62.1	61.1	61.4	61.6	62.0
Male	80.1	77.4	74.7	77.0	77.5	78.7
Female	47.2	48.1	48.9	47.4	47.1	46.9

Source: Department of Labor, Bureau of Labor Statistics

sider the opportunity cost of *not* working. As defined earlier, opportunity cost is the value of a forgone alternative. In this case, it is the alternative use value of a person's time or resources. If the wage rate goes up from, say, $2 to $3 and you have the opportunity of working at the higher wage rate, your opportunity cost for *not* working is considered to be at least $3 an hour.

In our hypothetical supply curve for the steel industry in Figure 22-2, we see that, at a wage rate of $1 an hour, the supply of workers in steel is only 300,000. At higher wage rates, the quantity of workers willing to work in steel increases.

Putting Demand and Supply Together

Now we want to put the demand and supply of labor in the steel industry together on one graph. We have done this in Figure 22-3. The equilibrium established by the forces of supply and demand is at point E, the intersection of those two schedules. The wage rate established there is $4 an hour, and the quantity of workers both supplied and demanded at that rate is 700,000. If, for some reason, the wage rate fell to $2 an hour, we would find, in our hypothetical example, that there was an *excess demand* for 400,000 steelworkers. Conversely, if the wage rate rose to $6 an hour, there would be an *excess supply* of 400,000 steelworkers —that is, unemployed steelworkers.

Standard supply-demand analysis indicates that, if all workers in a nonunionized steel industry were suddenly unionized and the steel union succeeded in raising the wage rate above that established by the unrestricted forces of supply and demand, an excess supply of workers wanting to make steel would result. Looking at Figure 22-3 we would say, therefore, that the

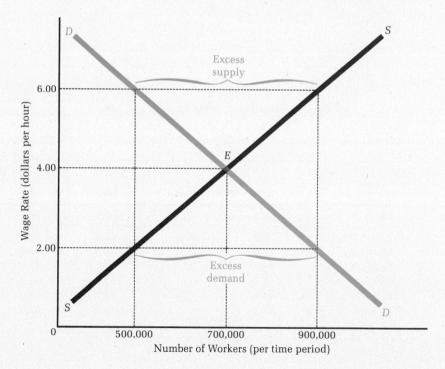

FIGURE 22-3 Demand and Supply of Labor in the Steel Industry

The demand schedule is *DD* and the supply schedule is *SS*. The forces of demand and supply establish an equilibrium at point *E*, with a wage rate of $4 and a number of workers both demanded and supplied at 700,000. At a wage rate of $6 per hour, an excess supply of 400,000 steel workers would result. At a wage rate of $2, there would be an excess demand for 400,000 steel workers.

short-run effect of the union raising the wage rate to $6 an hour would be 400,000 willing steelworkers unable to get a job. In such a situation, the union would somehow have to ration the available number of jobs to an excess supply of eager workers. Some economists maintain this is why unions have been discriminatory and have historically barred minority groups from their ranks. In terms of actual unemployment of steelworkers, we see that 200,000 formerly employed workers would have to seek employment in some other sector of the economy.

Limiting Entry

Unions can limit entry to the size of the employed work force when the union is first or-

ganized. No workers are put out of work at the time of the formation of the union. As demand for more workers in a particular industry increases, these original members receive larger wage increases than otherwise would be the case. We see this in Figure 22-4. Union members limit entry into their union, thereby obtaining a wage of $6 per hour instead of allowing a wage of $5 per hour with no restriction on labor supply.

What Do Unions Maximize?

To predict the effects of unions on wages and employment, we have to be able to assert *what* unions are maximizing. If, for example, they are maximizing the wage rate and nothing else, we would predict that the size of unions should

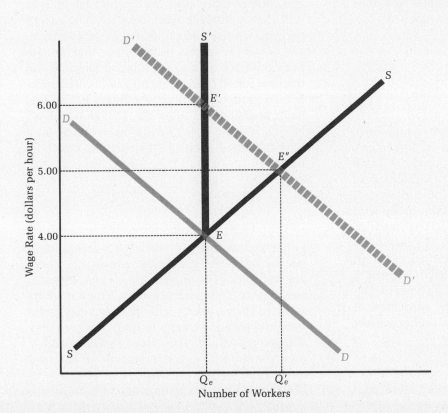

FIGURE 22-4 Restricting Supply Over Time

When the union was formed, it didn't affect wage rates or employment, which remained at $4 and Q_e (the wage rate and quantity demanded and supplied in equilibrium). However, as demand increased—that is, as the demand schedule *shifted* out to $D'D'$ from DD—the union restricted entry to its original level of Q_e. The new supply curve is SS', which intersects $D'D'$ at E', or at a wage rate of $6. Without the union, equilibrium would be at E'' with a wage rate of $5 and employment of Q'_e.

be getting smaller and smaller relative to the total labor force. Note here that we are referring to unions as only a part of the labor force, not to a unionization of the entire labor force. Currently, only about 22 percent of all workers are in unions. We can imagine, therefore, that union members might want to raise their wages relative to the wages of nonunion workers. Some economists believe that unions can raise union wages but cannot raise the wages of all workers. These economists assert that any increase in the wages of union workers will result in lower wages for nonunion workers because unemployed union members will go into nonunion work, increasing the supply of nonunion laborers. According to our usual supply-demand analysis, the only way all workers in a larger supply of nonunion laborers can find jobs is for some of them to accept lower wages; the demand schedule for nonunion labor slopes downward, just as that for union labor.

Has the Labor Movement Helped Workers?

There should be some way that we can measure the effectiveness of the labor union movement. It would be a mistake to look merely at wage rates for they were growing before unions ever had many members in the United States. It would, furthermore, be a mistake to look at money wages because we would first want to eliminate the effects of inflation. If your wages go up from $2 to $4 an hour, but prices go up by 100 percent during the same time period, your real wage rate has remained constant. We can define **real wages** as wages expressed in constant purchasing power or, in other words,

$$\text{Real wages} = \frac{\text{money wages}}{\text{price index}}$$

Often unions will boast that they have suc-

ceeded in getting large wage gains for their members. But these wage gains are expressed in terms of money, or *nominal* dollars, instead of *real* dollars and can, therefore, be misleading. In addition, we must not consider wage increases an effect of unions if these increases would have occurred even without unions. Nonunion workers do, after all, get wage increases too. Moreover, increases in the productive nature of workers may not be related to whether they belong to unions.

One possible approach to establishing the effectiveness of unions is to look at the distribution of income in the United States. We want to examine the distribution between income which comes from labor services and income which comes from capital—that is, rents, profits, and interest rates. In Table 22-3 we show the share of net national income that has gone to labor over the past 40 years. It is remarkably stable, hovering between 64 and 75 percent. On the basis of this type of evidence, we would be forced to conclude that unions have not been able to get a larger share of the total pie for all labor. This may be a very superficial way of establishing whether or not unions have benefited all workers. The share of all labor's income going to union workers may have increased, thereby making union members better off.

Problems in the Labor Market

Other characteristics of the labor market should be discussed. As mentioned previously, there are such things as *information costs, transactions costs,* and *search costs.* When workers are fired from a job or laid off, they must spend time and perhaps money in finding where they can get other jobs. They have to expend their own resources to get information on the best alternative source of work. The problem of obtaining this information may be more dif-

Table 22-3 Share of Total National Income Going to Workers

The percentage of national income paid as compensation to employees has remained between 64 and 75 percent since 1933. In less-developed countries this percentage is much smaller for much of national income is paid in rents and interest to landowners.

YEAR	PERCENTAGE OF NATIONAL INCOME AS COMPENSATION TO EMPLOYEES
1933	73.2
1935	65.2
1940	64.2
1945	67.8
1947	64.8
1950	64.1
1955	67.8
1960	71.0
1965	69.8
1967	71.5
1968	72.1
1969	73.3
1970	74.9
1974	73.7

Source: Department of Commerce, Office of Business Economics

ficult the more complex our society becomes. The Labor Department is presumably aware of this problem and has started a series of computerized job-information centers so that unemployed workers and workers seeking better employment can get information at a reasonably low cost to both themselves and the government.

A certain percentage of unemployment can be considered the result of information costs. This is what we term **frictional unemployment.** When workers leave one job voluntarily or involuntarily, they usually proceed to look for another job. They may not take the first job they are offered because they think they can find a job that is better either in wages or working conditions. However, a better job may not exist, or they may not be able to obtain the information that would lead them to the better job. These workers are counted as unemployed by the Bureau of Labor Statistics, an organization that estimates our unemployment rate every month by interviewing 52,000 people selected at random. A person is counted as unemployed if he or she is currently looking for work and is unable to find a job. The Bureau of Labor Statistics, of course, has no way of knowing what kind of wage rate the unemployed worker is demanding or holding out for.

Seeking Highest Valued Employment

We probably do not want to reduce unemployment below some level that is considered "normal" because, in so doing, we would reduce the productivity of our work force. Labor's productivity is increased when workers move from areas or jobs where they are of low value to their employers to jobs where they are of high value to their employers. We know that this happens because workers are continually moving from low wage jobs to higher wage jobs. Assuming that workers are paid only the amount they are worth to employers, we can conclude that a switch from a low paying job to a higher paying job means the worker has switched from a job where her or his contribution to economic production is low to a job where her or his contribution is higher. While in the process of moving, however, this worker will appear in the labor statistics as unemployed.

Unemployment also serves a useful purpose to workers who are seeking better alternatives. When persons are unemployed, they can devote all their time to searching for better alternatives. That is, the cost to them of obtaining this information is low. If they are employed, they have very little time to do this, making the information cost high. This is, of course, a rather cavalier statement to be made about unemployment for it implies that unemployment is voluntary. Most unemployed persons state that they would rather be working than not working.

The problem of information may be useful in explaining high levels of unemployment during periods of economic slowdown. If workers do not realize that economic activity has slowed down when they are put out of work, they will not go back to work for a wage

rate that is below what they are used to making. Only after a lengthy waiting period do these unemployed workers realize they must accept a lower wage rate if they wish to be reemployed. Their expectations are changed by the painful experience of not receiving a paycheck every 2 weeks. Expectations, though, take a long time to change. Studies of unemployed engineers around Cape Kennedy and Seattle, Washington, where the Boeing plant is located, showed that many engineers would choose to remain without work for several years before accepting a salary lower than the one they were used to making.

Unions: Organizations of workers that usually seek to secure economic improvements for their members.

Craft Unions: Labor unions composed of workers who engage in a particular trade or skill, such as baking, carpentry, or plumbing.

Collective Bargaining: Bargaining between management of a company or of a group of companies and management of a union or a group of unions for the purpose of setting a mutually agreeable contract on wages, fringe benefits, and working conditions for *all* employees in the union(s). Different from *individual* bargaining, where each employee strikes a bargain with his or her employer individually.

Industrial Unions: Labor unions that consist of workers from a particular industry, such as automobile manufacturing or steel manufacturing.

Right-to-Work Laws: Laws that make it illegal to require union membership as a precondition of employment in a particular firm.

Closed Shop: A business enterprise in which an employee must belong to the union before he or she can be employed. That employee must remain in the union after he or she becomes employed.

Union Shop: A business enterprise that allows nonunion members to become employed, conditional upon their joining the union by some specified date after employment begins.

Derived Demand: A demand that is derived from the demand for a final product.

Participation Rate: The percentage of the population in the labor force.

Real Wages: Money wages divided by the price index. Real wages are different from money or nominal wages because they represent the true purchasing power of the dollars paid to workers.

Frictional Unemployment: Temporary unemployment by people who are between jobs. Frictional unemployment results from imperfect knowledge of job opportunities and imperfect labor mobility.

Chapter Summary

1. The American labor movement started with local craft unions but was very small until the twentieth century. The history of labor in the United States involves the Knights of Labor, the American Federation of Labor, and the Congress of Industrial Organizations.

2. The Great Depression saw President Roosevelt get the National Industrial Recovery Act passed. This act allowed for the right of labor to bargain collectively. It was later supplanted by the Wagner Act, which is called labor's Magna Carta.

3. All fringe benefits must be included in the actual wages paid workers if we want to analyze the effects of unions. Fringe benefits include health insurance, better working conditions, life insurance, and so on.

4. The demand for labor is a demand derived from the demand for the products produced. At higher wage rates, less quantity of labor is demanded. That is, the demand curve for labor is downward sloping. We should always express our demand curves in terms of constant quality units.

5. The supply curve of labor is upward sloping because at higher rates, participation rates are higher and people are willing to work longer hours—that is, give up more leisure.

6. The short-run effect of a particular union raising the wage rate above the equilibrium rate is an excess supply of workers in that particular industry or firm.

7. In analyzing the effects of the labor movement, we must be careful to distinguish between money wages and real wages because it is the latter that represents the true purchasing power of money earned. Real wages are equal to money wages divided by the price index. For all labor taken together, the evidence is not overwhelming that the union movement has allowed workers to receive an increasing share of total national income. In fact, the share of national income going to labor has remained fairly constant for the last 40 years.

8. Information about job opportunities in the labor market are not perfect. We therefore find frictional unemployment where workers are temporarily between jobs.

1. Put yourself in the shoes of a union leader. What arguments could you use to support your demands for higher wages? What kind of fringe benefits would you want to negotiate? Would it matter which ones you did?
2. Should public servants such as fire fighters and police personnel have the right to strike?
3. Contrast university opposition to student activism with early firm opposition to union activism.
4. If you are a college student seeking only part-time or summer work, do you think your chances will be better or worse if the wages you can get in a particular factory, summer resort, or store are set by collective bargaining engaged in by a union consisting only of current full-time employees?
5. Why do you think unions are against the right-to-work laws?

Selected
References

Cohen, Sanford, *Labor in the United States*, 3d ed., Columbus, Ohio: Charles E. Merrill, 1970.

Rowan, Richard L. and Herbert R. Northrup, eds., *Readings in Labor Economics and Labor Relations*, rev. ed., Homewood, Ill.: Irwin, 1972.

Wortman, Max S., Jr., *Critical Issues in Labor*, New York: Macmillan, 1969.

Lobbyist for the Organized

GEORGE MEANY
President, AFL-CIO

Photo by Fabian Bachrach

The headquarters of the AFL-CIO is located two blocks from the White House, and over the years there has been frequent communication between the president of the union federation and the President of the United States. Golf with Nixon, rocking chair conversations with Kennedy, scores of discussions with Johnson—through all these meetings, George Meany has attempted to steer governmental policies in a direction favorable to his conception of the needs of organized labor. Whatever their political disagreements, recent presidents have usually consulted Meany before making appointments to labor-related jobs or introducing legislation that would affect labor.

As president of a giant but rather loose federation of labor unions, Meany acts as chief lobbyist and sets the tone for official labor union policy. Though he is often looked to as *the* spokesman of organized labor, some of the largest unions like the United Auto Workers and the Teamsters pursue independent policies outside the purview of the AFL-CIO. The extent of Meany's power even within his own organization is sometimes overestimated, stemming perhaps from his personal sway over other labor leaders. Said a biographer of Meany, explaining his difficulty in doing research for the book, "The presidents of some large unions, supposedly fearless labor leaders, are frightened silly at offending Meany, and would talk about him only in generalities, or off the record."

The son of an Irish plumber and local union president from the Bronx, Meany rose to power through union bureaucracies. He gained his first important union post in 1922, when he was elected business agent of Local 463 of the plumbers union, after working 7 years as a journeyman plumber. In 1934 he was elected president of both his local and the New York State Federation of Labor. Named secretary-treasurer of the AFL in 1939, Meany was chosen by the AFL executive council in November 1952 to succeed William Green as president, and in the following year he was unanimously reelected at the AFL convention. Meany encouraged the unification of the AFL with the CIO, which was headed by Walter Reuther. When the two labor federations did merge in 1955, Meany was made president, a post he has held ever since.

Meany has long been a fervent anticommunist, at home and abroad. Although he supported Humphrey in the 1968 elections, he was more sympathetic to Nixon's policies on Vietnam and the cold war. After the election, Meany grew disillusioned with Nixon's pursuit of détente with the Soviet Union and China. "This was the Number One anticommunist that this country had," Meany said of Nixon. "I know because I was Number Two." The AFL-CIO maintains a host of foreign union programs whose independence from government influence has been a point of pride to Meany, although he did once describe the Foreign Affairs Department of the AFL-CIO as "an arm of the United States Government."

Domestically, Meany's interest in expanding union membership is minimal. In a 1972 interview (with *U.S. News & World Report*), Meany was asked why union membership was not growing as fast as the country's labor force. "I don't know. I don't care," said Meany. "Quite a few years ago I just stopped worrying about it because to me it doesn't make any difference. It's the organized voice that counts." Despite the small degree of national unionization, Meany believes that the AFL-CIO has "delivered more to the American worker than any labor movement that ever existed."

An advocate of binding arbitration, Meany hopes it soon will become accepted practice. He also favors a guaranteed annual wage, but he expects this to come through labor contracts, industry by industry, rather than through legislation. In response to charges that union demands are inflationary, Meany replies, "I think it can be documented that labor has not caused this inflationary spiral . . . I think labor's got to do what they can to keep pace with it and I don't know any other approach."

Long before many professional analysts would admit there was a recession in 1974, Meany was already worried about a depression. A sharp and witty critic of President Ford's 1975 economic program, Meany urged the government to lower interest rates to help finance home building, enlarge the tax cut, put restrictions on the export of United States capital, and exercise greater control over commodity speculators. The way out of recession, Meany thought, was through government-sponsored programs aimed at full employment, not through a sacrifice of union contracts and established gains.

Sexism in the Labor Market

EMPLOYERS' AND CUSTOMERS' SEXUAL DISCRIMINATION

The Lord spoke to Moses saying: Speak to the Israelite people and say to them: When a man explicitly vows to the Lord the equivalent for a human being, the following scales shall apply: If it is a male from 20 to 60 years of age, the equivalent is 50 shekels of silver by the sanctuary weight; if it is female, the equivalent is 30 shekels.

—LEVITICUS, 27:1-4

Women's Wages

The Lord in the time of Moses, according to the *Five Books of Moses,* valued women at 60 percent of the going rate for men. In the job market today things have not changed. In 1975, women earned about 60 percent of the median income for men. Women now constitute more than 40 percent of the total civilian labor force in the United States. Despite this fact, they earn far less than 40 percent of the total wage payments made to that labor force. How do we explain such a large disparity between the wages of men and women? Sex discrimination on the

job is believed to be the culprit. "So widespread and pervasive are discriminatory practices against women that they have come to be regarded, more often than not, as normal"—so maintained the Presidential Task Force on Women's Rights and Responsibilities.

Tastes for Discrimination

One way to analyze the problem of discrimination against women is to assume, for the moment, that male employers have **tastes for discrimination.** This is merely a polite way to say "Let's assume male employers are sexists." When a male employer has tastes for discrimination, he must be compensated before he will hire a female worker. The easiest way for him to be compensated is for the female to offer her services at wages that are below those demanded by her male counterparts (or to work more for the same pay). Sexist male employers essentially have two demand schedules for workers: one for women and one for men. In Figure I-26.1, the solid line depicts the demand schedule for

men, the dashed line depicts the demand schedule for women. This reflects the male employers' discriminatory preferences. For example, if one has to pay workers $4 per hour, this employer would be willing to hire 26 men but only 14 women. For the male employer to hire 26 women, he would have to be compensated; the women would have to work for $2.50 per hour. The differential in this particular example is assumed to be solely due to male employers' tastes for discrimination.

Other Explanations for Male-Female Wage Differences

The graphic analysis presented above *assumed* that all differences in wages between men and women were due to the sexist behavior of male employers. If we begin an analysis with the assumption that discrimination causes wage differentials, then we can go no further since we do not allow for the possibility that other factors may determine wage differences. Among the increasingly large number of economists who have devoted some of their research time to the sex discrimination problem, Professor Victor R. Fuchs of Stanford University has done a careful analysis of the

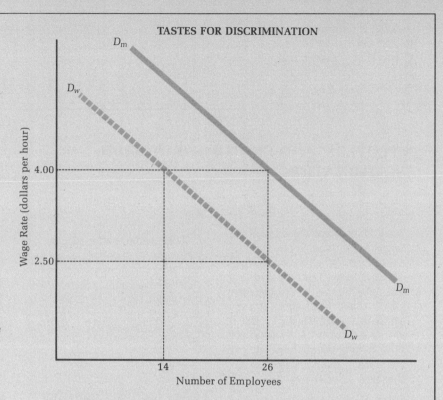

TASTES FOR DISCRIMINATION

FIGURE I-26.1

The sexist employer essentially has two labor demand schedules: one for women and one for men. The one for men, D_mD_m, is outside and to the right of the one for women, D_wD_w. If the going wage rate for men is $4 per hour, our sexist employer would hire 26 men but only 14 women. To induce him to hire the same number of women as men, women would have to accept a wage rate of only $2.50 per hour.

1960 Census of Population and Housing. His results shed a good deal of light on the causes of the sex differential in hourly earnings.[1]

Employer As Chief Sexist

One of the first things that Dr. Fuchs looked at was the theory that the male employer or supervisor is the principle source of discrimination against women. He reasoned that, if this were the case, we should expect the male-female differential in

[1]Victor R. Fuchs, "Differences in Hourly Earnings between Men and Women," *Monthly Labor Review*, May 1971, pp. 9–15.

earnings to be smaller for self-employed women because, by definition, no such discrimination could take place. We would also presume that the differential would be smaller in the private sector than in the government sector because we would assume that the pursuit of profit and survival would cause more "sex blindness" in private firms. This last statement probably needs a little clarification. If a private, profit-seeking firm is owned by a sexist, it will hire women only if the women compensate the firm by working for lower wages than a man. A firm run by a sexist and competing against nonsexist firms will eventually face higher labor costs because the non-

sexist firm can hire women away from the sexist employer by paying them just a little more than the sexist pays, but still less than what a man gets. The nonsexist firms will get all women in the labor force and thereby have lower labor costs than the sexist firms. Nonsexists will be able to cut prices and drive sexist firms out of business—or so goes the theory.

There is no such mechanism, however, in nonprofit institutions like government agencies. The sexists running the show in government should be able to get away with discriminating against women in the labor market because there are no competitive forces to drive any par-

tion of employer discrimination. These results are not due to current civil rights laws since the data were collected a year before that legislation was even introduced.

Customer Discrimination

Fuchs points out that this particular pattern of earnings differentials and employment distribution is consistent with the hypothesis of **customer discrimination.** Customers may not want to have their sink fixed by a female plumber or their television repaired by a female electrician, regardless of her training and experience. Furthermore, restaurant customers may want to be served by a waiter instead of a waitress.

Women are currently attempting to fight such customer discrimination. Females have been entering the plumbing and electrical fields in addition to the carpentry, truck driving, housepainting, and moving trades. Still, women in heavy construction trades are so rare that the Bureau of Labor Statistics doesn't bother to keep track of them. In early 1972, the Consolidated Edison Company of New York let a woman work in a manhole for the first time in the electric utilities' history. Also, women find it difficult to break into traditionally male-dominated trade unions and, therefore, start their own businesses. New York City, for example, has Lady Carpenter Enterprises, Mother Truckers, Lady Killers (exterminators), Women's Woodwork, and many other female-owned and operated trade businesses. According to many of the females involved, though, these businesses run into a tremendous amount of customer discrimination and incredulity.

ticularly sexist government agency out of business.

The data, however, refute the hypothesis of male employer discrimination. On the one hand, the wages of self-employed females equal 41 percent of those of their male counterparts. On the other hand, females who work for others in the private sector earn wages equal to 58 percent of their male counterparts' wages. The hypothesis of male employer discrimination, however, predicts the reverse will be true. Additionally, government-employed females earn 81 percent of what their male counterparts earn. This is further evidence to refute the proposition of employer discrimination.

"*I just want you to know, R.B., how much I admire the way you out-maneuvered Allied on that takeover without losing your femininity.*"

Marital Status and Age

Another important determinant of the differential in male-female wages seems to be marital status and age. Women who have never married and who are therefore much more likely to stay in the labor force have average hourly earnings that are 88 percent of those of their male counterparts; this percentage differs considerably from the general figure given for all women. In Figure I-21.2, we plot Fuchs' findings for women who never marry and for women who are married, with the spouse present. The earnings differential increases for married women but remains fairly constant for those who never marry, even as they get older. This type of evidence is cited by Fuchs as support for the argument that much of the wage differential between men and women is due to such economic factors as higher variability of employment and less investment in themselves after formal schooling has finished. Apparently women who never marry have more incentive to invest in themselves to improve their employment prospects than do women who marry. Furthermore, Fuchs cites evidence that the turn-

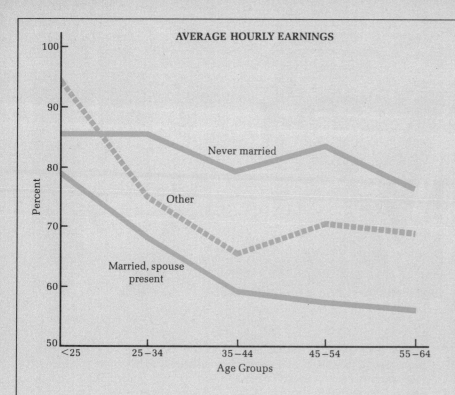

AVERAGE HOURLY EARNINGS

Never married

Other

Married, spouse
present

Percent

Age Groups

FIGURE I-26.2
Average hourly earnings of women,
as a percentage of earnings and
hours of men, by marital status and
age group. (Whites only; adjusted
for schooling, city size, class of
workers, and length of trip to work.)
(*Sources:* Bureau of the Census;
Fuchs.)

over rate of single women is much lower than that of married women, especially those with a husband present.

Role Differentiation

Dr. Fuchs presented his results as preliminary findings and certainly not as definitive ones. In any event, Fuchs concluded:

Most of the [differential] can be explained by the different *roles* assigned to men and women. Role differentiation, which begins in the cradle, affects the choice of occupation, labor force attachment, location of work, post-school investment, hours of work, and other variables that influence earnings. Role differentiation can, of course, result from discrimination. Given the changes that have been and are occurring in our society—such as the reduction in infant mortality, the improvements in family planning, and the shift from an industrial to a service economy—it appears to many [including Fuchs] that some reduction in role differentiation is desirable. Such reduction would require the combined efforts of men and women at home and in school, as well as the marketplace, and probably would result in a narrowing of earnings differences over the long run.

Evidence from other countries supports Fuchs' contention that role differentiation may be one of the reasons behind male-female wage differentials. We know in America that one reason women do not earn a percentage of total wage payments which equals the percentage of their participation in the labor force is that many of them are in low-paying, low-productivity work. Part of the reason why women are not in higher paying jobs is probably due to our value system. In Germany, more than 12 percent of all executive positions are held by women; in France, the figure is at least 9 percent. In the United States, however, women executives represent only 2 percent of the total executive population.

Even in terms of physically demanding labor, role playing seems to be rampant in the United States. We don't find American women doing stevedoring. In many African countries, however, very heavy physical labor is regarded as "woman's work." If you ever took a trip to Russia, you saw women sweeping the streets and using pneumatic drills to break up sidewalks. In Asia, you saw women tilling the fields. Obviously, occupational distribution by sex is not strictly a function of the physical differences between men and women.

The Effects of Legislation

It is now illegal to pay men and women different wage rates for the same work. Advocates of "equal pay for equal work" contend that those who do the same job should be paid the same wages. We cannot quarrel with such a value judgment. What we can do, however, is point out what will result from this legislation if, in fact, it is stringently enforced.

If we assume that discrimination against women exists, either because of employer prejudice, fellow-worker prejudice, or customer prejudice, then we know that the result of equal pay for equal work will not be necessarily higher wages for women but rather more work for men and less for women. How can that be, you might ask? The answer is not hard to find. If discrimination exists, then the only way for women to compete with men for the same job is by offering to work for lower wages. If employers must pay the same wages to women as to men, then women can no longer effectively compete. Thus, given the choice between a man and a woman, an employer, who is either catering to personal prejudice, worker prejudice or customer prejudice, will hire men. (The assumption is that the principal barrier to increasing female employment is on the demand rather than the supply side of the market.)

Now will come into play legislation affecting equal opportunity. If the equal-opportunity provisions of our various laws are stringently enforced, then we would expect the equal-pay provision to be skirted more than otherwise. It goes without saying, however, that the equal-opportunity legislation on the books can and is gotten around by employers. It is literally impossible to force all employers to give exactly equal opportunity to both men and women and to both majority and minority workers. Nonetheless, it can be said that equal-opportunity legislation makes it more expensive for employers to discriminate. Thus, there will be a lower quantity of discrimination demanded by employers. It is also possible that equal-opportunity legislation can affect employers' attitudes. Although many may engage in token compliance and many others may evade completely the legislation, some will comply, even if unwillingly, and still others will be shown by their experience in complying with the new law that their initial prejudice against women or against minority group workers was indeed unwarranted. From a social and normative point of view, this is perhaps ultimately the intention of such legislation.

Definitions of New Terms

Tastes for Discrimination: Employers may hold certain values according to which they will not hire women at the same wage rate as men. These employers have tastes for discrimination.

Customer Discrimination: Discrimination by customers against service by females.

Questions for Thought and Discussion

1. Do you believe in equal pay for equal work? Why? Can your views be considered positive or normative economics?
2. Why do you think women's roles are so different in the Soviet Union, Africa, and Asia as compared with the United States?
3. How can a male employer measure the cost to him of his tastes and discrimination?

Selected References

Becker, Gary, *The Economics of Discrimination,* 2d ed., Chicago: University of Chicago Press, 1971.

Fuchs, Victor R., "Differences in Hourly Earnings between Men and Women," *Monthly Labor Review,* May 1971, pp. 9–15.

Gilman, C. P., *Women and Economics,* Boston: Maynard & Co., 1898.

Morgan, Robin (ed.), *Sisterhood Is Powerful: An Anthology of Writing from the Women's Liberation Movement,* New York: Vintage Books, 1970.

23 The Decision to Hire and Fire

When a firm decides to fire an employee, the employee usually suffers. The costs of unemployment are not insignificant in our economy. Conversely, when employers decide to hire new workers, the workers usually feel they are better off; otherwise, they probably would not have accepted the job. If employers are willing to pay higher wages to workers, those workers are also obviously better off. If employers can get away with paying very low wages, then perhaps the employers will be better off, making higher profits. How much people are paid and the extent to which their labor resources are used are crucial issues in economics because they determine who is rich and who is poor. These factors determine what percentage of national income goes to wages and what percentage goes to interest, profits, and dividends.

Before analyzing the distribution of income, we first will develop a model that predicts the amount of a particular input firms will demand and the price they will pay for it. In our discussion, we will consider only one variable factor of production: labor. We will assume all other factors of production are fixed; in other words, the firm has a fixed number of machines but can hire or fire workers.

A firm's demand for inputs can be studied in much the same manner as we studied demands for outputs in different types of market situations. Again different types of market situations will be examined. Our analysis will always end with the same conclusion: A firm will hire employees up to the point where it isn't profitable to hire any more. It will hire employees to the point where the marginal revenue of hiring a worker will just equal the marginal cost. The best way for us to start is to assume that everything is perfectly competitive.

A Competitive Market

Let's take as our example a prerecorded tape manufacturing firm that is in competition with many companies selling the same kind of product. Assume that the laborers hired by our tape manufacturing firm do not need any special skills. This firm sells its product in a perfectly competitive market and also buys its variable input—labor—in a competitive market. The firm can influence neither the price of its product nor the price that it must pay for its variable input; it can purchase all the labor it wants at the going market wage without affecting that wage. The "going" wage is established by the forces of supply and demand in the labor market. The demand comes from all the individual firms' demands.

Constant Factor Costs

The cost of adding one more worker to the production line is the same whether our tape firm hires 50 workers or 500. Thus, it faces a constant marginal input cost (cost of a factor of production) that is exactly equal to the wage rate set by market forces which are out of its control. Since it can do nothing about the wage rate, the only variable it has left to play with is the total number of workers that it decides to employ. That is, it takes the wage rate as fixed and decides how many workers to hire, given that fixed wage rate. As you might expect, it will be profitable to hire more workers as long as they can make the firm more profits. When additional workers don't bring in more profits, our firm will stop hiring. It's fairly easy to figure out at what point hiring should stop.

Marginal Physical Product

To find the point at which hiring stops, we have to know the additional output or **marginal physical product** of each worker. We'll assume that all workers have the same education and

ability. They can all do the same type of job with the same results; each worker can produce the same amount; and each is paid the same wage. But each worker does *not* work alone. They work together to produce the tapes, and a new worker may not be able to produce as much as her or his coworkers.

We are assuming that everything else is held constant. So if our tape manufacturing firm wants to add one more worker to an assembly line, it has to crowd all the existing workers a little closer together because it did not increase its capital stock (the assembly line equipment) at the same time it increased the work force. Therefore, as we add more workers, each one has a smaller and smaller fraction of the available capital stock to work with. If one worker uses one machine, adding another worker usually won't double the output because the machine can run only so fast and for so many hours per day. This notion was introduced previously in connection with diminishing marginal returns. The returns from adding more of a variable factor of production first rose, then fell, and finally became negative.

Thus, for a variable factor of production, such as labor, the increased output made possible by hiring additional workers may be expected to become smaller. The increased output made possible by an additional worker is the worker's marginal physical product or **productivity.** If 10 workers can produce 1000 tapes and 11 workers can produce 1090 tapes, then the marginal physical product of the 11 workers is 90 tapes. Remember, we are assuming the only thing that varies is the number of workers. That's how we find their respective marginal physical product, or what their particular productivity is.

Value of Marginal Physical Product

We now know that as more workers are added, their marginal physical product falls. However, we still don't know how many workers our tape firm should hire. It should hire workers as long as the additional tapes each worker produces are worth more than the wages the worker receives. That way the firm ends up making a profit. But it is difficult to compare a physical product, such as a number of tapes, with a wage rate that is expressed in dollars. We somehow have to translate the physical product into a dollar value. This is done easily by multiplying the physical product times the market price of the tapes. If 11 workers' marginal physical product is 90 tapes and each tape sells for $3, then the value of the workers' marginal physical product (VMP) is 90 times $3, or $270. If that is the workers' value of marginal product per month and the wage rate per month is only $249, it behooves our tape maker to hire 11 workers for the difference between the workers' wage rate and contribution to total revenues **(value of marginal physical product)** is going to be $20.

Rule for Hiring

A general rule, then, for the hiring decision of a firm is: *The firm hires workers up to the point where the additional costs associated with hiring the last worker are exactly equal to or slightly less than the additional revenues generated by that worker.* In a perfectly competitive situation, this is the point where the wage rate just equals the value of marginal physical product. If the firm hired more workers, the additional wages would not be covered by additional increases in total revenue. If the firm hired fewer workers, it would be forfeiting the contributions that additional workers could make to increasing total profits. A simple example is outlined in Table 23-1, which shows that the firm should pay for only 12 worker-months because with that number the value of the workers' marginal physical product just

equals the going wage rate. (Actually the firm would be indifferent as to whether or not a twelfth worker was hired since that worker would neither increase nor decrease profits.)

We can plot the numbers in Table 23-1 on a simple graph called the *value of marginal physical product curve,* which is downward sloping. As more workers are hired, the value of the workers' marginal physical product decreases for only one reason: diminishing returns. The price of the tapes remains the same because the firm is selling in a competitive market. The firm is a price taker and cannot influence the market price.

Using Figure 23-1 we can find how many workers our firm should hire. First, we draw a straight line across from the going wage rate, which is determined by demand and supply on the labor market. This intersects the value of marginal physical product curve at 12 worker-months. At the intersection, *E,* the wage rate is equal to the value of marginal physical product. This value of marginal physical product curve is also a *factor demand curve,* assuming only one variable factor of production and competition in both the buying of the variable factor and the selling of the product.

Derived Demand

This demand curve is *derived*—it shows a **derived demand**—because the tape firm does not want to purchase the services of workers just for the services themselves. Factors of production are rented or purchased not because they give satisfaction per se but because they can be used to produce products that can be sold at a profit. This is different from a consumer's desire to buy a product, for example. The product is bought because it will give satisfaction.

Because it is derived, the value of marginal physical product curve will shift whenever the demand for the final product the workers are

Table 23-1 **The Value of Marginal Physical Product**

In the first column is the number of workers. In the second column is their marginal physical product per month. When we add one worker to an already existing work force of eight workers, the marginal physical product falls from 111 tapes per month to 104 tapes per month. We find in the third column the value of the marginal physical product of each worker. We multiply the marginal physical product times the price, which in our example is $3 per tape. Here we assume that the wage rate is $249 per month. In such a situation, the profit-maximizing employer will pay for only 12 worker-months because then the value of marginal physical product is just equal to the wage rate or monthly salary.

LABOR INPUT, NUMBER OF WORKER-MONTHS	MARGINAL PHYSICAL PRODUCT (TAPES PER WORKER-MONTH)	PRICE OF TAPE × MARGINAL PHYSICAL PRODUCT = VMP ($ PER WORKER-MONTH)
7	118	354
8	111	333
9	104	312
10	97	291
11	90	270
12	83	249
13	76	228

making changes. (Other reasons will cause this curve to shift, also, but we won't go into them here.) If, for example, the market price of tapes goes down, the value of marginal physical product schedule will shift inward to VMP′, as shown in Figure 23-2. If the market price of tapes goes up, the value of marginal physical product schedule will shift outward to the right to VMP″. After all, we know that VMP equals MP times price. If price falls, so too does VMP; at the same going wage rate, the firm will require fewer workers. Conversely, if price rises, VMP will also rise, and the firm will demand more workers.

Input Demand Curve for All Firms Taken Together

An individual firm's value of marginal physical product curve is also its demand schedule for the variable factor of production—in our example, labor. Is it possible to add up these individual demand curves for labor and come up with a market demand curve for labor? The answer is no because this is a derived demand—derived from the demand for the final product being produced. Therefore, if all firms together react to a reduction in the price of labor (the wage rate) by hiring more workers and producing more of the good, the only way *all firms combined* will be able to sell that increased production is by lowering the price. If the supply curve of the prerecorded tape industry shifts out to the right, the equilibrium price that will be established for tapes will be lower than it was before. If, for example, we go from a wage rate of $249 per month to $200 per month in the tape industry, we cannot simply look at how many more workers each individual firm wants to hire because then we would be *overestimat-*

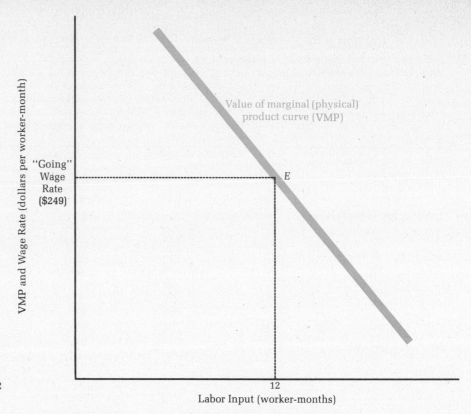

FIGURE 23-1 **Value of Marginal Physical Product Curve**

Here we have plotted the value of marginal physical product curve from Table 23-1. On the horizontal axis is the number of workers hired. On the vertical axis is the value of marginal physical product and the wage rate ($249 per month in this figure). We find how many workers the firm will want to hire by adding the wage rate that is established by the forces of supply and demand in the entire labor market. The employer in a competitive situation takes this wage rate as given and hires workers up to the point where the value of marginal physical product equals the wage rate. In our case, it is 12 workers.

VMP and Wage Rate (dollars per worker-month)

Value of marginal (physical) product curve (VMP)

"Going" Wage Rate ($249)

E

12

Labor Input (worker-months)

ing their total demand for labor. As firms hire more workers and expand production, the price of tapes will start to fall. This will shift the value of marginal physical product curve inward to the left, which means that, for the tape industry as a whole, the increased employment will be less than we would have predicted by looking at the original VMP curves for each firm. *The industry's price elasticity of demand for labor is less than the individual firm's price elasticity of demand for labor.*

We can see this in Figure 23-3. The original value of marginal physical product curve for the firm is VMP. At a wage rate of $249 a month, it demands quantity q_1 of workers. Let's now add together all the firms and put their total demand for workers at a wage rate of $249 on

the accompanying graph in Figure 23-4. Total market demand for the quantity of workers is Q_1. At a wage rate of $249, the entire industry demands Q_1 workers.

Now we assume that the market wage rate falls to $200. On the original VMP curve our firm will demand q_2 workers. But, when it hires more workers, it produces more; so too do all the other firms in the industry. But all this increased production cannot be sold without lowering the price of the product. Therefore, we have to draw a new VMP curve, which we will call VMP', and which is constructed using a *lower* price for the product. Now the firm's equilibrium demand for workers is q_3 when the wage rate drops to $2 an hour. We find all the workers demanded at this lower wage rate and

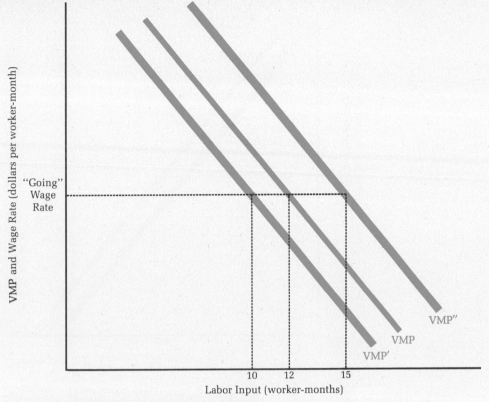

FIGURE 23-2 **Demand for Labor, a Derived Demand**

The demand for labor is a derived demand—derived from the demand for the final product being produced. Therefore, the value of marginal physical product curve will shift whenever the price of the product changes. If we start with the value of marginal physical product curve VMP, predicated on a price of tapes of $3 per reel, we know that at the going wage rate of $249 per month, 12 workers will be hired. If the price of tapes goes down, the value of marginal physical product curve will shift to VMP′ and the number of workers hired might fall to 10. If the price of tapes goes up, the value of marginal physical product curve might shift to VMP″ and the number of workers hired would increase to 15.

plot it in Figure 23-4. It happens to be at quantity Q_3. Notice one important thing again: *The market elasticity of demand for an input is smaller than the firm elasticity of demand for the same input at the market price for the input.* The firm's demand curve for labor is drawn assuming that product price is constant; the market's demand curve for labor allows for changes in the product price.

Our hypothetical derived demand schedule for the variable input "labor" has been drawn with the assumption of a certain elasticity of demand for labor.

We don't know the exact elasticity of the demand for labor, but there are a few rules of thumb that can be followed for a general idea. It is important to know labor demand elasticity if we want, for example, to forecast

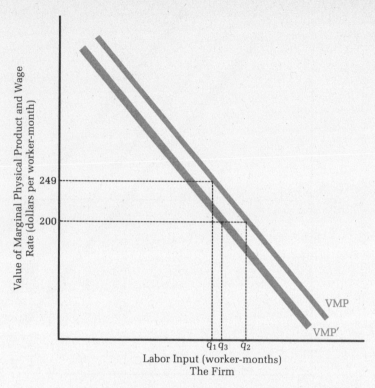

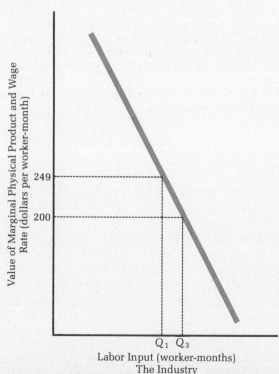

FIGURES 23-3, 23-4 The Firm and Market Demand Curves for Labor

In Figure 23-3 we draw the value of marginal physical product curve for the individual firm at VMP. The going wage rate is $249 per month. The total quantity of workers demanded by the firm is therefore q_1. We add up all the individual demands for workers at that wage rate and find it is equal to Q_1 in Figure 23-4. Now the wage rate falls to $200 per month. The value of marginal physical product curve dictates that q_2 number of workers would be hired by the firm. But all firms do the same thing. Therefore, they all increase production and the price of the product has to fall for all goods to be sold. This means that the value of marginal physical product curve will shift down to VMP'. At a wage rate of $200 per month, the quantity of workers demanded will fall from q_2 to q_3 for the firm. We add up all the q_3 quantities and find that the market demand for labor at a price of $200 per month is Q_3. Notice that the market demand curve for labor in Figure 23-4 is less elastic than the individual firm demand curve for labor in Figure 23-3.

the employment (or unemployment) effects of a new union movement in a specific occupation. So we should be aware of some of the determinants of this elasticity and not merely assume elasticity is the same for all industries and for all types of inputs. A long time ago, a well-known economist named Alfred Marshall came up with some determinants of the elasticity of demand for an input.

Determinants of Demand Elasticity for Inputs

There are basically five determinants of the price elasticity of demand for an input:

1. The easier it is for a particular variable input to be replaced by other inputs, the more price elastic the demand for that variable input will be.
2. The greater the price elasticity of demand for the final product, the greater the price elasticity of demand for the variable input.
3. The greater the price elasticity of supply of all other inputs, the greater the price elasticity of demand for a particular variable input.
4. The smaller the proportion of total costs accounted for by a particular variable input, the lower its price elasticity of demand.
5. A determinant not mentioned by Marshall is that the price elasticity of demand for a variable input will be larger in the long run than in the short run.

The first determinant seems obvious. If one particular input can be substituted very easily for another, then an increase in the price of one input will lead to much more extensive use of the other. For example, sleeping bag manufacturers can use either plastic or metal zippers on their bags. Both are equally useful and equally productive in doing the same job. They are also equally expensive, and are used, let's say, in equal proportions. For some reason, the price of plastic zippers rises by 20 percent. How many plastic zippers do you think a firm will use? Probably none; it will switch to metal zippers because they work just as well. On the other hand, thread is absolutely necessary for sewing the seams of the sleeping bags, and it cannot be replaced by anything else. We would expect the elasticity of demand for thread to be very low indeed. A rise in its price will not lead to a very large decrease in quantity demanded because no other inputs can be used instead.

The second determinant of factor demand elasticity is the elasticity of demand for the final product. It is probably the easiest to understand because we have already seen that the demand for an input is a *derived* demand. Since it is derived from the demand for the final output, we would expect that the elasticity of the derived demand would mirror the elasticity of the demand for the final product.

Assume the elasticity of demand for electricity is very low. If the wages of skilled workers in the electricity industry are forced up by strong unions, the companies can pass on part of the increase in costs to customers in the form of higher prices. But since the elasticity of demand for electricity is relatively low, customers will not reduce by very much the quantity of electricity demanded. The electricity companies will lay off very few workers. The low elasticity of demand for the final product leads to a low elasticity of demand for the factors of production. The converse is also true.

The third determinant is the price elasticity of the supply of other inputs. This determinant is probably somewhat less obvious. The elasticity of supply of an input is defined as the percentage increase in the quantity supplied of an input resulting from a 1 percent increase in the price of that input. Now, if all other inputs have very high price elasticities of supply, a very small increase in their prices will yield a very large increase in quantity supplied. If this is the case, then the demand for the variable input in question will be more price elastic than usual because the industry as a whole can obtain much more of all the other inputs by offering a slightly higher price. The competition from other inputs is therefore greater, and, hence, the price elasticity for the variable input under study must be relatively higher.

The fourth elasticity determinant is the proportion of total costs accounted for by the input under study. This determinant merely points out that if a factor of production accounts for only a very small part of the total cost of the product, any given price change will not affect total costs by much. Take the example of electricity as an input of manufacturing. On the average, the cost of electricity accounts for less than 1 percent of the total cost of manufactured goods. However, we'll assume that it accounts for exactly 1 percent. If electricity prices now go up by 100 percent, only 1 percent would be added to the total costs.

The fifth determinant concerns the difference between the short run and the long run. The long run is usually defined as the time period during which businesspersons adjust to a change in their business environment. As pointed out previously, the more time there is for adjustment, the more elastic both the supply and demand curves will be. This assertion holds for input demand curves as well. The longer the time allowed for adjustment to take place, the more responsive firms will be to a change in the price of a factor of production. Particularly in the long run, firms can reorganize their production process to minimize the use of a factor of production that has become more expensive relative to other factors of production.

Monopoly

Thus far, we've considered only a perfectly competitive situation, both in selling the final product and in buying factors of production. Now we'll consider other possibilities. One situation occurs when the firm buys factors of production in a competitive market but sells its product in a monopolistic situation. Remember that a monopolistic firm faces a downward-sloping demand curve for its product; thus, if it wants to sell more of its product, it has to lower the price *not only on the last unit but on all preceding units.* The marginal revenue received from selling an additional unit is continuously falling as the firm attempts to sell more and more. Now, in reconstructing our demand schedule for an input, we must account for the facts that (1) the marginal *physical product* falls because of the law of diminishing returns as more workers are added, and (2) the price received for the product sold also falls as more is produced and sold. That is, we have to account for both the diminishing marginal physical product and the diminishing marginal revenue.

In Table 23-2, we see that the change in total revenues gives us the **marginal revenue product** (MRP). This gives the firm a quantitative notion of how profitable additional workers and additional production actually are. In Figure 23-5, the marginal revenue product curve has been plotted. Just as the VMP curve is the input demand curve for a competitor, the MRP curve is the input demand curve for a monopolist.

Why does the MRP curve represent the monopolist's input demand curve? Our profit-maximizing monopolist will continue to hire labor as long as additional profits result. Profits are made as long as the additional cost of more workers is outweighed by the additional revenues made from selling the output of those workers. When the wage rate equals these ad-

Table 23-2 Finding Marginal Revenue Product

To find marginal revenue product, we must calculate total revenue for the output provided by different rates of use of the labor input.

(1) LABOR INPUT (WORKER-MONTHS)	(2) TOTAL PHYSICAL PRODUCT	(3) MARGINAL PHYSICAL PRODUCT (MPP)	(4) PRICE OF PRODUCT	(5) TOTAL REVENUE (2) × (4)	(6) MARGINAL REVENUE PRODUCT (MRP) CHANGE IN (5) / CHANGE IN (1)
7	1,000	118	$4.00	$4,000.00	$332.90
8	1,111	111	3.90	4,332.90	284.10
9	1,215	104	3.80	4,617.00	237.40
10	1,312	97	3.70	4,854.40	192.80
11	1,402	90	3.60	5,047.20	150.30
12	1,485	83	3.50	5,197.50	109.90
13	1,561	76	3.40	5,307.40	

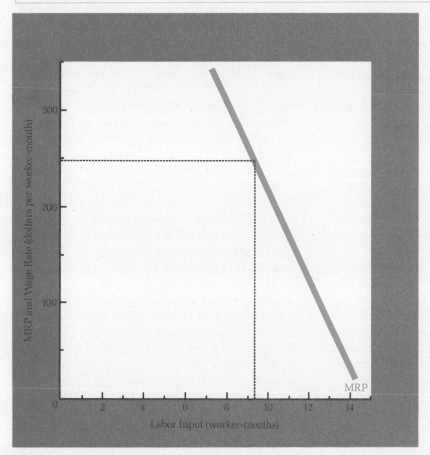

FIGURE 23-5 Marginal Revenue Product: Firm's Input Demand Curve

Here we plot the marginal revenue product, MRP, from Table 23-2. The monopolist hires just enough workers to make marginal revenue product equal to the going wage rate. If the going wage rate is $249 per month, the monopolist would want to hire somewhere between 9 and 10 worker-months.

ditional revenues, the monopolist stops hiring. That is, he or she stops hiring when the wage rate is equal to the marginal revenue product.

Monopsony: A Buyer's Monopoly

Let's again assume that the firm is a perfect competitor in the product market. The firm cannot alter the price of the product it sells and it faces a horizontal demand curve for its product. However, we will now assume that the firm is the only buyer of a particular input. Although this situation may not frequently occur, it is useful to consider. Let's think in terms of a "company town." There are numerous examples in the mining industry. One company not only hires the miners but also owns the businesses in the community and hires the clerks, waiters, paymaster, and all other personnel. This buyer of labor is called a **monopsonist,** which is Greek for "single buyer."

A monopsonist faces an *upward-sloping supply curve* for labor. The market supply curve has also generally been shown as upward sloping. However, firms don't usually face the market curve; they can buy all the workers they want at the going wage rate and thus usually face a fairly horizontal supply curve for factors of production.

What does an upward-sloping supply curve mean to monopsonists in terms of the costs of hiring extra workers? It means that if they want to hire more workers, they have to offer higher wages. Only if they face a horizontal supply curve would things be otherwise. Our monopsonist firm cannot hire all the labor it wants at the going wage rate. If it wants to hire 10 percent more workers, it may have to raise wages 3 percent. Not only does it have to raise wages to attract new workers, but it also has to raise the wages of all its current workers.

It therefore has to take account of these increased costs when deciding how many more workers to hire.

Marginal Factor Costs

To find out how a monopsonist decides the number of workers to hire, we need to look at the supply and demand for labor. Figure 23-6 shows an upward-sloping supply curve of labor. Above the supply line is the **marginal factor cost** curve, or MFC. This curve is similar to a marginal revenue curve, but now it is for buying rather than selling. The MFC curve indicates the increased costs that are incurred when a (nondiscriminating) monopsonistic firm wants to hire more of the variable input labor. It lies above the supply curve because whenever a monopsonistic firm wishes to hire one more worker, not only does it have to pay a higher wage to that worker but it also has to raise wages for all other workers. The marginal factor cost for that last worker is, therefore, his or her wages plus the increase in the wages for all other existing workers.

An Example

Let's take a simple example. Assume that our monopsonistic firm has 10 workers. It pays them each $100 a week. That means the total wage bill is $1000 per week. Since the firm faces an upward-sloping supply curve of labor, if it wants to hire one more worker, it has to pay that worker $101 to entice him or her to work. But it also has to pay more to all the other workers. They're not going to stand by and see a new worker make more than they do. Our monopsonist, therefore, has to pay them each $1 more a week. The increase in cost due to hiring one more worker is equal to his or her wage rate, $101, plus the increase in all the other wage rates, or $10 ($1 times 10). In this particu-

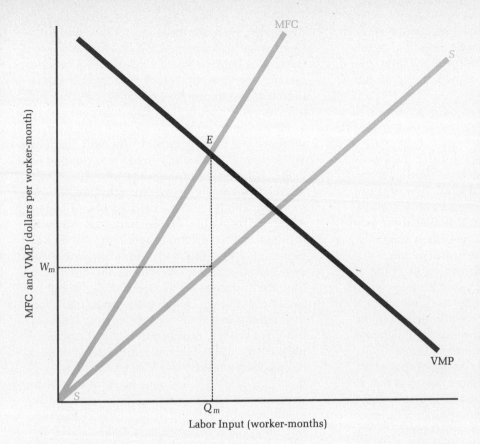

FIGURE 23-6 **Marginal Factor Cost Curve for a Monopsonist**
The monopsonistic firm's demand curve for labor is its value of marginal physical product curve—assuming it is in a competitive product market. Since the firm is monopsonistic, it faces an upward-sloping supply curve instead of a horizontal one as in the previous situation. It therefore knows that to hire more workers it has to pay higher wage rates. It looks at a marginal factor cost curve, MFC, which slopes upward and is above its supply curve, SS. It finds how many workers to hire by seeing that marginal factor cost equals the value of marginal physical product at point E. It therefore hires Q_m workers and has to pay them only W_m in wages.

lar example, the marginal factor cost for hiring one more worker is equal to $101 plus $10, or $111 a week.

We still haven't found how the monopsonistic firm determines the number of workers it wants to hire. It does this by comparing its demand curve for labor with the marginal factor cost curve for labor. How does it get its demand curve? Since it is perfectly competitive in selling its product, its demand curve for labor is the value of its marginal physical product curve, VMP in Figure 23-6. The intersection of the marginal factor cost curve and the demand curve for labor tells the monopsonist how many workers to hire because this is the point at which the marginal cost of hiring a worker is

exactly equal to the value of the marginal physical product produced by that additional worker.

How much is this firm going to pay these workers? In a normal situation, it would be faced with a given wage rate in the labor market. But since it is monopsonistic, it can determine the wage rate itself, depending on how many units of labor are hired. It sets the wage rate so it will get exactly that quantity supplied to it by a captive labor force. We find that that wage rate is W_m.

There is no reason to pay the workers any more than W_m because, at that wage rate, the firm can get exactly the quantity it demands. The quantity demanded is established at the intersection of the marginal factor cost curve and the demand curve for labor—that is, at the point where the marginal revenue from expanding employment just equals the marginal cost of doing so.

The Monopsony Model and Minimum Wages

The monopsony model has been used as a justification for **minimum wages.** A minimum wage is a wage level legislated by states, cities, or the federal government. It is illegal for employers to pay their employees less than that wage. In Figure 23-7, the firm's demand for labor schedule has been drawn as its value of marginal physical product curve because we're considering that it is selling its product in a competitive market. We have also drawn in the supply curve of labor and the marginal factor cost curve that the monopsonistic firm actually faces because it is the only buyer of that labor supply. If it wants to get more labor, it has to raise wages, not only for the additional workers but also for all the preceding ones. The marginal factor cost curve is always above the supply curve. The desired level of employment from the monopsonist's profit-maximizing point of view is at the intersection of the marginal factor cost curve and the value of marginal physical product curve. That is, the monopsonist will desire q_m number of workers. To get q_m number of workers, he has to pay only W_1.

Now suppose a minimum wage is established at W_2. We draw a horizontal line at W_2. It extends to and then merges with the supply curve. The monopsonist now faces a new supply curve, $S'S$, that starts at W_2, moves horizontally to the old supply curve, and then merges with it.

What is the new marginal factor cost curve? It is also the horizontal portion of the new supply curve—that is, the horizontal portion at the minimum wage rate, W_2. When the minimum wage rate line hits the old supply curve, we're also back to the old marginal factor cost curve. The new marginal factor cost curve therefore jumps up to coincide with the old one; as can be seen, it is discontinuous.

How do we figure out what quantity of workers the monopsonistic firm will demand when there is a minimum wage rate slapped on it that is higher than the wage rate it has been paying? Obviously, it will hire that amount of labor at which its marginal factor cost is just equal to the value of the marginal physical product of the additional workers. We find in Figure 23-7 that this happens to be where the new marginal factor cost curve—the horizontal line at W_2—jumps up to meet the old marginal factor cost curve. This is where marginal revenue equals marginal cost in hiring workers. Employment will now expand from the original level of q_m to q_1. Here is a situation where a rise in wages results in an increase in employment, contrary to the normal situation. The imposition of a minimum wage rate will cause employment to expand. It will benefit workers, not only those who already have a job, but others who will be hired.

The monopsony argument for minimum wages might, in special circumstances, be applicable to a company town. However, it is difficult for us to imagine that a sufficient percentage of the labor force would actually be employed in a company town so that an increase in minimum wages throughout the nation would cause an increase in employment. Even if we take a very broad definition of a company town, we find that the fraction of the labor force employed in a monopsonistic situation is very small indeed. For example, one researcher found that the fraction of counties in the United States where the 30 largest firms employed 50 percent of the labor force was extremely small.

Moreover, the minimum wage applies to the

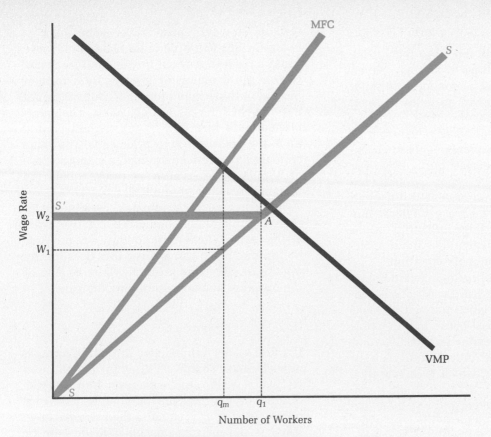

FIGURE 23-7 Minimum Wages and the Monopsony Model

A monopsonist looks at his or her marginal factor cost curve and, in the absence of restrictions, hires q_m workers and pays them a wage rate of W_1. However, if minimum wages are set, it is possible that we can get the monopsonist to hire more workers at a higher wage rate. Assume that the minimum wage rate is set at W_2. What is the effective supply curve now? It is equal to the horizontal line from W_2 to the old supply curve, SS. The new supply curve, then, is $S'S$. What is the marginal factor cost curve for this situation? For the horizontal part of the supply curve, the marginal factor cost curve is exactly the same line. But when the supply curve starts to slope up at point A, the marginal factor cost curve jumps up to its original line. We have shown that as the heavily shaded part of MFC. How many workers does the monopsonist hire in this minimum wage situation? He or she hires the number of workers that allows him or her to set marginal factor cost equal to value of marginal physical product. That's a q_1, where the marginal factor cost curve jumps up to its higher level. The minimum wage in this situation causes an increase in the quantity of workers hired from q_m to q_1.

lowest paid, least skilled workers in our economy. All other workers are making wages well above the minimum. It is equally hard to imagine that any firms actually have to offer higher than the going wage rate to get more unskilled workers. Hence, the firms affected by the minimum wage law can hardly be considered monopsonists.

Bilateral Monopoly

Now let's assume that in the labor market we have a single seller selling to a single buyer. In other words, we have a monopolistic seller of labor (one that can exert an influence over wage rates) facing a monopsonistic employer (one who can also affect wage rates)—that is, we have a **bilateral monopoly.** This is an extreme example, but it occurs quite often. For example, when the major league baseball club owners confront the major league Baseball Players Association, we have a bilateral monopoly situation. Often, large industrial unions will meet large industrial employers, and, again, we have a bilateral monopoly situation.

The bilateral monopoly is depicted in Figure 23-8. The monopolistic firm faces an upward-sloping supply curve of labor. It therefore looks at its marginal factor cost curve that is above its supply curve to determine how many workers it should hire. The intersection with its demand curve for labor, which is its marginal revenue product curve, is at Q_m. It would therefore like to hire Q_m workers and pay them just enough that they would be willing to work. That wage rate would be W_m. On the other hand, the monopolistic seller of labor, say a strong union, would presumably like to have a much higher wage rate. If we further assume that it would not want to decrease employment, then the maximum wage would be W_1. We don't really know where the wage will be, but we can hypothesize that it will be somewhere between W_m and W_1, depending on the bargaining skills of the two sides and on what the union wants to maximize.

When There are Other Factors of Production

The analysis in this chapter has been given in terms of the demand for a variable input called "labor." However, exactly the same analysis holds for any other variable factor input. We could have talked about the demand for fertilizer or the demand for tractors by a farmer, instead of the demand for labor, but we would have reached the same conclusions. The entrepreneur will hire or buy any variable input, up to the point where its price equals its value of marginal physical product, or, in the case of a monopolist, where its price equals the marginal revenue product.

A further question remains. How much of each variable factor should the firm use when all the variable factors are combined to produce the product? We can answer this question by looking at either the profit-maximizing side of the question or the cost-minimizing side.

Profit Maximization

If a firm wants to maximize profits, how much of each factor should be hired (or bought)? As we just saw, the firm will never hire a factor of production unless the marginal benefit from hiring that factor is equal to the marginal cost. What is the marginal benefit? In the case of a perfect competitor, it is the value of marginal physical product or VMP. In the case of a monopolist, it is the marginal revenue product or MRP. What is the marginal cost? In the case of a firm buying in a competitive market, it is the price of the variable factor—or the wage rate if we are referring to labor. If the firm is buying in a monopsonistic market, then the price of the variable factor is the marginal factor cost or MFC.

The profit-maximizing equilibrium point, then, will be where

$$\text{MRP of labor} = \text{MFC of labor}$$
$$\text{MRP of land} = \text{MFC of land}$$
$$\text{MRP of machines} = \text{MFC of machines}$$
$$\text{and so on}$$

We add that in a competitive market MRP can

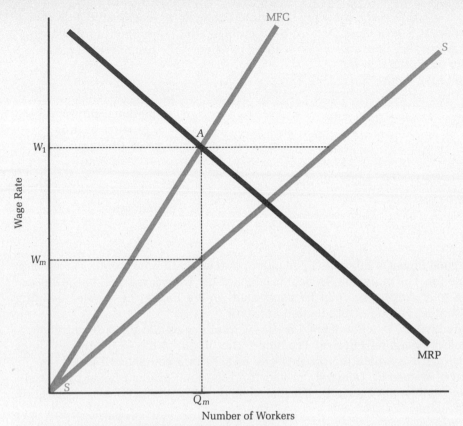

FIGURE 23-8 **Bilateral Monopoly in the Labor Market**

Here we show a monopsonist buying labor from a monopolistic seller of labor. The monopsonist might be a big company, and the monopolist seller of labor might be a union. The monopsonistic firm wants to hire Q_m workers where the marginal factor cost curve intersects the marginal revenue product curve. It would like to pay a wage rate of W_m. However, the union will want a higher wage than W_m. Moreover, it probably will not want a decrease in employment. This means that the range of wages will be between W_m and W_1. The solution here is logically indeterminate. Bargaining will, however, lead to an intermediate solution, with the wage rate certainly greater than W_m and probably less than W_1.

be replaced by VMP, and MFC can be replaced by the going wage rate.

Cost Minimization

From the cost-minimization point of view, how can the firm minimize its total costs for a given output? The answer should, by now, be obvious. Assume you are an entrepreneur attempt-

ing to minimize costs. If you spent a dollar more on labor you would get 20 more units of output, but if you spent a dollar more on machines you would get only 10 more units of output. What do you think you would do? You would probably want to hire more workers or sell off some machines. In other words, you would want to employ relative amounts of every factor of production so that the marginal product per last dollar spent on each is equal. Thus, the least-cost, or cost-minimization, rule will be as follows (we will analyze the way a very unusual firm puts together its factors of production by using the cost-minimization rule in the next issue):

To minimize total costs for a particular rate of production, the firm will hire factors of production up to the point where the marginal physical product per last dollar spent on each factor of production is equalized; or,

$$\frac{\text{Marginal physical product of labor}}{\text{Price of labor}} = \frac{\text{marginal physical product of machines}}{\text{price (rental value) of machines}}$$

$$= \frac{\text{marginal physical product of land}}{\text{price (rental value) of land}}$$

$$= \text{and so on}$$

Definitions of New Terms

Marginal Physical Product: The output that an additional worker is responsible for. The marginal physical product of the worker is equal to the change in total output that can be accounted for by hiring the worker, holding all other factors of production constant.

Productivity: Usually defined as the worker's marginal physical product.

Value of Marginal Physical Product: The marginal physical product times the price at which the product can be sold in a competitive market.

Derived Demand: Demand derived from the final product being produced.

Marginal Revenue Product: The marginal physical product times the marginal revenue.

Monopsonist: Single buyer.

Marginal Factor Cost: The cost of using more of a factor; that is, the additional cost of using a factor.

Minimum Wage: A legal minimum wage rate below which employers cannot pay workers.

Bilateral Monopoly: A situation in the labor market where a single seller of labor confronts a single buyer or monopsonist.

Chapter Summary

1. In a competitive situation where the firm is a very small part of the entire product and labor market, the firm will want to hire workers up to the point where the value of their marginal physical product just equals their going wage rate.

2. In such a situation, the value of marginal physical product curve for the individual firm is equal to the firm's demand curve for labor. However, the summation of all the value of marginal physical product curves does not equal the market demand curve for labor. The market demand curve for labor is less elastic because as more workers are hired, output is

increased and the price of the product must fall, thereby lowering the value of marginal physical product.

3. The demand for labor is a derived demand, derived from the demand for the product produced.

4. The elasticity of demand for an input is a function of several very obvious determinants, including the elasticity of demand for the final product and the elasticity of supply of other factors of production. Moreover, the price elasticity of demand for a variable input will usually be larger in the long run than it is in the short run because there is time for adjustment.

5. In a monopoly situation, the demand curve for labor is no longer the value of marginal physical product curve but the marginal revenue product curve, which is derived from the marginal physical product of workers times the marginal revenue. It slopes downward, just like the value of marginal physical product curve, but is usually steeper.

6. In a situation where there is only one buyer of a particular input, a monopsony arises. The single buyer faces an upward-sloping supply curve and therefore must pay higher wages to get more workers to work. The single buyer faces a marginal factor cost curve that is upward sloping and above the supply curve. The buyer hires workers up to the point where the value of marginal physical product equals the marginal factor cost. Then the buyer would find out how low a wage rate could be paid to get that many workers.

7. Often the monopsony model is used to justify a minimum wage, which in the monopsony situation will result in greater employment at higher wages.

8. A firm minimizes total costs by equating the marginal physical product of labor divided by the price of labor with the marginal physical product of machines divided by the price of machines with all other such ratios of all the different factors of production.

Questions for Thought and Discussion

1. Unions want to raise wages. Does the theory developed in this chapter tell us anything about the possible employment effects of "excessive" wage increases?

2. Since the demand curve for labor is the value of marginal physical product curve in a competitive situation, more workers would be hired if the value of marginal physical product curve shifted to the right. This can be accomplished by either raising the marginal product or increasing the price of the product sold. How can workers help in shifting the VMP curve to the right?

3. Many businesspersons maintain that they have no idea what the value of marginal physical product is for their workers, that they just hire their

workers at the going wage rate and hire as many as they "need." How can you reconcile the theoretical presentation in this chapter with what businesspersons say they do?

4. Look back at the five determinants of the price elasticity of demand for inputs. After reviewing them, figure out where you would want to unionize—that is, where you would think unionization could have the most effect.

5. Look at the outcome of some bilateral monopoly situations. Can you tell who had the better hand?

6. The minimum wage law has been called "the most anti-Negro law on the books." Why? Discuss.

7.

Quantity of Labor	Total Product Per Week	MP	MRP
1	250		
2	450		
3	600		
4	700		
5	750		
6	750		

Assume the above product sells for $2 per unit.

(a) Use the information above to derive a demand curve for labor.

(b) What would this firm be willing to pay each worker if five workers were hired?

(c) If the going salary for this quality of labor is $200 per week, how many workers would be hired?

Selected References

Cartter, Allan M. and F. Ray Marshall, *Labor Economics: Wages, Employment, and Trade Unionism,* rev. ed., Homewood, Ill.: Irwin, 1972.

Galenson, Walter, *A Primer on Employment and Wages,* 2d ed., New York: Random House, 1970.

Kreps, Juanita M. et al., *Contemporary Labor Economics,* Belmont, Calif.: Wadsworth, 1974.

Rees, Albert, *Economics of Trade Unions,* Chicago: University of Chicago Press, 1962.

Crime and Punishment

THE ECONOMICS OF CRIMINAL DETERRENCE

The Costs of Crime

The economic costs of crime in the United States probably exceed $65 billion a year. Perhaps $11 billion of those total costs are spent on police, prosecution, courts, jails, and certain private methods of preventing crime. Crime—in terms of both an activity committed by individuals and an activity whose prevention is attempted by the public and individuals—is big business and it may be getting even bigger. There is evidence that major felonies per capita have grown since the early 1930s. The FBI reported that in the 1960s the national crime rate rose over 100 percent. This is seen in Figures I-27.1 and I-27.2. The rise has strained the capacity of courts and police to a point that literally approaches chaos in some cities. It is estimated that in New York, for example, policepersons and courts are so overworked that a person who commits a felony faces only 1 chance in 200 of actually going to jail for it.

There is no doubt that crime is a complex social problem. It is a problem we have to deal with at national, state, and local levels. However, we will show in this issue

that it is possible to analyze how resources can be spent optimally on preventing crime and punishing offenders. We will use the laws of supply and demand, as well as our analysis of how a business operates, to do some theorizing about actual criminal enforcement procedures. Let's start our discussion with the dilemma that every police chief faces.

Constraining the Chief of Police

The head of any law enforcement department is usually faced with a fixed budget. In the city of New York, it might be $125 million. In the city of Dry Gulch, it might be $10,000. In any and all cases, the fixed budget will be a constraint imposed on the behavior of the chief of police. The chief knows that he or she has been hired to prevent crime, to prevent citizens in the area from suffering the economic, social, and psychological costs of crime. If the number of rapes, murders, and assaults increases drastically during the reign of a chief of police, he or she will

usually be replaced. Let's therefore look at the chief as if he or she were the manager of a large firm given a specific budget and told to maximize production.

Measuring Output

In this case production or output is very difficult to measure. Is it the number of robbers apprehended? Is it the decrease in the number of rapes during the chief's administration? Is it measured by the number of embezzlers who have been apprehended and prosecuted? Nobody really knows how the output of a police department can be measured, but the chief of police does have some idea as to what superiors want. The chief knows, for example, that he or she should not spend all the resources giving parking tickets. Some resources have to go to preventing robberies, preventing murders, apprehending felony criminals, and so on.

Allocating a Fixed Budget

The chief of police takes the given budget, then, and decides how it should be allocated. The chief has to figure out, for example, how many police cars, computers, and other machines to buy and how many persons to hire. Let's assume for the

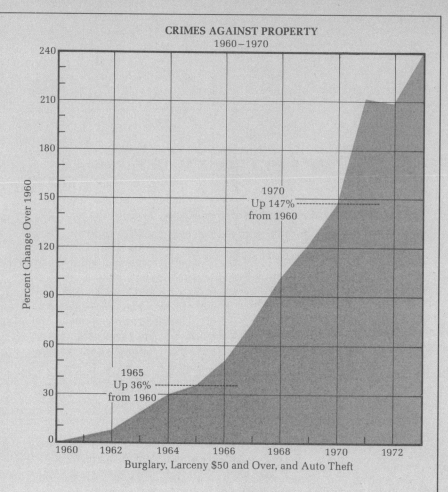

CRIMES AGAINST PROPERTY
1960–1970

1970
Up 147%
from 1960

1965
Up 36%
from 1960

Percent Change Over 1960

Burglary, Larceny $50 and Over, and Auto Theft

FIGURE I-27.1

The 1960s saw a 147 percent increase in crimes against property. Crime has become and continues to be big business. *(Source: FBI Crime Reports, 1973.)*

moment that the factors of production the chief wants to purchase can be divided into labor and machines. If the chief finds that by spending one more dollar on machines, a higher amount of crime deterrence can be obtained than by spending that dollar on labor, then the proportion of the budget spent on machines should be increased. Of course, even the best of police chiefs could not hope to measure the product made available from spending an additional $1 either on labor or on machines. The chief must work in much grosser figures; but the principle still holds. For a given budget, the chief of police will maximize the output of the firm (police department) if he or she uses the different inputs, such as labor and machines, in such quantities that the marginal product made possible by spending $1 on one input is just equal to the marginal product made possible by spending $1 on every one of the other inputs. The amount of crime deterrence that a chief of police can attain will be maximized with a given budget only if the marginal amount of crime deterrence made possible by $1 is the same for every input used in this crime-preventing firm.

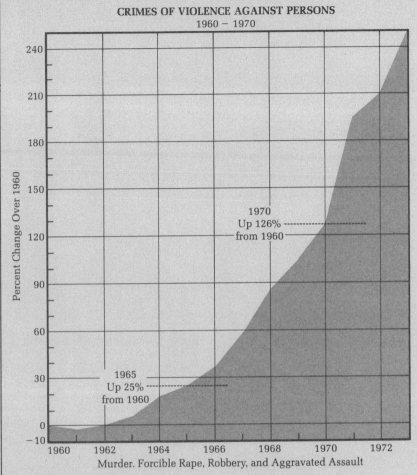

CRIMES OF VIOLENCE AGAINST PERSONS
1960 – 1970

Percent Change Over 1960

1970
Up 126% ------------------------
from 1960

1965
Up 25% ------------------
from 1960

Murder. Forcible Rape, Robbery, and Aggravated Assault

FIGURE I-27.2

Crimes of violence increased 126 percent from 1960 to 1970, slightly less than the increase in crimes against property. *(Source: FBI Crime Reports, 1973.)*

Eliminate Vice or Theft?

Not only is our chief of police faced with the problem of equalizing marginal products per dollar spent on all inputs, he or she also has to decide how much should be spent on the vice patrol, how much should be spent on the homicide division, how much should be spent on the traffic division, and so on. Somehow the chief has got to allocate this fixed budget among the different divisions. Here the problem becomes somewhat more difficult. The solution will be to allocate monies so that the marginal output of each is equalized per dollar spent.

The relative *value* of the marginal product or output for any particular crime-prevention detail is decided by society. If, in general, the majority of citizens are more disturbed by youths smoking marijuana than by robberies, an increase in the amount spent on deterrence of robberies will be worth less than an equal increase devoted to stopping marijuana smokers. The chief of police most likely gets signals about the value of different types of crime deterrence from political superiors (like the mayor). In some cities, for example, the voting public apparently places a very high value on the apprehension of young people who behave "inappropriately." It is not uncommon to see several police cars questioning a pair of youthful, long-haired hitchhikers at just about every freeway on-ramp in some cities. But, given a fixed-budget constraint, the use of police resources to apprehend illegal hitchhikers reduces the amount of resources that could be used, for example, to patrol residential districts to reduce the number of burglaries.

In any event, in some way or another the chief of police must allocate this budget among different departments within the police system so that the marginal product per dollar spent in each detail is equalized. Otherwise the chief could alter the spending among details and increase the total output of the department. A change in public sentiment concerning certain crime would force a change in the chief's budget allocation. For example, if the public became less incensed about the evils of prostitution, we would expect the chief of police to reduce the prostitution detail and add more police-persons to other divisions. He or she would have to do this to equalize the value of marginal product per dollar spent on the prostitution detail with that spent in all the other departments. This relates to the law of diminishing returns. If we assume the police department is operating in the area of diminishing returns, a decrease in the amount of resources used to apprehend prostitutes would increase the marginal product of those resources.

The City Council

The problems faced by a chief of police in allocating a fixed budget are no different from the problems faced by a city council headed by the mayor when budget time comes around every year. There are only so many dollars in the kitty; these have to be spent for street maintenance, hospitals, and other things, as well as for crime prevention. The city council must attempt in one way or another to allocate parts of the fixed budget to the police department, fire department, sanitation department, and so on in such a way that the value of the marginal physical products from each of these endeavors is equalized. A change in social attitude would obviously lead to a change in budget allocation. If, for instance, law and order becomes

a bigger issue relative to sanitation, we would expect the portion of the city's budget going to crime prevention to increase. This is exactly what has happened in some cases.

Deterring Crime

Some people believe that the more money spent on crime deterrence, the less crime there will be. However, the relationship between the money spent on deterrence and the actual number of crimes *not* committed because of that money is not known. It would take an extremely clever pollster to discover how many times an individual *didn't* break the law. We are even less certain about the effectiveness of the different methods used to deter crime. Is it best to have policepersons everywhere? Or, is it best to have a system of paid informants in lieu of those policepersons? Should we allow innocent parties to be apprehended and prosecuted merely because a larger absolute number of the guilty will thereby be convicted? Also, what are the available alternatives to punishing guilty offenders? Should we allow large fines instead of incarceration? Should we have public whippings? Should capital punishment be allowed? In terms of establishing a system of crime deterrence, we might want to assess carefully the real value of different deterrents.

Hard Drug Problem

As an example we might suspect that the larger the potential jail sentence, the smaller the number of attempted crimes. But this is not always correct. For physiologically addicted drug addicts, increased penalties do nothing to deter the commission of these "crimes." Also, if uniformly heavy punishments are made the rule for all crimes, thus expanding the category of major crimes, then we should expect to find a larger number of major crimes being committed.

Looking at the Margin

Let's look at the reasoning. All decisions are made on the margin. If an act of theft will be punished by hanging and an act of murder will be punished by the same fate, there is no marginal deterrence to murder. (In fact, it might be logical to murder the theft victim since no risk of greater punishment is involved.) If a theft of $5 is met with a punishment of 10 years in jail and a theft of $50,000 also incurs a 10-year sentence, then why not steal $50,000? Why not go for broke? There is no marginal deterrence to prevent one from doing so.

A very serious question exists as to how our system of justice can establish penalties appropriate from a social point of view. To establish the correct (marginal) deterrences, we must observe empirically how criminals respond to changes in punishments. This leads us to the question of how people decide whether to commit a "crime." We need a theory as to what determines the supply of criminal offenses.

Offensive Supplies

Adam Smith once said:

The affluence of the rich excites the indignation of the poor, who are often both driven by want, and prompted by envy, to invade his possessions. It is only under the shelter of the civil magistrate that the owner of that valuable property, which is acquired by the labour of many years, or perhaps by many successive generations, can sleep a single night in security. He is at all times surrounded by unknown enemies, whom, though he never provokes, he can never appease, and from whose injustice he can be protected only by the powerful arm of the civil magistrate continually held up to chastise it. The acquisition of valuable and extensive property,

. . . , necessarily requires the establishment of civil government. Where there is no property, or at least none that exceeds the value of two or three day's labour, civil government is not so necessary.[1]

Smith is pointing out that the professional criminals look for wealth. If they are looking for wealth, then their decision-making process can be viewed as any other economic activity. They look at the expected returns and expected costs of criminal activity and then compare them with the net returns from legitimate activities. The expected costs of crime involve the probabilities of apprehension, defense, conviction, jail, and so on. This is analogous to the costs that athletes may encounter when they are injured.

Viewing the supply of offenses thus, we can come up with methods by which society can lower the net expected rate of return for committing any illegal activity. That is, we can figure out how to reduce crime most effectively. We have talked about one particular aspect: the size of penalties. We also briefly mentioned the other—that is, the probability of detection for each offense. When either of these costs of crime goes up, the quantity of crime supplied goes down; that is, less crime is committed.

Increasing the Probability of Detection

How can the probability of detection be increased? There are numerous

[1] Adam Smith, *The Wealth of Nations*, 1776.

methods, increased police activity being only one. Individuals too can privately increase the probability of detecting people attempting to rob their homes. The market for individual burglar alarm systems is a growing one indeed. There is also a large amount of technologically sophisticated equipment that can be used to increase detection and apprehension through methods such as wiretapping. This approach, however, presents a problem of infringing on individual liberties—a cost that must be reckoned with whenever it is used. It is also possible for certain "traps" to be set to apprehend more criminals. For example, if money were made in a much more complicated manner, it would be more difficult for counterfeiters to copy it successfully and go undetected.

The Courts

The probability of conviction is very important in increasing the net expected cost of committing an illegal activity. This involves our system of courts, which today is in a sorry state. If a person knows that, even if apprehended, he or she will probably not be convicted, then of course the expected cost to that person of committing a crime is decreased. The likelihood of conviction is apparently an important factor in the prevention of crime. Currently, the probability of conviction for a crime is quite low in the United States. As mentioned, in New York City it is estimated that a person who commits a felony faces less than 1 chance in 200 of going to jail. One major reason for this is that the courts lack adequate facili-

ties to handle the large number of cases facing them. The court calendars in many cities are clogged beyond belief. Many court calendars are booked for 2, 3, or even 4 years into the future. The average time lapse between filing a civil suit and getting it to trial is 40 months in New York City. What do you think happens? An overworked prosecuting attorney and his team of crime-busting assistants increasingly arrange pretrial settlements rather than put an additional weight on the already overburdened courts. Eighty to 90 percent of criminal charges are settled before trial. Money might be spent better streamlining court proceedings than making more arrests. The district attorneys would not be forced to make so many "deals" with suspects. There are many inequities, of course, on the other side as well.

No Compensation for the Innocent

If someone is wrongfully convicted of a crime and later found innocent, he or she is not compensated—except in rare cases—for the pain, suffering, and lost income that was caused. For example, in 1964 four youths were apprehended in New York for a suspected murder. They were convicted, but then an appellate court ruled a mistrial. They were tried three more times but the juries never reached a unanimous verdict. If they are eventually found innocent, they will most likely be paid absolutely nothing for all the years they spent behind bars. A "just" system of justice should involve not only punishing the guilty but also making

full and just retribution to the innocent convicted of crimes they did not commit. If the court system is not faced with the full and true costs of its own mistakes, it is not operating in an optimal manner.

Civil Suits

Courts handling noncriminal proceedings are just as overworked as those handling criminal ones. An economically efficient system of courts would charge the full opportunity cost of that scarce resource to those who use it. Instead of paying jurors a nominal fee for the days they spend in court, the courts would pay them their full opportunity cost. And the payment would be made by the party who loses in the civil action. At present, taxpayers subsidize lawyers and their clients in the use of the courts. Since the courts are relatively free of charge, they are used more often than if the lawyer and his or her client had to pay the full cost. This is an inefficient use of resources.

The Victims

It is difficult to assess the social value that people place on the prevention of different types of crimes. For this reason, chiefs of police, legislators, mayors, and other officials find it difficult to decide how resources should be expended in different areas of crime deterrence. However, it is possible to improve the information being used by decision makers. Currently, there is almost no compensation to the victim or to the victim's dependents in the case of violent crimes. If you were knocked

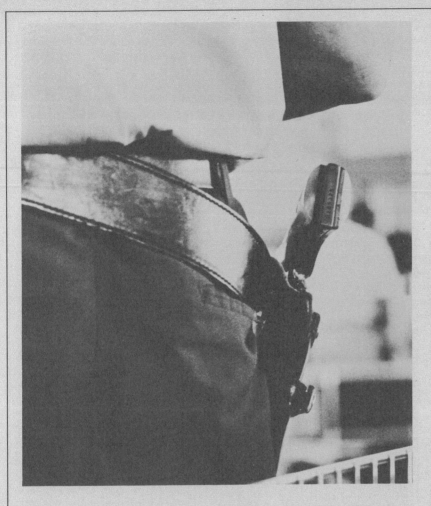

ments to assume responsibility for the complete liability of anyone within their geographical territory. If unlimited liability were assessed against the state in the case of criminal assaults and crimes against property, then the taxpayers would find a portion of their taxes going to compensate victims of crimes. This would eventually come back through the political process as a demand for better law enforcement in those areas that were most expensive to taxpayers.

Most likely, fewer resources would be spent on apprehending and convicting victimless criminals, such as prostitutes and marijuana smokers, and more resources would be spent on preventing robberies, assaults, rapes, and murders. We would expect an optimal allocation of resources to prevail within police departments. Also, there might be an effort to streamline the courts in order to increase the probability of conviction. Furthermore, our prisons might be turned into rehabilitation institutions instead of schools for improved future criminal activities.

However, full liability should include a deductible. If people were fully compensated for all losses, then some homeowners, for example, might not bother to lock their houses against potential robbers. And some automobile owners might not lock their cars. If a deductible of, for example, $250, were to be included, then individuals would still have an incentive to protect their persons and property, but the local government would compensate victims of crime for all damages sustained in excess of $250.

over the head on the street by a robber, you would probably try to sue the offender—if he or she were apprehended. But in most cases you certainly wouldn't get much money. Also, if somebody is supporting you and that person is killed by a crazy gangster, you as the dependent would be able to collect nothing from the gangster, the state, or the government. In fact, you would probably end up paying because the criminal might be apprehended and sent to jail. You, as a taxpayer, would end up paying for his or her care while in jail. In short, you get it coming and going.

A Solution—Full Liability

What is the solution? One solution might be for individual local govern-

and $1,000 is paid to the Dodgers. If the $1,000 per annum exceeds the player's net value to the Dodgers after paying his $20,000 a year salary, then it will be in the Dodgers' best interest to sell his contract to the Giants. On the other hand, if this particular player is worth more to the Dodgers than $21,000, which is equal to the $1,000 offer from the Giants plus this player's $20,000 salary, it will refuse to sell his contract.

Surprisingly enough, under the reserve clause, the condition under which this player will be transferred to the Giants is exactly the condition under which he will decide himself to transfer to the Giants when not subject to the reserve clause. He transfers to the Giants if the Giants find his services more valuable than the Dodgers *whether or not the reserve clause is effective.* We must conclude that the reserve clause does not cause a different distribution of players among teams than would obtain otherwise. This is a surprising result, indeed, but it does serve to discredit the absurd allegations of baseball club owners. They want to keep the reserve clause because they, not the players, are the ones who reap the benefits of the services of exceptional players.

Monopsony and Monopoly

This is a classic monopsony situation. However, the only way it can persist is for there to be some sort of monopoly in the baseball business. After all, competition among teams would cause the starting salaries of players to go up. For a while

"side payments" or bonuses were paid to new players. But then the draft system was inaugurated and no such payments were allowed. The impact of the reserve clause on players' salaries was, for quite a time, augmented by the effects of a compact between the National and American Leagues *not* to compete for each other's players. Such an arrangement would obviously suggest a potential for a third league to bid the best players away from the other two by offering higher salaries. However, no third United States league could have succeeded because players who might have signed with it would have been barred forever from the American and National Leagues. Apparently not enough players are willing to take this chance and no other major league has appeared.

Baseball can get away with such obvious restraints of trade because Supreme Court Justice Oliver Wendell Holmes wrote a decision in 1922 which said that professional baseball was outside the scope of federal antitrust laws. The decision pointed out that baseball games were not trade or commerce in the accepted uses of these words. He supposed that Congress had not intended to subject baseball to antitrust regulation. He went on to say that baseball exhibitions were purely local affairs to which the interstate transportation of players was merely incidental. Again in 1953 the Supreme Court reviewed the antitrust implications of baseball's restraints of trade. Then it did not even examine the underlying issue of interstate commerce; instead, it reaffirmed Holmes' earlier decision. The Court stated: "That

decision determines that Congress had no intention of including the business of baseball within the scope of the federal antitrust laws."

Graphic Analysis

The professional baseball world fits very nicely into the monopsony model developed previously. We can show how much the players lose by the monopolization of baseball and the ability of the clubs to act as monopsonists in their hiring by looking at Figure I-28.1. (The analysis is strictly correct if teams are nondiscriminating monopsonists.) Here we have drawn the value of marginal physical product curve for all baseball players, but we are assuming that the teams have banded together to form a cartel arrangement sanctioned by the Supreme Court rulings. Therefore, the teams will look at their marginal revenue product curve, MRP, and not their VMP curve. We've also drawn the supply curve of baseball players, but that is not what the teams will look at. They will look at the marginal factor cost curve, MFC. They're acting as monopsonists. A competitive situation would find us at point *E*. Here the players would obtain a salary of $20,000 and there would be 1500 professional players. However, the equilibrium wage rate is established by the baseball monopoly first equating the marginal revenue product with the marginal factor cost at point *E'*. That determines the quantity of players demanded. Then the teams figure out how much they have to pay to get that quantity. We'll say they happen to pay $18,000. The

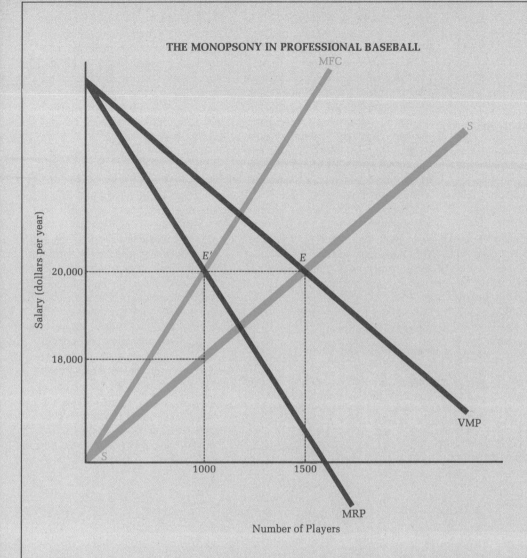

THE MONOPSONY IN PROFESSIONAL BASEBALL

FIGURE I-28.1

The number of players in the entire baseball industry is on the horizontal axis and the salary per year on the vertical axis. The demand curve for players is represented by the marginal revenue product curve, MRP, because the baseball club owners have banded together to form a monopoly. These baseball club owners face an upward-sloping supply curve, *SS*, and therefore look at their marginal factor cost curve, MFC. They decide how many players to hire at the intersection, *E'*, where the marginal factor cost curve and the marginal revenue product curve intersect. They hire 1000 players and pay them a salary of $18,000 per year. In an unrestricted or competitive situation, the equilibrium intersection would be at *E*, with 1500 players working for a salary of $20,000 per year.

monopolist clubs end up paying their players less than they would in a competitive situation; they also end up employing fewer players than they would in a competitive situation.

Other Professional Sports

The analysis we just applied to professional baseball is essentially the same, with minor institutional variations, for football, basketball, hockey, and soccer. We have examples of players' salaries rising astronomically when a competing league comes into being. When the World Hockey League started competing with the National Hockey League, for example, the salaries of hockey players skyrocketed. When the American Basketball Association was formed in 1967, the salaries of first-year players in the competing National Basketball Association jumped from $13,000 to $17,000 a year. By the 1970 to 1971 season, average rookie salaries in the National Basketball Association were nearly $45,000. As one could predict using simple economic theory, there were many attempts by the NBA to merge with the ABA. In fact, by the time you read this, that merger may have been consummated.

The same thing happened in football when the American Football League sprang up to compete with the National Football League. After 6 years of competition, the AFL and the NFL decided to merge. A rider to an investment tax bill allowed the merger—a strategic move worked out by Representative Hale Boggs, a Democrat from Louisiana.[1]

When the World Football League formed in 1974, football players' salaries again began to skyrocket. If the WFL succeeds, we can predict that similar attempts at merging will appear in a few years.

Conclusion

Professional sports are big businesses; they are owned by men and women who have invested large sums of money and who wish to make profits on their investments.

[1]Curiously, New Orleans got a new franchise that year and was also the site of the Superbowl.

Many onlookers maintain that there is nothing wrong with professional sports clubs being business concerns, but these onlookers feel that sports should operate under the same laws as other businesses. The trustbusters have taken on professional sports to that end. Senator Warren G. Magnuson of Washington introduced for several consecutive years a bill that would have included baseball under the Sherman Antitrust Act. Senator Sam Ervin and Representative Emanuel Celler of New York introduced identical bills in the Senate and the House that would have stripped professional basketball and professional football of their antitrust exemptions. The time may be ripe for introducing more competition into professional spectator sports. Whether you think that is "good" or "bad" must ultimately depend on your particular value judgment. The distribution of players among competing clubs will not change, as we explained above. However, the distribution of total earnings from games like baseball will change: The players will get higher salaries and the clubowners will get smaller profits.

Definitions of New Terms

Reserve Clause: A clause in the contract of a professional athlete that essentially transfers the ownership of his playing talents to the first club which hires him. He is reserved to them and cannot change unless they want to allow him to change. They can trade him just like any other asset.

Draft: A system of choosing new players for professional teams. In a draft system teams are not allowed to bid for the best players by offering higher amounts of money. Rather, they draft players in sequence, the worst teams being allowed the first choice.

1. Some baseball players support the reserve clause. They maintain that if it did not exist, competiton among teams would drive salaries so high that many teams would go out of business. If this reasoning is correct, which kind of players should support the reserve clause: the best ones or the worst ones?
2. Do you think that professional sports should be exempt from antitrust laws? Why?
3. Professional teams have agreed not to seduce college stars away from college until 4 years after they enter. Why do you think professional teams agree to this? *(Hint: What services are colleges providing professional teams?)*
4. A few college players have started to go to work for Canadian teams. What are the implications for the future of professional sports in the United States?

**Selected
Reference**

Rottenberg, Simon, ''The Baseball Players' Labor Market,'' *Journal of Political Economy*, June 1956.

24

Wealth, Capital, and Savings

Some people have lots of wealth: yachts, big houses, several cars, big bank accounts, stocks, bonds, and businesses. Some people have very little wealth. How do people obtain wealth? Why is it that some people have more than others? What's the difference between wealth and income? Do savings enter into this picture? These are some of the questions we will answer in this chapter.

Concentration of Wealth

In the United States, wealth is concentrated among a relatively small number of people. Data from the Internal Revenue Service were used by the Urban Institute to study the concentration of wealth among the "superrich." According to these data (which were for 1969), the superrich, defined as the top 4.4 percent of the total adult population in the United States, own

1. 35.6 percent of the nation's wealth
2. 27 percent of all privately owned real estate
3. 33 percent of all cash
4. 40 percent of all noncorporation business assets
5. 63 percent of privately held corporation stock

The study shows that if the nation's total wealth of $3.5 trillion were to be divided equally among all adults over the age of 21, then everyone would have a net worth of approximately $25,000. In reality, an estimated half of the population in 1969 had a net worth of only $3,000, and 4.4 percent of the population had a net worth in excess of $200,000 apiece. The very superrich—the millionaires—represent only 8/100ths of 1 percent of the adult population, yet they hold 8.1 percent of the nation's wealth. Figure 24-1 shows the average amount of wealth held by various income groups.

Wealth

Wealth includes more than tangible objects, such as buildings, machinery, land, cars, and houses. People are wealth also. They have skills, knowledge, initiative, talents, and comprise what is called the human wealth part of our nation's **capital stock.** Capital stock refers to anything that can generate utility to individuals in the future. A fresh ripe tomato is not part of our capital stock. It has to be eaten before it gets rotten, and after it is eaten it can no longer generate utility. The nonhuman aspect of our capital stock has a market value of over $3 trillion. But it is difficult to estimate the value of the human aspect. Human beings do not usually sell themselves like capital goods, and since the abolition of slavery, they have not been auctioned off to the highest bidders.

People can invest in themselves, however. That is, they can engage in human capital investment. One increases one's future productive ability by investing in training or schooling. By going to college, a person is sacrificing current income and consumption in order to be more productive later and to make his or her human capital worth more. Once a person acquires a particular skill or additional education, it is embodied in that person. No one else can take it away (although it can become obsolete).

How to Get Wealth

Let's say that you have no wealth at all except your body. You decide to get a job. You start making income. How do you acquire nonhuman wealth? If you spend everything that you make on consumption goods, you won't be able to get any wealth at all. That is, if you consume everything, nothing will be left over with which to acquire nonhuman wealth like stocks and bonds, houses, and so on. Thus, the way to obtain wealth is to save—that is, to not spend your income on perishable goods. (Of course, you can also obtain wealth either by inheritance or by stealing.) You have to buy durable goods or you have to lend your income to someone else in exchange for the promise to be repaid in the future with interest. At this point, we

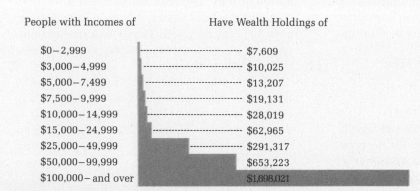

People with Incomes of   Have Wealth Holdings of

$0–2,999	$7,609
$3,000–4,999	$10,025
$5,000–7,499	$13,207
$7,500–9,999	$19,131
$10,000–14,999	$28,019
$15,000–24,999	$62,965
$25,000–49,999	$291,317
$50,000–99,999	$653,223
$100,000– and over	$1,698,021

FIGURE 24-1 Average Amount of Wealth Held by Income Groups

The largest amount of wealth is held by the 700,000 consuming units with incomes of $25,000 or more. A great amount of wealth is held by consuming units with incomes of over $100,000. Even individuals with incomes of less than $3,000 when this survey was done had wealth holdings of almost $8,000. However, many individuals in this category are retired with little or no current income but with a life savings that they are drawing down.

should probably make the distinction between perishable or nondurable goods and nonperishable or durable goods.

Durable and Nondurable Goods

Economists usually call goods that are used up in the very near future "nondurables." When used by consumers, they are also called "consumer nondurable goods." Examples are food, movies, trips to Europe, pencils, and cigarettes. These are goods and services that are bought for non-wealth-increasing purposes. Durable goods cannot be used up right away. They last; they give utility in the future. These durable goods, like houses and cars and stereos, are also called "consumer capital goods." It is these durable or capital goods that add to one's wealth position.

Saving

We mentioned that the only way to acquire wealth is to save. Saving is the process of not consuming part of one's current income. Any time you buy something that lasts—that is, any time you buy a durable or capital good—you are actually saving. This means that people who go out and buy houses and cars aren't really consuming all their income; they are actually saving part of it because they will receive, well into the future, the services of the houses and cars they buy. One of the easiest ways to realize that the purchase of durable goods is actually a form of saving is to see what happens when you go to the bank to take out a loan.

Net Worth

The bank will try to determine your **net worth** position. That is, it will try to determine how much wealth you own outside of your body. You will be asked whether you have any stereos, cameras, cars, and things that could be sold if you were in a pinch. In other words, your durable goods will be treated as part of your net worth or wealth position. If you recently saved up money and bought a car, your wealth position would be higher than if you had not bought the car but, rather, had spent the money on a Caribbean vacation. In determining your wealth position, the bank does not ask you how many trips to the Caribbean you took. If you default on your loan, the bank cannot get you to sell a trip you already took. Obviously, a trip you already took has no market value because it is a consumption good already consumed. Nobody else can have it.

When referring to wealth and capital, we have been talking about a **stock.** We have already discussed the difference between a stock and a flow, but the subject is important enough to go over again.

Stocks and Flows

When the bank tries to determine your wealth position, it tries to determine how much you are worth at a point in time. The wealth that you have is a stock. (Note here we're not talking about stock in a company.) Lots of other things are stocks, too, such as a building you might own. Stocks are defined independently of time although they are assessed at a point in time. A car dealer can have a stock or inventory of cars that may be worth $500,000. A timber company may have 5 acres of $3,000 worth of trees; this is a stock of trees.

On the other hand, the income you make is a flow. Remember, a **flow** is an ongoing concept, a stream of things through time. It is a certain number of things per time period. You receive so many dollars a week or so many dollars per month or so many dollars per year. The number of trees (that is, the change in board-feet) which grow in a forest is a flow of trees; it is a certain number of trees per time period, such as a year. The number of cars that a car dealer sells per week is a flow. Flows, in other words, are defined for a specific period of time.

If you want to add to your stock of wealth or capital, you must save. That is, you must not consume part of your income. The act of saving is a flow that makes your stock of wealth larger. You should not confuse the act of saving with how much you have in savings. Savings is a stock concept akin to wealth, as we have defined it. If you have $5,000 in a savings account, you have a stock of $5,000 of accumulated savings. If you want to increase that stock, you have to save more. You have to add a flow of saving to your stock of savings.

There is a big difference, for example, between a millionaire and someone who makes $1 million a year. The person who makes $1 million a year is probably much richer than the former. The millionaire has a stock of wealth worth $1 million; however, individuals who make $1 million a year have a flow of income equal to $1 million per year—year in and year out. They could easily save a big chunk of that $1 million each year to add to their wealth or savings so that in time they would be much more than mere millionaires. They could become multimillionaires in very short order. We can translate a flow of income or saving into a stock of wealth through a procedure called **present value** discounting.

Present Values

If someone gave you a choice between receiving $1 a year for the rest of your life or $20 today, which would you prefer? You might be hard-pressed to decide which was the better deal. It's hard to assess the value of dollars coming in at the end of each year, year in and year out. A dollar 10 years from now will certainly not be as desirable as a dollar today. In fact, you might even be dead 10 years from now, so the dollar would do you no good at all. The point is that dollars today are worth more than dollars tomorrow. You have to *discount* future dollars to figure out what they're worth to you today.

Discounting is a term we apply to the procedure of reducing *future* values to show how much they are actually worth today. We reduce them by a discount factor that depends on the discount rate we use. The discount rate we use is some interest rate. Let's say that you could take your money and put it in a savings and loan institution. At the savings and loan institution you might get a 5 percent rate of return on your savings. If you put in $1 today, you would have $1.05 a year from now. The discounted value of $1.05 to be received a year hence, using a discount rate of 5 percent, is only $1. Or, put another way, the discounted value of $1 one year from now at a 5 percent rate is about 95¢. You could put your 95¢ in today and get about $1 in a year. Two years from now, a dollar would be worth even less. You could put in about 91¢ today and have a dollar 2 years from now. The point is that *a dollar received in the future is worth less than a dollar received today*. In Table 24-1 we show various present values of future dollars at the end of specified years for particular interest rates. The higher the interest rate (that is, the higher the amount you could actually get by investing your savings), the lower the value of dollars in the future. Moreover, the farther in the future you get those dollars, the smaller the present value.

Annuities

We still haven't answered the question of whether you would want to take $20 today or

Table 24-1 Present Values of a Future Dollar

Each column shows how much a dollar received at the end of a certain number of years in the future (identified on the extreme left-hand or right-hand column) is worth today. For example, at 5 percent a year, a dollar to be received 20 years in the future is worth only 37.7¢. At the end of 50 years, it isn't even worth a dime today. To find out how much $10,000 would be worth a certain number of years from now, just multiply the figures in the columns by 10,000. For example, $10,000 received at the end of 10 years discounted at a 5 percent rate of interest would be equal to $6,140.

NUMBER OF YEARS	3%	4%	5%	6%	8%	10%	20%	NUMBER OF YEARS
1	0.971	0.962	0.952	0.943	0.926	0.909	0.833	1
2	0.943	0.925	0.907	0.890	0.857	0.826	0.694	2
3	0.915	0.890	0.864	0.839	0.794	0.751	0.578	3
4	0.889	0.855	0.823	0.792	0.735	0.683	0.482	4
5	0.863	0.823	0.784	0.747	0.681	0.620	0.402	5
6	0.838	0.790	0.746	0.705	0.630	0.564	0.335	6
7	0.813	0.760	0.711	0.665	0.583	0.513	0.279	7
8	0.789	0.731	0.677	0.627	0.540	0.466	0.233	8
9	0.766	0.703	0.645	0.591	0.500	0.424	0.194	9
10	0.744	0.676	0.614	0.558	0.463	0.385	0.162	10
11	0.722	0.650	0.585	0.526	0.429	0.350	0.134	11
12	0.701	0.625	0.557	0.497	0.397	0.318	0.112	12
13	0.681	0.601	0.530	0.468	0.368	0.289	0.0935	13
14	0.661	0.577	0.505	0.442	0.340	0.263	0.0779	14
15	0.642	0.555	0.481	0.417	0.315	0.239	0.0649	15
16	0.623	0.534	0.458	0.393	0.292	0.217	0.0541	16
17	0.605	0.513	0.436	0.371	0.270	0.197	0.0451	17
18	0.587	0.494	0.416	0.350	0.250	0.179	0.0376	18
19	0.570	0.475	0.396	0.330	0.232	0.163	0.0313	19
20	0.554	0.456	0.377	0.311	0.215	0.148	0.0261	20
25	0.478	0.375	0.295	0.232	0.146	0.0923	0.0105	25
30	0.412	0.308	0.231	0.174	0.0994	0.0573	0.00421	30
40	0.307	0.208	0.142	0.0972	0.0460	0.0221	0.000680	40
50	0.228	0.141	0.087	0.0543	0.0213	0.00852	0.000109	50

have $1 a year for the rest of your life. What if you could put that $20 in a savings account? If it yielded 5 percent, you could get a dollar a year forever. So at an interest rate of 5 percent, and assuming you will live quite a while, you would be indifferent to receiving $20 or receiving an **annuity** of $1 a year forever. How-

ever, if you thought you could get 10 percent if you invested or saved that $20, you would prefer getting the $20 today rather than $1 a year. At a 10 percent rate a year, you could get $2 a year in interest: You'd obviously be better off.

In Table 24-2 we show the present value of

Table 24-2 **Present Value of an Annuity of $1**

Here we show the present value of $1 received at the end of each year for a specified number of years. For example, the present value of a dollar received at the end of each year for 10 years at an interest rate of 5 percent would be $7.72. If it were received for 50 years, it would have a present value of $18.30.

NUMBER OF YEARS	3%	4%	5%	6%	8%	10%	20%	NUMBER OF YEARS
1	0.971	0.962	0.952	0.943	0.926	0.909	0.833	1
2	1.91	1.89	1.86	1.83	1.78	1.73	1.53	2
3	2.83	2.78	2.72	2.67	2.58	2.48	2.11	3
4	3.72	3.63	3.55	3.46	3.31	3.16	2.59	4
5	4.58	4.45	4.33	4.21	3.99	3.79	2.99	5
6	5.42	5.24	5.08	4.91	4.62	4.35	3.33	6
7	6.23	6.00	5.79	5.58	5.21	4.86	3.60	7
8	7.02	6.73	6.46	6.20	5.75	5.33	3.84	8
9	7.79	7.44	7.11	6.80	6.25	5.75	4.03	9
10	8.53	8.11	7.72	7.36	6.71	6.14	4.19	10
11	9.25	8.76	8.31	7.88	7.14	6.49	4.33	11
12	9.95	9.39	8.86	8.38	7.54	6.81	4.44	12
13	10.6	9.99	9.39	8.85	7.90	7.10	4.53	13
14	11.3	10.6	9.90	9.29	8.24	7.36	4.61	14
15	11.9	11.1	10.4	9.71	8.56	7.60	4.68	15
16	12.6	11.6	10.8	10.1	8.85	7.82	4.73	16
17	13.2	12.2	11.3	10.4	9.12	8.02	4.77	17
18	13.8	12.7	11.7	10.8	9.37	8.20	4.81	18
19	14.3	13.1	12.1	11.1	9.60	8.36	4.84	19
20	14.9	13.6	12.5	11.4	9.82	8.51	4.87	20
25	17.4	15.6	14.1	12.8	10.7	9.08	4.95	25
30	19.6	17.3	15.4	13.8	11.3	9.43	4.98	30
40	23.1	19.8	17.2	15.0	11.9	9.78	5.00	40
50	25.7	21.5	18.3	15.8	12.2	9.91	5.00	50
∞	33.3	25.0	20.0	16.7	12.5	10.0	5.00	∞

an annuity of $1 received at the end of each year. Various interest rates for assessing that annuity and various time periods are shown. You can see that the higher the interest rate, the lower the value of the annuity. That's because at higher interest rates, the present value of a dollar in the future is worth less than at lower interest rates. At higher interest rates, you would often be better off getting a lump sum payment today than an annuity. This is similar to the first example, where you'd be better off getting $20 today than $1 a year forever if the interest rate exceeds 5 percent.

Now you see how a future stream of income can be translated into a present value of wealth figure. Businesspersons determine how much they should pay for an investment by similar procedures. They look at expected profits on a potential investment through the years and discount these profits back to the present. This tells them how much the investment is worth and the maximum amount they should pay for it. If the person selling the investment wants more than the present value of the discounted future profits, it probably would be a mistake for our businessperson to buy it.

Let's take a specific example. Assume that a McDonald's hamburger stand is expected to yield a profit of $10,000 for 50 years. How much would a businessperson pay for that McDonald's hamburger stand? Look at Table 24-2. We have to multiply everything by 10,000 because the table is based on $1 per year. Then we have to decide on an appropriate rate of interest for discounting purposes. The discount rate will be determined by what we could do with our money if we invested it in something else. Let's say we thought we could make 10 percent by investing in something else. At an interest rate of 10 percent, $1 per year for 50 years is worth only $9.91 today. Therefore, $10,000 every year for 50 years is worth, at a 10 percent interest, $99,100. If the prospective seller of the McDonald's wanted more than $99,100, it wouldn't be worthwhile to buy the hamburger stand. If he or she wanted less than this amount, it would.

The Nature of Compound Interest

The opposite of discounting dollars into the future is **compounding** dollars into the future. If you decide to add to your capital stock or wealth position by not consuming all your income, you can take what you save and (loosely speaking) invest it. You can put it in the stock market or you can buy bonds—that is, lend money to businesses. You can also put it in your own business. In any event, you might expect to make a profit or interest every year

in the future for a certain amount of time. To figure out how much you will have at the end of any specified time period, you have to *compound* your savings yield, and, just as in discounting, you have to use a specified interest rate. Let's go back to the simple case of putting money in a savings and loan association that yields 5 percent per year (ignoring personal income taxes). At the end of 1 year, you have $1.05. At the end of 2 years, you have $1.05 plus 5 percent of $1.05—$0.0525—or $1.1025. And this continues every year.

The power of compound interest is, indeed, truly amazing. Look at Table 24-3. Here we show $1 compounded every year for 1 to 50 years at different interest rates. At an interest rate of 10 percent, $1 at the end of 50 years will equal $117. This means that if you inherited a modest $10,000 when you were 20 years old and put it in an investment which paid 10 percent after taxes every year compounded, you would end up at 70 years of age with $1,170,000. Now it's not hard to understand how some people become millionaires. It usually doesn't take much brains or much business acumen to get a 10 percent rate of return on your savings. If somebody had invested in the stock market 50 years ago, he or she would have received a lot more than 10 percent. A number of people inherit moderate amounts of money when they are quite young. If this money is put into the stock market and left there to compound itself, it grows to quite unbelievable amounts after 30 or 40 years. One should be careful about analyzing the astuteness of elderly millionaires; they could have been very conservative and done nothing with the money they inherited except put it into the stock market and leave it there. No business sense would have been needed at all and the person could easily have become a millionaire by the age of 65.

The power of compound interest should also

Table 24-3 $1 Compounded Annually at Different Interest Rates

Here we show the value of the dollar at the end of a specified period after it has been compounded annually at a specified interest rate. For example, if you took $1 today and invested it at 5 percent, it would yield $1.05 at the end of the year. At the end of 10 years, it would be equal to $1.63, and at the end of 50 years, it would be equal to $11.50.

NUMBER OF YEARS	3%	4%	5%	6%	8%	10%	20%	NUMBER OF YEARS
1	1.03	1.04	1.05	1.06	1.08	1.10	1.20	1
2	1.06	1.08	1.10	1.12	1.17	1.21	1.44	2
3	1.09	1.12	1.16	1.19	1.26	1.33	1.73	3
4	1.13	1.17	1.22	1.26	1.36	1.46	2.07	4
5	1.16	1.22	1.28	1.34	1.47	1.61	2.49	5
6	1.19	1.27	1.34	1.41	1.59	1.77	2.99	6
7	1.23	1.32	1.41	1.50	1.71	1.94	3.58	7
8	1.27	1.37	1.48	1.59	1.85	2.14	4.30	8
9	1.30	1.42	1.55	1.68	2.00	2.35	5.16	9
10	1.34	1.48	1.63	1.79	2.16	2.59	6.19	10
11	1.38	1.54	1.71	1.89	2.33	2.85	7.43	11
12	1.43	1.60	1.80	2.01	2.52	3.13	8.92	12
13	1.47	1.67	1.89	2.13	2.72	3.45	10.7	13
14	1.51	1.73	1.98	2.26	2.94	3.79	12.8	14
15	1.56	1.80	2.08	2.39	3.17	4.17	15.4	15
16	1.60	1.87	2.18	2.54	3.43	4.59	18.5	16
17	1.65	1.95	2.29	2.69	3.70	5.05	22.2	17
18	1.70	2.03	2.41	2.85	4.00	5.55	26.6	18
19	1.75	2.11	2.53	3.02	4.32	6.11	31.9	19
20	1.81	2.19	2.65	3.20	4.66	6.72	38.3	20
25	2.09	2.67	3.39	4.29	6.85	10.8	95.4	25
30	2.43	3.24	4.32	5.74	10.0	17.4	237	30
40	3.26	4.80	7.04	10.3	21.7	45.3	1470	40
50	4.38	7.11	11.5	18.4	46.9	117	9100	50

tip you off as to the true worth of many investment schemes. Take high-priced paintings. Often art dealers will tell you that paintings are good investments. They will cite, for example, a Picasso that somebody purchased for only $5,000 and then sold for $15,000. You should find out, however, the dates when it was purchased and sold. Looked at in this way, the actual gain in value might be very modest, say only 3 percent a year. After all, if the painting cost $1,000 in 1950, at a 3 percent compound interest, it would be worth over $2,000 in 1975. The person who sold it in 1975 could boast that the investment was doubled, whereas she or he probably could have done better if, in 1950, the $1,000 had been put into a savings account that yielded 4 or 5 percent; he or she would have done even better if the money had been put into the stock market because then the rate of return would have been 8 to 12 percent on the average. Usually paintings yield a lower rate of return than savings accounts or the stock market because people get some consumption pleasure from having the paintings in their houses. They are, therefore, willing to receive a lower rate of return than they would if they had put the money in some other type of investment.

The Unkind Truth

Even though the power of compound interest is indeed staggering, particularly at higher in-terest rates, the fact remains that the only way to increase wealth is not to consume all of what you make as income. Unless you plan on inheriting something or stealing wealth from others, you will not be a wealthy person if you consume everything you earn. The larger the percentage of your income you decide to save, the larger your wealth will be in the future. The better the investment, the higher the rate of return, and, again, the larger your wealth will be in the future. You do have the option of investing in your own personal human wealth or capital and that's exactly what one does by going to college. You will probably be wealthier because of this investment since your productivity and, hence, the wage rate you will make in the future will be higher.

Definitions of New Terms

Capital Stock: The sum total of all human and nonhuman wealth in the United States. Included are buildings, machinery, land, cars, houses, and the productive talents of human beings.

Net Worth: The difference between the assets and liabilities of an individual or a business. Your net worth position can be found by adding up the value of everything you own and subtracting the amount you owe. The difference is your net worth.

Stock: The quantity of something at a point in time. An inventory of goods is a stock. A bank account at a point in time is a stock. Stocks are defined independently of time although they are assessed at a point in time. Different from a flow.

Flow: Something defined per unit time period. Income is a flow that occurs per week, per month, or per year. Consumption is a flow. So is saving.

Present Value: The value of something that occurs in the future. The present value of a dollar tomorrow is less than a dollar today. Present values are obtained by discounting future dollar figures.

Discounting: The procedure used to reduce future values to their present values. Discounting requires the use of a discount rate, which is the interest rate decided upon as appropriate for each particular case.

Annuity: A specified income payable at stated intervals for a fixed period.

Compounding: The process of allowing the interest on an investment or savings to yield interest itself, thereby being compounded.

1. The total wealth of the United States consists of the nonhuman wealth and the human wealth, the human wealth being the productive capacities of individuals.
2. The only way to obtain wealth besides stealing it or inheriting it is by not consuming everything that you make. In other words, you have to save to acquire wealth. Your wealth is then your accumulated savings.
3. It is useful to distinguish between stocks and flows. A stock of wealth is something you have accumulated and can measure at a point in time. You obtain a flow of income, however, for a specific period. Your income is so many dollars per week or per month. Your saving is also a flow concept. You save at a rate of so many dollars per week or per month or per year. On the other hand, your savings is a stock, the result of your past saving.
4. To assess the value of future dollars, it is necessary to reduce those future dollars by discounting them to the present value; discounting requires using an appropriate interest rate.
5. Compound interest is exceedingly powerful. A small amount of money left in a savings account at 5 percent a year ends up being quite a large amount of money at the end of, for example, 50 years.

1. In some universities and colleges you can receive loans at interest rates that are very low relative to what you would have to pay in the open market. If you could borrow money at 5 percent per year on these special loans even though you didn't need it, do you think it would be worthwhile to take advantage of it? Why? (*Hint:* Could you earn more than the 5 percent interest if you invested the money?)
2. If you decide to save all your income over the next 2 years, what happens to the value of your wealth position right now? In 1 year? In 2 years?
3. Are there any people around with no wealth at all?
4. Would you rather be given $1 million today or $100,000 a year for the rest of your life?

Restrictions on Rates of Return

USURY LAWS AND SELECTIVE CREDIT CONTROLS

Savers and Borrowers Getting Together

When individuals save—when they do not consume—they usually seek to obtain a positive rate of return on their savings. A positive rate of return often (but not always) can be obtained by investing in the stock market or by lending money to corporations or the government by buying their bonds. Alternatively, individuals can put money in savings and loan associations and receive an interest on those savings. There are many savings outlets where the wealth of individuals increases because of interest earned or a positive rate of return obtained.

On the other side of the picture is the process of dissaving, or borrowing. We know that since the total quantity of resources in the economy is fixed at any point in time, for every borrower there must be a saver, at least in quantitative terms. The market where savers and borrowers get together is called the *credit market*. In this issue, we won't go into the operation of the credit market in great detail; rather, we'll look at what happens when restrictions are placed on both (1) the prices that

can prevail in the credit market, and (2) the rate of return that individuals can receive in different types of savings outlets.

Usury Laws

The price charged in the credit market for borrowing money is called the *interest rate*. When ceilings are put on interest rates, **usury laws** have been applied—**usury** meaning lending money at "unreasonable rates." The history of usury laws is long indeed.

Babylonians permitted credit but restricted the rate of interest. The Bible (Deuteronomy 23:19–20) tells us that "Unto a stranger thou mayest lend upon usury; but unto thy brother thou shalt not lend upon usury." In Luke 6:35 of the New Testament we are told that we must "lend freely, hoping nothing thereby."

One of the earliest economists, Aristotle, considered money to be sterile. The "breeding" of money from money was unnatural and justly to be hated. During the Roman republic, no interest charges were permitted, but by the time of the

Roman Empire, this restriction was relaxed.

During the Middle Ages, the Catholic Church had very specific rules against lending money at interest. Such a pursuit of wealth was considered sinful because humility and charity were the greatest virtues that could be obtained. Secular legislation responded to the Church's influence at that time, and interest and usury were regarded as synonymous.

In the United States, most usury laws were inherited during the Colonial days, from the British. It is interesting to note that most of these usury laws still remain in force in the United States, but Great Britain repealed them in 1854.

Let's take a look at a specific instance where a usury law was passed in a state.

The Case of Washington State

Prior to 1968, interest rates on consumer loans from the credit card companies—BankAmericard, Master Charge, and so on—as well as revolving credit loans from the big stores—Sears and others—were generally 18 percent per annum, or 1.5 percent per month, in the state of Washington. Many consumer advocates and concerned citizens felt that this rate of interest was much too high. At that time, commercial bank loans to some customers were going for as low as 9 percent. It was felt that poor people were the ones being discriminated against because they could not "afford" the high interest charge. They therefore had to forgo the benefits of being able to buy on time. A movement was started to pass legislation against such usurious interest rates.

In 1968 a motion was put on the ballot to set the maximum legal interest rate on consumer loans at 12 percent instead of 18 percent. It was felt that lowering the interest rate would benefit those who could not afford the higher rate.

The measure passed quite successfully, and all the credit card companies and stores in the state were forced to lower their rates to 1 percent per month, or 12 percent a year. We should be able to analyze and predict what happens after such legislation is enacted.

Supply and Demand Analysis

Let's simplify our analysis and assume that the only money market which existed in the state of Washington was the consumer credit market represented by the major credit card companies and the individual stores that offered their own revolving credit cards. Let's further assume that, during the period under study, there is no technological change in the credit card business. That is, no new computerized technique lowers the cost of being able to process bills and so on.

Figure I-29.1 shows the demand and supply of credit in the state of Washington. At higher interest rates, credit card institutions will be willing to lend more money. At lower interest rates they will want to lend less money. Obviously, the reverse relationship holds for the demand side. If the price of credit falls, more credit is demanded, and we move down our downward-sloping demand schedule (*DD*). Here we see that the supply and demand schedules intersect at an interest rate of 18 percent per year. This is the equilibrium or market

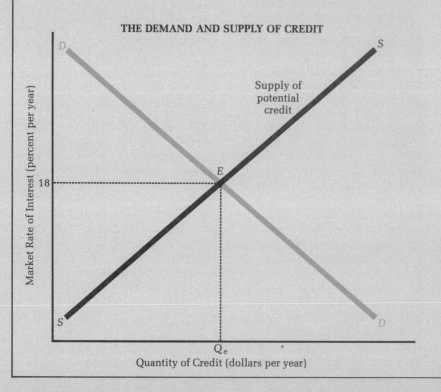

THE DEMAND AND SUPPLY OF CREDIT

FIGURE I-29.1

At a lower price, more credit will be demanded. The supply curve slopes upward. At higher interest rates, more credit will be supplied. The equilibrium is established at the intersection of the demand and supply curves, *E*. The quantity supplied and demanded at that equilibrium interest rate of 18 percent is Q_e.

clearing rate. Now obviously it is true that at 18 percent, some people will feel they cannot "afford" credit. These people will not partake in obtaining command over goods and services today by promising to pay back the principle and an interest rate in future days. They will consume only when they have enough current income to do so. Many people who feel they cannot afford to borrow are indeed less wealthy than most of those who do borrow.

Borrowing As a Form of Dissaving

We define *saving* as a method of obtaining optimal consumption over a lifetime. Borrowing can be viewed both as a form of dissaving and also as a form of obtaining optimal consumption over one's lifetime. The decision to borrow to buy today depends upon how much one values getting something today rather than in the future. In economic parlance, we call this the person's personal *discount* rate. A person's discount rate is determined subjectively by his or her own impatience. If you have a high discount rate, you are very impatient; you want to consume now. If you have a very low discount rate, you are willing to wait longer before consuming. If your personal discount rate is substantially higher than the rate of interest you will be charged for borrowing, then you will probably end up borrowing—provided you have sufficient credit worthiness.

Your credit worthiness is usually based upon the probability that you will be able to pay off your loan as it comes due. Obviously, you could have an extremely high discount rate

(be very impatient) and not be able to borrow anything because the prospects of your paying the loan back might be very low. No one would want to lend you money, which is usually the case with students. They want to borrow—buy on credit—but have difficulty doing so because they have no credit rating, no job, and so on.

If we assume that the supply schedule presented in Figure I-29.1 is representative of the actual situation, then the equilibrium price of 18 percent for credit represents the lowest price possible in Washington state, given the then current technology and the desire of savers to forgo present consumption.

Setting the Maximum Rate below the Equilibrium Rate

Now a new law sets the maximum rate below the market clearing equilibrium rate. Now only 12 percent per year, or 1 percent per month can be charged on loans. We see in Figure I-29.2 that, at 12 percent, there is an excess demand for credit equal to the difference between Q_d and Q_s. At an interest rate of 12 percent, suppliers of credit are willing to give out only Q_s in loans, but demanders want much more. How are things resolved?

The first thing which happens is that those who lend money seek out ways to get around the legal limit. Many companies that were formerly not imposing a service charge on small amounts of borrowed money start doing so. Companies also begin to set other rules. Some start charging a fee for opening an account, for example. There are numerous

methods of skirting the law, but these are insignificant compared to what happens after things are sorted out. At a rate of 12 percent, lenders eventually find that their profits aren't as high as before. If we assume the equilibrium was at 18 percent before the legislation, a credit price of 12 percent means that the less efficient lenders now earn less than the normal or competitive rate of return. Their costs are now high relative to the revenues made from lending money. These companies, and some of the others too, attempt to find ways to cut their costs. One way to do this is to eliminate some of the bad (potential and actual) accounts—the ones that don't pay up. But how do companies decide which are the bad accounts when people come to apply for loans? They look at past behavior and at future earnings possibilities. Who do you think are the people denied credit at 12 percent?

The Poor Lose Out Again

Obviously, the people who have the worst credit worthiness are the ones denied credit at 12 percent. Welfare mothers, people with records of unstable employment, easily distinguishable minority groups, such as blacks and Puerto Ricans, students, and very old people fall into this category. The fact is that this list includes just about every group of people which the legislation was originally supposed to help.

Who Benefits?

Surprise! The people who benefit from lower interest rates on con-

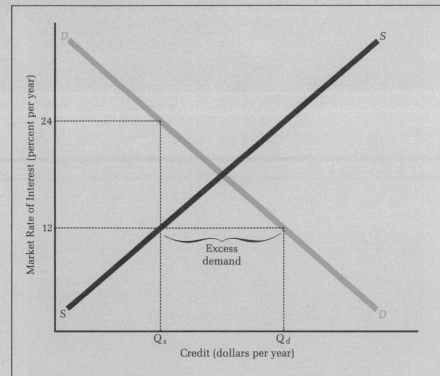

FIGURE I-29.2

When a legal maximum interest rate of 12 percent is imposed on credit cards, the quantity demanded will be Q_d but the quantity supplied will be Q_s. The difference will be excess demand. How is this excess demand taken care of? Credit companies will find out how to charge higher prices for credit, and some borrowers will seek out other sources of credit that will cost more—such as the friendly local finance company.

sumer credit are the ones who have the best credit worthiness. They are the ones with the most money, the best jobs, and the highest probability of being able to pay off. These are the people who gain, and the poor are once again left out.

The Lesson To Be Learned

Usury laws have pernicious long-run effects. Our simplified example of the state of Washington ignored all the other credit markets available to high-risk borrowers. If, for example, these high-risk borrowers are refused credit from BankAmericard, they can go to their local finance company or, worse, to the local loan shark, where interest rates are not restricted. The borrowers end up paying a much higher price. We see in Figure I-29.2 that the quantity of credit supplied at 12 percent can be sold at, say, 24 percent interest rates. That is, if suppliers are willing to lend only at Q_s, credit-hungry demanders will be willing to pay 24 percent to get some of that smaller supply. This means that many people will go to finance companies and other credit institutions and end up paying more than they would have paid if the legal maximum had not been set.

You Have to Pay to Get Money

Money will usually be lent if the lender is compensated enough. (The compensation is, of course, interest.) Also, there is no reason to believe that people will forgo consumption today unless they are paid for it. In other words, people who save or who provide the money that goes into credit must be compensated. In addition, there are costs to distributing credit and costs to making sure that contracts are fulfilled. Since there are many different money markets and credit institutions, we can be reasonably sure there is some sort of competition among them. Therefore, the price one is charged for credit probably represents the opportunity cost of providing that credit (including, as always, the normal rate of return for the lending institutions). Most of the time it is not the disadvantaged groups in our society who are helped when the government sets maximum legal interest rates for lending. In fact, as we have seen, these groups may be worse off.

This same analysis holds for government restrictions on how much borrowers can offer lenders in order to control their money.

Selective Credit Controls

For many years now there have also been restrictions in our economy on the amount of interest that banks can *pay* to savers. The reasons for these selective credit controls are varied. One is to prevent "destructive competition" in the banking industry.

The yield offered by savings banks for your dollars are certainly higher than your dollars can earn in your wallet. However, if it were not for government regulation, savings (time) account yields would be even higher. This has not always been true, but certainly it is true today with our high inflation. The Federal Reserve regulates all interest rates paid by member banks via **Regulation Q.** During the current period of rising interest rates, the ceilings established by Regulation Q have created a large differential between government security yields and the yields offered by member banks.

Graphic Analysis of Zero Interest Rate for Checking Accounts

We can use our tools of supply and demand analysis to analyze the effect of a zero interest rate restriction on checking account balances. We

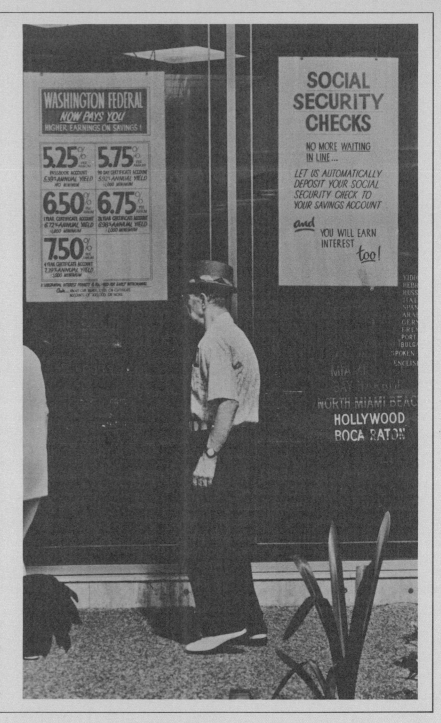

see in Figure I-29.3 that the demand curve for checking account balances is downward sloping. At higher interest rates, banks demand fewer deposits; at lower prices, they demand more. The supply curve is upward sloping. The equilibrium interest rate that exists without restrictions occurs at a rate of i_e; the quantity both supplied and demanded is Q_e. However, at a zero interest rate, the quantity demanded by the various banks is greater than the quantity supplied by the public. There is a gap between the two, which creates excess demand. Banks want more deposits than the public is willing to give them. Something obviously has to give—and it does.

Competition in Banking

Competing banks attempt to lure you to their doors by offering you "free" checking accounts and checks with pretty pictures on them. Also, the banks put branches in every block so you don't have to walk too far. These little competitive gimmicks on the part of regulated banks serve to

THE DEMAND AND SUPPLY FOR CHECKING ACCOUNT BALANCES

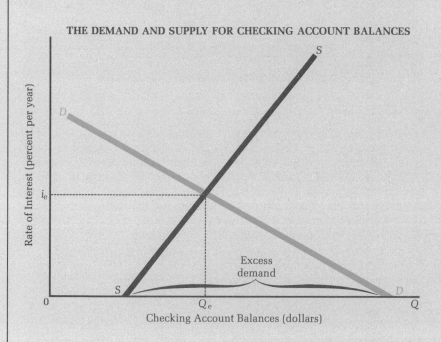

FIGURE I-29.3

Banks demand checking account balances because they can use the proceeds to purchase earning assets such as loans or government bonds. They have a demand schedule for checking account balances, *DD*, which is downward sloping. The supply schedule is upward sloping, and it represents the amount of checking account balances that individuals are willing to leave in banks. Notice that at a zero interest rate, the quantity supplied is positive. That means that individuals would be willing to leave a positive amount of money in a checking account balance even if they were paid nothing for doing so because there are benefits from being able to write checks. The equilibrium rate of interest is established at the intersection of *DD* and *SS*. It occurs at rate i_e. The equilibrium quantity of checking account balances is Q_e. At a zero interest rate, there's an excess demand for checking account balances by banks. This excess demand leads to nonprice competition in the banking industry. You get free checking accounts and other free services from the bank. This effectively raises the rate of interest you are paid on your checking account balance. Banks also compete by opening up branch offices near you.

raise the "price" paid for your supplying deposits and raise the costs to the banks as well. Eventually an equilibrium will be established. In some cities, this equilibrium occurs when banks can no longer fit more branches into the downtown area without demolishing all the hotels.

Destructive Competition

Interest rate ceilings such as those described here were established with the hope that there would be no destructive competition in the banking industry. It was hoped that if no interest rate wars (not unlike gas wars) were allowed to occur in the banking industry, there would be less chance of bank failures. The rationale for such laws was that if banks had to pay higher interest rates, they would be forced to take on riskier loans, that is, loans with a high degree of risk for which they would thus charge higher interest rates to get the higher income to pay a higher yield to their depositors. If enough high-risk loans did default, the banks might fail.

However, with the development of federal insurance for all deposits in member banks under the **Federal Deposit Insurance Corporation (FDIC),** the likelihood of widespread bank failures was greatly reduced. Why would you withdraw your money from a bank if you knew it was completely insured? You would withdraw your money only if you wanted to spend it.

Housing Hurt

The effects of Regulation Q have been painfully obvious in the past

several years, with market interest rates greatly exceeding ceiling rates. One particularly obvious example concerns the housing industry, which did very poorly during the latter part of the 1960s and early 1970s. Since ceiling rates for savings and loan associations were below comparable market interest rates available on securities with similar risks, few savings flowed into savings and loan associations despite the "free" gifts they offered.[1] Although these institutions were able to rent out mortgage money at a high rate of 9 percent, they were still unable to obtain people's savings to increase the supply of mortgages because they could still offer only 5 percent yields to savers. Had they not been regulated, they could have

[1]Effective regulation can cause economic agents specializing in one endeavor to expand into other areas. Thus, savings and loan associations have on occasion become small-appliance distributors.

raised the yields offered to savers and obtained more funds with which to buy mortgages. Mortgage interest rates would not have risen as high and more mortgage money would have been available.

Regulating Bank Credit

Current attempts at regulating interest rates are sometimes justified by policymakers as a necessary control on bank credit for the purpose of economic stabilization. But Regulation Q cannot control total credit in the economy. Funds that leave bank savings deposits because of the rate differential will be channeled into unregulated markets. Although the growth of total credit is probably little affected by Regulation Q, the allocation of credit most certainly is. Funds do not flow into the regulated financial intermediaries such as savings and loan associations and mutual savings banks; they flow into unregulated markets where lucky borrowers are able to obtain funds more cheaply.

All those borrowers who must rely on regulated institutions are forced to pay a higher price or find that funds are simply unavailable. Those who wish to save are put in a similar situation. People with large amounts of liquid funds and a knowledge of capital markets can receive a high rate of return. Those who must rely on regulated institutions to hold and accumulate their savings end up receiving a much lower return than if all banks were free to compete.

Interest rate restrictions on finan-cial markets impose inequities in the economy. These restrictions dis-criminate against the regulated fi-nancial institutions, housing, and small savers. If this were generally realized, monetary authorities might wish to reevaluate them. The people hurt by usury laws are the same ones hurt by credit controls!

Definitions of New Terms	**Usury Laws:** Laws prohibiting the charging of an interest rate in excess of a statutory maximum; usually set by the individual states and varying with the type of loan (that is, the use to which the borrowed money will be put).
	Usury: The lending of money at an exorbitant interest rate or one that exceeds the legal maximum.
	Regulation Q: A Federal Reserve regulation listing the maximum interest rate that member banks can pay on such things as savings accounts and checking accounts. The maximum Regulation Q ceiling rate on checking accounts is zero percent.
	Federal Deposit Insurance Corporation (FDIC): An agency set up in 1933 to insure the deposit liabilities of member banks and qualify nonmember banks that voluntarily become members of the FDIC. Almost 100 percent of all depositors have their deposits insured up to a maximum of $40,000 by the Federal Deposit Insurance Corporation.

Questions for Thought and Discussion	1. Why do some people pay for checking accounts?
	2. Can you think of an instance where a usury law would be appropriate?
	3. Who are the people who benefit from the regulation of savings and loan associations?

Selected References	Board of Governors of the Federal Reserve System, *The Federal Reserve System: Purposes and Functions,* 5th ed., Washington, D.C.: U.S. Government Printing Office, 1963.
	Homer, Sidney, *A History of Interest Rates,* New Brunswick, N.J.: Rutgers University Press, 1963.
	Seidl, John M., "Let's Compete with Loan Sharks," *Harvard Business Review,* May–June 1970, pp. 69–77.

The Distribution of Income

Everyone knows there are a lot of rich people around, and everyone knows there are a lot of poor people, too. However, not many of us know why some people make more money than others. Why is the **distribution of income** the way it is? Economists have devised different theories to explain this distribution. In this chapter we will present some of these theories. In addition, we will present some of the more obvious institutional reasons why income is not distributed evenly in the United States.

Income Distribution—Past and Present

The easiest way to talk about the distribution of income is to divide income earners into groups—in this case, we'll divide them into five groups. Then we can talk about how much the bottom fifth makes compared to the top fifth, and so on. Table 25-1 shows that in 1947 the bottom fifth of the population was receiving 5.0 percent of total personal income, while the top fifth was reaping 43.1 percent. Today, the figures haven't changed very much, as shown by the data for 1974.

Lorenz Curve

We can graphically represent the distribution of income by the use of what is called a **Lorenz curve.** Look at Figure 25-1. On the horizontal axis we measure the accumulated percentage of families. Starting at the left-hand corner there are zero families. On the right-hand corner we have 100 percent of the families,

Table 25-1 The Distribution of Income, 1947 to 1974

When we divide all households into five groups, we see that the distribution of income has not changed very much since just after World War II.

| | PERCENTAGE OF NATIONAL INCOME | |
PERCENTAGE OF HOUSEHOLDS	1947	1974
Lowest 5th	5.0	5.6
Second 5th	11.8	12.1
Third 5th	17.0	17.2
Fourth 5th	23.1	23.0
Highest 5th	43.1	42.1
	100.0	100.0

Source: Department of Commerce

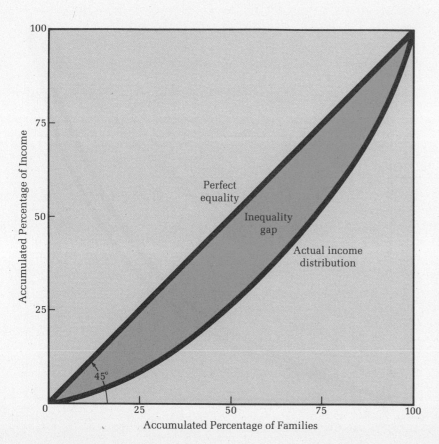

FIGURE 25-1 The Lorenz Curve

The horizontal axis measures the accumulated percentage of families from 0 to 100 percent. The vertical axis measures the accumulated percentage of income from 0 to 100. A straight line at a 45 degree angle cuts the box in half and represents a line of perfect income equality, where 25 percent of the families get 25 percent of the income, 50 percent get 50 percent, and so on. The Lorenz curve, showing actual income distribution, is not a straight line but, rather, a curved line as shown. The difference between perfect income equality and the Lorenz curve is the inequality gap.

and in the middle we have 50 percent of the families. The vertical axis represents the accumulated percentage of total income. The line between the lower left-hand corner and the upper right-hand corner of the Lorenz box (a 45 degree line) represents perfect equality. At the middle of the box we have 50 percent of the families obtaining 50 percent of total income. Of course, no real-world situation is such that there is perfect equality of income; no Lorenz curve will be a straight line. Rather, it will be the curved line.

Figure 25-2 shows that the actual distribution of income in the United States is certainly not equal. Compared to 1929, however, it is improving (a value judgment) in the sense of becoming more equal. It might be interesting to compare the United States today with other countries in the world. We see in Figure 25-3 that the Lorenz curve for Sweden is closer to the straight line than is the curve for the United States. Just as we would have expected, Sweden has a more equal distribution of income than we do. This has been accomplished in Sweden by extremely progressive taxes. On the other hand, we see that the distribution of income in Thailand is much more unequal than in the United States. The bottom 80 percent of families receive less than 40 percent of all income, whereas the top 10 percent of families receives more than 40 percent of all income.

As an aside, it might be noted that the more industrialized a nation becomes, the larger is the percentage of national income that is paid

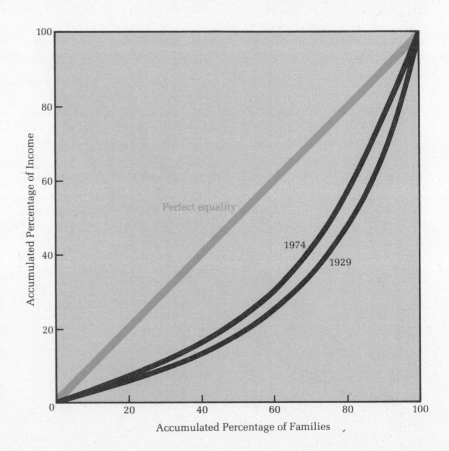

FIGURE 25-2 Lorenz Curves of Income Distribution, 1929 and 1974

We notice that the Lorenz curve has come slightly in toward the straight line of perfect income equality since 1929. (*Source:* U.S. Department of Commerce.)

in wages. In less developed countries, much of the national income goes to rent, interest, and profits. In countries such as the United States, Britain, France, Germany, Sweden, and the rest of Western Europe, the majority of national income does not originate from capital but, rather, from labor services. In the United States today, for example, over three-fourths of national income is paid in wages; less than one-fourth is paid as returns to investment in land, buildings, companies, and so on.

Measuring the Degree of Income Inequality

We can obtain a more or less precise measure of the degree of income inequality by using the Gini coefficient of inequality. A diagram showing a Lorenz curve, such as the one in Figure 25-1, can also show the Gini coefficient. We compare the area between the 45 degree straight line and the Lorenz curve of actual income distribution to the entire area under the diagonal, that is, to the triangle which represents one-half of the box in Figure 25-1. In other words:

$$\text{Gini coefficient of inequality} = \frac{\text{area between diagonal and Lorenz curve of actual income distribution}}{\text{triangular area under diagonal line}}$$

What does this mean? This means that the Gini coefficient will range from 0·to 1. If we

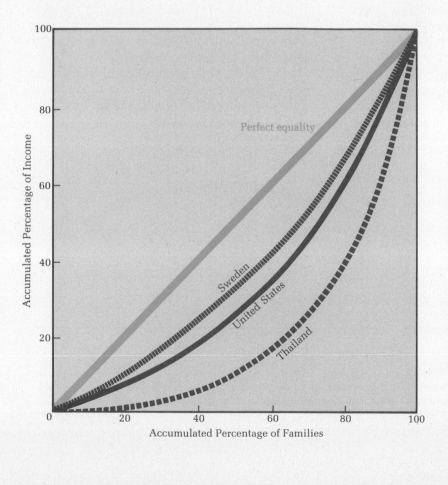

FIGURE 25-3 **International Comparisons of income Distribution**
Here we show the Lorenz curves for the United States, Sweden, and Thailand. As can be expected, Sweden has a Lorenz curve which is closer to the straight line of perfect income equality than that of the United States. Sweden has a much more progressive system of income tax. Thailand, on the other hand, has a much more unequal distribution of income. (*Source*: United States data from U.S. Department of Commerce. Data for Thailand from *Statistical Yearbook of Thailand*. Data for Sweden from *Statistical Abstract of Sweden*, 1968.)

had perfect equality, the Gini coefficient would obviously be 0 because there would be no area between the diagonal line, or curve of absolute equality, and the curve of actual distribution of income. The greater that area becomes, however, the greater becomes the Gini coefficient and hence the measure of inequality.

Do you know what the Lorenz curve would look like if the Gini coefficient were 1?

The Age-Earnings Cycle

Within every class of income earners, there seem to be regular cycles of earning behavior. Most people earn much more when they are middle-aged than when they are either younger or older. This is called the **age-earnings cycle.** Every occupation has its own age-earnings cycle, and every individual will probably experience some variation from the average. Nonetheless, we can characterize the typical age-earnings cycle graphically in Figure 25-4. Here we see that at age 18 the lowest income is made. Income gradually rises until it peaks at about

ages 45 to 50. Then it falls until retirement when it becomes zero—that is, earned income becomes zero although retirement payments may then commence. The answer as to why there is such a regular cycle in earnings is fairly straightforward.

When individuals start working at a young age, they typically have no work-related experience. Their ability to produce is lower than that of more experienced workers. That is, their productivity is lower. As they become older, they attain more training and more experience. Their productivity rises, and they are therefore paid more. Moreover, they start to work longer hours, in general. At the age of 45 or 50 the productivity of individual workers usually peaks. So, too, do the number of hours per week that are worked. After this peak in the age-earnings cycle, the detrimental effects of aging usually outweigh any increases in training or experience. Moreover, hours worked usually start to fall for older people. Finally, as a person reaches retirement age, his or her productivity and hours worked fall rather drastically relative to, say, 15 or 20 years earlier.

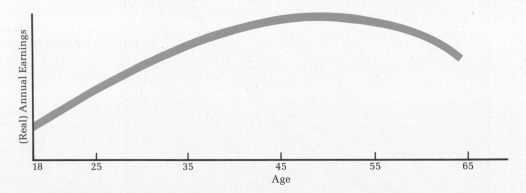

FIGURE 25-4 Typical Age-Earnings Profile

Within every class of income earners, there is usually a typical age-earnings profile. Earnings are lowest when starting out to work at age 18, reach their peak at around 45 to 50, then taper off until retirement at around 65 when they become zero for most people. The rise in earnings up to age 45 to 50 is usually due to more experience, working longer hours, and better training and schooling. (We abstract from economywide productivity changes that would shift this curve.)

Note that inflation and general increases in overall productivity for the entire work force will raise upward the typical age-earnings profile given in Figure 25-4. Thus, even at the end of the age-earnings cycle, when the worker is just about to retire, he or she would not receive a really "low" wage compared with what he or she started out with 45 years earlier. The wage would be much higher due to inflation and other factors that contribute to rising wages for everyone, regardless of where they are in their age-earnings cycle.

Now we have some idea why individuals earn different incomes at different times in their lives, but we have yet to explain why different people are paid different amounts of money for their individual labors. One way to explain this is to fall back onto the marginal productivity theory developed in Chapter 23.

Marginal Productivity Theory

When trying to determine how many workers a firm would hire, we had to construct a value of marginal physical product curve. We found that as more workers were hired, the value of marginal physical product fell since the marginal productivity of the work force fell due to diminishing returns. If the forces of supply and demand established a certain wage rate, workers would be hired until the value of their marginal physical product was equal to the wage rate. Then the hiring would stop. This analysis suggests what persons can expect to be paid in the labor market. *They can expect to be paid the value of their marginal product*—assuming, of course, that there are good information flows and that everything is competitive.

Process of Competition

In most situations the value of marginal physical product theory gives us a rough idea of what workers will be paid. In a competitive situation, with mobility of labor resources (at least on the margin), workers who are being paid less than the value of their marginal product will be bid away to better employment opportunities. Either they will seek better employment themselves or employers, in an attempt to lower labor costs, will try to find workers who are being paid below the value of their marginal physical product. This process will continue until each worker is paid his or her value of marginal physical product. In general, employers will not want to keep workers if the workers' wage rate is greater than the VMP. In such a situation it would pay an entrepreneur to fire or lay off those workers who are being paid more than the worth of their contribution to total output. It would be unusual, then, to find situations where large numbers of workers were being privately employed at wages exceeding their VMPs. (This assertion may not hold for government employment situations.)

Full Adjustment Is Never Obtained

You may balk at the suggestion that people are paid the value of their marginal physical product because you may personally know individuals who are seemingly worth more than they are being paid. Such a situation may, in fact, exist because we do not live in a world with perfect information. Employers cannot always seek out the most productive employees available. It takes resources to research the past records of potential employees, their training, their education, and their abilities. You may know musicians, artists, photographers, singers, and other talented people who are being paid much less than more well-known, publicized "stars." But this does not mean that marginal physical product theory is invalid. It merely indicates that information is costly. It is not always possible for talent scouts to find out exactly who the next superstars are going to be, which means that lots of potential stars never fulfill their dreams.

If we accept value of marginal physical product theory, then we have a way to find out how people can, in fact, earn higher incomes. If they can manage to increase the value of their marginal physical product, they can expect to be paid more. Some of the determinants of marginal physical product are innate intelligence, schooling, experience, and training. These are means by which marginal product can be increased. Let's examine them in greater detail.

Innate Abilities and Attributes   These factors are obviously the easiest to explain and the hardest to acquire if you don't have them. Innate abilities and attributes can be very strong, if not overwhelming, determinants of a person's potential productivity. Strength, good looks, coordination, mental alertness, and so on are all facets of nonacquired human capital and thus have some bearing on one's ability to earn income. If one is born without "brains," he or she has a smaller chance of "making it" in the economic world than does an individual who is born "smart." The determinants of intelligence are, of course, not a topic for economic discussion. It is no longer believed, however, that intelligence is purely innate. Some sociologists and educators think that intelligence can be changed by the environment. Nevertheless, whether a change in intelligence due to a "better" environment leads to higher incomes in the future is a debatable and as yet untested contention.

Schooling   Schooling is usually placed under the heading of "investment in human capital," a topic we will go into later. For the moment, suffice it to say that schooling or education improves one's productivity by increasing the human capital one has available for use

in the labor market. If you have been taught to read, write, work with mathematics, understand scientific problems, do engineering, drafting, lay out advertisements, design clothes, or edit manuscripts, you obviously are of more value to a potential employer than a person who is illiterate and unknowledgeable about anything except manual labor. Schooling usually allows an individual to be more versatile in the things he or she can do.

Experience   Additional experience at particular tasks is another way to increase one's productivity. Experience can be linked to the well-known *learning curve* that occurs when the same task is done over and over. Take an example of a person going to work on an assembly line at General Motors. At first he or she is able to screw on only three bolts every 2 minutes. Then the worker becomes more adept and can screw on four bolts in the same time plus insert a rubber guard on the bumper. After a few more weeks even another task can be added. Experience allows this individual to improve his or her productivity. The better people learn to do something, the quicker they can do it and the more efficient they are. Hence, we would expect experience to lead to higher rates of productivity. And we would expect people with more experience to be paid more than those with less experience.

Training   Training is similar to experience but is more formal. Much of a person's increased productivity is due to on-the-job training. Many companies have training programs for new workers. They learn to operate machinery, fill out forms, and do other things required for the new job. On-the-job training is perhaps responsible for as much of an increase in productivity as is formal schooling.

There are, of course, other determinants of people's wage incomes that we have not yet discussed. One of the most fascinating is the uniqueness of individual resources. If you have a unique resource—a singing voice, a beautiful face and body, a creative mind, athletic prowess—you may be able to earn "surplus" income or **economic rents.** But, of course, in your attempt to capture those rents, you will run into much risk, which is what we will talk about now.

Earning Too Much

Some people earn "too" much. That is, they are paid more income than is required to get them to do the amount of work they actually perform. These people are receiving what economists call "economic rents." These rents have nothing to do with the rents that must be paid on apartments. *Economic rents are the income over and above what is required that are paid to get someone to do a specific kind and amount of work.*

How can you possibly get into a situation where you are paid more than you actually require to do the work that someone wants you to do? All you have to do is have a unique resource. Just ask Bob Dylan, or the Rolling Stones, or Joan Baez, or Catherine Deneuve, or Linda Lovelace, or Marlon Brando. They are making fantastic incomes. Most likely, they would be willing to work for less if they had to. But they don't have to, and the reason they don't have to is because the demand for their special talents is relatively high. No one else can take their place. That is, there are very few substitutes for people who have unique resources or unique talents.

We can formally define economic rent for workers as that portion of the price paid for a person's labor services which does not influence the amount of the services offered. If, for example, the supply curve of Bob Dylan's talents was the vertical line in Figure 25-5, then the amount of economic rent he would receive

would be exactly equal to whatever he was paid. If the demand curve happened to be D_1D_1, the rent he would receive would equal the intersection price times the quantity of services he offered. This is because he would presumably be willing to offer that same amount of services at a zero price.

Economic Rent Cannot Be Eliminated

There is no way to get rid of economic rents, or economic surplus (except perhaps by taxation). The demand and supply curves intersect at the point E in Figure 25-5. *Economic rent serves a rationing function.* The only way people can obtain the services of Bob Dylan is by bidding those services away from someone else. Since a lot of people want to bid for the same services, the price goes up, and the economic rent that Bob Dylan receives goes up accordingly. Since price serves as a rationing mechanism, it has to be high enough to allocate a scarce resource. If we do not allow price (wages) to rise to the point where the quantity supplied just equals the quantity demanded, then some other form of rationing must be used.

Joan Baez's "Peculiar" Habit

A good example of this need for another form of rationing concerns a "peculiar" habit of singer Joan Baez. Often she requests that her concert tickets be sold at $2 or $3 apiece and no higher. However, the quantity of tickets demanded at that relatively low price far exceeds the quantity available for any given performance. We find that fans line up a day in advance to get the low-priced tickets. Instead of paying a higher *money* price to get in the door to see Joan Baez, devoted fans pay a combination of time cost and relatively low price for the tickets. The point is that when the price is below the market clearing one, some form

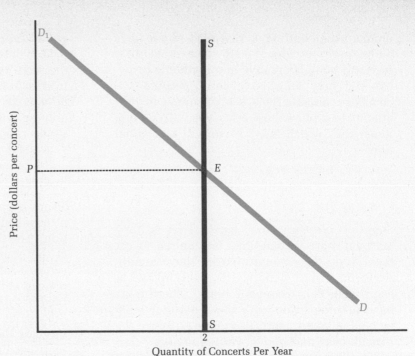

FIGURE 25-5 **Economic Rents Accruing to Bob Dylan**

If we assume that Bob Dylan's supply curve of concerts is a vertical line at, say, two concerts per year, then the economic rents that Bob Dylan would receive would equal the price, P_1, times the quantity of concerts that he gave. (Note that the vertical SS assumes that Dylan would be willing to work for nothing if necessary.)

of rationing must take place. In this particular example, it is a long wait in line.

People who attempt to make extraordinary incomes on the basis of their artistic talents usually start out at the bottom making almost nothing. The Beatles were a relatively poorly paid Liverpool rock group for a number of years before they became stars and started collecting economic rents. During those Liverpool years they probably could have made more money in some alternative occupation, such as driving a truck.

Risk Factor

A high risk is involved with occupations that promise fantastic incomes. There are a lot of superbeautiful $80-a-week waitresses and carhops in Hollywood. These budding starlets could probably make more money if they did office work in another city. However, they want

to take a chance on making it big, of breaking into the movies or singing. Many would-be actors, actresses, singers, musicians, painters, photographers, and authors voluntarily remain relatively poor throughout their lives because they do not seek alternative employments where they could make more money. Rather, they attempt to eke out a living doing bit parts, for example, or writing infrequently published short stories in the hope that eventually they will break into the big time. If they do, you can be sure they will make economic rents—they will be paid more than is required to get them to work. But that's one of the considerations that makes the risk acceptable.

Exploitation and Discrimination

Exploitation and discrimination also affect the distribution of income. Even with equal educational achievement, both in quality and quantity, certain disadvantaged groups may not and empirically do not receive incomes equal to those of other groups. We know, for example, that urban nonwhite males earn approximately 40 percent less than urban white males. We know that blacks obtain lower rates of return, on the average, from investing in a college education than do whites. Are minority groups, and especially blacks, being exploited? Are minority groups being discriminated against in the labor market?

Exploitation

The economist's definition of **exploitation** is somewhat more restrictive than the common one. We usually say that a person is being exploited if he or she is being paid less than the value of his or her labor services to an employer.

How can exploitation exist in the labor market? Lack of information can allow it. If employees (on the margin) are ignorant of better job opportunities, they may be exploited by employers. Also, if laborers experience restricted entry into an industry, they may be exploited. Professional sports leagues, for example, try to prevent the entry of competing leagues into the system because the price of professional athletes would be bid up. We say that a player may be exploited because of the monopsony power of the employers in the single existing major league. Another possible cause of exploitation is restricted mobility. If a lawyer is prevented from practicing in states other than the one where he or she now works, he or she may be exploited because of the impossibility of going where the value of his or her services and potential income is the highest.

Note, however, that we have talked about the possibility but not the certainty of exploitation. Stress should be placed on the possibility, because the lack of information, the lack of free entry, and the lack of mobility do not offer *prima facie* evidence of exploitation. More evidence is needed.

In terms of information, *all* employees concerned must be unaware of the facts, not just the average employee. But we know, for example, that even non-English-speaking immigrants arriving in America can be exploited only when they first set foot on shore because afterward there are brokers who specialize in providing them with translated information. Competition among brokers for immigrants ensures that non-English-speaking employees receive wages equal to the value of their marginal physical product. (It should not be forgotten that the value of their marginal physical product is, on the average, lower than for the native born because the ability to use English increases productivity.) The point is that information does not have to be obtained directly by the employee. Competition among employers will provide sufficient information, at least at the margin, to ensure nonexploitation.

The mere lack of free entry into a new industry is not a surefire way to exploit workers. To exploit workers, those participating on the restrictive side of the market must also agree *among themselves* not to compete with one another. This, as we saw, is exactly what has happened in the professional sports leagues—a draft system prevents teams from bidding against each other. Without this draft system, there would be incentives for individual teams to compete for the best players. Players would no longer be exploited. They would receive incomes equal to the value of their services to club owners.

Exploitation, then, requires restrictions on information, entry, and mobility plus additional arrangements which will ensure that such restrictions affect *all* employees.

Discrimination

How can we define discrimination now that we have analyzed exploitation? Discrimination is usually defined in almost the same way as exploitation, but it may also include not being able to find a job and not being able to buy certain products, such as housing in particular neighborhoods. Usually we say that employers have "tastes for discrimination" when they act as if there were nonmonetary costs associated with the hiring of blacks or other minority group members. This type of behavior leads to lower incomes for blacks than they would receive otherwise. In fact, there is quite a bit of evidence of discrimination in the labor market, particularly in restricted situations such as those caused by union activities.

In a theoretical and empirical study of discrimination against blacks, Professor Gary S. Becker found that discrimination was related to a number of readily observable variables. In the study, discrimination is defined by wage differentials not accounted for by different VMPs between whites and blacks in similar job situations. Becker found the following relationships:

1. Discrimination is positively related to the relative number of blacks and whites. For a given sized city, the larger the proportion of blacks, the more discrimination there will be. This is sometimes called the "propinquity" theorem. Further, discrimination is more prevalent when large numbers of blacks are involved in nonmarket activities such as attaining a formal education. This means that the larger the number of blacks relative to whites, the more discrimination we would expect to see.
2. Discrimination is less evident for those seeking temporary as opposed to permanent work.
3. Discrimination is greater for those who are older and better educated.

4. Discrimination has deterred blacks from entering professions such as law because of their competitive disadvantage in arguing before white juries.

Becker also found that black incomes were reduced by 16 percent as a result of discrimination.[1]

There appears to be quite a bit of discrimination against blacks and other minorities in the acquisition of human capital. That is, the amount and quality of schooling offered blacks has been detrimentally inferior to that offered to whites. We find that even if minorities attend school as long as whites, their scholastic achievement is usually less because they typically are allotted more meager school resources than their white counterparts. Analysis of census data reveals that a large portion of white/nonwhite income differentials resulted from differences in both the quantity of education received and in scholastic achievement, which is more or less a function of the quality of education received. One study showed that nonwhite urban males receive between 23 and 27 percent less income than white urban males because of lower quality education. This would mean that even if employment discrimination is substantially reduced, we would still expect to see a difference between white and nonwhite income because of the low quality of schooling received by the nonwhites and the resulting lower level of productivity. We say, therefore, that, among other things, blacks and certain other minority groups, such as Chicanos, suffer from too small an investment in human capital. Even when this difference in human capital is taken into account, however, there still appears to be an income differential that cannot be explained. The unexplained income differential between whites and blacks is often attributed to discrimination in the labor market. Until a

[1] Gary Becker, *The Economics of Discrimination*, rev. ed., Chicago: University of Chicago Press, 1971.

better explanation is offered, we will stick with the notion that discrimination does indeed exist in it.

Investment in Human Capital

Investment in human capital is just like investment in any other thing. If you invest in a building, you expect to realize a profit later on by receiving a rate of return for your investment. You expect to receive some reward for not consuming all your income today. The same is true for investment in human capital. If you invest in yourself by going to college rather than going to work after high school and being able to spend more money, you presumably will be rewarded in the future by a higher income and a more interesting job. This is exactly the motivation that usually underlies the decision of many college-bound students to obtain a formal higher education. Undoubtedly, there would be students going to school even if the rate of return to formal education was zero or negative. After all, college is fun, right? (And it's certainly better than going to work.) But we do expect that the higher the rate of return on investing in oneself, the more investment there will be. And we find that the investment in a college education does pay off. Figure 25-6 shows the

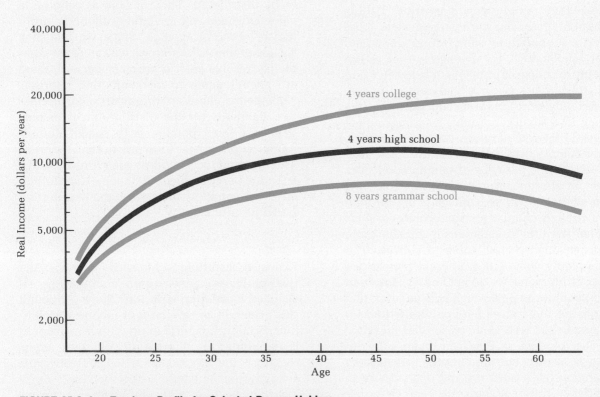

FIGURE 25-6 Age-Earnings Profile for Selected Degree Holders
The age-earnings cycle jumps up for each increase in formal education. It is obvious that the investment in human capital eventually "pays off." (*Source:* U.S. Department of Commerce, Consumer Income, ser. P60, no. 74.)

age-earnings cycle of grade school graduates, high school graduates, and college graduates. The age-earnings cycle jumps up for each increase in formal education. The investment in human capital does pay off.

To figure out the rate of return on an investment in a college education, we first have to figure out the costs of going to school. The main cost is not what you have to pay for books, fees, and tuition but, rather, the income you forgo. *The main cost of education is the income forgone or the opportunity cost of not working.* That may amount to as much as $5,000 to $10,000 a year. In addition, of course, you have to pay for the direct expenses (or, rather, your parents do in many cases). Of course, not all students forgo income during their college years. Many people work part-time. Taking account of those who work part-time and those who are supported by state tuition grants and other scholarships, the average rate of return of going to college is somewhere between 8 and 12 percent. This is not a bad rate of return. It's certainly more than you could get by putting money in a savings account. It's about equal, in fact, to the rate of return you would receive by randomly selecting stocks in the stock market. Of course, this type of computation does leave out all the consumption benefits you get from attending college. College is not *all* pain even though economics sometimes is. Also omitted from the calculations is the change in one's personality after going to college. You undoubtedly come out a different person (for better or for worse we do not know). However, most people who go through college think that they better themselves both culturally and intellectually, as well as increase their marginal physical product so they can make more income. How does one measure the benefit from expanding one's horizons and one's desire to experience different things in life? Certainly

this is not easy to measure, and such nonpecuniary benefits from investing in human capital are not included in our normal calculations.

The fact that the rate of return on investing in human capital is higher than one can get by putting money in a savings and loan association does not mean, however, that everybody "should" go to college. And it does not mean that there "should" be more public higher education for more people.

Theories of Income Distribution

We have talked about the factors affecting the distribution of income, but we have not mentioned the normative issue of how income *ought* to be distributed. This, of course, requires a value judgment. We are talking about the problem of economic justice. Since we live in a society of limited resources, we can never completely resolve such a problem because there are always going to be conflicting interests. Nonetheless, there are three particular normative standards for the distribution of income that have been popular with social philosophers, economists, and politicians as well. These normative standards are (1) income distribution based on need, (2) income distribution based on equality, and (3) income distribution based on productivity.

Need

"To each according to his needs." So goes the distributive principle of pure communism, associated most often with Karl Marx. Although this principle, or standard, of income distribution certainly has little to do with how income is distributed in this country, it does apply roughly to the way income is distributed within a family unit and also to the way income is distributed within a geographical area during wartime or other period of emergency. There is little doubt that this distribution standard has a great appeal to many individuals. However, its implementation poses a number of extremely thorny problems. The most difficult problem perhaps is the establishment of an unbiased objective, an operational mechanism for measuring need. In general, the only way we can determine need is by using subjective judgment. Furthermore, it is very difficult for us to establish just what is a necessity for each individual.

Another problem concerns the full utilization of society's resources. If we added up all the "needs," we might possibly end up with surpluses in some areas and shortages in others—we wouldn't be fully using society's resources.

Equality

The egalitarian principle of income distribution can be simply stated as "to each exactly the same." In other words, everyone would have exactly the same amount of income. This criterion of distribution has been debated as far back as biblical times. Just as with the need criterion, the equality criterion has problems.

If there were an equal distribution of income, the incentive of rewards would be eliminated. What would motivate people to develop and apply their skills and productive capacities to the most productive uses? What incentive would there be for individuals to use economic resources efficiently? If we used the equality principle in the distribution of income, this nation would probably suffer a decline in economic growth. However, this does not necessarily mean that the equality criterion should be eliminated—the benefits from equalizing income may still outweigh the costs. As we saw in Issue I-3, mainland China has basically

adopted this criterion for the distribution of income, but the U.S.S.R. seems to be moving away from it.

Productivity

The productivity standard for the distribution of income can be stated simply as "to each according to what he produces." This is also called a *contributive* standard because it is based on the principle of being rewarded according to the contribution one makes to society's total output. It is also sometimes referred to as a merit standard and is one of the oldest concepts of justice known to man. People are rewarded according to merit, and merit is judged by one's ability to produce that which is considered useful by society. However, just as the other two standards are value judgments, so is the contributive or productivity standard. The productivity standard is rooted in the capitalist ethic, though, and has been attacked vigorously by some economists and philosophers, including Karl Marx who, as we pointed out, felt that people should be rewarded according to need and not according to productivity.

We measure one's productive contribution in a capitalist system by the market value of one's output. We have already referred to this as the marginal productivity theory of wage determination.

Do not immediately jump to the conclusion that in a world of income distribution determined by productivity, society will necessarily allow the aged, infirm, and disabled to die from starvation because they are unproductive. In the United States today, the productivity standard is mixed with the need standard so that the aged, disabled, involuntarily unemployed, very young, and other unproductive (in the market sense of the word) members of the economy are provided for.

Distribution of Income: The way income is distributed in a particular country. For example, a perfectly equal distribution of income would find that the lowest 20 percent of income earners would make 20 percent of national income and the top 20 percent would also make 20 percent of national income. The middle 60 percent of income earners would receive 60 percent of national income.

Lorenz Curve: A geographic representation of the distribution of income. A Lorenz curve that is perfectly straight represents perfect income equality. The more bowed a Lorenz curve, the more unequally income is distributed.

Age-Earnings Cycle: The regular earnings behavior of an individual throughout her or his lifetime. The age-earnings cycle usually starts with a low income, builds gradually to a peak at around 45 to 50, and then gradually curves down until it becomes zero at retirement age.

Economic Rents: That amount of payment for an individual's services over and above what the individual would be willing to accept to provide that same quantity of services. Sometimes called surplus.

Exploitation: The payment to a person of wages or income that is less than the value of his or her services to the employer.

1. The distribution of income in the United States has remained fairly constant since after World War II. The lowest fifth of income earners still receives only about 5 percent of total personal income while the top fifth of income earners receives over 40 percent.

2. We can represent the distribution of income graphically with a Lorenz curve. The extent to which the line is bowed from a straight line shows how unequal the distribution of income is.

3. Most individuals face a particular age-earnings cycle or profile. Earnings are lowest when starting out to work at age 18 to 24. They gradually rise and peak at about 45 to 50, then fall until retirement. They go up usually because of increased experience, increased training, and working longer hours.

4. Marginal productivity theory of the distribution of income indicates that workers can expect to be paid the value of their marginal product. For this theory to be exactly correct, we must have competition with fairly minimal information costs. Otherwise there will always be people who are being paid more or less than the value of their marginal product.

5. The value of marginal product is usually determined by innate intelligence, schooling, experience, and training.

6. Some people can be paid economic rents if they have a unique resource, such as a beautiful singing voice, a beautiful face or body, or a creative mind. Economic rents or surplus cannot be eliminated without rendering

the rationing function of the price system ineffective and creating a need for an alternative system of rationing the resource.

7. Exploitation can be defined as a situation where a worker is paid less than his or her value to the employer. Exploitation may occur in situations where monopsony power exists on the part of the employer, where information is restricted, or where entry into the industry is also restricted.

8. Discrimination is usually defined as a situation where a certain minority group is paid a lower wage for the same work than other groups.

9. You can invest in your own human capital by going to school. The investment usually pays off for the rate of return is somewhere between 8 and 12 percent.

1. What kind of changes do you think will tend to make the distribution of income more equal?

2. Do you think that exploitation and discrimination are responsible for the inequality of the distribution of income in the United States? If not, what are the main determinants?

3. Do you think that in a capitalistic system there will always be rich people and poor people?

4. "If we took all the income in the United States and all the wealth and divided it equally among everybody in the country, within 10 years rich people would be rich again and poor people would be poor again." Do you agree?

5. "To each according to his needs, from each according to his means." What kind of distribution of income would result from such a system?

Selected References

Becker, Gary, *The Economics of Discrimination,* rev. ed., Chicago: University of Chicago Press, 1971.

Budd, Edward, *Inequality and Poverty,* New York: W. W. Norton, 1968.

Ferman, Louis A., J. L. Kornbluh, and A. Haber (eds.), *Poverty in America,* rev. ed., Ann Arbor: The University of Michigan Press, 1968.

Harrington, Michael, *The Other America: Poverty in the United States,* rev. ed., New York: Macmillan, 1970.

Soltow, Lee (ed.), *Six Papers on the Size Distribution of Wealth and Income,* New York: Columbia University Press for the National Bureau of Economic Research, 1969.

Will, Robert E. and Harold G. Vatter (eds.), *Poverty in Affluence,* 2d ed., New York: Harcourt, Brace Jovanovich, 1970.

Poverty and the Poor

FINDING ALTERNATIVES TO WELFARE

Poverty Still Around

Throughout the history of the world, mass poverty has been an accepted inevitability. However, this nation and others, particularly in the Western world, have sustained enough economic growth in the last several hundred years so that *mass* poverty can no longer be said to be a problem for these fortunate countries. As a matter of fact, the residual of poverty in the United States appears to be bizarre—an anomaly. How is it that there can still be so much poverty in a nation of so much abundance? Having talked about the determinants of the distribution of income, we now have at least some ideas of why some people are destined to remain low-income earners throughout their lives.

There are methods of transferring income from the relatively well to do to the relatively poor, and as a nation, we have begun attempting to use them. Today we are saddled with a vast array of welfare programs set up for the purpose of redistributing income and for that purpose alone. However, we know that these programs have not been entirely successful. The relative distribution of

income has not changed appreciably in the last 30 or 40 years. Are there alternatives to our current welfare system? Is there a better method of helping the poor? Before we answer these questions let's look at the concept of poverty in more detail and at the characteristics of the poor.

The Low-Income Population

We see in Figure I-30.1 that the number of individuals classified as poor fell rather steadily from 1959 to 1969. Since 1969, although there has been very little change in the number, the percentage of the population classified as poor actually has been falling slightly because the total population has grown.

Defining Poverty

The threshold income level, which is used to determine who falls into the poverty category, was originally based on the cost of a nutritionally adequate food plan designed by the Department of Agriculture for emergency or temporary use. The threshold was determined by multiplying

the food plan cost times 3 on the assumption that food expenses comprise approximately one-third of the family income. In 1969 a federal interagency committee looked at the calculations of the threshold and decided to set new standards. Until then annual revisions of the threshold level were based purely on price changes in the food budget only. After 1969, the adjustments were made on the basis of changes in the Consumer Price Index.

The low-income threshold thus represents an absolute measure of income needed to maintain a specified standard of living as of 1963, with the real dollar value, or the purchasing power value, increased year by year in relation to the general increase in prices. For 1975, for example, the low-income threshold budget for a nonfarm family of four was $5,390. By the time you read this book, it will have gone up by whatever the change in the Consumer Price Index has been during the period. (It varies for families of different size.)

The Relative Nature of Poverty

Since the low-income threshold is an absolute measure, we know that if it never changes in real terms, we will eliminate poverty even if we do

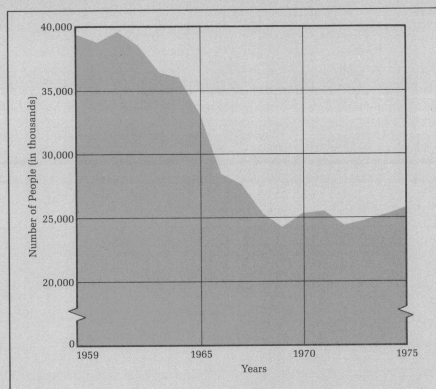

FIGURE I-30.1
The number of individuals classified as poor has fallen steadily from 1959 through 1969. But since then there has been little change in number classified as poor. This indicates, though, that the percentage of the population classified as poor fell dramatically in the 1960s and continues to fall at a much smaller rate in the 1970s. (*Source:* U.S. Department of Labor.)

nothing. How can that be? The reasoning is rather straightforward. Real incomes in the United States have been growing at a compounded annual rate of about 1.5 percent per capita for the last 100 or more years and at about 2.5 percent since World War II. If we define the poverty line at a specified real level, more and more individuals will make incomes that exceed that poverty line. Thus, in absolute terms we will eliminate poverty. However, one should be careful with this analysis. Poverty has generally been defined in relative terms; that is, it is defined in terms of the income levels of individuals or families relative to what exists in the rest of the population. As long as there is a distribution of income

that is not perfectly equal, there will always be some who make less income than others, some who have a relatively low income—even if that relatively low income is high by historical standards. Thus, in a relative sense, the problem of poverty will always exist.

Who Are the Poor?

Individuals who are classified as poor share some general characteristics. They usually fall into one or more of the following classifications.

Minority Groups

Minority groups—blacks, Puerto Ricans, Mexicans, and so on—have

a relatively high incidence of poverty. It is interesting to note that the poverty rate among black families is more than three times that of white families. This is also true—usually more so—for native Americans and Chicanos.

The Elderly

Family units headed by individuals over 65 years of age often have very low levels of income also. Of every five poor families, one is headed by an elderly person. (Note, however, that their situation is often mitigated by the fact that they own their own homes and therefore don't need income for housing.)

The Young

The young, especially black teenagers, usually suffer high rates of unemployment. As indicated earlier, the minimum wage law is often responsible for this situation. The younger members of society are generally not as educated or experienced as the older groups and therefore they are not as productive. Hence, their value is often not sufficient to induce employers to pay the statutory minimum wage to hire them.

Rural Population

Poverty is far more common among families living in rural areas than among those living in the city or in an urban area. Poverty rates among families living on farms are almost twice as high as among those in urban areas. (Note, however, that rural families often grow much of their own food and therefore do not require as much food income.)

Households Headed by Women

Nearly 40 percent of all women heading a household and providing for their children are defined as poor. If we look at the nonwhite population of fatherless families, this figure rises to nearly 60 percent.

Now that we have some idea as to how individuals are classified as poor or nonpoor, and who those individuals are, let's look at some current means of helping low-income families.

The Welfare Mess

Current welfare programs are a labyrinth of state and local legislation. Nonetheless, over 90 percent of national welfare payments are made through programs that are partly or largely federally funded. Each month perhaps 10 million persons are given some form of welfare. These recipients include:

1. 3 million who are over 65, blind, or otherwise severely handicapped.
2. 4 million who are children in the Aid to Dependent Children program, whose parents do not or cannot provide financial support.
3. 1.5 to 2.5 million who are the parents of children on Aid to Families with Dependent Children (AFDC). Of these, over 1 million are mothers and the rest are fathers. About two-thirds of the fathers are incapacitated.

Public Assistance

Public assistance programs are designed to meet, at least partially, the needs of certain categories of the poor. Some public assistance programs are Aid to Families with Dependent Children, old age assistance, aid to the permanently and totally disabled, aid to the blind, and a general assistance program. Only about one-third of poor families and one-quarter of poor persons receive public assistance (PA). Many of the poor do not receive PA because they fail to pass the so-called means tests. These are tests that the state uses to compare a budget plan of expenditures with potential resources of the persons applying for aid. In the past, poor people often could not obtain public assistance because they failed to meet local or state residency qualifications. Of course, there are many who do not know their possible eligibility, and some are frightened off by the stigma they feel is attached to going on relief. There are many more poor people who receive no public assistance merely because they do not fall into one of the prescribed categories.

Disparity of Payments

Different states pay different amounts for different public assistance programs. Take, for example, the AFDC program. State and local governments contribute on average about 45 percent of the costs of supporting this program. Each state sets the level of grants for its own residents. We find that monthly payments range from a low of less than $20 in Mississippi to a high of over $100 in New York City. AFDC programs cost approximately $4.5 billion a year. In many states and cities the case loads are increasing, particularly in times when unemployment is high. As can be expected, the burden of welfare and of the increase in case loads falls principally on our central cities, particularly New York, Chicago, St. Louis, Detroit, Cleveland, and Los Angeles. Examination of current programs provides one with an insight into the relatively high cost of giving away money under certain systems and the disadvantages of doing it in such a manner.

Disadvantages of Current Public Assistance

The amount of paperwork involved in providing public assistance is in-deed appalling. In many cities, five, six, or even seven copies of each form must be made and filed. Welfare workers have to go out to interview prospective and current welfare recipients to make sure they are eligible—to find out if, indeed, the recipients are spending their welfare money in the correct way. In most welfare situations, for example, it is not possible for the recipients to have phones. That is considered a frivolous expense. Moreover, and perhaps even more appalling, is the fact that many welfare programs are cut off once a person who receives money finds a job—no matter how poor the pay for that job might be. Until recently, all amounts earned on outside jobs by adult welfare recipients were deducted directly from the welfare payments they would have otherwise received. This practice was required at one time by federal law.

Incentives Not to Work

How do these rules affect the incentive of welfare recipients to seek part-time or full-time employment? Most likely, the laws have succeeded in reducing the work effort on the part of welfare recipients. Put yourself in the unenviable position of someone on public assistance. You know that if you find a job for a few hours a week, your welfare payment will be reduced by exactly the amount you make. In such a situation the rate of return for working rather than not working is zero. In fact, you would have to find a job that paid you quite a bit more than you get for doing nothing and remaining on public assistance. Oth-erwise, it really wouldn't pay you to work. New York City finally started to experiment with a program that allowed welfare mothers to keep the first $85 of earnings each month and a percentage of the amounts above that. This particular type of system, at least, does not generate an incentive *not* to work as did previous systems.

Man-in-the-House Rule

An additional, somewhat disconcerting feature of most public assistance programs is that the money is cut off if both parents live in the same household. In other words, in some states one parent has to be absent from the home for the family unit to be eligible for AFDC. This is called the **man-in-the-house rule** and was intended to prevent payments to children who have an alternative potential source of support. But what has probably been the actual effect of such a rule? Most likely it has fostered the breakup of homes and perpetuated reliance on welfare. The irritation caused by this rule has been aggravated in some states by regular searches of recipients' homes to ferret out violations. Some cities have actually employed "spies" to snoop around AFDC homes to make sure a man is not present.

This sort of degradation of one's human dignity is another detrimental aspect of the current public assistance programs. In some cases, the amount of questioning that welfare recipients have to go through to receive their payments is appalling. In Chicago, for example, welfare workers are usually required to ask

mothers who apply for AFDC monies to explain when, with whom, and how they last had intercourse.

In addition to public assistance, there are social insurance programs that to some extent also provide income redistribution.

Social Insurance

For the retired and unemployed, certain social insurance programs exist that provide income payments in prescribed situations. The most well known is Social Security, which includes what has been called old age, survivors, disability and health insurance—or OASDHI. This is essentially a program of compulsory saving financed from compulsory payroll taxes levied on both employers and employees. One pays for Social Security while working and receives the benefits later after retirement. The benefit payments are usually made to those reaching retirement age. When the insured worker dies, benefits accrue to the survivors, including widows and children. There are also special benefits that provide for disabled workers. Over 90 percent of all employed persons in the United States are covered by OASDHI.

Since it is a social insurance program that is supposedly paid for by the workers themselves, the actual size of the benefit payment varies according to the amount which the worker has contributed to the program, to the number of dependents, and so on. In 1975, there were more than 28 million people receiving OASDHI checks averaging about $208 a month. Benefit payments from OASDHI redistribute income to some degree. However, benefit payments typically are not based on the recipient's need. Participants' contributions give them the right to benefits even if they would be financially secure without them. In fact, Social Security appears to be a system whereby the relatively young subsidize the relatively old. One pays in when one is younger and receives payment when one is older. Social Security is not really an insurance program, however, because people are not guaranteed that the benefits they receive will be in line with the contributions they have made. The benefits are legislated by Congress. In the future, Congress may not be as sympathetic toward older people as it is today. It could legislate for lower benefits instead of higher ones.

Food Stamps

The food stamp program has become a major part of the welfare system in the United States. It was started in 1964 and, in retrospect, seems to have been used mainly to shore up the nation's agricultural sector by distributing "surplus" food through retail channels. In addition, of course, the food stamp program was and continues to be a method of supporting better nutrition among the poor.

In 1964, 367,000 Americans received food stamps. By 1975 there were over 14 million. The annual cost jumped from $860,000 to more than $4 billion per year. The eligibility requirements for the program in 1975 were such that a family of four with an income of $230 a month could obtain $150 worth of food stamps by paying $60. Individuals who find themselves on strike, and also many college students, are eligible for the food stamp program.

A congressional committee found that in 1975, 1 in every 14 persons was estimated to be using food stamps. At the current rate of expansion, by the end of this decade 1 in every 4 Americans could be eligible to receive some type of food stamp allotment.

An alternative to food stamps is, of course, direct payments in cash. However, the food stamp program will probably remain a major aspect of our welfare system because of its direct tie to the purchase of agricultural products. The agricultural sector of the nation certainly benefits from welfare aid in the form of stamps that can be used only to purchase agricultural products.

Some Alternative Ways to Eliminate Poverty

Two of the most popular alternatives to the current morass of welfare programs are a guaranteed annual income and negative income taxes.

Guaranteed Annual Income

For many years now a number of economists, sociologists, and social workers have been suggesting that a guaranteed annual income be instituted so that all families under the "poverty line" could obtain a straight cash payment, varying perhaps according to the size of the family. As the family's income rose, the payments would of course be reduced.

Under this system, although families are still not as well off as they would be if they were working, there is a significant disincentive to work. After all, if the gain from working were small because of the consequent loss in guaranteed annual income, there would be fewer people who would be willing to work. This would not have much effect on those making substantially higher than poverty-line income, but it certainly would have an effect on those making incomes around and below the poverty line. There are also a number of critics who maintain that it smacks of government "paternalism."

Negative Taxes

The other suggested alternative to welfare programs involves the individual income tax. Through a system of negative taxation, the actual income of poor families could be raised to the income that society stipulates as the poverty line. The money would be paid directly out of the federal Treasury according to a schedule based on family size, actual income earned, and other attributes. Notice that we're talking not about setting up a new system but of extending an already existing, fully computerized income taxation setup.

With a **negative income tax,** a family of four, for example, making

an income of $1,000 might be said to have a *poverty income gap* of $2,000. Their income is $2,000 below a poverty line of $3,000. The $1,000 of earned income also falls below the total of personal tax exemptions and minimum standard deductions allowed under current income tax laws. Under current laws, each person is allowed, say, a $750 exemption for each member of the family. For a family of four, total ex-emptions would be $3,000. In this particular situation, with an income of only $1,000, there would be $2,000 of unused exemptions. This is the negative base to which one would apply a tax rate to compute a negative tax. In this particular ex-ample, the negative tax base would be $2,000. If the negative tax rate was 50 percent, then the family of four would receive a check for $1,000.

Advantages of the Negative Income Tax Proponents of the neg-ative income tax point out that it has many advantages—particularly in relation to a guaranteed annual in-come. In the first place, it could be administered very efficiently by using the Internal Revenue Service. Sec-ondly, there would be no problem of determining who was the ''worthy'' poor. The decision would be based purely on income. (This

There are, in general, two ways of providing welfare to those in need: through income and wealth transfers, which are direct, and through transfers in kind. A transfer in kind is, for example, a food stamp program, a housing program, or a medical care program where those in need are given assistance in kind. A direct transfer system provides only money income to the poor. If we look only at the level of satisfaction obtained by the recipients of welfare, the direct transfer system is the most efficient because the recipients have the option of purchasing exactly the same bundle of goods that might have been provided by a transfer in kind but, in addition, they have other options open to them as well.

However, it would be naive to take into account only the satisfaction levels of recipients. We must also take into account the preferences of the taxpaying members of the community. It is probably true that taxpayers want to support poverty elimination—not so much for the elimination of poverty per se, but because they want to eliminate the overt manifestations of poverty. The relatively more fortunate members of the community may not want to see substandard housing and starving children. It is thus understandable that welfare programs in kind, such as food stamps, will elicit less opposition from the taxpaying community than will any system of direct welfare payments, such as guaranteed annual or negative income taxes.

does not mean some individuals wouldn't cheat by accepting income only in cash—and then not reporting it.) Lastly, there would be less disincentive to work because the payment scheme from the government would decrease gradually, not abruptly as would the guaranteed annual income.

Disadvantages of the Negative Income Tax Critics of the negative income tax point out that it would be extremely costly. Perhaps more importantly, there would be criticisms from middle-income groups who would receive no benefits. These groups would probably resent paying taxes to subsidize the incomes of families who, for example, earned only a few hundred dollars less than they did. In other words, equity problems would undoubtedly come up.

A Final Note

Even the most hardhearted citizen will probably agree that certain forms of poverty should be eliminated. Even the most misanthropic of us will agree that people unable to earn income because of disabilities should be provided for. And those who do not like to see poverty in the midst of plenty want to have a much more comprehensive program of income redistribution from the rich to the poor—even if the poor are working. Currently, we have a complex, often ineffective system of helping those in need—and of helping many who are not in need, such as the bureaucrats who run these programs.

Few economists will agree on the "correct" approach to income redistribution. However, we have been quite unsuccessful in effecting any real redistribution of income in the United States. Also, with our public assistance programs, we have probably perpetuated a class of welfare recipients who have been encouraged to remain unemployed. Quite clearly, there are alternatives to the current welfare mess. All plans will cause some deterioration of the work incentive. That is an inescapable fact and the cost society must bear for any type of income redistribution. Apparently, however, society thinks the cost of such programs are outweighed by the benefits.

Definitions of New Terms

Public Assistance: Programs designed to meet, at least partially, the needs of certain categories of the poor. Public assistance programs included Aid to Families with Dependent Children, old age assistance, and others.

Man-in-the-House Rule: A rule that has usually been applied to families who want to become eligible for Aid to Families with Dependent Children. There can be no man in the house if AFDC is to be given.

Negative Income Tax: A system of transferring income to the relatively poor by taxing them negatively—that is, giving them an income subsidy which varies depending upon how far below a minimum income their earned income lies.

Questions for Thought and Discussion

1. Do you think poverty is a relative concept, or is there an absolute standard on which we can judge whether people are poor?
2. What method of eliminating poverty do you favor? Why? Is it economically efficient?
3. "We have socialism for the rich and free enterprise for the poor." Explain.
4. Do you believe in forcing unemployed workers to take any job given to them?
5. If a negative income tax program were instituted, would it be necessary to have special welfare programs or special subsidy programs for individual groups in the economy?

Selected References

Gans, Herbert J., *More Equality,* New York: Pantheon Books, 1973.

Hamilton, David, *A Primer on the Economics of Poverty,* New York: Random House, 1968.

Kershaw, Joseph A., *Government Against Poverty,* Washington, D.C.: Brookings Institution, 1970.

Levitan, Sar A., *Programs in Aid of the Poor for the 1970s,* Baltimore: Johns Hopkins University Press, 1970.

Sachery, Charles, *The Political Economy of Urban Poverty,* New York: W. W. Norton, 1973.

Theobald, Robert (ed.), *Guaranteed Income,* New York: Doubleday, 1965.

Tuckman, Howard P., *The Economics of the Rich,* New York: Random House, 1973.

Wilcox, Clair, *Toward Social Welfare,* Homewood, Ill.: Irwin, 1969.

Economics as a Moral Science

GUNNAR MYRDAL
Swedish Economist and Nobel Laureate

Photo, copyright—Sven-Gösta Johansson

"I am well aware that I am often considered
. . . not a part of the profession of establishment economists, though sometimes given
credit for what I did during the first decade
of my working life," wrote Myrdal, distinguished economist and social scientist, 2
years before he received the 1974 Nobel
Prize in economics for "pioneering work in
the theory of money and economic fluctuations." What Myrdal wrote reflects the intellectual distance he has traveled from when
he developed his ideas of monetary equilibrium to his later, more famous studies of
world poverty and American race relations.

Now chairman of the board of two new
research institutes, Myrdal founded and
directed the Institute of International Economic Studies in Stockholm. He served as
executive secretary of the UN Economic
Commission for Europe and taught for many
years at Stockholm University. Influenced by
the important Swedish economist, Knut
Wicksell, Myrdal provided the theoretical
justification for Sweden's expansionary fiscal

policy during the Depression. Myrdal also played a formative role in the development of Sweden's welfare state during the 1930s and 1940s as a Social Democratic member of the Swedish Senate, government adviser, and minister of commerce.

During the 1930s Myrdal turned his attention to the issues of poverty and equality, first in Sweden, where he and his wife directly influenced reform programs for the welfare of children and the family, and later in America. He changed, he says, from a "theoretical" to an "institutional" economist, that is, an economist whose analysis includes such "noneconomic" factors as politics, social structure, institutions, and attitudes.

From this "institutional" perspective Myrdal wrote *An American Dilemma: The Negro Problem and Modern Democracy* (1946). Now a classic, *An American Dilemma* is a study of "American society from the viewpoint of the most disadvantaged group." Myrdal saw a dilemma between a sincere belief in the ideals of justice, liberty, and equality and the specific ways in which whites actually conceived and acted toward black people in contradiction to those ideals. Myrdal is now at work on a sequel to *An American Dilemma,* which he envisions will be more policy oriented than its forerunner.

Myrdal considers himself working in the tradition of classical and neoclassical economists who viewed economics as a moral science. There is no "objective" economics, says Myrdal. Since values are implicit in the questions economists ask and in the viewpoint from which they approach the world, Myrdal argues that economists must make their premises explicit and justify these premises' relevance to the reality under study.

Economics can never hope to establish the type of constant, universal laws evident in the natural sciences, Myrdal believes, because economics, like other social sciences, is rooted in human behavior, which varies over time and in response to different conditions. To Myrdal, economists who ignore the importance of these variances are apt to distort reality, especially when they concentrate on the study of underdeveloped countries. The aggregate categories economists use in the developed world—GNP, savings, income, unemployment—and the assumptions underlying these concepts make little sense in the study of underdeveloped countries where conditions are so different and markets are imperfect or nonexistent. A purely "economic" approach, Myrdal says, "abstracts from most . . . conditions . . . not only peculiar to the underdeveloped countries but are largely responsible for their underdevelopment and for the particular difficulties they meet in developing." This critique of conventional economics pervades Myrdal's *Asian Drama* (1968) and *The Challenge of World Poverty* (1970).

Asian Drama is a monumental synthesis of the social, political, and economic factors that retard development in South Asia. Myrdal believes that mass poverty in South Asia, as in the United States, is a consequence of the underutilization of the labor force. The sympathies of the developed countries, he argues, have been with the privileged classes, not the impoverished masses who alone can become the vehicle for the needed radical reforms and genuine development. Only by finding ways to utilize what has become an ever more superfluous labor force and by increasing equality can true and lasting development be accomplished. This belief elaborates a theme evident in Myrdal's writings since the 1930s. Although many economists assume that the aims of economic growth and equality are in conflict, Myrdal believes that egalitarian social reforms are not only a moral imperative but, by increasing productivity, a necessary condition for economic development.

SEVEN

ECOLOGY, POLITICS, AND GROWTH

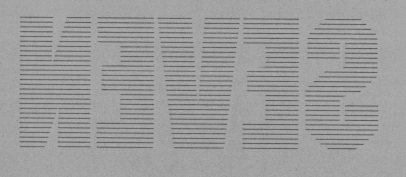

26 Social Costs and the Ecology

Today there seems to be an appalling amount of air, water, noise, and olfactory and visual pollution. At first glance, it seems that the market solution to the problem of allocating our scarce resources has gone awry. In fact, as pollution increases, so too do people's fears that the free working of supply and demand will bring about the ultimate destruction of the world as we know it. Perhaps there is a way we can alter some of the existing signals in our market economy so as to bring about a more rational use of resources and a less polluted environment. We will see in this chapter that some fairly straightforward improvements, which might bring about the desired reduction in pollution, could be made in the institutional setup in our economy. After this chapter, we will examine some of the most pressing ecological issues. First, however, we must establish why some economic agents (polluters) can harm our environment without paying for the consequences.

Social vs. Private Costs

Thus far, we've been dealing with situations where the costs of an individual's actions are fully recognized and, indeed, quite explicit. When a business firm has to pay wages to workers, it knows exactly what its labor costs are. When it has to buy materials or build a plant, it knows quite well what it will cost. When an individual has to pay for car repairs, or shoe repairs, or for a theater ticket, he or she knows exactly what the cost will be. These very explicit costs are what we term *private costs*. Private costs are those borne solely by the individuals who incur them. They are *internal* in the sense that the firm or household must explicitly take account of them.

Social Costs

What about a situation where a business firm dumps the waste products from its production process into a nearby river? Or where an individual litters a public park or beach? Obviously, a cost is involved in these actions. When the business firm pollutes the water, people downstream suffer the consequences. They may not want to drink the polluted water or swim and bathe in it. They may also be unable to catch as many fish as before because of the pollution. In the case of littering, the people who come along after our litterer has cluttered the park or the beach are the ones who bear the costs. The scenery certainly will be less attractive. The cost of these actions is borne by people other than those who commit the actions. That is, the creator of the cost is not the sole bearer. The costs are not internalized; they are external. When we add *external* costs to *internal* or private costs, we get **social costs.** They are called social costs because it is society in general who bears them, not just the individuals who create them. Pollution problems and, indeed, all problems pertaining to the environment may be viewed as situations where social costs are different from private costs. Since some economic agents don't pay the full social costs of their actions, but rather only the smaller private costs, their actions are socially excessive.

Polluted Air

Why is the air in cities so polluted from automobile exhaust fumes? When automobile drivers step into their cars, they bear only the private costs of driving. That is, they must pay for the gas, maintenance, depreciation, and insurance on their automobiles. However, they cause an additional cost—that of air pollution—which they are not forced to take account of when they make the decision to drive. The air pollution created by automobile exhaust is a social cost that, as yet, individual operators of automobiles do not bear *directly*. The social cost of driving includes all the private costs plus the cost of air pollution, which society bears. Decisions made on the basis of private costs only lead to too much automobile driving or, alternatively, too little money spent on the reduction of automobile pollution.

Externalities

When private costs differ from social costs, we usually term the situation a problem of **externalities** because individual decision makers are not *internalizing all* the costs that society is bearing. Rather, some of these costs are remaining external to the decision-making process. We might want to view the problem as it is presented in Figure 26-1. Here we have the market demand curve for product X and a supply curve for product X. The supply curve, however, is equivalent to the horizontal summation of the marginal cost curves of all individual firms and includes only internal or private costs. The intersection of the demand and supply curves as drawn will be at price P_e and quantity Q_e. However, we will assume that the production of good X involves externalities which the private business firms did not take into account. Those externalities could be air pollution or water pollution or scenery destruction or anything of that nature.

We know that the social costs of producing X exceed the private costs. We show this by drawing the supply curve $S'S'$. It is above the original supply curve SS because it includes the externalities, or the full social costs of producing the product. Now the "correct" market equilibrium price is P_1 and the quantity supplied and demanded is Q_1. The inclusion of external costs in the decision-making process

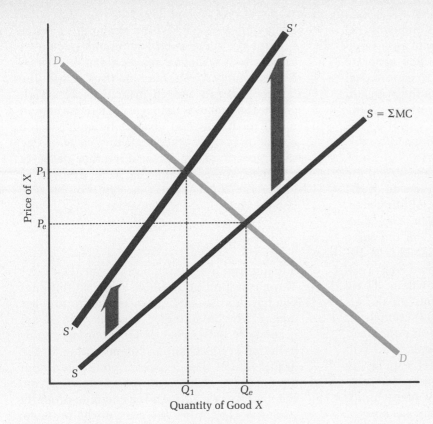

FIGURE 26-1 Adding Social Costs

Here we show the demand for good X as *DD*. The supply curve, *SS*, is equal to the horizontal summation of the individual marginal cost curves of all the firms producing that good. These individual marginal cost curves include only internal or private costs; they do not include any social costs such as pollution of the air or water. If the social costs were included and added to the private costs, the supply curve would shift up to *S'S'*. In the uncorrected situation, the equilibrium price would be P_e and the quantity demanded and supplied would be Q_e. In the corrected situation, the equilibrium price would rise to P_1 and the quantity demanded and supplied would fall to Q_1.

leads to a higher-priced product and less of a quantity produced. We can say, therefore, that in an unrestricted situation where social costs are not being fully borne by the creators of those costs, the quantity produced is "excessive."

Correcting the Signals

We can see here an "easy" method of reducing the amount of pollution and environmental degradation that exists. Somehow the signals in the economy must be changed so that decision makers will take into account all the costs of their actions. In the case of automobile pol-

lution, we might want to devise some method whereby motorists are taxed according to the amount of pollution they cause. In the case of a firm, we might want to devise a system whereby businesses are taxed according to the amount of pollution they are responsible for. In this manner, they would have an incentive to install pollution-abatement equipment.

However, it may not be appropriate to levy a *uniform* tax according to physical quantities of pollution. After all, we're talking about social costs. Such costs are not necessarily the same everywhere in the United States for the same action. If you drive your smelly, belching car in the middle of the Mojave Desert, you will inflict little or no damage on anyone else. No one will be there to complain; the natural cleansing action of the large body of air around you will eliminate the pollution you generate to such an extent that it creates no economical harm. If a business firm pollutes the water in a lake that is used by no other parties and the lake is, in fact, inaccessible to everyone else, the external economic damages created by this pollution may be negligible

Essentially, we must establish the size of the *economic damages* rather than the size of the *physical* amount of pollution. A polluting electric steam-generating plant in New York City will cause much more damage than the same plant in, say, Nowhere, Montana. This is because the concentration of people in New York City is much higher than in Nowhere. There are already innumerable demands on the air in New York City, so that the pollution from smokestacks will not naturally be cleansed away. There are millions of people who will breathe that smelly air and thereby incur the costs of sore throats, sickness, emphysema, and even early death. There are many, many buildings that will become dirtier faster because of the pollution, and many cars and clothes that will also become dirtier faster. The list goes on and on, but it should be obvious that a given quantity of pollution will cause more harm in concentrated urban environments than it will in less-dense rural environments. If we were to establish some form of taxation to align social costs with private costs and to force people to internalize externalities, we would somehow have to come up with a measure of economic costs instead of physical quantities.

Property Rights

Now let's find out why there will be a divergence between social costs and private costs. Why do certain situations create externalities while others do not? For an example, consider some of the things you own. Suppose you own a bicycle. If someone comes along and alters it unfavorably by slashing the tires or bending the spokes, you can, in principle, press civil charges and recover damages. The damages you might recover would at least be equal to the reduction in the market value of your bike. The same goes for your car or any other property you own. Anyone damaging your property is liable for those damages. The courts will uphold your right to compensation.

Common Property

Suppose you live next to a smelly steel factory? The air around you—which is something that you have to use—is damaged. You, in turn, are damaged by breathing it. However, you do not necessarily have grounds for stopping the air pollution or for obtaining compensation for the destruction of the air around you. You do not have *property rights* in the air surrounding you, nor does anyone else. Air is a **common property** resource. Herein lies the crux of the problem: Whenever property rights are indefinite or nonexistent, social costs may be different from private costs, particularly in the situations we will outline below. This is as you would expect. When no one owns a particular resource, people do not have an incentive to consider their particular despoliation of that resource. In fact, a person would be foolish to do so. If one person decides not to pollute the air, there will be no significant effect on the total level of pollution. If one person decides not to pollute the ocean, there will still be approximately the same amount of ocean pollution, provided of course that the individual is only a small part of the total number of polluters.

When property rights are in existence, individuals have legal recourse to any damages sustained through the misuse of their property.

When property rights are well defined, the use of property—that is, the use of resources—will generally involve contracting between the owners of those resources. If you own any land, you might contract with another person who wants to use your land for raising cows. The contract would most likely be written in the form of a rental agreement. Whenever contracting becomes exceedingly expensive or difficult, social and private costs will probably diverge. Whenever contracting is relatively costless, social costs and private costs will end up being one and the same thing, as we will see. In fact, this is why externalities are only problems in certain areas of activity in our society. We don't worry about social and private costs with the majority of activities that occur in our economy because almost all of what occurs involves contracting among individuals and the transference (whether temporary or permanent) of property rights.

When Private Costs Equal Social Costs

Surprisingly enough, even when property rights do not exist, it is sometimes possible for private costs to equal social costs. In such situations, there is no misallocation of resources. Let's take a simple example. Suppose you live in a house with a nice view of a lake. The people living below you plant a tree. Over the years the tree grows larger and larger, and eventually it cuts off your view. In most cities, nobody has property rights to views, and therefore, you usually cannot go to the courts for relief. You cannot file suit against your downhill neighbors for obstructing your view.

Contracting   You do have an alternative, however. You can, as it were, bribe your neighbors (contract with them) to top their tree (make it shorter). What kind of bribe would you offer them? You could start with a small money

figure and keep going up until either they agree or you reach your limit. Your limit will be equal to the value you place on having an unobstructed view of the lake. The neighbors will be willing to top their tree if the payment is at least equal to the reduction in (intrinsic) property value due to a stunted tree. In this manner, you make them aware of the social cost of their action; you inform them of the social cost of their growing a large tree that blocks your view and thereby lowers the value of your property. But you do this in a rather odd way—essentially, you bribe them. Nonetheless, they are still informed of the true cost of their actions. Alternatively, your neighbors could come to you and ask you how much you would be willing to pay to have them top their tree.

Now, let's take a hypothetical situation. Suppose property rights were actually vested in views. If the property right to your view was vested in you, anybody destroying your view would have to pay the consequences. In this particular case, the downhill landowner would have to bribe you to be able to let the tree grow higher than you would want it. The bribe to you would have to be at least equal to the reduction in the value of your property because of an obstructed view. (This will, of course, be a measure of the value of the view itself.) If the downhill landowner doesn't offer a high enough bribe, he or she will have to top the tree because you will not go for the deal.

Opportunity Costs   Now let's change the situation. Assume that your neighboring landowners have the property right in your view—a strange situation indeed but actually equivalent to the example where no one had the property right. If your neighbors have the property right in your view, will the assets called "view" and "tree" be used differently from when you had the property right? If you think so, you're wrong. Just because your neighbors now own the view does not mean they will ignore the cost they are imposing on you. After all, your neighbors would be giving up the opportunity of perhaps making some money in a deal with you. Your neighbors could gingerly walk to your house and ask you how much you would be willing to pay to have the tree topped. If you were willing to pay enough, they would do so. If not, they would leave it as is.

In other words, your neighbors would take account of the *opportunity cost*. This is the key to understanding why private costs equal social costs in all three of the above situations—in the first instance where there were no property rights, in the second case where property rights were given to the uphill landowner, and in the third case where property rights were given to the downhill landowners. In each situation, opportunity costs exist and will be taken into account. The contracting involved is relatively simple: Only two parties are concerned and verbal agreements can be made relatively easily. These particular examples lead us to a strange but, nonetheless, correct conclusion:

When transactions costs are minimal, it does not matter who has the property rights in the resources under study. They will be used in exactly the same way.

Otherwise stated:

The allocation of resources does not depend on who has property rights if transactions costs are small.

Wealth Distribution   Note also in this example that the distribution of wealth differs. *The person who gets the property rights to some resource that was formerly common property will obviously be better off because that person's wealth will be higher.* If a large untopped tree is more valuable than the view of the uphill

landowner, the tree will not be topped. Think about this. In the case where the uphill landowner has the property right in the view, the landowner will accept a bribe that is at least equal to the reduction in the property value due to the large tree. The downhill landowners will offer a sum that does not exceed the increase in their property value due to an untouched tree. If the view is more valuable than the untouched tree, they will not be able to bribe the uphill landowner; they will have to top the tree.

On the other hand, if the downhill landowners have the property rights in the view, they will have to be bribed to top the tree. If the increased value of the unobstructed view leads the uphill landowner to offer a sum that is greater than the value of the untouched tree to the downhill landowners, the downhill landowners will accept the bribe and top the tree. In either case, the two resources—the view and the tree—will be used such that they generate the highest economic value.

When Transactions Costs Are High   Our example so far is pretty simple. It involves only two parties and the contracting or transactions costs are small. What about a case where the transactions costs aren't as small? Take the example of a factory polluting a city of several million people. It would be difficult for the several million people to get together to somehow bribe the factory into reducing its pollution. The transactions costs here would be extremely high. Therefore, we cannot predict that private costs will equal social costs for the factory. This is probably true with many environmental problems.

There are indefinite property rights that in and of themselves are not always a problem if contracting can be done easily. However, when large numbers of people are involved, contracting is difficult, and, in many instances, the actual costs are hard to measure and/or the creators of those costs are difficult to identify. If ships are spilling excess oil into the ocean, how do we police them to find out which ones are doing it? The costs of such policing may be high. This discussion of property rights leads us to another possible solution to our environmental problems.

Pinpointing Property Rights

Instead of attempting to tax polluters in proportion to the economic damages caused by their pollution, we could define property rights more precisely so that contracting would have to take place. As concerns the view of the lake, it did not really matter who had property rights in the view. In fact, indefinite property rights really were inconsequential to the outcome of the situation except, of course, with reference to the wealth positions of the individuals. This is not the case with other environmental problems. For example, we might want to make factories liable for the pollution that they create. When we do that, we are implicitly vesting property rights in the common property resources of water and air surrounding the factories. The individuals living near it will implicitly be the owners of that air and water. The factory will therefore be liable for its use of water and air if its use imposes costs on others.

In a sense, this is not really "fair." After all, a common property resource is, by definition, owned by everyone. We would be arbitrary in assigning property rights in a common property resource to the homeowners, just as we would be arbitrary in assigning the property rights to the factory. But, because it is easier to make the individual factory owner pay, we still might want to go ahead with this arbitrary assignment of property rights.

In essence, the government may have to act

in behalf of the homeowners when dealing with the polluting factory. The government would somehow have to determine the value of the economic damages that the factory's pollution is causing and require the factory to make due compensation or install pollution-abatement equipment. The compensation would have to be distributed to the homeowners in a manner that reflected the economic cost sustained by each of them. That, of course, is a difficult problem. It might be simpler to use the "bribe" money to clean up some of the pollution caused by the factory instead of trying to compensate the losers (the individual homeowners). Note here that the optimal level of pollution is not zero. The optimal level is that point where the social benefits of further reducing pollution just equal the social costs of doing so.

What about External Benefits?

So far we've discussed external costs that were not internalized by individual decision makers. We should note that there are also situations with external benefits. In cases where the social benefits of an action exceed the private benefits, we would expect that individual decision makers would do too little of such an action from society's point of view. In fact, it is often argued that many endeavors involve large social benefits that are not internalized. It is further argued that government subsidization of such activity is in order. This is often the argument used to justify public education. An educated citizenry presumably votes more wisely, commits less crime, and so on. Therefore, it behooves society to furnish public education below marginal cost.

In many cases, the mere fact that an external benefit exists does not economically justify government subsidization of the activity. A well-dressed, attractive person generates a considerable amount of external benefits. Does that mean that we are underproducing attractive persons? Should the government subsidize attractive clothes so that more persons can generate more external benefits? Well-developed individuals also generate external benefits, but should the government, therefore, subsidize gyms? When someone has a beautiful garden, passersby benefit from that garden yet do not pay anything. Does that mean that we should subsidize beautiful gardens so that there will be more of them?

The key to understanding when an external benefit is relevant is in finding out whether those people who are benefiting from the externality would be willing to pay, on the margin, for one more unit. For example, it is argued that when electricity wires are put underground, more people than just the property owners benefit. People driving or walking in a neighborhood that has no overhead wires benefit because they are looking on a more beautiful neighborhood. That does not necessarily mean, however, that underground electricity wires should be subsidized (paid for by the government instead of the property owners). We would somehow have to find out if people who do not live in the area but who enjoy walking, bicycling, and driving through it would nonetheless be willing to pay something for the privilege of seeing the neighborhood without electricity wires. If they are unwilling, then in this particular situation it is probably not economically meaningful to consider the externality problem as a real problem.

External Benefits and Nonpayers

When external benefits exist, we usually find that those who obtain those external benefits cannot be excluded from obtaining them. Otherwise, the benefits wouldn't be external; they would be internal. A theater could generate external benefits if, in fact, there were no way to exclude viewers. After all, once the picture is being shown, everybody can benefit from the picture as long as there is sufficient space. But since theater owners like to capture profits, they construct walls and doors to exclude nonpayers. The exclusion of nonpayers is important to making sure that all benefits from an action are internalized.

This is not the case in all situations. Consider, for example, fireworks displays. They can be seen for many, many blocks, and it is difficult to exclude nonpayers. Here is a case where social or external benefits actually exist because nonpayers will not be excluded and can get value from the production of a fireworks display. However, business firms in general are quite ingenious in finding ways to exclude nonpayers. To the extent that they are successful, we need not worry about external benefits. Football stadiums have high walls, theaters have closed doors, and so on.

There are situations, however, where, although it is relatively costless to exclude nonpayers, it might be socially beneficial if no one were excluded.

Public Goods

There is a class of goods that economists have labeled **public goods.** With such goods, the amount that one individual uses of the good or service does not take away from the amount which any other individual can use of the good, *once it has already been produced.* If you write a poem, anybody can read the poem without preventing anybody else from doing the same thing. If you develop a theory, anybody else can use the theory without reducing others use of that theory. The marginal cost, once the good or service is produced, is zero. Indeed, pricing on the basis of marginal cost, we would see that once the good is produced there is no price!

This is the situation with television and radio signals. Once they are produced, they are a public good. Anyone who wants to use them can do so without taking away from any other person's ability to use them. Furthermore, the marginal cost to the television or radio generating station is zero when a new person decides to use the waves. The marginal cost of providing TV or radio programs, once they are produced, is usually zero, and, in that sense, the price should be zero. However, if the price were zero, then you would not expect much to be produced, would you? Entrepreneurs usually don't like to sell their products at a zero price.

In such cases, and for most public goods, there has to be some way to transform the public good into a private good. Otherwise, the government would have to take on the production itself. In the case of television, we now have a *semi*public good because television stations allow advertisers to buy time. The advertising pays for the production of the signals. You pay for the TV programs you watch when you buy the products that are advertised. If you buy none of the products advertised on TV, then in essence you are being subsidized by those people who do. In the case of national defense, another classic public good, government has taken on the production of the service. (With that particular public good, it would be very expensive to exclude nonpayers from the benefits.)

Sometimes there are ways of transforming a public good into a private good by setting up a system that will exclude nonpayers. That's exactly what cable television or pay TV is all about. People who do not pay do not obtain the TV signal, or if they do, it is scrambled. In this case, the private good means we do not have to see so many commercials on television because we pay directly for the service.

The area of public goods is new in economics and not very well defined. At this point, we can say that it is inappropriate to blindly carry over the principles we have laid out for private goods to public goods. We have, however, established a fairly comprehensive theory in this chapter that we can apply to various ecological and social issues. We shall turn to these issues next.

Definitions of New Terms

Social Costs: The costs of an action, including all those that society bears. Social costs differ from private costs whenever there are externalities.

Externalities: Positive or negative effects on third parties that are not taken into account by individual decision makers. An externality to the production of steel might be the pollution put into the air for which neither the producer nor the consumer has to pay.

Common Property: Property owned by no one, that can be used by all.

Public Goods: Goods for which the marginal cost of an additional person using them once they have been produced is zero. National defense is a good example of a public good.

1. Up until this chapter we had been dealing implicitly with situations where the costs of individual actions are fully recognized. These are called private costs, and they are borne privately by people making voluntary exchanges in the economy. In some sense they are internal to the firm or the household and must explicitly be taken care of.

2. In some situations there are social costs that do not equal private costs. That is, there are costs to society which exceed the cost to the individual. These social costs may include such things as air and water pollution, for which private individuals do not have to pay. Society, however, does bear the costs of these externalities.

3. One way to analyze the problem of pollution is to look at it in terms of an externality situation. Individual decision makers do not take account of the negative externalities they impose on the rest of society. In such a situation, they produce "too much" pollution and too many polluting goods.

4. It might be possible to ameliorate the situation by imposing a tax on polluters. The tax, however, should be dependent upon the extent of the economic damages created rather than upon the physical amounts of pollution. This tax, therefore, will be different for the same level of physical pollution in different parts of the country because the economic damages differ, depending upon the location and the density of the population, and on other factors.

5. Another way of looking at the externality problem is to realize that it involves the lack of definite property rights. We are talking about common property resources such as air and water. No one owns them, and, therefore, no one takes account of the long-run pernicious effects of excessive pollution.

6. In situations where transaction costs are minimal, the same allocation of resources will result whether the property in question is common or privately owned. The distribution of wealth, however, will change depending on who is able to appropriate what, until now, have been common property rights.

7. External benefits arise when individual actions generate benefits to other individuals without those other individuals having to pay for them. It is often thought that whenever external benefits exist, subsidization is desirable in order to achieve a socially optimal rate of production.

8. In economics we have a body of theory devoted to public goods. These are defined as goods for which the cost of providing service to an additional individual is zero, once the good has already been produced. National defense and radio and TV signals are examples of public goods.

1. Are there any actions you engage in for which no external benefits or costs arise? What are they?
2. Invitingly dressed members of the opposite sex generate external benefits. Should the government subsidize such clothing?
3. If you were in a jury and a houseowner was suing an airport for noise pollution, in whose favor would you decide? Would it depend on who got there first, the homeowner or the airport? Does this bother you?
4. If you were the economic consultant to a nation that was just created, would you tell the government to prohibit private property rights in land or allow private property rights? Why?
5. Is it true that property rights often interfere with human rights?
6. When Charles de Gaulle was head of the French government, he decided not to support NATO. Do you think there was a free-rider problem involved here? Why? Is NATO a public good?

Selected
References

Coase, Ronald H., "The Problem of Social Costs," *Journal of Law and Economics,* October 1961.
——, "The Federal Communications Commission," *Journal of Law and Economics,* October 1962, pp. 111–140.
Commoner, Barry, *The Closing Circle: Nature, Man and Technology,* New York: Knopf, 1971.
Edel, Matthew, *Economics and the Environment,* Englewood Cliffs, N.J.: Prentice-Hall, 1973.
Kneese, Allen V., *Economics and the Quality of the Environment,* Washington, D.C.: Resources for the Future, April 1968.
McKean, Roland M., *Public Spending,* New York: McGraw-Hill, 1968, pp. 67–75.

Who Gets the Ocean's Wealth?

THE COMMON HERITAGE OF ALL NATIONS

Resources from the Sea

Since before the beginning of civilization, the ocean has provided human beings with food and other forms of wealth. The ocean has been and continues to be one of our most important resources. Millions make their living by fishing and millions live on the food the ocean provides. Nations are increasingly obtaining oil and gas from under the waters surrounding the continents, and in the future many minerals will be mined from the seabeds. Until recently, the ocean appeared "big enough" to satisfy all the activities on and in it. However, as both population and the consumption demands of the world have increased, the ocean's resources have been severely strained. Several species of fish have died out, for example, and traditional fishing grounds have been destroyed because of overfishing. But even perhaps more important than population and consumption demands is the fact that today many nations, especially those who do not border on the sea, feel they too deserve a share of the ocean's resources. In 1957, the ambassador from Malta to the United Nations gave an impassioned 3½-hour speech in which he pointed out that two-thirds of the earth's surface (the oceans) was being grabbed up by a very few nations, leaving all the landlocked nations to a destiny of poverty, or at least of lower economic status. He outlined in his speech a dream. The dream was that the living and nonliving resources outside each nation's territorial limits be formally declared the "common heritage of mankind." The ambassador wanted a new regime to be established to exploit these resources and apportion them "for the benefit of everyone." In particular, he pointed out the needs of developing nations.

Since 1957 there have been a number of international conferences on the law of the seas. In this issue we will discuss some of the proposals that have been made to apportion the sea's resources to the various competing and conflicting interests throughout the world. We will also discuss the probable outcomes of these proposals. In addition, we'll take a brief look at how the United States has treated the oceans.

Territorial Waters

In 1945 President Truman declared that the United States was the sole owner of mineral resources in its underwater continental shelf. Most other nations followed suit. At the same time we decided to go from the traditional 3-mile limit as the delineation of our territorial waters to a 12-mile limit. Today, although most nations have a 12-mile limit, many are even starting to extend their territorial waters far beyond this limit. Some Latin American countries, for example, with large schools of fish in their offshore waters, have decided that a 200-mile limit is more appropriate. Ecuador, Peru, and Chile declared this limit a number of years ago. Since then, the American government has paid millions of dollars in fines to the governments of these nations for infringing on their unilaterally declared 200-mile limit. And a number of Americans have been jailed for trespassing on these waters.

The concept of freedom of the seas has generally been restricted to international waters—recently the concept has been diminishing along with these "international" waters.

Economic Zones

At the various international conferences dealing with this problem of

resource apportionment, one suggestion that has been made, by the United States and by other countries, is that economic zones of 200 miles offshore should be set up. In other words, the oceans should be divided among the owners of any land touching a body of water. This would mean that small islands would have economic rights within a 200-mile radius of their shore. The plan has been much heralded in the United States as the savior of financially troubled fishing interests along the northwestern and Atlantic coasts.

American fishing interests have been outclassed in these areas by Soviet and Japanese fishing units. In certain instances entire fishing grounds are being threatened by the very efficient methods they are using on what are now regarded as the high seas. For example, the Bristol Bay fishing area in Alaska is threatened by a severe reduction in total catch because of the efficiency of Japanese gill-net techniques used in outlying international waters.

Unfortunately, the goals and desires of the fishermen in the north-west and the northeast are at variance with those of the fishing fleets operating out of California and the Gulf states. These fleets go after shrimp and tuna—usually in foreign waters. If the 200-mile economic zone were put into effect, these fishing interests would undoubtedly lose out. They would then, at the very minimum, be forced to pay foreign countries for the right to fish in what would then be territorial waters but which are now international waters.

Also, if the suggested 200-mile economic zone were incorporated into international law, landlocked nations would probably try to gain control over small islands so as to have access to ocean resources.

In addition, there is speculation that such a limit could disrupt navigation. However, navigation that is not for the purpose of resource exploitation could be left free as it is now except within the traditional 3- or 12-mile territorial limits.

Suggestions for Mining "Nodules"

One of the greatest potential sources of minerals in the world today is called the "manganese nodule." These black and potato-shaped nodules cover much of the ocean's floor. They contain significant quantities of copper, nickel, and cobalt, as well as trace quantities of a number of other minerals. As of the middle of the 1970s, they have not yet been commercially mined, but as the relative price of raw materials continues to rise and/or new and more technologically efficient means are developed to "suck up" these nodules for processing, it will only be a matter of time until commercial mining begins.

Who owns these nodules? If we are to take into consideration the notion of the "common heritage of mankind," then the nodules belong to everyone. But of course that does not tell us how they should be mined or who should profit from them. The less-developed nations have devised a scheme whereby a central licensing authority, probably a unit of the United Nations, would divide all potential nodule-producing seabeds

into well-defined geographical units and then issue licenses granting the right to mine those units to all comers. Of course, if this were done, and if the licensing were done on a highest-bid basis, then maximum economic value would be obtained from these resources, and they would be mined in the most efficient way possible. However, if a political process were used to give out the licensing rights, or if there were a first-come, first-serve situation where the ownership rights could *not* be transferred, then we would not be ensured of an economically efficient solution.

As can be expected, the less-developed nations are not in favor of these latter suggestions for licensing. They want a central authority to retain control of production, marketing, and prices. They want, in other words, the central authority—probably the United Nations—to let out service contracts but continue to own the entire resource. The important mineral-producing nations of Chile, Peru, Zaire, and Zambia are particularly in favor of a central authority having control over prices. These countries fear that massive mining of magnesium nodules would put a downward pressure on the world prices of the minerals they export, whereas a central authority for the nodules could probably help keep prices relatively high.

Not too many years ago, the American Mining Congress attempted to get a bill through Congress that would have involved the United States government in the nodule-mining process. Montana's Senator Lee Metcalf introduced the bill. If passed, the United States gov-

ernment would have been mining nodules in international waters. The proposal, to be sure, shocked most underdeveloped nations. It would have meant their not sharing in these resources.

The Fishing Problem Revisited

There are many suggestions about how to solve the "fishing problem," but each faces difficulties. The development of economic zones faces a difficulty concerned with the difference between migrating fish and bottom fish. The economic zones would solve any problem of overfishing bottom fish, but they would not solve the problem of overfishing migrating schools of fish, such as tuna and the like.

Since international agreements don't seem to be working, perhaps other solutions to overfishing should be tried. One such solution could be for nations that own waters where migrating fish spawn to obtain property rights on those migrating fish. It is now possible to monitor the movement of schools of fish, so these countries could, in fact, keep a close watch on the fish they "owned." They could sell licenses or charge specific fees to fishing interests that wanted to take part in exploiting this migrating fish resource. In this manner, a generally more efficient harvesting of the fish would take place since there would be no overfishing. The owners of the migrating fish would find it in their own best interest to limit the catch so that population size would not go below a critical level, which might

spell destruction for the entire species.

Another Problem—Ocean Spills

Many oil tankers and other such vessels ply the seas, and occasionally they have accidents. When they do, they cause countless millions of dollars worth of damage to beaches, wildlife, and the like. How can we possibly hope to solve such a problem? One solution is to somehow measure the actual economic damage caused by ocean spills and, if possible, find the responsible vessel so that the guilty party could be assessed liability. Some economists feel that the liability should be unlimited. If a supertanker wants to take the chance of going into the Puget Sound region and perhaps cracking up, spilling millions of gallons of crude oil along 2000 miles of beaches, it would have to take the financial responsibility of unlimited liability. With such an economic incentive hanging over their heads, the owners of oil-carrying vessels would improve methods of preventing oil spills, improve methods of minimizing the economic damages caused by oil spills, and in general probably reduce the amount of destruction involved in ocean shipping.

This is not the complete answer, however, because the problem of ocean dumping and oil spills on the high seas are still difficult to detect.

The Real Issue—The Distribution of Wealth

The real issue here is: Who owns the oceans and their wealth? As of now, they are, by and large, common property. Everyone owns them and no one owns them. The fish in those waters are a common-property resource, as the oil and gas have been. But until ownership rights over these now common-property resources are established, we can be fairly sure they will be overutilized, particularly as world population, demand, and income grow. It is not surprising that certain species of fish will die out, for example, before ownership rights are established. It is in no nation's best interest at any one time to stop fishing. Nations know that other nations will continue fishing and will ruin the catch for the future anyway.

Since we now have the electronic equipment necessary to monitor—relatively cheaply—vast expanses of ocean waters, it is not impossible for us to establish economic zones of 200 miles or even 1000 miles and actually police those zones. What we will be doing is arbitrarily vesting ownership rights in an, until now, common-property resource. The owners of these rights will make sure that the maximum economic value is extracted from the resource in question.

In other words, resources would be allocated in an economically efficient manner. But what about the distribution of wealth from these ocean resources? The less-developed nations, as we mentioned, would like to have a share of that wealth and certainly will make a great effort to get it. Whether or not we call it a "just" share, and whether or not we call the oceans a part of the "common heritage of mankind," depends on each individual's value judgments. In any event, we must keep in mind the distinction between an "equitable" distribution of wealth and an efficient allocation of resources. No doubt, something can, and from a value-judgment point of view should, be done about overfishing, ocean pollution, and the extraction of minerals from the seabed in a rational manner. But the question of who should own the wealth in the ocean involves us in the area of normative economics. Positive or value-free economics cannot give us an answer.

Questions for Thought and Discussion

1. Which resources are not the "common heritage of mankind"? How do we decide which resources are?
2. Is it possible to police ocean waters to prevent overfishing?
3. "Now that transactions costs are lower, it is possible to solve the overfishing problem." Evaluate this quote.
4. Do you think it is technologically possible to police oil spills?

Selected References

Crutchfield, J. A. and G. Pontecorvo, *The Pacific Salmon Fisheries,* Baltimore: Johns Hopkins University Press, 1969.

Dales, J. H., "Land, Water, and Ownership," *Canadian Journal of Economics,* vol. 1, November 1968, pp. 791–804.

Garvey, Gerald, *Energy, Ecology, Economy: A Framework for Environmental Policy,* New York: W. W. Norton, 1972, pp. 99–106.

Conservation and Energy

HOW SHOULD WE UTILIZE OUR RESOURCES?

The Debate

Conservation is a loaded word. The first head of the U.S. Forest Service, Gifford Pinchot, felt that "conservation means the greatest good for the greatest numbers, and that for the longest time." Members of the Sierra Club and the Wilderness Society believe that the government should take a vastly increased interest in preserving our natural wilderness areas and in preserving Mother Earth in general. Some businesspersons think that Sierra Club members are fanatical and unknowledgable about the economics of conservation. After all, trees have to be cut to make houses, and iron ore has to be taken out of the ground to make steel for buildings. We can look at these economic aspects of the conservation question to find what the real issue is.

What Conservation Really Means

Let's look carefully at Gifford Pinchot's quotation. We should ask whether this is really an operational definition of conservation. Is this really what conservationists believe should be the *modus operandi* of the government in conserving our natural resources? The answer is probably no.

Limited Resources

We know that at any particular moment, the total amount of resources in the United States is fixed. Therefore, with the exception of public goods, whatever you use of a resource, your friends cannot use. Whatever your friends use, you cannot use. This makes it difficult to talk about the greatest good for the greatest number, and this is what economists refer to as erroneous and impossible double maximization. It is like saying you want the best for the least. Either you seek out the highest-quality product you can buy for a given price, or for a given quality you seek out the lowest-priced brand. A firm either takes production as given and tries to minimize costs, or it takes costs as given and tries to maximize production. The same holds for conservation. It is impossible to have the greatest good for the greatest number because what one person has, another person doesn't have.

Also consider the clause, "and that for the longest time." What does this mean? What could it possibly lead to in terms of the use of resources? Doesn't it imply that no resources should be used at all today and forever after? That, of course, is how we use our resources for the longest time—by never using them up at all! We can keep coal in the ground from now to eternity by never taking any out. But does conservation mean that we should limit the amount of resources we use so that they will last the longest? If so, we should stop consuming resources today. Then our grandchildren and their grandchildren and their grandchildren will inherit the largest amount of natural resources.

An Operational Definition

Another definition of conservation must be found if we are to have a rational, objective standard by which to judge current actions involving our natural resources. Let's take the simple example of 1 acre of land with some trees on it. Suppose you are the owner of that land. How would you decide whether to cut the trees or let them grow? If you decide to cut the trees, when should you cut them and how many should you cut?

Should you cut one tree, two trees, or all the trees?

Let's make the problem simple and assume that the trees are located in an area that no one ever sees. We will assume you get no pleasure from the mere fact of owning trees. You are a wealth-maximizer and look only at the monetary return on the piece of property that you own. If you wanted to maximize wealth, you would decide how to use your trees by looking at how profitable it would be either to cut them or let them grow. It's a hard decision but really no different from the decisions facing any property owner. You must decide the optimal use of your resource. With natural resources, this also involves the optimal *timing* of the use of the resource.

If you thought you could build a road to your stand of trees and charge campers a certain amount of money to use the area, you would consider this alternative. Or you could cut down the trees today, sell them on the open market, and receive a certain price per tree. If you waited another year, you could sell them on the open market and perhaps receive a different price. Since the trees would have grown during that time, there would be more board-feet of lumber to sell. Obviously, if you thought the price was going to rise in the future and the trees were going to grow bigger, you might wait to cut them. But obviously you shouldn't wait forever. At some point, you will maximize your net wealth position by cutting the trees or, if camping becomes very lucrative, by making your tree stand into a private campground. The point is that you must compare the benefits of not

cutting the trees with the costs of not cutting the trees. The benefits of not cutting is the fact that they could be used as a campground. Moreover, if you do not cut, you might get a higher price for them in the future.

Your costs are the opportunity costs of not cutting the trees and selling them for what you could get.

If, for example, you could sell them for $1 million this year and invest that money in a comparatively risk-free government bond that yielded an 8 percent rate of return, the opportunity cost of not cutting the trees is going to equal 8 percent of $1 million, or $80,000. The combined benefits of not cutting the trees—that is, the benefits of a potential higher price in the future with bigger trees to sell—must at least equal the $80,000. Otherwise, you would cut the trees right away. (You also have the alternative of cutting now and then replanting. You might want to sell the timberland with small young trees on it.)

Discounting

To maximize the value of a piece of property that has natural resources on it, you should time your use of those resources so as to maximize their *discounted* value. Let's review the concept of discounting. If you get a dollar today, it's worth a dollar; but if you get a dollar 1 year from now, in today's terms it is not worth $1. It is worth less. You must discount tomorrow's dollar back to today to find out what it is really worth to you. After all, today's dollars could be put in a savings and loan association to earn interest. If somebody said you had to pay them $1 a year from now, you could probably put 95¢ in the bank and earn interest so that in 1 year, you would be able to pay the dollar. Thus, *costs that are borne in the future are less of a burden than those which must be paid today.*

The same is true of benefits. In this particular case the benefits will be the income received from cutting the timber. Money that will be forthcoming a year from now is worth less than money today. Even if you didn't want to invest the money you have today, you would be better off having it today than in the future because this way you have the opportunity to invest it or spend it during the interim if you desire.

Benefits are worth less the farther away they are in the future. If you had 1 acre of trees, you could estimate how much money you would receive for each time profile of cutting them. (You could sell the land and trees, too.) It could be that you should never cut them if the money you could make from turning the acre into a private campground exceeded the money you could make from cutting the trees. That, in fact, has happened in this country. As public campgrounds (for which users are usually charged a lower than market clearing price) become more and more crowded, private campgrounds become more attractive to individuals, and therefore more and more have sprung up throughout the United States. There was an 11 percent increase in such campgrounds from 1973 to 1974.

Conservation Defined Operationally

Conservation now takes on a very definite meaning. The definition we will use will be that *conservation means the optimal timing of the use of our known reserves of resources based upon present technology and preferences.* What does optimal timing involve? It involves utilizing re-

sources in such a way that the present value of the streams of net benefits from those resources is maximized. We can apply this definition to many of the problems of conserving our natural resources. Let's do that now.

Depletion of Nonrenewable Resources

There is much concern about using up all the natural gas under the earth. There's also much concern about using up the iron ore, coal, oil, and other nonrenewable (or renewable, but only very slowly) minerals and resources found in the earth. Many conservationists believe that because the resources cannot be renewed, their use should be limited. Using our newly found definition of conservation, we can agree that the use of such resources should indeed be limited, but not to the degree of *never* using them. After all, if the coal in the earth is never used, the present value of that coal will be zero. We'll never obtain any benefits from it. Neither will our grandchildren nor their grandchildren because they will never be able to use it to furnish energy. If it will never yield a benefit in the future, then there is nothing to discount, and present value is zero.

The question really is: "How fast should we use our coal?" How fast should we use our natural gas? Inevitably, we will eventually run out of many of our natural resources if we consume them forever at some constant rate. Any finite use of resources will eventually deplete nonrenewable resources unless their quantity is infinite. The only true thing is that the slower we use them, the longer they'll last. But how do we decide the rate at which we should actually use these resources?

Correct Timing

Again we can go back to a wealth-maximizing situation, and assume that it is the wealth of the entire world that is important. Here we can use our same criterion. The value from nonrenewable resources is maximized if they are used at different periods in time so that the net present value of these resources is highest. You might immediately scream ''bloody murder'' at this criterion because it leads to an eventual depletion of the kinds of resources you are familiar with. Let's take the case of natural gas. We may indeed eventually run out of natural gas if we continue using it. However, we will not continue using it at its same rate if the Federal Power Commission allows the price to rise as a reflection of the interaction of supply and demand. As the price of natural gas becomes higher, people will seek cheaper alternatives. This is one key to understanding why there is a limit as to how much of a natural resource will be used. After a point, the resource becomes so expensive that nobody uses it. In fact, we may never run out of natural gas because it will become so prohibitively expensive to take out of the ground that people will use substitutes.

Using Substitutes

The use of substitutes is another key to understanding why it might be

better to use up some of our natural resources rather than limit their use today. If we do not use natural gas, for example, we will use oil, coal, or some other form of energy. If we restrict the production and consumption of any one of our natural resources, we can be sure that some others will be used more intensively or other substitutes will be developed. That means that they will be used up faster than otherwise. It is impossible to conserve *everything* because that means that we would have to cease to exist. It is also somewhat naïve to talk in terms of conserving only one or a selected few natural resources because then other resources will be used up more quickly. If, in fact, we want to maximize the benefits from our available resources, we would be wise to use up the cheapest ones first and then go on to the more inaccessible and

less readily available ones. This can perhaps be best illustrated by another example.

Using Too Little May Mean Less for the Future

Assume the government has $1 million to invest in the economy. If the government decides to invest the $1 million in a project that yields a 5 percent rate of return, and the rate of return in the private (nongovernmental) sector is 10 percent, future generations will not be better off by the government investment. They would inherit a larger capital stock—that is, more wealth—if the government had not used the $1 million—which it got from the private sector in the first place—and had allowed the private sector to use it in private investment where it would have yielded a 10 percent rate of return. The same goes for use of natural resources.

If we decide to use a combination of natural resources that has a higher cost than some other combination, we will be cheating future generations, not helping them out. It may be that if we decide to use less natural gas and hence more of other energy sources, the wealth which future generations will inherit will be less than it would be otherwise. We will be doing future generations a disfavor by being "conservationist-minded." Admittedly, this is a hard concept to accept because it does mean allowing nonrenewable resources to be depleted if this is in fact the cheapest way to provide consumption and investment that the present generation wishes to engage in. But acting in any other way would leave future generations worse off, contrary to the notion of most conservationists. Conservation cannot mean limiting the use of our resources; it has to mean maximizing the net benefit from our limited resources.

The Energy Question

The basic analysis in this issue is applicable to all resources. However, there is an additional aspect to the resource called *energy*. Many people believe that an energy "crisis" has occurred (or will soon occur). Energy can be obtained from many sources: fossil fuels, nuclear fission and fusion, the sun, rivers, tides, and so forth. For now, we will combine these sources and refer to them all, simply, as "energy."

In the last few years we have seen a series of crises caused by the insufficient amount of energy in various forms that were available to the consuming public, at least in the United States. In 1973 and 1974 the energy crisis mainly affected automobile gasoline consumption and, to a lesser extent, heating-oil consumption. There were also sporadic problems with electric utilities not having enough fuel for their generating systems. When these problems—which, by the way, resulted from the embargo of the United

States and other countries by the Organization of Petroleum Exporting Countries—arose, there was a lot of talk about the need to conserve energy because we were "using it up" at a faster rate than we could supply it.

Generally the argument was presented in the following manner. We see in Figure I-32.1 the two lines "Energy Demand" and "Energy Supply." The difference between these two lines is the "Energy Deficit." Basically, the lines were obtained by using historical trends. That is, the lines are based on the historical rate of growth of the quantity of energy demanded and the historical increase in the supply of energy, taking into account predicted improvements in technology. In any event, an energy deficit clearly exists.

If we look at the energy question from the long-run point of view, however, we might have a difficult time accepting the reasoning behind Figure I-32.1. It does not take into account changing *relative* prices. We

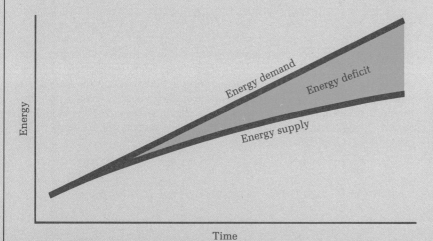

FIGURE I-32.1 The Energy Deficit
If we put time on the horizontal axis and energy on the vertical axis, we can look at projected quantities of energy supplied and demanded. In the typical scenario, there is a line called "Energy Supply" below the line called "Energy Demand." In other words, the energy supply grows over time at a smaller rate than energy demand. The difference is the "Energy Deficit."

have seen throughout this text that in unrestricted situations, relative prices will change so as to bring into equality the quantity of any particular good or service demanded and the quantity supplied. Since energy, in principle, is no different from any other resource, in a long-run unrestricted situation we would expect that the relative price of energy, or more specifically, of the various components of total energy consumption, would change so as to bring total quantity supplied with total quantity demanded into accord. If, in fact, a "deficit" was developing, the relative price of energy would rise so that the quantity demanded would fall. At the same time, this rise in the relative price of energy would bring additional investment, and eventually additional supplies, to that particular area.

Nonetheless, such an analysis is not usually presented by those who favor severe cutbacks to keep us from consuming "too much" energy. They present, instead, a fixed formula showing energy "needs." In economics, however, it is difficult to talk in terms of "need" when we use a demand schedule because a demand schedule shows that the quantity "needed" depends on the relative price. At higher relative prices of gasoline, for example, consumers of gasoline consume less. They consume less by reducing their use of the resource. They voluntarily reduce the number of trips they take, increase the number of car tuneups, reduce the horsepower and size of their cars, and alter the manner in which they drive. They may also voluntarily switch to public transportation, ride in car pools, and the like. In other words, the analysis of the demand for gasoline is no different, in principle, from the analysis of the demand for any other commodity. Changing relative prices of gasoline elicit changing relative intensities of use by consumers.

The Problem of Dependency

Although the economic analysis may tell us that energy should not be treated in any special manner, we still may be faced with a political aspect of the issue which is beyond the realm of economic analysis. Specifically, if we depend on foreign nations for significant amounts of energy sources—particularly crude oil—then we are more vulnerable to short-run disruptions in our sources of energy, depending on the political atmosphere in these countries. It is understandable that some people would prefer the United States not to have to depend on imported crude oil for so much of its energy need. But how do we reduce the quantity of imports demanded?

One of the most frequently discussed (and perhaps by now implemented) solutions has been the forced conservation of gasoline by rationing or other techniques. Another alternative is a tax, such as the 1975 one, on the import of petroleum products. This would seem to be the most efficient method. It raises the price that domestic oil companies can charge for their own crude oil products (unless an excise tax were added) thus stimulating greater production of domestic oil, and, at the same time, the relatively higher price causes oil to be conserved in all its uses, not in just some—as would be the case with a gasoline rationing system.

Further Energy Considerations

Many other considerations—a number of them political—would have to be brought into our analysis if we were to get a complete picture of the energy problem. It is extremely easy to look only at the supply and demand relationships for the different sources of energy and ignore all these other questions. As we said, if we do this, we find that energy, particularly in the long run, is no different from any other resource and, from a policy point of view, does not necessarily have to be treated differently. But politicians live in the short run and must contend with short-run problems, such as an oil embargo from oil-exporting nations. And although economic analysis is a useful basis for policy considerations, policymakers must look at all other aspects of the energy problem as well.

Definition of New Term	**Conservation:** The optimal timing of the use of our limited resources such that their present value is maximized.

Questions for Thought and Discussion

1. If we extended our territorial limits in ocean waters to the territorial limits of other nations, what would happen to the doctrine of "freedom of the seas?"
2. If private property rights were standard to all ocean waters, does that mean that only the nation that owned a particular segment of the ocean would be allowed to use it?
3. Do you think there is a relationship between property rights and economic incentives even in a socialist country?
4. If the dodo bird had been privately owned, do you think that it would have become extinct? If dinosaurs had been owned by someone, do you think they would have been exterminated? Why?
5. In comparing a private lake with a public lake, what do you think would be the average age of the fish caught in the private one as compared with the public one? In which lake do you think there would be overfishing?
6. Would you favor $10,000 fines for anyone caught shooting a bald eagle? A condor? Or a bighorn mountain sheep?

Selected References

Campbell, Rex R. and Jerry L. Wade, *Society and Environment,* Boston: Allyn and Bacon, 1972.

Ehrlich, Paul R. and Anne H. Ehrlich, *Population, Resources, Environment,* 2d ed., San Francisco: W. H. Freeman, 1972.

Falk, Richard A., *This Endangered Planet,* New York: Random House, 1971.

Miller, Roger LeRoy, *The Economics of Energy: What Went Wrong?,* Glenridge, N.J.: Horton, 1974.

Schwartz, William (ed.), *Voices for the Wilderness,* New York: Ballantine Books, 1969.

Zurhorst, Charles, *The Conservation Fraud,* New York: Cowles, 1970.

27 Politics and Public Choice

Much of what goes on in our economy is directly affected by political decisions made by elected officials or government bureaucrats. In our current political situation, we elect various senators and representatives as well as presidents, governors, mayors, and the like. We also elect judges, city councilpersons, and, in some cases, sheriffs. All these elected individuals can influence our economic, as well as our social and psychological, well-being. In principle, we live in a democracy where most of us have a franchise—that is, the right to vote. In this chapter we will look at how an ideal democracy would operate and, more specifically, how economic decisions would be made and what their effect on individuals would be. Then we will look at our actual political system and try to come up with theories as to why voters vote the way they do, why elected individuals make policies the way they do, and why bureaucrats make the decisions they do.

The Ideal Political Democracy

An ideal political democracy has much in common with a perfectly competitive, or ideal, market situation. In a perfectly competitive market situation, you will remember, no individual firm can influence quantities and prices, no individual buyer has any influence, and resources are allocated in such a way that maximum economic value is obtained from those fixed resources at any point in time.

Defining an Ideal Political Democracy

Our definition of an ideal political democracy draws heavily on the one presented by Joseph Schumpeter in his seminal work, *Capitalism, Socialism* and Democracy.[1] Basically, an ideal political democracy is defined as an institutional situation used to obtain political decisions in which individuals attempt to be elected to political office through perfectly free competition for votes from a broadly based electorate.

What does the phrase, "perfectly free competition for votes" mean? It means exactly the same thing that the phrase "perfect competition for goods" means in the marketplace. Individual producers attempt to sell their product to a large number of individuals acting in competition with numerous other sellers of that same good. The same is true of candidates seeking political office in our ideal political democracy. Because transactions costs are minimal so as not to prevent entry into the business of politics, candidates find it easy to compete against other potential officeholders.

As with a firm, the short-run aim of a political party or a political candidate is to be chosen by the electorate. But, again as with a firm, the long-run aim, at least by the assumptions we have used throughout this book, is to maximize profits. So, for the perfectly competitive firm, for example, fraudulent advertising and grossly defective products are not worthwhile because they mean a loss of business and hence profits in the long run. The same is true of a political party or a political candidate offering a platform grossly inconsistent with what that party or individual will do once elected because in a perfectly competitive market for political office, voters, in the long run, would learn of the incorrectness of their decisions and vote in another party.

The Equilibrium Point

The above analysis is seen more easily when we assume that all voters have the same prefer-

[1] Joseph Schumpeter, *Capitalism, Socialism and Democracy,* New York: Harper & Row, 1942, p. 269.

ences or tastes. Whenever the party in office does not adopt policies preferred by the voters, another party can gain popular support by offering a platform that more closely coincides with these preferences. Thus the only "equilibrium" platform would be one that perfectly satisfied the tastes of the voters since these tastes are assumed to be alike. In such a situation, an ideal political democracy would be perfectly responsive to the "will" of all individuals in the society. Thus, even though the immediate and ultimate aims of each political party is to acquire and keep political power, there is going to be only one equilibrium political party and that will be the one which offers a platform most closely matching the tastes of the community. Political officials in such a situation have no room for choice because their choices are determined by the electorate's preferences.

Actual Democracies

Just as the model of perfect competition is not always the most useful for analyzing what happens in the real marketplace, so too the model of the ideal political democracy is not always the most useful for analyzing what happens in the real political marketplace. Perhaps most importantly in the real world, political competition is reduced by the large scale effort and financial resources required to organize political parties and activities. This certainly has to be true for presidential and gubernatorial offices, where literally millions of voters must be reached. Even under the most ideal of real-world situations, many groups that would like to compete for political office do not and will not have sufficient resources to reach a large number of voters. In the following issue, we will see the effect that public financing of political campaigns has on this particular aspect of political competition.

Tie-In Activities

It is, of course, possible for firms to specialize in the production of a single good. That is, it is not generally necessary for a firm to produce products which are tied to each other. This is typically known as the "nonnecessity of activity tie-ins." In an ideal democracy, the same is true for potential and actual political candidates—they can specialize in an activity, or area of knowledge. But in the real world of political democracy, such is not the case. Candidates must know, or at least appear to know, something about a tremendous variety of problems and economic and social activities to be elected. Voters probably prefer such an arrangement because, since they have a limited amount of political information, they find it easier, that is, less costly, to place one individual in charge of many activities rather than one individual in charge of each separate activity.

Coalitions and Cartels

In the world of perfect competition, there are no coalitions because they are unnecessary. In the real world of politics, however, there are coalitions—by necessity. In a democracy we can best understand collective decision making or public choice as decisions made by partnerships or coalitions of individuals. To understand why some individuals participate in these partnerships or coalitions and others do not (that is, some vote and some do not vote), we must look at two aspects of the real world: the fixed amount of resources available and the way in which individuals can evaluate political information.

Politics and the Size of the Pie

Throughout this book we have stressed the point that scarcity exists no matter where we are, who we are, or what we are doing. Every action has an opportunity cost, even if it is not explicit. The same analysis of course, holds for collective decision making. Any attempt by a collective body of individuals to alter the economic landscape will, by necessity, mean that some lose and some gain, *given majority rule.* That is, when some benefit by collective action, others lose. (There are exceptions to this statement, but we will ignore them for the moment.) Now, any collective body contemplating the selection of a budget has two problems: (1) how big should that fixed budget be, and (2) how should the fixed budget be allocated once its size is determined? Economic political theorists sometimes lump these two decisions into one because if voters can control the composition of the budget, then they can control its size.

The Question of Ignorance

For most political decisions, majority rule prevails. Only a coalition of voters representing slightly more than 50 percent of those who vote is needed. Whenever a vote is taken, the result is going to involve costs and benefits. Voters, then, must evaluate their share of the costs and benefits of any budgetary expenditure. Voters, however, are not perfectly informed. That is one of the crucial characteristics of the real world—information is a resource that is costly to obtain. Rational voters will, in fact, decide to "purchase" some level of ignorance about government programs because the benefits from being fully informed are not worth the cost of fully informing themselves, given their extremely limited impact as individual voters. For the same reason, voters will fail to inform themselves about taxes or other revenue sources to pay for proposed expenditures because they know that, for any specific expenditure program, the cost to them individually will be small. At this point it might be useful to

contrast the above situation with what exists in the nonpolitical or private sector of the economy. In the private sector, the individual chooses the *mix* of his or her selection of purchases. Moreover, the individual bears fully the consequences of such a selection. (We abstract for the moment from the problem of externalities.)

Such analysis leads us to conclude that voters as consumers generally will not be concerned with potential expenditure programs which affect them only slightly. Rather, only those voters who are directly involved in a particular expenditure program will take the time and the resources to be better informed. We therefore find much more success in producer-oriented ("special-interest") coalitions than in consumer-oriented coalitions. And, as a result, we find that special-interest legislation abounds, whereas legislation affecting consumers in general does not. How many con-

sumers would rise in anger and actually take the time to write their elected representatives if a bill were introduced requiring that 20 percent of foreign crude oil be shipped in American vessels? Not very many, because the effect on any individual American consumer of petroleum products would be insignificant. However, American shipping interests and, in particular, unions whose members would be directly affected by a shift to American vessels would have an incentive to influence such legislation. Its passage, then, would be highly likely.[2]

Ignorance, it would seem, causes many voters to favor or be indifferent about proposals

[2]There is a limit, however, to special-interest legislation because as it increases, the cost to consumers also increases. This, in turn, increases the likelihood of the rise of a political entrepreneur to protect the general group of consumers. All we can really say is that the ratio of special- to general-interest legislation is higher than in an ideal world with zero information costs.

that they might oppose if they had perfect information about costs and benefits. It is costly for voters to let themselves be informed, and voters are continuously bombarded by fraudulent political advertising. Such "rational" ignorance may also explain why the average voter declares himself or herself a conservative or middle-of-the-roader. The average voter wants to avoid risk. The average voter also has adjusted to living with the "devils" of the moment. Thus it is possible to argue with him or her that the government should, for example, allow competition in the selling of postal services, banish certain types of regulation that harm the consumer, and undertake many other acts which might marginally benefit the average voter. But why should this average voter believe such an argument? He or she has no evidence that it is correct, and since this average voter tries to avoid risk and has adjusted to living with what is happening at the moment, his or her support is unlikely. As Mark Twain once said, "The free traders win the debate, but the protectionists win the vote."

We can further extend this argument to consider the nature of bureaucracies.

Bureaucracy and Public Choice

Much of government today—federal, state, and local—is run by well-established bureaucracies. Bureaucracies can exert great influence on matters concerning themselves—the amount of funding granted them, the activities they engage in. In the political marketplace, well-organized bureaucracies can even influence the articulation of public demand itself. In many cases, they will organize their clientele, coach that clientele on what is appropriate, and stick up for the "rights" of the clientele. More importantly perhaps, many bureaucrats belong to organized groups, such as public service unions, who vote for and support sympathetic political entrepreneurs. For example, public school teachers form a potent political group that can often influence public decision making regarding the size of the public school budget. And teachers are very active when bond issues for financing current or future educational expenses are being debated. As another example, we pointed out in Issue I-22 that the Postal Service Workers' union filed suit against competitors to the U.S. Postal Service. From the public's point of view, competition in postal services would be beneficial, but from the postal workers' point of view, this is not the case. Notice that no coalition of Postal Service consumers has been formed to push through legislation allowing competition with the post office. But notice, too, that significant, and in some cases effective, coalitions have been formed, mainly by members of the Postal Service union, to stop competition that would take away their jobs.

The Gains to Political Entrepreneurship

It would be easy for us to suggest that individuals enter politics in order to do "good" for the people. However, it may be more appropriate to use as a model of political activities the same model we used throughout the rest of this text. Individuals enter the political marketplace to maximize income, which may in this case, of course, be in the form of political power, prestige, or other nonpecuniary return. Now if we assume that there is a tolerably competitive market for political office, we will immediately conclude that potential and actual office seekers will not be able to obtain monopoly rents. That is, all they will obtain from their efforts is a competitive rate of return. However, this is probably not correct. Even in a perfectly competitive market for products, there are firms

that make a higher than normal rate of return and no other firm can compete away that higher than normal rate of return. In other words, even in perfect competition, differentially more efficient firms do make economic rents. If, however, you attempt to buy the more efficient firm in a competitive situation (or even a monopoly), you will have to pay the "full" price, which includes the discounted, future above-normal profits. In other words, economic rents are discounted immediately and included in the price of an asset. The same could be said for political offices. Political entrepreneurs are not all the same. Some of them are differentially more efficient than others. On the margin, it is true

that political entrepreneurs make only a normal rate of return. But intramarginally, some are going to make what might be called economic rents in the marketplace of politics.

This argument illustrates a most important economic principle concerning competition for economic gains via political processes. Whenever a potentially profitable asset is going to be made available via the political process, there is going to be competition for its acquisition: Resources will be used to acquire resources. Consider new TV licenses offered by the Federal Communications Commission. When a new license is to be issued, there are usually numerous applicants for it. Resources

will be spent by these applicants to obtain that license. In fact, the firm or individual who does obtain that license may spend such a quantity of resources that the real price of the license is such that the anticipated rate of return will be no higher than normal.

Concluding Remarks

There is no good theory of political behavior and public choice. No one, for example, has a theory that can explain when or why voters will favor legislation which has been shown again and again to harm most of them—as is apparently the case with wage and price controls. Most assessments of past attempts at wage

and price controls conclude that such controls ultimately impose a net cost on society. Nonetheless, voters seem to favor politicians who want them. In any event, only now are economists attempting to develop models that can predict such seemingly "irrational" behavior on the part of voters.

What we do know is that there is competition in the market for political office. We also know that voters do not attempt to obtain complete information on all political platforms or proposed budget expenditures because of the costs involved. And lastly, we know that special-interest legislation abounds in our political democracy. Some of the theories presented above may help you understand why these facts are so.

1. It is possible to construct a model of a perfectly competitive political market in an ideal democracy.
2. In an ideal democracy, political decisions would be made through perfectly free competition for votes; these votes would come from a broadly based electorate.
3. In a perfectly competitive market for political offices, political platforms would not deviate dramatically from the "will of the people."
4. In actual democracies, political competition is limited by the large-scale effort required for organizing political parties and activities. Moreover, politicians cannot specialize. They must make decisions on a broad range of issues.
5. In actual political situations, coalitions and cartels are the rule.
6. In a majority-rule system of democracy, coalitions of voters representing only slightly more than 50 percent of the votes will, in fact, control the society.
7. Average voters find it advantageous to be "ignorant" of most political issues and political candidates because the benefits of becoming politically "informed" are small relative to the costs.
8. When potentially profitable assets are made available via a political process, there will be competition for ownership rights to those assets. Thus assets conferred by the state are often obtained by parties who have used up large amounts of resources to obtain them.

Questions for
Thought
and Discussion

1. If you have taken a course in political science, how does an economic theory of politics compare with what you learned?
2. Compare a model of an ideal political democracy with a model of pure competition. Are the two "pure" models useful for anything?
3. What is the difference between saying that voters are ignorant and voters are stupid?
4. Why is ignorance on the part of the average voter rational?

Selected
References

Haveman, Robert H. and Robert D. Hamrin (eds.), *The Political Economy of Federal Policy,* New York: Harper & Row, 1973.

Key, V. O., Jr., *Politics, Parties and Pressure Groups,* 5th ed., New York: Crowell, 1964.

The Mathematics of Uncertainty

KENNETH J. ARROW

Economist, Harvard University, and Nobel Laureate

In an age when many prominent economists frequent the halls of government, advising and criticizing presidential budgets and congressional bills, Nobel laureate Kenneth J. Arrow is most conspicuous by his absence. When awarded the 1972 Nobel Prize in economics for his "pioneering contributions to general economic equilibrium theory and welfare theory," Arrow said he was gratified the award had been given for theoretical work in light of the contemporary demand "for relevance . . . I'm thoroughly in favor of action," he said, "but I think everything needs to be seen in broader relations that perhaps are not obvious to the eye."

At home in highly mathematical areas as well as in classical economic theory—Samuelson called him "an economist's economist"— Arrow's ground-breaking contributions to economics have been many and varied. He has developed a model of risk bearing that takes into account different possible economic conditions, devised theorems for optimal resource allocation and for systems in equilibrium, and developed a theory of welfare. Despite Arrow's conceptual approach, his complex mathematical formulas, and his abstruse reasonings, he has applied his theories to the most "relevant" of social problems: income redistribution, voting, medical care, education, race relations, public information, and water distribution.

Educated at City College of New York and Columbia, Arrow served as a RAND Corporation consultant in 1948 and worked for a brief time as an economist for the Council of Economic Advisers during Kennedy's administration. Although a professor of economics at Harvard since 1968, it was during his years of teaching at Stanford, from 1949 to 1968, that Arrow established his reputation and developed many of his most important ideas.

In one of his most well-known works, *Social Choice and Individual Values* (1951, 1963), Arrow established his impossibility theorem for ideal democratic resolution of divergent preferences. In this, he demonstrated that no democratic method of social choice would always be responsive to the preferences of individual citizens and, at the same time, result in a coherent and rational collective choice. Samuelson said of Arrow's work in this field, "Aristotle must be turning over in his grave. The theory of democracy can never be the same (actually, it never was!) since Arrow."

Theories of social choice and theories of general equilibrium seem worlds apart, but Arrow sees some significant links between them. In his 1972 Nobel speech at Stockholm, Arrow put them together: "General competitive equilibrium above all teaches the extent to which a social allocation of resources can be achieved by independent private decisions coordinated through the market [but] there is nothing in the process which guarantees that the distribution be just. . . . If we want to rely on the virtues of the market but also to achieve a more just distribution, the theory [of general competitive equilibrium] suggests the strategy of changing the initial distribution rather than interfering with the allocation process at some later stage."

This reasoning has led Arrow to a concern about income redistribution. In his article "Taxation and Democratic Values: A Case for Redistributing Income" in the *New Republic,* Arrow argues that an "unequal distribution of property and of income is inherently an unequal distribution of freedom."

Currently, Arrow is engaged in research on how information, or its lack, affects the decisions of business people, workers, and consumers. "The uncertainties about economics," he suggests, "are rooted in our need for a better understanding of the economics of uncertainty; our lack of economic knowledge is, in good part, our difficulty in modeling the ignorance of the economic agent." As with earlier work leading to important discoveries, Arrow starts from an obvious, but often overlooked fact—that no one has perfect information—and proceeds to explore the meaning and consequences of this presumption for contemporary economic theory. "The fact that one side is ignorant means the whole system [of general equilibrium] changes," says Arrow. Although his new research is still in a speculative stage, Arrow sees possible wide applications of it, particularly in the fields of consumer knowledge, job finding, and investment decisions.

Should Political Campaigns Be Publicly Financed?

ON PREVENTING FUTURE WATERGATES

The American Public Is Shocked

The revelations surrounding Watergate shocked the American public. It seemed apparent that "something" had to be done about the ability of presidential candidates to acquire funds for such devious purposes as "dirty tricks," burglary, and the like. Even before Watergate, it was obvious that many campaign contributions were obtained, implicitly or explicitly, in exchange for favors that rewarded the campaign contributors. According to articles in the *Wall Street Journal* and elsewhere, for example, the dairy industry provided large quantities of money to the reelection campaign of President Nixon in exchange for a rise in price supports for milk and milk products. In an attempt to reform such campaign financing and spending, Congress passed, and President Ford signed, the Federal Campaign Reform Act, which became effective on January 1, 1975.

The Federal Campaign Reform Act

The act has put some very specific restrictions on campaign financing.

No person may contribute more than $1,000 directly to a candidate for federal office or spend more than $1,000 directly on the candidate's behalf. In addition, a citizen can contribute up to $500 in drink, food, and travel expenses for volunteer workers, but all such contributions, direct or indirect, must be recorded and are applied against the candidate's own spending limit. Also, any organization doing anything to influence an election—such as publishing the voting record of an incumbent—must file a report as a political committee.

The spending limits for the federal offices of senator and congressperson (in states entitled to only one congressperson) were set at $100,000 per election during the primary campaign and $150,000 for the general election. In states where two or more congresspersons were allowed, then the spending limit for that office was to be $70,000 per election at the primary level and $70,000 for the general election. Various states have, or are passing, similar legislation.

Not everyone is happy with the campaign reform act. In fact, on

January 2, 1975, conservative Senator James L. Buckley (Con., New York) and former presidential hopeful and liberal Senator Eugene McCarthy (Dem., Minnesota), joined together in a suit seeking to have most of the act held void. They maintained the new law trampled First Amendment freedoms, one of which, they contended, is that a citizen has a right to express a political opinion, and to do so, if desired, by giving money to the candidate of his or her choice.

What is at issue here? Is it merely a question of free speech? Will campaign reform prevent future Watergates? These are the questions we consider in the rest of this issue.

Private Campaign Money

Most losing candidates contend that they lost because they couldn't obtain enough money for their primary campaign. In our political system, many citizens, recognizing their social and economic dependence on government decisions, will make contributions to candidates, hoping to obtain personal favors if these candidates win the election. For this reason, from a normative ("moral") point of view, the use of private campaign money seems undesirable to many.

to the donor—or, in fact, that a donor is requesting favors. For example, a congressperson receiving a large union contribution will not necessarily then support union causes. It is possible that this congressperson received the contribution because the union shared his or her convictions. (He or she may, of course, be more "vocal" about such convictions if unions were to contribute more money.)

Does More Money Ensure Winning?

It is often felt that with a sufficient amount of money a candidate can win an election. According to this, then, with a sufficient number of campaign contributions, even the most nefarious candidate should be able to get into office. The facts, however, do not seem to support this contention. Six of the top ten spenders in the 1972 races for the House of Representatives were defeated. Money seems to be only one variable in a typical campaign. It gives candidates a better chance to get their message across, but it certainly does not ensure victory.

At the same time, the personal wealth of a candidate may also not be sufficient to ensure the candidate's election. In 1972, Howard Metzenbaum of Ohio and Richard Ottinger of New York supported their own candidacies with their own personal wealth and both failed in the general election. On the other hand, the political careers of the Kennedys and Nelson Rockefeller were and are based on somewhat more than personal wealth.

On the other hand, campaign contributions are a means of expression for donors seeking to persuade other citizens on public issues. If you have a particular conviction but are not yourself a politician, you can contribute to the campaign of a political candidate who shares your convictions and can spread them to a wider audience. Also, a contribution does not necessarily mean that favors will be given

The Problems of Regulating Campaign Financing

Even if it were possible to strictly limit campaign financing to the specific amounts given in the Federal Campaign Reform Act, we would still have problems. No clear dividing line separates election campaigns from the propaganda and political activities that occur between elections. If we regulate the spending of candidates' election committees, should we not also regulate the advocacy organizations that publicize their own views on political issues between elections? These include many of the Ralph Nader groups, such as the Center for Auto Safety, and other organizations, such as the Committee on Political Education of the AFL-CIO. In other words, laws that regulate only campaign financing and not advocacy organization financing force an accounting distinction that is arbitrary and unfair.

We should also realize that campaign spending limits will not necessarily deter large implicit contributions. A large contributor can still "give" to the campaign of a political candidate by, for example, hiring the candidate's law firm. Try to think of all the devices that can be used to skirt the campaign spending limit. When you are done, you will probably have thought of only a small fraction of the possibilities that will be tried.

Incumbents and Campaign Spending Limits

With a limit on campaign spending for federal offices, we can make one firm prediction. We can predict with a fair degree of certainty that these limitations will favor incumbents. How is that so? In the first place, more than 97 percent of all congresspersons who entered the House in the three general elections prior to 1974 were returned to office in 1974 despite opinion polls that showed congresspersons to be held in less esteem than undertakers or used car salespersons.

Historically, incumbents seem to have had the edge on other candidates anyway. This edge has been increasing since the 1930s when TV and radio began giving the incumbents added exposure. In addition, incumbents have the right to send out "official" newsletters at government expense. The postage for these newsletters alone must be worth $25,000 to $50,000 a year. And when incumbents send out mailings, they are bringing their messages to every household. The incumbent's name becomes very well known.

Anyone running against an incumbent has to fight an uphill battle just to become known, let alone liked and voted into office. Imagine the cost of covering the Thirteenth Congressional District in Texas. It has 31,000 square miles and 470,000 people living in 35 counties. Any candidate wishing to gain office has to travel by private plane to get around and has to advertise in seven daily newspapers and on five television stations. In 1972 it was not surprising that the Republican candidate, Robert Price, spent over $200,000 in that district just to win the general election. A limit on the spending of a potential candidate wanting to unseat Price is essentially going to guarantee that Price will remain in office.

A statistical study of 1972 Senate races by a Harvard graduate student, Roland Cole, confirmed the above contentions. His results suggested that "Only incumbents win when expenditures are very low and things are much more even when expenditures are relatively high." He further concluded that present expenditure limitation proposals are "far too low to achieve any conceivable purpose other than to maintain incumbents in office."

Although one study doesn't make an irrefutable case, the argument that limits on campaign spending favor incumbents is certainly not weak.

Public Financing

The Pros

Financially subsidizing political candidates with public funds has been offered as a way to reduce illegal activities in campaigns. Advocates suggest that subsidies will lead to more meaningful participation in electoral contests because candidates won't have to worry about financial resources.

The question of special-interest influence on legislation is also considered by proponents of public financing. They suggest that subsidies will reduce the pressure on congressional candidates to accept large campaign contributions from private sources. If this pressure is reduced, congressional candidates will not have to "repay" private

donors with special-interest legislation.

There are certainly numerous other arguments in favor of public financing, but for every pro argument there seems to be a con.

The Cons

The experience in Puerto Rico, where subsidies for political campaigns are given, shows that they seem to be used up well before an election. And after the subsidies are used up, the illegal solicitation of funds, especially from government employees, ensues.

More important perhaps is the argument contesting the idea that subsidies will allow more meaningful participation. This is the problem of who could become a candidate if we subsidize campaigns. Almost any formula will discriminate against some individuals. If the criteria for eligibility for public subsidy in political campaigns are strict, the result will be a closed system—no outsider will have a chance. That is, if only candidates of the two major parties are subsidized, third-party and independent candidates will lose out. Alternatively, if the criteria are lax, there may be a proliferation of parties and/or candidates who will be attracted by the easy availability of public money.

Finally, reducing the need to cater to special-interest groups for contributions may lead to a curious situation. If candidates receive campaign money from the government, why would they have to face up to the issues? Wouldn't they then be able to do things strictly for window dressing and/or attention-getting?

The Future of Reform

We are about to see a stream of bills modifying those already passed concerning campaign policies. Many who were disgusted with the revela- tions of the Watergate episode put a tremendous amount of faith in the campaign reforms that have already become law. As we have pointed out here, however, these laws may have some negative results that reformers did not anticipate. In addition, campaign reform may not dramatically change the future of politics in the United States because the incentive structure surrounding the political process really hasn't changed.

Questions for Thought and Discussion

1. Do you think limitations on campaign financing can work?
2. What effect does public financing of political campaigns have on the growth of third parties?
3. "Money may not win elections, but it helps." Evaluate this quote.

Selected References

Committee for Economic Development, *Financing a Better Election System,* New York, 1968.

Heidenheimer, Arnold J. (ed.), *Comparative Political Finance: The Financing of Party Organizations and Election Campaigns,* Indianapolis: D. C. Heath, 1970.

Key, V. O., Jr., *Politics, Parties and Pressure Groups,* 5th ed., New York: Crowell, 1964.

Leuthold, David A., *Electioneering in a Democracy: Campaigns for Congress,* New York: Wiley, 1968.

Plattner, Marc F., "Campaign Financing: The Dilemmas of Reform," *The Public Interest,* no. 37, Fall 1974, pp. 112–130.

Rosenthal, A., *Federal Regulation of Campaign Finance: Some Constitutional Questions,* Princeton, N.J.: Citizens' Research Foundation, 1972.

The Twentieth Century Fund, Task Force on Financing Congressional Campaigns, *Electing Congress: The Financial Dilemma,* New York, 1970.

Whells, Henry and Robert Anderson, *Government Financing of Political Parties in Puerto Rico: A Supplementary Study,* no. 4, Princeton, N.J.: Citizens' Research Foundation, 1966.

28 Population Economics

Just about everybody has heard that there is a population explosion. Many books and articles tell us that the world will come to an end if we don't cut back the growth of population. The arithmetic of population economics is not hard to figure out, but it is deceiving, as we will see in this chapter when we talk about the economic and social consequences of zero population growth. First, however, we'll see how demographers—those who study population—measure trends in population growth. We'll also look at the economic variables that determine fertility and mortality. By doing this, then perhaps we will be better equipped to analyze the arguments presented by those who advocate zero population growth.

The Arithmetic of Population Growth

Demographers like to look at the difference between birth rates and death rates. They calculate for a given country and a given year what is called the **crude birth rate**—the number of babies born per 1000 people in the population. Then they look at the **crude death rate,** which is the number of deaths per 1000 people in the population. When we subtract the crude death rate from the crude birth rate, we come up with the change in population per 1000 people in that year. If we divide that by 10, we get the result as a percentage, and we have the annual **population rate of growth.** Let's look at a few examples. In Table 28-1, we listed the crude death rate and the crude birth rate for several countries. When the difference is divided by 10, we find that the rate of increase of population in these countries varies from 3.31 percent per year to a low of −0.02 percent per year in East Germany.

Table 28-1 Birth and Death Rates and Rate of Increase of Population for Selected Countries

Column 2 shows the crude birth rate per 1000 people per year in each of these countries. Column 3 shows the crude death rate per year. Column 4 is the difference between the crude birth rate and the crude death rate divided by 10. It represents the percentage annual rate of change per year of population.

COUNTRY	CRUDE BIRTH RATE	CRUDE DEATH RATE	RATE OF INCREASE
United States	15.6	9.4	0.62
Canada	15.9	7.4	0.85
Costa Rica	45.1	7.6	0.38
Denmark	15.2	10.1	0.51
France	16.9	10.8	0.61
Germany—East	11.8	13.8	−0.20
Iceland	21.9	6.9	1.50
Israel	27.8	7.2	2.06
Japan	19.3	6.6	1.27
Mexico	43.2	8.9	3.43
Pakistan	50.9	18.4	3.25
Poland	17.4	8.0	0.94
South Africa	40.3	16.6	2.37
Sweden	13.8	10.4	0.34
U.S.S.R.	18.0	8.5	0.95
Venezuela	40.9	7.8	3.31
Vietnam	37.5	16.1	2.14

Source: Statistical Office of the United Nations

The rate of growth of population is not, therefore, just a function of the birth rate, but also a function of the death rate. We would expect that any improvement in death control, as it were, would lead to an increase in population growth.

Doubling Time

Population experts like to translate rates of population growth per annum into what is called the **doubling time.** In other words, if the population of Luxembourg is growing at 0.4 percent a year, how many years will it take for the population to double? In the case of Luxembourg, this would take almost 175 years!

In Table 28-2 we see the doubling time for the populations of the countries in Table 28-1. A good rule to use to figure out the doubling time is the *rule of 72.* If you divide the percentage rate of increase in population into 72, you get an approximate doubling time. In our example of Luxembourg, the growth rate of population is 0.4 percent a year. Thus, 72 divided by 0.4 equals 180 years, just about the figure we got before.

Doubling times are fascinating numbers because if we extend them indefinitely into the future, we find that the population of very small

Table 28-2 The Doubling Time for Selected Countries' Populations

Here we show how many years it takes for each country's population to double. The range is immense, from Mexico's 21 years to Sweden's 212 years.

COUNTRY	DOUBLING TIME
United States	116
Canada	85
Costa Rica	189
Denmark	191
France	118
Iceland	48
Israel	35
Japan	57
Mexico	21
Pakistan	22
Poland	77
South Africa	30
Sweden	212
U.S.S.R.	76
Venezuela	27
Vietnam	34

Source: Statistical Office of the United Nations

Latin American countries will increase until there are so many people there will no longer be a place to walk. The countries literally will be covered with people. Even if the doubling time is 175 years, as in Luxembourg, if you extend that rate of growth far enough into the future, the result is one horrendously large number. That's one reason Zero Population Growth people are so adamant about the necessity of limiting the number of births not only in countries where the populations are unbelievably dense, as in Hong Kong, but also in countries where population is much less dense.

Net Reproduction Rate

Demographers also like to talk in terms of **net reproduction rate.** This rate is calculated on the basis of the total number of female children born to every 1000 mothers. If every mother has exactly one daughter in her lifetime, then the net reproduction rate will be exactly 1. What do you think will happen to the population? It will eventually stabilize (assuming life expectancy doesn't change). If mothers tend to have more than one daughter throughout their child-bearing years, then the net reproduction rate will be in excess of 1 and the population will grow.

The net reproduction rate is probably the most important statistic to look at when you want to find what the future holds for a particular country. Japan is a good example. There, the crude birth rate is about 19 per 1000, and the crude death rate is about 6.6 per 1000. The rate of growth in population is therefore in excess of 1 percent per annum. Even a 1 percent annual growth rate in population leads to a doubling every 72 years. But Japan really isn't worried about that. In fact, Japan's worries are in the opposite direction. The net reproduction rate is now less than 1 in Japan. The Japanese have legalized abortion, and there is widespread birth control. Given that the net reproduction rate is less than 1, after a few more years of growth, the Japanese population will begin a long steady decline. In fact, by extending net reproduction rates into the future forever without any change, you would find that the population of Japan will eventually disappear. Some time ago, Japanese businesspersons were publicized as complaining that their profits were going to fall in the future because of a diminishing labor supply. They would have to start paying higher wages to have a sufficient number of workers.

Where the People Are

It is interesting to note that even though population seems to be exploding all around us, the centers of population are really the only places where this is the case. Historically, we find that people moved where jobs were. Jobs were usually in ports or places with many natural resources. After transportation became relatively cheap, people started to live where they wanted to, and jobs then followed people. And people are going to the cities. Indeed, the percentage of people in urban centers has increased from 5 to 74 percent in the last 185 years. Additionally, in the United States, population has shifted out of the central areas to the south and to the west. The south and the west happen to have more agreeable climates.

If people did not find benefits from living in large cities, there would probably be a much more even population distribution throughout our entire land area. Presumably, if this were the case, there would be less concern over population explosion. Indeed, one need only take a drive or a plane trip across the United States to realize how sparsely populated these United States really are. This is not to say that we should or should not do something about population growth. Rather, the paucity of people in certain areas may merely serve to demonstrate that overpopulation is really only a problem in overcrowded urban environments.

The Population Curve

If we were to examine population growth in other animal species, we would find that there are natural limits to the total population a particular species can obtain. An experiment can be run with a pair of willing fruit flies in a small enclosure. At first, the population grows by leaps and bounds. It increases at a geometric rate: first 2, then 4, then 8, then 16, and so on. If this geometric progression of the fruit fly population were extended way into the future, we would find that their mass would eventually overcome the earth. However, this geometric growth rate does not continue for very long. Eventually it peters out because there just aren't enough resources for the flies to continue growing.

In our particular example, one resource that holds the fruit flies back is the size of the container. For other populations, it might be the food supply. In any event, reproduction slows down, and at some point, a ceiling is reached. The growth curve for the fruit fly population in our container can be plotted as an S, as shown in Figure 28-1. The ceiling is called the *natural population limit*. It is determined by the supply of the resources that are needed for survival.

In Figure 28-2, however, the growth line of population has for some reason just kept going up and up. This is what seems to have happened with the world population. Instead of slowing down, the growth rate has actually increased. Doubling time has fallen from 2000 years to 1000 years to 500 years, down to its present 35 years. However, we know that there has to be a ceiling somewhere. As one famous economist characterized the earth, it is a spaceship; it can only hold so many people because it has a fixed amount of space and a fixed number of resources. (And we can live under- and aboveground, too.) Population obviously cannot continue to grow forever.

Why Has the S Curve Gone Awry?

World population growth has, according to some, departed from the S curve. The natural population limit seems to be a long way into the future. One of the most obvious reasons for this departure lies in our ability to alter our environment—an ability that fruit flies do not possess. Medical science can change the course of population. We have been successful

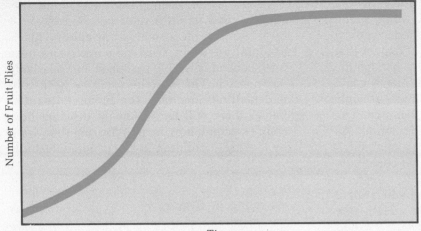

FIGURE 28-1 **S Curve for Fruit Fly Population**

FIGURE 28-1 **S Curve for Fruit Fly Population**

The population of fruit flies in a container might grow very rapidly at first, but it will level off and reach its natural limit at some specific number. The growth in population looks like an S curve, as depicted in this diagram.

in decreasing the crude death rate tremendously in the last few decades. We have also been extending our medical knowledge to underdeveloped countries where the birth rate has remained the same for many, many years but the death rates have fallen drastically. The growth rate of population in those countries has consequently increased dramatically.

Numerous studies have been done on what determines the death rate in different countries. The economic determinants of that variable are quite obvious. We would expect that the larger

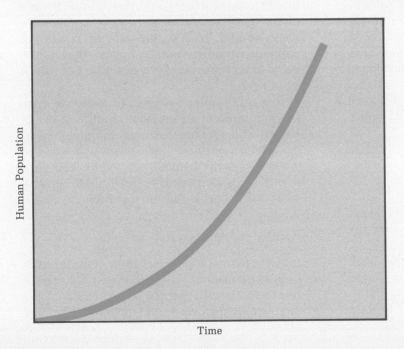

FIGURE 28-2 **The S Curve for Human Beings Gone Awry**

Here we show what has happened to the population of human beings in the world. Instead of following a typical S curve where the natural limit is eventually reached, there seems to be no end in sight.

the real income per capita, the lower would be the death rate because people would spend more money on more nutritious foods, medical care, and the like. We would also expect that the larger the number of doctors per capita, the lower would be the death rate. Literacy and the educational level also determine to some extent the level of deaths in a country. The more educated and literate the population, the more knowledgable it is about hygiene, nutrition, exercise, and other things that contribute to a healthy life.

Improvements in economic and educational determinants would not lower the death rate forever, however. Some sort of S curve would obtain for each determinant. At first, improvements in education and literacy, as well as increases in real income and the number of doctors per capita, might decrease the death rate dramatically. After a while, however, it would become more and more difficult to reduce mortality and morbidity rates in the population. For most segments of the population in the United States, we may have already reached the lower limit on the death rate per 1000. Only very large increases in spending on medical care could lower it even further. This, of course, is not the case in underdeveloped countries, where life expectancy is still extremely short by American standards and where infant mortality is very high by world standards.

Birth Control

Even before the advent of modern birth control techniques, couples had ways to determine the number of children they would have. Also, when marriage occurs at a later age, the birth rate will be lower. Celibacy, of course, is always an effective method of birth control, and it doesn't require modern techniques.

In any event, economists have found that fertility rates or birth rates can be explained by a number of economic variables. This is especially true in Western countries where birth control is widely practiced and relatively inexpensive. The more inexpensive birth control methods become, the fewer unwanted babies there will be. We might discover how couples decide how many offspring they want by looking at children in an economic fashion.

Investing in Children

If we treat children as an investment, the rate of return on that investment will most likely be an important determinant of how many children are desired. This is especially true for agricultural societies where children become productive members of the family at a very young age. In the past, it was not uncommon for 5- and 6-year-old children to be picking cotton, olives, grapes, or strawberries on the family farm. Most probably, the higher the price of the farm products, the more farm babies were desired because the rate of return on children would have been higher—that is, the value of their marginal physical product would have risen.

It is quite ludicrous now, however, to consider children as an investment (at least in the United States). Some parents do, nonetheless, get a return on their "investment" later in life when their retirement is provided by their children. This is increasingly rare, though, because of Social Security and other retirement plans.

Children As Consumption

It might be more appropriate to consider children as a consumption good. We would expect, therefore, that the normal determinants of the quantity demanded would prevail. What are those determinants? In the main, they are the price of the good and the income of the demander. There will be an income elasticity of the demand for children and also a price elasticity. The price elasticity most likely will be negative; that is, the higher the price (cost) of raising children, the lower the quantity demanded. The income elasticity will be positive, but it may be less than unity. As real incomes go up, the quantity of children demanded may not go up in proportion. In any event, we can easily determine the cost of raising children, and this is exactly what the Insurance Institute of America has done.

Cost of Children

Surprising as it may seem, the cost of raising children through college has risen to about $80,000 per child (undiscounted). That means that $80,000 in income which the parents could have used will be used instead to raise the child. This, of course, does not indicate the total cost of raising children, however, as any parent can vouch for. There is a tremendous time cost involved. The higher the wage rate that a parent makes, the higher the opportunity cost of the time which must be devoted to the child. This perhaps is where the term "a millionaire's family" comes from. The millionaire's family is one boy and one girl—only two children. It becomes too expensive in terms of opportunity cost for the high-income individual to have more children. The opportunity cost of spending time with your children—playing baseball, going to the movies—is the amount of income you could have earned using this time to work. (He or she could, of course, purchase the services of a surrogate parent at less than the opportunity cost. But then, why have children?)

Given the rapidly rising cost of higher education and the larger and larger portion of young people attending college, one would expect that *ceteris paribus* the number of children desired should fall. For this or for some other reason, the net reproduction rate in the United States has done just that: Zero population growth may be a reality in the United States within the next few decades, if the trend in net reproduction does not reverse itself. In fact, in the long run, our current reproduction trend may lead to below ZPG.

The Economic and Social Consequences of ZPG

Zero Population Growth people believe that the only way to prevent increasing amounts of pollution is to check our rapidly growing population. In fact, some maintain that the underlying cause of pollution is too large a population. In a ZPG ad appearing in a major magazine, the assumption was made that if we stabilize our population we will have "Clear skies. Clean water." There is a problem with this line of reasoning that you should be aware of. If we had a population of one-half our current size but the income per capita was somehow double what it is today, the level of total production would remain the same. Given our current set of institutions—property laws, pricing systems, and so on—we would expect that the same level of pollution would prevail regardless of population (within limits, of course) because pollution output is a function of consumption levels and consumption levels are a function of income or real standards of living. The problems of despoiling our environment are really not problems of overpopulation. When the problems of conservation, ecological destruction, pollution, and so on were covered in previous discussions, we saw that much of the problem of pollution is due to the fact that nobody owns natural resources such as air and water. It is perhaps misguided, then, to think that without solving the common property problem, or the problem of equating social costs and private costs, the reduction in population growth will somehow create a cleaner environment. In fact, we would imagine that if property rights became more indefinite, we could have more pollution with a smaller population even if income fell.

Crowding

One of the inevitable consequences of the population explosion is overcrowding. In fact, all you need do is try to get to work on the subway at 8 A.M. in New York City to find out what crowding is, or travel to Hong Kong to see how closely people can pack themselves into a restricted space. But are these really the problems of overpopulation?

The density per square mile in the United States is quite small relative to other countries. Does the United States, then, face a problem of overcrowding due to a population explosion? No. The United States faces a problem of too many people in too concentrated an area. That is, we find that 98 percent of the people live on only 2 percent of the available land. We know, of course, that lots of the land in the United States is uninhabitable, but still, much land is left that generally does not have people living on it. Perhaps instead of attempting to control the population, we should consider attempting to control its location to ameliorate overcrowding in big cities.

And big cities are becoming more and more crowded despite the horrendous distresses created by them. Of course, when you think about it, it should not be too surprising. *Specialization is a function of the size of the market.* How many operas, symphonies, and playhouses can be supported in small rural towns? Even when you go to a relatively large city, you cannot always find what you want in terms of entertainment and cultural activity. Seattle is one of the largest cities in the United States, but the variety of cultural activities available to its inhabitants is unbelievably small relative to what is available in, say, New York City. This may explain why people like to live in New York City despite the tremendous cost of doing so: The benefits are also tremendous—thousands of restaurants, hundreds of theaters, and everything else imaginable that one might want to do.

An Unexpected Result of ZPG—A Geriatric Population

If we accept the premises of Zero Population Growth advocates, then our population should indeed stabilize. If we accept some of the more radical suggestions, such as the one that Paul Ehrlich made in a *Playboy* interview some years back, then we should have a net reproduction rate of less than 1 so that population will decline to about 50 million people in the United States. A consequence of either course on the age structure of the population is a little talked about and less understood aspect of population control.

Right now, the median age in the United States is somewhere between 20 and 30. As the population growth rate increases, the median age falls, as you would expect. However, if we were to go to a stable population, the median age would jump by a full 10 years. That is, it would lie somewhere between 30 and 40. Some demographers estimate that it would be 37. There would be an aging of the population, and if we were to go from our current 200 million plus to Ehrlich's desired 50 million, the age distribution of the population would be skewed dramatically toward older people. That is, the median age would go from its current 27 to 37 to 47 or even to 57, depending upon how fast we reached the magic number of 50 million.

The thought of a geriatric population may be somewhat discomforting to you, but, of course, that is a noneconomic problem. In any event, we would find that there would be less chance for rapid advancement in the job market. There would be very few young people who would be as successful as they can be now, and there would be almost no presidents of corporations in their 30s, as there are now. Everything would become much more stabilized in terms of job advancement. Perhaps the benefits from population stabilization or reduction would be worth the costs. But in any event, the costs would be there and there would be no way to avoid them. The age structure of the population must change; it's an arithmetic certainty if we stabilize the population. No doubt the country would be a much less exciting place to live in, unless, of course, medical science improved the mental and physical well-being of older people so that aging would not be as noticeable.

Depopulation

While the United States concerns itself with limiting population growth, there are other countries in the world that concern themselves with how to *increase* population growth. Believe it or not, populating is a problem in certain countries of the world such as France.

France has had a population "problem" for many years. Various methods have been tried to increase average family size and prevent France's total population from declining. The government has even given special family allowances to encourage larger families. Family size increased for a few years after World War II and after incentives were presented to French families, but it again started to go down. The government increased family allotments and used other monetary methods to encourage larger families. For most countries, it is frightening to think that population size is actually getting smaller (except, of course, in India, Pakistan, or some other non-Western nations).

In any event, France's methods for increasing family size should give us a hint as to what might be done in the United States to encourage smaller families, if indeed that is what we want to do. Currently, there is an incentive to have larger families—a $750 deduction per dependent when paying income taxes. For every child in the family, the parent is allowed to deduct $750 from income before computing taxes. Obviously, eliminating this deduction would raise the price of having children. And we would expect (at least on the margin) that there would be fewer children born because of the increase. Perhaps Zero Population Growth sympathizers might suggest this as a start toward finding out what the natural population growth rate in the United States would be without any special inducements. It may turn out that there is no need to worry about a population explosion because the natural reproduction rate is 1.

| Definitions of New Terms | **Crude Birth Rate:** The number of births per 1000 people in the population per year. |
| | **Crude Death Rate:** The number of deaths per 1000 people in the population per year. |

Population Rate of Growth: The crude birth rate minus the crude death rate divided by 10; the percentage rate of growth per year in a population.

Doubling Time: The number of years it takes for the population in a specific country to double.

Net Reproduction Rate: The number of daughters born to every mother. When the net reproduction rate is 1, the population will remain stable.

Chapter Summary

1. The arithmetic of population growth is rather simple. To find out the rate of increase in population per year in percentage terms, we subtract the crude death rate from the crude birth rate and divide by 10. We can translate the rate of increase in population into a doubling time, which is equal to the number of years it takes the population to double.

2. The easiest way to find the doubling time of a population is to use the rule of 72. We divide the percentage rate of increase of population into 72 and get an approximate doubling time.

3. Another important population statistic is the net reproduction rate. When it is equal to 1, it means that one mother has one female child and the population will remain stable.

4. People are moving to the cities in increasing numbers. Urban centers account for about 75 percent of all the population in the United States.

5. Although animal species reach a natural population limit, human beings apparently have not reached one yet. The S curve of population growth has turned out to be an incorrect predictor of human population. One of the reasons is because of the drastic increases in preventing the premature death of human beings.

6. We might explain fertility rates using economic variables. The children of agricultural societies can be looked on as an investment because by the age of 5 or 6 they become productive. However, in an industrial society such as ours, children are much more a consumption item.

7. Like any other consumption item, the demand for children should be a function of income and the price of raising them. The price of raising children has been increasing rapidly.

Questions for Thought and Discussion

1. Do you think that human beings will necessarily procreate until they reach the natural population limit?

2. East Germany has a negative rate of population growth. Do you believe that this is because the death rate is greater than the birth rate or because of other reasons? What are they?

3. "The $750 tax exemption for dependent children should be eliminated because it encourages large families." Do you agree? Why or why not? If you do not agree, why do you think that the demand for children is price inelastic?

Selected
References

Ehrlich, Paul and Anne Ehrlich, *Population, Resources, Environment*, 2d ed., San Francisco: W. H. Freeman, 1972.
Hardin, Garrett, *Population, Evolution and Birth Control*, 2d ed., San Francisco: W. H. Freeman, 1969.

Was Malthus Right?

THE EXPLODING POPULATION

Essay on Population

In 1798, a little-known English minister named Thomas Robert Malthus published *An Essay on the Principle of Population, As It Affects the Future Improvement of Society*. The uncomfortable and, indeed, depressing conclusion of that 50,000-word treatise was that "population, when unchecked, goes on doubling every 24 years or increases in the geometric ratio," but according to Reverend Malthus, food production—or more generally, the means of subsistence—only increases at an arithmetic ratio. We can see what Malthus meant about geometric as opposed to arithmetic rates by looking at Figure I-34.1. Here the gold line would represent something, say, population, rising at a geometric rate. Notice that it starts slowly and then gradually gets steeper and steeper. Compare this with the blue line, which represents, say, food growing at an arithmetic rate. It remains equally steep throughout its path.

A few years later, in 1803, Malthus put out a second edition of his now famous essay on population. Instead of talking about population increasing at a geometric ratio, he

indicated that the human species was destined to poverty and a life of misery unless the rate of population growth was retarded by **positive checks** or **preventive checks.** He listed as preventives such things as late marriages or no marriage at all, sexual abstinence, and moral restraint.

Even though Malthus preached moral restraint, he realized that "hot passion leads to surplus souls and cold reason leads to sin." And since he was of strong moral character, he appeared unimpressed by the low fertility of prostitutes because

". . . a promiscuous intercourse to such a degree as to prevent the birth of children seems to lower, in the most marked manner, the dignity of human nature. It cannot be without its effect on men, and nothing can be more obvious than its tendency to degrade the female character, and to destroy all of its most amiable and distinguished characteristics."

It's understandable, then, that Malthus put much more faith in such positive checks as wars, pestilence, and famine. (Preventive checks de-

crease the birth rate, and positive checks increase the death rate.)

As you can imagine, Malthus was criticized severely. His fellow clergymen thought he was crazy; politicians and journalists called him a heretic. But others, especially a famous economist of the time named David Ricardo, made good use of the Malthusian theory. Let's delve a little more deeply into why Malthus came up with such heretical ideas. We will see that although his theories didn't describe the industrial society of his time very well, they did do a great job of describing preindustrial Europe.

A Product of Traditional Europe

Although the Reverend Malthus grew up during the Industrial Revolution, he was a product of traditional Europe—that is, preindustrial, pregrowth society. He believed, as did Adam Smith, the father of much modern economic thinking, that economic life depended on the productivity of land, so that ultimately it was the land which determined the level of existence.

Positive Checks

Malthus was convinced, being the clergyman that he was, that the

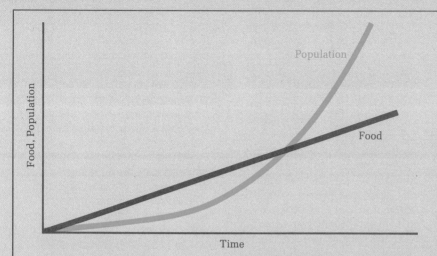

FIGURE I-34.1 The Malthusian Dilemma

Population increases at an exponential or geometrically increasing rate, as evidenced by the heavy gold line, whereas food production increases only linearly or arithmetically. Eventually population outstrips the food supply.

"passion between sexes" would cause men and women to breed, and as long as there was enough food around to feed a growing family, the family size would increase. We can depict the Malthusian cycle, as it is called, graphically as in Figure I-34.2. Here we show the population size on the horizontal axis and the real wage rate per person on the vertical axis. Notice here the emphasis on the word *real*. The real wage rate is essentially the wage rate expressed in purchasing power over real goods and services. Real wage rates are, therefore, an indication of a person's ability to purchase the things he wants. By using real wage rates, we don't have to worry about problems of inflation, or rather, general changes in the price level. Notice that we have drawn in a heavily shaded line that we call subsistence. This is the so-called subsistence level of income, or real wages—the amount necessary for a family to survive. Presumably, if the family does not obtain at least this level of income, the children will die because the parents cannot feed or clothe them. Real wages first increase, but after **diminishing returns** set in, they fall. Once they reach point *D*, widespread famines occur and there are numerous deaths in the society, according to the Malthusian doctrine. This was the period of "positive" checks: disease, famine, wars, plus an increase in vice (including birth control!) that, according to Malthus, was degrading but resulted in fewer births.

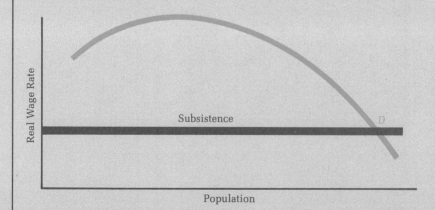

FIGURE I-34.2 The Malthusian Cycle

Population is on the horizontal axis and the real wage rate or standard of living on the vertical axis. The heavy horizontal line indicates the subsistence level of real wages that the population must receive to survive. Real wages will first increase, but after diminishing returns set in, they will fall until point *D*. Then positive checks come into account: famines, pestilence, and the like.

Key Assumption

The key assumption that Malthus made was that there was a fixed technology. As we said before, Malthus grew up in the Industrial Revolution, when this assumption certainly did not hold, but he was a product of an era when technology in fact did not change very quickly. This was certainly true with agricultural societies, when technological changes were very slow. For example, English crop rotation and fertilization methods were only slowly adopted during the commercial revolution. This is one of the reasons that Malthus viewed agricultural output as growing at an arithmetic rate, instead of at a geometric rate like the population. But, according to Malthus, even if there were some once-and-for-all increase in the food base of a society, it would only lead to inexorable pressure of the population on the increased resources. He felt that when everything got sorted out, the average level of living would be just as low as it was before the great increase in the food base.

What Went Wrong?

What was wrong with Malthus' thesis was that he assumed, as we mentioned, a fixed technology. He also assumed that population size was a function only of real income, and in fact that survival rates were a function of income level. As to the first assumption, we know that starting in the seventeenth and eighteenth centuries the technological capacity of society increased; whether it was due to the Industrial Revolution, to increased schooling of the population, or to other determinants, it did increase.

Malthus also ignored the possibility that the curve in Figure I-34.2 could rise. Look at Figure I-34.3. Here we show three separate curves, each with a different productivity of the population. The increases in productivity that are indicated are a result of increases in technology. The real income per capita of the population can rise even though the population is growing if the curves shift up fast enough. In this particular simplified model, there need never be a Malthusian positive check, as long as the curve keeps shifting upward.

Additionally, in many situations, as real income rises, the survival rate of children may increase, but the demand for children might fall, or at least might not rise as fast as income does. Stable populations are not unknown in the world today—witness, for example, Japan and France. However, we do still find the Malthusian cycle acting in various less-developed countries in the world today.

"Passion between the Sexes" Not the Answer

Remember that Malthus maintained that passion between the sexes produced population growth at a geo-

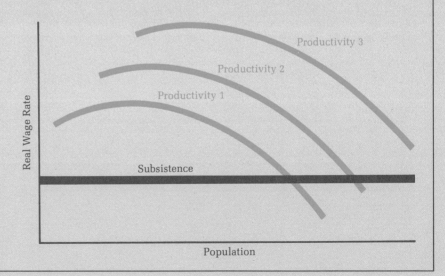

FIGURE I-34.3 Possibility of Improved Technology

In this diagram, the curves move to the right as technology improves productivity. We labeled these curves successively Productivity 1, 2, and 3. If productivity rises fast enough, the population can grow without real wages falling to subsistence levels.

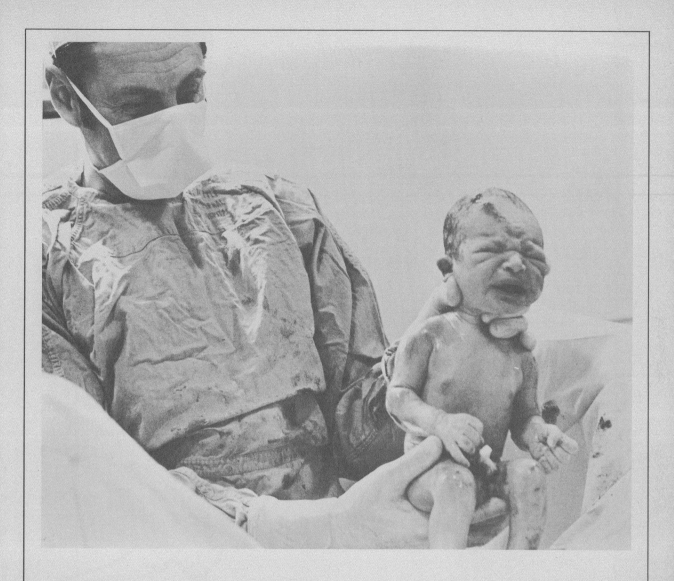

metric rate, whereas food production would grow only at an arithmetic rate. This isn't what has really happened in underdeveloped countries. In fact, the developed nations may be more at fault for the rapid population rise in these countries than the countries themselves. For example, in Figure I-34.4 look at the birth rate in three selected underdeveloped countries: Mexico, Mauritius, and Barbados.

The birth rate in Mexico has been steady; the one in Mauritius has started to fall, as it has in Barbados. However, the big change has been in the death rate. It has fallen dramatically and persistently since the 1930s. Obviously, if the birth rate remains fairly constant and the death rate falls, the rate of population growth is going to rise dramatically, just as it has done. Population increases of 1 percent a year were considered fairly high in years past, but today in countries like Costa Rica, Mexico, Pakistan, and Vene-

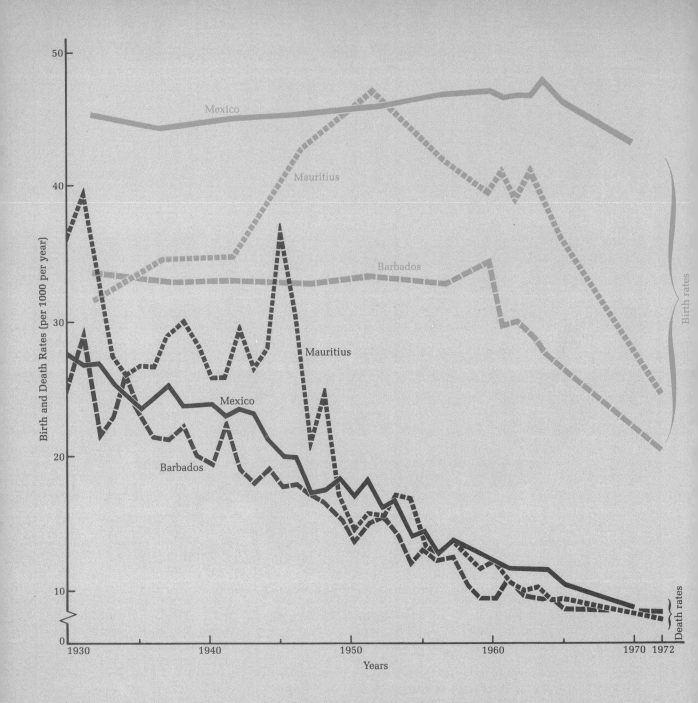

FIGURE I-34.4 Death Rates Fall Dramatically in Three Selected Underdeveloped Countries

Although the birth rates in Mexico, Mauritius, and Barbados have remained constant or fallen slightly, the dramatic change has been in death rates, which have fallen since the 1930s in all these countries. This has caused a widening gap between birth and death rates and, hence, higher rates of growth in population. (*Source:* Statistical Office of the United Nations.)

zuela growth rates of 3 and 4 percent a year are not unknown. It all has to do with the improved chances of people to live a longer and healthier life. Crude death rates in many developing countries are lower than in European countries. And in a number of these developing countries, life expectancies have risen by 1 year or more per annum for a decade. In Taiwan, for example, the life expectancy is well over 60 years for men and women. In Puerto Rico, it is over 70 for women, and not much less for men! Mortality and morbidity have decreased so rapidly because public health knowledge has been imported into the Third World to eradicate disease and pestilence. Also, developed countries have exported their knowledge of nutrition and the living standards most amenable to healthy lives.

Falling Mortality Rate a Mixed Blessing

In other words, the developed countries have helped the underdeveloped countries improve their health science and gain more healthful living conditions. The result is a population boom in these countries, which is a mixed blessing at best. There are, of course, other reasons why the mortality rate has fallen in developing countries—better education, a rising income level, and so on. All these contribute to a lower death rate.

Breaking Out of the Malthusian Cycle

There is no question of what developing countries must do to raise the per capita standard of living at a faster rate than currently. (Since population is growing just as fast as output in some of these countries, the per capita real income is essentially standing still.) We can hardly suggest that crude death rates be allowed to rise again, so there is only one variable left to change, and that is the birth rate. Fertility among underdeveloped populations must fall if there is ever to be any hope of contradicting Malthus in these countries. We are all aware of how this can be accomplished: later marriages, more widespread use of birth control techniques, subsidizing legalized abortion—in short, whatever available birth reduction techniques a country is willing to use. The results of such techniques are indeed amazing. In Hong Kong and Singapore, crude birth rates per 1000 fell from 36 and 38.7 respectively in 1960 to 24.9 and 29.9 in 1966. That is an amazing reduction, probably unprecedented in the history of modern times. Another country that has been successful in reducing its birth rate is Japan, as we've seen. At the moment, the net reproduction rate in Japan is less than unity. In other words, eventually, if nothing changes, its population will contract.

The conclusion: Reducing birth rates and, hence, reducing the population growth rate is possible now for many, if not all, developing nations. The implementation of the necessary policies is up to them.

Definitions of New Terms

Positive Checks: According to Malthus, these were the necessary checks on population growth that came about whenever the subsistence level of living was reached. These included famines, plagues, and the like.

Preventive Checks: These, according to Malthus, involved abstinence, late marriage and other actions that would prevent population from outstripping the food supply. If enough preventive checks were taken, positive checks would not occur.

Diminishing Returns: Usually called the law of diminishing returns: After some point, successive increases in labor, for example, added to fixed amounts of land and capital used for production, will not cause a proportionate increase in output.

Questions for Thought and Discussion

1. Why did Malthus' predictions go awry?
2. After the plague in the Middle Ages, workers' wages (whether explicit or implicit) increased. Why do you think this occurred? (*Hint:* Remember the law of demand and turn it around.)
3. Why do you think there might be a correlation between population growth and the start of wars?

Selected References

Brunner, John, *Stand on Zanzibar,* New York: Ballantine Books, 1968.

Coale, A. J. and E. M. Hoover, *Population Growth and Economic Development in Low-Income Countries,* Princeton, N.J.: Princeton University Press, 1958.

Hardin, G., *Population, Evolution and Birth Control,* 2d ed., San Francisco: W. H. Freeman, 1969.

Malthus, Thomas Robert, *First Essay on Population* (1798), London: Rural Economic Society Reprint, 1926.

Stanford, Quentin H., *The World's Population: Problems of Growth,* New York: Oxford University Press, 1973.

29

Development of the Less-Developed Countries

The world consists of the haves and the have-nots. In this chapter we'll look at some of the problems facing these have-nots—the so-called less-developed countries, or LDCs. Then in the issue following we will look at the question of whether or not foreign aid can actually help the LDCs to become more developed, that is, richer.

How Do We Define an LDC?

The term *less-developed country* doesn't have a very definite meaning—what does "less developed" mean as opposed to "more developed?" The answer, of course, is relative. We usually define this term by comparing the per capita incomes of different countries and arbitrarily classifying those with a per capita income of around $500 or less as "less-developed countries." Look at Table 29-1. Here we show countries classified by the level of their per capita income: those with per capita income in excess of $1,000; those with per capita income between $501 and $1,000; and those with per capita income of $500 or less. Notice that the final category fits our definition of LDCs. It includes most of the Middle East and southeastern Europe, all Africa except South Africa, all Asia except for a few countries, and most of Latin America.

The Problems of the Information Explosion

The LDCs today are not as content with their economic lot as they were in the past. One of the reasons for this is that information about how the inhabi-

Table 29-1 Level of Per Capita Income in Selected Countries in Three Categories

Here we see which countries are classified as developed and which are classified as less developed by arbitrarily separating those countries with per capita incomes in excess of $1,000 from those countries where per capita income is less than $500. In between these two figures are countries that are in the process of development.

PER CAPITA INCOME OVER $1,000	PER CAPITA INCOME OF $501 TO $1,000	PER CAPITA INCOME OF LESS THAN $500
Australia	Argentina	Most of Latin America
Austria	Chile	All of Africa (except South Africa)
Canada	Cuba	All of Asia (except for a few
Czechoslovakia	Greece	countries)
East Germany	Most of the Middle	Mexico
Denmark	East and Southeast	Panama
Finland	Europe	Poland
France		Portugal
Ireland		Spain
Italy		Rumania
Japan		
Netherlands		
New Zealand		
Norway		
Sweden		
Switzerland		
United States		
U.S.S.R.		
Venezuela		
West Germany		

Source: Statistical Office of the United Nations

tants of rich countries live is now known in even the remotest villages of the most backward nation. Everybody knows about the comforts of modern Western living. The relative poverty of the world's masses is not as accepted as it used to be. These masses know that a better life exists elsewhere, and this is the life they are striving for. What do they want? They want all the good things in life: better health conditions, better housing, a more equal distribution of the wealth, perhaps starting with land reform, and so on.

And the poor people of the world are demanding that their governments do something about poverty and substandard living conditions. The governments, on the other hand, are relying on various political and economic theories to determine which policies will be the most appropriate to achieve these desired ends. But before we look into this matter, let us first take a look at why living standards are different throughout the world. Why, in other words, do some nations develop, but other nations do not?

Geographical Theories of Economic Development

One of the earliest and most simplistic theories of growth concerns geographical location. This might also be called the north/south theory of economic development. Nations that are in the colder climates will be more developed than nations in the warmer climates. This north/south theory works in some places today. In the United States, the north is more developed than the south. (However, this was not the case before the Civil War and might not be the case now had the institution of slavery been *gradually* abolished.) In Italy too, the north is more developed than the south; and the same is also true in France. It is not the case, however, in other countries.

In addition, if this theory had any relevance or validity, it should apply also to the past. It doesn't. Some of the first civilizations were in the southern, hot regions of the world. Look at the Mayas in Central America and all the great civilizations in the Mediterranean area and the Near East. The Germans and the Saxons were far behind the Greeks in development, even though the Greeks endured a warmer climate.

As an offshoot of this north/south theory, some economists have hypothesized that the geographical distribution of natural resources is important: where the oil and ore deposits are, where the best soil is, where the most useful rainfall is, and so on. However, although this may have had some validity in the past when trade was not as widespread as it is today, Japan, Denmark, and Israel demonstrate successful counterexamples of this theory.

The Race Theory of Development

Even more simplistic and certainly less easily defended is the race theory of development.

Prosperity, according to this theory, is a matter of race: the whiter the race, the more productive the economy. There are so many counterexamples to this theory that they cannot all be mentioned here. The incredible success of the Japanese population in raising its standard of living is the most currently obvious example. However, the great development of the Egyptian, Greek, and Indian cultures, as well as the development of ancient China, also contradict this theory. Ethiopia too developed to a relatively high degree on its own. Race per se does not seem to be a very useful device for explaining why or predicting where prosperity will occur in the world economy.

More Modern Theories

More modern and more sophisticated theories of development are presented by today's economists. One of the most widely discussed concerns the need for balanced growth.

Balancing Industry with Agriculture

One characteristic of most developed countries is their high degree of industrialization. In general, nations with relatively high standards of living are more industrialized than countries with low standards of living. Some economists have taken this to mean that industrialization can be equated with economic development. The policy prescription is then obvious: So-called backward nations in which a large percentage of the total resources are devoted to agricultural pursuits should attempt to obtain a more balanced growth; they should industrialize.

Although the theory is fairly acceptable at first glance, it leads to some absurd results. We find in many LDCs with steel factories and automobile plants that the people are actually worse off because of this attempted industrialization. The reason is not hard to find. Most LDCs currently do not have a comparative advantage in producing steel or automobiles. They can engage in such industrial activities only by a heavy subsidization of the industry itself and by massive restrictions on competitive imports from other countries. For example, in India a steel mill may produce steel at two or three times the resource cost that would be required if the steel were imported. It seems quite apparent that the country is worse off, not better off, because of the steel mill. It may have the national prestige of owning a large, smoke-producing factory, but its citizens get less economic value out of their given resources than they would otherwise. This circumstance occurs throughout the entire less-developed world. Import restrictions abound, preventing the purchase of foreign, mostly cheaper, substitutes for the industrial products that the country itself produces in a usually subsidized environment. Sometimes the subsidization is not grossly obvious, but it usually exists in one form or another. In general, when an industry must be subsidized to exist, the subsidy leads to a misallocation of resources and a lower economic welfare for the country as a whole. The owners in the subsidized industry and the workers with skills specific to that industry are obviously better off. But the consumer ends up paying a higher *total* cost for the domestically made goods, and the total output of the nation remains less than it could be if the resources were reallocated.

The Stages of Development

If we look at the development of modern nations, we find that they go through three stages. First there is the agricultural stage, when most of the population is involved in agriculture. Then there is the manufacturing stage, when much of the population becomes involved in the industrialized sector of the economy. And finally there is a shift toward services. That is exactly what is happening in the United States: The so-called tertiary or service sector of the economy is growing by leaps and bounds, whereas the manufacturing sector, and its percentage employment, is declining.

However, it is important to understand the need for early specialization in one's comparative advantage. We have continuously referred to the doctrine of comparative advantage, and it is even more appropriate for the LDCs of the world. If trading is allowed among nations, a nation is best off if it produces what it has a comparative advantage at producing and imports the rest. This means that many LDCs should continue to specialize in agricultural production.

Agriculture Subsidized

There is a problem here, to be sure, and it is that modern Western countries have continually subsidized their own agricultural sectors to allow them to compete more easily with the comparative advantage that LDCs might have in this area. If we lived in a world of no subsidization, we would probably see much less food being produced in the highly developed Western world and much more being produced in the less-developed nations of the rest of the world. They would trade food for manufactured goods, and we would do the opposite. It would appear, then, that one of the most detrimental aspects of our economic policy for the Third World has been the continued subsidization of the American farmer. The United States, of course, is not alone; Germany, France, and England do exactly the same thing.

Even with this situation, however, a policy of balanced growth, or increased industrialization, in the LDCs of the world may lead

to more harm than good. Industrialization is generally only beneficial if it comes about naturally—that is, when the economic market conditions are such that the countries' entrepreneurs freely decide to build factories instead of increasing farm output.

Planning for Development in the LDCs

In many LDCs the governments have established specific development plans with specific targets and goals for the economy. In all cases, the purpose of these plans is to allocate resources so as to achieve a more rapid rate of economic growth. Capital, for example, may be allocated for specific purposes to encourage the development of well-defined sectors of the economy such as industry, education, or agriculture.

Development plans, however, should be carefully scrutinized before a decision is made as to their value. Some plans, for example, are merely window dressing. They are not based on careful investigation and some are not even actually put into effect. Other planning depends on such tools of modern economic analysis as linear programming and input-output analysis. These tools have been used extensively in certain situations and have been considered successful by some observers. However, their importance should not be exaggerated. No matter how good a plan is, it must be put into effect in a realistic and useful manner. Some of the

LDCs that have experienced the most development have tended to put aside their early development plans. Planning in these particular countries has become either modest or nonexistent. And although this is not to say that planning cannot help in development, nevertheless, some countries may find it difficult to formulate realistic plans and put them into effective action.

of stagnation. The degree of ability and certainty with which one can reap the gains from investing also determines the extent to which businesspersons in *other* countries will invest capital in LDCs. The threat of nationalization that hangs over many Latin American nations probably prevents a great amount of the foreign investment which might be necessary to allow these nations to become more developed.

Property Rights and Economic Development

If you were in a country where bank accounts and businesses were periodically expropriated by the government, how willing would you be to leave your money in a savings account or to invest in a business? Certainly you would be less willing than if such things never occurred. A good rule of thumb is: The more certain private property rights are, the more capital accumulation there will be. People are more willing to invest the money that they do not spend in endeavors which will increase their wealth in future years. They have property rights in their wealth that are sanctioned and enforced by the government. In fact, some economic historians have attempted to show that it was the development of well-defined private property rights which allowed Western Europe to increase its growth rate after many centuries

What Hope Is There for LDCs?

We have no perfect plan or theory for development. There have been few spectacular examples of development in the last 25 years—that is, few countries have shifted from the less-developed to the developed category. Israel is one that has. But there is no guaranteed model of economic development—no guaranteed process by which LDCs can become developed.

The future, however, may be different. Economists may become better attuned to the actual determinants of growth in different situations so that specific models can be made and applied in specific situations. The economics of development and growth is perhaps one of the least well-defined disciplines in the entire study of economics, despite the large number of books written on the subject. Economists still have many deep disagreements regarding a theory of economic development.

Chapter Summary
1. There are numerous theories of why nations grow. Some of the most simplistic are the north/south theory, the race theory, the natural resources theory, and so on.
2. One of the modern theories is that of balanced growth—agriculture and industry should grow in a balanced manner for the whole nation to develop. However, this often involves heavy subsidization of industrial projects against the dictates of comparative advantage, thus leading to reduced total output of the nation.

3. Modern Western nations have continuously subsidized their own agricultural sectors, thus putting a crimp in the apparent comparative advantage that LDCs might have in agricultural pursuits.

Questions for Thought and Discussion

1. It is often said that the rich are getting richer and the poor poorer. Do you agree?
2. Why do you think there is so much disagreement about what LDCs should do to grow faster?
3. Do you think that the prestige value of industrial development is so important as to negate certain economic arguments against that development?
4. Some people have stated that since we have given LDCs death control, we have a moral obligation to help them out today. Do you agree?

Selected References

Bauer, Peter T., *Dissent on Development: Studies and Debates in Development Economics,* Cambridge, Mass.: Harvard University Press, 1972.

Elkan, Walter, *An Introduction to Development Economics,* Middlesex, England: Penguin Books, 1973.

Gill, Richard T., *Economic Development: Past and Present,* Englewood Cliffs, N.J.: Prentice-Hall, 1973.

Myrdal, Gunnar, *Challenge of World Poverty: A World Poverty Program in Outline,* New York: Pantheon Books, 1970.

Ranis, Gustav (ed.), *The United States and the Developing Economies,* rev. ed., New York: W. W. Norton, 1973.

The Economist as Evangelist

BARBARA WARD

English Economist

Photo by V. Sladon, W. W. Norton & Co., Inc.

At the age of 26, Barbara Ward was named honorary secretary of the Sword of the Spirit movement, the purpose of which she said was "to remind English Catholics of the fifth precept of Pope Pius' encyclical which inveighed against the division of the world into have and have-not nations." The year was 1940 and Ward was already well launched on what has become a distinguished career devoted to bridging the gap between rich lands and poor. She had already written her first book, a study of the colonial question, titled *The International Share-Out*. The same year she was made foreign editor of *The Economist*. By 1949, having written two more books, worked for the British Ministry of Information during World War II, and served on the staff of the BBC, she was awarded an honorary degree at Smith as "one of the most widely read and most influential persons in the entire Western world."

Born in England and educated in France, Germany, and England, Ward was named Albert Schweitzer Professor of International Economic Development at Columbia University in 1968 and is now president of the International Institute for Environment and Development. She is the author of numerous books on economic development and the necessity for aid to poor countries, including *The West at Bay* (1948), *Policy for the West* (1951), *Faith and Freedom* (1954), *The Interplay of East and West* (1957), *Five Ideas that Change the World* (1959), *India and the West* (1961), *Nationalism and Ideology* (1966), *Spaceship Earth* (1966), *The Lopsided World* (1968), and with others, *The Widening Gap* (1971).

In one of her most influential books, *The Rich Nations and the Poor Nations* (1962), the popular development economist draws on themes from her earlier work. Noting that communism provides a coherent and appealing program for development, Ward urges the Western industrialized nations to formulate a cooperative strategy of their own toward developing nations. She calls for a spiritual revival of the Marshall Plan and proposes that each country contribute 1 percent of its annual income to foreign aid. The gap between the rich lands and the poor is widening, she says, because the nations of the West have already achieved a "momentum of sustained growth" while the poor countries—because they are poor—have not been able to accumulate sufficient capital "to get off the ground."

Since the thirst for modernization, as well as many current dilemmas in the poor countries are directly attributable to the impact of the "Western colonial system," Ward argues that it is therefore the responsibility of the capitalist nations of the "Atlantic arena" to finish the task of development. A foe of the haphazard nature of most foreign aid programs, she criticizes the colonial system of the past and foreign aid programs of the present for creating only partial modernization, when what is needed is enough capital to transform the entire economies of the poor nations. "All parts of the economy have to change if the economic pattern as a whole is to change," she says.

In recent years Ward has become more critical of the private enterprise system and economic nationalism. She has become increasingly involved in projects and commissions of the United Nations, and she emphasizes the need for planning and international cooperation in economic development. Though still concerned with the gap between rich lands and poor that endangers political and economic stability, and still critical of Western foreign aid programs, Ward has broadened her scope to include the ecological consequences of different strategies of development.

In her latest book, *Only One Earth* (1972), written with microbiologist René Dubos and based on the United Nations Conference on the Human Environment, Ward and Dubos ask what would happen if all the world's peoples lived like Europeans or Japanese. If the rates of energy use, consumption of foodstuffs and raw materials, urbanization, and population continue their present degree of acceleration, "the natural system of the planet upon which biological survival depends" will be altered "dangerously and perhaps irreversibly." Outlining the major worldwide "external diseconomies" that "pass on a hidden and heavy cost to the community," Ward and Dubos conclude that economic growth is still imperative but feasible in the long run only if more vigorous and conscious planning is exercised. They call for a new vision of unity, based on the realization that all nations and all peoples are interdependent and that such unity is necessary for human survival.

Can Foreign Aid Help Less-Developed Countries?

CAN DEVELOPMENT ASSISTANCE WORK?

The Rationale behind Foreign Aid

The United States and other countries have been giving assistance to less-developed countries for many years now. Why? Four basic reasons are usually given to justify this assistance, which can be in the form of grants, food, military supplies, or technical expertise. We will look at these reasons now.

Security

Foreign aid during the 1950s was provided by the United States principally under the amended Mutual Security Act of 1951. It was justified primarily as a national security measure needed to strengthen allies and to build up low-income countries to make them less vulnerable to communist invasion or takeover. Throughout the 1960s, the long-term security argument remained the underpinning of the official rationale. Basically, America wanted allies and lots of them. Economic aid was, so to speak, a down payment on a military alliance with a less-developed country. Through such alliances, the United States obtained foreign bases that could be used for military intelligence gathering and for United States forces. In the age of intercontinental ballistic missiles, Trident submarines, and spy satellites, however, the importance of such bases has seriously diminished, and although the United States may want military allies, it certainly is less in need of foreign bases for its own internal security.

Economics

Economically, extending foreign aid to help develop other countries can be good business. Developing other countries presumably widens the market for American exports and also provides new opportunities for international investment by American capitalists. In addition, lower-cost sources of raw materials can also be developed. Really poor LDCs tend to be unreliable sources of raw materials. However, if they can be developed, then both reliability and quantity supplied may grow.

Also, higher levels of production and trade in LDCs will strengthen international trade and international financial transactions. Countries with undiversified, weak economies are often feeble members in the network of international trading institutions on which all nations must ultimately rely for international trade.

Politics

It used to be thought that development assistance would have an obvious political payoff in that it would help win friends for the United States. Although not completely dead, such a view is certainly highly discredited today. In its place is a longer-range view of the world political situation. If we help develop, then the world will have greater order and the international political climate will be improved. In this sense, foreign aid is only one of many tools that are helping fashion an international environment that will be less polarized and less divisive.

Humanitarianism

The humanitarian argument in support of foreign aid remains a strong and potent rationale. In the United States itself, the problem of poverty has not gone unnoticed. If we feel that our citizens should not starve or live in despicable conditions, then we can justify foreign aid by merely extending these humanitarian views to the rest of the world. One might say that our world has become too small for feelings of kinship between individuals to be stopped at political frontiers.

In its most elementary form, the humanitarian appeal is quite clearly a plea for the relief of suffering. At this level then, aid would be for consumption only rather than for investment. But immediate consumption relief is only a short-run palliative and not a cure. The humanitarian rationale would be better served in the long run if aid were in the form of investments in industry, agriculture, and education.

A Brief Rundown of American Foreign Aid

Look at Table I-35.1. Here we show the total amount of economic and military aid that the United States has extended to other nations. We also break down that aid into its military component and its economic components consisting of grants and loans. The numbers are given in constant dollars, with 1967 as a base year. One thing strikes us immediately: Foreign aid, in real terms, has been falling dramatically over the last several decades.

To get a better idea of how much aid each individual country receives, we show in Table I-35.2 the net receipts of economic aid per capita for the years 1960 to 1965. Note that these are current dollars rather than constant dollars. In any event, we see that many countries have received minute amounts of aid in terms of aid per person per year.

Table I-35.1

Foreign Economic and Military Aid Program, 1949–1975 (In Billions of 1967 Dollars)

In the last 2½ decades, the amount of foreign aid, both military and economic, has trended downward, if we express it in constant 1967 dollars.

YEAR	TOTAL AID	YEAR	TOTAL AID
1949	8.8	1964	3.9
1950	5.1	1965	3.5
1951	4.6	1966	3.8
1952	4.5	1967	3.2
1953	7.6	1968	2.6
1954	6.8	1969	2.1
1955	5.2	1970	2.1
1956	5.4	1971	2.9
1957	4.4	1972	3.0
1958	4.7	1973	2.2
1959	4.6	1974	2.6
1960	4.0	1975	2.5
1961	3.8		
1962	4.4		
1963	4.6		

Source: Statistical Abstract of the United States

Table I-35.2

Receipt of Economic Aid Per Capita in Selected Countries

Here we show the net receipts of economic aid per capita from 1960 to 1965 for selected countries. If we were to correct for inflation, the amount of aid per person would be much smaller.

COUNTRY	PER-CAPITA AID RECEIVED (DOLLARS PER YEAR)	COUNTRY	PER-CAPITA AID RECEIVED (DOLLARS PER YEAR)
Argentina	1.6	Mexico	1.3
Ceylon	1.6	Pakistan	3.6
Chile	13.2	Peru	1.8
Colombia	3.7	Philippines	1.7
Egypt	8.7	Spain	1.3
Greece	5.5	Taiwan	6.3
India	2.0	Thailand	1.4
Israel	46.2	Venezuela	2.5
Malaya	2.1	Yugoslavia	6.1

Source: OECD

The Marshall Plan

After World War II, American financial assistance to other countries in the world became quite impressive. The United States financed approximately three-quarters of the United Nations Relief and Rehabilitation Program, which extended $4 billion worth of food, clothing, and medical services to war-ravaged European economies. In fact, in the 3 years following the end of the war, the United States provided about $17 billion in aid to Europe. That, however, did not seem to be enough.

By 1948 it became clear to Secretary of State George Marshall that more was needed to stimulate the European economies. In a famous address at Harvard University in June 1948, Marshall outlined a plan to speed Europe's recovery—and so we got the Marshall Plan. The plan established the European Recovery Program, which granted over $10 billion in foreign assistance to Europe. Most of this $10 billion was in the form of outright grants. Many observers contend that the Marshall Plan was instrumental in allowing Europe's productive capacity to grow dramatically during the late 1940s and early 1950s.

A Shift in Emphasis

After European economies got back on their feet, United States foreign aid began to go to LDCs. About one-third of this was military aid and the other two-thirds was nonmilitary aid. Much of it, however, was in the form of loans or grants of money that were ''tied''—that is, the aid had to be spent on American goods and services. In other words, much of it was a form of subsidy to American

"A trillion-dollar economy is all right with me, but will it buy happiness?"

exporters rather than purely and simply aid for other nations.

We also gave aid under Public Law 480, which allowed for the transfer of ''surplus'' commodities, such as wheat, to selected countries. India, for example, obtained more than $3.3 billion worth of agricultural surplus commodities during the period 1953 to 1956. Public Law 480, however, has been greatly criticized. We'll look at these criticisms shortly.

The Case of India

It is interesting to examine the foreign aid situation of a country where such aid has accounted for a large percentage of that nation's gross national product. Take the case of India. In 1951, foreign assistance was about 1 percent of GNP. By 1958 such assistance had risen to 2.7 percent, and by 1970 it had increased to over 4 percent. We have given India surplus wheat and other aid in the form of grants and loans. Other Western countries, international agencies, and communist-bloc countries, have also given aid to India. Almost all noncommunist aid to India has been channeled through the Aid India Consortium. This consortium is composed of Canada, Japan, the United States, the United Kingdom, Belgium, France, West Germany, Italy, Holland, and others. India has also received long-term loans at preferential interest rates from Japan, Germany, the United Kingdom, and other countries.

Problems with Assistance to Less-Developed Countries

We have now given over $100 billion total in foreign aid to Europe and LDCs. The Marshall Plan seemed to show all involved that foreign aid could be extremely effective. However, critics of foreign aid pointed out that the Marshall Plan's apparent success could not be duplicated in other countries. Under the Marshall Plan, money was given to countries who already had advanced economic organizations, skilled labor forces, and experienced, as well as relatively efficient, government bureaucracies. Hence, the Marshall Plan was essentially an aid system to help restore or replace physical plants and equipment destroyed during the war. Proponents of the Marshall Plan, who saw its success as justification for further foreign aid, must agree that perhaps the major factor in that success was the United States' provision of the one ingredient—physical resources—missing from an economic environment ready to generate its own recovery.

The Situation in Less-Developed Countries

The LDCs in the world today cannot be compared to those war-torn European countries at the end of World War II. The modernization of LDCs is a much more complicated task than the restoration of postwar Europe. There are many barriers to economic growth: a lack of technical skills and capacities, poorly organized markets, political and social elites who are unreceptive to change, non-growth-oriented foreign trade policies, and so on.

If we look back at Table I-35.2, we see that the foreign aid impact on per capita income in recipient countries has been small, both in absolute terms and relative to existing levels of per capita income. Israel, for example, received approximately $29.10 in aid per capita from the United States in 1968, but the country's 1968 per capita income was over $1,000. The contribution of foreign aid to per capita income has to be quite small.

Critics of foreign aid contend that the only countries in which foreign aid may have caused a substantial percentage increase in national income are those countries where military and political motives dominated. These countries include Taiwan, Laos, Jordan, Libya, and Liberia.

The Rate of Return on Investment

Even if we assume that every dollar given as foreign aid is put into an investment in a less-developed country, the end result is still not that significant. Much research has been done on the rate of return on invest-

ments in underdeveloped countries, and at the most, we are talking in terms of a 10 percent annual figure. Although such a rate of return is not bad, given the per capita levels of foreign aid we are talking about, we cannot expect miracles from our foreign aid dollars.

Destroying Relative Prices

We have talked throughout the microeconomic section of this book about the role of relative prices. Relative prices indicate the relative scarcity and desirability of the various goods and services available in our economy and throughout the world. Relative prices will also determine the amount of resources that will go into producing a particular good or service. If the relative price of one good goes up and everything else remains the same, generally the profitability of increasing production of that good will go up also. This is the notion of a long-run competitive equilibrium, where economic profits are competed away by new producers entering the industry when the going market price yields a higher than normal rate of return.

Critics of foreign aid have pointed out that Public Law 480 has in many instances hurt countries like India more than it has helped them. Why? Simply because when we give our "surplus" food products to another nation, we destroy the system of relative prices that is supposed to signal individual farmers or would-be farmers in such countries that increased production would be profitable in the future. Think about it this way: When there is a reduction in the supply of agricultural commodities during any one year for whatever reason—drought, pestilence, or whatever—the relative price of agricultural commodities will rise. When the relative price rises, the profitability of engaging in agricultural pursuits rises also. More individuals will go into the farming sector of the economy, and those already in that sector will expend more energy and resources to provide food for the future. However, if, when there is a reduction in agricultural supplies due to some natural calamity, the United States or any other nation ships large quantities of food products to the stricken nation, then the relative price of food products will not rise as abruptly. The incentive to put more resources into the farming sector will be destroyed. In the short run, those recipients of ''free'' surplus food commodities from the United States will be better off. In the long run, however, the agricultural sector will not expand as much as it would have otherwise, and the nation will be worse off.

A Final Note

A former president of the International Finance Corporation, Robert L. Gardner, has succinctly stated the probable impact of foreign aid:

Over the post-war period immense sums have been made available to the developing areas. Some of these funds have been well applied and have produced sound results, others have not . . . if [foreign aid] is applied to uneconomic purposes, or if good projects are poorly planned and executed, the result will be minus, not plus. The effective spending of large funds requires experience, competence, honesty and organization. Lacking any of these factors, large injections of capital into developing countries can cause more harm than good. The test of how much additional capital is required for development is how much a country can effectively apply within any given period, not how much others are willing to supply.

The game of foreign aid is indeed a difficult one. It has not been and will not be enough for the United States and other more developed countries merely to transfer funds to countries in need. Foreign aid can help, but only to a limited extent and only if it is applied wisely, as Gardner pointed out.

Questions for Thought and Discussion

1. Is foreign aid as essential today in the development of the LDCs as it was 50 years ago?
2. Some observers contend that the Marshall Plan was not the key to Western Europe's development after World War II. Rather, they assert it was the tremendous amount of human capital that already existed in Western Europe which allowed such rapid rebuilding after the war. Do you agree or disagree?
3. Several rationales for foreign aid were given in this issue. Can you think of others?
4. What do you think is the effect of ''tied'' foreign aid? (Tied foreign aid requires the recipient to spend the proceeds on United States products.)

Selected References

Bauer, Peter T., *Dissent on Development: Studies and Debates in Development Economics,* Cambridge, Mass.: Harvard University Press, 1972.

Bhagwati, Jagdish and R. S. Eckhaus (eds.), *Foreign Aid,* Baltimore: Penguin Books, 1970.

Raffaele, Joseph A., *The Economic Development of Nations,* New York: Random House, 1971.

30 Economic Growth

Economic growth is an important policy variable that concerns the governments of all nations. Today in the United States there is an increasing clamor to *reduce* our current economic growth rate. We will touch on this in greater detail in the following and final issue of this text. Here we will discuss the general theory of growth. Zero economic growth may seem desirable to many in the United States, but LDCs in the world today are struggling for higher standards of living and are therefore still interested in the problems of economic growth.

What Is the Meaning of Economic Growth?

Most of you probably have a general idea what the term *economic growth* means. When a nation grows, its citizens are in some ways better off—at least in terms of material well-being. A formal definition of economic wealth might be as follows:

Economic growth is the rate of change in an economy's real level of output over time.

Generally, economic growth is measured by the rate of change of some measure of output. In this nation, and in most other nations today, the most commonly used measure of economic output is gross national product (GNP). In discussing the rate of change of actual output, we have to correct GNP for changes in prices. When we do this, we get what is called *real GNP*. Hence, one measure of economic growth is the rate of change in real GNP over time. This measure may be misleading, however, if the population is growing rapidly at the same time that real GNP is growing. In this case, economic growth is measured by the rate of change in per capita real GNP over time.

Growth and the Production-Possibilities Curve

We can graphically show economic growth by using the production-possibilities curve presented in Chapter 2. Figure 30-1 shows the production-possibilities curve for 1977. On the horizontal axis are agricultural goods and on the vertical axis are manufactured goods. If there is economic growth between 1977 and 1980, then the production-possibilities curve

will shift outward to the heavy line. The distance that it shifts represents the amount of economic growth—that is, the increase in the productive capacity of the nation.

The Importance of Growth Rates

Look at the growth rates in per capita income for selected countries in Table 30-1. The difference between the growth rates of different countries is not large; generally it varies by only 1 to 3 percentage points. You might want to know why such small differences in growth rates are important. What does it matter, you could say, if we grew at 3 percent or at 4 percent per year?

It matters a lot—not for next year or the year after—but for the future. The power of com-

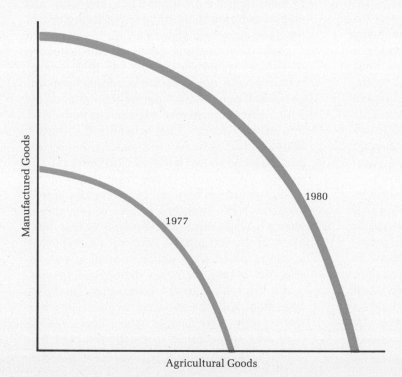

FIGURE 30-1 **Economic Growth**
We can see economic growth in terms of production-possibilities curves. If there is growth between 1977 and 1980, then the production-possibilities curve for the entire economy will shift outward from the line labeled 1977 to the heavier curve labeled 1980. The distance that it shifts represents an increase in the productive capacity of the nation.

Table 30-1 Per Capita Growth Rates—Various Countries

Here we show the average annual rate of growth of GNP per capita for various countries.

COUNTRY	AVERAGE ANNUAL RATE OF GROWTH OF INCOME PER CAPITA (1929–1970)
United States	1.9%
France	2.0
Italy	2.5
United Kingdom	1.7
Germany	3.0
Canada	2.1
Greece	5.2
Brazil	1.8

Source: Statistical Abstract of the United States and Statistical Office of the United Nations

pound interest is overwhelming. Let's see what happens with three different growth rates: 3 percent, 4 percent, 5 percent. We start with $1 trillion, which is approximately equal to the gross national product of the United States in 1971. We then compound or grow this $1 trillion into the future at these three different growth rates. The difference is huge. In 50 years, $1 trillion becomes $4,380,000,000,000 if compounded at 3 percent per year. Just one percentage point more in the growth rate—that is, 4 percent—results in a GNP almost double that amount. Two percentage points difference in the growth rate—that is, 5 percent per year—results in a GNP of $11,500,000,000,000 in 50 years. Obviously, there is a great difference in the results of economic growth for very small differences in growth rates. That is why nations are concerned if the growth rate falls even by a very small amount in absolute percentage terms.

It is often asserted that income and wealth in the United States are so great relative to other countries because we were endowed with such a large amount of valuable natural resources. This factor, however, is neither a necessary nor a sufficient condition for rapid economic growth.

Natural Resources and Economic Growth

A large amount of natural resources is not sufficient to guarantee economic growth. Many Latin American countries are fantastically rich in natural resources. However, they have not been overly successful in exploiting these resources. Natural resources must be converted to useful forms. Even in the United States, the Indians had more natural resources available to them than we have now, but they were unable to increase their standard of living or experience economic growth.

Only if we include people in the category of natural resources can we say that natural resources are required for economic growth; obviously, *people* must devise the methods by which other natural resources can be converted into useable forms. This is where the United States was more fortunate than other countries, particularly those with similar natural resources. (We also benefited from large capital investments from England and other Old World countries.) The founding fathers of our nation were a biased sample of the people at that time. Many of the "criminals" who were transported to the colonies were guilty of such crimes as religious heresy, being in debt, evading economic laws made by the government, and disagreement with the government itself. In other words, they were people who either wanted to or who were forced to escape the regimentation of a much more structured society. These are just the type of people who would attempt to devise new methods to utilize the natural resources in America. And that they did.

This is not to say, of course, that if we transplanted a cross section of Americans to some Latin American country, the growth rate in that country would suddenly take off. However, we can assert that the United States required more than just abundant natural resources to reach its current level of development; it required people who could devise ways to form those resources into something useful. Less-developed nations will also require this type of human resource.

Capital Accumulation

It is often asserted that a necessary prerequisite for economic development is a large capital stock—machines and other durable goods which can be used to aid in the production of consumption goods and more capital goods in the future. It is true that developed countries have larger capital stocks per capita than less-developed countries. It is also true that the larger the capital stock for any given population, the higher the possible level of real income. This fact is one of the bases of many foreign aid programs. The United States and other nations have attempted to add capital stocks to less-developed countries so that they, too, might grow. However, the amount of capital that we have actually given is, as we saw in Issue I-35, quite small.

What is the relationship between capital and a nation's growth rate?

Let's look at a production-possibilities curve for a country as a whole. We want to find the trade-off between goods today and goods tomorrow, or between present consumption and future consumption. Therefore, in Figure 30-2 we label the horizontal axis as present goods and the vertical axis as future goods. The pro-

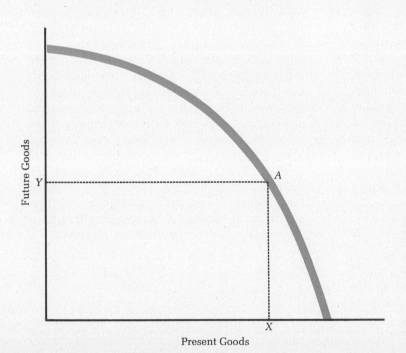

FIGURE 30-2 **The Trade-Off between Present Goods and Future Goods**

Here we show the production-possibilities curve between present goods and future goods. If we want to have more goods in the future, we have to sacrifice goods today. In other words, there has to be more saving if we are to have more future goods. At a point in time—for example, at point A—we could consume X present goods and still have Y future goods.

duction-possibilities curve, as you will remember, represents the *maximum* amount of each of the two goods that a nation can produce at any point in time. If, for example, we were at point A, we could, with our present resources, consume X amount of present goods and Y amount of future goods. By decreasing the amount of present goods, we can increase the amount of future goods. This means that if we consume less today, we will have more tomorrow. We have to sacrifice present consumption to have more future consumption.

All individuals, of course, are faced with this decision. It is a decision they must make with respect to how much they want to save. If they want a lot of future consumption, they cut back on current consumption; they save more. More income can go into a savings and loan association or into the stock market so that later, perhaps when they retire, they will be able to consume more than otherwise. In terms of the economy as a whole, the decision as to whether there should be present consumption or future consumption translates into a decision as to whether there should be more movies and food consumed today or more buildings and machines constructed today. When you decide not to consume but to save part of your income, you will perhaps put it in a savings and loan association. That money will then be available to borrowers for new housing. Or you might invest your savings in a new company or in the expansion of an old one. This way, the money you save provides the money capital for businesspersons to construct and purchase physical capital—machines and equipment.

Why Is Capital Important?

The size of the capital stock determines the maximum amount of income that can be produced at any point in time. Obviously, if very few machines can be used to make goods and services, we will be able to make fewer and our income will be lower. The more machines there are, the more income can be generated. Therefore, the larger the capital stock, the larger the income pie. But how does the capital stock grow? It grows by people making the decision not to consume today but to save and invest. The more saving and investment there are as a percentage of total income, the higher will be the capital stock, and therefore, the higher will be possible future income. We can perhaps demonstrate this decision by again using our production-possibilities curve.

In Figure 30-3, we show a production-possibilities curve for 1984. The horizontal axis is again labeled as present consumption, but now the vertical axis is labeled capital goods. "Capital goods" is just another way of describing future consumption. We would expect that if our economy is operating at A, where there are relatively more capital goods being produced than at B, the production-possibilities curve in 1984 would be farther to the right than it would be if we were producing at B. We have labeled the outside curve AA and the middle curve BB. Obviously, the rate of growth starting from point A is greater than the rate of growth starting from point B. The pie gets potentially larger the more people are willing to save today. In fact, we might be able to increase the rate of growth in the United States drastically if we somehow increased the saving rate of the population. This could be done by government taxation. That is, taxes could be increased, and the proceeds from those increased taxes could be put into investment goods that, in turn, would yield increased income in the future. Let's now turn from investment to saving.

Saving Decisions

Saving decisions are based on many things. However, one key determinant is what we call

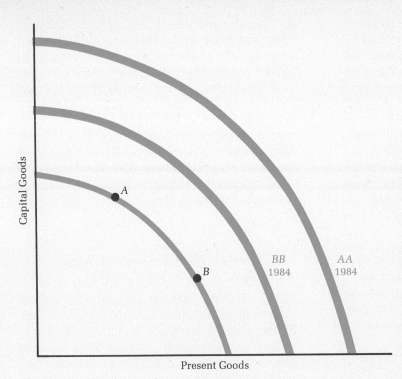

FIGURE 30-3 **The Importance of Capital for Growth**

Here we show a production-possibilities curve with two points on it, A and B. At point A we are consuming less today and providing more consumption for tomorrow in the form of capital goods. At point B we are consuming more today and providing less in the form of future consumption. If we operate at point A, we may end up on a production-possibilities curve of AA in 1984. However, if we are at point B, we may end up at a production-possibilities curve of only BB in 1984. In other words, there will be less growth during the next decade if we consume more goods today instead of saving and investing in capital goods that provide for more future consumption.

a person's **personal discount rate.** If you just can't wait to consume all the income you make, you have a relatively high discount rate. If you are not so impatient and can wait longer, you have a relatively low discount rate. The lower your discount rate, the more you'll be willing to save at any given yield on those savings. Whenever your personal discount rate exceeds the yield you can get on savings, you will not save; you have to be offered a yield that is higher than your discount rate. Otherwise you'll be better off by consuming today. The saving behavior of economies taken as a whole depends therefore on the collective discount rate of the population and the average rate of return on saving. Note here that we are talking about the rate of saving—that is, how much of current income people put away per period of time.

Saving and the Poor

It is often stated that people in less-developed countries cannot save because they are barely subsisting. This is not actually true. Many anthropological studies—of villages in India, for example—have revealed that saving is in fact going on, but it takes forms that we don't recognize in our money economy. In some places, saving may involve storing dried onions. In any event, saving does take place even in the most poverty-stricken areas.

The Hard Facts

Look at it this way: Even if you are very, very poor and just barely making a living, you know that sometime in the future you will no longer be able to work. You will either reach mandatory retirement or you will become so debilitated and unproductive that nobody will be willing to hire you. Your income stream will be cut off. Unless there is a benevolent government or some charitable people (perhaps your family) who will take care of you, you will starve. There is a way out: You can have accumulated savings, the income and principal of which you can live on. Therefore, today you must make the decision as to how much of your current income you want to set aside for those retirement years, or for those years when you are sick or debilitated and cannot work. Unless it is literally true that you will starve if you reduce your current level of consumption, you probably will attempt to save a little bit out of your income. Most people are willing to reduce current consumption by a small amount to, at least, exist after they no longer can work. If this is not done, they face certain starvation when their income stream falls to zero.

Basically, then, saving is a method by which individuals can realize an optimal consumption stream throughout their expected lifetimes. Be careful. The word optimal here does not mean adequate or necessary or decent. It means most desirable from the *individual's* point of view.

Improving Technology

When people save, there has to be a profitable outlet for those savings so that the capital stock will grow and future incomes will be higher. Otherwise, saving would not lead to higher economic growth. One of the main ways that less-developed countries have been able to increase their capital stock and productivity in general is by adapting foreign techniques to their own situation. The most obvious and helpful technological advances that less-developed countries have been able to borrow from the developed world involve those in

agriculture—improved pesticides, hybrid seeds, improved irrigation techniques. One of the most striking examples of these technological breakthroughs that have aided less-developed countries is the development of "miracle" rice.

When we see the importance of technological progress in the growth of an underdeveloped country (or a developed country), we might come to a tentative conclusion that technological progress, along with the *associated* accumulation of human and material capital, is *the* crucial aspect of successful development.

Can We Tell Which Factor Is Most Important?

Is it possible to find out which factor is most important in determining a nation's economic growth rate? The answer is difficult. One way to simplify the problem, though, is to talk only in terms of the three economic growth determinants that can be measured—at least in theory:

1. Growth of capital stock
2. Growth of the labor force
3. Technological progress

Economists have found it relatively easy to measure the first two determinants. And in the past they have had a tendency to attribute any economic growth not accounted for by these determinants to technological progress. However, this is a very questionable procedure. In fact, recently economists have found that a large part of economic growth can be attributed to improvements in the labor force or, otherwise stated, improvements in human capital. This may also be true in the measurement of the capital stock. To the extent that the measurement of the growth in capital and labor does not take account of the growth in quality of these two factors, any residual measure of technological progress will be seriously biased upward.

Economic Growth—A Policy Objective

After World War II, governments throughout the world made economic growth a distinct policy objective. When, in the 1950s and early 1960s, American economists and politicians re-alized that the American rate of economic growth was slower than that of other nations, an explicit policy directive was issued by President Kennedy. He set a target of a 4½ percent annual increase in total real output during the 1960s. Presumably, government stimulation of

the rate of economic growth was necessary because of our political desire to stay ahead of the communist countries, the Soviet Union in particular. Economic growth was also considered important for national prestige as well as national defense. In addition, some economists, including John Kenneth Galbraith, pointed out that there was underinvestment in public sector spending. Hence, economic growth was called for to increase the funds available for public expenditures on urban renewal, hospitals, and public transportation.

Recently, political stress on increasing the rate of economic growth in the United States has greatly diminished. There are many economists who have pointed out that economic growth brings with it serious environmental problems in addition to depleting natural relevels. They point out that higher levels of economic growth may cause higher levels of congestion and noise in our cities and the destruction of our natural heritage. We will take up these very important problems in the following issue.

Definition of New Term

Personal Discount Rate: The rate at which you as an individual discount future pleasure or future consumption. If you have a high personal discount rate, you will want to consume a lot today because you don't want to wait until tomorrow. If you have a low personal discount rate, you will be willing to wait in order to have more consumption in the future. You will be willing to save more.

Chapter Summary

1. Just as there are different levels of per capita income in the world, there are different rates of growth. There seems to be no correlation between the level of per capita income and the rate of growth, however. It is the rate of growth that we are concerned with in this chapter.
2. A slight difference in the compound rate of growth can cause a tremendous difference in the per capita income or GNP many years in the future. For example, a jump from a 3 percent to a 5 percent per year rate of growth results in, at the end of 50 years, a difference in total income of almost 250 percent.
3. While natural resources are important for allowing economic growth, we must include in the concept of natural resources people and their productive services in order to come up with factors necessary for economic growth.
4. Even though people are important, so is capital accumulation or capital from other countries. We find that the more saving there is today, the larger is the capital stock and the larger will be the amount of possible future consumption. Hence, in economies where the people save a large percentage of their income, we would expect, *ceteris paribus,* a higher

rate of growth than in economies where people do not save as much. The use to which this capital is put is also important. If it is not used for investments that allow for future production and consumption, then the rate of growth may not be high even if the rate of saving is high.

5. Saving is a way to reach an optimal rate of consumption throughout one's life. Even poor people may want to save, to provide for future consumption when they are no longer working and making an income.

1. Do you think Latin America is going to be better off by discouraging foreign investment through numerous nationalizations and expropriations of foreign property? Why?

2. Many less-developed countries put extreme restrictions on the purchase of imported luxury goods. Do you think this is a helpful policy for increasing the rate of growth in these countries?

3. If you were the economic policy adviser to a less-developed country, where would you suggest the government start investing? Why?

4. Many people contend that in most less-developed countries, the population is too poor to be able to save. Go back to our definition of saving as a way to distribute consumption optimally throughout one's lifetime. Do you think it is true that poorer people are unable to save as much as rich people in percentage terms? What is the relevant determinant of desired saving?

Selected
References

Baldwin, Robert E., *Economic Development and Growth*, 2d ed., New York: Wiley, 1972.

Fabricant, Solomon, *A Primer on Productivity*, New York: Random House, 1969.

Mansfield, Edwin, *The Economics of Technological Change*, New York: W. W. Norton, 1968.

Mishan, E. J., *Technology and Growth*, New York: Praeger, 1970.

Rostow, W. W., *The Stages of Economic Growth*, New York: Cambridge University Press, 1960.

Should Growth Be Stopped?

WHAT DOES THE FUTURE HOLD?

The Economic Problem

The economic problem occurs because we live in a world of scarcity. John Maynard Keynes, however, wrote an article in 1930 in which he concluded that "[a]ssuming no important wars and no important increase in population, the economic problem may be solved, or be at least within sight of solution within a hundred years."[1] Keynes felt that within 100 years, we would be eight times better off economically.

Keynes didn't see this opulence as such a good thing. In fact, he felt that "[for] the first time since his creation man will be faced with his real, permanent problem—how to use his freedom from pressing economic cares, how to occupy his leisure, . . . to live wisely and agreeably and well."

It would be nice if that were our only problem. Serious doubt has been expressed about Keynes' forecast by those who are worried that if we continue growing at the same

[1]John Maynard Keynes, "Economic Possibilities for Our Grandchildren," rep. in *Essays in Persuasion,* London: Macmillan, 1933.

rate we have in the past, the world will no longer be livable.

Stopping GNP Growth

We've noted some of the various theories that explain why nations grow, and we've shown some of the strategies less-developed nations might want to follow to increase their rate of economic growth so their inhabitants might enjoy higher standards of living. Recently, though, there has been a cry that economic growth should be stopped, at least in advanced areas of the world. Ecologically minded scientists, laypersons, academicians, and public officials have declared that we must end our fetish with GNP growth. They argue that growth in GNP should be stopped because it depletes our natural resources, pollutes our environment, and makes us into materialistic money grubbers. Furthermore, lurking somewhere in the future is a maximum limit that will be reached sooner or later. A fast growth rate in GNP just makes us reach it sooner. And when it is reached, then GNP will fall, and liv-

ing standards will go down instead of up.

To Zero Economic Growth enthusiasts, there is no hope. Those concerned with the environment attack GNP as a digital idol worshipped by materialistic gluttons. GNP measures, of course, only the output of goods and services. It ignores the pollution and industrial grime that growth generates.

So some maintain that there must be a limit to growth. In fact, in the hands of several scientists, the computer has shown that growth will reach a limit. An 18-month study sponsored by the Club of Rome arrived at this very conclusion. We will discuss it now.

The Limits to Growth

Look at Figure I-36.1. It's pretty wild, isn't it? But the conclusion, if those lines mean anything, is that food supplies are going to prove inadequate, even with ample natural resources, pollution controls, and a falling population. The question is: "Who drew those curves and how did they do it?" Several scientists at the Massachusetts Institute of Technology set up mathematical equations using information on what determines industrial output, food production, pollution, population,

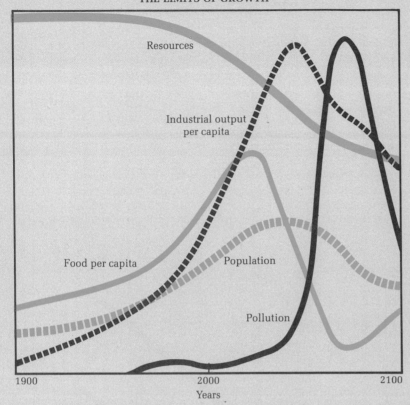

Resources

Industrial output
per capita

Food per capita

Population

Pollution

1900   2000   2100

Years

FIGURE I-36.1

Here we look into the twenty-first century. The prediction is that even though we will have ample natural resources, sufficient pollution controls, and better birth control, we will still run out of food. Malthus revisited. (*Source:* Potomac Associates.)

and so on, and the relationships between these factors. A computer was then used to calculate and project the behavior of each of these trends as they related to each other.

The M.I.T. computer forecast dramatic events for the world if the current trends in these variables continued. Before the year 2100, the world as a system would reach a point where the population could no longer be supported by existing resources. These grim findings apparently hold even if important advances are made in birth control

and food production, in natural resources output and pollution control.

The equations show exponential (geometric) growth for everything except food production. Even breakthroughs in technology will not prevent the final collapse of the world. Take, for example, one computer run that the M.I.T. scientists experimented with. This is the one that actually underlies the curves shown in Figure I-36.1. These curves assume that recycling technology will reduce the input of raw material per unit of output to 25 percent of

the amount now used. It is also assumed that birth control will eliminate unwanted children. Additionally, pollution will be 75 percent below its present level. What happens? Resources are sufficient; that's no problem. But the growth of industry is so great that higher output soon offsets the 75 percent decline in pollution. That is, even with the smaller amount of pollution per unit of output, the tremendous increases in output result in an overwhelming absolute amount of unwanted waste. Population, of course, even when all unwanted pregnancies are eliminated, gets out of hand so that there is a food crisis. Even increases in agricultural technology apparently will not save us. There will still be overuse of land, which will lead to erosion, causing food production to drop. This, at least, is what the computer predicted.

The M.I.T. authors of *Limits to Growth* point out that even if there are tremendous scientific breakthroughs, they must be matched by equally dramatic changes in the world's social institutions. Otherwise, these breakthroughs, whether they be birth-control devices or high grain yields, will not be effectively distributed to those in need of them. Needed changes, in other words, won't appear.

Changing the Equation

Not everyone was happy with the way in which the Club of Rome's first model of the future was put together. It seemed to have left out some critical variables. One of these was relative prices.

An economic fact that you are all aware of by now was completely forgotten in the model established by the scientist-authors. When specific resources become scarce, their price goes up. People are motivated to find substitutes or, if necessary, to do without the more expensive goods and services. That's something that many ecologists seem to forget, but it is an immutable economic fact of life. If a good becomes scarcer, the supply curve shifts inward. With a stable demand curve, we expect a rise in price. The quantity sold falls, as we see in Figure I-36.2. If timber becomes scarcer we

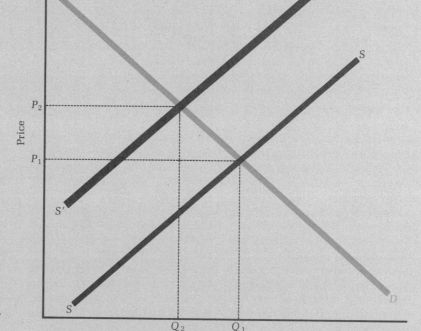

SCARCITY ALTERS PRICE

FIGURE I-36.2

If some particular resource becomes scarcer, its supply curve will shift from SS to S'S' and its price will rise from P_1 to P_2. The quantity demanded and supplied will fall from Q_1 to Q_2. This change in the relative price of resources that become scarcer is something that modern-day doomsayers do not discuss.

expect its price to rise and substitutes to be found. The same holds for steel, coal, copper, and anything else. The history of any economy is in part a history of how changing relative prices reflect relative scarcity. Production and innovation respond to changes in relative prices. If the price of steel goes up because iron ore is becoming scarcer and more expensive, more attempts will be made at finding steel substitutes. Perhaps there will be an increased use of plastics. In any event, such is the way of the economic world.

A new study published in 1974 by the Club of Rome, *Mankind at the Turning Point,* did in fact take into account some changing relative prices. Aiming specifically at problems concerned with energy and the presumed lack of oil in the future, researchers compiling the new report found that a relative rise in the price of oil might, in the long run, help the economies of both the oil producers and the consuming nations. In the consuming nations, individuals would learn to use fewer petroleum products and alternatives would be found.

On the subject of food, the report points out that the only way to avoid a tragic situation where 500 million children starve by the year 2025 is for the developed nations to tighten their own belts and to invest heavily in building up the industries of poorer nations.

The Club of Rome's second report tells us, in other words, that with a concerted effort the world can devise solutions to its shortages of goods and excesses of people. Nonetheless, this second report still predicts horrifying scenarios of what might happen in the future if "something" isn't done.

The Problem with Gloom and Doom Projections

We have to be careful about projections into the future which tell us that the future of the world, the future of humankind, is one of mass starvation, overwhelming pollution, or total destruction. The *Economist* of London pointed out, for example, that

"... if a Club of Rome has rightly forecast Britain's present quantum of travel, industry, and urban work force exponentially forward from 1850, it would have proved that this plague-ridden, industrial maimed nation must long since have disappeared beneath several hundred feet of horse manure."

We just cannot assume that things won't change in the future. It is possible to cite numerous examples of situations that have gotten better, not worse—such as the pollution level in London, which has been reduced by 85 percent in the last 15 years, doubling the hours of winter sunshine and adding 55 species of fish to the once mordant Thames. Concerning the problem of the psychological well-being of the human species, a University of Utah medical sociologist, Dr. John Collett, contends, based on the results of a massive study of urban stress, that the mental and physical well-being of city dwellers exceeds that of backwoodspersons and plainspersons.

Planning for Planning

In spite of a history of solutions to technological, sociological, and ec-

onomic problems, numerous concerned scientists, including economists, feel that the only way we can solve our problems in the future is by planning. In other words, instead of allowing unrestricted market forces to allocate scarce resources, we must institute planning on a massive scale never before considered in the United States. Planning would involve coordinating the use of resources in different critical areas in the economy to prevent bottlenecks and disrupting shortages. Planning, presumably, would also attempt to bring the rate of economic growth into line with the supposed reality of dwindling natural resource supplies.

Does the future of civilization require that planning take over the role that relative prices play in our market economy? Is planning required to reduce the rate of economic growth in this nation and elsewhere? Do we have to provide for the poorer nations of the world so that they can reach the level of material well-being that we in the United States have attained? These are important questions that we cannot attempt to answer here. A complete study of the pros and cons of a planned economy would require an examination of the success or failure of current planned economies, an analysis of why prices should not be used to allocate scarce resources, and whether a blueprint for the practical and operational aspects of planning is possible.

In the United States, perhaps a less-dramatic approach to these problems can be taken. Perhaps we can just redirect the growth equation so that it concerns itself with specific areas in the economy which we want to grow. Neither the United States' nor any other economy was built in a day. It seems inappropriate to talk about changing it overnight.

Questions for Thought and Discussion

1. Why is growth a problem today but wasn't a problem in the past?
2. Do you think that growth should be stopped?
3. Why are relative prices important in predicting what will happen to resources in the future?
4. Are predictions of the future demise of civilization new?

Selected References

Adelman, Morris A. et al., *No Time to Confuse,* San Francisco, Calif.: Institute for Contemporary Studies, 1975.

Barnett, H. and C. Morse, *Scarcity and Growth,* Baltimore: Johns Hopkins University Press, 1963.

Mishan, E. J., *The Cost of Economic Growth,* London: Staples Press, 1967.

Olson, Mancur and Hans H. Landsberg (eds.), *The No Growth Society,* New York: W. W. Norton, 1973.

Weintraub, Andrew et al. (eds.), *The Economic Growth Controversy,* White Plains, N.Y.: International Arts and Sciences, 1973.

Index

Numbers in **bold** indicate pages where terms are defined.

A

Ability-to-pay principle, 100
Abortion, 670
Abraham, W. I., 85
Absolute advantage, 312, **318**
Acceleration principle, 216–218
Accelerator, and multiplier, 218
Accounting identity, 178
Action time lag, 298
Actual democracy, 638–639
Adams, W., 325, 439, 498
Adelman, M. A., 701
Advertising, 65, 67, 488, 491–495, 497
  by doctors, 448
  as investment, 493
  political, 642
  postal rates for, 479
Advisory Board on Economic Growth
  and Stability, 264
AFL-CIO, 514, 515
  Committee on Political Education,
  650
Age and sexism in labor market, 530
Age-earnings cycle, 590–591, **600**
Aggregate demand, 198–200, **211**
  function, 199
  government purchases and, 219–221
Aggregate supply, 200–201, **211**
  excess, 203
  function, 200

Agricultural and Consumer Protection
  Act (1973), 422
Agriculture, 416–423
  in China, 38–39
  subsidized, 674–675
Aid to Families with Dependent
  Children (AFDC), 604, 605
Aid India Consortium, 684
Air pollution, 616
Airlines, 465–466
Aldridge-Vreeland Act, 248
Aliber, R., 174, 350
Alliance for Labor Action, 515
Allocation of scarce resources, 9
Alternative cost (see Opportunity
  cost)
Aluminum, 455
Aluminum Company of America, 426
American Economics Association, 111,
  237
American Federation of Labor (AFL),
  513
American Institute of Public Opinion,
  23
American League, 564
American Medical Association,
  444–450
  Council on Medical Education, 446
American Mining Congress, 628
American Stock Exchange, 10, 407, 408

American Telephone and Telegraph,
  32, 425, 462, 500
American Temperance Society, 64
American Tobacco Company, 470
Americans for Democratic Action, 505
Anderson, R., 652
Anderson, W. H., 109, 243
Andreano, R. L., 508
Andrews, P. W., 7
Angell, N., 262
Annuity, 571–574, **576**
Antitrust legislation, 96, 449, 458,
  466–471
  and consumer protection legislation,
  476
  enforcement of, 502–503
  and sports, 564
Antitrust policy, 466–469
Appreciation, 335, **341**
Aristotle, 578, 647
Arrow, K. J., 646–647
Artificial wants, 494
Asset:
  liquid, 188, **195**
  paper, 178
Assumption, 14–15
Athletics, 561–567, 595
Australia, 314
Automatic fiscal policy, 219–230
Autonomous consumption, 182

Autonomous investment function, 199
Average fixed costs, 380, **383**
Average propensity to consume (APC), 182, 184, **195**
Average propensity to save (APS), 182, 184, **195**
Average total costs, 378–379, **383**
Average unit cost, 380–381
Average variable costs, 380, **383**
Avis Rental, 470

B

Bach, G. L., 283
Baez, J., 593
Bain, J., 500
Balance:
  of payments, 332–333, **340**
    deficit, 332, 346–347
  of trade, 331–332, **340**
Balanced-budget multiplier, 223–224, **228**
Banana, 453
Bank credit, 584–585
Bank rate, 258
Banking, competition in, 583, 584
Banking holiday, 147
Banking system:
  and money, 244–262
  protecting, 267–268
Baratz, M. S., 478n
Barnes, P., 235
Barnett, H., 701
Barriers to entry, 396, **403**, 425–426, **436**, 497
Barter, 10, **16**, 245, **260**
Basic balance, 333
Bauer, P. T., 677, 685
Bauxite, 453, 454, 455, 457
Becker, G., 533, 596, 601
Behrman, J. N., 350
Benefits-received principle, 100
Bennett, P. D., 360
Bergsten, C. F., 457
Berki, S. E., 473
Bhagwati, J., 685
Bilateral monopoly, 548, **550**
Binding arbitration, 526
Birth control, 658, 670, 697
Birth rate, 667, 670
  (See also Crude birth rate)
Bish, R. L., 109
Black market, 169, **174**
Blair, J. M., 503
Boggs, H., 566

Bolshevik Revolution, 35
Bond, 408
  government, 165–166, 167, 188
  tax-exempt, 121–122
Bond price, 271
Boom, 127
Bornstein, M., 37
Borrowing, 578, 580
  from abroad, 240
  vs. taxation, 240
Bottom, 127
Boulding, K. E., 17
Bowen, W. G., 243
Bradburn, N. M., 23n
Brannan, C. F., 422
Brazil, 164–165
Break-even point, 393
Brimmer, A. F., 162
British Columbia, 145
The Brookings Institution, 11, 120, 159
Brooks, D. B., 7
Brown, L. R., 7
Brunner, J., 670
Buckley, J. L., 648
Budd, E., 601
Budget:
  federal, 98
    and fiscal policy, 226–228
  local, 98–99
  state, 98–99
Budget constraint, 361, 364–365
Burden of inflation, 154–155, 157
Bureaucracy, 642
Burke-Hartke Foreign Trade and Investment Proposal, 320, 324
Burns, A. F., 88, 111, 263–264
Business:
  costs of, 372–386
  defined, 372–373
Business activity, indicators of, 127–130
Business Conditions Digest, 126, 127
Business cycle, 126–141, **139**
  phases in, 127
  theories, 130–132
Business Cycle Developments, 126
Business tax, 191–192
Butz, E. L., 422

C

Cable television, 623
Campaign financing, 648–652
  public, 650–651

Campaign financing *(cont'd.):*
  regulation, 650
Campbell, R. R., 637
Capital, 30, **36,** 131
Capital accumulation, 689–690
Capital consumption allowance *(see* Depreciation)
Capital costs, 426
Capital equipment, 35
Capital formation, 35
Capital gains, 124, 408, **415**
  tax, 105, 165
Capital goods, 30, 178, 191, **194,** 690
Capital-intensive production, 132
Capitalism, 25, **36**
  American, 32–33
  and competition, 32–33
  theory, 30–32
Capitalization, 409, **415**
Capital loss, 408
Capital stock, 239, **243,** 569, **576**
Capper-Volstead Act, 469
Career, in China, 41
Carnegie Foundation, 444, 445
Carson, R. B., 109
Cartel, 452–**457**
Cartter, A. M., 552
Cash income maintenance, 98
Caves, R., 439, 503
Celler, E., 566
Center for Auto Safety, 650
Center for the Study of Responsive Law, 488, 489
Ceteris paribus, 44, 47, 192, 659
Chain Store Act, 468
Chamberlin, E., 490–491, 498
Chandler, L. V., 141, 262
Charting, 411, **415**
Cheating, 454, 455, 562
Chen, Nai-Ruenn, 42
Children, 658–659
China, 38–42, 599
Chromium, 455
Chrysler, 495, 501
Circular flow, 179
  of income, 74–75, **83**
Citizen Action Group, 489
City, in China, 41
Civil Aeronautics Board (CAB), 465, 466
Clark, J. M., 216
Clayton Act, 467–468
  (See also Antitrust Laws)
Closed shop, 514, **522**

Club of Rome, 696, 698, 699, 700
Coal Mine Health and Safety Act
  (1969), 489
Coale, A. J., 670
Coalition, 640, 641
Coase, R. H., 625
Coffee, 453
Cohen, S., 524
Coincidental indicators, 127, 129
Cole, R., 650
Collective bargaining, 513, 515, **522**
Collectivist economic planning, 38
Collett, J., 700
Collusion, 466, 562
Columbia University, 264, 679
Combination, 467
Command economy, 30, 33, 35, **36**
Commercial bank, subsidization of,
  265–269
Committee for Economic
  Development, 228
Commodities market, 367, 368
Commodity Credit Corporation, 421
Commodity currency, 244, **260**
Common property, 618–619, **623**
Commoner, B., 625
Communal farming, in China, 39
Community Nutrition Institute, 4
Company town, 544, 546
Comparative advantage, 12–13, **16,**
  312, 313–315, **318,** 320, 321, 674
  and opportunity cost, 314, 315
Competition:
  and capitalism, 32–33
    destructive, 584
    perfect, 401–402
Competitive firm, 387, **403**
Compounding, 574, **576**
Compound interest, 574–576
Concentration ratio, 470, 499–500
Conglomerates, 470, **472**
Congress, 125, 167, 168, 264, 284, 296,
  371, 421, 422, 442, 450, 475, 477,
  514, 564, 607
  and tax loopholes, 120–121
Congress of Industrial Organizations
  (CIO), 514
Conservation, 5, 631–635, **637**
Consol, 271, **281**
Consolidated Edison, 529
Constant dollars, 81, **83,** 149
Constant quality, 44
Constant-quality units, 47, 68
Consumer choice, 353–366

Consumer choice (cont'd.):
  and demand, 353–360
Consumer equilibrium, 365
Consumer goods, 76
Consumerism, 482–487
Consumer Price Index, 150–151, 156,
  160, 442, 443, 602
Consumer-protection legislation, 476,
  482–487, 641
Consumer sovereignty, 485–486, **487**
Consumption, 177–197
  autonomous, 182, 185, 187
  defined, **194**
  determinants of, 188–189
Consumption function, 180, 182, 183,
  185, 186, **195,** 222
  fitted, 187
  short-run vs. long-run, 187–188
Consumption goods, 30, 177, **194**
Contract, 163, 166
Cooper, I. B., 562
Cooperative Marketing Act, 469
Cootner, P. H., 415
Copper, 453, 455
Copyright, 79
Corporate income tax, 103–105, 165
Corporate structure, 506–508
Corporation, 372, 373, **383,** 499–503
Corporation restructuring, 507–508
Corporation structure, 506–508
Cost minimization, 549–550
Cost-push inflation, 153–154, **160**
Cost-of-service regulation, 462, **471**
Costs:
  of business, 372–386
  of crime, 553
  depreciation, 123
  external, 616
  fixed, 378, **383**
  internal, 616
  minimum, 382–383
  social, 615–**623**
    and private, 615–616, 619–621
  start-up, 425
  sunk, 378
  total, 378, **383,** 389, **403**
    and total revenues, 389, 392
  variable, 379, **383**
Council of Economic Advisers (CEA),
  92, 93, 110, 118, 159, 171, 172, 231,
  232, 233, 264, 647
Council on Medical Education, 444
Coupon rate, 271
Court system, 558

Craft union, 512, **522**
Cream skimming, 478, 479, **481**
Credit:
  vs. money, 247
  price of, 180
Credit card company, 578–580
Credit controls, selective, 578, 582–584
Credit market, 578
Creditor, 154–155
Cressey, D. R., 560
Crime:
  deterrence, 556–558
  against property, 554
  and punishment, 553–560
  victim of, 558–559
  of violence, 555
Crook, F. W., 42
Crowding, and population explosion,
  660
Crude birth rate, 653, 654, **661**
Crude death rate, 653, 654, 657, **661,**
  669
Crutchfield, J. A., 630
Currency, 246–247
Currency crisis, 337–338, **341**
Current account, 333
Current disposable personal income,
  187
Current dollar, 149
Current income, 188
Customer discrimination, 529, **533**
Cyclical unemployment, 137, **139**

D

Dales, J. H., 630
Data Resources, Inc., 118
Davidson, I., 350
Death rate, 667
  (See also Crude death rate)
DeBeers Company, 426
Debt, public, 238–243
Debtor, 154–155
Decentralization, 34
Defense, 98
Defense spending, 112–114
Deficit, 226, **228**
  full-employment, 226
Deficit financing, 238–243
Deficit spending, 226, **228**
Deflationary gap, 209–**211,** 221–222
Demand:
  aggregate, 198–200, **211**
  and consumer choice, 353–360
  derived, 327, 328, **522,** 536, **550**

Demand *(cont'd.):*
  effective, 215
  elastic, 54–55, **61**
  inelastic, 55, **61**, 68, 69
  law of, 43–44, 54, **60**
  for money, 270–271
  perfectly elastic, 55
  shifting, 50–52
  and supply, 43–63
Demand curve, 45, **60**, 357–358
  kinked, 496–497
  for labor, 515–516
  single-firm, 388–389
Demand-pull inflation, 153, **160**, 173
Demand schedule, 45, **60**
Democracy:
  actual, 638–639
  ideal, 639–640
Demographer, 653
Depopulation, 661
Depreciation, 77, 78, 79, **83**, 335, **341**
Depreciation costs, 123
Depression, 127n
  (See also Great Depression)
Derived demand, 327, 328, **522**, 536,
  550
  for labor, 515
Determinants of investment, 189–192
Devaluation, 338
Development:
  geographic theory of, 673
  of less-developed countries, 671–677
    planning for, 675–676
  race theory of, 673
  theories of, 673–675
  (See also Growth)
Dillard, D., 213
Diminishing marginal utility, law of,
  354, **359**, 362–363
Diminishing (marginal) returns, **383**,
  665, **670**
  law of, 26–28, **36**, 375–378, 556
  measuring, 377
"Dirty" float, 348, **350**
Disadvantaged, 234–235
Discomfort index, 159
Discounting, 571, **576**, 633
Discount rate, 258, **260**, 265–267, 571
  personal, 580, 691, **694**
Discouraged worker, 135, 136
Discretionary fiscal policy, 224–225
Discrimination, 445, 595–596, 597–598
  customer, 529, **533**
  against minorities, 519, 596

Discrimination *(cont'd.):*
  price, 447–448, 461–462, 463, 468, 479
  tastes for, 527, 533
  against women, 527–533
Disposable personal income, 81, **83**,
  178, 180, 185, 186, 225
  current, 187
Disposable personal income
  hypothesis, 188
Dissaving, 180, 187, 578, 580
Distribution, of income, 586–**600**
Dividend, 408
Division of labor, 11
  (See also Specialization)
Dollar, 149
Doubling time, 654–655, **662**
Dow Jones Industrial Average, 412,
  414, **415**
Draft, 114, 116, 562, **566**, 595
Dry hole, 123, 124
Dubos, R., 679
du Pont Company, 489
Durable consumer goods, 76, **83**, 570
Dynamic process, 402, **403**

E

Eckhaus, R. S., 685
Eckstein, A., 42
Eckstein, O., 109, 118–119
Ecology, and social costs, 615–625
Econometrics, 297, **302**
Economic activity:
  regulation of, 95–96
  tax on, 106–107
Economic efficiency, 401
Economic good, 9, **16**
Economic growth, 686–701
Economic rents, 593–594, **600**
Economic system, 29
Economic warfare, 452–457
Economics, 8, **16**
  as core of socialism, 33
  and foreign aid, 680
  new, 93, 231
Economies:
  of mass production, 426, **436**
  of scale, 426, **436**, 503
Economist, 700
Economy Act (1933), 164
Edel, M., 625
Education, 96, 98–99, 592, 597–598
  in China, 40
Effect time lag, 298
Effective demand, 215
Effective tax rate, 101, **108**

Ehrlich, A. H., 637, 663
Ehrlich, P. R., 637, 660, 663
Eisenhower, D.D.
  administration of, 119, 263, 264
  policies of, 231
Elastic demand, 54–55, **61**
Elasticity, 53–59
  of demand for investment, 190
  extreme, 55
  kinds of, 54–55
  long-run, 58
  short-run, 58
  and slope, 57, 59
Electric utilities, 32, 462
Electrical conspiracy, 455, 470
Elkan, W., 677
Emergency Employment Act (1971),
  233, 234
Employment:
  full, 221, 226, **228**, 297
  and income determination, 198–213
  public service, 233–235
Employment Act (1946), 296, 297, 302
Employment and Training Act (1973),
  233
Energy, 635–636
Energy crisis, 3, 6
Engel, L., 415
Entrepreneur, 373
Environment, 98
  social costs and, 615–625
Equal-opportunity legislation, 532
Equality, 599
Equilibrium, 201–202, 329, 355–357
  consumer, 365
  of income, 201
  international, 310–**311**
  static, 441
Equilibrium exchange rate, 327–329
Equilibrium price, 49, **60**
Equities, 408, **415**, 463
Ervin, S., 566
Escalator clause, 163–164
Estate tax, 106
Evans, J. W., 344
Excess aggregate supply, 200–201, **211**
Excess demand schedule, 307–308, **317**
Excess reserves, 249–250, **260**
Excess supply schedule, 308, **318**
Exchange, 9–14
Exchange rate:
  fixed, 333, **340**
  flexible, 329–332, **340**
  floating, 329–332, 347–348

Exchange rate *(cont'd.)*:
  foreign, 326, **340**
  and monetary policy, 348–349
Excise tax, 79, 106
Exclusion, principle of, 95
Exemption, fixed, 165
Expansionary fiscal policy, 224
Expansion multiplier, 255–256
Expectation, 286, 287–288, 290
  and consumption, 189
  and demand, 52
  and investment, 190, 191
  and supply, 53
Expectation argument, 173
Expenditure approach, 75–78, **83**
Exploitation, 595–596, **600**
Exports, 77, 306–309
External benefit, 621–622
External costs, 616
External economies of scale, 426, **436**
External effect, 486
External public debt, 240, **243**
Externalities, 616–617, **623**
Extreme elasticity, 55

F

Fabricant, S., 695
Fair-trade agreement, 469
Falk, R. A., 637
Fallacy of composition, 209
Farming sector *(see Agriculture)*
Federal budget, 98
  and fiscal policy, 226–228
Federal Campaign Reform Act, 648, 650
Federal deposit insurance, 267–269
Federal Deposit Insurance
  Corporation (FDIC), 268–269, 584, **585**
Federal Energy Administration, 6, 7
Federal Farm Board, 419
Federal Funds Market, 258, **260**, 265
Federal Insurance Contribution Act
  (FICA), 106–107
Federal Open Market Committee
  (FOMC), 248, 251, 256, 263, 299
Federal Reserve, 271, 284, 582
  borrowing from, 265–269
  policies, 259
Federal Reserve Act, 248
Federal Reserve Bank of New York,
  251, 256, 265, 298
Federal Reserve Board, 119, 232, 263,
  264, 294

Federal Reserve Discount Window,
  257, 265–266
Federal Reserve System, 88, 93,
  247–251, 254, 256, 298
Federal unemployment tax, 106–107
Feige, E. L., 174
Feldstein, M., 143, 145, 146
Fellner, W., 233
Ferman, L. A., 601
Fiduciary monetary system, 244, **260**
Firing, 534–552
Firm, 373, **383**
  in competition, 387–406
  short-run costs of, 378–383
Fiscal policy, 219–230
  automatic, 225–226
  and the budget, 226–228
  discretionary, 224–225
  expansionary, 224
  and full-employment budget, 226, **228**
Fisher, I., 164
Fishlow, A., 166n
Fixed costs, 378, **383**
Fixed exchange rate, 333, **340**
Fixed exemption, 165
Flat tax, 100
Fleetwood, W., 163
Flexible exchange rates, 329–332, **340**
  and worldwide inflation, 345–350
  (See also Floating exchange rate)
Flexner, A., 444
  report of, 445
Floating exchange rate, 329–332,
  347–348
  and oil prices, 350
  (See also Flexible exchange rate)
Flood, C., 561, 562
Flow, 26, **36**, 178, **194**, 570, **576**,
  circular, 179
  of income, 74–75, **83**
Food crisis, 3–4
Food shortage, in China, 38
Food stamps, 81, 113, 143, 163, 607
Food Research Institute, 371
Ford, G., 111, 119, 232, 237, 526, 648
  administration of, 160, 263, 264, 295
Ford Motor Company, 495, 501
Ford Foundation, 4
Foreign aid:
  critics of, 684
  and less-developed countries,
  680–685
Foreign exchange market, 326, **340**

Foreign exchange rate, 326, **340**
Foreign sector, 77
Fortune, 505
Fractional reserve banking system,
  249, **260**
France, 661, 673
Franklin, B., 477
Franklin National, 266–267
Fraud, 482, 483
Free enterprise, 31
Freedom of the seas, 626
Free goods, 9, **16**
Free rider, 95, 100
Free trade, 315–317, 320–321
Frictional unemployment, 137, **139**,
  297, 521, **523**
Friedman, M., 293, 294–295, 299, 344
Fuchs, V. R., 526, 531, 532
Full employment, 221, 226
  defined, **297**
  Full-employment budget, 221
  and fiscal policy, 226, **228**
Full-employment deficit, 226, **228**
Full-employment government budget,
  228
Full-employment surplus, 226, **228**
Full unemployment, 137
Fussfeld, D. R., 37
Future test year, 463
Futures contract, 367, **371**
Futures market, 367–371
Futures trading, 371

G

Galbraith, J. K., 173, 233, 498, 504–508,
  694
Galenson, W., 42, 552
Gans, H. J., 610
Gardner, R. L., 685
Garvey, G., 630
General congestion, 179–180
  (See also Overproduction)
General Motors, 426, 485, 489, 495, 500
Geographic mobility, in Russia, 34
Geriatric population, 660–661
Germany, 321
Gill, R. T., 677
Gilman, C. P., 533
Gini coefficient, of inequality, 589
Global natural resources, 6–7
Gold, 153, 347–348
  paper, 338, 346
Gold standard, 333–335, **341**
Goldsmith, R., 91
Goldwater, B., 295

Gompers, S., 513
Goods and services account, 332
Gordon, R. A., 141
Government:
  economic functions of, 94–97
  growth of, 97
  role of, 32
Government bonds, 165–166, 167, 188
Government expenditures, 76–77
Government purchases and aggregate
  demand, 219–221
Government spending and taxation,
  94–108
Great Britain, 157, 449–450
Great Depression, 126, 142, 147, 187,
  188, 233, 264, 267, 268, 280, 296,
  305, 419, 441, 513, 612
Great Leap Forward, 38
Great Society, 237
Green, M. J., 499n
Green, W., 526
Greenbackism, 147
Gross investment, 217
Gross National Product (GNP), 75–82,
  83, 86–91, 97, 686
  deflator, 152
  growth rate in China, 39
  income approach and, 78–81
  per capita, 81–82
  stopping growth of, 696
Gross private investment, **189**
  domestic, 77
Gross public debt, 238, **243**
Group health plan, 448–449
Groves, H. M., 109
Growth:
  balanced 673–674
  economic, 686–701
  of public debt, 238
  (See also Development, Population
    growth)
Grubel, H. G., 146
Guaranteed annual income, 607
Guaranteed annual wage, 526
Guideposts, 171–172, **174**
Guild, 511
Gurley, J. W., 39, 41, 42

H

Haber, A., 601
Hamilton, D., 610
Hamilton, M., 288
Hamrin, R. D., 645
Hansen, A., 213

Hard-core unemployment, 138
Hard drug, 557
Hardin, G., 663, 670
Harrington, M., 601
Harrod, R., 215
Harshbarber, C. E., 423
Hart, P. A., 475–476
Haveman, R. H., 645
Hay Market Riot, 512
Haynes, W. W., 386
Heady, E. O., 423
Health care, 442–451
Health insurance, national, 449–450
Health plan, group, 448–449
Heidenheimer, R. J., 652
Heilbroner, R. L., 7
Heller, W., 110, 118, 230, 231–232, 233
Henderson, H., 63
Hicks, J., 218
Hidden unemployment, 135
Hiring, 534–552
Historic test year, 463
Hoffman, C., 42
Hollister, R. G., 156n
Holmes, O. W., 564
Home Stake Production Company,
  124
Homer, S. A., 585
Hoover, E. M., 670
Horizontal addition, 358
Hot tip, 410
Housewife, services of, 86–87
Housing, 505
Housing market, 271
Housing vouchers, 113
Houthakker, H. S., 423
Humanitarianism, and foreign aid,
  680–681
Humphrey, H., 526
Hungary, 148
Hunger, 4
Hyperinflation, 148

I

Ideal democracy, 639–640
Ideology, and education in China, 40
Illegal activity, 64–69, 87, 95
Immigrant, 595
Implicit price deflator, 152, **160**
Imports, 77, 295, 307–308, 321
Income:
  current, 188
  disposable, 81, **83**, 178, 180, 185, 186
    current, 187

Income (cont'd.):
  hypothesis, 188
  permanent, 188
Income approach, 75, **83**
Income distribution, 586–**600**
  theories of, 598–599
Income elasticity, 416–418, **423**
  and employment determination,
    198–213
  fixed, 155
Income inequality, measuring, 589–590
Income maintenance, 32
Income redistribution, 92–93, 96, 103,
  113–114, 240–241
Income and substitution effects, 366
Income tax, 100–103
  corporate, 103–105, 165
  personal, 102–103, 165
Income velocity, 153
Incomes policy, 170
Independent Postal Service of
  America, 480, 481
Indexing, 163–167
  taxes, 165
  (See also Monetary correction)
India, 683–684
Indifference curve, 361
Indifference map, 363–364
Indirect business taxes, 79, **83**
Industrial deconcentration, 476
Industrial Revolution, 664, 665
Industrial unions, 514, **522**
Inefficiency, and underemployment, 26
Inelastic demand, 55, **61**, 68, 69
Infant industry argument, 315–316, **318**
Inflation, 73, **160**
  burden of, 154–155, 157
  cost-push, 153–154, **160**, 173
  demand-pull, 153, **160**, 173
  and indexing, 163–167
  and the poor, 155–156
  rate of, 149–150
  repressed, 169–170
  and stagflation, 147–162
  theories of, 152–154
  unemployment and, 157–160
  worldwide, and flexible exchange
    rates, 345–350
Inflationary gap, 209–**211**, 222, 278
Inflationary recession, 285, **292**
Information:
  inside, 409, **415**
  on the margin, 484
  public, 409

Information (cont'd.):
  suppression of, 371
Information costs, 482, 483, 520–522
Information-dissemination activity, 10
Information explosion, 671–672
Information time lag, 298, 640–641, 647
Inheritance tax, 31
Innate ability, 592
Innovation, 191
Innovation theory, 130–131, **139**
Input, and output, 375
Inside information, 409, **415**
Institute of International Economic
  Studies, 611
Institute for Research on Poverty, 156
Institution, 29
Insurance Institute of America, 659
Intangible drilling costs (IDC), 124,
  125
Interest, 79, 180, 687–688
  compound, 574–576
  on national debt, 98, 240
  on public debt, 240
Interest rate, 271–273, 578
Interlocking directorate, 468
Internal costs, 616
Internal economies of scale, 426, **436**
Internal public debt, 240
International Brotherhood of
  Teamsters, 514–515, 525
International commodity cost, 452–457
International equilibrium, 310–**311**
International finance, 326–345
International Institute for
  Environment and Development,
  679
International Monetary Fund (IMF);
  338, 345–346, **350**
  quota system, 346
International monopoly, 452–457
International Telephone and
  Telegraph (ITT), 470
International trade, 305–319
  financing, 326–345
International Typographical Union,
  512
Interstate Oil Compact (1935), 469
Invention, 130
Inventories, 77, **83**
Investment, 77, **83,** 177–197
  defined, 178, **194**
  determinants of, 189–192
  elasticity of demand for, 190
  gross, 217

Investment (cont'd.):
  gross private, 189
    domestic, 77
  in human capital, 597–598
  and saving, 192–194, 203–204
Investment inventory change, 178
Investment plan, 412
Investment spending, 198
Involuntary loan, 338
Iran, 456
Irrigation, in China, 38
Israel, 455

J

Japan, 314, 315, 321, 324, 627, 655, 670,
  673
Jawboning, 172, **174**
Jevons, S. W., 167
Job-information center, 521
Joint Economic Committee, 116–117,
  119
Johns Hopkins University, 445
Johnson, D. G., 421
Johnson, L. B., 110, 119, 172, 232, 237,
  505, 525
  administration of, 504
Johnston, J. F., 481
Joint costs, 463, **471**
Justice, administration of, 96

K

Kahn, A. E., 473
Kassarjian, H. H., 360
Kefauver, E., 439, 475
Kenen, P. B., 319
Kennedy, J. F., 93, 119, 171, 172, 232,
  237, 525, 649, 693
  administration of, 231, 264, 298, 504,
  505, 647
Kershaw, J. H., 616
Kessel, R., 451
Key, V. O., 645, 652
Keynes, J. M., 180, 187, 214–215, 270,
  279, 345, 441, 696
Keynesian model, 270–283
Kneese, A. V., 625
Knight, F. H., 406
Knights of Labor, 512–513
Knowles, J. H., 444
Kornbluh, J. L., 601
Kreps, J. M., 552
Krieger, R. A., 167
Kuwait, 452

L

Labor, demand for, 515–516
Labor-force participation rate, 135,
  136
Labor Management Relations Act, 514
  (See also Taft-Hartley Act)
Labor market, 511–524
  sexism in, 527–533
  unrestricted, 561–562
Labor movement, 324, 511–515, 520
Labor shortage, 170
Labor supply, 516–518
Lagging indicator, 127, 129
Laisez-faire economics, 30, 31
Land reform, in China, 38
Landsberg, H. H., 7, 701
Law:
  of demand, 43–44, 54, **60**
    and leisure, 142–143
  of diminishing marginal utility, 354,
    359, 362–363
  of diminishing returns, 26–28, **36,**
    375–378, 556
  of equal marginal utilities per
    dollar, 356, **359**
  of substitution, 363
  of supply, 45–53, 56, **60**
  of the seas, 626
Leading indicator, 127, 129
Leading link, 35
Legislation:
  antitrust, 96, 449, 458, 466–471
  consumer-protection, 476, 482–487,
    641
  equal-opportunity, 532
  producer-oriented, 641
  safety, 486
Leisure, 88
  law of demand and, 142–143
Lekachman, R., 91, 162, 197, 213
Leonard, W. N., 474
Lerman, 234, 235
Less-developed country (LDC),
  671–677
  and foreign aid, 680–685
Leuthold, D. A., 652
Levitan, S., 616
Lewis, J. L., 514
Libya, 452
Licensing, 450
Limited natural resources, 631–633
  depletion of, 633–634
Liquid assets, 188, **195**

Liquidity, 245, **260**
Liquidity preference function, 272, 273, 274, **281**
Liquidity trap, 279, *280*, **281**
Local budget, 98–99
Long-run average total cost curve (LATC), 458–459
Long-run elasticity, 58
Long-run marginal cost curve (LMC), 459
Loophole (*see* Tax loophole)
Lorenz curve, 586–589, **600**
Lubitz, R., 319
Luck, 412
Luxembourg, 654, 655

M

MacAvoy, P. W., 474
Macroeconomics, 73, **82**
Mafia, 65, 67
Magnuson, W. G., 566
Maher, J. E., 17
Maisel, S. J., 262
Majority rule, 640
Maki, D., 146
Malpractice, 447
Malthus, T. R., 664–670
Man-in-the-house rule, 605–606, **610**
Manager, 373
Manganese, 455
Manne, H. G., 350
Mao Tse-Tung, 38
Mansfield, E., 498, 695
Marginal analysis, 392–393, 484–485
Marginal cost pricing, 401, **403**
Marginal costs, 381–382, **384**
  and average costs, 382
Marginal factor cost (MFC), 544, **550**
Marginal physical product, 377, **383**, 535, **550**
  value of, 535–536, 550
Marginal productivity theory, 591–593
Marginal propensity to consume (MPC), 184, **195**, 221–222
Marginal rate of substitution, 363
Marginal revenue, 392, **403**
  of competitor, 427
  and elasticity, 430
  of monopolist, 427
Marginal revenue product, 542, **550**
Marginal tax rate, 101, **107**
Marginal utility analysis, 358–359, 367
Marijuana, 555, 559

Marital status, and sexism in labor market, 530
Market, 10, **16**
  basket, 150
  labor, 511–524
    sexism in, 527–533
Market clearing price, 49, **60**
Market system, traditional, 506
Marshall, A., 164
Marshall, F. R., 552
Marshall, G., 682
Marshall Plan, 346, 679, 682, 684
Martin, J. P., 560
Martin. W. M., 264
Marx, K., 131–132, 598, 599
Marxist economic theory, 440
Massachusetts Institute of Technology, 236, 696, 697
Mass production, 426
Mass transport, 505
Masterpiece, 511
Maximization, 14
Mayer, T., 283
McCarthy, E., 648
McCormick Harvester Works, 512
McFarlane, B., 42
McGuire Act, 469
McKean, R. M., 625
McKenzie, R., 561
McMillan, R. A., 302
Meadows, D., 7
Meany, G., 514, 525–526
Measure of economic welfare (MEW), 89–90, 93
Measures of satisfaction, 87–88
Medicaid, 442, 451
Medical care, 98, 156, 442–451, 505
Medical school, 443, 447
Medicare, 442, 447–448, 450
Meier, G. M., 325
Meiselman, D., 293
Merchandise trade balance, 332
Merger, 467, 470
  of AFL and CIO, 514–515
Metcalf, L., 628
Metzenbaum, H., 649
Microeconomics, 73, **82**
Mikesell, R. F., 344, 457
Miller, R. L., 302, 350, 457, 637
Miller-Tydings Act, 469
  (*See also* Antitrust laws)
Minimum costs, 382–383
Minimum wage, 546, **550**
Mining nodule, 628

Minority group, 603
Mishan, E. J., 7, 695, 701
Mixed capitalist system, 31, **36**
Mobility:
  geographic, in Russia, 34
  job, in China, 38
Monetarist, 284
Monetary correction, 164–165
  (*See also* Indexing)
Monetary policy, 275, 277, 335
  dynamics of, 259
  and exchange rates, 348–349
  restrictive, 289
  tools of, 256–259
Monetary rule, 299
Monetary standard, 244–245
Money:
  and banking system, 244–262
  vs. credit, 246
  functions of, 245–246
  in Keynesian model, 270–283
  quantity theory of, 152–153, 160, 294
  role of, 284–293
Money creation, 240
Money supply, 246–247, 251–256
Monopolist, 424, **436**
Monopolistic competition, 490–**497**
Monopoly, 32, 542, 564
  bilateral, 548, **550**
  international, 452–457
  natural, 458, **471**
    post office as, 477–481
  power, 154
  regulation of, 458–474
    in sports, 561–567
Monopoly management, 424–439
Monopsonist, 544, **550**
Monopsony, 544–547, 564
  in sports, 561–567
Moore, G. H., 141
Moore, T. G., 174
Morgan, R., 533
Morley, S. A., 162
Mortgage market, 271
Motor Vehicle Safety Act (1966), 489
Movement, and shift, 184–186
Mueller, W. F., 503
Multiplier, 205–207, **211**, 234
  balanced-budget, 223–224, **228**
  expansion, 255–256
  net export, 339, **341**
Multiplier-accelerator theory, 218
Mundell, R. A., 17
Mutual fund, 412, **415**

Mutual Security Act (1951), 680
Myrdal, G., 611–612, 677
Mystery, 511

N

Nader, R., 476, 485, 487, 488–489, 490, 650
  task force, 499, 501
National Bureau of Economic Research, 263, 264
National debt, 98
National Defense Advisory Commission, 504
National Football League Players' Association, 561
National health insurance, 449–450
National income, 73–85, **83**
National income accounting, 73, 80–81, **83**, 86
National Industrial Recovery Act, 513
National Labor Relations Act (NLRA), 513–514
  (See also Wagner Act)
National League, 564
National Monetary Commission, 248
National Opinion Research Center, 23
National priorities, 112–117
National product, 73–85, **83**
  (See also Gross National Product)
National Prohibition Act, 64, 67
  (See also Volstead Act)
National security, and free trade, 316
National Typographic Union, 512
Nationalization, 505, 676
Natural gas, 462, 634
Natural Gas Pipeline Safety Act (1968), 489
Natural monopoly, 458, **471**
  post office as, 477–481
Natural population limit, 656
Natural resources:
  and economic growth, 688–689
  global, 6–7
  limited, 631–633
    depletion of, 633–634
  nonrenewable, 5
Need, 598–599
Negative check, 664, **670**
Negative externalities, 96, **107**
Negative income tax, 607–609, **610**
Net export multiplier, 339, **341**
Net exports, 339, **341**
Net liquidity balance, **333**
Net public debt, 238, **243**

Net national product, 77–78, **83**, 90
Net reproduction rate, 655, **662**
Net worth, 570, **576**
Netherlands, 170–171
New Deal, 512
New Economic Policy, 38
New economics, 93, 231
New Frontier, 231
New unemployment, 145–146
New York State Federation of Labor, 526
New York Stock Exchange, 10, 245, 407, 408, 412
New York Times, 409
Newsweek, 237
Nichols, D. M., 283
Nixon, R., 172, 232, 237, 264, 295, 442, 525, 526, 648
  administration of, 92, 111, 263, 294, 505
Nondurable consumer goods, 76, **83**, 570
Nordhaus, W., 90, 93
Normal rate of return, 374
Norris-LaGuardia Act, 469
Northrup, H. R., 524

O

O'Bannon, H. B., 269
Obsolete skill, 138
Ocean, 626–630
Occupational Safety and Health Act (1970), 489
Official settlements balance, 333
Office of Price Administration (OPA), 93, 168, 169, 504
Oil, 122–124
  importation of, 321–322
Oil depletion allowance, 122–123, 123
Oil exploration, 316
Oil-import quota system, 310
Oil prices, 350
Oil spills, 629
Okner, B. A., 120n, 121n
Okun, A., 110–111, 159, 162, 243
Oligopoly, 490, 495–**497**, 499
Olson, M., 7, 701
On-the-job training, 592
Open-market operation, 256–257
Opportunity cost, 13–14, **16**, 27, 47, 401, 402, 412, 518, 581, 598, 619–620, 632, 640, 659
  of capital, 374, **383**

Opportunity cost (con't.):
  and comparative advantage, 314–315
  of labor, 374
  of not working, 142–143
  of money, 246
  and tax shelter, 124–125
Optimal timing, 632, 633
Organization of Petroleum Exporting Countries (OPEC), 452, 455, 456, 457, 635
Ottinger, R., 649
Output, and input, 375
Overfishing, 626, 628
Overproduction, 180
  (See also General congestion)
Ozaki, R. S., 162

P

Palmer, J. L., 156n
Paper asset, 178
Paper gold, 338, 346
Paradox of thrift, 208, 209, **211**
Paramedic, 450
Parity, 421, **423**
Participation rate, 516, 517, **522**
Partnership, 372, 373, **383**
Patent, 79, 425, 497
Payroll tax, 142
Pechman, J. A., 109, 120n, 121n
Pelzman, S., 486n, 500n
Pen, J., 319
Per se violation, 468, **471**
Percentage oil depletion allowance, 123, **125**
Perfect competition, 401–402
Perfectly elastic demand, 55
Permanent-income hypothesis, 187–188, **195**
Personal discount rate, 580, 691, **694**
Personal income, 81, **83**
  disposable, 81
Personal income tax, 102–103, 165
Peterson, W. C., 197
Phillips, A. W., 157
Phillips curve, 157–158, **160**, 288–292, 300
Pinchot, G., 631
Planning system, 506–**508**
Plattner, M. F., 652
Pohlman, J. E., 174
Police power, 513
Policymaking, model, 160
Politics:
  and financing, 648–652

Politics (cont'd.):
  and foreign aid, 680
  and public choice, 638–645
Pollution, 88–89, 96, 615, 616, 697
  and consumption, 659
  of the ocean, 629–630
Pollution-abatement equipment, 617
Pontecorvo, G., 630
Poor, 580, 602–610
  characteristics of, 602–604
  and saving, 691
Poor man's price index, 156
Population:
  geriatric, 660–661
  stable, 666
Population curve, 656
Population economics, 653–663
Population explosion, 653, 660,
  664–670
Population growth, zero, 653, 655, 659,
  696
Population rate of growth, 653, **662**
Population limit, natural, 656
Positive checks, 664, **670**
Postal Reorganization Act, 477
Poverty, 602–610, 680
Poverty line, 607
Power:
  and concentration, 499–501
  police, 513
  union, 154, 511–515
Power monopoly, 154
Preference formation, 67
Present value, 571, **576**
President's Aide on Consumer Affairs,
  483
President's Commission on Postal
  Reorganization, 478
President's Commission on Product
  Safety, 485
President's Reemployment Agreement,
  513
Presidential Commission on Antitrust
  Activities, 470
Presidential Task Force on Women's
  Rights and Responsibilities, 527
Preventive checks, 664, **670**
Price:
  of credit, 180
  market clearing, 49, **60**
  relative, 43, **60**, 353
Price Control Act (1942), 168
Price determination, 399

Price differentiation, 462, **471**
Price-discriminating monopolist, **436**
Price discrimination, 447–448, 461–462,
  463, 468, 479
Price elasticity, 416, 417
  of demand, 53, 56–57, **60**
  defined, 53
  of supply, 56–57, 418
Price Emergency Regulation, 168
Price index, 149–152
  consumer, 150–151, **160**
  poor man's, 156
  wholesale, 148, 151–152, **160**
Price, R., 650
Price responsiveness, 53, 54
Price setter, 496
Price supports, 295, 419–422, **423**
Price system, 31–32
Price taker, 387, **403**, 496
Principle of exclusion, 95
Priorities, national, 112–117
Private Express Statutes, 477, 478, 481
Private property, 31
Private property rights, 96–97
Private sector, 166
Producer goods, 33, **36**
  (See also Capital goods)
Producer-oriented legislation, 641
Product group, 491
Production function, 202, *203*, **211**, 375,
  383
Production-possibility frontier, 26, **36**
Productive resource, 30
Productivity, 535, **550**, 599
Profit, 79, 373–375, 433
  short-run, 393
Profit maximization, 393, 548–549
  model, 389
Profitability, in Russia, 34
Progressive taxation, 100–101, 121, 165,
  588
  and income redistribution, 103
Prohibition, 64–69
Proletariat, in China, 40–41
Property rights, 31, 32, **36**, 618, 621
  and economic development, 676
Property tax, 79
Propinquity theorem, 596
Proportional taxation, 100
Proprietorship, 372, 373, **383**
Prostitution, 556, 559
Protectionism, 320
Psychological theory, 131, **139**

Public assistance, 604, **610**
  residency qualifications for, 604
Public Citizen, Inc., 489
Public debt, **243**
  alternatives to, 239–240
  burden of, 238–**243**
  external, 240, **243**
  gross, 238, **243**
  growth of, 238
  interest on, 240
  internal, 240
  net, 238, **243**
Public goods, 94, **107**, 622–**623**
Public information, 409
Public Law, 480, 683, 684
Public service employment, 233–235
Public utility, 464
Punishment, 556–558
Purchasing power, conservation of,
  179

Q

Quantity theory of money and prices,
  152–153, **160**, 294
Quota, 35, **318**, 321–323
Quota system:
  in China, 38
  oil-import, 316
  of International Monetary Fund, 346

R

Radio, 623
Raffaele, J. A., 685
RAND Corporation, 647
Random walk, 411, 412, **415**
Ranis, G., 677
Rate of inflation, 149–150
Rate of investment and capital
  expansion, 215
Rate of population growth, 653, **662**
Rate-of-return regulation, 463, **471**
Ration book, 169
Rationing, 5, **7**
  functioning of, 593
Raw material, 306, 426
Rawski, T. G., 39
Rayack, E., 451
Real-income adjustment mechanism,
  334–335
Real wages, 520, **522**
Recession, 127
Recognition lag, 298
Recovery, 127

Recycling, 4
Rees, A., 288, 552
Rees, R. D., 423
Regressive taxation, 101
Regulation:
    of economic activity, 95–96
    and inflation, 464
    of monopolies, 458–474
Regulation Q, 582, 584, **585**
Regulatory agency, 488
Regulatory commission, 460, 463, 464
Relative price, 43, **60**, 353
Rent, 79
Repressed inflation, 169–170
Resale price maintenance, 469, **471**, 502
Reserve army of the unemployed, 131, **139**
Reserve clause, 561, 562, **566**
Reserve position, 346, **350**
Reserve, 249–250
    excess, 249–250, **260**
Resource allocation, 35
Resource apportionment, 627
Resource base, 314
Restrictive monetary policy, 289
Restraint of trade, 466, 467
Retained earnings, 105, **108**
Reuther, W., 515, 526
Revenue sharing, 98, 232
Ricardo, D., 664
Rich, W. E., 481
Richman, B. M., 42
Right-to-work laws, 514, **522**
Risk factor, 594
Ritter, L. S., 262, 283
Robertson, D. H., 262
Robinson, E. A., 406
Robinson, E. A. G., 439
Robinson, J., 440–441, 490n, 498
Robinson-Patman Act, 468–469
    (See also Antitrust laws)
Rockefeller, N., 649
Role differentiation, 531
Role of money, 284–293
Roosa, R. U., 344
Roosevelt, F. D., 147, 215, 505, 513
    administration of, 142
Rosen, S., 85
Rosenthal, A., 652
Ross, L., 93
Rostow, W. W., 695
Rottenberg, S., 567

Rowan, R. L., 524
Royalty, 79
Rule of '72, 654
Russia, 34, 599
Ruttan, V. W., 423

S

Sachery, C., 610
Sachs, S., 146
Safety, 485
Safety legislation, 486
Sales tax, 79, 106
Samuelson, P., 218, 236–237, 295, 646, 647
Sandor, R. I., 371
Satisfaction, measures of, 87–88
Saturday Review, 444
Saudi Arabia, 452
Saunders, C., 91
Saving, 177–179, 207–209, 570, 580, 690–692
    defined, **194**
    and investment, 192–194, 203–204
    and the poor, 691
    and savings, 178, 571
Saving decisions, 690–692
Savings and loan association, 188, 271, 578, 584, 690
Savings and saving, 178, 571
Savings function, 182, *183*
Say's law, 179–180
Scarcity, 8, **16**, 25, 640, 696, 698, 699
    government and, 112
Scarcity society, 3–7
Scheele, C., 481
Schooling (see Education)
Schultz, G. P., 174
Schumpeter, J. A., 439, 638, 639n
Schur, E. M., 560
Schwartz, W., 637
Search cost, 520
Sea, 626–630
    freedom of, 626
    law of, 626
Seasonal unemployment, 137–138, **139**, 144–145
Sectoral advantage, 321
Sectoral effect, 339
Securities and Exchange Commission, 410
Security, 408
    and foreign aid, 680
Seidl, J. M., 585

Self-exploitation, 506
Seligman, R. A., 106
Seniority, inverse, 144
Services, 76, **83**
    of housewife, 86–87
Severn, W., 69
Sexism, in the labor market, 527–533
Shaffer, H. G., 42
Sheahan, J., 174
Sherman Antitrust Act, 449, 467, 470, 566
    (See also Antitrust laws)
Shift, and movement, 184–186
Shifting demand, 50–52
Shifting supply, 52–53
Short-run break-even point, 393, **403**
Short-run costs of firm, 378–383
Short-run elasticity, 58
Short-run profit, 393
Short-run shutdown point, 397, **403**
Short-run stabilization, 296–302
Shortage:
    energy, 3, 6
    food, 3–4
Shortage society, 3–7
Shortfall, 3, **7**
Shutdown point, 397–398
Sierra Club, 631
Silber, W. L., 262, 283
Simon, J., 498
Sinclair, A., 69
Skolnick, 560
Slavery, 9, 673
    athletic, 561–567
Small Business Act (1953), 469
Smith, A., 11, 30, 32, 40, 358, 441, 557, 664
Snider, D. A., 319, 344
Social costs, 615–**623**
Social programs, 98
Social Security, 96, 98, 157, 219, 295, 606–607, 658
    benefits, 155–156, 163
    tax, 106–107
Socialism, 25, 33–34, **36**
Solomon, E., 233
Soltow, L., 601
Special Drawing Rights, 346
Specialization, 10, 11, **16**, 312, 314, 320, 377
    in China, 40
    and exchange, 10–14
Speculation, 367–**371**

Speculation *(cont'd.)*:
  and price stability, 370–371
  and total utility, 368–369
Speculative motive, 273
Sports *(see* Athletics)
Spot price, 367, 368, **371**
Sprinkel, B. W., 415
Stability, and free trade, 316
Stabilization, short-run, 296–302
Stagflation, **160**
Standard Oil, 467, 470
Stanford, D., 487
Stanford, Q. H., 670
Stanford University, 264, 371, 527, 647
Start-up costs, 425
Starvation *(see* Hunger)
State budget, 98–99
Static equilibrium, 441
Stelzer, I. M., 474
Sterilization policies, 337, **341**
Stern, P. M., 120, 124, 125
Stevens, N. A., 371
Stevens, R. W., 350
Stewart, M., 197, 213
Stock, 26, **36,** 178, 194, 408, 570, **576**
Stockbroker, 10
Stockholder, 372
Stock market, 214, 407–415
Strata, 132
Structural unemployment, 138, **139**
Subjective utility, 354
Subsidization, 461
  of agriculture, 674–675
  of industry, 674
Subsidy, 116, 295
  explicit, 125
  to producers, 98, 112–113
Substitution, 464–465, 501, 634
  law of, 363
  marginal rate of, 363
Substitution effects, 366
Sunk costs, 378
Sunspot theory, 130, **139**
Superrich, 568
Supply:
  and demand, 43–63
  excess, of money, 274–275
  of labor, 516–518
  law of, 45–53, 56
  price elasticity of, 56–57
  shifting, 52–53
  unitary elasticity of, 57
Supply curve, 47, **60,** 398–399

Supply schedule, 47, **60**
Supreme Court, 467, 469, 513–514, 564
Surplus, 226, **228**
  full-employment, 226
Surplus value, 131
Surtax, 105, **108,** 165, 299
Sweden, 486, 588

T

T account, 251, 253, 256
Tabular standard, 164
Taft, W. H., 13
Taft-Hartley Act (1947), 514
  (See also Labor Management
    Relations Act)
Take-home pay, 225
  (See also Disposable income)
Target price, 422, **423**
Tariff, 323–325, 419
Tastes for discrimination, 527, **533**
Tax:
  business, 191–192
  capital gains, 105, 165
  effect of changing, 222–223
  estate, 106
  excise, 79, 106
  flat, 100
  income, 100–103
    corporate, 103–105, 165
    personal, 102–103, 165
    negative, 295, 607–609, **610**
  progressive, 100–101, 121, 165, 225
  proportional, 100
  sales, 79, 106
  Social Security, 106–107
  on wealth, 105–106
  withholding, 232
Taxation, 99–107, 690
  vs. borrowing, 240
  and pollution, 617–618
  progressive, 100–101, 121, 165, 588
    and income redistribution, 103
  proportional, 100
  regressive, 101
  theories of, 100
  types of, 100–101
Tax loophole, 120–121
Taxpayer, rape of, 120–125
Tax shelter, 120, 124–125
Technical analysis, 411, **415**
Technological unemployment, 138, **139**
Technology, 191, 692
Technostructure, 507, **508**

Television, 623
Territorial waters, 626
Thailand, 588
Theft, 555
Theobald, R., 610
Theories of inflation, 152–154
Theories of taxation, 100
Theory of income analysis, 177
Theory of income and employment
    determination, 177
Third-party effect, 486, **487**
Thrift, paradox of, *208,* 209, **211**
Thurow, L. C., 230
Time dimension, 44
Time lag, 298–299
Tin, 453
Tobacco, 421–422
Tobin, J., 90, 92–93
Tomerlin, J., 487
Total costs, 378, **383,** 389, **403**
  and total revenues, 389, 392, **403**
Total utility:
  maximizing, 369–370
  speculation and, 368–369
Trade:
  balance of, 331–332, **340**
  free, 315–317, 320–321
  international, 305–319
    financing, 326–345
  voluntary, 307
Trade-off, 26, 158–159
Training, 592–593
Transactions cost, 10, **16,** 520
Transactions demand, 284–285
Transfer in kind, 609
Transfer payments, 81, **83,** 96, 139,
    155, 219, **228**
Transmission mechanism, 278–279, 285
Trezise, P. H., 457
Triffin, R., 350
Trough, 127
  (See also Bottom)
Truman, H., 264, 422, 626
Truth:
  in labeling, 485
  in packaging, 476
Tuckman, H. P., 610
Tullock, G., 560

U

Underemployment, and inefficiency,
    26
Unemployment, 93, 132–139, 167, 288

Unemployment (cont'd.):
cyclical, 137, **139**
duration of, 134–135
frictional, 137, **139**, 297, 521, **522**
full, 137
hidden, 135
and inflation, 157–160
new, 145–146
seasonal, 137–138, **139**, 144–145
structural, 138, **139**
technological, 138, **139**
types of, 137–138
voluntary, 133–134
Unemployment compensation, 139,
142–146, 219, 225
Unemployment rate, 73, 521
Unemployment tax, 106–107
Union power, 154, 511–515
Union shop, 514, **522**
Unions, 511–**522**
craft, 512, **522**
Unitary elasticity:
of demand, 55
of supply, 57
United Automobile Workers (UAW),
515, 525
United Mine Workers (UMW), 514
United Nations, 4
Conference on the Human
Environment, 679
Economic Commission, 611
Relief and Rehabilitation Program,
682
United Parcel Service, 479
U.S. Bureau of the Budget, 132
U.S. Department of Agriculture, 371,
602
U.S. Department of Commerce, 85, 86,
126, 127
U.S. Department of Defense, 113
U.S. Department of Health,
Education, and Welfare, 113
U.S. Department of Justice, 470
antitrust division, 500, 503
U.S. Department of Labor, 521
Bureau of Labor Statistics, 81, 132,
135, 151, 152, 156, 521, 529
U.S. Department of the Treasury, 119,
124, 125, 231
U.S. Federal Communications
Commission, 643
U.S. Federal Power Commission, 634
U.S. Federal Trade Commission, 489

U.S. Forest Service, 631
U.S. Internal Revenue Service, 232,
247, 568, 608
U.S. Post Office, 463, 465, 477–481, 642
U.S. Senate:
Antitrust and Monopoly
Subcommittee, 475
Environment Subcommittee, 475,
476
United States Steel, 172, 497
University of Chicago, 294
University of Minnesota, 231, 232
University of Wisconsin, 156
Urban Institute, 568
Usury, 578, **585**
Usury laws, 578, 581, **585**
Utility, subjective, 354
Utility analysis, 353
marginal, 367
Utility maximization, 14
Utility theory, 353–355

V

Value of marginal physical product,
535–536, **550**
Variable costs, 379, **383**
Vatter, H. G., 601
Veen, R. V., 234
Vice, 555
Vietnam, 93
Vietnam conflict, 111, 264
Volstead Act, 64, 65, 68
Voluntary trade, 307
Voluntary unemployment, 133–134

W

Wade, J. L., 637
Wage, minimum, 564, **550**
Wage and price controls, 111, 159,
168–174, 508, 644
Wage differential, 527–528
Wage earner, 155
Wage-price review board, 264
Wages, 79, 373
Wagner Act, 513–514
(See also National Labor Relations
Act)
Wall Street Journal, 407, 409, 648
War on Poverty, 505
War Production Board, 93
Ward, B., 678–679
Watson, D. S., 63, 360, 386
Wealth, 568–577

Wealth (cont'd.):
concentration of, 568–569
of the ocean, 626–630
tax on, 105–106
Wealth distribution, 620, 629
Wealth maximization, 14
Webb-Pomerane Act, 469
Weil, G. L., 350
Weintraub, A., 701
Weiss, L. W., 498
Welfare, 81, 295, 647
alternatives to, 602–610
Welfare services, 33
Well-being:
and GNP, 82
material, 23–24
Wheelwright, E. L:, 42
Whells, H., 652
White, H. D., 346
White House Task Force on Antitrust
Policy, 500
Wholesale price index, 148, 151–152,
160
Wholesome Meat Act (1967), 489
Wicksell, K., 611
Wilcox, C., 474, 610
Wilderness Society, 631
Will, R. E., 601
Williams, R. M., 302
Wilson, G., 560
Wilson, W., 248
Wiretapping, 558
Withholding tax system, 232
Women, 508
discrimination against, 527–533
self-employed, 529
Worker, 373
Working, H., 371
Works Progress Administration
(WPA), 233
World Bank, 455
World Food Conference, 4
World trade (see International trade)
Worldwide inflation, and flexible
exchange rates, 345–350
Wortman, M. S., 524

Z

Zero economic profit, 393–395, 491
Zero population growth, 653, 655, 659,
696
Zero trade point, 309, **318**
Zuhorst, C., 637